Praise for *Learning MySQL*, Second Edition

It's been a long time since a good book covering MySQL and its ecosystem has been published, and many changes have occurred since then. Many topics are clearly covered with examples, from installation and database design to maintenance and architecture for HA and cloud. Many third-party tools are also covered, like dbdeployer and ProxySQL, which are MySQL DBA's very good friends but are often not covered in the literature. Very nice job from Vinicius and Sergey. Don't miss the last chapter—it's very interesting!

—*Frederic Descamps, MySQL evangelist at Oracle*

First of all, I want to thank Vinicius and Sergey for making possible my dream book for all beginners of MySQL while I work on the developer edition. This book offers the most comprehensive details on MySQL, not only how to get started but also for complex topics like high availability and load balancing. It's a smooth read with well-organized content befitting the quality of O'Reilly publishing. I highly recommend this book to all readers, from developers to operations.

—*Alkin Tezuysal, senior technical manager at PlanetScale*

This book is a terrific resource, whether you're installing MySQL for the first time, learning load balancing, or migrating your database to the cloud. I highly recommend it.

—*Brett Holleman, software engineer*

This book is essential for anyone who wants to dive into the MySQL ecosystem. With clear and objective communication, it covers topics from basic to advanced. Simply an indispensable book to increase MySQL knowledge.

—*Diego Hellas, CEO, PerformanceDB*

Walks the reader through all the important MySQL concepts, from the foundation of SQL and data modeling to advanced topics like high availability and cloud, using clear, concise, direct language.

—*Charly Batista, Percona*

SECOND EDITION

Learning MySQL

Get a Handle on Your Data

Vinicius M. Grippa and Sergey Kuzmichev

Beijing · Boston · Farnham · Sebastopol · Tokyo

Learning MySQL

by Vinicius M. Grippa and Sergey Kuzmichev

Published by O'Reilly Media, Inc., 1005 Gravenstein Highway North, Sebastopol, CA 95472.

O'Reilly books may be purchased for educational, business, or sales promotional use. Online editions are also available for most titles (*http://oreilly.com*). For more information, contact our corporate/institutional sales department: 800-998-9938 or *corporate@oreilly.com*.

Acquisitions Editor: Andy Kwan	**Indexer:** Sue Klefstad
Development Editor: Corbin Collins	**Interior Designer:** David Futato
Production Editor: Beth Kelly	**Cover Designer:** Karen Montgomery
Copyeditor: Rachel Head	**Illustrator:** Kate Dullea
Proofreader: Kim Wimpsett	

November 2006:	First Edition
September 2021:	Second Edition

Revision History for the Second Edition

2021-09-09:   First Release

See *http://oreilly.com/catalog/errata.csp?isbn=9781492085928* for release details.

978-1-492-08592-8

[LSI]

Table of Contents

Preface

Database management systems are part of the core of many companies. Even if a business is not technology-focused, it needs to store, access, and manipulate data in a fast, secure, and reliable way. Because of the COVID-19 pandemic, many areas that had traditionally resisted digital transformation, like the judiciary systems in many countries, are now being integrated through technology due to travel and meeting restrictions, and online shopping and working from home are more popular than ever before.

But it's not just disasters that have propelled such far-reaching changes. With the advent of 5G, we will soon have many more machines connected to the internet than humans. Vast amounts of data are already being harvested, stored, and used to train machine learning models, artificial intelligence, and much more. We are living at the beginning of the next revolution.

Several database types have emerged to help with the mission of storing more data—especially unstructured data—including NoSQL databases like MongoDB, Cassandra, and Redis. However, traditional SQL databases remain popular, and there is no sign that they will vanish in the near future. And in the SQL world, undoubtedly the most popular open source solution is MySQL.

Both of the authors of this book have worked with many customers from all parts of the world. Along the way, we have learned lots of lessons and experienced a vast number of use cases, ranging from mission-critical monolith applications to simpler microservices applications. This book is full of the tips and advice we think most readers will find helpful for their daily activities.

Who This Book Is For

This book is primarily for people using MySQL for the first time or learning it as a second database. If you are entering the database arena for the first time, the first chapters will introduce you to the database design concepts and show you how to deploy MySQL into different operating systems and in the cloud.

For those coming from another ecosystem, like Postgres, Oracle, or SQL Server, the book covers backup, high availability, and disaster recovery strategies.

We hope all readers will also find this book to be a good companion for learning or reviewing fundamentals, from the architecture to advice for the production environment.

How This Book Is Organized

We introduce many topics, from the basic installation process, database design, backups, and recovery to CPU performance analysis and bug investigation. We've divided the book into four main parts:

1. Starting with MySQL
2. Using MySQL
3. MySQL in Production
4. Miscellaneous Topics

Let's look at how we've organized the chapters.

Starting with MySQL

Chapter 1, *Installing MySQL* explains how to install and configure the MySQL software on different operating systems. This chapter provides far more detail than most books do. We know that those initiating their career with MySQL are often unfamiliar with various Linux distributions and installation options, and running the MySQL "hello world" requires far more steps than compiling a hello world in any programming language does. You will see how to set up MySQL on Linux, Windows, macOS, and Docker, and how to deploy instances quickly for testing.

Using MySQL

Before we dive into creating and using databases, we look at proper database design in Chapter 2, *Modeling and Designing Databases*. You will learn how to access your database's features and see how the information items in your database relate to each other. You will see that lousy database designs are challenging to change and can lead to performance problems. We will introduce the concept of strong and weak entities and their relationships (*foreign keys*) and explain the process of normalization. This chapter also shows how to download and configure database examples such as `sakila`, `world`, and `employees`.

In Chapter 3, *Basic SQL*, we explore the famous SQL commands that are part of the CRUD (create, read, update, and delete) operations. You will see how to read data from an existing MySQL database, store data in it, and manipulate existing data.

In Chapter 4, *Working with Database Structures*, we explain how to create a new MySQL database and create and modify tables, indexes, and other database structures.

Chapter 5, *Advanced Querying* covers more advanced operations such as using nested queries and using different MySQL database engines. This chapter will give you the ability to perform more complex queries.

MySQL in Production

Now that you know how to install MySQL and manipulate data, the next step is to understand how MySQL handles simultaneous access to the same data. The concepts of isolation, transaction, and deadlocks are explored in Chapter 6, *Transactions and Locking*.

In Chapter 7, *Doing More with MySQL*, you will see more complex queries that you can perform in MySQL as well as how to observe the query plan to check whether the query is efficient or not. We'll also explain the different engines available in MySQL (InnoDB and MyISAM are the most famous ones).

In Chapter 8, *Managing Users and Privileges*, you will learn how to create and delete users in the database. This step is one of the most important in terms of security since users with more privileges than they need can cause considerable damage to the database and the company's reputation. You will see how to establish security policies, give and remove privileges, and restrict access to specific network IPs.

Chapter 9, *Using Option Files* covers the MySQL configuration files, or *option files*, which contain all the necessary parameters to start MySQL and optimize its performance. Those familiar with MySQL will recognize the */etc/my.cnf* configuration file. You will also see that it is possible to configure user access using special option files.

Databases without backup policies are headed for disaster sooner or later. In Chapter 10, *Backups and Recovery* we discuss the different types of backups (*logical* versus *physical*), the options available to execute this task, and the ones that are more appropriate for large production databases.

Chapter 11, *Configuring and Tuning the Server* discusses the essential parameters you need to pay attention to when setting up a new server. We provide formulas for that and help you to identify whether a parameter value is the correct one for the database workload.

Miscellaneous Topics

With the essentials established, it is time to go beyond. Chapter 12, *Monitoring MySQL Servers* teaches you how to monitor your database and collect data from it. Since database workload behavior can change according to the volume of users, transactions, and data being manipulated, identifying which resource is saturated and what is causing the problem is crucial.

Chapter 13, *High Availability* explains how to replicate servers to provide high availability. We also introduce the cluster concept, highlighting two solutions: InnoDB Cluster and Galera/PXC Cluster.

Chapter 14, *MySQL in the Cloud* expands the MySQL universe to the cloud. You will learn about the database-as-a-service (DBaaS) option and how to use the managed database services provided by the most prominent three cloud providers: Amazon Web Services (AWS), Google Cloud Platform (GCP), and Microsoft Azure.

In Chapter 15, *Load Balancing MySQL*, we'll show you the most commonly used tools to distribute queries among different MySQL servers to extract even more performance from MySQL.

Finally, Chapter 16, *Miscellaneous Topics* introduces more advanced analysis methods and tools, and a bit of programming. In this chapter we'll talk about MySQL Shell, flame graphs, and how to analyze bugs.

Conventions Used in This Book

The following typographical conventions are used in this book:

Italic
> Indicates new terms, URLs, email addresses, filenames, and file extensions.

`Constant width`
> Used for program listings, as well as within paragraphs to refer to program elements such as variable or function names, databases, data types, environment variables, statements, and keywords.

`Constant width bold`
> Shows commands or other text that should be typed literally by the user.

`Constant width italic`
> Shows text that should be replaced with user-supplied values or by values determined by context.

This element signifies a tip or suggestion.

 This element signifies a general note.

 This element indicates a warning or caution.

Using Code Examples

Code examples are available for download at *https://github.com/learning-mysql-2nd/learning-mysql-2nd*.

If you have a technical question or a problem using the code examples, please send email to *bookquestions@oreilly.com*.

This book is here to help you get your job done. In general, if an example code is offered with this book, you may use it in your programs and documentation. You do not need to contact us for permission unless you're reproducing a significant portion of the code. For example, writing a program that uses several chunks of code from this book does not require permission. Selling or distributing examples from O'Reilly books does require permission. Answering a question by citing this book and quoting example code does not require permission. Incorporating a significant amount of example code from this book into your product's documentation does require permission.

We appreciate, but generally do not require attribution. An attribution usually includes the title, author, publisher, and ISBN. For example: "*Learning MySQL*, 2nd ed., by Vinicius M. Grippa and Sergey Kuzmichev (O'Reilly). Copyright 2021 Vinicius M. Grippa and Sergey Kuzmichev, 978-1-492-08592-8."

If you feel your use of code examples falls outside fair use or the permission given above, feel free to contact us at *permissions@oreilly.com*.

O'Reilly Online Learning

 For more than 40 years, *O'Reilly Media* has provided technology and business training, knowledge, and insight to help companies succeed.

Our unique network of experts and innovators share their knowledge and expertise through books, articles, and our online learning platform. O'Reilly's online learning platform gives you on-demand access to live training courses, in-depth learning paths, interactive coding environments, and a vast collection of text and video from O'Reilly and 200+ other publishers. For more information, visit *http://oreilly.com*.

How to Contact Us

Please address comments and questions concerning this book to the publisher:

> O'Reilly Media, Inc.
> 1005 Gravenstein Highway North
> Sebastopol, CA 95472
> 800-998-9938 (in the United States or Canada)
> 707-829-0515 (international or local)
> 707-829-0104 (fax)

We have a web page for this book, where we list errata, examples, and any additional information. You can access this page at *https://oreil.ly/learn-mysql-2e*.

Email *bookquestions@oreilly.com* to comment on or ask technical questions about this book.

For news and information about our books and courses, visit *http://oreilly.com*.

Find us on Facebook: *http://facebook.com/oreilly*

Follow us on Twitter: *http://twitter.com/oreillymedia*

Watch us on YouTube: *http://youtube.com/oreillymedia*

Acknowledgments

From Vinicius Grippa

Thanks to the following people who helped improve this book: Corbin Collins, Charly Batista, Sami Ahlroos, and Brett Holleman. Without them, this book would not have achieved the excellence we strove for.

Thanks to the MySQL community (especially Shlomi Noach, Giuseppe Maxia, Jeremy Cole, and Brendan Gregg) and all the bloggers on Planet MySQL (*https://oreil.ly/ MSFP1*), Several Nines (*https://oreil.ly/X1UZN*), Percona Blog (*https://oreil.ly/rsrAA*), and MySQL Entomologist (*https://oreil.ly/yXkuy*) who have contributed so much material and so many great tools.

Thanks to everyone at Percona who provided the means to write this book, notably Bennie Grant, Carina Punzo, and Marcelo Altmann, and who have helped me grow as a professional and human being.

Thanks to the O'Reilly staff who do such a classy job of publishing books and running conferences.

I want to thank my parents Divaldo and Regina, my sister Juliana, and my girlfriend Karin for having patience and supporting this project in many ways. A special thanks to Paulo Piffer, who gave me my first opportunity to work with what I love.

And last, to Sergey Kuzmichev, the cowriter of this book. Without his expertise, dedication, and hard work, this book would not have been possible. I am grateful for having him as a colleague and for having had the honor of working with him on this project.

From Sergey Kuzmichev

I would like to thank my wife, Kate, for supporting and helping me on every step of this difficult but rewarding project. From ruminating about whether to take on writing this book, to many sometimes difficult days of writing it, she was there. Our first child was born while the book was in writing, and yet Kate found time and strength to continue motivating and helping me.

Thanks to my parents, relatives, and friends, who over the years helped me grow as a person and as an expert. Thank you for supporting me in this project.

Thanks to the amazing people of Percona for helping me with all the technical and non-technical questions and issues I had while writing this book: Iwo Panowicz, Przemyslaw Malkowski, Sveta Smirnova, and Marcos Albe. Thanks to Stuart Bell and everyone in Percona's support management for the amazing level of assistance we received every step of the way.

Thanks to everyone at O'Reilly for leading us and helping us to create this edition. Thanks to Corbin Collins for helping to mold the structure of the book and keeping us firmly on our path. Thanks to Rachel Head for finding myriad issues during the copyedit phase and for spotting problems with the technical details of MySQL in our writing. Without you, and everyone at O'Reilly, this book wouldn't be a book, but merely a collection of loosely related words.

Special thanks to our technical editors Sami Ahlroos, Brett Holleman, and Charly Batista. They were instrumental in making the technical and non-technical contents of this book of the highest quality.

Thanks to everyone in the MySQL community for being open, helpful, and sharing their knowledge in every way possible. The world of MySQL is not a walled garden, but is open for everybody. I'd like to mention Valerii Kravchuk, Mark Callaghan, Dimitri Kravchuk, and Jeremy Cole for helping me through their blogs to understand MySQL's internals better.

I want to thank the authors of the first edition of this book: Hugh E. Williams and Seyed M.M. Tahaghoghi. We built this project on top of a solid foundation thanks to their work.

Last but not least, I would like to thank Vinicius Grippa for being a great coauthor and colleague. This wouldn't be the same book without him.

I dedicate this edition to my son Grigorii.

## CHAPTER 1

Installing MySQL

Let's begin our learning path by installing MySQL and accessing it for the first time.

Note that we do not rely on a single version of MySQL for this book. Instead, we have drawn on our collective knowledge of MySQL in the real world. The book's core is focused on Linux operating systems (mostly Ubuntu/Debian and CentOS/RHEL or its derivatives) and on MySQL 5.7 and MySQL 8.0, because those are what we consider the "current" versions capable of production workloads. The MySQL 5.7 and 8.0 series are still under development, which means that newer versions with bug fixes and new features will continue to be released.

With MySQL becoming the most popular (*https://oreil.ly/pPG4q*) open source database (Oracle, which ranks first, is not open source), the demand for having a fast installation process has increased. You can think of installing MySQL from scratch as similar to baking a cake: the source code is the recipe. But even with the source code available, the recipe for building software is not easy to follow. It takes time to compile, and usually, it is necessary to install additional development libraries that expose production environments to risk. Say you want a chocolate cake; even if you have the instructions for how to make it yourself, you may not want to mess up your kitchen, or you may not have the time to bake it, so you go to a bakery and buy one instead. For MySQL, when you want it ready to use without the effort involved in compiling it, you can use the *distribution packages*.

Distribution packages for MySQL are available for diverse platforms, including Linux distributions, Windows, and macOS. These packages provide a flexible and fast way to start using MySQL. Returning to the chocolate cake example, suppose you want to change something. Maybe you want a white chocolate cake. For MySQL, we have what are called forks, which include some different options. We'll look at a few of these in the next section.

MySQL Forks

In software engineering, a *fork* occurs when someone copies the source code and starts their own path of independent development and support. The fork can follow a track close to that of the original version, as the Percona distribution of MySQL does, or drift away, like MariaDB. Because the MySQL source code is open and free, new projects can fork the code without permission from its original creator. Let's take a look at a few of the most notable forks.

MySQL Community Edition

MySQL Community Edition, also known as the *upstream* or *vanilla* version of MySQL, is the open source version distributed by Oracle. This version drives the development of the InnoDB engine and new features, and it is the first one to receive updates, new features, and bug fixes.

Percona Server for MySQL

The Percona distribution of MySQL is a free, open source, drop-in replacement for MySQL Community Edition. The development closely follows that version, focusing on improving performance and the overall MySQL ecosystem. Percona Server also includes additional enhancements like the MyRocks engine, an Audit Log plugin, and a PAM Authentication plugin. Percona was cofounded by Peter Zaitsev (*https:// oreil.ly/MfiKb*) and Vadim Tkachenko (*https://oreil.ly/283nR*).

MariaDB Server

Created by Michael "Monty" Widenius (*https://oreil.ly/PRoMh*) and distributed by the MariaDB Foundation, MariaDB Server is by far the fork that has drifted the furthest away from vanilla MySQL. In recent years it has developed new features and engines such as MariaDB ColumnStore, and it was the first database to integrate Galera 4 clustering functionality.

MySQL Enterprise Edition

MySQL Enterprise Edition is currently the only version with a commercial license (which means you need to pay to use it, like a Windows license). Also distributed by Oracle, it contains all the functionality of the Community Edition plus exclusive features for security, backup, and high availability.

Installation Choices and Platforms

First, you must choose the MySQL version compatible with your operating system (OS). You can verify compatibility with the MySQL website (*https://oreil.ly/DTRSR*). The same support policies are available for Percona Server (*https://oreil.ly/1ahne*) and MariaDB (*https://oreil.ly/7SYE4*).

We often hear the question: is it possible to install MySQL on an OS that is not supported? Most of the time, the answer is yes. It is possible to install MySQL on Windows 7, for example, but the risks of hitting a bug or facing unpredictable behavior (like memory leaks or underperformance) are high. Because of these risks, we do not recommend doing this for production environments.

The next step is to decide whether to install a *development* or *General Availability* (GA) release. Development releases have the newest features, but we do not recommend them for production because they are not stable. GA releases, also called *production* or *stable* releases, are meant for production use.

> We highly recommend using the most recent GA release because this will include the latest stable bug fixes and performance improvements.

The last thing to decide is which distribution format to install for the operating system. For most use cases, a binary distribution fits. Binary distributions are available in native format for many platforms, such as *.rpm* packages for Linux or *.dmg* packages for macOS. The distributions are also available in generic formats, such as *.zip* archives or compressed *.tar* files (*tarballs*). On Windows, you can use the MySQL Installer to install a binary distribution.

> Watch out for whether the version is 32-bit or 64-bit. The rule of thumb is to pick the 64-bit version. Unless you are working with an ancient OS, you should *not* select the 32-bit version. This is because 32-bit processors can handle only a limited amount of RAM (4 GB or less), whereas 64-bit processors are capable of addressing much more memory.

The installation process consists of four major steps, outlined in the following sections. It's essential to follow these correctly and to set the minimum security requirements for the MySQL database.

1. Download the Distribution that You Want to Install

Each distribution has its owner and, by consequence, its source. Some Linux distributions provide default packages in their repositories. For example, on CentOS 8, the MySQL vanilla distribution is available from the default repositories. When the OS has default packages available, it is unnecessary to download MySQL from a website or configure a repository yourself, which facilitates the installation process.

We will demonstrate how to install the repositories and download the files without the need to go to the website during the installation process. However, if you do want to download MySQL yourself, you can use the following links:

- MySQL Community Server (*https://oreil.ly/sBR5i*)
- Percona Server for MySQL (*https://oreil.ly/R9oO4*)
- MariaDB Server (*https://oreil.ly/a78XW*)

2. Install the Distribution

Installing consists of the elementary steps to make MySQL functional and bring it online, but not securing MySQL. For example, at this point, the MySQL root user can connect without a password, which is quite hazardous since the root user has privileges to perform every action, including dropping a database.

3. Perform Any Necessary Post-Installation Setup

This step is about making sure the MySQL server is working correctly. It is essential to make sure that your server is secure, and the first step for this is executing the *mysql_secure_installation* script. You'll change the password for the root user, disable access for the root user from a remote server, and remove the test database.

4. Run Benchmarks

Some DBAs run benchmarks for each deployment to measure whether the performance is suitable for the project they are using it for. The most common tool for this is sysbench (*https://oreil.ly/ioyXF*). It's essential to highlight here that sysbench performs a *synthetic workload*, whereas when the application is running, we call it the *real workload*. Synthetic workloads usually provide reports about the maximum server performance, but they can't reproduce the real-world workload (with its inherent locks, different query execution times, stored procedures, triggers, and so on).

In the next section we'll walk through the details of the installation process for a few of the most commonly used platforms.

Installing MySQL on Linux

The Linux ecosystem is diverse and has many variants, including Red Hat Enterprise Linux (RHEL), CentOS, Ubuntu, Debian, and others. This section focuses on only the most popular ones—otherwise, this book would be entirely about the installation process!

Installing MySQL on CentOS 7

CentOS, short for Community Enterprise Linux Operating System, was founded in 2004, and Red Hat acquired it in 2014. CentOS is the community version of Red Hat, so they're pretty much identical, but CentOS is free, and support comes from the community instead of Red Hat itself. CentOS 7 was released in 2014, and its end-of-life date is in 2024.

Installing MySQL 8.0

To install MySQL 8.0 on CentOS 7 using the *yum* repository, complete the following steps.

Log in to Linux server.   Usually, for security reasons, users log into Linux servers as nonprivileged users. Here is an example of a user logging into Linux from a macOS terminal using a private key:

```
$ ssh -i key.pem centos@3.227.11.227
```

After you've successfully connected, you'll see something like this in the terminal:

```
[centos@ip-172-30-150-91 ~]$
```

Become root in Linux.   Once you're connected to the server, you need to become root:

```
$ sudo su - root
```

You will then see a prompt like the following in your terminal:

```
[root@ip-172-30-150-91 ~]#
```

Becoming root is important because to install MySQL it is necessary to perform tasks such as creating the MySQL user in Linux, configuring directories, and setting permissions. It is also possible to use the sudo command for all examples we will show that should be executed by the root user. However, if you forget to prefix a command with sudo, the installation process will be incomplete.

This chapter will use the Linux root user in the majority of the examples (represented by the prompt # in the code lines). Another advantage of the # representation is that this is also the comment character in Linux. If you blindly copy/paste lines from the book, you won't run any real commands in the shell.

Configure the yum repository. Execute the following command to configure the MySQL *yum* repository:

```
# rpm -Uvh https://repo.mysql.com/mysql80-community-release-el7.rpm
```

Install MySQL 8.0 Community Server. Because the MySQL *yum* repository has repositories for multiple MySQL versions (5.7 and 8.0 major versions), first we have to disable all repositories:

```
# sed -i 's/enabled=1/enabled=0/'
/etc/yum.repos.d/mysql-community.repo
```

Next, we need to enable the MySQL 8.0 repository and execute the following command to install MySQL 8.0:

```
# yum --enablerepo=mysql80-community install mysql-community-server
```

Start the MySQL service. Now, start the MySQL service with the systemctl command:

```
# systemctl start mysqld
```

It is also possible to start the MySQL process manually, which can be useful to troubleshoot initialization problems when MySQL is refusing to start. To start manually, indicate the location of the *my.cnf* file and which user can manipulate the database files and the process:

```
# mysqld --defaults-file=/etc/my.cnf --user=mysql
```

Discover the default password for the root user. When you install MySQL 8.0, MySQL creates a temporary password for the root user account. To identify the password of the root user account, execute the following command:

```
# grep "A temporary password" /var/log/mysqld.log
```

The command provides output like the following:

```
2020-05-31T15:04:12.256877Z 6 [Note] [MY-010454] [Server] A temporary
password is generated for root@localhost: #z?hhCCyj2aj
```

Secure the MySQL installation. MySQL provides a shell script that you can run on Unix systems, *mysql_secure_installation*, that enables you to improve the security of your server installation in the following ways:

- You can set a password for the root account.
- You can disable root access from outside the localhost.
- You can remove anonymous user accounts.
- You can remove the test database, which by default can be accessed by anonymous users.

Execute the command `mysql_secure_installation` to secure the MySQL server:

```
# mysql_secure_installation
```

It will prompt you for the current password of the root account:

```
Enter the password for user root:
```

Enter the temporary password obtained in the previous step and press Enter. The following message will appear:

```
The existing password for the user account root has expired. Please
set a new password.

New password:
Re-enter new password:
```

 This section will cover only the basics of changing the root password to grant access to the MySQL server. We will show more details about granting privileges and creating a password policy in Chapter 8.

You will need to enter the new password for the root account twice. More recent MySQL versions come with a validation policy, which means that the new password needs to respect minimal requirements to be accepted. The default requirements are that passwords must be at least eight characters long and include:

- At least one numeric character
- At least one lowercase character
- At least one uppercase character
- At least one special (nonalphanumeric) character

Next, it will prompt you with some yes/no questions about whether you want to make some initial setup changes. To ensure maximum protection, we recommend removing anonymous users, disabling remote root login, and removing the test database (i.e., answering *yes* for all options):

```
Remove anonymous users? (Press y|Y for Yes, any other key for No) : y

Disallow root login remotely? (Press y|Y for Yes, any other key for No) : y

Remove test database and access to it? (Press y|Y for Yes, any other key
for No) : y

Reload privilege tables now? (Press y|Y for Yes, any other key for No) : y
```

Connect to MySQL. This step is optional, but we use it to verify that we executed all the steps correctly. Use this command to connect to the MySQL server:

```
# mysql -u root -p
```

It will prompt for the password of the root user. Type the password and press Enter:

```
Enter password:
```

If successful, it will show the MySQL command line:

```
mysql>
```

Start MySQL 8.0 upon server start (optional). To set MySQL to start whenever the server boots up, use the following command:

```
# systemctl enable mysqld
```

Installing MariaDB 10.5

To install MariaDB 10.5 on CentOS 7, you'll need to execute similar steps as for the vanilla MySQL distribution.

Become root in Linux. First, we need to become root. See the instructions in "Installing MySQL 8.0" on page 5.

Install the MariaDB repository. The following set of commands will download the MariaDB repo and configure it for the next step. Note that in the yum commands, we are using the -y option. This option tells Linux to assume the answer is *yes* for all subsequent questions:

```
# yum install wget -y
# wget https://downloads.mariadb.com/MariaDB/mariadb_repo_setup
# chmod +x mariadb_repo_setup
# ./mariadb_repo_setup
```

Install MariaDB. With the repository configured, the next command will install the latest stable version of MariaDB and its dependencies:

```
# yum install MariaDB-server -y
```

The end of the output will be similar to this:

```
Installed:
  MariaDB-compat.x86_64 0:10.5.8-1.el7.centos

Dependency Installed:
  MariaDB-client.x86_64 0:10.5.8-1.el7.centos MariaDB-common.x86_64
  0:10.5.8-1.el7.centos boost-program-options.x86_64 0:1.53.0-28.el7
  galera-4.x86_64 0:26.4.6-1.el7.centos         libaio.x86_64
  0:0.3.109-13.el7         lsof.x86_64 0:4.87-6.el7
  pcre2.x86_64 0:10.23-2.el7               perl.x86_64
  4:5.16.3-299.el7_9         perl-Carp.noarch 0:1.26-244.el7
  ...

Replaced:
  mariadb-libs.x86_64 1:5.5.64-1.el7

Complete!
```

The *Complete!* at the end of the log indicates a successful installation.

Start MariaDB. With MariaDB installed, initialize the service with the systemctl command:

```
# systemctl start mariadb.service
```

You can use this command to verify its status:

```
# systemctl status mariadb

  mariadb.service - MariaDB 10.5.8 database server
    Loaded: loaded (/usr/lib/systemd/system/mariadb.service; disabled;
    vendor preset: disabled)
  ...
  Feb 07 12:55:04 ip-172-30-150-91.ec2.internal systemd[1]: Started
  MariaDB 10.5.8 database server.
```

Secure MariaDB. At this point, MariaDB will be running in insecure mode. In contrast to MySQL 8.0, MariaDB will have an empty root password so you can access it instantly:

```
# mysql

Welcome to the MariaDB monitor.  Commands end with ; or \g.
Your MariaDB connection id is 44
Server version: 10.5.8-MariaDB MariaDB Server

Copyright (c) 2000, 2018, Oracle, MariaDB Corporation Ab and others.
```

```
Type 'help;' or '\h' for help. Type '\c' to clear the current input
statement.

MariaDB [(none)]>
```

You can execute `mysql_secure_installation` to secure MariaDB just like you would for MySQL 8.0 (see the previous section for details). There is a slight variation in output, with one extra question:

```
Switch to unix_socket authentication [Y/n] y
Enabled successfully!
Reloading privilege tables..
 ... Success!
```

Answering *yes* changes the connection from TCP/IP to Unix socket mode. We will discuss the different connection types in "MySQL 5.7 Default Files" on page 41.

Installing Percona Server 8.0

Install Percona Server 8.0 on CentOS 7 using the following step.

Become root in Linux.   First, you need to become root. See the instructions in "Installing MySQL 8.0" on page 5.

Install the Percona repository.   You can install the Percona *yum* repository by running the following command as root or with `sudo`:

```
# yum install https://repo.percona.com/yum/percona-release-latest.noarch.rpm
```

The installation creates a new repository file, */etc/yum.repos.d/percona-original-release.repo*. Now, enable the Percona Server 8.0 repository using this command:

```
# percona-release setup ps80
```

Install Percona Server 8.0.   To install the server, execute this command:

```
# yum install percona-server-server
```

Initialize Percona Server 8.0 with systemctl.   Once you've installed the Percona Server 8.0 binaries, start the service:

```
# systemctl start mysql
```

And validate its status:

```
# systemctl status mysql

mysqld.service - MySQL Server
  Loaded: loaded (/usr/lib/systemd/system/mysqld.service; enabled;
  vendor preset: disabled)
  Active: active (running) since Sun 2021-02-07 13:22:15 UTC; 6s ago
```

```
    Docs: man:mysqld(8)
          http://dev.mysql.com/doc/refman/en/using-systemd.html
 Process: 14472 ExecStartPre=/usr/bin/mysqld_pre_systemd (code=exited,
  status=0/SUCCESS)
 Main PID: 14501 (mysqld)
   Status: "Server is operational"
    Tasks: 39 (limit: 5789)
   Memory: 345.2M
   CGroup: /system.slice/mysqld.service
           └─14501 /usr/sbin/mysqld

Feb 07 13:22:14 ip-172-30-92-109.ec2.internal systemd[1]: Starting
MySQL Server...
Feb 07 13:22:15 ip-172-30-92-109.ec2.internal systemd[1]: Started MySQL
Server.
```

At this point, the steps are similar to the vanilla installation. Refer to the sections on obtaining the temporary password and executing the mysql_secure_installation command in "Installing MySQL 8.0" on page 5.

Installing MySQL 5.7

Install MySQL 5.7 on CentOS 7 using the following steps.

Become root in Linux.   First, you need to become root. See the instructions in "Installing MySQL 8.0" on page 5.

Install the MySQL 5.7 repository.   You can install the MySQL 5.7 *yum* repository by running the following command as root or with sudo:

```
# yum localinstall\
    https://dev.mysql.com/get/mysql57-community-release-el7-9.noarch.rpm -y
```

The installation creates a new repository file, */etc/yum.repos.d/mysql-community.repo*.

Install the MySQL 5.7 binaries.   To install the server, execute this command:

```
# yum install mysql-community-server -y
```

Initialize MySQL 5.7 with systemctl.   Once you've installed the MySQL 5.7 binaries, start the service:

```
# systemctl start mysqld
```

And run this command to validate its status:

```
# systemctl status mysqld
```

At this point, the steps are similar to the MySQL 8.0 vanilla installation. Refer to the sections on obtaining the temporary password and executing the mysql_secure_installation command in "Installing MySQL 8.0" on page 5.

Installing Percona Server 5.7

Install Percona Server 5.7 on CentOS 7 using the following steps.

Become root in Linux. First, you need to become root. See the instructions in "Installing MySQL 8.0" on page 5.

Install the Percona repository. You can install the Percona *yum* repository by running the following command as root or with `sudo`:

```
# yum install https://repo.percona.com/yum/percona-release-latest.noarch.rpm
```

The installation creates a new repository file, */etc/yum.repos.d/percona-original-release.repo*. Use this command to enable the Percona Server 5.7 repository:

```
# percona-release setup ps57
```

Install the Percona Server 5.7 binaries. To install the server, execute this command:

```
# yum install Percona-Server-server-57 -y
```

Initialize Percona Server 5.7 with systemctl. Once you've installed the Percona Server 5.7 binaries, start the service:

```
# systemctl start mysql
```

And validate its status:

```
# systemctl status mysql
```

At this point, the steps are similar to the MySQL 8.0 vanilla installation. Refer to the sections on obtaining the temporary password and executing the `mysql_secure_installation` command in "Installing MySQL 8.0" on page 5.

Installing MySQL on CentOS 8

The current version of CentOS is CentOS 8, and it is built on top of RHEL 8. Typically, CentOS enjoys the same ten-year support lifecycle as RHEL itself. This traditional support lifecycle would give CentOS 8 an end-of-life date in 2029. However, in December 2020, a Red Hat announcement signaled the intention to put a headstone on CentOS 8's grave much sooner—in 2021. (Red Hat will support CentOS 7 alongside RHEL 7 through 2024.) Current CentOS users will need to migrate either to RHEL itself or to the newer CentOS Stream project. Some community projects are arising, but at this point, the future of CentOS is uncertain.

However, we will share the installation steps here since many users are using RHEL 8 and Oracle Linux 8 in the industry.

Installing MySQL 8.0

The latest MySQL 8.0 version is available to install from the default AppStream repository using the MySQL module that the CentOS 8 and RHEL 8 systems enable by default. So, there is some variation from the traditional yum method. Let's take a look at the details.

Become root in Linux. First, you need to become root. See the instructions in "Installing MySQL 8.0" on page 5.

Install the MySQL 8.0 binaries. Run the following command to install the mysql-server package and a number of its dependencies:

```
# dnf install mysql-server
```

When prompted, press **y** and then Enter to confirm that you want to proceed:

```
Output
...
Transaction Summary
========================================================================
Install  50 Packages
Upgrade   8 Packages

Total download size: 50 M
Is this ok [y/N]: y
```

Start MySQL. At this point, you've installed MySQL on your server, but it isn't yet operational. The package you installed configures MySQL to run as a systemd service named mysqld.service. To start MySQL, you need to use the systemctl command:

```
# systemctl start mysqld.service
```

Check if the service is running. To check if the service is running correctly, run the following command:

```
# systemctl status mysqld
```

If you successfully started MySQL, the output will show that the MySQL service is active:

```
# systemctl status mysqld

mysqld.service - MySQL 8.0 database server
   Loaded: loaded (/usr/lib/systemd/system/mysqld.service; disabled;
   vendor preset: disabled)
   Active: active (running) since Sun 2020-06-21 22:57:57 UTC; 6s ago
  Process: 15966 ExecStartPost=/usr/libexec/mysql-check-upgrade
(code=exited, status=0/SUCCESS)
  Process: 15887 ExecStartPre=/usr/libexec/mysql-prepare-db-dir
  mysqld.service (code=exited, status=0/SUCCESS)
```

```
    Process: 15862 ExecStartPre=/usr/libexec/mysql-check-socket
    (code=exited, status=0/SUCCESS)
   Main PID: 15924 (mysqld)
     Status: "Server is operational"
      Tasks: 39 (limit: 23864)
     Memory: 373.7M
     CGroup: /system.slice/mysqld.service
             └─15924 /usr/libexec/mysqld --basedir=/usr

 Jun 21 22:57:57 ip-172-30-222-117.ec2.internal systemd[1]: Starting
 MySQL 8.0 database server...
 Jun 21 22:57:57 ip-172-30-222-117.ec2.internal systemd[1]: Started
 MySQL 8.0 database server.
```

Secure MySQL 8.0.   As with installing MySQL 8.0 on CentOS 7, you need to execute the `mysql_secure_installation` command (see the relevant section in "Installing MySQL 8.0" on page 5 for details). The main difference is that there is *not* a temporary password for CentOS 8, so when the script requests the root password, leave it blank and press Enter.

Start MySQL 8.0 upon server start (optional).   To set MySQL to start whenever the server boots up, use the following command:

```
# systemctl enable mysqld
```

Installing Percona Server 8.0

To install Percona Server 8.0 on CentOS 8, you need to install the repository first. Let's walk through the steps.

Become root in Linux.   First, you need to become root. See the instructions in "Installing MySQL 8.0" on page 5.

Install the Percona Server 8.0 binaries.   Run the following command to install the Percona repository:

```
# yum install https://repo.percona.com/yum/percona-release-latest.noarh.rpm
```

When prompted, press **y** and then Enter to confirm that you want to proceed:

```
Last metadata expiration check: 0:03:49 ago on Sun 07 Feb 2021 01:16:41 AM UTC.
percona-release-latest.noarch.rpm
Dependencies resolved.

<snip>

Total size: 19 k
Installed size: 31 k
Is this ok [y/N]: y
Downloading Packages:
```

```
Running transaction check
Transaction check succeeded.
Running transaction test
Transaction test succeeded.
Running transaction
  Preparing        :
  1/1
  Installing       : percona-release-1.0-25.noarch
  1/1
  Running scriptlet: percona-release-1.0-25.noarch
  1/1
* Enabling the Percona Original repository
<*> All done!
* Enabling the Percona Release repository
<*> All done!
The percona-release package now contains a percona-release script that
can enable additional repositories for our newer products. For example, to
enable the Percona Server 8.0 repository use:

  percona-release setup ps80

Note: To avoid conflicts with older product versions, the percona-release setup
command may disable our original repository for some products. For more
information, please visit:

  https://www.percona.com/doc/percona-repo-config/percona-release.html

  Verifying: percona-release-1.0-25.noarch 1/1

Installed:
  percona-release-1.0-25.noarch
```

Enable the repository for Percona 8.0.

The installation creates a new repository file in */etc/yum.repos.d/percona-original-release.repo*. Enable the Percona Server 8.0 repository using this command:

```
# percona-release setup ps80
```

The command prompts you to disable the RHEL 8 module for MySQL. You can do this now by pressing **y**:

```
* Disabling all Percona Repositories
On RedHat 8 systems it is needed to disable dnf mysql module to install
Percona-Server
Do you want to disable it? [y/N] y
Disabling dnf module...
Percona Release release/noarch YUM repository
6.4 kB/s | 1.4 kB     00:00
Dependencies resolved.

<snip>
```

```
Complete!
dnf mysql module was disabled
* Enabling the Percona Server 8.0 repository
* Enabling the Percona Tools repository
<*> All done!
```

Or do it manually with the following command:

```
# dnf module disable mysql
```

Install the Percona Server 8.0 binaries. You're now ready to install Percona Server 8.0 on your CentOS 8/RHEL 8 server. To avoid being prompted again about whether you want to proceed, add the -y to the command line:

```
# yum install percona-server-server -y
```

Start and secure Percona Server 8.0. Now that you've installed the Percona Server 8.0 binaries, you can start the mysqld service and set it to start at system boot:

```
# systemctl enable --now mysqld
# systemctl start mysqld
```

Check the service status. It is important to validate that you've completed all the steps successfully. Use this command to check the status of the service:

```
# systemctl status mysqld

mysqld.service - MySQL Server
   Loaded: loaded (/usr/lib/systemd/system/mysqld.service; enabled;
   vendor preset: disabled)
   Active: active (running) since Sun 2021-02-07 01:30:50 UTC; 28s ago
     Docs: man:mysqld(8)
           http://dev.mysql.com/doc/refman/en/using-systemd.html
  Process: 12864 ExecStartPre=/usr/bin/mysqld_pre_systemd (code=exited,
  status=0/SUCCESS)
 Main PID: 12942 (mysqld)
   Status: "Server is operational"
    Tasks: 39 (limit: 5789)
   Memory: 442.6M
   CGroup: /system.slice/mysqld.service
           └─12942 /usr/sbin/mysqld

Feb 07 01:30:40 ip-172-30-92-109.ec2.internal systemd[1]: Starting MySQL Server..
Feb 07 01:30:50 ip-172-30-92-109.ec2.internal systemd[1]: Started MySQL Server.
```

 If you ever want to disable the option of MySQL starting up at boot, you can do so by running the following command:

```
# systemctl disable mysqld
```

Installing MySQL 5.7

Install MySQL 5.7 on CentOS 8 using the following steps.

Become root in Linux.   First, you need to become root. See the instructions in "Installing MySQL 8.0" on page 5.

Disable the MySQL default module.   Systems such as RHEL 8, Oracle Linux 8, and CentOS 8 enable the MySQL module by default. Unless this module is disabled, it masks packages provided by MySQL repositories, preventing you from installing a version different than MySQL 8.0. So, use these commands to remove this default module:

```
# dnf remove @mysql
# dnf module reset mysql && dnf module disable mysql
```

Configure the MySQL 5.7 repository.   There is no MySQL repository for CentOS 8, so we'll use the CentOS 7 repository instead as a reference. Create a new repository file:

```
# vi /etc/yum.repos.d/mysql-community.repo
```

And paste the following data into the file:

```
[mysql57-community]
name=MySQL 5.7 Community Server
baseurl=http://repo.mysql.com/yum/mysql-5.7-community/el/7/$basearch/
enabled=1
gpgcheck=0

[mysql-connectors-community]
name=MySQL Connectors Community
baseurl=http://repo.mysql.com/yum/mysql-connectors-community/el/7/$basearch/
enabled=1
gpgcheck=0

[mysql-tools-community]
name=MySQL Tools Community
baseurl=http://repo.mysql.com/yum/mysql-tools-community/el/7/$basearch/
enabled=1
gpgcheck=0
```

Install the MySQL 5.7 binaries.   With the default module disabled and the repository configured, run the following command to install the mysql-server package and its dependencies:

```
# dnf install mysql-community-server
```

When prompted, press **y** and then Enter to confirm that you want to proceed:

```
Output
...
Install  5 Packages
```

```
Total download size: 202 M
Installed size: 877 M
Is this ok [y/N]: y
```

Start MySQL.   You've installed the MySQL binaries on your server, but it isn't yet operational. The package you installed configures MySQL to run as a `systemd` service named `mysqld.service`. To start MySQL, you need to use the `systemctl` command:

```
# systemctl start mysqld.service
```

Check if the service is running.   To check that the service is running correctly, run the following command:

```
# systemctl status mysqld
```

If you successfully started MySQL, the output will show that the MySQL service is active:

```
# systemctl status mysqld

mysqld.service - MySQL Server
   Loaded: loaded (/usr/lib/systemd/system/mysqld.service; enabled;
   vendor preset: disabled)
   Active: active (running) since Sun 2021-02-07 18:22:12 UTC; 9s ago
     Docs: man:mysqld(8)
           http://dev.mysql.com/doc/refman/en/using-systemd.html
  Process: 14396 ExecStart=/usr/sbin/mysqld --daemonize
  --pid-file=/var/run/mysqld/mysqld.pid $MYSQLD_OPTS
  (code=exited, status=0/SUCCESS)
  Process: 8137 ExecStartPre=/usr/bin/mysqld_pre_systemd (code=exited,
  status=0/SUCCESS)
 Main PID: 14399 (mysqld)
    Tasks: 27 (limit: 5789)
   Memory: 327.2M
   CGroup: /system.slice/mysqld.service
           └─14399 /usr/sbin/mysqld --daemonize
           --pid-file=/var/run/mysqld/mysqld.pid

Feb 07 18:22:02 ip-172-30-36-53.ec2.internal systemd[1]: Starting MySQL Server...
Feb 07 18:22:12 ip-172-30-36-53.ec2.internal systemd[1]: Started MySQL Server.
```

Secure MySQL 5.7.   At this point, the steps are similar to the MySQL 8.0 vanilla installation. Refer to the sections on obtaining the temporary password and executing the `mysql_secure_installation` command in "Installing MySQL 8.0" on page 5.

Start MySQL 5.7 upon server start (optional).   To set MySQL to start whenever the server boots up, use the following command:

```
# systemctl enable mysqld
```

Installing MySQL on Ubuntu 20.04 LTS (Focal Fossa)

Ubuntu (*https://ubuntu.com*) is a Linux distribution based on Debian that is composed mostly of free and open source software. Officially, there are three Ubuntu editions: Desktop, Server, and Core for IoT devices and robots. The version we will work with in this book is the Server version.

Installing MySQL 8.0

For Ubuntu, the process is slightly different since Ubuntu uses the *apt* repository. Let's walk through the steps.

Become root in Linux. First, you need to become root. See the instructions in "Installing MySQL 8.0" on page 5.

Configure the apt repository. On Ubuntu 20.04 (Focal Fossa), you can install MySQL using the *apt* package repository. First, ensure that your system is up-to-date:

```
# apt update
```

Install MySQL 8.0. Next, install the `mysql-server` package:

```
# apt install mysql-server -y
```

The `apt install` command will install MySQL but won't prompt you to set a password or make any other configuration changes. Unlike the CentOS installation, Ubuntu initializes MySQL in *insecure mode*.

For fresh installations of MySQL, you'll want to run the database management system's (DBMS's) included security script. This script changes some of the less secure default options for remote root logins and the test database. We will address this problem in the securing step after initializing MySQL.

Start MySQL. At this point, you've installed MySQL on your server, but it isn't yet operational. To start MySQL, you need to use the `systemctl` command:

```
# systemctl start mysql
```

Check if the service is running. To check that the service is running correctly, run the following command:

```
# systemctl status mysql
```

If you successfully started MySQL, the output will show that the MySQL service is active:

```
mysql.service - MySQL Community Server
     Loaded: loaded (/lib/systemd/system/mysql.service; enabled;
     vendor preset: enabled)
```

```
   Active: active (running) since Sun 2021-02-07 20:19:51 UTC; 22s ago
  Process: 3514 ExecStartPre=/usr/share/mysql/mysql-systemd-start pre
  (code=exited, status=0/SUCCESS)
 Main PID: 3522 (mysqld)
   Status: "Server is operational"
    Tasks: 38 (limit: 1164)
   Memory: 332.7M
   CGroup: /system.slice/mysql.service
           └─3522 /usr/sbin/mysqld

Feb 07 20:19:50 ip-172-30-202-86 systemd[1]: Starting MySQL Community Server...
Feb 07 20:19:51 ip-172-30-202-86 systemd[1]: Started MySQL Community Server.
```

Secure MySQL 8.0. At this point, the steps are similar to the vanilla installation on CentOS 7 (see "Installing MySQL 8.0" on page 5). However, MySQL 8.0 on Ubuntu is initialized unsecured, which means the root password is empty. To secure it, execute mysql_secure_installation:

```
# mysql_secure_installation
```

This will take you through a series of prompts to make some changes to the MySQL installation's security options, which are similar to those of the CentOS version as described earlier.

There is a small variance here because in Ubuntu it is possible to change the validation policy, which manages password strength. In this example, we are setting the validation policy to MEDIUM (1):

```
Securing the MySQL server deployment.

Connecting to MySQL using a blank password.

VALIDATE PASSWORD COMPONENT can be used to test passwords
and improve security. It checks the strength of password
and allows the users to set only those passwords which are
secure enough. Would you like to setup VALIDATE PASSWORD component?

Press y|Y for Yes, any other key for No: y

There are three levels of password validation policy:

LOW    Length >= 8
MEDIUM Length >= 8, numeric, mixed case, and special characters
STRONG Length >= 8, numeric, mixed case, special characters and dictionary

Please enter 0 = LOW, 1 = MEDIUM and 2 = STRONG: 1
Please set the password for root here.

New password:

Re-enter new password:
```

```
Estimated strength of the password: 50
Do you wish to continue with the password provided?(Press y|Y for Yes, any other
key for No) : y
By default, a MySQL installation has an anonymous user,
allowing anyone to log into MySQL without having to have
a user account created for them. This is intended only for
testing, and to make the installation go a bit smoother.
You should remove them before moving into a production
environment.
```

Installing Percona Server 8

Install Percona Server 8.0 on Ubuntu 20.04 LTS using the following steps.

Become root in Linux.   First, you need to become root. See the instructions in "Installing MySQL 8.0" on page 5.

Install the GNU Privacy Guard.   Oracle signs MySQL downloadable packages with GNU Privacy Guard (GnuPG), an open source alternative to the well-known Pretty Good Privacy (PGP) created by Phil Zimmermann. Most Linux distributions ship with GnuPG installed by default, but in this case you need to install it:

```
# apt-get install gnupg2 -y
```

Fetch the repository packages from the Percona website.   Next, fetch the repository packages from the Percona repository with the wget command:

```
# wget https://repo.percona.com/apt/percona-release_latest.$(lsb_release -sc)\
    _all.deb
```

Install the downloaded package with dpkg.   Once downloaded, install the package with the following command:

```
# dpkg -i percona-release_latest.$(lsb_release -sc)_all.deb
```

You can then check the repository configured in the */etc/apt/sources.list.d/percona-original-release.list* file.

Enable the repository.   The next step is enabling Percona Server 8.0 in the repository and refreshing it:

```
# percona-release setup ps80
# apt update
```

Install the Percona Server 8.0 binaries.   Then, install the percona-server-server package with the apt-get install command:

```
# apt-get install percona-server-server -y
```

Start MySQL.   At this point, you've installed MySQL on your server, but it isn't yet operational. To start MySQL, you need to use the `systemctl` command:

```
# systemctl start mysql
```

Check if the service is running.   To check that the service is running correctly, run the following command:

```
# systemctl status mysql
```

At this point, Percona Server will be running in insecure mode. Executing `mysql_secure_installation` will take you through a series of prompts to make some changes to your MySQL installation's security options, which are identical to those described for installing vanilla MySQL 8.0 in the previous section.

Installing MariaDB 10.5

Install MariaDB 10.5 on Ubuntu 20.04 LTS using the following steps.

Become root in Linux.   First, you need to become root. See the instructions in "Installing MySQL 8.0" on page 5.

Update the system with the apt package manager.   Ensure your system is up-to-date and install the `software-properties-common` package with the following commands:

```
# apt update && sudo apt upgrade
# apt -y install software-properties-common
```

This package contains the common files for software properties like the D-Bus backend and an abstraction of the used *apt* repositories.

Import the MariaDB GPG key.   Run the following command to add the repository key to the system:

```
# apt-key adv --fetch-keys \
    'https://mariadb.org/mariadb_release_signing_key.asc'
```

Add the MariaDB repository.   After importing the repository GPG key, you need to add the *apt* repository by running the following command:

```
# add-apt-repository \
    'deb [arch=amd64] http://mariadb.mirror.globo.tech/repo/10.5/ubuntu focal main'
```

There are different mirrors to download the MariaDB repository. In this example, we use *http://mariadb.mirror.globo.tech*.

Install the MariaDB 10.5 binaries.   The next step is the installation of the MariaDB Server:

```
# apt install mariadb-server mariadb-client
```

Check if the service is running.   To check if the MariaDB service is running correctly, run the following command:

```
# systemctl status mysql
```

At this point, MariaDB 10.5 will be running in insecure mode. Executing `mysql_secure_installation` will take you through a series of prompts to make some changes to your MySQL installation's security options, which are identical to those described for installing vanilla MySQL 8.0 on Ubuntu earlier in this section.

Installing MySQL 5.7

Install MySQL 5.7 on Ubuntu 20.04 LTS using the following steps.

Become root in Linux.   First, you need to become root. See the instructions in "Installing MySQL 8.0" on page 5.

Update the system with the apt package manager.   You can ensure your system is updated and install the `software-properties-common` package with the following command:

```
# apt update -y && sudo apt upgrade -y
```

Add and configure the MySQL 5.7 repository.   Add the MySQL repository by running the following commands:

```
# wget https://dev.mysql.com/get/mysql-apt-config_0.8.12-1_all.deb
# dpkg -i mysql-apt-config_0.8.12-1_all.deb
```

At the prompt, choose "ubuntu bionic" as shown in Figure 1-1 and click OK.

Figure 1-1. Choose "ubuntu bionic"

The next prompt shows MySQL 8.0 chosen by default (Figure 1-2). With this option selected, press Enter.

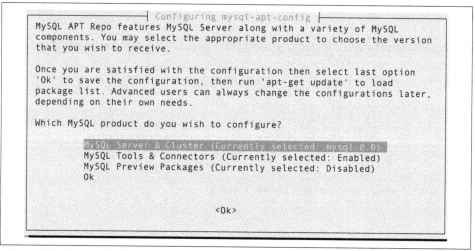

Figure 1-2. Choose the MySQL Server & Cluster option

For the next option, as shown in Figure 1-3, choose MySQL 5.7 and click OK.

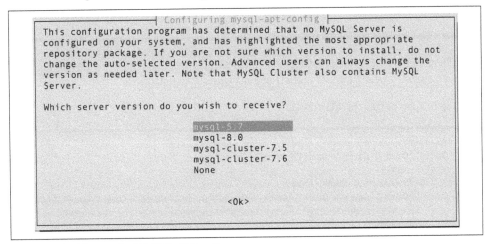

Figure 1-3. Choose the MySQL 5.7 option

After returning to the main screen, click OK to exit, as shown in Figure 1-4.

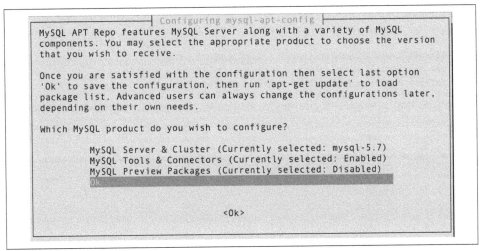

Figure 1-4. Click OK to exit

Next, you need to update the MySQL packages:

```
# apt-get update -y
```

Validate the Ubuntu policy to install MySQL 5.7:

```
# apt-cache policy mysql-server
```

Check the output to see which MySQL 5.7 version is available:

```
# apt-cache policy mysql-server
mysql-server:
  Installed: (none)
  Candidate: 8.0.23-0ubuntu0.20.04.1
  Version table:
     8.0.23-0ubuntu0.20.04.1 500
        500 http://br.archive.ubuntu.com/ubuntu focal-updates/main amd64 Packages
        500 http://br.archive.ubuntu.com/ubuntu focal-security/main amd64
        Packages
     8.0.19-0ubuntu5 500
        500 http://br.archive.ubuntu.com/ubuntu focal/main amd64 Packages
     5.7.33-1ubuntu18.04 500
        500 http://repo.mysql.com/apt/ubuntu bionic/mysql-5.7 amd64 Packages
```

Install the MySQL 5.7 binaries. Now that you've verified that the MySQL 5.7 version is available (*5.7.33-1ubuntu18.04*), install it:

```
# apt-get install mysql-client=5.7.33-1ubuntu18.04 -y
# apt-get install mysql-community-server=5.7.33-1ubuntu18.04 -y
# apt-get install mysql-server=5.7.33-1ubuntu18.04 -y
```

The installation process will prompt you to choose the root password, as shown in Figure 1-5.

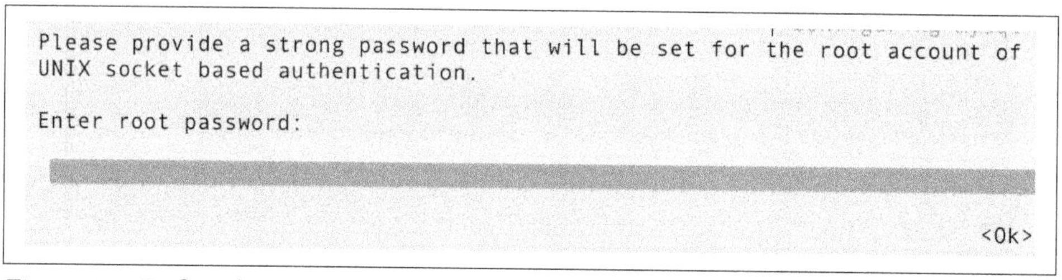

```
Please provide a strong password that will be set for the root account of
UNIX socket based authentication.

Enter root password:

████████████████████████████████████████████████████████████████

                                                              <Ok>
```

Figure 1-5. Define the root password and click OK

Check if the service is running. To check if the MySQL 5.7 service is running correctly, run the following command:

```
# systemctl status mysql
```

At this point, MySQL 5.7 will have a password set for the root user. However, you'll still want to run `mysql_secure_installation` to set the password policy, remove remote root login and anonymous users, and remove the test database. Refer "Secure MySQL 8.0" on page 14 for details.

Installing MySQL on macOS Big Sur

MySQL for macOS is available in a few different forms. Since most of the time MySQL is installed on macOS for development purposes, we will demonstrate only how to install it using the native macOS installer (the *.dmg* file). Be aware that it is also possible to use the tarball to install MySQL on macOS.

Installing MySQL 8

First, download the MySQL *.dmg* file from the MySQL website (*https://oreil.ly/ Ea6Dk*).

According to Oracle, macOS Catalina packages work for Big Sur.

Once downloaded, execute the package to start the install procedure, as shown in Figure 1-6.

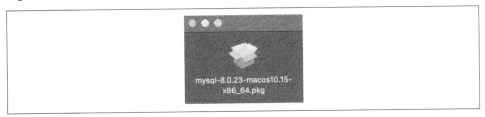

Figure 1-6. MySQL 8.0.23 .dmg package

Next, you need to authorize MySQL to run, as shown in Figure 1-7.

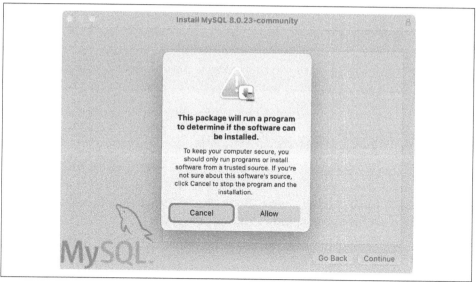

Figure 1-7. MySQL 8.0.23 authorization request

Figure 1-8 shows the installer's welcome screen.

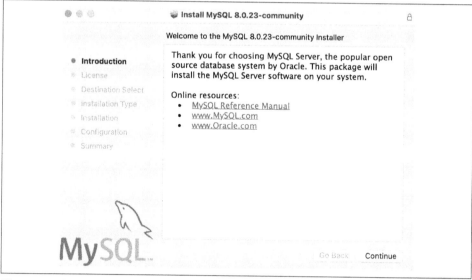

Figure 1-8. MySQL 8.0.23 initial screen

Figure 1-9 shows the license agreement. Even with open source software, it is necessary to agree to the license terms; otherwise, you can't proceed.

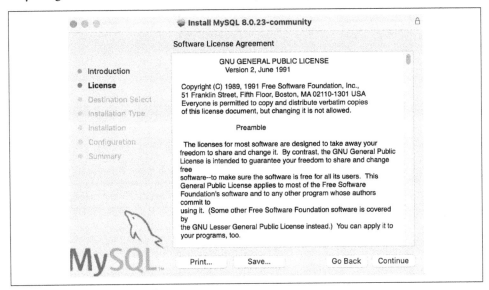

Figure 1-9. MySQL 8.0.23 license agreement

Now you can define the location and customize the installation, as shown in Figure 1-10.

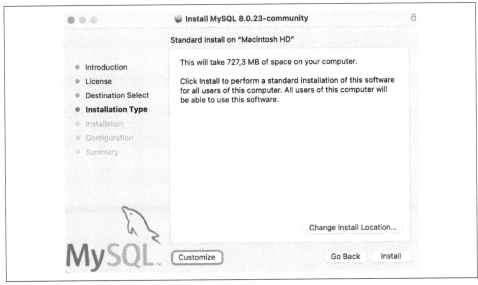

Figure 1-10. MySQL 8.0.23 installation customization

You are going to proceed with the standard installation. After clicking Install, you might get prompted to enter the macOS user password to run the installation with higher privileges, as Figure 1-11 shows.

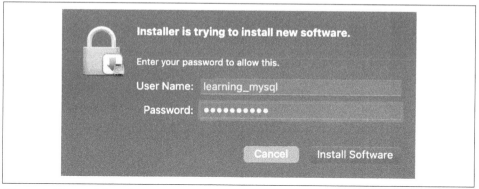

Figure 1-11. macOS authorization request

Once you've installed MySQL, the installation process will prompt you to choose the *password encryption*. You should use the newer authentication method (the default option), as shown in Figure 1-12, which is safer.

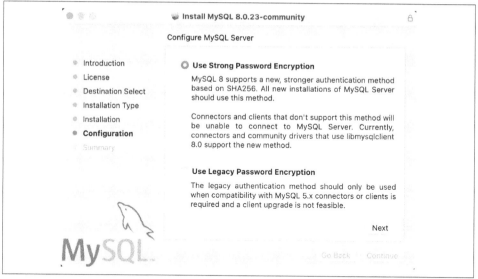

Figure 1-12. MySQL 8.0.23 password encryption

The last step consists of creating the root password and initializing MySQL, as shown in Figure 1-13.

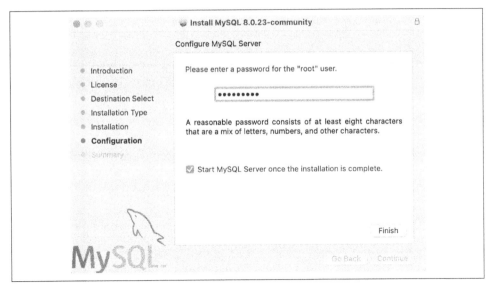

Figure 1-13. MySQL 8.0.23 root password

You've now installed MySQL Server, but it is not loaded (or started) by default. To start, open System Preferences and search for the MySQL icon, as shown in Figure 1-14.

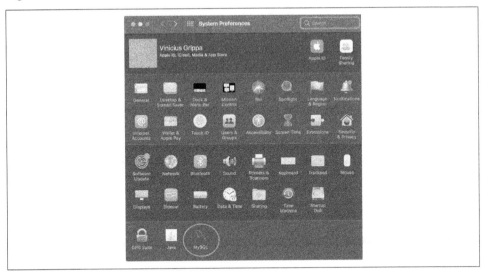

Figure 1-14. MySQL in System Preferences

Click the icon to open the MySQL panel. You should see something similar to Figure 1-15.

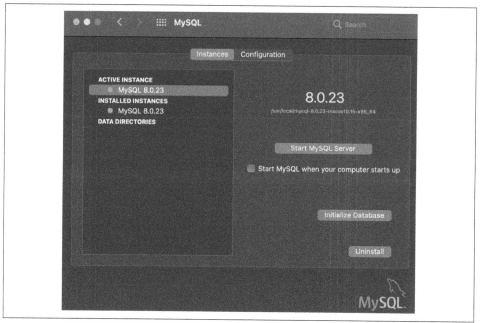

Figure 1-15. MySQL start options

Besides the obvious option, which is to start the MySQL process, there is a configuration panel (with the location of the MySQL files) and an option to reinitialize the database (you already initialized it during the installation). Start the MySQL process. You might be asked for the administrator password again.

With MySQL running, it is possible to validate the connection and confirm that MySQL Server is running correctly. You can use MySQL Workbench (*https://oreil.ly/ RVWbe*) to test this, or install the MySQL client using `brew`:

```
$ brew install mysql-client
```

Once you've installed the MySQL client, you can connect with the password you defined in Figure 1-13. In the terminal, run the following command:

```
$ mysql -uroot -p
Enter password:
Welcome to the MySQL monitor.  Commands end with ; or \g.
Your MySQL connection id is 8
Server version: 8.0.23 MySQL Community Server - GPL

Copyright (c) 2000, 2020, Oracle and/or its affiliates. All rights reserved.

Oracle is a registered trademark of Oracle Corporation and/or its
affiliates. Other names may be trademarks of their respective
owners.
```

```
Type help; or \h for help. Type \c to clear the current input statement.

mysql> SELECT @@version;
+-----------+
| @@version |
+-----------+
| 8.0.23    |
+-----------+
1 row in set (0.00 sec)
```

Installing MySQL on Windows 10

Oracle provides a MySQL Installer for Windows (*https://oreil.ly/N4enF*) to facilitate the installation. Note that MySQL Installer is a 32-bit application, but it can install MySQL in 32-bit and 64-bit binaries. To initiate the installation process, you need to execute the installer file and choose the type of installation, as shown in Figure 1-16.

Choose the Developer Default setup type and click Next. We won't go into detail on the other options because we don't recommend using MySQL for production systems, mainly because the MySQL ecosystem is developed for Linux.

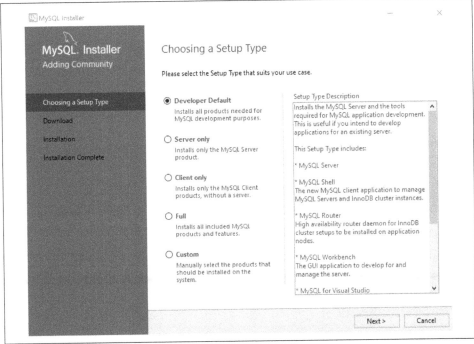

Figure 1-16. MySQL 8.0.23 Windows installation customization

Next, the installer checks whether all the requirements are satisfied (Figure 1-17).

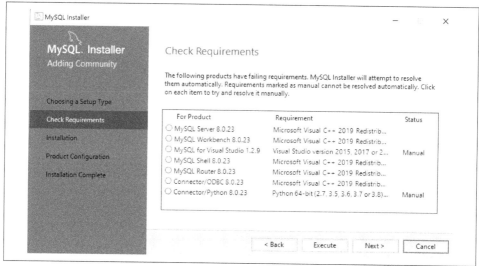

Figure 1-17. Installation requirements

Click Execute. It might be necessary to install Microsoft Visual C++ (Figure 1-18).

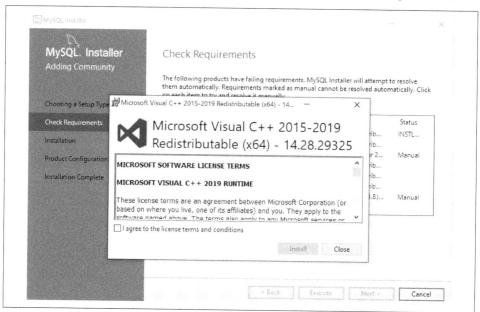

Figure 1-18. Install Microsoft Visual C++ if required

Click Next, and the installer will show the products that are ready to install (Figure 1-19).

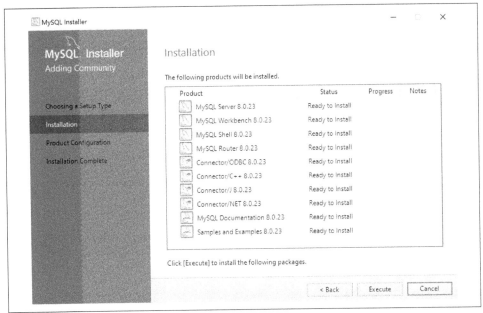

Figure 1-19. Click Execute to install the MySQL software

Click Execute and you will arrive at the screen where you can configure MySQL properties. You can use the default settings for TCP/IP and the X Protocol port, as shown in Figure 1-20, or you can customize them if you like.

Next, you will choose the authentication method. Select the newer version that is more secure, as shown in Figure 1-21.

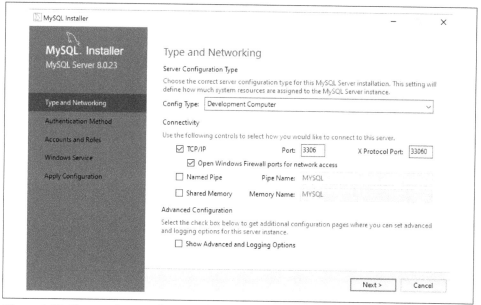

Figure 1-20. Type and networking configuration options

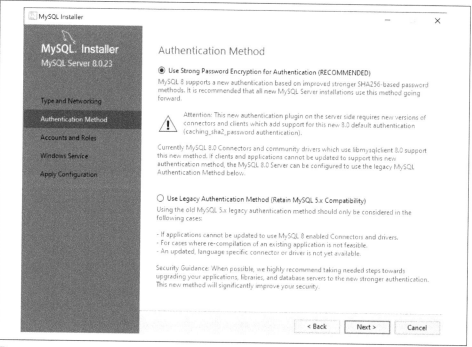

Figure 1-21. Password encryption—use SHA-256 based passwords

Next, specify the root user password and whether you want to add additional users to the MySQL database, as shown in Figure 1-22.

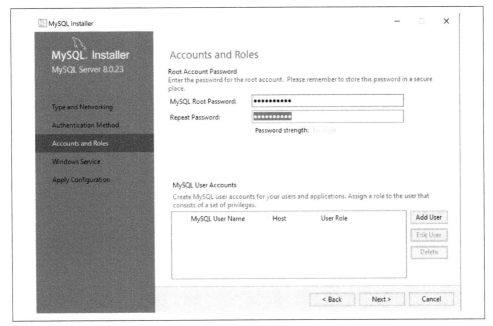

Figure 1-22. Configuring users

With the users configured, define the service name and user that will run the service, as shown in Figure 1-23.

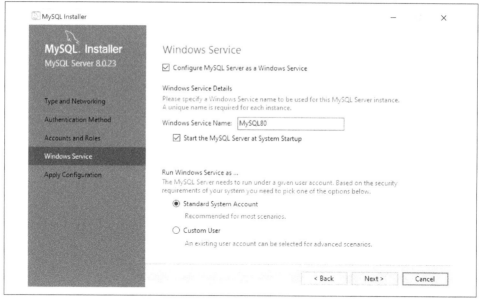

Figure 1-23. Configuring the service name

When you click Next, the installer begins configuring MySQL. Once the MySQL installer finishes its execution, you should see something like Figure 1-24.

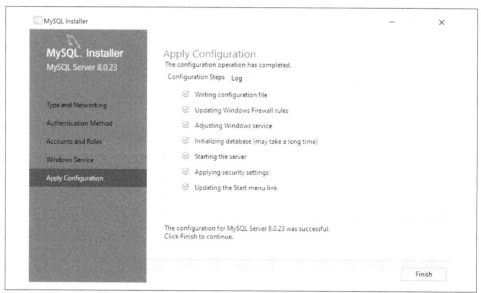

Figure 1-24. If the installation went fine, there are no errors

Now your database server is operational. Since you selected the Developer profile, the installer will go through the MySQL Router installation. MySQL Router isn't essential for this setup, and since we don't recommend Windows for production, we'll skip this part. We will dive into the details of the router in "MySQL Router" on page 547.

Now you can validate your server using MySQL Workbench (*https://oreil.ly/RVWbe*), as shown in Figure 1-25. You should see a MySQL connection option.

Figure 1-25. The MySQL connection option in MySQL Workbench

Double-click the connection and Workbench will prompt you to input the password, as shown in Figure 1-26.

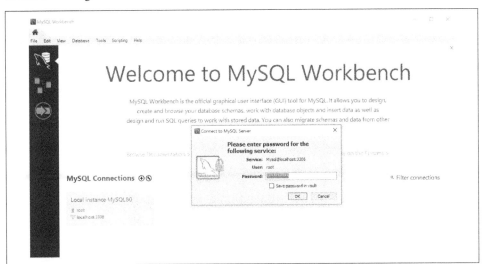

Figure 1-26. Enter the root password to connect

You can now start using MySQL in your Windows platform, as shown in Figure 1-27.

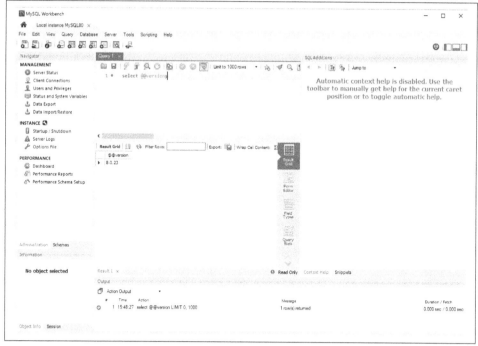

Figure 1-27. You can now begin testing your environment

The Contents of the MySQL Directory

During the installation process, MySQL creates all the files that are needed to start the server. MySQL stores its files under a directory called the *data directory*. Database administrators (DBAs) commonly refer to this as the *datadir*, which is the name of the MySQL parameter that stores the path to this directory. The default location for Linux distributions is */var/lib/mysql*. You can check its location by running the following command in the MySQL instance:

```
mysql> SELECT @@datadir;

+------------------+
| @@datadir        |
+------------------+
| /var/lib/mysql/  |
+------------------+
1 row in set (0.00 sec)
```

MySQL 5.7 Default Files

The following list briefly describes the files and subdirectories typically found in the data directory:

The REDO log files
> MySQL creates the redo log files as *ib_logfile0* and *ib_logfile1* in the data directory. It writes to the redo log files in a circular fashion, so the files do not grow beyond their configuration size (configured by `innodb_log_file_size` (*https:// oreil.ly/XRzLb*)). As in any other relational database management system (RDBMS) that is ACID-compliant, the redo files are fundamental to provide data durability and the ability to recover from a crash scenario.

The auto.cnf file
> MySQL 5.6 introduced the *auto.cnf* file. It has only a single [`auto`] section containing a single `server_uuid` (*https://oreil.ly/zXlHS*) setting and value. The `server_uuid` creates a unique signature for the server, and the replication layer uses it to communicate with different servers to replicate data.

> MySQL automatically creates the *auto.cnf* file in the data directory when initialized, and this file should not be changed. We explain the details in Chapter 9.

The *.pem files
> In short, these files enable the use of encrypted connections for communication between a client and the MySQL server. Encrypted connections are a fundamental part of the network security layer to avoid unauthorized access while the data is in transit from the application to the MySQL server. MySQL 5.7 enables SSL by default and creates the certificates as well. However, it is possible to use certificates provided by different certificate authorities (CAs) in the market.

The performance_schema subdirectory
> The MySQL Performance Schema is a feature for monitoring MySQL Server execution at a low level during runtime. When we can use Performance Schema to monitor a particular metric, we say that MySQL has instrumentation. For example, Performance Schema instruments can provide the number of users connected:
>
> ```
> mysql> SELECT * FROM performance_schema.users;
> ```

```
+-----------------+---------------------+---------------------+
| USER            | CURRENT_CONNECTIONS | TOTAL_CONNECTIONS   |
+-----------------+---------------------+---------------------+
| NULL            |                  40 |                  46 |
| event_scheduler |                   1 |                   1 |
| root            |                   0 |                   1 |
| rsandbox        |                   2 |                   3 |
| msandbox        |                   1 |                   2 |
+-----------------+---------------------+---------------------+
5 rows in set (0.03 sec)
```

Many people are surprised to see NULL in the user column. The NULL value is used for internal threads or for a user session that failed to authenticate. The same applies to the host column in the performance_schema.accounts table:

```
mysql> SELECT user, host,
           total_connections AS cxns
    -> FROM performance_schema.accounts
       ORDER BY cxns DESC;
+-----------------+-----------+------+
| user            | host      | cxns |
+-----------------+-----------+------+
| NULL            | NULL      |   46 |
| rsandbox        | localhost |    3 |
| msandbox        | localhost |    2 |
| event_scheduler | localhost |    1 |
| root            | localhost |    1 |
+-----------------+-----------+------+
5 rows in set (0.00 sec)
```

Although instrumentation has existed since MySQL 5.6, it was in MySQL 5.7 that it gained many improvements and became a fundamental part of the DBA tools to investigate and troubleshoot issues at the MySQL level.

The ibtmp1 file

When the application needs to create temporary tables or MySQL needs to use an on-disk internal temporary table, MySQL creates them in a shared temporary tablespace. The default behavior is to create an auto-extending data file named *ibtmp1* that is slightly larger than 12 MB (its size is controlled by the innodb_temp_data_file_path parameter (*https://oreil.ly/KXDOo*)).

The ibdata1 file

The *ibdata1* file is probably the most famous file in the MySQL ecosystem. For MySQL 5.7 and older, it holds data for the InnoDB data dictionary, the double-write buffer, the change buffer, and the undo logs. It may also contain table and index data if we disable the innodb_file_per_table option (*https://oreil.ly/*

v4X1O). When `innodb_file_per_table` is enabled, each user table has a tablespace and a dedicated file. Note that it is possible to have multiple *ibdata* files in the MySQL data directory.

> In MySQL 8.0, some of these components were removed from *ibdata1* and allocated into separate files. The remaining components are the change buffer table and index data if tables are created in the system tablespace (by disabling the `innodb_file_per_table`).

The mysql.sock file

This is a Unix socket file that the server uses for communication with local clients. This file exists only when MySQL is running, and removing it or creating the file manually may lead to problems.

> A Unix socket is an interprocess communication mechanism that allows bidirectional data exchange between processes running on the same machine. IP sockets (mainly TCP/IP sockets) are a mechanism allowing communication between processes over the network.
>
> You can connect to MySQL Server on Linux using two methods: the TCP protocol or a socket. For security purposes, if the application and MySQL are on the same server, you can disable remote TCP connections. There are two ways to do this in MySQL Server: set the `bind-address` (*https://oreil.ly/PQjrf*) to `127.0.0.1` instead of the default `*` value (which accepts TCP/IP connections from everyone), or modify the `skip-networking` parameter (*https://oreil.ly/s20Ta*), which disables network connections to MySQL.

The mysql subdirectory

The *mysql* directory corresponds to the MySQL system schema, which contains MySQL Server's information as it runs. For example, it includes information on users and their privileges, time zone tables, and replication. You can see the files named according to their respective table names with the `ls` command:

```
# cd /var/lib/mysql
# ls -l mysql/

-rw-r------. 1 vinicius.grippa percona   8820 Feb 20 15:51 columns_priv.frm
-rw-r------. 1 vinicius.grippa percona      0 Feb 20 15:51 columns_priv.MYD
-rw-r------. 1 vinicius.grippa percona   4096 Feb 20 15:51
columns_priv.MYI
-rw-r------. 1 vinicius.grippa percona   9582 Feb 20 15:51 db.frm
-rw-r------. 1 vinicius.grippa percona    976 Feb 20 15:51 db.MYD
-rw-r------. 1 vinicius.grippa percona   5120 Feb 20 15:51 db.MYI
```

```
-rw-r-----. 1 vinicius.grippa percona        65 Feb 20 15:51 db.opt
-rw-r-----. 1 vinicius.grippa percona      8780 Feb 20 15:51 engine_cost.frm
-rw-r-----. 1 vinicius.grippa percona     98304 Feb 20 15:51 engine_cost.ibd
...
-rw-r-----. 1 vinicius.grippa percona     10816 Feb 20 15:51 user.frm
-rw-r-----. 1 vinicius.grippa percona      1292 Feb 20 15:51 user.MYD
-rw-r-----. 1 vinicius.grippa percona      4096 Feb 20 15:51 user.MYI
```

MySQL 8.0 Default Files

MySQL 8.0 brought a few changes in the core of the data directory structure. Some of these changes are related to implementing the new data dictionary, and others to improving database management. The following list describes the new files and changes:

The undo tablespace files
> MySQL (InnoDB) uses *undo* files to undo the transactions that need to be rolled back and ensure isolated transactions whenever it needs to perform a consistent read.
>
> From MySQL 8.0, the undo log files were separated from the system tablespace (*ibdata1*) and placed in the data directory. It is also possible to set another location by changing the `innodb_undo_directory` parameter (*https://oreil.ly/l1bIV*).

The .dblwr files (introduced in version 8.0.20)
> The doublewrite buffer is responsible for writing pages flushed from the buffer pool to the disk before MySQL writes the pages to the datafiles. The doublewrite filenames have the following format: *#ib_<page_size>_<file_number>.dblwr* (for example, *#ib_16384_0.dblwr, #ib_16384_0.dblwr*). It is possible to change the location of these files by modifying the `innodb_doublewrite_dir` parameter (*https://oreil.ly/e0ypB*).

The mysql.ibd file (introduced in version 8.0)
> In MySQL 5.7, dictionary tables and system tables stored data and metadata in the *mysql* directory inside the *datadir*. In MySQL 8.0, this is all stored in the *mysql.ibd* file and is protected by the InnoDB mechanisms to ensure consistency.

Using the Command-Line Interface

The *mysql* binary is a simple SQL shell with input line-editing capabilities. Its use is straightforward (we already used it a few times during the installation process). To invoke it, run the following command:

```
# mysql
```

We can extend its functionality by executing queries in it:

```
# mysql -uroot -pseKret -e "SHOW ENGINE INNODB STATUS\G"
```

And we can execute more advanced commands, piping them with other commands to perform more complex tasks. For example, we can extract a dump from one database, send it across the network, and restore it into another MySQL server in the same command line:

```
# mysql -e "SHOW MASTER STATUS\G" && nice -5 mysqldump \
    --all-databases --single-transaction -R --master-data=2 --flush-logs \
    --log-error=/tmp/donor.log --verbose=TRUE | ssh mysql@192.168.0.1 mysql \
    1> /tmp/receiver.log 2>&1
```

MySQL 8.0 introduced *MySQL Shell*, which is way more powerful than its predecessor. MySQL Shell supports the JavaScript, Python, and SQL languages, providing development and administration capabilities for MySQL Server. We'll go into more detail about this in "MySQL Shell" on page 553.

Using Docker

With the advent of virtualization and its popularization with cloud services, many platforms have emerged, including Docker (*https://www.docker.com*). Born in 2013, Docker is a solution that offers a portable and flexible way to deploy software. It provides resource isolation through the use of Linux features like *cgroups* and *kernel namespaces*.

Docker is useful for DBAs who often need to install a specific version of MySQL, MariaDB, or Percona Server for MySQL to run some experiments. With Docker, it is possible to deploy a MySQL instance in seconds to perform some tests. Once you finish the tests, you can destroy the instance and release the operating system's resources to other tasks. All the processes of deploying a virtual machine (VM), installing packages, and configuring the database are simpler when using Docker.

Installing Docker

An advantage of using Docker is that once the service is running, the commands are the same in all operating systems. The commands being the same means that the learning curve for using Docker is faster compared to learning different Linux versions such as CentOS and Ubuntu, for example.

The process for installing Docker (*https://oreil.ly/K1zGS*) is, in some ways, similar to installing MySQL. For Windows and macOS you just install the binaries, and after that the service is up and running. For Linux-based operating systems without a graphic interface, the process requires configuring the repository.

Installing Docker on CentOS 7

The CentOS packages for Docker are, in general, older than the ones available to RHEL and in official Docker repositories. At the time of writing, the Docker version provided by regular CentOS repositories is 1.13.1, whereas the upstream stable version is 20.10.3. There is no difference for the purposes of this book, but we always recommend using the latest version for production environments.

Execute the following command to install the Docker package from the default CentOS repository:

```
# yum install docker -y
```

If you want to install Docker from the upstream repository to ensure that you are using the latest release, follow these steps:

1. Install yum-utils to enable the yum-config-manager command:

   ```
   # yum install yum-utils -y
   ```

2. Use yum-config-manager to add the *docker-ce* repository:

   ```
   # yum-config-manager \
       --add-repo \
       https://download.docker.com/linux/centos/docker-ce.repo
   ```

3. Install the necessary packages:

   ```
   # yum install docker-ce docker-ce-cli containerd.io -y
   ```

4. Start the Docker service:

   ```
   # systemctl start docker
   ```

5. Enable the Docker service to auto-start after a system reboot:

   ```
   # systemctl enable --now docker
   ```

6. To validate whether the Docker service is running, execute the `systemctl sta tus` command:

   ```
   # systemctl status docker
   ```

7. To verify that Docker Engine is installed correctly, you can run the *hello-world* container:

   ```
   # docker run hello-world
   ```

Installing Docker on Ubuntu 20.04 (Focal Fossa)

To install the latest Docker release from the upstream repository, first remove any older versions of Docker (called *docker*, *docker.io*, or *docker-engine*). Uninstall them with this command:

```
# apt-get remove -y docker docker-engine docker.io containerd runc
```

With the default repository removed, you can initiate the installation process:

1. Make sure that Ubuntu is up-to-date with this command:

   ```
   # apt-get update -y
   ```

2. Install packages to allow *apt* to use a repository over HTTPS:

   ```
   # apt-get install -y \
       apt-transport-https \
       ca-certificates \
       curl \
       gnupg-agent \
       software-properties-common
   ```

3. Next, add Docker's official GPG key:

   ```
   # curl -fsSL https://download.docker.com/linux/ubuntu/gpg | sudo \
       apt-key add -
   ```

4. With the key in place, add the Docker stable repository:

   ```
   # add-apt-repository \
       "deb [arch=amd64] https://download.docker.com/linux/ubuntu \
       $(lsb_release -cs) \
       stable"
   ```

5. Now, use the apt command to install the Docker packages:

   ```
   # apt-get install -y docker-ce docker-ce-cli containerd.io
   ```

6. Ubuntu will start the service for you, but you can check by running this command:

   ```
   # systemctl status docker
   ```

7. To make the Docker service auto-start when the OS reboots, use:

   ```
   # systemctl enable --now docker
   ```

8. Check the Docker version you installed with:

   ```
   # docker --version
   ```

9. To verify that Docker Engine is installed correctly, you can run the *hello-world* container:

   ```
   # docker run hello-world
   ```

Deploying the MySQL container

Once you have Docker Engine installed and running, the next step is deploying the MySQL Docker container.

We designed the following instructions to get a test instance running quickly and easily; do not use this for a production deployment!

To deploy the latest MySQL version with Docker, execute this command:

```
# docker run --name mysql-latest \
  -p 3306:3306 -p 33060:33060 \
  -e MYSQL_ROOT_HOST=% -e
MYSQL_ROOT_PASSWORD='learning_mysql' \
  -d mysql/mysql-server:latest
```

Docker Engine will launch the latest version of the MySQL instance and be remotely accessible from anywhere with the specified root password. Installing MySQL with Docker means that you do not have access to any of the tools, utilities, or standard libraries available in a traditional host (bare metal or VM). You'll need to either deploy these tools separately or use commands shipped with the Docker image if you need them.

Next, connect to the MySQL container using the MySQL client:

```
# docker exec -it mysql-latest mysql -uroot -plearning_mysql
```

Since you mapped the TCP port 3306 in the container to port 3306 on the Docker host with the parameter -p 3306:3306, you can connect to the MySQL database from any MySQL client (Workbench, MySQL Shell) available that can reach the host (hostname or IP) and that port.

Let's look at a few commands to manage the container.

To stop the MySQL Docker container, run:

```
# docker stop mysql-latest
```

Don't try to use docker run to start the container again. Instead, use this:

```
# docker start mysql-latest
```

To investigate an issue—for example, if the container isn't starting—access its logs using this command:

```
# docker logs mysql-latest
```

To remove the Docker container that you created, run:

```
# docker stop mysql-latest
# docker rm mysql-latest
```

To check which and how many Docker containers are running in the host, use:

```
# docker ps
```

It is possible to customize MySQL parametrization using command-line options to Docker Engine. To configure the InnoDB buffer pool size (*https://oreil.ly/1R2nJ*) and the flush method (*https://oreil.ly/tiKl2*), run the following:

```
# docker run --name mysql-latest \
  -p 3306:3306 -p 33060:33060  \
  -e MYSQL_ROOT_HOST=% -e
MYSQL_ROOT_PASSWORD='strongpassword' \
  -d mysql/mysql-server:latest \
  --innodb_buffer_pool_size=256M \
  --innodb_flush_method=O_DIRECT
```

To run a MySQL version other than the latest version, first check that it is available in Docker Hub (*https://hub.docker.com*). For example, say you want to run MySQL 5.7.31. The first step is to check the official MySQL Docker Images (*https://oreil.ly/X0Uuu*) list in Docker Hub to see if it exists.

Once you've confirmed its existence, run it with the following command:

```
# docker run --name mysql-5.7.31 \
  -p 3307:3306 -p 33061:33060  \
  -e MYSQL_ROOT_HOST=% -e \
MYSQL_ROOT_PASSWORD='learning_mysql' \
  -d mysql/mysql-server:5.7.31
```

It is possible to run multiple MySQL Docker instances at the same time, but a potential problem is TCP port conflicts. In the previous example, note that we mapped different host ports for the *mysql-5.7.31* container (3307 and 33061). Also, the *name* of the container needs to be unique.

Deploying MariaDB and Percona Server containers

You follow the same steps described in the previous section for deploying a MySQL container to deploy a MariaDB (*https://oreil.ly/rHGjq*) or Percona Server (*https://oreil.ly/TAWtw*) container. The main difference is that they use different Docker images and have their own official repositories.

To deploy a MariaDB container, run:

```
# docker run --name maria-latest \
  -p 3308:3306 \
  -e MYSQL_ROOT_HOST=% -e \
MYSQL_ROOT_PASSWORD='learning_mysql' \
  -d mariadb:latest
```

And for Percona Server, run:

```
# docker run --name ps-latest \
  -p 3309:3306 -p 33063:33060 \
  -e MYSQL_ROOT_HOST=% -e \
MYSQL_ROOT_PASSWORD='learning_mysql' \
  -d percona/percona-server:latest \
```

```
--innodb_buffer_pool_size=256M \
--innodb_flush_method=O_DIRECT
```

 We are mapping different ports for MariaDB (-p 3308:3306) and Percona (-p 3309:3306) because we are deploying all the containers in the same host:

```
# docker ps

CONTAINER ID              IMAGE
5e487dd41c3e              percona/percona-server:latest

COMMAND                    CREATED          STATUS
"/docker-entrypoint..." About a minute ago Up 51 seconds
"docker-entrypoint..."  2 minutes ago      Up 2 minutes

PORTS                      NAMES
0.0.0.0:3309->3306/tcp, ps-latest
0.0.0.0:33063->33060/tcp
f5a217f1537b              mariadb:latest
0.0.0.0:3308->3306/tcp  maria-latest
```

If you are deploying a single container, you can use port 3306 or any custom port you might want to use.

Using Sandboxes

In software development, a *sandbox* is a testing environment that isolates code changes and allows experimentation and testing before deploying to production. DBAs primarily use sandboxes for testing new software versions, performance tests, and bug analysis, and the data present in MySQL is disposable.

 It is common in the context of MySQL databases to hear the terms *master* and *slave*. The origins of these words are clearly negative. Oracle, Percona, and MariaDB have therefore decided to change this terminology and instead use *source* and *replica*. In this book, we will use both sets of terms because you will encounter both of them, but be aware that these companies will implement the following terminology for the upcoming releases:

Old	New
master	source
slave	replica
blacklist	blocklist
whitelist	allowlist

In 2018, Giuseppe Maxia (*https://oreil.ly/0wLPk*) introduced DBdeployer (*https://oreil.ly/lZK98*), a tool that provides an easy and fast way to deploy MySQL and its forks. It supports diverse MySQL topologies such as master/slave (source/replica), master/master (source/source), Galera Cluster, and Group Replication.

Installing DBdeployer

The tool is developed in the *Go* language and works with macOS and Linux (Ubuntu and CentOS), and standalone executables are provided. Get the latest version here:

```
# wget https://github.com/datacharmer/dbdeployer/releases/download/v1.58.2/ \
    dbdeployer-1.58.2.linux.tar.gz
# tar -xvf dbdeployer-1.58.2.linux.tar.gz
# mv dbdeployer-1.58.2.linux /usr/local/bin/dbdeployer
```

If you have your */usr/local/bin/* directory in the $PATH variable, you should now be able to run the dbdeployer commands:

```
# dbdeployer --version
dbdeployer version 1.58.2
```

Using DBdeployer

The first step in using DBdeployer is to download the MySQL binary you want to run and unpack it into the directory where you store your binaries. We will use *Linux - Generic* tarballs (*https://oreil.ly/DoI1c*) since they are compatible with most Linux distributions, and we will store our binaries in the */opt/mysql* directory:

```
# wget https://dev.mysql.com/get/Downloads/MySQL-8.0/ \
    mysql-8.0.11-linux-glibc2.12-x86_64.tar.gz
# mkdir /opt/mysql
# dbdeployer --sandbox-binary=/opt/mysql/ unpack \
    mysql-8.0.11-linux-glibc2.12-x86_64.tar.gz
```

The unpack command will extract and move the files to the specified directory. The expected output of this operation is:

```
# dbdeployer --sandbox-binary=/opt/mysql/ unpack

mysql-8.0.11-linux-glibc2.12-x86_64.tar.gz
Unpacking tarball mysql-8.0.11-linux-glibc2.12-x86_64.tar.gz to
/opt/mysql/8.0.11
.........100.........200........289
Renaming directory /opt/mysql/mysql-8.0.11-linux-glibc2.12-x86_64 to
/opt/mysql/8.0.11
```

We can now use the following command to create a new standalone MySQL sandbox with the newly extracted binary:

```
# dbdeployer --sandbox-binary=/opt/mysql/ deploy single 8.0.11
```

And we can observe DBdeployer initializing MySQL:

```
# dbdeployer --sandbox-binary=/opt/mysql/ deploy single 8.0.11

Creating directory /root/sandboxes
Database installed in $HOME/sandboxes/msb_8_0_11
run 'dbdeployer usage single' for basic instructions'
. sandbox server started
```

Confirm that MySQL is running with the ps command:

```
# ps -ef | grep mysql

root      4249     1  0 20:18 pts/0    00:00:00 /bin/sh bin/mysqld_safe
--defaults-file=/root/sandboxes/msb_8_0_11/my.sandbox.cnf
root      4470  4249  1 20:18 pts/0    00:00:00 /opt/mysql/8.0.11/bin/mysqld
--defaults-file=/root/sandboxes/msb_8_0_11/my.sandbox.cnf
--basedir=/opt/mysql/8.0.11 --datadir=/root/sandboxes/msb_8_0_11/data
--plugin-dir=/opt/mysql/8.0.11/lib/plugin --user=root
--log-error=/root/sandboxes/msb_8_0_11/data/msandbox.err
--pid-file=/root/sandboxes/msb_8_0_11/data/mysql_sandbox8011.pid
--socket=/tmp/mysql_sandbox8011.sock --port=8011
root      4527  3836  0 20:18 pts/0    00:00:00 grep --color=auto mysql
```

We can now connect to MySQL using DBdeployer's use command:

```
# cd sandboxes/msb_8_0_11/
# ./use
```

or using the default root credentials:

```
# mysql -uroot -pmsandbox -h 127.0.0.1 -P 8011
```

 We got the port information from the previous ps command. Remember that there are two ways to connect to MySQL: via TCP/IP or using a socket. We can also get the socket file location from the output of the ps command and connect with that, as shown here:

```
# mysql -uroot -pmsandbox -S/tmp/mysql_sandbox8011.sock
```

If we want to set up a replication environment with a source/replica topology, we can do it with the following command line:

```
# dbdeployer --sandbox-binary=/opt/mysql/ deploy replication 8.0.11
```

And we will have three mysqld processes running:

```
# ps -ef | grep mysql

root      4673     1  0 20:26 pts/0    00:00:00 /bin/sh bin/mysqld_safe
--defaults-file=/root/sandboxes/rsandbox_8_0_11/master/my.sandbox.cnf
root      4942  4673  1 20:26 pts/0    00:00:00
/opt/mysql/8.0.11/bin/mysqld
...
```

```
--pid-file=/root/sandboxes/rsandbox_8_0_11/master/data/mysql_sandbox201
12.pid --socket=/tmp/mysql_sandbox20112.sock --port=20112

root      5051     1 0 20:26 pts/0    00:00:00 /bin/sh bin/mysqld_safe
--defaults-file=/root/sandboxes/rsandbox_8_0_11/node1/my.sandbox.cnf
root      5320  5051 1 20:26 pts/0    00:00:00
/opt/mysql/8.0.11/bin/mysqld
--defaults-file=/root/sandboxes/rsandbox_8_0_11/node1/my.sandbox.cnf
...
--pid-file=/root/sandboxes/rsandbox_8_0_11/node1/data/mysql_sandbox2011
3.pid --socket=/tmp/mysql_sandbox20113.sock --port=20113

root      5415     1 0 20:26 pts/0    00:00:00 /bin/sh bin/mysqld_safe
--defaults-file=/root/sandboxes/rsandbox_8_0_11/node2/my.sandbox.cnf
root      5684  5415 1 20:26 pts/0    00:00:00
/opt/mysql/8.0.11/bin/mysqld
...
--pid-file=/root/sandboxes/rsandbox_8_0_11/node2/data/mysql_sandbox2011
4.pid --socket=/tmp/mysql_sandbox20114.sock --port=20114
```

Another topology that DBdeployer can configure is Group Replication. For this example, we will define a base-port. By doing this, we will order DBdeployer to configure our servers starting from port 49007:

```
# dbdeployer deploy --topology=group replication --sandbox-binary=/opt/mysql/\
    8.0.11 --base-port=49007
```

Now let's see an example of the deployment of Galera Cluster using Percona XtraDB Cluster 5.7.32. We will indicate the base-port, and we want our nodes configured with the log-slave-updates option (*https://oreil.ly/oMhOY*):

```
# wget https://downloads.percona.com/downloads/Percona-XtraDB-Cluster-57/\
    Percona-XtraDB-Cluster-5.7.32-31.47/binary/tarball/Percona-XtraDB-Cluster-\
    5.7.32-rel35-47.1.Linux.x86_64.glibc2.17-debug.tar.gz
# dbdeployer --sandbox-binary=/opt/mysql/ unpack\
    Percona-XtraDB-Cluster-5.7.32-rel35-47.1.Linux.x86_64.glibc2.17-debug.tar.gz
# dbdeployer deploy --topology=pxc replication\
    --sandbox-binary=/opt/mysql/ 5.7.32 --base-port=45007 -c log-slave-updates
```

As we've seen, it is possible to customize MySQL parameters. One interesting option is enabling MySQL replication using *global transaction identifiers* (*https://oreil.ly/QNCBh*), or GTIDs (we'll discuss GTIDs in more detail in Chapter 13):

```
# dbdeployer deploy replication --sandbox-binary=/opt/mysql/ 5.7.32 --gtid
```

Our last example shows that it is possible to deploy multiple standalone versions at once—here, we create five standalone instances:

```
# dbdeployer deploy multiple --sandbox-binary=/opt/mysql/ 5.7.32 -n 5
```

The previous examples are just a small sample of DBdeployer's capabilities. The full documentation is available on GitHub (*https://oreil.ly/5ygE0*). Another option to understand the universe of possibilities is to use --help in the command line:

```
# dbdeployer --help
```

dbdeployer makes MySQL server installation an easy task.
Runs single, multiple, and replicated sandboxes.

Usage:
  dbdeployer [command]

Available Commands:
    admin   sandbox management tasks
    cookbook   Shows dbdeployer samples
    defaults   tasks related to dbdeployer defaults
    delete   delete an installed sandbox
    delete-binaries delete an expanded tarball
    deploy   deploy sandboxes
    downloads   Manages remote tarballs
    export   Exports the command structure in JSON format
    global   Runs a given command in every sandbox
    help   Help about any command
    import   imports one or more MySQL servers into a sandbox
    info   Shows information about dbdeployer environment samples
    sandboxes   List installed sandboxes
    unpack   unpack a tarball into the binary directory
    update   Gets dbdeployer newest version
    usage   Shows usage of installed sandboxes
    versions   List available versions

Flags:
      --config string   configuration file (default
                                   "/root/.dbdeployer/config.json")
  -h, --help   help for dbdeployer
      --sandbox-binary string   Binary repository (default
                                   "/root/opt/mysql")
      --sandbox-home string   Sandbox deployment directory (default
                                   "/root/sandboxes")
      --shell-path string   Which shell to use for generated
                                   scripts (default "/usr/bin/bash")
      --skip-library-check   Skip check for needed libraries (may
                                   cause nasty errors)
      --version   version for dbdeployer

Use "dbdeployer [command] --help" for more information about a command.

Upgrading MySQL Server

If the most common question to arise is about replication, the second most common
is about how to upgrade a MySQL instance. If the procedure is not well tested before
it's done in production, the chances of having a problem are high. There are two types
of upgrades that you can perform:

- A *major upgrade* in MySQL would be changing versions from 5.6 to 5.7 or 5.7 to 8.0. Such an upgrade is trickier and more complex than a minor upgrade because the changes to the architecture are more substantial. For example, a considerable change in MySQL 8.0 involved modifying the data dictionary, which is now transactional and encapsulated by InnoDB.

- A *minor upgrade* would be changing from MySQL 5.7.29 to 5.7.30 or MySQL 8.0.22 to MySQL 8.0.23. Most of the time, you'll need to install the new version using your distribution's package manager. A minor upgrade is simpler than a major one because it does not involve any changes in the architecture. The modifications are focused on fixing bugs, improving the performance, and optimizing the code.

To start planning for an upgrade, first choose between two strategies. These are the recommended strategies according to the documentation and are the ones we use:

In-place upgrade
This involves shutting down MySQL, replacing the old MySQL binaries or packages with the new ones, restarting MySQL in the existing data directory, and running mysql_upgrade.

 As of MySQL 8.0.16, the *mysql_upgrade* binary is deprecated, and the MySQL server itself executes its functionality (you can think of it as a "server upgrade"). MySQL added this change alongside the data dictionary upgrade (DD upgrade), which is a process to update the data dictionary table definitions. Benefits of the new process include:

- Faster upgrades
- Simpler process
- Better security
- Significant reduction in upgrade steps
- More easily automated
- No restarts
- Plug and play

Logical upgrade
This involves exporting the data in SQL format from the old MySQL version using a backup or export utility such as *mysqldump* or *mysqlpump*, installing the new MySQL version, and applying the SQL data to the new MySQL version. In other words, this process involves rebuilding the entire data dictionary and the user data. A logical upgrade usually takes longer than an in-place upgrade.

Regardless of your chosen strategy, it is essential to establish a rollback strategy in case something goes wrong. The rollback strategy will vary based on the upgrade plan you choose, and the database size and the topology present (if you're using replicas or Galera Cluster, for example) will influence this decision.

Here are some additional points to take into consideration when planning an upgrade:

- Upgrading from MySQL 5.7 to 8.0 is supported. However, the upgrade is only supported between GA releases. For MySQL 8.0, it is required that you upgrade from a MySQL 5.7 GA release (5.7.9 or higher). Upgrades from non-GA releases of MySQL 5.7 are not supported.

- Upgrading to the latest release is recommended before upgrading to the next version. For example, upgrade to the latest MySQL 5.7 release before upgrading to MySQL 8.0.

- Upgrades that skip versions are not supported. For example, upgrading directly from MySQL 5.6 to 8.0 is not supported.

> Based on our experience, moving from MySQL 5.6 to MySQL 5.7 is the upgrade that causes the most performance issues, especially if the application is using *derived tables* (see "Nested Queries in the FROM Clause" on page 231). MySQL 5.7 modified the `opti mizer_switch` system variable (*https://oreil.ly/m0Ky3*), enabling the `derived_merge` setting (*https://oreil.ly/JROqc*) by default, and this can hurt query performance.
>
> Another complicating change is that MySQL 5.7 implements network encryption by default (SSL). Applications that were not using SSL in MySQL 5.6 may suffer a substantial performance hit.
>
> Finally, MySQL 5.7 changed the `sync_binlog` (*https://oreil.ly/Khh3Q*) default to synchronous mode. This mode is the safest but can harm performance due to the increased number of disk writes.

Let's go through an example of upgrading from MySQL 5.7 upstream to MySQL 8.0 upstream using the in-place method:

1. Stop the MySQL service. Perform a clean shutdown using `systemctl`:

    ```
    # systemctl stop mysqld
    ```

2. Remove the old binaries:

    ```
    # yum erase mysql-community -y
    ```

This process only removes the binaries and does not touch the *datadir* (see "The Contents of the MySQL Directory" on page 40).

3. Follow the regular steps for the installation process (see "Installing MySQL on Linux" on page 5). For example, to use MySQL 8.0 Community Version on CentOS 7 using yum:

```
# yum-config-manager --enable mysql80-community
```

4. Install the new binaries:

```
# yum install mysql-community-server -y
```

5. Start the MySQL service:

```
# systemctl start mysqld
```

We can observe in the logs that MySQL upgraded the data dictionary and that we're now running MySQL 8.0.21:

```
# tail -f /var/log/mysqld.log

2020-08-09T21:20:10.356938Z 2 [System] [MY-011003] [Server] Finished
populating Data Dictionary tables with data.
2020-08-09T21:20:11.734091Z 5 [System] [MY-013381] [Server] Server
upgrade from '50700' to '80021' started.
2020-08-09T21:20:17.342682Z 5 [System] [MY-013381] [Server] Server
upgrade from '50700' to '80021' completed.
...
2020-08-09T21:20:17.463685Z 0 [System] [MY-010931] [Server]
/usr/sbin/mysqld: ready for connections. Version: '8.0.21'  socket:
'/var/lib/mysql/mysql.sock'  port: 3306  MySQL Community Server - GPL.
```

 We highly recommend before upgrading MySQL that you check the release notes. They contain a summary of the changes made and the bug fixes. Release notes are available for MySQL upstream (*https://oreil.ly/FcOVq*), Percona Server (*https://oreil.ly/Mtt2J*), and MariaDB (*https://oreil.ly/T8M9z*).

A common question is whether it's safe to upgrade to the latest major release. The answer is...it depends. As with any new product in the industry, early adopters tend to benefit from the new features, but they are testers as well, and they may discover and be affected by new bugs. When MySQL 8.0 was released, our recommendation was to wait for three minor releases before considering moving. The golden rule of this book is to test everything in advance before executing the next step. If you learn just that from this book, we will consider our mission accomplished.

CHAPTER 2

Modeling and Designing Databases

When implementing a new database, it's easy to fall into the trap of quickly getting something up and running without dedicating adequate time and effort to the design. This carelessness frequently leads to costly redesigns and reimplementations down the road. Designing a database is like drafting the blueprints for a house; it's silly to start building without detailed plans. Notably, good design allows you to extend the original building without pulling everything down and starting from scratch. And as you will see, bad designs are directly related to poor database performance.

How Not to Develop a Database

Database design is probably not the most exciting task in the world, but indeed it is becoming one of the most important ones. Before we describe how to go about the design process, let's look at an example of database design on the run.

Imagine we want to create a database to store student grades for a university computer science department. We could create a Student_Grades table to store grades for each student and each course. The table would have columns for the given names and the surname of each student and each course they have taken, the course name, and the percentage result (shown as Pctg). We'd have a different row for each student for each of their courses:

```
+-------------+---------+----------------------+------+
| GivenNames  | Surname | CourseName           | Pctg |
+-------------+---------+----------------------+------+
| John Paul   | Bloggs  | Data Science         |   72 |
| Sarah       | Doe     | Programming 1        |   87 |
| John Paul   | Bloggs  | Computing Mathematics|   43 |
| John Paul   | Bloggs  | Computing Mathematics|   65 |
| Sarah       | Doe     | Data Science         |   65 |
| Susan       | Smith   | Computing Mathematics|   75 |
+-------------+---------+----------------------+------+
```

```
| Susan      | Smith   | Programming 1          |   55 |
| Susan      | Smith   | Computing Mathematics  |   80 |
+------------+---------+------------------------+------+
```

The list is nice and compact, we can easily access grades for any student or any course, and it looks similar to a spreadsheet. However, we could have more than one student with the same name. For instance, there are two entries for Susan Smith and the Computing Mathematics course in the sample data. Which Susan Smith got 75% and which got 80%? A common way to differentiate duplicate data entries is to assign a unique number to each entry. Here, we can assign a unique `StudentID` number to each student:

```
+------------+-------------+---------+------------------------+------+
| StudentID  | GivenNames  | Surname | CourseName             | Pctg |
+------------+-------------+---------+------------------------+------+
| 12345678   | John Paul   | Bloggs  | Data Science           |   72 |
| 12345121   | Sarah       | Doe     | Programming 1          |   87 |
| 12345678   | John Paul   | Bloggs  | Computing Mathematics  |   43 |
| 12345678   | John Paul   | Bloggs  | Computing Mathematics  |   65 |
| 12345121   | Sarah       | Doe     | Data Science           |   65 |
| 12345876   | Susan       | Smith   | Computing Mathematics  |   75 |
| 12345876   | Susan       | Smith   | Programming 1          |   55 |
| 12345303   | Susan       | Smith   | Computing Mathematics  |   80 |
+------------+-------------+---------+------------------------+------+
```

Now we know which Susan Smith got 80%: the one with the student ID number 12345303.

There's another problem. In our table, John Paul Bloggs has two scores for the Computing Mathematics course: he failed it once with 43%, and then passed it with 65% on his second attempt. In a relational database, the rows form a set, and there is no implicit ordering between them. Looking at this table we might guess that the pass happened after the failure, but we can't be sure. There's no guarantee that the newer grade will appear after the older one, so we need to add information about when each grade was awarded, say by adding a year (`Year`) and semester (`Sem`):

```
+------------+-------------+---------+------------------------+------+-----+------+
| StudentID  | GivenNames  | Surname | CourseName             | Year | Sem | Pctg |
+------------+-------------+---------+------------------------+------+-----+------+
| 12345678   | John Paul   | Bloggs  | Data Science           | 2019 |  2  |  72  |
| 12345121   | Sarah       | Doe     | Programming 1          | 2020 |  1  |  87  |
| 12345678   | John Paul   | Bloggs  | Computing Mathematics  | 2019 |  2  |  43  |
| 12345678   | John Paul   | Bloggs  | Computing Mathematics  | 2020 |  1  |  65  |
| 12345121   | Sarah       | Doe     | Data Science           | 2020 |  1  |  65  |
| 12345876   | Susan       | Smith   | Computing Mathematics  | 2019 |  1  |  75  |
| 12345876   | Susan       | Smith   | Programming 1          | 2019 |  2  |  55  |
| 12345303   | Susan       | Smith   | Computing Mathematics  | 2020 |  1  |  80  |
+------------+-------------+---------+------------------------+------+-----+------+
```

Notice that the `Student_Grades` table has become a bit bloated. We've repeated the student ID, given names, and surname for every year. We could split up the information and create a `Student_Details` table:

```
+------------+------------+---------+
| StudentID  | GivenNames | Surname |
+------------+------------+---------+
| 12345121   | Sarah      | Doe     |
| 12345303   | Susan      | Smith   |
| 12345678   | John Paul  | Bloggs  |
| 12345876   | Susan      | Smith   |
+------------+------------+---------+
```

And we could keep less information in the `Student_Grades` table:

```
+------------+----------------------+------+-----+------+
| StudentID  | CourseName           | Year | Sem | Pctg |
+------------+----------------------+------+-----+------+
| 12345678   | Data Science         | 2019 |  2  |  72  |
| 12345121   | Programming 1        | 2020 |  1  |  87  |
| 12345678   | Computing Mathematics | 2019 |  2  |  43  |
| 12345678   | Computing Mathematics | 2020 |  1  |  65  |
| 12345121   | Data Science         | 2020 |  1  |  65  |
| 12345876   | Computing Mathematics | 2019 |  1  |  75  |
| 12345876   | Programming 1        | 2019 |  2  |  55  |
| 12345303   | Computing Mathematics | 2020 |  1  |  80  |
+------------+----------------------+------+-----+------+
```

To look up a student's grades, we would need to first look up their student ID from the `Student_Details` table and then read the grades for that student ID from the `Student_Grades` table.

There are still issues we haven't considered, though. For example, should we keep information on a student's enrollment date, postal and email addresses, fees, or attendance? Should we store different types of postal addresses? How should we store addresses so that things don't break when students change their addresses?

Implementing a database in this way is problematic; we keep running into things we hadn't thought about and have to keep changing our database structure. We can save a lot of reworking by carefully documenting the requirements up front and then working through them to develop a coherent design.

The Database Design Process

There are three major stages in the database design, each producing a progressively lower-level description:

Requirements analysis

First, we determine and write down what we need from the database, what data we will store, and how the data items relate to each other. In practice, this might involve a detailed study of the application requirements and talking to people in various roles that will interact with the database and application.

Conceptual design

Once we know the database requirements, we distill them into a formal description of the database design. Later in this chapter we'll see how to use modeling to produce the conceptual design.

Logical design

Finally, we map the database design onto an existing database management system and database tables.

At the end of the chapter, we'll look at how we can use the open source MySQL Workbench tool to convert the conceptual design to a MySQL database schema.

The Entity Relationship Model

At a basic level, databases store information about distinct objects, or *entities*, and the associations, or *relationships*, between these entities. For example, a university database might store information about students, courses, and enrollment. A student and a course are entities, whereas enrollment is a relationship between a student and a course. Similarly, an inventory and sales database might store information about products, customers, and sales. A product and a customer are entities, and a sale is a relationship between a customer and a product. It is common to get confused between entities and relationships when you're starting out, and you may end up designing relationships as entities and vice versa. The best way to improve your database design skills is by practicing a lot.

A popular approach to conceptual design uses the *Entity Relationship* (ER) model, which helps transform the requirements into a formal description of the entities and relationships in the database. We'll start by looking at how the ER modeling process works and then observe it in "Entity Relationship Modeling Examples" on page 77 for three sample databases.

Representing Entities

To help visualize the design, the ER modeling approach involves drawing an ER diagram. In the ER diagram, we represent an entity set by a rectangle containing the entity name. For our sales database example, our ER diagram would show the product and customer entity sets, as shown in Figure 2-1.

Figure 2-1. An entity set is represented by a named rectangle

We typically use the database to store specific characteristics, or *attributes*, of the entities. We could record the name, email address, postal address, and telephone number of each customer in a sales database. In a more elaborate customer relationship management (CRM) application, we could also store the names of the customer's spouse and children, the languages the customer speaks, the customer's history of interaction with our company, and so on. Attributes describe the entity they belong to.

We may form an attribute from smaller parts; for example, we compose a postal address from a street number, city, zip code, and country. We classify attributes as *composite* if they're composed of smaller parts in this way, and as *simple* otherwise.

Some attributes can have multiple values for a given entity—for example, a customer can provide several telephone numbers, so the telephone number attribute is *multivalued*.

Attributes help distinguish one entity from other entities of the same type. We could use the name attribute to differentiate between customers, but this could be an inadequate solution because several customers could have identical names. To tell them apart, we need an attribute (or a minimal combination of attributes) guaranteed to be unique to each customer. The identifying attribute or attributes form a unique key, and in this particular case, we call it a *primary key*.

In our example, we can assume that no two customers have the same email address, so the email address can be the primary key. However, when designing a database, we need to think carefully about the implications of our choices. For example, if we decide to identify customers by their email addresses, how will we handle a customer having multiple email addresses? Any applications we build to use this database might treat each email address as a separate person. It could be hard to adapt everything to allow people to have more than one. Using the email address as the key also means that every customer must have an email address; otherwise, we can't distinguish between customers who don't have one.

Looking at the other attributes for one that can serve as an alternative key, we see that while it's possible that two customers could have the same telephone number (and so we cannot use the telephone number as a key), it's likely that people who have the same telephone number will not have the same name, so we can use the combination of the telephone number and the name as a composite key.

Clearly, there may be several possible keys that could be used to identify an entity; we choose one of the alternatives, or *candidate* keys, to be our main or *primary* key. We usually choose based on how confident we are that the attribute will be nonempty and unique for each entity and how small the key is (shorter keys are faster to maintain and to use to perform lookup operations).

In the ER diagram, attributes are represented as labeled ovals connected to their entity, as shown in Figure 2-2. Attributes comprising the primary key are shown underlined. The parts of any composite attributes are drawn connected to the composite attribute's oval, and multivalued attributes are shown as double-lined ovals.

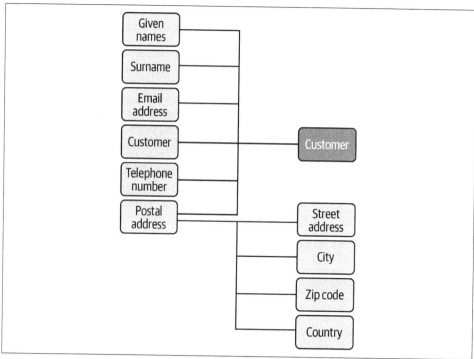

Figure 2-2. The ER diagram representation of the customer entity

Attribute values are chosen from a domain of legal values. For example, we could specify that a customer's given names and surname attributes can each be a string of up to 100 characters, while a telephone number can be a string of up to 40 characters. Similarly, a product price could be a positive rational number.

Attributes can be empty; for example, some customers may not provide their telephone numbers. However, the primary key of an entity (including the components of a multiattribute primary key) must never be unknown (technically, it must be NOT NULL). So, if it's possible for a customer to not provide an email address, we cannot use the email address as the key.

You should think carefully when classifying an attribute as multivalued: are all the values equivalent, or do they in fact represent different things? For example, when listing multiple telephone numbers for a customer, would they be more usefully labeled separately as the customer's business phone number, home phone number, cell phone number, and so on?

Let's look at another example. The sales database requirements may specify that a product has a name and a price. We can see that the product is an entity because it's a distinct object. However, the product's name and price aren't distinct objects; they're attributes that describe the product entity. Note that if we want to have different prices for different markets, then the price is no longer just related to the product entity, and we will need to model it differently.

For some applications, no combination of attributes can uniquely identify an entity (or it would be too unwieldy to use a large composite key), so we create an artificial attribute that's defined to be unique and can therefore be used as a key: student numbers, Social Security numbers, driver's license numbers, and library card numbers are examples of unique attributes created for various applications. In our inventory and sales application, it's possible that we could stock different products with the same name and price. For example, we could sell two models of "Four-Port USB 2.0 Hub," both at $4.95 each. To distinguish between products, we can assign a unique product ID number to each item we stock; this would be the primary key. Each product entity would have name, price, and product ID attributes. This is shown in the ER diagram in Figure 2-3.

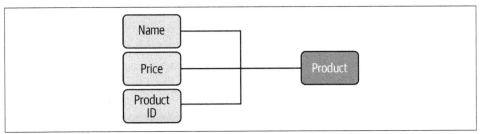

Figure 2-3. The ER diagram representation of the product entity

Representing Relationships

Entities can participate in relationships with other entities. For example, a customer can buy a product, a student can take a course, an employee can have an address, and so on.

Like entities, relationships can have attributes: we can define a sale to be a relationship between a customer entity (identified by the unique email address) and a given number of the product entity (identified by the unique product ID) that exists at a particular date and time (the timestamp).

Our database could then record each sale and tell us, for example, that at 3:13 p.m. on Wednesday, March 22, Marcos Albe bought one "Raspberry Pi 4," one "500 GB SSD M.2 NVMe," and two sets of "2000 Watt 5.1 Channel Sub-Woofer Speakers."

Different numbers of entities can appear on each side of a relationship. For example, each customer can buy any number of products, and each product can be bought by any number of customers. This is known as a *many-to-many* relationship. We can also have *one-to-many* relationships. For example, one person can have several credit cards, but each credit card belongs to just one person. Looking at it the other way, a *one-to-many* relationship becomes a *many-to-one* relationship; for example, many credit cards belong to a single person. Finally, the serial number on a car engine is an example of a *one-to-one* relationship; each engine has just one serial number, and each serial number belongs to just one engine. We use the shorthand terms *1:1*, *1:N*, and *M:N* for one-to-one, one-to-many, and many-to-many relationships.

The number of entities on either side of a relationship (the *cardinality* of the relationship) define the *key constraints* of the relationship. It's important to think about the cardinality of relationships carefully. There are many relationships that may at first seem to be one-to-one, but turn out to be more complex. For example, people sometimes change their names; in some applications, such as police databases, this is of particular interest, and so it may be necessary to model a many-to-many relationship between a person entity and a name entity. Redesigning a database can be costly and time-consuming if you assume a relationship is simpler than it really is.

In an ER diagram, we represent a relationship set with a named diamond. The cardinality of the relationship is often indicated alongside the relationship diamond; this is the style we use in this book. (Another common style is to have an arrowhead on the line connecting the entity on the "1" side to the relationship diamond.) Figure 2-4 shows the relationship between the customer and product entities, along with the number and timestamp attributes of the sale relationship.

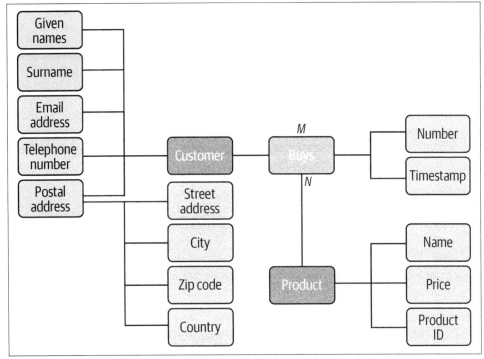

Figure 2-4. The ER diagram representation of the customer and product entities, and the sale relationship between them

Partial and Total Participation

Relationships between entities can be optional or compulsory. In our example, we could decide that a person is considered to be a customer only if they have bought a product. On the other hand, we could say that a customer is a person whom we know about and whom we hope might buy something—that is, we can have people listed as customers in our database who never buy a product. In the first case, the customer entity has *total participation* in the bought relationship (all customer have bought a product, and we can't have a customer who hasn't bought a product), while in the second case it has *partial participation* (a customer can buy a product). These are referred to as the *participation constraints* of the relationship. In an ER diagram, we indicate total participation with a double line between the entity box and the relationship diamond.

Entity or Attribute?

From time to time, we encounter cases where we wonder whether an item should be an attribute or an entity on its own. For example, an email address could be modeled as an entity in its own right. When in doubt, consider these rules of thumb:

Is the item of direct interest to the database?
> Objects of direct interest should be entities, and information that describes them should be stored in attributes. Our inventory and sales database is really interested in customers, not their email addresses, so the email address would be best modeled as an attribute of the customer entity.

Does the item have components of its own?
> If so, we must find a way of representing these components; a separate entity might be the best solution. In the student grades example at the start of the chapter, we stored the course name, year, and semester for each course that a student takes. It would be more compact to treat the course as a separate entity and to create a class ID number to identify each time a course is offered to students (the "offering").

Can the object have multiple instances?
> If so, we must find a way to store data on each instance. The cleanest way to do this is to represent the object as a separate entity. In our sales example, we must ask whether customers are allowed to have more than one email address; if they are, we should model the email address as a separate entity.

Is the object often nonexistent or unknown?
> If so, it is effectively an attribute of only some of the entities, and it would be better to model it as a separate entity rather than as an attribute that is often empty. Consider a simple example: to store student grades for different courses, we could have an attribute for the student's grade in every possible course, as shown in Figure 2-5. But because most students will have grades for only a few of these courses, it's better to represent the grades as a separate entity set, as in Figure 2-6.

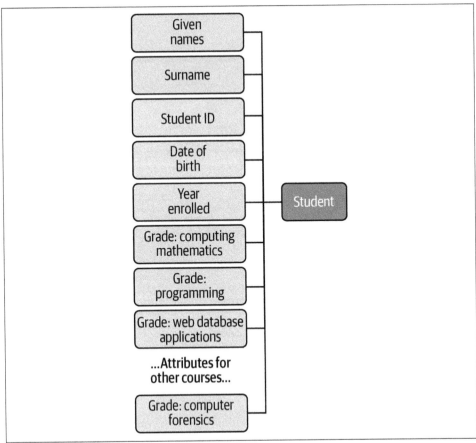

Figure 2-5. The ER diagram representation of student grades as attributes of the student entity

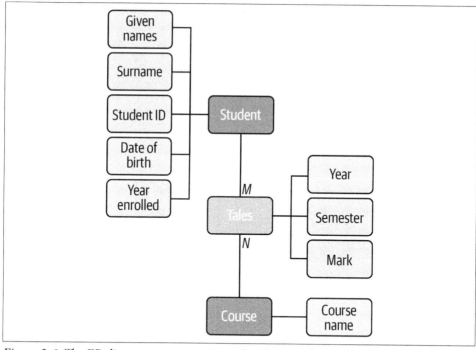

Figure 2-6. The ER diagram representation of student grades as a separate entity

Entity or Relationship?

An easy way to decide whether an object should be an entity or a relationship is to map nouns in the requirements to entities, and map verbs to relationships. For example, in the statement "A degree program is made up of one or more courses," we can identify the entities "program" and "course," and the relationship "is made up of." Similarly, in the statement "A student enrolls in one program," we can identify the entities "student" and "program," and the relationship "enrolls in." Of course, we can choose different terms for entities and relationships than those that appear in the relationships, but it's a good idea not to deviate too far from the naming conventions used in the requirements so that the design can be checked against the requirements. All else being equal, try to keep the design simple, and avoid introducing trivial entities where possible. That is, there's no need to have a separate entity for the student's enrollment when we can model it as a relationship between the existing student and program entities.

Intermediate Entities

It is often possible to conceptually simplify a many-to-many relationship by replacing it with a new *intermediate* entity (sometimes called an *associate* entity) and connecting the original entities through a many-to-one and a one-to-many relationship.

Consider this statement: "A passenger can book a seat on a flight." This is a many-to-many relationship between the entities "passenger" and "flight." The related ER diagram fragment is shown in Figure 2-7.

Figure 2-7. A passenger participates in an M:N relationship with a flight

However, let's look at this from both sides of the relationship:

- Any given flight can have many passengers with a booking.
- Any given passenger can have bookings on many flights.

Hence, we can consider the many-to-many relationship to be in fact two one-to-many relationships, one each way. This points us to the existence of a hidden intermediate entity, the booking, between the flight and passenger entities. The requirement could be better worded as: "A passenger can make a booking for a seat on a flight." The updated ER diagram fragment is shown in Figure 2-8.

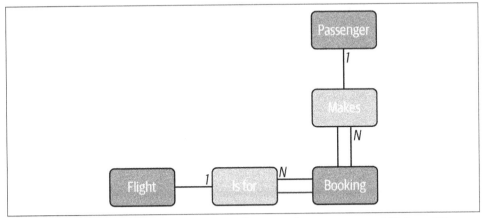

Figure 2-8. The intermediate booking entity between the passenger and flight entities

Each passenger can be involved in multiple bookings, but each booking belongs to a single passenger, so the cardinality of this relationship is 1:N. Similarly, there can be many bookings for a given flight, but each booking is for a single flight, so this relationship also has cardinality 1:N. Since each booking must be associated with a particular passenger and flight, the booking entity participates totally in the relationships with these entities (as described in "Partial and Total Participation" on page 67 on page 77). This total participation could not be captured effectively in the representation in Figure 2-7.

Weak and Strong Entities

Context is very important in our daily interactions; if we know the context, we can work with a much smaller amount of information. For example, we generally call family members by only their first name or nickname. Where ambiguity exists, we add further information such as the surname to clarify our intent. In database design, we can omit some key information for entities that are dependent on other entities. For example, if we wanted to store the names of our customers' children, we could create a child entity and store only enough key information to identify it in the context of its parent. We could simply list a child's first name on the assumption that a customer will never have several children with the same first name. Here, the child entity is a *weak* entity, and its relationship with the customer entity is called an *identifying relationship*. Weak entities participate totally in the identifying relationship, since they can't exist in the database independently of their owning entity.

In the ER diagram, we show weak entities and identifying relationships with double lines and the partial key of a weak entity with a dashed underline, as in Figure 2-9. A weak entity is uniquely identified in the context of its owning (or *strong*) entity, and so the full key for a weak entity is the combination of its own (partial) key with the key of its owning entity. To uniquely identify a child in our example, we need the first name of the child and the email address of the child's parent.

Figure 2-10 shows a summary of the symbols we've explained for ER diagrams.

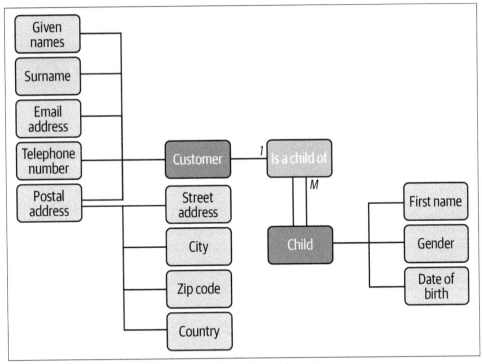

Figure 2-9. *The ER diagram representation of a weak entity*

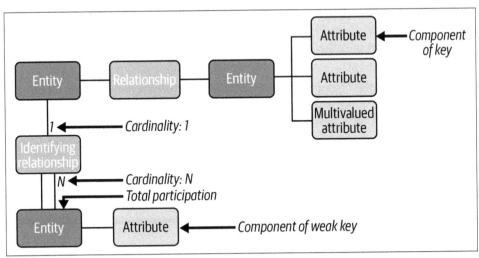

Figure 2-10. *A summary of the ER diagram symbols*

Database Normalization

Database normalization is an important concept when designing the relational data structure. Dr. Edgar F. Codd, the inventor of the relational database model, proposed the normal forms in the early '70s, and these are still widely used by the industry nowadays. Even with the advent of the NoSQL databases, there is no evidence in the short or medium term that relational databases will disappear or that the normal forms will fall into disuse.

The main objective of the normal forms is to reduce data redundancy and improve data integrity. Normalization also facilitates the process of redesigning and extending the database structure.

Officially, there are six normal forms, but most database architects deal only with the first three forms. That is because the normalization process is progressive, and we cannot achieve a higher level of database normalization unless the previous levels have been satisfied. Using all six norms constricts the database model too much, however, and in general, they become very complex to implement.

In real workloads, usually there are performance issues. This is one reason for extract, transform, load (*ETL*) jobs to exist: they denormalize the data to process it.

Let's take a look at the first three normal forms:

The first normal form (1NF) has the following goals
- Eliminate repeating groups in individual tables.
- Create a separate table for each set of related data.
- Identify each set of related data with a primary key.

  If a relation contains composite or multivalued attributes, it violates the first normal form. Conversely, a relation is in first normal form if it does not contain any composite or multivalued attributes. So, a relation is in first normal form if every attribute in that relation has a single value of the appropriate type.

The goals of second normal form (2NF) are
- Create separate tables for sets of values that apply to multiple records.
- Relate these tables with a foreign key.

  Records should not depend on anything other than a table's primary key (a compound key, if necessary).

Third normal form (3NF) adds one more goal
- Eliminate fields that do not depend on the key.

  Values in a record that are not part of that record's key do not belong in the table. In general, any time the contents of a group of fields may apply to more than a single record in the table, you should consider placing those fields in a separate table.

Table 2-1 lists the normal forms, from the least normalized to the most normalized. The unnormalized form (UNF) is a database model that does not meet any of the database normalization conditions. Other normalization forms exist, but they are beyond the scope of this discussion.

Table 2-1. The normal forms (from least to most normalized)

	UNF (1970)	1NF (1970)	2NF (1971)	3NF (1971)	4NF (1977)	5NF (1979)	6NF (2003)
Primary key (no duplicate tuples)	Maybe	Yes	Yes	Yes	Yes	Yes	Yes
No repeating groups	No	Yes	Yes	Yes	Yes	Yes	Yes
Atomic columns (cells have single value)	No	Yes	Yes	Yes	Yes	Yes	Yes
Every nontrivial functional dependency either does not begin with a proper subset of a candidate key or ends with a prime attribute (no partial functional dependencies of nonprime attributes on candidate keys)	No	No	Yes	Yes	Yes	Yes	Yes
Every nontrivial functional dependency begins with a superkey or ends with a prime attribute (no transitive functional dependencies of nonprime attributes on candidate keys)	No	No	No	Yes	Yes	Yes	Yes
Every nontrivial functional dependency either begins with a superkey or ends with an elementary prime attribute	No	No	No	No	Yes	Yes	N/A
Every nontrivial functional dependency begins with a superkey	No	No	No	No	Yes	Yes	N/A
Every nontrivial multivalued dependency begins with a superkey	No	No	No	No	Yes	Yes	N/A
Every join dependency has a superkey component	No	No	No	No	No	Yes	N/A
Every join dependency has only superkey components	No	No	No	No	No	Yes	N/A
Every constraint is a consequence of domain constraints and key constraints	No	No	No	No	No	No	N/A
Every join dependency is trivial	No	No	No	No	No	No	Yes

Normalizing an Example Table

To make these concepts clearer let's walk through an example of normalizing a fictional student table.

We'll start with the unnormalized table:

```
Student#   Advisor   Adv-Room   Class1   Class2   Class3
1022       Jones     412        101-07   143-01   159-02
4123       Smith     216        201-01   211-02   214-01
```

First Normal Form: No Repeating Groups

Tables should have only a single field for each attribute. Since one student has several classes, these classes should be listed in a separate table. The fields `Class1`, `Class2`, and `Class3` in our unnormalized table are indications of design trouble.

Spreadsheets often have multiple fields for the same attribute (e.g., `address1`, `address2`, `address3`), but tables should not. Here's another way to look at this problem: with a one-to-many relationship, don't put the one side and the many side in the same table. Instead, create another table in first normal form by eliminating the repeating group—for example, with `Class#`, as shown here:

```
Student#   Advisor   Adv-Room   Class#
1022       Jones     412        101-07
1022       Jones     412        143-01
1022       Jones     412        159-02
4123       Smith     216        201-01
4123       Smith     216        211-02
4123       Smith     216        214-01
```

Second Normal Form: Eliminate Redundant Data

Note the multiple `Class#` values for each `Student#` value in the previous table. `Class#` is not functionally dependent on `Student#` (the primary key), so this relationship is not in second normal form.

The following two tables demonstrate the conversion to second normal form. We now have a `Students` table:

```
Student#   Advisor   Adv-Room
1022       Jones     412
4123       Smith     216
```

and a `Registration` table:

```
Student#   Class#
1022       101-07
1022       143-01
1022       159-02
```

```
4123     201-01
4123     211-02
4123     214-01
```

Third Normal Form: Eliminate Data Not Dependent on Key

In the previous example, Adv-Room (the advisor's office number) is functionally dependent on the Advisor attribute. The solution is to move that attribute from the Students table to a Faculty table, as shown next.

The Students table now looks like this:

```
Student#  Advisor
1022      Jones
4123      Smith
```

And here's the Faculty table:

```
Name   Room  Dept
Jones  412   42
Smith  216   42
```

Entity Relationship Modeling Examples

In the previous sections, we walked though hypothetical examples to help you understand the basics of database design, ER diagrams, and normalization. Now we're going to look at some ER examples from sample databases available for MySQL. To visualize the ER diagrams, we are going to use *MySQL Workbench* (*https://oreil.ly/ 1971c*).

MySQL Workbench uses a physical ER representation. Physical ER diagram models are more granular, showing the processes necessary to add information to a database. Rather than using symbols, we use tables in the ER diagram, making it closer to the real database. MySQL Workbench goes one step further and uses *enhanced entity-relationship (EER) diagrams*. EER diagrams are an expanded version of ER diagrams.

We won't go into all the details, but the main advantage of an EER diagram is that it provides all the elements of an ER diagram while adding support for:

- Attribute and relationship inheritance
- Category or union types
- Specialization and generalization
- Subclasses and superclasses

Let's start with the process to download the sample databases and visualize their EER diagrams in MySQL Workbench.

The first one we'll use is the `sakila` database. Development of this database began in 2005. Early designs were based on the database used in the Dell whitepaper "Three Approaches to MySQL Applications on Dell PowerEdge Servers" (*https://oreil.ly/aDDlO*), which was designed to represent an online DVD store. Similarly, the `sakila` sample database is designed to represent a DVD rental store, and it borrows film and actor names from the Dell sample database. You can use the following commands to import the `sakila` database to your MySQL instance:

```
# wget https://downloads.mysql.com/docs/sakila-db.tar.gz
# tar -xvf sakila-db.tar.gz
# mysql -uroot -pmsandbox < sakila-db/sakila-schema.sql
# mysql -uroot -pmsandbox < sakila-db/sakila-data.sql
```

`sakila` also provides the EER model, in the *sakila.mwb* file. You can open the file with MySQL Workbench, as shown in Figure 2-11.

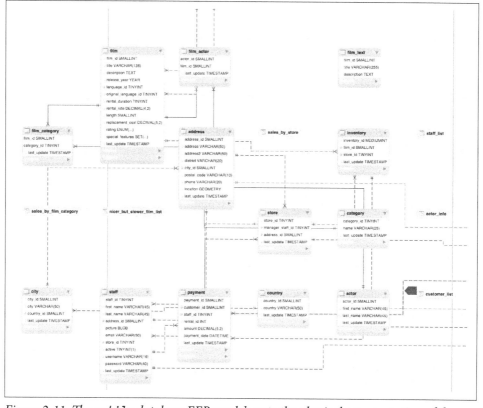

Figure 2-11. The `sakila` database EER model; note the physical representation of the entities instead of using symbols

Next is the `world` database, which uses sample data from Statistics Finland (*https://oreil.ly/0Y9tZ*).

The following commands will import the `world` database to your MySQL instance:

```
# wget https://downloads.mysql.com/docs/world-db.tar.gz
# tar -xvf world-db.tar.gz
# mysql -uroot -plearning_mysql < world-db/world.sql
```

The `world` database does not come with an EER file as `sakila` does, but you can create the EER model from the database using MySQL Workbench. To do this, select Reverse Engineer from the Database menu, as in Figure 2-12.

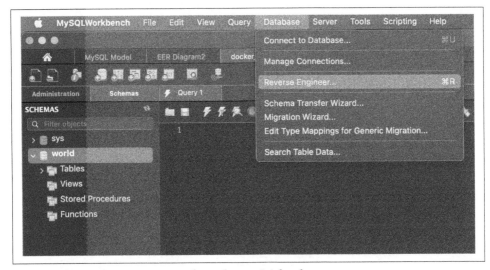

Figure 2-12. Reverse engineering from the `world` database

Workbench will connect to the database (if not connected already) and prompt you to choose the schema you want to reverse engineer, as shown in Figure 2-13.

Click Continue, and then click Execute on the next screen, shown in Figure 2-14.

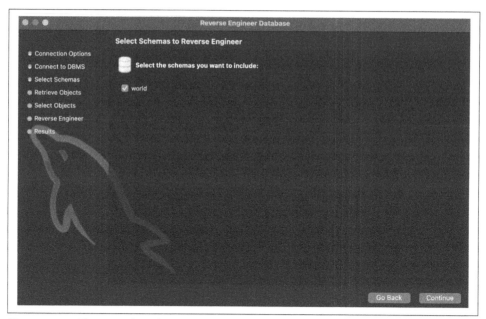

Figure 2-13. Choosing the schema

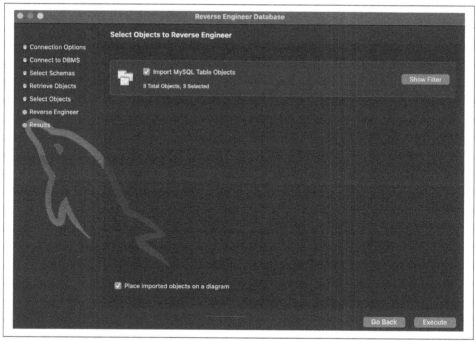

Figure 2-14. Click Execute to start the reverse-engineering process

This produces the ER model for the `world` database, shown in Figure 2-15.

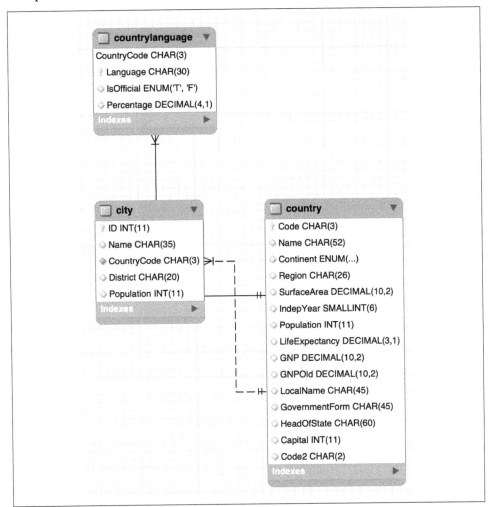

Figure 2-15. The ER model for the `world` database

The last database you'll import is the `employees` database. Fusheng Wang and Carlo Zaniolo created the original data (*https://oreil.ly/1rvPc*) at Siemens Corporate Research. Giuseppe Maxia made the relational schema, and Patrick Crews exported the data in relational format.

To import the database, first you need to clone the Git repository:

```
# git clone https://github.com/datacharmer/test_db.git
# cd test_db
# cat employees.sql | mysql -uroot -psekret
```

Then you can use the reverse engineering procedure in MySQL Workbench again to create the ER model for the employees database, as shown in Figure 2-16.

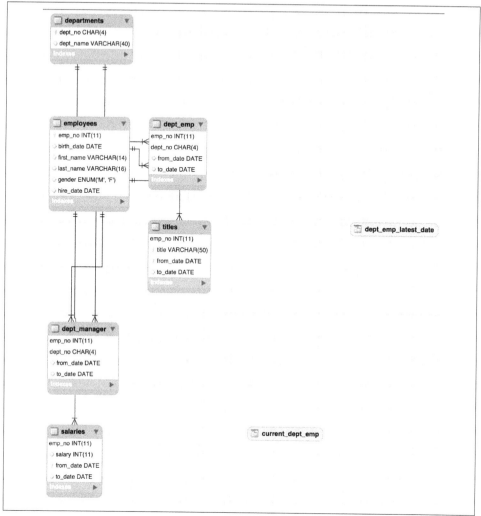

Figure 2-16. The ER model for the employees database

It is important that you carefully review the ER models shown here so you understand the relationships between entities and their attributes. Once the concepts are solidified, start practicing. You will see how to do that in the next section. We'll show you how to create a database on your MySQL server in Chapter 4.

Using the Entity Relationship Model

This section looks at the steps required to create an ER model and deploy it into database tables. We saw previously that MySQL Workbench lets us reverse engineer an existing database. But how do we model a new database and deploy it? We can automate this process with the MySQL Workbench tool.

Mapping Entities and Relationships to Database Tables

When converting an ER model to a database schema, we work through each entity and then through each relationship according to the rules discussed in the following sections to end up with a set of database tables.

Map the entities to database tables

For each strong entity, create a table comprising its attributes and designate the primary key. The parts of any composite attributes are also included here.

For each weak entity, create a table comprising its attributes and including the primary key of its owning entity. The owning entity's primary key is a foreign key here because it's a key not of this table but another table. The table's primary key for the weak entity is the combination of the foreign key and the partial key of the weak entity. If the relationship with the owning entity has any attributes, add them to this table.

For each entity's multivalued attribute, create a table comprising the entity's primary key and the attribute.

Map the relationships to database tables

Each one-to-one relationship between two entities includes the primary key of one entity as a foreign key in the table belonging to the other. If one entity participates totally in the relationship, place the foreign key in its table. If both participate totally in the relationship, consider merging them into a single table.

For each nonidentifying one-to-many relationship between two entities, include the entity's primary key on the "1" side as a foreign key in the table for the entity on the "N" side. Add any attributes of the relationship in the table alongside the foreign key. Note that identifying one-to-many relationships (between a weak entity and its owning entity) are captured as part of the entity-mapping stage.

For each many-to-many relationship between two entities, create a new table containing each entity's primary key as the primary key and add any attributes of the relationship. This step helps to identify intermediate entities.

For each relationship involving more than two entities, create a table with the primary keys of all the participating entities, and add any relationship attributes.

Creating a Bank Database ER Model

We've discussed database models for student grades and customer information, plus the three open source EERs available for MySQL. Now let's see how we could model a bank database. We've collected all the requisites from the stakeholders and defined our requirements for the online banking system, and we've decided we need to have the following entities:

- Employees
- Branches
- Customers
- Accounts

Now, following the mapping rules as just described, we are going to create the tables and attributes for each table. We established primary keys to ensure every table has a unique identifier column for its records. Next, we need to define the relationships between the tables.

Many to many relationships (N:M)

We've established this type of relationship between branches and employees, and between accounts and customers. An employee can work for any number of branches, and a branch could have any number of employees. Similarly, a customer could have many accounts, and an account could be a joint account held by more than two customers.

To model these relationships, we need two more intermediate entities. We create them as follows:

- account_customers
- branch_employees

The account_customers and branch_employees entities will be the bridges between account and customer entities and branch and employee entities, respectively. We are converting the N:M relationship into two 1:N relationships. You will see how the design looks in the next section.

One to many relationship (1:N)

This type of relationship exists between branches and accounts and between customers and account_customers. This brings up the concept of the *nonidentifying relationship*. For example, in the `accounts` table, the `branch_id` field is not part of the primary key (one reason for this is that you can move your bank account to another branch). It is common nowadays to keep a surrogate key as the primary key in each table; therefore, a genuine identifying relationship where the foreign key is also part of the primary key in a data model is rare.

Because we're creating a physical EER model, we are also going to define the primary keys. It is common and recommended to use auto-incrementing unsigned fields for the primary key.

Figure 2-17 shows the final representation of the bank model.

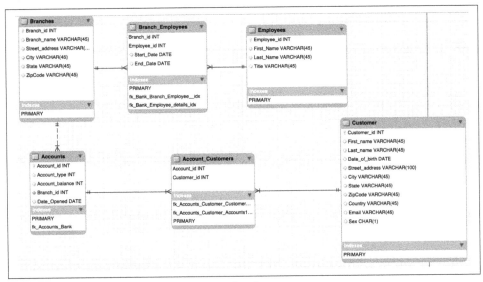

Figure 2-17. The EER model for the bank database

Note that there are items we haven't considered for this model. For example, our model does not support a customer with multiple addresses (say, a work address and a home address). We did this intentionally to emphasize the importance of collecting the requisites prior to database deployment.

You can download the model from the book's GitHub repository (*https://oreil.ly/FJm12*). The file is *bank_model.mwb*.

Converting the EER to a MySQL Database Using Workbench

It's a good idea to use a tool to draw your ER diagrams; this way, you can easily edit and redefine them until the final diagrams are clear and unambiguous. Once you're comfortable with the model, you can deploy it. MySQL Workbench allows the conversion of the EER model into data definition language (DDL) statements to create a MySQL database, using the Forward Engineer option in the database menu (Figure 2-18).

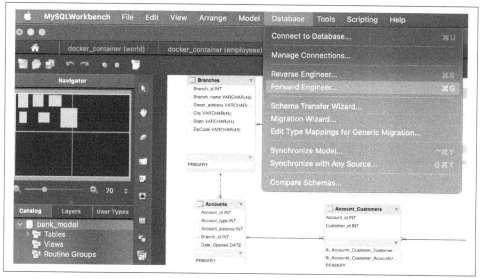

Figure 2-18. Forward Engineering a database in MySQL Workbench

You'll need to enter the credentials to connect to the database, and after that MySQL Workbench will present some options. For this model, we are going to use the standard options as shown in Figure 2-19, with all but the last option unchecked.

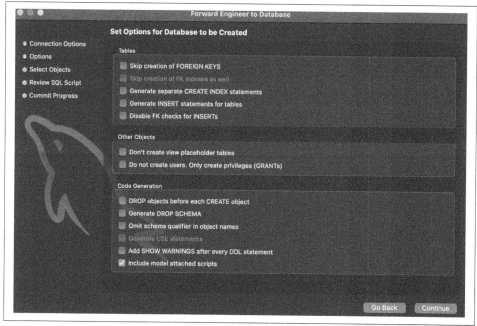

Figure 2-19. Database creation options

The next screen will ask which elements of the model we want to generate. Since we do not have anything special like triggers, stored procedures, users, and so on, we will only create the table objects and their relationships; the rest of the options are unchecked.

MySQL Workbench will then present us with the SQL script that will be executed to create the database from our model, as shown in Figure 2-20.

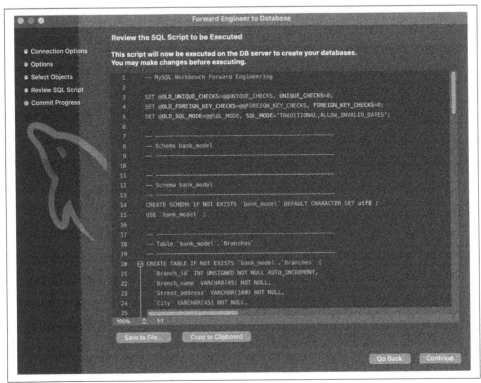

Figure 2-20. The script generated to create the database

When we click Continue, MySQL Workbench will execute the statements on our MySQL server, as shown in Figure 2-21.

We cover the details of the statements in this script in "Creating Tables" on page 130.

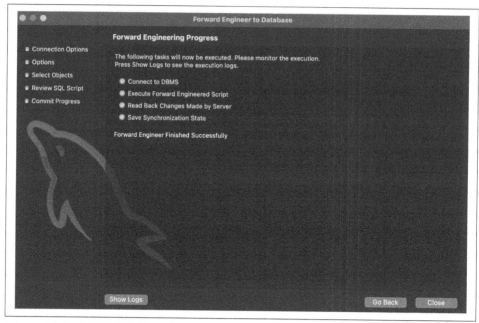

Figure 2-21. MySQL Workbench starts running the script

## CHAPTER 3

Basic SQL

As mentioned in Chapter 2, Dr. Edgar F. Codd conceived the relational database model and its normal forms in the early 1970s. In 1974, researchers at IBM's San Jose lab began work on a major project intended to prove the relational model's viability, called System R. At the same time, Dr. Donald Chamberlin and his colleagues were also working to define a database language. They developed the Structured English Query Language (SEQUEL), which allowed users to query a relational database using clearly defined English-style sentences. This was later renamed Structured Query Language (SQL), for legal reasons.

The first database management systems based on SQL became available commercially by the end of the '70s. With the growing activity surrounding the development of database languages, standardization emerged to simplify things, and the community settled on SQL. Both the American and international standards organizations (ANSI and ISO) took part in the standardization process, and in 1986 the first SQL standard was approved. The standard was later revised several times, with the names (SQL: 1999, SQL:2003, SQL:2008, etc.) indicating the versions released in the corresponding years. We will use the phrase *the SQL standard* or *standard SQL* to mean the current version of the SQL standard at any time.

MySQL extends the standard SQL, providing extra features. For example, MySQL implements the STRAIGHT_JOIN (*https://oreil.ly/rAHrZ*), which is syntax not recognized by other DBMSs.

This chapter introduces MySQL's SQL implementation, which we often refer to as the *CRUD* operations: create, read, update, and delete. We will show you how to read data from a database with the SELECT statement and choose what data to retrieve and in which order it is displayed. We'll also show you the basics of modifying your databases with the INSERT statement to add data, UPDATE to change data, and DELETE to remove data. Finally, we'll explain how to use the nonstandard SHOW TABLES and SHOW COLUMNS statements to explore your database.

Using the sakila Database

In Chapter 2, we showed you the principles of how to build a database diagram using the ER model. We also introduced the steps you take to convert an ER model to a format that makes sense for constructing a relational database. This section will show you the structure of the MySQL sakila database so you can start to get familiar with different database relational models. We won't explain the SQL statements used to create the database here; that's the subject of Chapter 4.

If you haven't imported the database yet, follow the steps in "Entity Relationship Modeling Examples" on page 77 to perform the task.

To choose the sakila database as our current database, we will use the USE statement. Type the following command:

```
mysql> USE sakila;

Database changed
mysql>
```

You can check which is the active database by typing the **SELECT DATABASE();** command:

```
mysql> SELECT DATABASE();
+------------+
| DATABASE() |
+------------+
| sakila     |
+------------+
1 row in set (0.00 sec)
```

Now, let's explore what tables make up the sakila database using the SHOW TABLES statement:

```
mysql> SHOW TABLES;
+----------------------------+
| Tables_in_sakila           |
+----------------------------+
| actor                      |
| actor_info                 |
| ...                        |
| customer                   |
| customer_list              |
| film                       |
| film_actor                 |
| film_category              |
| film_list                  |
```

```
| film_text                 |
| inventory                 |
| language                  |
| nicer_but_slower_film_list |
| payment                   |
| rental                    |
| sales_by_film_category    |
| sales_by_store            |
| staff                     |
| staff_list                |
| store                     |
+---------------------------+
23 rows in set (0.00 sec)
```

So far, there have been no surprises. Let's find out more about each of the tables that make up the sakila database. First, let's use the SHOW COLUMNS statement to explore the actor table (note that the output has been wrapped to fit with the page margins):

```
mysql> SHOW COLUMNS FROM actor;
+-------------+-------------------+------+-----+-------------------+...
| Field       | Type              | Null | Key | Default           |...
+-------------+-------------------+------+-----+-------------------+...
| actor_id    | smallint unsigned | NO   | PRI | NULL              |...
| first_name  | varchar(45)       | NO   |     | NULL              |...
| last_name   | varchar(45)       | NO   | MUL | NULL              |...
| last_update | timestamp         | NO   |     | CURRENT_TIMESTAMP |...
+-------------+-------------------+------+-----+-------------------+...
   ...+------------------------------------------------+
   ...| Extra                                          |
   ...+------------------------------------------------+
   ...| auto_increment                                 |
   ...|                                                |
   ...|                                                |
   ...| DEFAULT_GENERATED on update CURRENT_TIMESTAMP  |
   ...+------------------------------------------------+
4 rows in set (0.01 sec)
```

The DESCRIBE keyword is identical to SHOW COLUMNS FROM, and we can abbreviate it to just DESC, so we can write the previous query as follows:

```
mysql> DESC actor;
```

The output produced is identical. Let's examine the table structure more closely. The actor table contains four columns, actor_id, first_name, last_name, and last_update. We can also extract the types of the columns: a smallint for actor_id, varchar(45) for first_name and last_name, and timestamp for last_update. None of the columns accepts NULL (empty) value, actor_id is the primary key (PRI), and last_name is the first column of a nonunique index (MUL). Don't worry about the details; all that's important right now are the column names we will use for the SQL commands.

Next let's explore the `city` table by executing the DESC statement:

```
mysql> DESC city;
+-------------+-------------------+------+-----+-------------------+...
| Field       | Type              | Null | Key | Default           |...
+-------------+-------------------+------+-----+-------------------+...
| city_id     | smallint unsigned | NO   | PRI | NULL              |...
| city        | varchar(50)       | NO   |     | NULL              |...
| country_id  | smallint unsigned | NO   | MUL | NULL              |...
| last_update | timestamp         | NO   |     | CURRENT_TIMESTAMP |...
+-------------+-------------------+------+-----+-------------------+...
...+------------------------------------------------+
...| Extra                                          |
...+------------------------------------------------+
...| auto_increment                                 |
...|                                                |
...|                                                |
...| DEFAULT_GENERATED on update CURRENT_TIMESTAMP  |
...+------------------------------------------------+
4 rows in set (0.01 sec)
```

 The DEFAULT_GENERATED that you see in the Extra column indicates that this particular column uses a default value. This information is a MySQL 8.0 notation particularity, and it is not present in MySQL 5.7 or MariaDB 10.5.

Again, what's important is getting familiar with the columns in each table, as we'll make frequent use of these later when we discuss querying.

The next section shows you how to explore the data that MySQL stores in the `sakila` database and its tables.

The SELECT Statement and Basic Querying Techniques

The previous chapters showed you how to install and configure MySQL and use the MySQL command line, and introduced the ER model. Now you're ready to start learning the SQL language that all MySQL clients use to explore and manipulate data. This section introduces the most commonly used SQL keyword: the SELECT keyword. We explain the fundamental elements of style and syntax and the features of the WHERE clause, Boolean operators, and sorting (much of this also applies to our later discussions of INSERT, UPDATE, and DELETE). This isn't the end of our discussion of SELECT; you'll find more in Chapter 5, where we show you how to use its advanced features.

Single-Table SELECTs

The most basic form of SELECT reads the data in all rows and columns from a table. Connect to MySQL using the command line and choose the `sakila` database:

```
mysql> USE sakila;

Database changed
```

Let's retrieve all of the data in the `language` table:

```
mysql> SELECT * FROM language;
+-------------+----------+---------------------+
| language_id | name     | last_update         |
+-------------+----------+---------------------+
|           1 | English  | 2006-02-15 05:02:19 |
|           2 | Italian  | 2006-02-15 05:02:19 |
|           3 | Japanese | 2006-02-15 05:02:19 |
|           4 | Mandarin | 2006-02-15 05:02:19 |
|           5 | French   | 2006-02-15 05:02:19 |
|           6 | German   | 2006-02-15 05:02:19 |
+-------------+----------+---------------------+
6 rows in set (0.00 sec)
```

The output has six rows, and each row contains the values for all the columns present in the table. We now know that there are six languages, and we can see the languages, their identifiers, and the last time each language was updated.

A simple SELECT statement has four components:

1. The keyword SELECT.
2. The columns to be displayed. The asterisk (*) symbol is a wildcard character meaning all columns.
3. The keyword FROM.
4. The table name.

So in this example, we've asked for all columns from the `language` table, and that's what MySQL has returned to us.

Let's try another simple SELECT. This time, we'll retrieve all columns from the `city` table:

```
mysql> SELECT * FROM city;
```

```
+---------+----------------------+------------+---------------------+
| city_id | city                 | country_id | last_update         |
+---------+----------------------+------------+---------------------+
|       1 | A Corua (La Corua)   |         87 | 2006-02-15 04:45:25 |
|       2 | Abha                 |         82 | 2006-02-15 04:45:25 |
|       3 | Abu Dhabi            |        101 | 2006-02-15 04:45:25 |
|     ... |                      |            |                     |
|     599 | Zhoushan             |         23 | 2006-02-15 04:45:25 |
|     600 | Ziguinchor           |         83 | 2006-02-15 04:45:25 |
+---------+----------------------+------------+---------------------+
600 rows in set (0.00 sec)
```

There are 600 cities, and the output has the same basic structure as in our first example.

This example provides some insight into how the relationships between the tables work. Consider the first row of the results. In the column `country_id`, you will see the value 87. As you'll see later, we can check the `country` table to find out that the country with code 87 is Spain. We'll discuss how to write queries on relationships between tables in "Joining Two Tables" on page 109.

If you look at the complete output, you'll also see that there are several different cities with the same `country_id`. Having repeated `country_id` values isn't a problem since we expect a country to have many cities (a one-to-many relationship).

You should now feel comfortable choosing a database, listing its tables, and retrieving all of the data from a table using the `SELECT` statement. To practice, you might want to experiment with the other tables in the `sakila` database. Remember that you can use the `SHOW TABLES` statement to find out the table names.

Choosing Columns

Earlier, we used the * wildcard character to retrieve all the columns in a table. If you don't want to display all the columns, it's easy to be more specific by listing the columns you want, in the order you want them, separated by commas. For example, if you want only the `city` column from the `city` table, you'd type:

```
mysql> SELECT city FROM city;

+----------------------+
| city                 |
+----------------------+
| A Corua (La Corua)   |
| Abha                 |
| Abu Dhabi            |
| Acua                 |
| Adana                |
+----------------------+
5 rows in set (0.00 sec)
```

If you want both the city and city_id columns, in that order, you'd use:

```
mysql> SELECT city, city_id FROM city;
```

```
+----------------------+---------+
| city                 | city_id |
+----------------------+---------+
| A Corua (La Corua)   |       1 |
| Abha                 |       2 |
| Abu Dhabi            |       3 |
| Acua                 |       4 |
| Adana                |       5 |
+----------------------+---------+
5 rows in set (0.01 sec)
```

You can even list columns more than once:

```
mysql> SELECT city, city FROM city;
```

```
+----------------------+----------------------+
| city                 | city                 |
+----------------------+----------------------+
| A Corua (La Corua)   | A Corua (La Corua)   |
| Abha                 | Abha                 |
| Abu Dhabi            | Abu Dhabi            |
| Acua                 | Acua                 |
| Adana                | Adana                |
+----------------------+----------------------+
5 rows in set (0.00 sec)
```

Although this may seem pointless, it can be useful when combined with aliases in more advanced queries, as you'll see in Chapter 5.

You can specify database, table, and column names in a SELECT statement. This allows you to avoid the USE command and work with any database and table directly with SELECT; it also helps resolve ambiguities, as we'll show in "Joining Two Tables" on page 109. For example, suppose you want to retrieve the name column from the lan guage table in the sakila database. You can do this with the following command:

```
mysql> SELECT name FROM sakila.language;
```

```
+----------+
| name     |
+----------+
| English  |
| Italian  |
| Japanese |
| Mandarin |
| French   |
| German   |
+----------+
6 rows in set (0.01 sec)
```

The `sakila.language` component after the FROM keyword specifies the `sakila` database and its `language` table. There's no need to enter **USE sakila;** before running this query. This syntax can also be used with other SQL statements, including the UPDATE, DELETE, INSERT, and SHOW statements we discuss later in this chapter.

Selecting Rows with the WHERE Clause

This section introduces the WHERE clause and explains how to use operators to write expressions. You'll see these in SELECT statements and other statements such as UPDATE and DELETE; we'll show you examples later in this chapter.

WHERE basics

The WHERE clause is a powerful tool that allows you to filter which rows are returned from a SELECT statement. You use it to return rows that match a condition, such as having a column value that exactly matches a string, a number greater or less than a value, or a string that is a prefix of another. Almost all our examples in this and later chapters contain WHERE clauses, and you'll become very familiar with them.

The simplest WHERE clause is one that exactly matches a value. Consider an example where you want to find out the English language's details in the `language` table. Here's what you'd type:

```
mysql> SELECT * FROM sakila.language WHERE name = 'English';
+-------------+---------+---------------------+
| language_id | name    | last_update         |
+-------------+---------+---------------------+
|           1 | English | 2006-02-15 05:02:19 |
+-------------+---------+---------------------+
1 row in set (0.00 sec)
```

MySQL returns all rows that match your search criteria—in this case, just the one row and all its columns.

Let's try another exact match example. Suppose you want to find out the first name of the actor with an `actor_id` value of 4 in the `actor` table. You would type:

```
mysql> SELECT first_name FROM actor WHERE actor_id = 4;
+------------+
| first_name |
+------------+
| JENNIFER   |
+------------+
1 row in set (0.00 sec)
```

Here you provide a column and a row, including the column `first_name` after the SELECT keyword and specifying the WHERE `actor_id` = 4.

If a value matches more than one row, the results will contain all the matches. Suppose you want to see all the cities belonging to Brazil, which has a country_id of 15. You would type in:

```
mysql> SELECT city FROM city WHERE country_id = 15;
```

```
+----------------------+
| city                 |
+----------------------+
| Alvorada             |
| Angra dos Reis       |
| Anpolis              |
| Aparecida de Goinia  |
| Araatuba             |
| Bag                  |
| Belm                 |
| Blumenau             |
| Boa Vista            |
| Braslia              |
| ...                  |
+----------------------+
28 rows in set (0.00 sec)
```

The results show the names of the 28 cities that belong to Brazil. If we could join the information we get from the city table with information we get from the country table, we could display the cities' names with their respective countries. We'll see how to perform this type of query in "Joining Two Tables" on page 109.

Now let's retrieve values that belong to a range. Retrieving multiple values is simple for numeric ranges, so let's start by finding all cities' names with a city_id less than 5. To do this, execute the following statement:

```
mysql> SELECT city FROM city WHERE city_id < 5;
```

```
+---------------------+
| city                |
+---------------------+
| A Corua (La Corua)  |
| Abha                |
| Abu Dhabi           |
| Acua                |
+---------------------+
4 rows in set (0.00 sec)
```

For numbers, the frequently used operators are equal (=), greater than (>), less than (<), less than or equal (<=), greater than or equal (>=), and not equal (<> or !=).

Consider one more example. If you want to find all languages that don't have a language_id of 2, you'd type:

```
mysql> SELECT language_id, name FROM sakila.language
    -> WHERE language_id <> 2;
```

```
+-------------+----------+
| language_id | name     |
+-------------+----------+
|           1 | English  |
|           3 | Japanese |
|           4 | Mandarin |
|           5 | French   |
|           6 | German   |
+-------------+----------+
5 rows in set (0.00 sec)
```

The previous output shows the first, third, and all subsequent languages in the table. Note that you can use either the <> or != operator for the *not-equal* condition.

You can use the same operators for strings. By default, string comparisons are not case-sensitive and use the current character set. For example:

```
mysql> SELECT first_name FROM actor WHERE first_name < 'B';
+------------+
| first_name |
+------------+
| ALEC       |
| AUDREY     |
| ANNE       |
| ANGELA     |
| ADAM       |
| ANGELINA   |
| ALBERT     |
| ADAM       |
| ANGELA     |
| ALBERT     |
| AL         |
| ALAN       |
| AUDREY     |
+------------+
13 rows in set (0.00 sec)
```

By "not case-sensitive" we mean that B and b will be considered the same filter, so this query will provide the same result:

```
mysql> SELECT first_name FROM actor WHERE first_name < 'b';
+------------+
| first_name |
+------------+
| ALEC       |
| AUDREY     |
| ANNE       |
| ANGELA     |
| ADAM       |
| ANGELINA   |
| ALBERT     |
| ADAM       |
```

```
| ANGELA   |
| ALBERT   |
| AL       |
| ALAN     |
| AUDREY   |
+------------+
13 rows in set (0.00 sec)
```

Another common task to perform with strings is to find matches that begin with a prefix, contain a string, or end in a suffix. For example, we might want to find all album names beginning with the word "Retro." We can do this with the LIKE operator in a WHERE clause. Let's see an example where we are searching for a film with a title that contains the word family:

```
mysql> SELECT title FROM film WHERE title LIKE '%family%';

+-----------------+
| title           |
+-----------------+
| CYCLONE FAMILY  |
| DOGMA FAMILY    |
| FAMILY SWEET    |
+-----------------+
3 rows in set (0.00 sec)
```

Let's take a look at how this works. The LIKE clause is used with strings and means that a match must meet the pattern in the string that follows. In our example, we've used LIKE '%family%', which means the string must contain family, and it can be preceded or followed by zero or more characters. Most strings used with LIKE contain the percentage character (%) as a wildcard character that matches all possible strings. You can use it to define a string that ends in a suffix—such as "%ing"—or a string that starts with a particular substring, such as "Corruption%".

For example, "John%" would match all strings starting with John, such as John Smith and John Paul Getty. The pattern "%Paul" matches all strings that have Paul at the end. Finally, the pattern "%Paul%" matches all strings that have Paul in them, including at the start or at the end.

If you want to match exactly one wildcard character in a LIKE clause, you use the underscore character (_). For example, if you want the titles of all movies starring an actor whose name begins with the three letters NAT, you use:

```
mysql> SELECT title FROM film_list WHERE actors LIKE 'NAT_%';

+-----------------------+
| title                 |
+-----------------------+
| FANTASY TROOPERS      |
| FOOL MOCKINGBIRD      |
| HOLES BRANNIGAN       |
```

```
| KWAI HOMEWARD       |
| LICENSE WEEKEND     |
| NETWORK PEAK        |
| NUTS TIES           |
| TWISTED PIRATES     |
| UNFORGIVEN ZOOLANDER |
+---------------------+
9 rows in set (0.04 sec)
```

In general, you should avoid using the percentage (%) wildcard at the beginning of the pattern, like in the following example:

```
mysql> SELECT title FROM film WHERE title LIKE '%day%';
```

You will get the results, but MySQL will not use the index under this condition. Using the wildcard will force MySQL to read the entire table to retrieve the results, which can cause a severe performance impact if the table has millions of rows.

Combining conditions with AND, OR, NOT, and XOR

So far, we've used the WHERE clause to test one condition, returning all rows that meet it. You can combine two or more conditions using the Boolean operators AND, OR, NOT, and XOR.

Let's start with an example. Suppose you want to find the titles of sci-fi movies that are rated PG. This is straightforward with the AND operator:

```
mysql> SELECT title FROM film_list WHERE category LIKE 'Sci-Fi'
    -> AND rating LIKE 'PG';

+----------------------+
| title                |
+----------------------+
| CHAINSAW UPTOWN      |
| CHARADE DUFFEL       |
| FRISCO FORREST       |
| GOODFELLAS SALUTE    |
| GRAFFITI LOVE        |
| MOURNING PURPLE      |
| OPEN AFRICAN         |
| SILVERADO GOLDFINGER |
| TITANS JERK          |
| TROJAN TOMORROW      |
| UNFORGIVEN ZOOLANDER |
| WONDERLAND CHRISTMAS |
+----------------------+
12 rows in set (0.07 sec)
```

The AND operation in the WHERE clause restricts the results to those rows that meet both conditions.

The OR operator is used to find rows that meet at least one of several conditions. To illustrate, imagine now that you want a list of movies in the Children or Family categories. You can do this with OR and two LIKE clauses:

```
mysql> SELECT title FROM film_list WHERE category LIKE 'Children'
    -> OR category LIKE 'Family';

+------------------------+
| title                  |
+------------------------+
| AFRICAN EGG            |
| APACHE DIVINE          |
| ATLANTIS CAUSE         |
...
| WRONG BEHAVIOR         |
| ZOOLANDER FICTION      |
+------------------------+
129 rows in set (0.04 sec)
```

The OR operation in the WHERE clause restricts the answers to those that meet either of the two conditions. As an aside, we can observe that the results are ordered. This is merely a coincidence; in this case, they're reported in the order they were added to the database. We'll return to sorting output in "The ORDER BY Clause" on page 105.

You can combine AND and OR, but you need to make it clear whether you want to first AND the conditions or OR them. Parentheses cluster parts of a statement together and help make expressions readable; you can use them just as you would in basic math. Let's say that now you want sci-fi or family movies that are rated PG. You can write this query as follows:

```
mysql> SELECT title FROM film_list WHERE (category like 'Sci-Fi'
    -> OR category LIKE 'Family') AND rating LIKE 'PG';

+------------------------+
| title                  |
+------------------------+
| BEDAZZLED MARRIED      |
| CHAINSAW UPTOWN        |
| CHARADE DUFFEL         |
| CHASING FIGHT          |
| EFFECT GLADIATOR       |
...
| UNFORGIVEN ZOOLANDER   |
| WONDERLAND CHRISTMAS   |
+------------------------+
30 rows in set (0.07 sec)
```

The parentheses make the evaluation order clear: you want movies from either the Sci-Fi or the Family category, but all of them need to be PG-rated.

With the use of parentheses, it is possible to change the evaluation order. The easiest way to see how this works is by playing around with calculations:

```
mysql> SELECT (2+2)*3;

+---------+
| (2+2)*3 |
+---------+
|      12 |
+---------+
1 row in set (0.00 sec)

mysql> SELECT 2+2*3;

+-------+
| 2+2*3 |
+-------+
|     8 |
+-------+
1 row in set (0.00 sec)
```

 One of the most difficult problems to diagnose is a query that is running with no syntax errors, but it is returning values different from those expected. While the parentheses do not affect the AND operator, the OR operator is significantly impacted by them. For example, consider the result of this statement:

```
mysql> SELECT * FROM sakila.city WHERE city_id = 3
    -> OR city_id = 4 AND country_id = 60;

+---------+-----------+------------+---------------------+
| city_id | city      | country_id | last_update         |
+---------+-----------+------------+---------------------+
|       3 | Abu Dhabi |        101 | 2006-02-15 04:45:25 |
|       4 | Acua      |         60 | 2006-02-15 04:45:25 |
+---------+-----------+------------+---------------------+
2 rows in set (0.00 sec)
```

If we change the ordering of the operators, we will obtain a different result:

```
mysql> SELECT * FROM sakila.city WHERE country_id = 60
    -> AND city_id = 3 OR city_id = 4;

+---------+------+------------+---------------------+
| city_id | city | country_id | last_update         |
+---------+------+------------+---------------------+
|       4 | Acua |         60 | 2006-02-15 04:45:25 |
+---------+------+------------+---------------------+
1 row in set (0.00 sec)
```

Using parentheses makes the queries much easier to understand and increases the likelihood that you'll get the results you're expecting. We recommend that you use parentheses whenever there's a chance MySQL could misinterpret your intention; there's no good reason to rely on MySQL's implicit evaluation order.

The unary NOT operator negates a Boolean statement. Earlier we gave the example of listing all languages with a language_id not equal to 2. You can also write this query with the NOT operator:

```
mysql> SELECT language_id, name FROM sakila.language
    -> WHERE NOT (language_id = 2);
```

```
+-------------+----------+
| language_id | name     |
+-------------+----------+
|           1 | English  |
|           3 | Japanese |
|           4 | Mandarin |
|           5 | French   |
|           6 | German   |
+-------------+----------+
5 rows in set (0.01 sec)
```

The expression in parentheses, (language_id = 2), gives the condition to match, and the NOT operation negates it, so you get everything but those results that match the condition. There are several other ways you can write a WHERE clause with the same idea. In Chapter 5, you will see that some have better performance than others.

Consider another example using NOT and parentheses. Suppose you want to get a list of all movie titles with an FID less than 7, but not those numbered 4 or 6. You can do this with the following query:

```
mysql> SELECT fid,title FROM film_list WHERE FID < 7 AND NOT (FID = 4 OR FID = 6);
```

```
+------+-----------------+
| fid  | title           |
+------+-----------------+
|    1 | ACADEMY DINOSAUR |
|    2 | ACE GOLDFINGER  |
|    3 | ADAPTATION HOLES |
|    5 | AFRICAN EGG     |
+------+-----------------+
4 rows in set (0.06 sec)
```

Understanding operator precedence can be a little tricky, and sometimes it takes DBAs a long time to debug a query and identify why it is not returning the requested values. The following list shows the available operators in order from the highest priority to the lowest. Operators that are shown together on a line have the same priority:

- INTERVAL
- BINARY, COLLATE
- !
- - (unary minus), ~ (unary bit inversion)

- ^

- *, /, DIV, %, MOD

- -,+

- <<, >>

- &

- \|

- = (comparison), <=>, >=, >, <=, <, <>, !=, IS, LIKE, REGEXP, IN, MEMBER OF

- BETWEEN, CASE, WHEN, THEN, ELSE

- NOT

- AND, &&

- XOR

- OR, \|\|

- = (assignment), :=

It is possible to combine these operators in diverse ways to get the desired results. For example, you can write a query to get the titles of any movies that have a price range between $2 and $4, belong to the Documentary or Horror category, and have an actor named Bob:

```
mysql> SELECT title
    -> FROM film_list
    -> WHERE price BETWEEN 2 AND 4
    -> AND (category LIKE 'Documentary' OR category LIKE 'Horror')
    -> AND actors LIKE '%BOB%';

+------------------+
| title            |
+------------------+
| ADAPTATION HOLES |
+------------------+
1 row in set (0.08 sec)
```

Finally, before we move on to sorting, note that it is possible to execute queries that do not match any results. In this case, the query will return an empty set:

```
mysql> SELECT title FROM film_list
    -> WHERE price BETWEEN 2 AND 4
    -> AND (category LIKE 'Documentary' OR category LIKE 'Horror')
    -> AND actors LIKE '%GRIPPA%';

Empty set (0.04 sec)
```

The ORDER BY Clause

We've discussed how to choose the columns and which rows are returned as part of the query result, but not how to control how the result is displayed. In a relational database, the rows in a table form a set; there is no intrinsic order between the rows, so we have to ask MySQL to sort the results if we want them in a particular order. This section explains how to use the ORDER BY clause to do this. Sorting does not affect *what* is returned; it only affects *what order* the results are returned in.

 InnoDB tables in MySQL have a special index called the *clustered index* that stores row data. When you define a primary key on a table, InnoDB uses it as the clustered index. Suppose you are executing queries based on the primary key. In that case, the rows will be returned ordered in ascending order by the primary key. However, we always recommending using the ORDER BY clause if you want to enforce a particular order.

Suppose you want to return a list of the first 10 customers in the sakila database, sorted alphabetically by name. Here's what you'd type:

```
mysql> SELECT name FROM customer_list
    -> ORDER BY name
    -> LIMIT 10;
+-------------------+
| name              |
+-------------------+
| AARON SELBY       |
| ADAM GOOCH        |
| ADRIAN CLARY      |
| AGNES BISHOP      |
| ALAN KAHN         |
| ALBERT CROUSE     |
| ALBERTO HENNING   |
| ALEX GRESHAM      |
| ALEXANDER FENNELL |
| ALFRED CASILLAS   |
+-------------------+
10 rows in set (0.01 sec)
```

The ORDER BY clause indicates that sorting is required, followed by the column that should be used as the sort key. In this example, you're sorting by name in alphabetically ascending order—the default sort is case-insensitive and in ascending order, and MySQL automatically sorts alphabetically because the columns are character strings. The way strings are sorted is determined by the character set and collation order that are being used. We discuss these in "Collation and Character Sets" on page 133. For most of this book, we assume that you're using the default settings.

Let's look at another example. This time, you'll sort the output from the `address` table in ascending order based on the `last_update` column and show just the first five results:

```
mysql> SELECT address, last_update FROM address
    -> ORDER BY last_update LIMIT 5;

+----------------------------+---------------------+
| address                    | last_update         |
+----------------------------+---------------------+
| 1168 Najafabad Parkway     | 2014-09-25 22:29:59 |
| 1031 Daugavpils Parkway    | 2014-09-25 22:29:59 |
| 1924 Shimonoseki Drive     | 2014-09-25 22:29:59 |
| 757 Rustenburg Avenue      | 2014-09-25 22:30:01 |
| 1892 Nabereznyje Telny Lane| 2014-09-25 22:30:02 |
+----------------------------+---------------------+
5 rows in set (0.00 sec)
```

As you can see, it is possible to sort different types of columns. Moreover, we can compound the sorting with two or more columns. For example, let's say you want to sort the addresses alphabetically, but grouped by district:

```
mysql> SELECT address, district FROM address
    -> ORDER BY district, address;

+-------------------------------------------+---------------------+
| address                                   | district            |
+-------------------------------------------+---------------------+
| 1368 Maracabo Boulevard                   |                     |
| 18 Duisburg Boulevard                     |                     |
| 962 Tama Loop                             |                     |
| 535 Ahmadnagar Manor                      | Abu Dhabi           |
| 669 Firozabad Loop                        | Abu Dhabi           |
| 1078 Stara Zagora Drive                   | Aceh                |
| 663 Baha Blanca Parkway                   | Adana               |
| 842 Salzburg Lane                         | Adana               |
| 614 Pak Kret Street                       | Addis Abeba         |
| 751 Lima Loop                             | Aden                |
| 1157 Nyeri Loop                           | Adygea              |
| 387 Mwene-Ditu Drive                      | Ahal                |
| 775 ostka Drive                           | al-Daqahliya        |
| ...                                       |                     |
| 1416 San Juan Bautista Tuxtepec Avenue    | Zufar               |
| 138 Caracas Boulevard                     | Zulia               |
+-------------------------------------------+---------------------+
603 rows in set (0.00 sec)
```

You can also sort in descending order, and you can control this behavior for each sort key. Suppose you want to sort the addresses by descending alphabetical order and the districts in ascending order. You would type this:

```
mysql> SELECT address,district FROM address
    -> ORDER BY district ASC, address DESC
    -> LIMIT 10;
```

```
+--------------------------+-------------+
| address                  | district    |
+--------------------------+-------------+
| 962 Tama Loop            |             |
| 18 Duisburg Boulevard    |             |
| 1368 Maracabo Boulevard  |             |
| 669 Firozabad Loop       | Abu Dhabi   |
| 535 Ahmadnagar Manor     | Abu Dhabi   |
| 1078 Stara Zagora Drive  | Aceh        |
| 842 Salzburg Lane        | Adana       |
| 663 Baha Blanca Parkway  | Adana       |
| 614 Pak Kret Street      | Addis Abeba |
| 751 Lima Loop            | Aden        |
+--------------------------+-------------+
10 rows in set (0.01 sec)
```

If a collision of values occurs and you don't specify another sort key, the sort order is undefined. This may not be important for you; you may not care about the order in which two customers with the identical name "John A. Smith" appear. If you want to enforce a certain order in this case, you need to add more columns to the ORDER BY clause, as demonstrated in the previous example.

The LIMIT Clause

As you may have noted, a few of the previous queries used the LIMIT clause. This is a useful nonstandard SQL statement that allows you to control how many rows are output. Its basic form allows you to limit the number of rows returned from a SELECT statement, which is useful when you want to restrict the amount of data communicated over a network or output to the screen. You might use it, for example, to get a sample of the data from a table, as shown here:

```
mysql> SELECT name FROM customer_list LIMIT 10;
```

```
+------------------+
| name             |
+------------------+
| VERA MCCOY       |
| MARIO CHEATHAM   |
| JUDY GRAY        |
| JUNE CARROLL     |
| ANTHONY SCHWAB   |
| CLAUDE HERZOG    |
| MARTIN BALES     |
| BOBBY BOUDREAU   |
| WILLIE MARKHAM   |
| JORDAN ARCHULETA |
+------------------+
```

The LIMIT clause can have two arguments. In this case, the first argument specifies the first row to return, and the second specifies the maximum number of rows to return. The first argument is known as the *offset*. Suppose you want five rows, but you want to skip the first five rows, which means the result will start at the sixth row. Record offsets for LIMIT start at 0, so you can do this as follows:

```
mysql> SELECT name FROM customer_list LIMIT 5, 5;
+-------------------+
| name              |
+-------------------+
| CLAUDE HERZOG     |
| MARTIN BALES      |
| BOBBY BOUDREAU    |
| WILLIE MARKHAM    |
| JORDAN ARCHULETA  |
+-------------------+
5 rows in set (0.00 sec)
```

The output is rows 6 to 10 from the SELECT query.

There's an alternative syntax that you might see for the LIMIT keyword: instead of writing LIMIT 10, 5, you can write LIMIT 10 OFFSET 5. The OFFSET syntax discards the *N* values specified in it.

Here's an example with no offset:

```
mysql> SELECT id, name FROM customer_list
    -> ORDER BY id LIMIT 10;
+----+-------------------+
| ID | name              |
+----+-------------------+
|  1 | MARY SMITH        |
|  2 | PATRICIA JOHNSON  |
|  3 | LINDA WILLIAMS    |
|  4 | BARBARA JONES     |
|  5 | ELIZABETH BROWN   |
|  6 | JENNIFER DAVIS    |
|  7 | MARIA MILLER      |
|  8 | SUSAN WILSON      |
|  9 | MARGARET MOORE    |
| 10 | DOROTHY TAYLOR    |
+----+-------------------+
10 rows in set (0.00 sec)
```

And here are the results with an offset of 5:

```
mysql> SELECT id, name FROM customer_list
    -> ORDER BY id LIMIT 10 OFFSET 5;
```

```
+----+----------------+
| ID | name           |
+----+----------------+
|  6 | JENNIFER DAVIS |
|  7 | MARIA MILLER   |
|  8 | SUSAN WILSON   |
|  9 | MARGARET MOORE |
| 10 | DOROTHY TAYLOR |
| 11 | LISA ANDERSON  |
| 12 | NANCY THOMAS   |
| 13 | KAREN JACKSON  |
| 14 | BETTY WHITE    |
| 15 | HELEN HARRIS   |
+----+----------------+
10 rows in set (0.01 sec)
```

Joining Two Tables

So far we've only been working with one table in our SELECT queries. However, the majority of cases will require information from more than one table at once. As we've explored the tables in the sakila database, it's become obvious that by using relationships, we can answer more interesting queries. For example, it'd be useful to know the country each city is in. This section shows you how to answer queries like that by joining two tables. We'll return to this issue as part of a longer, more advanced discussion of joins in Chapter 5.

We use only one join syntax in this chapter. There are two more (LEFT and RIGHT JOIN), and each gives you a different way to bring together data from two or more tables. The syntax we use here is the INNER JOIN, which is the most commonly used in daily activities. Let's look at an example, and then we'll explain more about how it works:

```
mysql> SELECT city, country FROM city INNER JOIN country
    -> ON city.country_id = country.country_id
    -> WHERE country.country_id < 5
    -> ORDER BY country, city;
+----------+----------------+
| city     | country        |
+----------+----------------+
| Kabul    | Afghanistan    |
| Batna    | Algeria        |
| Bchar    | Algeria        |
| Skikda   | Algeria        |
| Tafuna   | American Samoa |
| Benguela | Angola         |
| Namibe   | Angola         |
+----------+----------------+
7 rows in set (0.00 sec)
```

The output shows the cities in each country with a `country_id` lower than 5. You can see for the first time which cities are in each country.

How does the `INNER JOIN` work? The statement has two parts: first, two table names separated by the `INNER JOIN` keywords; and second, the `ON` keyword that specifies the required columns to compose the condition. In this example, the two tables to be joined are `city` and `country`, expressed as `city INNER JOIN country` (for the basic `INNER JOIN`, it doesn't matter what order you list the tables in, so using `country INNER JOIN city` would have the same effect). The `ON` clause (`ON city.country_id = country.country_id`) is where we tell MySQL the columns that hold the relationship between the tables; you should recall this from our design and our previous discussion in Chapter 2.

If in the join condition the column names in both tables used for matching are the same, you can use the `USING` clause instead:

```
mysql> SELECT city, country FROM city
    -> INNER JOIN country using (country_id)
    -> WHERE country.country_id < 5
    -> ORDER BY country, city;
+----------+----------------+
| city     | country        |
+----------+----------------+
| Kabul    | Afghanistan    |
| Batna    | Algeria        |
| Bchar    | Algeria        |
| Skikda   | Algeria        |
| Tafuna   | American Samoa |
| Benguela | Angola         |
| Namibe   | Angola         |
+----------+----------------+
7 rows in set (0.01 sec)
```

The Venn diagram in Figure 3-1 illustrates the inner join.

Before we leave `SELECT`, we'll give you a taste of one of the functions you can use to aggregate values. Suppose you want to count how many cities Italy has in our database. You can do this by joining the two tables and counting the number of rows with that `country_id`. Here's how it works:

```
mysql> SELECT COUNT(1) FROM city INNER JOIN country
    -> ON city.country_id = country.country_id
    -> WHERE country.country_id = 49
    -> ORDER BY country, city;
```

```
+-----------+
| count(1)  |
+-----------+
|        7  |
+-----------+
1 row in set (0.00 sec)
```

We explain more features of SELECT and aggregate functions in Chapter 5. For more on the COUNT() function, see "Aggregate functions" on page 193.

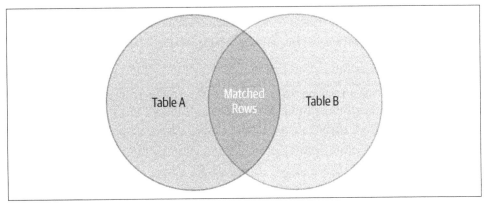

Figure 3-1. The Venn diagram representation of the INNER JOIN

The INSERT Statement

The INSERT statement is used to add new data to tables. This section explains its basic syntax and walks through some simple examples that add new rows to the sakila database. In Chapter 4, we'll discuss how to load data from existing tables or external data sources.

INSERT Basics

Inserting data typically occurs in two situations: when you bulk-load in a large batch as you create your database, and when you add data on an ad hoc basis as you use the database. In MySQL, different optimizations are built into the server for each situation. Importantly, different SQL syntaxes are available to make it easy for you to work with the server in both cases. We'll explain the basic INSERT syntax in this section and show you examples of using it for bulk and single-record insertion.

Let's start with the basic task of inserting one new row into the language table. To do this, you need to understand the table's structure. As we explained in "Using the sakila Database" on page 90, you can discover this with the SHOW COLUMNS statement:

```
mysql> SHOW COLUMNS FROM language;
```

```
+--------------+------------------+------+-----+-------------------+...
| Field        | Type             | Null | Key | Default           |...
+--------------+------------------+------+-----+-------------------+...
| language_id  | tinyint unsigned | NO   | PRI | NULL              |...
| name         | char(20)         | NO   |     | NULL              |...
| last_update  | timestamp        | NO   |     | CURRENT_TIMESTAMP |...
+--------------+------------------+------+-----+-------------------+...

...+-----------------------------------------------+
...| Extra                                         |
...+-----------------------------------------------+
...| auto_increment                                |
...|                                               |
...| DEFAULT_GENERATED on update CURRENT_TIMESTAMP |
...+-----------------------------------------------+
3 rows in set (0.00 sec)
```

This tells you that the `language_id` column is auto-generated, and the `last_update` column is updated every time an UPDATE operation happens. You'll learn more about the AUTO_INCREMENT shortcut to automatically assign the next available identifier in Chapter 4.

Let's add a new row for the language Portuguese. There are two ways to do this. The most common is to let MySQL fill in the default value for the `language_id`, like this:

```
mysql> INSERT INTO language VALUES (NULL, 'Portuguese', NOW());
Query OK, 1 row affected (0.10 sec)
```

If you we execute a SELECT on the table now, we'll see that MySQL inserted the row:

```
mysql> SELECT * FROM language;
+-------------+------------+---------------------+
| language_id | name       | last_update         |
+-------------+------------+---------------------+
|           1 | English    | 2006-02-15 05:02:19 |
|           2 | Italian    | 2006-02-15 05:02:19 |
|           3 | Japanese   | 2006-02-15 05:02:19 |
|           4 | Mandarin   | 2006-02-15 05:02:19 |
|           5 | French     | 2006-02-15 05:02:19 |
|           6 | German     | 2006-02-15 05:02:19 |
|           7 | Portuguese | 2020-09-26 09:11:36 |
+-------------+------------+---------------------+
7 rows in set (0.00 sec)
```

Note that we used the function NOW() (*https://oreil.ly/5YBth*) in the `last_update` column. The NOW() function returns the current date and time of the MySQL server.

The second option is to insert the value of the `language_id` column manually. Now that we already have seven languages, we should use 8 for the next value of the `language_id`. We can verify that with this SQL instruction:

```
mysql> SELECT MAX(language_id) FROM language;
```

```
+------------------+
| max(language_id) |
+------------------+
|                7 |
+------------------+
1 row in set (0.00 sec)
```

The MAX() function tells you the maximum value for the column supplied as a parameter. This is cleaner than using SELECT language_id FROM language, which prints out all the rows and requires you to inspect them to find the maximum value. Adding an ORDER BY and a LIMIT clause makes this easier, but using MAX() is much simpler than SELECT language_id FROM language ORDER BY language_id DESC LIMIT 1, which returns the same answer.

We're now ready to insert the row. In this INSERT, we are going to insert the last_update value manually too. Here's the needed command:

```
mysql> INSERT INTO language VALUES (8, 'Russian', '2020-09-26 10:35:00');

Query OK, 1 row affected (0.02 sec)
```

MySQL reports that one row has been affected (added, in this case), which we can confirm by checking the contents of the table again:

```
mysql> SELECT * FROM language;
+-------------+------------+---------------------+
| language_id | name       | last_update         |
+-------------+------------+---------------------+
|           1 | English    | 2006-02-15 05:02:19 |
|           2 | Italian    | 2006-02-15 05:02:19 |
|           3 | Japanese   | 2006-02-15 05:02:19 |
|           4 | Mandarin   | 2006-02-15 05:02:19 |
|           5 | French     | 2006-02-15 05:02:19 |
|           6 | German     | 2006-02-15 05:02:19 |
|           7 | Portuguese | 2020-09-26 09:11:36 |
|           8 | Russian    | 2020-09-26 10:35:00 |
+-------------+------------+---------------------+
8 rows in set (0.00 sec)
```

The single-row INSERT style detects primary key duplicates and stops as soon as it finds one. For example, suppose we try to insert another row with the same lan guage_id:

```
mysql> INSERT INTO language VALUES (8, 'Arabic', '2020-09-26 10:35:00');

ERROR 1062 (23000): Duplicate entry '8' for key 'language.PRIMARY'
```

The INSERT operation stops when it detects the duplicate key. You can add an IGNORE clause to prevent the error if you want, but note that the row still will not be inserted:

```
mysql> INSERT IGNORE INTO language VALUES (8, 'Arabic', '2020-09-26 10:35:00');

Query OK, 0 rows affected, 1 warning (0.00 sec)
```

In most cases you'll want to know about possible problems, though (after all, primary keys are supposed to be unique), so this IGNORE syntax is rarely used.

It is also possible to insert multiple values at once:

```
mysql> INSERT INTO language VALUES (NULL, 'Spanish', NOW()),
    -> (NULL, 'Hebrew', NOW());

Query OK, 2 rows affected (0.02 sec)
Records: 2  Duplicates: 0  Warnings: 0
```

Note that MySQL reports the results of bulk insertion differently from single insertion.

The first line tells you how many rows were inserted, while the first entry in the second line tells you how many rows (or records) were actually processed. If you use INSERT IGNORE and try to insert a duplicate record (one for which the primary key matches that of an existing row), MySQL will quietly skip inserting it and report it as a duplicate in the second entry on the second line:

```
mysql> INSERT IGNORE INTO language VALUES (9, 'Portuguese', NOW()),
    (11, 'Hebrew', NOW());

Query OK, 1 row affected, 1 warning (0.01 sec)
Records: 2  Duplicates: 1  Warnings: 1
```

We discuss the causes of warnings, shown as the third entry on the second line of output, in Chapter 4.

Alternative Syntaxes

There are several alternatives to the VALUES syntax demonstrated in the previous section. This section walks through them and explains the advantages and drawbacks of each. If you're happy with the basic syntax we've described so far and want to move on to a new topic, feel free to skip ahead to "The DELETE Statement" on page 117.

There are some advantages to the VALUES syntax we've been using: it works for both single and bulk inserts, you get an error message if you forget to supply values for all the columns, and you don't have to type in the column names. However, it also has some disadvantages: you need to remember the order of the columns, you need to provide a value for each column, and the syntax is closely tied to the underlying table structure. That is, if you change the table's structure, you need to change the INSERT statements. Fortunately, we can avoid these disadvantages by varying the syntax.

Suppose you know that the actor table has four columns, and you recall their names, but you've forgotten their order. You can insert a row using the following approach:

```
mysql> INSERT INTO actor (actor_id, first_name, last_name, last_update)
    -> VALUES (NULL, 'Vinicius', 'Grippa', NOW());

Query OK, 1 row affected (0.03 sec)
```

The column names are included in parentheses after the table name, and the values stored in those columns are listed in parentheses after the VALUES keyword. So, in this example, a new row is created, and the value 201 is stored as the actor_id (remember, actor_id has the auto_increment property), Vinicius is stored as the first_name, Grippa is stored as the last_name, and the last_update column is populated with the current timestamp. This syntax's advantages are that it's readable and flexible (addressing the third disadvantage we described) and order-independent (addressing the first disadvantage). The burden is that you need to know the column names and type them in.

This new syntax can also address the second disadvantage of the simpler approach—that is, it can allow you to insert values for only some columns. To understand how this might be useful, let's explore the city table:

```
mysql> DESC city;
+-------------+----------------------+------+-----+-------------------+...
| Field       | Type                 | Null | Key | Default           |...
+-------------+----------------------+------+-----+-------------------+...
| city_id     | smallint(5) unsigned | NO   | PRI | NULL              |...
| city        | varchar(50)          | NO   |     | NULL              |...
| country_id  | smallint(5) unsigned | NO   | MUL | NULL              |...
| last_update | timestamp            | NO   |     | CURRENT_TIMESTAMP |...
+-------------+----------------------+------+-----+-------------------+...

...+-----------------------------------------------+
...| Extra                                         |
...+-----------------------------------------------+
...| auto_increment                                |
...|                                               |
...|                                               |
...| on update CURRENT_TIMESTAMP                   |
...|-----------------------------------------------+

4 rows in set (0.00 sec)
```

Notice that the last_update column has a default value of CURRENT_TIMESTAMP. This means that if you don't insert a value for the last_update column, MySQL will insert the current date and time by default. This is just what we want: when we store a record, we don't want to bother checking the date and time and typing it in. Let's try inserting an incomplete entry:

```
mysql> INSERT INTO city (city, country_id) VALUES ('Bebedouro', 19);
Query OK, 1 row affected (0.00 sec)
```

We didn't set a value for the city_id column, so MySQL defaults it to the next available value (because of the auto_increment property), and last_update stores the current date and time. You can check this with a query:

```
mysql> SELECT * FROM city where city like 'Bebedouro';
```

```
+---------+-----------+------------+---------------------+
| city_id | city      | country_id | last_update         |
+---------+-----------+------------+---------------------+
|     601 | Bebedouro |         19 | 2021-02-27 21:34:08 |
+---------+-----------+------------+---------------------+
1 row in set (0.01 sec)
```

You can also use this approach for bulk insertion, as follows:

```
mysql> INSERT INTO city (city,country_id) VALUES
    -> ('Sao Carlos',19),
    -> ('Araraquara',19),
    -> ('Ribeirao Preto',19);

Query OK, 3 rows affected (0.00 sec)
Records: 3  Duplicates: 0  Warnings: 0
```

In addition to needing to remember and type in column names, a disadvantage of this approach is that you can accidentally omit values for columns. MySQL will set the omitted columns to the default values. All columns in a MySQL table have a default value of NULL, unless another default value is explicitly assigned when the table is created or modified.

When you need to use default values for the table columns, you might want to use the DEFAULT keyword (supported by MySQL 5.7 and later). Here's an example that adds a row to the country table using DEFAULT:

```
mysql> INSERT INTO country VALUES (NULL, 'Uruguay', DEFAULT);

Query OK, 1 row affected (0.01 sec)
```

The keyword DEFAULT tells MySQL to use the default value for that column, so the current date and time are inserted in our example. This approach's advantages are that you can use the bulk-insert feature with default values, and you can never accidentally omit a column.

There's another alternative INSERT syntax. In this approach, you list the column names and values together, so you don't have to mentally map the list of values to the earlier list of columns. Here's an example that adds a new row to the country table:

```
mysql> INSERT INTO country SET country_id=NULL,
    -> country='Bahamas', last_update=NOW();

Query OK, 1 row affected (0.01 sec)
```

The syntax requires you to list a table name, the keyword SET, and then column-equals-value pairs, separated by commas. Columns for which values aren't supplied are set to their default values. Again, the disadvantages are that you can accidentally omit values for columns and that you need to remember and type in column names. A significant additional disadvantage is that you can't use this method for bulk insertion.

You can also insert using values returned from a query. We discuss this in Chapter 7.

The DELETE Statement

The DELETE statement is used to remove one or more rows from a table. We explain single-table deletes here and discuss multitable deletes—which remove data from two or more tables through one statement—in Chapter 7.

DELETE Basics

The simplest use of DELETE is to remove all the rows in a table. Suppose you want to empty your rental table. You can do this with:

```
mysql> DELETE FROM rental;
Query OK, 16044 rows affected (2.41 sec)
```

The DELETE syntax doesn't include column names since it's used to remove whole rows and not just values from a row. To reset or modify a value in a row, you use the UPDATE statement, described in "The UPDATE Statement" on page 120. Note that the DELETE statement doesn't remove the table itself. For example, having deleted all the rows in the rental table, you can still query the table:

```
mysql> SELECT * FROM rental;
Empty set (0.00 sec)
```

You can also continue to explore its structure using DESCRIBE or SHOW CREATE TABLE, and insert new rows using INSERT. To remove a table, you use the DROP statement described in Chapter 4.

Note that if the table has a relationship with another table, the delete might fail because of the foreign key constraint:

```
mysql> DELETE FROM language;
ERROR 1451 (23000): Cannot delete or update a parent row: a foreign key
constraint fails (`sakila`.`film`, CONSTRAINT `fk_film_language` FOREIGN KEY
(`language_id`) REFERENCES `language` (`language_id`) ON UPDATE CASCADE)
```

Using WHERE, ORDER BY, and LIMIT

If you deleted rows in the previous section, reload your `sakila` database now by following the instructions in "Entity Relationship Modeling Examples" on page 77. You'll need the rows in the `rental` table restored for the examples in this section.

To remove one or more rows, but not all rows in a table, use a `WHERE` clause. This works in the same way as it does for `SELECT`. For example, suppose you want to remove all rows from the `rental` table with a `rental_id` less than 10. You can do this with:

```
mysql> DELETE FROM rental WHERE rental_id < 10;

Query OK, 9 rows affected (0.01 sec)
```

The result is that the nine rows that match the criterion are removed.

Now suppose you want to remove all the payments from a customer called Mary Smith from the database. First, perform a `SELECT` with the `customer` and `payment` tables using `INNER JOIN` (as described in "Joining Two Tables" on page 109):

```
mysql> SELECT first_name, last_name, customer.customer_id,
    -> amount, payment_date FROM payment INNER JOIN customer
    -> ON customer.customer_id=payment.customer_id
    -> WHERE first_name like 'Mary'
    -> AND last_name like 'Smith';

+------------+-----------+-------------+--------+---------------------+
| first_name | last_name | customer_id | amount | payment_date        |
+------------+-----------+-------------+--------+---------------------+
| MARY       | SMITH     |           1 |   2.99 | 2005-05-25 11:30:37 |
| MARY       | SMITH     |           1 |   0.99 | 2005-05-28 10:35:23 |
| MARY       | SMITH     |           1 |   5.99 | 2005-06-15 00:54:12 |
| MARY       | SMITH     |           1 |   0.99 | 2005-06-15 18:02:53 |
...
| MARY       | SMITH     |           1 |   1.99 | 2005-08-22 01:27:57 |
| MARY       | SMITH     |           1 |   2.99 | 2005-08-22 19:41:37 |
| MARY       | SMITH     |           1 |   5.99 | 2005-08-22 20:03:46 |
+------------+-----------+-------------+--------+---------------------+
32 rows in set (0.00 sec)
```

Next, perform the following `DELETE` operation to remove the row with a *customer_id* of 1 from the `payment` table:

```
mysql> DELETE FROM payment where customer_id=1;

Query OK, 32 rows affected (0.01 sec)
```

You can use the `ORDER BY` and `LIMIT` clauses with `DELETE`. You usually do this when you want to limit the number of rows deleted. For example:

```
mysql> DELETE FROM payment ORDER BY customer_id LIMIT 10000;

Query OK, 10000 rows affected (0.22 sec)
```

We highly recommend using DELETE and UPDATE operations for small sets of rows, due to performance issues. The appropriate value varies depending on the hardware, but a good rule of thumb is around 20,000–40,000 rows per batch.

Removing All Rows with TRUNCATE

If you want to remove all the rows in a table, there's a faster method than removing them with DELETE. When you use the TRUNCATE TABLE statement, MySQL takes the shortcut of dropping the table, removing the table structures, and then re-creating them. When there are many rows in a table, this is much faster.

As a curiosity, there is a bug in MySQL 5.6 that can cause it to stall MySQL when performing a TRUNCATE operation when MySQL is configured with a large InnoDB buffer pool (200 GB or more). See the bug report for details (*https://oreil.ly/I40U9*).

If you want to remove all the data in the payment table, you can execute this:

```
mysql> TRUNCATE TABLE payment;
Query OK, 0 rows affected (0.07 sec)
```

Notice that the number of rows affected is shown as zero: to speed up the operation, MySQL doesn't count the number of rows that are deleted, so the number shown does not reflect the actual number of rows deleted.

The TRUNCATE TABLE statement differs from DELETE in a lot of ways, but it is worth mentioning a few:

- TRUNCATE operations drop and re-create the table, which is much faster than deleting rows one by one, particularly for large tables.
- TRUNCATE operations cause an implicit commit, so you can't roll them back.
- You cannot perform TRUNCATE operations if the session holds an active table lock.

Table types, transactions, and locking are discussed in Chapter 5. None of these limitations affects most applications in practice, and you can use TRUNCATE TABLE to speed up your processing. Of course, it's not common to delete whole tables during regular operation. An exception is temporary tables used to store query results for a particular user session temporarily, which can be deleted without losing the original data.

The UPDATE Statement

The UPDATE statement is used to change data. In this section, we show you how to update one or more rows in a single table. Multitable updates are discussed in "Updates" on page 286.

If you've deleted rows from your sakila database, reload it before continuing.

Examples

The simplest use of the UPDATE statement is to change all the rows in a table. Suppose you need to update the amount column of the payment table by adding 10% for all payments. You could do this by executing:

```
mysql> UPDATE payment SET amount=amount*1.1;

Query OK, 16025 rows affected, 16025 warnings (0.41 sec)
Rows matched: 16049  Changed: 16025  Warnings: 16025
```

Note that we forgot to update the last_update status. To make it coherent with the expected database model, you can fix this by running the following statement:

```
mysql> UPDATE payment SET last_update='2021-02-28 17:53:00';

Query OK, 16049 rows affected (0.27 sec)
Rows matched: 16049  Changed: 16049  Warnings: 0
```

 You can use the NOW() function to update the last_update column with the current timestamp of the execution. For example:

```
mysql> UPDATE payment SET last_update=NOW();
```

The second row reported by an UPDATE statement shows the overall effect of the statement. In our example, you see:

```
Rows matched: 16049  Changed: 16049  Warnings: 0
```

The first column reports the number of rows that were retrieved as matches; in this case, since there's no WHERE or LIMIT clause, all rows in the table match the query. The second column reports how many rows needed to be changed, which is always equal to or less than the number of rows that match. If you repeat the statement, you'll see a different result:

```
mysql> UPDATE payment SET last_update='2021-02-28 17:53:00';

Query OK, 0 rows affected (0.07 sec)
Rows matched: 16049  Changed: 0  Warnings: 0
```

This time, since the date is already set to 2021-02-28 17:53:00 and there is no WHERE condition, all the rows still match the query but none are changed. Note also the number of rows changed is always equal to the number of rows affected, as reported on the first line of the output.

Using WHERE, ORDER BY, and LIMIT

Often, you don't want to change all the rows in a table. Instead, you want to update one or more rows that match a condition. As with SELECT and DELETE, the WHERE clause is used for the task. In addition, in the same way as with DELETE, you can use ORDER BY and LIMIT together to control how many rows are updated from an ordered list.

Let's try an example that modifies one row in a table. Suppose that the actress Penelope Guiness has changed her last name. To update it in the actor table of the database, you need to execute:

```
mysql> UPDATE actor SET last_name= UPPER('cruz')
    -> WHERE first_name LIKE 'PENELOPE'
    -> AND last_name LIKE 'GUINESS';

Query OK, 1 row affected (0.01 sec)
Rows matched: 1  Changed: 1  Warnings: 0
```

As expected, MySQL matched one row and changed one row.

To control how many updates occur, you can use the combination of ORDER BY and LIMIT:

```
mysql> UPDATE payment SET last_update=NOW() LIMIT 10;

Query OK, 10 rows affected (0.01 sec)
Rows matched: 10  Changed: 10  Warnings: 0
```

As with DELETE, you would do this because you either want to perform the operation in small chunks or modify only some rows. Here, you can see that 10 rows were matched and changed.

The previous query also illustrates an important aspect of updates. As you've seen, updates have two phases: a matching phase, where rows are found that match the WHERE clause, and a modification phase, where the rows that need changing are updated.

Exploring Databases and Tables with SHOW and mysqlshow

We've already explained how you can use the SHOW command to obtain information on the structure of a database, its tables, and the table columns. In this section, we'll review the most common types of the SHOW statement with brief examples using the sakila database. The mysqlshow command-line program performs the same functions as several SHOW command variants, but without you needing to start the MySQL client.

The SHOW DATABASES statement lists the databases you can access. If you've followed our sample database installation steps in "Entity Relationship Modeling Examples" on page 77 and deployed the bank model in "Creating a Bank Database ER Model" on page 84, your output should be as follows:

```
mysql> SHOW DATABASES;

+--------------------+
| Database           |
+--------------------+
| information_schema |
| bank_model         |
| employees          |
| mysql              |
| performance_schema |
| sakila             |
| sys                |
| world              |
+--------------------+
8 rows in set (0.01 sec)
```

These are the databases that you can access with the USE command (discussed in Chapter 4); if you have access privileges for other databases on your server, these will be listed too. You can only see databases for which you have some privileges, unless you have the global SHOW DATABASES privilege. You can get the same effect from the command line using the mysqlshow program:

```
$ mysqlshow -uroot -pmsandbox -h 127.0.0.1 -P 3306
```

You can add a LIKE clause to SHOW DATABASES. This is useful if you have many databases and want a short list as output. For example, to see only databases whose names begin with s, run:

```
mysql> SHOW DATABASES LIKE 's%';

+----------------+
| Database (s%)  |
+----------------+
| sakila         |
| sys            |
+----------------+
2 rows in set (0.00 sec)
```

The LIKE statement's syntax is identical to its use in SELECT.

To see the statement used to create a database, you can use the SHOW CREATE DATABASE statement. For example, to see how you created sakila, type:

```
mysql> SHOW CREATE DATABASE sakila;
```

```
*************************** 1. row ***************************
       Database: sakila
Create Database: CREATE DATABASE `sakila` /*!40100 DEFAULT CHARACTER SET
utf8mb4 COLLATE utf8mb4_0900_ai_ci */ /*!80016 DEFAULT ENCRYPTION='N' */
1 row in set (0.00 sec)
```

This is perhaps the least exciting SHOW statement; it only displays the statement. Note, though, that some additional comments are included, /*! and */:

```
40100 DEFAULT CHARACTER SET utf8mb4 COLLATE utf8mb4_0900_ai_ci
80016 DEFAULT ENCRYPTION='N'
```

These comments contain MySQL-specific keywords that provide instructions that are unlikely to be understood by other database programs. A database server other than MySQL will ignore this comment text, so the syntax is usable by both MySQL and other database server software. The optional number at the start of the comment indicates the minimum version of MySQL that can process this particular instruction (for example, 40100 indicates version 4.01.00); older versions of MySQL ignore such instructions. You'll learn about creating databases in Chapter 4.

The SHOW TABLES statement lists the tables in a database. To check the tables in sakila, type:

```
mysql> SHOW TABLES FROM sakila;

+----------------------------+
| Tables_in_sakila           |
+----------------------------+
| actor                      |
| actor_info                 |
| address                    |
| category                   |
| city                       |
| country                    |
| customer                   |
| customer_list              |
| film                       |
| film_actor                 |
| film_category              |
| film_list                  |
| film_text                  |
| inventory                  |
| language                   |
| nicer_but_slower_film_list |
| payment                    |
| rental                     |
| sales_by_film_category     |
| sales_by_store             |
| staff                      |
| ...              |         |
+----------------------------+
23 rows in set (0.01 sec)
```

If you've already selected the sakila database with the USE sakila command, you can use the shortcut:

```
mysql> SHOW TABLES;
```

You can get a similar result by specifying the database name to the mysqlshow program:

```
$ mysqlshow -uroot -pmsandbox -h 127.0.0.1 -P 3306 sakila
```

As with SHOW DATABASES, you can't see tables that you don't have privileges for. This means you can't see tables in a database you can't access, even if you have the SHOW DATABASES global privilege.

The SHOW COLUMNS statement lists the columns in a table. For example, to check the columns of country, type:

```
mysql> SHOW COLUMNS FROM country;
*************************** 1. row ***************************
  Field: country_id
   Type: smallint unsigned
   Null: NO
    Key: PRI
Default: NULL
  Extra: auto_increment
*************************** 2. row ***************************
  Field: country
   Type: varchar(50)
   Null: NO
    Key:
Default: NULL
  Extra:
*************************** 3. row ***************************
  Field: last_update
   Type: timestamp
   Null: NO
    Key:
Default: CURRENT_TIMESTAMP
  Extra: DEFAULT_GENERATED on update CURRENT_TIMESTAMP
3 rows in set (0.00 sec)
```

The output reports the names of all the columns, their types and sizes, whether they can be NULL, whether they are part of a key, their default values, and any extra information. Types, keys, NULL values, and defaults are discussed further in Chapter 4. If you haven't already chosen the sakila database with the USE command, then you can add the database name before the table name, as in sakila.country. Unlike with the previous SHOW statements, you can always see all column names if you have access to a table; it doesn't matter that you don't have certain privileges for all columns.

You can get a similar result by using `mysqlshow` with the database and table name:

```
$ mysqlshow -uroot -pmsandbox -h 127.0.0.1 -P 3306 sakila country
```

You can see the statement used to create a particular table using the SHOW CREATE TABLE statement (we'll also look at creating tables in Chapter 4). Some users prefer this output to that of SHOW COLUMNS, since it has the familiar format of a CREATE TABLE statement. Here's an example for the country table:

```
mysql> SHOW CREATE TABLE country\G
*************************** 1. row ***************************
       Table: country
Create Table: CREATE TABLE `country` (
  `country_id` smallint unsigned NOT NULL AUTO_INCREMENT,
  `country` varchar(50) NOT NULL,
  `last_update` timestamp NOT NULL DEFAULT CURRENT_TIMESTAMP ON UPDATE
  CURRENT_TIMESTAMP,
  PRIMARY KEY (`country_id`)
) ENGINE=InnoDB AUTO_INCREMENT=110 DEFAULT CHARSET=utf8mb4
  COLLATE=utf8mb4_0900_ai_ci
1 row in set (0.00 sec)
```

## CHAPTER 4

Working with Database Structures

This chapter shows you how to create your own databases, add and remove structures such as tables and indexes, and make choices about column types in your tables. It focuses on the syntax and features of SQL, and not the semantics of conceiving, specifying, and refining a database design; you'll find an introductory description of database design techniques in Chapter 2. To work through this chapter, you need to understand how to work with an existing database and its tables, as discussed in Chapter 3.

This chapter lists the structures in the sample sakila database. If you followed the instructions for loading the database in "Entity Relationship Modeling Examples" on page 77, you'll already have the database available and know how to restore it after you've modified its structures.

When you finish this chapter, you'll have all the basics required to create, modify, and delete database structures. Together with the techniques you learned in Chapter 3, you'll have the skills to carry out a wide range of basic operations. Chapters 5 and 7 cover skills that allow you to do more advanced operations with MySQL.

Creating and Using Databases

When you've finished designing a database, the first practical step to take with MySQL is to create it. You do this with the CREATE DATABASE statement. Suppose you want to create a database with the name lucy. Here's the statement you'd type:

```
mysql> CREATE DATABASE lucy;
Query OK, 1 row affected (0.10 sec)
```

We assume here that you know how to connect using the MySQL client, as described in Chapter 1. We also assume that you're able to connect as the root user or as another user who can create, delete, and modify structures (you'll find a detailed discussion on user privileges in Chapter 8). Note that when you create the database, MySQL says that one row was affected. This isn't in fact a normal row in any specific database, but a new entry added to the list that you see with the SHOW DATABASES command.

Once you've created the database, the next step is to use it—that is, choose it as the database you're working with. You do this with the MySQL USE command:

```
mysql> USE lucy;

Database changed
```

This command must be entered on one line and need not be terminated with a semicolon, though we usually do so automatically through habit. Once you've used (selected) the database, you can start creating tables, indexes, and other structures using the steps discussed in the next section.

Before we move on to creating other structures, let's discuss a few features and limitations of creating databases. First, let's see what happens if you try to create a database that already exists:

```
mysql> CREATE DATABASE lucy;

ERROR 1007 (HY000): Can't create database 'lucy'; database exists
```

You can avoid this error by adding the IF NOT EXISTS keyword phrase to the statement:

```
mysql> CREATE DATABASE IF NOT EXISTS lucy;

Query OK, 0 rows affected (0.00 sec)
```

You can see that MySQL didn't complain, but it didn't do anything either: the 0 rows affected message indicates that no data was changed. This addition is useful when you're adding SQL statements to a script: it prevents the script from aborting on error.

Let's look at how to choose database names and use character case. Database names define physical directory (or folder) names on disk. On some operating systems, directory names are case-sensitive; on others, case doesn't matter. For example, Unix-like systems such as Linux and macOS are typically case-sensitive, whereas Windows isn't. The result is that database names have the same restrictions: when case matters to the operating system, it matters to MySQL. For example, on a Linux machine, LUCY, lucy, and Lucy are different database names; on Windows, they refer to just one database. Using incorrect capitalization under Linux or macOS will cause MySQL to complain:

```
mysql> SELECT SaKilA.AcTor_id FROM ACTor;

ERROR 1146 (42S02): Table 'sakila.ACTor' doesn't exist
```

But under Windows, this will normally work.

 To make your SQL machine-independent, we recommend that you consistently use lowercase names for databases (and for tables, columns, aliases, and indexes). That's not a requirement, though, and as earlier examples in this book have demonstrated, you're welcome to use whatever naming convention you are comfortable with. Just be consistent and remember how MySQL behaves on different OSs.

This behavior is controlled by the `lower_case_table_names` parameter. If it's set to 0, table names are stored as specified, and comparisons are case-sensitive. If it's set to 1, table names are stored in lowercase on disk, and comparisons are not case-sensitive. If this parameter is set to 2, table names are stored as given but compared in lowercase. On Windows, the default value is 1. On macOS, the default is 2. On Linux, a value of 2 is not supported; the server forces the value to 0 instead.

There are other restrictions on database names. They can be at most 64 characters in length. You also shouldn't use MySQL reserved words, such as `SELECT`, `FROM`, and `USE`, as names for structures; these can confuse the MySQL parser, making it impossible to interpret the meaning of your statements. You can get around this restriction by enclosing the reserved word in backticks (`` ` ``), but it's more trouble remembering to do so than it's worth. In addition, you can't use certain characters in the names—specifically, the forward slash, backward slash, semicolon, and period characters—and a database name can't end in whitespace. Again, the use of these characters confuses the MySQL parser and can result in unpredictable behavior. For example, here's what happens when you insert a semicolon into a database name:

```
mysql> CREATE DATABASE IF NOT EXISTS lu;cy;
Query OK, 1 row affected (0.00 sec)

ERROR 1064 (42000): You have an error in your SQL syntax; check the manual
that corresponds to your MySQL server version for the right syntax to use
near 'cy' at line 1
```

Since more than one SQL statement can be on a single line, the result is that a database lu is created, and then an error is generated by the very short, unexpected SQL statement cy;. If you really want to create a database with a semicolon in its name, you can do that with backticks:

```
mysql> CREATE DATABASE IF NOT EXISTS `lu;cy`;
Query OK, 1 row affected (0.01 sec)
```

And you can see that you now have two new databases:

```
mysql> SHOW DATABASES LIKE `lu%`;
```

```
+----------------+
| Database (lu%) |
+----------------+
| lu             |
| lu;cy          |
+----------------+
2 rows in set (0.01 sec)
```

Creating Tables

This section covers topics on table structures. We show you how to:

- Create tables, through introductory examples.
- Choose names for tables and table-related structures.
- Understand and choose column types.
- Understand and choose keys and indexes.
- Use the proprietary MySQL AUTO_INCREMENT feature.

When you finish this section, you'll have completed all of the basic material on creating database structures; the remainder of this chapter covers the sample sakila database and how to alter and remove existing structures.

Basics

For the examples in this section, we'll assume that the database sakila hasn't yet been created. If you want to follow along with the examples and you have already loaded the database, you can drop it for this section and reload it later; dropping it removes the database, its tables, and all of the data, but the original is easy to restore by following the steps in "Entity Relationship Modeling Examples" on page 77. Here's how you drop it temporarily:

```
mysql> DROP DATABASE sakila;
Query OK, 23 rows affected (0.06 sec)
```

The DROP statement is discussed further at the end of this chapter in "Deleting Structures" on page 177.

To begin, create the database sakila using the statement:

```
mysql> CREATE DATABASE sakila;
Query OK, 1 row affected (0.00 sec)
```

Then select the database with:

```
mysql> USE sakila;
Database changed
```

We're now ready to begin creating the tables that will hold our data. Let's create a table to hold actor details. For now, we're going to have a simplified structure, and we'll add more complexity later. Here's the statement we use:

```
mysql> CREATE TABLE actor (
    -> actor_id SMALLINT UNSIGNED NOT NULL DEFAULT 0,
    -> first_name VARCHAR(45) DEFAULT NULL,
    -> last_name VARCHAR(45),
    -> last_update TIMESTAMP,
    -> PRIMARY KEY (actor_id)
    -> );
Query OK, 0 rows affected (0.01 sec)
```

Don't panic—even though MySQL reports that zero rows were affected, it created the table:

```
mysql> SHOW tables;
+------------------+
| Tables_in_sakila |
+------------------+
| actor            |
+------------------+
1 row in set (0.01 sec)
```

Let's consider all this in detail. The CREATE TABLE command has three major sections:

1. The CREATE TABLE statement, which is followed by the table name to create. In this example, it's actor.

2. A list of one or more columns to be added to the table. In this example, we've added quite a few: actor_id SMALLINT UNSIGNED NOT NULL DEFAULT 0, first_name VARCHAR(45) DEFAULT NULL, last_name VARCHAR(45), and last_update TIMESTAMP. We'll discuss these in a moment.

3. Optional key definitions. In this example, we've defined a single key: PRIMARY KEY (actor_id). We'll discuss keys and indexes in detail later in this chapter.

Notice that the CREATE TABLE component is followed by an opening parenthesis that's matched by a closing parenthesis at the end of the statement. Notice also that the other components are separated by commas. There are other elements that you can add to a CREATE TABLE statement, and we'll discuss some in a moment.

Let's discuss the column specifications. The basic syntax is as follows: name type [NOT NULL | NULL] [DEFAULT value]. The name field is the column name, and it has the same limitations as database names, as discussed in the previous section. It can be at most 64 characters in length, backward and forward slashes aren't allowed, periods aren't allowed, it can't end in whitespace, and case sensitivity is dependent on the underlying operating system. The type field defines how and what is stored in the column; for example, we've seen that it can be set to VARCHAR for strings, SMALLINT for numbers, or TIMESTAMP for a date and time.

If you specify NOT NULL, a row isn't valid without a value for the column; if you specify NULL or omit this clause, a row can exist without a value for the column. If you specify a *value* with the DEFAULT clause, it'll be used to populate the column when you don't otherwise provide data; this is particularly useful when you frequently reuse a default value such as a country name. The *value* must be a constant (such as 0, "cat", or 20060812045623), except if the column is of the type TIMESTAMP. Types are discussed in detail in "Column Types" on page 138.

The NOT NULL and DEFAULT features can be used together. If you specify NOT NULL and add a DEFAULT value, the default is used when you don't provide a value for the column. Sometimes, this works fine:

```
mysql> INSERT INTO actor(first_name) VALUES ('John');
Query OK, 1 row affected (0.01 sec)
```

And sometimes it doesn't:

```
mysql> INSERT INTO actor(first_name) VALUES ('Elisabeth');
ERROR 1062 (23000): Duplicate entry '0' for key 'actor.PRIMARY'
```

Whether it works or not is dependent on the underlying constraints and conditions of the database: in this example, actor_id has a default value of 0, but it's also the primary key. Having two rows with the same primary key value isn't permitted, and so the second attempt to insert a row with no values (and a resulting primary key value of 0) fails. We discuss primary keys in detail in "Keys and Indexes" on page 161.

Column names have fewer restrictions than database and table names. What's more, the names are case-insensitive and portable across all platforms. All characters are allowed in column names, though if you want terminate them with whitespace or include periods or other special characters, such as a semicolon or dash, you'll need to enclose the name in backticks (`). Again, we recommend that you consistently choose lowercase names for developer-driven choices (such as database, alias, and table names) and avoid characters that require you to remember to use backticks.

Naming columns and other database objects is something of a personal preference when starting anew (you can get some inspiration by looking at the example databases) or a matter of following standards when working on an existing codebase. In general, aim to avoid repetition: in a table named actor, use the column name first_name rather than actor_first_name, which would look redundant when preceded by the table name in a complex query (actor.actor_first_name versus actor.first_name). An exception to this is when using the ubiquitous id column name; either avoid using this or prepend the table name for clarity (e.g., actor_id).

It's good practice to use the underscore character to separate words. You could use another character, like a dash or slash, but you'd have to remember to enclose the names with backticks (e.g., `actor-id`). You can also omit the word-separating formatting altogether, but "CamelCase" is arguably harder to read. As with database and table names, the longest permitted length for a column name is 64 characters.

Collation and Character Sets

When you're comparing or sorting strings, how MySQL evaluates the result depends on the character set and collation used. Character sets, or charsets, define what characters can be stored; for example, you may need to store non-English characters such as ю or ü. A collation defines how strings are ordered, and there are different collations for different languages: for example, the position of the character ü in the alphabet is different in two German orderings, and different again in Swedish and Finnish. Because not everyone wants to store English strings, it's important that a database server be able to manage non-English characters and different ways of sorting characters.

We understand that discussion of collations and charsets may feel to be too advanced when you're just starting out learning MySQL. We also think, however, that these are topics worth covering, as mismatched charsets and collations may result in unexpected situations including loss of data and incorrect query results. If you prefer, you can skip this section and some of the later discussion in this chapter and come back to these topics when you want to learn about them specifically. That won't affect your understanding of other material in this book.

In our previous string-comparison examples, we ignored the collation and charset issue and just let MySQL use its defaults. In versions of MySQL prior to 8.0, the default character set is `latin1`, and the default collation is `latin1_swedish_ci`. MySQL 8.0 changed the defaults, and now the default charset is `utf8mb4`, and the default collation is `utf8mb4_0900_ai_ci`. MySQL can be configured to use different character sets and collation orders at the connection, database, table, and column levels. The outputs shown here are from MySQL 8.0.

You can list the character sets available on your server with the SHOW CHARACTER SET command. This shows a short description of each character set, its default collation, and the maximum number of bytes used for each character in that character set:

```
mysql> SHOW CHARACTER SET;
+----------+---------------------------+---------------------+--------+
| Charset  | Description               | Default collation   | Maxlen |
+----------+---------------------------+---------------------+--------+
| armscii8 | ARMSCII-8 Armenian        | armscii8_general_ci |      1 |
| ascii    | US ASCII                  | ascii_general_ci    |      1 |
| big5     | Big5 Traditional Chinese  | big5_chinese_ci     |      2 |
| binary   | Binary pseudo charset     | binary              |      1 |
```

```
| cp1250   | Windows Central European   | cp1250_general_ci   |   1 |
| cp1251   | Windows Cyrillic           | cp1251_general_ci   |   1 |
| ...      |                            |                     |     |
| ujis     | EUC-JP Japanese            | ujis_japanese_ci    |   3 |
| utf16    | UTF-16 Unicode             | utf16_general_ci    |   4 |
| utf16le  | UTF-16LE Unicode           | utf16le_general_ci  |   4 |
| utf32    | UTF-32 Unicode             | utf32_general_ci    |   4 |
| utf8     | UTF-8 Unicode              | utf8_general_ci     |   3 |
| utf8mb4  | UTF-8 Unicode              | utf8mb4_0900_ai_ci  |   4 |
+----------+----------------------------+---------------------+-------+
41 rows in set (0.00 sec)
```

For example, the latin1 character set is actually the Windows code page 1252 character set that supports West European languages. The default collation for this character set is latin1_swedish_ci, which follows Swedish conventions to sort accented characters (English is handled as you'd expect). This collation is case-insensitive, as indicated by the letters ci. Finally, each character takes up 1 byte. By comparison, if you use the default utf8mb4 character set, each character will take up to 4 bytes of storage. Sometimes, it makes sense to change the default. For example, there's no reason to store base64-encoded data (which, by definition, is ASCII) in utf8mb4.

Similarly, you can list the collation orders and the character sets they apply to:

```
mysql> SHOW COLLATION;
+---------------------+----------+-----+---------+...+---------------+
| Collation           | Charset  | Id  | Default |...| Pad_attribute |
+---------------------+----------+-----+---------+...+---------------+
| armscii8_bin        | armscii8 |  64 |         |...| PAD SPACE     |
| armscii8_general_ci | armscii8 |  32 | Yes     |...| PAD SPACE     |
| ascii_bin           | ascii    |  65 |         |...| PAD SPACE     |
| ascii_general_ci    | ascii    |  11 | Yes     |...| PAD SPACE     |
| ...                 |          |     |         |...|               |
| utf8mb4_0900_ai_ci  | utf8mb4  | 255 | Yes     |...| NO PAD        |
| utf8mb4_0900_as_ci  | utf8mb4  | 305 |         |...| NO PAD        |
| utf8mb4_0900_as_cs  | utf8mb4  | 278 |         |...| NO PAD        |
| utf8mb4_0900_bin    | utf8mb4  | 309 |         |...| NO PAD        |
| ...                 |          |     |         |...|               |
| utf8_unicode_ci     | utf8     | 192 |         |...| PAD SPACE     |
| utf8_vietnamese_ci  | utf8     | 215 |         |...| PAD SPACE     |
+---------------------+----------+-----+---------+...+---------------+
272 rows in set (0.02 sec)
```

The number of character sets and collations available depends on how the MySQL server was built and packaged. The examples we show are from a default MySQL 8.0 installation, and the same numbers can be seen on Linux and Windows. MariaDB 10.5, however, has 322 collations but 40 character sets.

You can see the current defaults on your server as follows:

```
mysql> SHOW VARIABLES LIKE 'c%';
+-------------------------+--------------------------------+
| Variable_name           | Value                          |
+-------------------------+--------------------------------+
| ...                     |                                |
| character_set_client    | utf8mb4                        |
| character_set_connection | utf8mb4                       |
| character_set_database  | utf8mb4                        |
| character_set_filesystem | binary                        |
| character_set_results   | utf8mb4                        |
| character_set_server    | utf8mb4                        |
| character_set_system    | utf8                           |
| character_sets_dir      | /usr/share/mysql-8.0/charsets/ |
| ...                     |                                |
| collation_connection    | utf8mb4_0900_ai_ci             |
| collation_database      | utf8mb4_0900_ai_ci             |
| collation_server        | utf8mb4_0900_ai_ci             |
| ...                     |                                |
+-------------------------+--------------------------------+
21 rows in set (0.00 sec)
```

When you're creating a database, you can set the default character set and sort order for the database and its tables. For example, if you want to use the utf8mb4 character set and the utf8mb4_ru_0900_as_cs (case-sensitive) collation order, you would write:

```
mysql> CREATE DATABASE rose DEFAULT CHARACTER SET utf8mb4
    -> COLLATE utf8mb4_ru_0900_as_cs;

Query OK, 1 row affected (0.00 sec)
```

Usually, there's no need to do this if you've installed MySQL correctly for your language and region and if you're not planning on internationalizing your application. With utf8mb4 being the default since MySQL 8.0, there's even less need to change the charset. You can also control the character set and collation for individual tables or columns, but we won't go into the details of how to do that here. We will discuss how collations affect string types in "String types" on page 144.

Other Features

This section briefly describes other features of the CREATE TABLE statement. It includes an example using the IF NOT EXISTS feature, and a list of advanced features and where to find more about them in this book. The statement shown is the full representation of the table taken from the sakila database, unlike the previous simplified example.

You can use the IF NOT EXISTS keyword phrase when creating a table, and it works much as it does for databases. Here's an example that won't report an error even when the actor table exists:

```
mysql> CREATE TABLE IF NOT EXISTS actor (
    -> actor_id SMALLINT UNSIGNED NOT NULL AUTO_INCREMENT,
    -> first_name VARCHAR(45) NOT NULL,
    -> last_name VARCHAR(45) NOT NULL,
    -> last_update TIMESTAMP NOT NULL DEFAULT
    -> CURRENT_TIMESTAMP ON UPDATE CURRENT_TIMESTAMP,
    -> PRIMARY KEY  (actor_id),
    -> KEY idx_actor_last_name (last_name));
Query OK, 0 rows affected, 1 warning (0.01 sec)
```

You can see that zero rows are affected, and a warning is reported. Let's take a look:

```
mysql> SHOW WARNINGS;
+-------+------+-------------------------------+
| Level | Code | Message                       |
+-------+------+-------------------------------+
| Note  | 1050 | Table 'actor' already exists  |
+-------+------+-------------------------------+
1 row in set (0.01 sec)
```

There are a wide range of additional features you can add to a CREATE TABLE statement, only a few of which are present in this example. Many of these are advanced and aren't discussed in this book, but you can find more information in the MySQL Reference Manual in the section on the CREATE TABLE statement (*https://oreil.ly/ZGQgq*). These additional features include the following:

The AUTO_INCREMENT feature for numeric columns
This feature allows you to automatically create unique identifiers for a table. We discuss it in detail in "The AUTO_INCREMENT Feature" on page 167.

Column comments
You can add a comment to a column; this is displayed when you use the SHOW CREATE TABLE command that we discuss later in this section.

Foreign key constraints
You can tell MySQL to check whether data in one or more columns matches data in another table. For example, the sakila database has a foreign key constraint on the city_id column of the address table, referring to the city table's city_id column. That means it's impossible to have an address in a city not present in the city table. We introduced foreign key constraints in Chapter 2, and we'll take a look at what engines support foreign key constraints in "Alternative Storage Engines" on page 297. Not every storage engine in MySQL supports foreign keys.

Creating temporary tables

If you create a table using the keyword phrase CREATE TEMPORARY TABLE, it'll be removed (dropped) when the connection is closed. This is useful for copying and reformatting data because you don't have to remember to clean up. Sometimes temporary tables are also used as an optimization to hold some intermediate data.

Advanced table options

You can control a wide range of features of the table using table options. These include the starting value of AUTO_INCREMENT, the way indexes and rows are stored, and options to override the information that the MySQL query optimizer gathers from the table. It's also possible to specify *generated columns*, containing data like sum of two other columns, as well as indexes on such columns.

Control over index structures

Some storage engines in MySQL allow you to specify and control what type of internal structure—such as a B-tree or hash table—MySQL uses for its indexes. You can also tell MySQL that you want a full-text or spatial data index on a column, allowing special types of search.

Partitioning

MySQL supports different partitioning strategies, which you can select at table creation time or later. We will not be covering partitioning in this book.

You can see the statement used to create a table using the SHOW CREATE TABLE statement introduced in Chapter 3. This often shows you output that includes some of the advanced features we've just discussed; the output rarely matches what you actually typed to create the table. Here's an example for the actor table:

```
mysql> SHOW CREATE TABLE actor\G
*************************** 1. row ***************************
       Table: actor
Create Table: CREATE TABLE `actor` (
  `actor_id` smallint unsigned NOT NULL AUTO_INCREMENT,
  `first_name` varchar(45) NOT NULL,
  `last_name` varchar(45) NOT NULL,
  `last_update` timestamp NOT NULL DEFAULT CURRENT_TIMESTAMP
        ON UPDATE CURRENT_TIMESTAMP,
  PRIMARY KEY (`actor_id`),
  KEY `idx_actor_last_name` (`last_name`)
) ENGINE=InnoDB DEFAULT CHARSET=utf8mb4
        COLLATE=utf8mb4_0900_ai_ci
1 row in set (0.00 sec)
```

You'll notice that the output includes content added by MySQL that wasn't in our original CREATE TABLE statement:

- The names of the table and columns are enclosed in backticks. This isn't necessary, but it does avoid any parsing problems that can be caused by the use of reserved words and special characters, as discussed previously.

- An additional default ENGINE clause is included, which explicitly states the table type that should be used. The setting in a default installation of MySQL is InnoDB, so it has no effect in this example.

- An additional DEFAULT CHARSET clause is included, which tells MySQL what character set is used by the columns in the table. Again, this has no effect in a default installation.

Column Types

This section describes the column types you can use in MySQL. It explains when each should be used and any limitations it has. The types are grouped by their purpose. We'll cover the most widely used data types and mention more advanced or less used types in passing. That doesn't mean they have no use, but consider learning about them as an exercise. Most likely, you will not remember each of the data types and its particular intricacies, and that's okay. It's worth rereading this chapter later and consulting the MySQL documentation on the topic to keep your knowledge up-to-date.

Integer types

We will start with numeric data types, and more specifically with integer types, or the types holding specific whole numbers. First, the two most popular integer types:

INT[(width)] [UNSIGNED] [ZEROFILL]
    This is the most commonly used numeric type; it stores integer (whole number) values in the range –2,147,483,648 to 2,147,483,647. If the optional UNSIGNED keyword is added, the range is 0 to 4,294,967,295. The keyword INT is short for INTEGER, and they can be used interchangeably. An INT column requires 4 bytes of storage space.

    INT, as well as other integer types, has two properties specific to MySQL: optional width and ZEROFILL arguments. They are not part of a SQL standard, and as of MySQL 8.0 are deprecated. Still, you will surely notice them in a lot of codebases, so we will briefly cover both of them.

    The width parameter specifies the display width, which can be read by applications as part of the column metadata. Unlike parameters in a similar position for other data types, this parameter has no effect on the storage characteristics of a particular integer type and does not constrain the usable range of values. INT(4) and INT(32) are the same for the purpose of data storage.

ZEROFILL is an additional argument that is used to left-pad the values with zeros up to the length specified by the *width* parameter. If you use ZEROFILL, MySQL automatically adds UNSIGNED to the declaration (since zero-filling makes sense only in the context of positive numbers).

In a few applications where ZEROFILL and *width* are useful, the LPAD() function can be used, or numbers can be stored formatted in CHAR columns.

BIGINT[(*width*)] [UNSIGNED] [ZEROFILL]

In the world of growing data sizes, having tables with counts of rows in the billions is getting more common. Even simple id-type columns might need a wider range than a regular INT provides. BIGINT solves that problem. It is a large integer type with a signed range of −9,223,372,036,854,775,808 to 9,223,372,036,854,775,807. An unsigned BIGINT can store numbers from 0 to 18,446,744,073,709,551,615. Columns of this type will require 8 bytes of storage.

Internally, all calculations within MySQL are done using signed BIGINT or DOUBLE values. The important consequence of that is that you should be very careful when dealing with extremely large numbers. There are two issues to be aware of. First, unsigned big integers larger than 9,223,372,036,854,775,807 should only be used with bit functions. Second, if the result of an arithmetical operation is larger than 9,223,372,036,854,775,807, unexpected results might be observed.

For example:

```
mysql> CREATE TABLE test_bigint (id BIGINT UNSIGNED);
Query OK, 0 rows affected (0.01 sec)

mysql> INSERT INTO test_bigint VALUES (18446744073709551615);
Query OK, 1 row affected (0.01 sec)

mysql> INSERT INTO test_bigint VALUES (18446744073709551615-1);
Query OK, 1 row affected (0.01 sec)

mysql> INSERT INTO test_bigint VALUES (184467440737095516*100);
ERROR 1690 (22003): BIGINT value
is out of range in '(184467440737095516 * 100)'
```

Even though 18,446,744,073,709,551,600 is less than 18,446,744,073,709,551,615, since a signed BIGINT is used for multiplication internally, the out-of-range error is observed.

The SERIAL data type can be used as an alias for BIGINT UNSIGNED NOT NULL AUTO_INCREMENT UNIQUE. Unless you must optimize for data size and performance, consider using SERIAL for your id-like columns. Even the UNSIGNED INT can run out of range much quicker than you'd expect, and often at the worst possible time.

Keep in mind that although it's possible to store every integer as a BIGINT, that's wasteful in terms of storage space. Moreover, as we discussed, the *width* parameter doesn't constrain the range of values. To save space and put constraints on stored values, you should use different integer types:

SMALLINT[(*width*)] [UNSIGNED] [ZEROFILL]
> Stores small integers, with a range from −32,768 to 32,767 signed and from 0 to 65,535 unsigned. It takes 2 bytes of storage.

TINYINT[(*width*)] [UNSIGNED] [ZEROFILL]
> The smallest numeric data type, storing even smaller integers. The range of this type is −128 to 127 signed and 0 to 255 unsigned. It takes only 1 byte of storage.

BOOL[(*width*)]
> Short for BOOLEAN, and a synonym for TINYINT(1). Usually, Boolean types accept only two values: true or false. However, since BOOL in MySQL is an integer type, you can store values from −128 to 127 in a BOOL. The value 0 will be treated as false, and all nonzero values as true. It's also possible to use special true and false aliases for 1 and 0, respectively. Here are some examples:

```
mysql> CREATE TABLE test_bool (i BOOL);
Query OK, 0 rows affected (0.04 sec)

mysql> INSERT INTO test_bool VALUES (true),(false);
Query OK, 2 rows affected (0.00 sec)
Records: 2  Duplicates: 0  Warnings: 0

mysql> INSERT INTO test_bool VALUES (1),(0),(-128),(127);
Query OK, 4 rows affected (0.02 sec)
Records: 4  Duplicates: 0  Warnings: 0

mysql> SELECT i, IF(i,'true','false') FROM test_bool;
+------+----------------------+
| i    | IF(i,'true','false') |
+------+----------------------+
|    1 | true                 |
|    0 | false                |
|    1 | true                 |
|    0 | false                |
| -128 | true                 |
```

```
|   127 | true                   |
+-------+------------------------+
6 rows in set (0.01 sec)
```

MEDIUMINT[(*width*)] [UNSIGNED] [ZEROFILL]

Stores values in the signed range of –8,388,608 to 8,388,607 and the unsigned range of 0 to 16,777,215. It takes 3 bytes of storage.

BIT[(*M*)]

Special type used to store bit values. *M* specifies the number of bits per value and defaults to 1 if omitted. MySQL uses a b'*value* syntax for binary values.

Fixed-point types

The DECIMAL and NUMERIC data types in MySQL are the same, so although we will only describe DECIMAL here, this description also applies to NUMERIC. The main difference between fixed-point and floating-point types is precision. For fixed-point types, the value retrieved is identical to the value stored; this isn't always the case with types that contain decimal points, such as the FLOAT and DOUBLE types described later. That is the most important property of the DECIMAL data type, which is a commonly used numeric type in MySQL:

DECIMAL[(*width*[,*decimals*])] [UNSIGNED] [ZEROFILL]

Stores a fixed-point number such as a salary or distance, with a total of *width* digits of which some smaller number are *decimals* that follow a decimal point. For example, a column declared as price DECIMAL(6,2) can be used to store values in the range –9,999.99 to 9,999.99. price DECIMAL(10,4) would allow values like 123,456.1234.

Prior to MySQL 5.7, if you tried to store a value outside this range, it would be stored as the closest value in the allowed range. For example, 100 would be stored as 99.99, and –100 would be stored as –99.99. Starting with version 5.7.5, however, the default SQL mode includes the mode STRICT_TRANS_TABLES, which prohibits this and other unsafe behaviors. Using the old behavior is possible, but could result in data loss.

SQL modes are special settings that control the behavior of MySQL when it comes to queries. For example, they can restrict "unsafe" behavior or affect how queries are interpreted. For the purpose of learning MySQL, we recommend that you stick to the defaults, as they are safe. Changing SQL modes may be required for compatibility with legacy applications across MySQL releases.

The *width* parameter is optional, and a value of 10 is assumed when it is omitted. The number of *decimals* is also optional, and when omitted, a value of 0 is assumed; the maximum value of *decimals* may not exceed the value of *width*. The maximum value of *width* is 65, and the maximum value of *decimals* is 30.

If you're storing only positive values, you can use the UNSIGNED keyword as described for INT. If you want zero-padding, use the ZEROFILL keyword for the same behavior as described for INT. The keyword DECIMAL has three identical, interchangeable alternatives: DEC, NUMERIC, and FIXED.

Values in DECIMAL columns are stored using a binary format. This format uses 4 bytes for every nine digits.

Floating-point types

In addition to the fixed-point DECIMAL type described in the previous section, there are two other types that support decimal points: DOUBLE (also known as REAL) and FLOAT. They're designed to store approximate numeric values rather than the exact values stored by DECIMAL.

Why would you want approximate values? The answer is that many numbers with a decimal point are approximations of real quantities. For example, suppose you earn $50,000 per annum and you want to store it as a monthly wage. When you convert this to a per-month amount, it's $4,166 plus 66 and 2/3 cents. If you store this as $4,166.67, it's not exact enough to convert to a yearly wage (since 12 multiplied by $4,166.67 is $50,000.04). However, if you store 2/3 with enough decimal places, it's a closer approximation. You'll find that it is accurate enough to correctly multiply to obtain the original value in a high-precision environment such as MySQL, using only a bit of rounding. That's where DOUBLE and FLOAT are useful: they let you store values such as 2/3 or pi with a large number of decimal places, allowing accurate approximate representations of exact quantities. You can later use the ROUND() function to restore the results to a given precision.

Let's continue the previous example using DOUBLE. Suppose you create a table as follows:

```
mysql> CREATE TABLE wage (monthly DOUBLE);
Query OK, 0 rows affected (0.09 sec)
```

You can now insert the monthly wage using:

```
mysql> INSERT INTO wage VALUES (50000/12);
Query OK, 1 row affected (0.00 sec)
```

And see what's stored:

```
mysql> SELECT * FROM wage;

+----------------+
| monthly        |
+----------------+
| 4166.666666666 |
+----------------+
1 row in set (0.00 sec)
```

However, when you multiply it to obtain a yearly value, you get a high-precision approximation:

```
mysql> SELECT monthly*12 FROM wage;

+--------------------+
| monthly*12         |
+--------------------+
| 49999.999999992004 |
+--------------------+
1 row in set (0.00 sec)
```

To get the original value back, you still need to perform rounding with the desired precision. For example, your business might require precision to five decimal places. In this case, you could restore the original value with:

```
mysql> SELECT ROUND(monthly*12,5) FROM wage;

+---------------------+
| ROUND(monthly*12,5) |
+---------------------+
|         50000.00000 |
+---------------------+
1 row in set (0.00 sec)
```

But precision to eight decimal places would not result in the original value:

```
mysql> SELECT ROUND(monthly*12,8) FROM wage;

+---------------------+
| ROUND(monthly*12,8) |
+---------------------+
|        49999.99999999 |
+---------------------+
1 row in set (0.00 sec)
```

It's important to understand the imprecise and approximate nature of floating-point data types.

Here are the details of the FLOAT and DOUBLE types:

FLOAT[(*width, decimals*)] [UNSIGNED] [ZEROFILL] *or*
FLOAT[(*precision*)] [UNSIGNED] [ZEROFILL]

> Stores floating-point numbers. It has two optional syntaxes: the first allows an optional number of *decimals* and an optional display *width*, and the second allows an optional *precision* that controls the accuracy of the approximation measured in bits. Without parameters (the typical usage), the type stores small, 4-byte, single-precision floating-point values. When *precision* is between 0 and 24, the default behavior occurs. When *precision* is between 25 and 53, the type behaves like DOUBLE. The *width* parameter has no effect on what is stored, only on what is displayed. The UNSIGNED and ZEROFILL options behave as for INT.

DOUBLE[(*width, decimals*)] [UNSIGNED] [ZEROFILL]

> Stores floating-point numbers. It allows specification of an optional number of *decimals* and an optional display *width*. Without parameters (the typical usage), the type stores normal 8-byte, double-precision floating-point values. The *width* parameter has no effect on what is stored, only on what is displayed. The UNSIGNED and ZEROFILL options behave as for INT. The DOUBLE type has two identical synonyms: REAL and DOUBLE PRECISION.

String types

String data types are used to store text and, less obviously, binary data. MySQL supports the following string types:

[NATIONAL] VARCHAR(*width*) [CHARACTER SET *charset_name*]
[COLLATE *collation_name*]

> Probably the single most commonly used string type, VARCHAR stores variable-length strings up to a maximum *width*. The maximum value of *width* is 65,535 characters. Most of the information applicable to this type will apply to other string types as well.

> The CHAR and VARCHAR types are very similar, but there are a few important distinctions. VARCHAR incurs one or two extra bytes of overhead to store the value of the string, depending on whether the value is smaller or larger than 255 bytes. Note that this size is different from the string length in characters, as certain characters might require up to 4 bytes of space. It might seem obvious, then, that VARCHAR is less efficient. However, that is not always true. As VARCHAR can store strings of arbitrary length (up to the *width* defined), shorter strings will require less storage space than a CHAR of similar length.

Another difference between CHAR and VARCHAR is their handling of trailing spaces. VARCHAR retains trailing spaces up to the specified column width and will truncate the excess, producing a warning. As will be shown later, CHAR values are right-padded to the column width, and the trailing spaces aren't preserved. For VARCHAR, trailing spaces are significant unless they are trimmed and will count as unique values. Let's demonstrate:

```
mysql> CREATE TABLE test_varchar_trailing(d VARCHAR(2) UNIQUE);

Query OK, 0 rows affected (0.02 sec)

mysql> INSERT INTO test_varchar_trailing VALUES ('a'), ('a ');

Query OK, 2 rows affected (0.01 sec)
Records: 2  Duplicates: 0  Warnings: 0

mysql> SELECT d, LENGTH(d) FROM test_varchar_trailing;

+------+-----------+
| d    | LENGTH(d) |
+------+-----------+
| a    |         1 |
| a    |         2 |
+------+-----------+
2 rows in set (0.00 sec)
```

The second row we inserted has a trailing space, and since the *width* for column d is 2, that space counts toward the uniqueness of a row. If we try inserting a row with two trailing spaces, however:

```
mysql> INSERT INTO test_varchar_trailing VALUES ('a  ');

ERROR 1062 (23000): Duplicate entry 'a '
for key 'test_varchar_trailing.d'
```

MySQL refuses to accept the new row. VARCHAR(2) implicitly truncates trailing spaces beyond the set *width*, so the value stored changes from "a " (with a double space after *a*) to "a " (with a single space after *a*). Since we already have a row with such a value, a duplicate entry error is reported. This behavior for VARCHAR and TEXT can be controlled by changing the column collation. Some collations, like latin1_bin, have the PAD SPACE attribute, meaning that upon retrieval they are padded to the *width* with spaces. This doesn't affect storage, but does affect uniqueness checks as well as how the GROUP BY and DISTINCT operators work, which we'll discuss in Chapter 5. You can check whether a collation is PAD SPACE or NO PAD by running the SHOW COLLATION command, as we've shown in "Collation and Character Sets" on page 133. Let's see the effect in action by creating a table with a PAD SPACE collation:

```
mysql> CREATE TABLE test_varchar_pad_collation(
    -> data VARCHAR(5) CHARACTER SET latin1
    -> COLLATE latin1_bin UNIQUE);

Query OK, 0 rows affected (0.02 sec)

mysql> INSERT INTO test_varchar_pad_collation VALUES ('a');

Query OK, 1 row affected (0.00 sec)

mysql> INSERT INTO test_varchar_pad_collation VALUES ('a ');

ERROR 1062 (23000): Duplicate entry 'a '
for key 'test_varchar_pad_collation.data'
```

The NO PAD collation is a new addition of MySQL 8.0. In prior releases of
MySQL, which you may still often see in use, every collation implicitly has the
PAD SPACE attribute. Therefore, in MySQL 5.7 and prior releases, your only
option to preserve trailing spaces is to use a binary type: VARBINARY or BLOB.

> Both the CHAR and VARCHAR data types disallow storage of val-
> ues longer than *width*, unless strict SQL mode is disabled (i.e.,
> if neither STRICT_ALL_TABLES or STRICT_TRANS_TABLES is
> enabled). With the protection disabled, values longer than
> *width* are truncated, and a warning is shown. We don't recom-
> mend enabling legacy behavior, as it might result in data loss.

Sorting and comparison of the VARCHAR, CHAR, and TEXT types happens according
to the collation of the character set assigned. You can see that it is possible to
specify the character set, as well as the collation for each individual string-type
column. It's also possible to specify the binary character set, which effectively
converts VARCHAR into VARBINARY. Don't mistake the binary charset for a BINARY
attribute for a charset; the latter is a MySQL-only shorthand to specify a binary
(_bin) collation.

What's more, it's possible to specify a collation directly in the ORDER BY clause.
Available collations will depend on the character set of the column. Continuing
with the test_varchar_pad_collation table, it's possible to store an ä symbol
there and then see the effect collations make on the string ordering:

```
mysql> INSERT INTO test_varchar_pad_collation VALUES ('ä'), ('z');

Query OK, 2 rows affected (0.01 sec)
Records: 2  Duplicates: 0  Warnings: 0

mysql> SELECT * FROM test_varchar_pad_collation
    -> ORDER BY data COLLATE latin1_german1_ci;
```

```
+------+
| data |
+------+
| a    |
| ä    |
| z    |
+------+
3 rows in set (0.00 sec)

mysql> SELECT * FROM test_varchar_pad_collation
    -> ORDER BY data COLLATE latin1_swedish_ci;
+------+
| data |
+------+
| a    |
| z    |
| ä    |
+------+
3 rows in set (0.00 sec)
```

The NATIONAL (or its equivalent short form, NCHAR) attribute is a standard SQL way to specify that a string-type column must use a predefined character set. MySQL uses utf8 as this charset. It's important to note that MySQL 5.7 and 8.0 disagree on what exactly utf8 is, however: the former uses it as an alias for utf8mb3, and the latter for utf8mb4. Thus, it is best to not use the NATIONAL attribute, as well as ambiguous aliases. The best practice with any text-related columns and data is to be as unambiguous and specific as possible.

```
[NATIONAL] CHAR(width) [CHARACTER SET charset_name]
[COLLATE collation_name]
```

CHAR stores a fixed-length string (such as a name, address, or city) of length *width*. If a *width* is not provided, CHAR(1) is assumed. The maximum value of *width* is 255. As with VARCHAR, values in CHAR columns are always stored at the specified length. A single letter stored in a CHAR(255) column will take 255 bytes (in the latin1 charset) and will be padded with spaces. The padding is removed when reading the data, unless the PAD_CHAR_TO_FULL_LENGTH SQL mode is enabled. It's worth mentioning again that this means that strings stored in CHAR columns will lose all of their trailing spaces.

In the past, the *width* of a CHAR column was often associated a size in bytes. That's not always the case now, and it's definitely not the case by default. Multibyte character sets, such as the default utf8mb4 in MySQL 8.0, can result in much larger values. InnoDB will actually encode fixed-length columns as variable-length columns if their maximum size exceeds 768 bytes. Thus, in MySQL 8.0, by default InnoDB will store a CHAR(255) column as it would a VARCHAR column. Here's an example:

```
mysql> CREATE TABLE test_char_length(
    ->   utf8char CHAR(10) CHARACTER SET utf8mb4
    -> , asciichar CHAR(10) CHARACTER SET binary
    -> );
```

Query OK, 0 rows affected (0.04 sec)

```
mysql> INSERT INTO test_char_length VALUES ('Plain text', 'Plain text');
```

Query OK, 1 row affected (0.01 sec)

```
mysql> INSERT INTO test_char_length VALUES ('的開源軟體', 'Plain text');
```

Query OK, 1 row affected (0.00 sec)

```
mysql> SELECT LENGTH(utf8char), LENGTH(asciichar) FROM test_char_length;
```

```
+------------------+-------------------+
| LENGTH(utf8char) | LENGTH(asciichar) |
+------------------+-------------------+
|               10 |                10 |
|               15 |                10 |
+------------------+-------------------+
```
2 rows in set (0.00 sec)

As the values are left-aligned and right-padded with spaces, and any trailing spaces aren't considered for CHAR at all, it's impossible to compare strings consisting of spaces alone. If you find yourself in a situation in which that's important, VARCHAR is the data type to use.

BINARY[(*width*)] *and* VARBINARY(*width*)

These types are very similar to CHAR and VARCHAR but store binary strings. Binary strings have the special binary character set and collation, and sorting them is dependent on the numeric values of the bytes in the values stored. Instead of character strings, byte strings are stored. In the earlier discussion of VARCHAR we described the binary charset and BINARY attribute. Only the binary charset "converts" a VARCHAR or CHAR into its respective BINARY form. Applying the BINARY attribute to a charset will not change the fact that character strings are stored. Unlike with VARCHAR and CHAR, *width* here is exactly the number of bytes. When *width* is omitted for BINARY, it defaults to 1.

Like with CHAR, data in the BINARY column is padded on the right. However, being a binary data, it's padded using zero bytes, usually written as 0x00 or \0. BINARY treats a space as a significant character, not padding. If you need to store data that might end in zero bytes that are significant to you, use the VARBINARY or BLOB types.

It is important to keep the concept of binary strings in mind when working with both of these data types. Even though they'll accept strings, they aren't synonyms for data types using text strings. For example, you cannot change the case of the letters stored, as that concept doesn't really apply to binary data. That becomes quite clear when you consider the actual data stored. Let's look at an example:

```
mysql> CREATE TABLE test_binary_data (
    ->    d1 BINARY(16)
    -> , d2 VARBINARY(16)
    -> , d3 CHAR(16)
    -> , d4 VARCHAR(16)
    -> );
```

Query OK, 0 rows affected (0.03 sec)

```
mysql> INSERT INTO test_binary_data VALUES (
    ->    'something'
    -> , 'something'
    -> , 'something'
    -> , 'something');
```

Query OK, 1 row affected (0.00 sec)

```
mysql> SELECT d1, d2, d3, d4 FROM test_binary_data;
```

*************************** 1. row ***************************
d1: 0x736F6D657468696E6700000000000000
d2: 0x736F6D657468696E67
d3: something
d4: something
1 row in set (0.00 sec)

```
mysql> SELECT UPPER(d2), UPPER(d4) FROM test_binary_data;
```

*************************** 1. row ***************************
UPPER(d2): 0x736F6D657468696E67
UPPER(d4): SOMETHING
1 row in set (0.01 sec)

Note how the MySQL command-line client actually shows values of binary types in hex format. We believe that this is much better than the silent conversions that were performed prior to MySQL 8.0, which might've resulted in misunderstanding. To get the actual text data back, you have to explicitly cast the binary data to text:

```
mysql> SELECT CAST(d1 AS CHAR) d1t, CAST(d2 AS CHAR) d2t
    -> FROM test_binary_data;
```

```
+-------------------+-----------+
| d1t               | d2t       |
+-------------------+-----------+
| something         | something |
+-------------------+-----------+
1 row in set (0.00 sec)
```

You can also see that BINARY padding was converted to spaces when casting was performed.

BLOB[(*width*)] *and*

TEXT[(*width*)] [CHARACTER SET *charset_name*] [COLLATE *collation_name*]

BLOB and TEXT are commonly used data types for storing large data. You may think of BLOB as a VARBINARY holding as much data as you like, and the same for TEXT and VARCHAR. The BLOB and TEXT types can store up to 65,535 bytes or characters, respectively. As usual, note that multibyte charsets do exist. The *width* attribute is optional, and when it is specified, MySQL actually will change the BLOB or TEXT data type to whatever the smallest type capable of holding that amount of data is. For example, BLOB(128) will result in TINYBLOB being used:

```
mysql> CREATE TABLE test_blob(data BLOB(128));
Query OK, 0 rows affected (0.07 sec)

mysql> DESC test_blob;
+-------+----------+------+-----+---------+-------+
| Field | Type     | Null | Key | Default | Extra |
+-------+----------+------+-----+---------+-------+
| data  | tinyblob | YES  |     | NULL    |       |
+-------+----------+------+-----+---------+-------+
1 row in set (0.00 sec)
```

For the BLOB type and related types, data is treated exactly as it would be in the case of VARBINARY. That is, no character set is assumed, and comparison and sorting are based on the numeric values of the actual bytes stored. For TEXT, you may specify the exact desired charset and collation. For both types and their variants, no padding is performed on INSERT, and no trimming is performed on SELECT, making them ideal for storing data exactly as it is. In addition, a DEFAULT clause is not permitted, and when an index is created on a BLOB or TEXT column, a prefix must be defined limiting the length of the indexed values. We talk more about that in "Keys and Indexes" on page 161.

One potential difference between BLOB and TEXT is their handling of trailing spaces. As we've shown already, VARCHAR and TEXT may pad strings depending on the collation used. BLOB and VARBINARY both use the binary character set with a single binary collation with no padding and are impervious to collation mixups and related issues. Sometimes, it can be a good choice to use these types for additional safety. In addition to that, prior to MySQL 8.0, these were the only types that preserved trailing spaces.

TINYBLOB *and*

TINYTEXT [CHARACTER SET *charset_name*] [COLLATE *collation_name*]

These are identical to BLOB and TEXT, respectively, except that a maximum of 255 bytes or characters can be stored.

MEDIUMBLOB *and*

MEDIUMTEXT [CHARACTER SET *charset_name*] [COLLATE *collation_name*]

These are identical to BLOB and TEXT, respectively, except that a maximum of 16,777,215 bytes or characters can be stored. The types LONG and LONG VARCHAR map to the MEDIUMTEXT data type for compatibility.

LONGBLOB *and*

LONGTEXT [CHARACTER SET *charset_name*] [COLLATE *collation_name*]

These are identical to BLOB and TEXT, respectively, except that a maximum of 4 GB of data can be stored. Note that this is a hard limit even in case of LONGTEXT, and thus the number of characters in multibyte charsets can be less than 4,294,967,295. The effective maximum size of the data that can be stored by a client will be limited by the amount of available memory as well as the value of the max_packet_size variable, which defaults to 64 MiB.

ENUM(*value1*[,*value2*[, …]]) [CHARACTER SET *charset_name*]
[COLLATE *collation_name*]

This type stores a list, or *enumeration*, of string values. A column of type ENUM can be set to a value from the list *value1*, *value2*, and so on, up to a maximum of 65,535 different values. While the values are stored and retrieved as strings, what's stored in the database is an integer representation. The ENUM column can contain NULL values (stored as NULL), the empty string ' ' (stored as 0), or any of the valid elements (stored as 1, 2, 3, and so on). You can prevent NULL values from being accepted by declaring the column as NOT NULL when creating the table.

This type offers a compact way of storing values from a list of predefined values, such as state or country names. Consider this example using fruit names; the name can be any one of the predefined values Apple, Orange, or Pear (in addition to NULL and the empty string):

```
mysql> CREATE TABLE fruits_enum
    -> (fruit_name ENUM('Apple', 'Orange', 'Pear'));
Query OK, 0 rows affected (0.00 sec)

mysql> INSERT INTO fruits_enum VALUES ('Apple');
Query OK, 1 row affected (0.00 sec)
```

If you try inserting a value that's not in the list, MySQL produces an error to tell you that it didn't store the data you asked:

```
mysql> INSERT INTO fruits_enum VALUES ('Banana');
ERROR 1265 (01000): Data truncated for column 'fruit_name' at row 1
```

A list of several allowed values isn't accepted either:

```
mysql> INSERT INTO fruits_enum VALUES ('Apple,Orange');
ERROR 1265 (01000): Data truncated for column 'fruit_name' at row 1
```

Displaying the contents of the table, you can see that no invalid values were stored:

```
mysql> SELECT * FROM fruits_enum;
+------------+
| fruit_name |
+------------+
| Apple      |
+------------+
1 row in set (0.00 sec)
```

Earlier versions of MySQL produced a warning instead of an error and stored an empty string in place of an invalid value. That behavior can be enabled by disabling the default strict SQL mode. It's also possible to specify a default value other than the empty string:

```
mysql> CREATE TABLE new_fruits_enum
    -> (fruit_name ENUM('Apple', 'Orange', 'Pear')
    -> DEFAULT 'Pear');
Query OK, 0 rows affected (0.01 sec)

mysql> INSERT INTO new_fruits_enum VALUES();
Query OK, 1 row affected (0.02 sec)

mysql> SELECT * FROM new_fruits_enum;
+------------+
| fruit_name |
+------------+
| Pear       |
+------------+
1 row in set (0.00 sec)
```

Here, not specifying a value results in the default value Pear being stored.

SET(*value1* [, *value2* [, ...]]) [CHARACTER SET *charset_name*]
[COLLATE *collation_name*]

This type stores a set of string values. A column of type SET can be set to zero or more values from the list *value1*, *value2*, and so on, up to a maximum of 64 different values. While the values are strings, what's stored in the database is an integer representation. SET differs from ENUM in that each row can store only one ENUM value in a column, but can store multiple SET values. This type is useful for storing a selection of choices from a list, such as user preferences. Consider this example using fruit names; the name can be any combination of the predefined values:

```
mysql> CREATE TABLE fruits_set
    -> ( fruit_name SET('Apple', 'Orange', 'Pear') );
Query OK, 0 rows affected (0.08 sec)

mysql> INSERT INTO fruits_set VALUES ('Apple');
Query OK, 1 row affected (0.00 sec)

mysql> INSERT INTO fruits_set VALUES ('Banana');
ERROR 1265 (01000): Data truncated for column 'fruit_name' at row 1

mysql> INSERT INTO fruits_set VALUES ('Apple,Orange');
Query OK, 1 row affected (0.00 sec)

mysql> SELECT * FROM fruits_set;
+--------------+
| fruit_name   |
+--------------+
| Apple        |
| Apple,Orange |
+--------------+
2 rows in set (0.00 sec)
```

Again, note that we can store multiple values from the set in a single field and that an empty string is stored for invalid input.

As with numeric types, we recommend that you always choose the smallest possible type to store values. For example, if you're storing a city name, use CHAR or VARCHAR rather than, say, the TEXT type. Having shorter columns helps keep your table size down, which in turns helps performance when the server has to search through a table.

Using a fixed size with the CHAR type is often faster than using a variable size with VARCHAR, since the MySQL server knows where each row starts and ends and can quickly skip over rows to find the one it needs. However, with fixed-length fields, any space that you don't use is wasted. For example, if you allow up to 40 characters in a city name, then CHAR(40) will always use up 40 characters, no matter how long the city name actually is. If you declare the city name to be VARCHAR(40), then you'll use up only as much space as you need, plus 1 byte to store the name's length. If the average city name is 10 characters long, this means that using a variable-length field will take up on average 29 fewer bytes per entry. This can make a big difference if you're storing millions of addresses.

In general, if storage space is at a premium or you expect large variations in the length of strings that are to be stored, use a variable-length field; if performance is a priority, use a fixed-length field.

Date and time types

These types serve the purpose of storing particular timestamps, dates, or time ranges. Particular care should be taken when dealing with time zones. We will try to explain the details, but it's worth rereading this section and the documentation later, when you need to actually work with time zones. The date and time types in MySQL are:

DATE

Stores and displays a date in the format *YYYY-MM-DD* for the range 1000-01-01 to 9999-12-31. Dates must always be input as year, month, day triples, but the format of the input can vary, as shown in the following examples:

YYYY-MM-DD or YY-MM-DD
It's optional whether you provide two-digit or four-digit years. We strongly recommend that you use the four-digit version to avoid confusion about the century. In practice, if you use the two-digit version, you'll find that 70 to 99 are interpreted as 1970 to 1999, and 00 to 69 are interpreted as 2000 to 2069.

YYYY/MM/DD, YYYY:MM:DD, YY-MM-DD, or other punctuated formats
MySQL allows any punctuation characters to separate the components of a date. We recommend using dashes and, again, avoiding two-digit years.

YYYY-M-D, YYYY-MM-D, or YYYY-M-DD
When punctuation is used (again, any punctuation character is allowed), single-digit days and months can be specified as such. For example, February 2, 2006, can be specified as 2006-2-2. The two-digit year equivalents are available, but not recommended.

YYYYMMDD or YYMMDD

Punctuation can be omitted in both date styles, but the digit sequences must be six or eight digits in length.

You can also input a date by providing both a date and time in the formats described later for DATETIME and TIMESTAMP, but only the date component is stored in a DATE column. Regardless of the input type, the storage and display type is always *YYYY-MM-DD*. The *zero date* 0000-00-00 is allowed in all versions and can be used to represent an unknown or dummy value. If an input date is out of range, the zero date is stored. However, only MySQL versions up to and including 5.6 allow that by default. Both 5.7 and 8.0 by default set SQL modes that prohibit this behavior: STRICT_TRANS_TABLES, NO_ZERO_DATE, and NO_ZERO_IN_DATE.

If you're using an older version of MySQL, we recommend that you add these modes to your current session:

```
mysql> SET sql_mode=CONCAT(@@sql_mode,
    -> ',STRICT_TRANS_TABLES',
    -> ',NO_ZERO_DATE', ',NO_ZERO_IN_DATE');
```

 You can also set the sql_mode variable on a global server level and in the configuration file. This variable must list every mode you want to be enabled.

Here are some examples of inserting dates on a MySQL 8.0 server with default settings:

```
mysql> CREATE TABLE testdate (mydate DATE);

Query OK, 0 rows affected (0.00 sec)

mysql> INSERT INTO testdate VALUES ('2020/02/0');

ERROR 1292 (22007): Incorrect date value: '2020/02/0'
for column 'mydate' at row 1

mysql> INSERT INTO testdate VALUES ('2020/02/1');

Query OK, 1 row affected (0.00 sec)

mysql> INSERT INTO testdate VALUES ('2020/02/31');

ERROR 1292 (22007): Incorrect date value: '2020/02/31'
for column 'mydate' at row 1

mysql> INSERT INTO testdate VALUES ('2020/02/100');

ERROR 1292 (22007): Incorrect date value: '2020/02/100'
for column 'mydate' at row 1
```

Once INSERT statements are executed, the table will have the following data:

```
mysql> SELECT * FROM testdate;

+------------+
| mydate     |
+------------+
| 2020-02-01 |
+------------+
1 row in set (0.00 sec)
```

MySQL protected you from having "bad" data stored in your table. Sometimes you may need to preserve the actual input and manually process it later. You can do that by removing the aforementioned SQL modes from the list of modes in the sql_mode variable. In that case, after running the previous INSERT statements, you would end up with the following data:

```
mysql> SELECT * FROM testdate;

+------------+
| mydate     |
+------------+
| 2020-02-00 |
| 2020-02-01 |
| 0000-00-00 |
| 0000-00-00 |
+------------+
4 rows in set (0.01 sec)
```

Note again that the date is displayed in the *YYYY-MM-DD* format, regardless of how it was input.

TIME [*fraction*]

Stores a time in the format *HHH:MM:SS* for the range –838:59:59 to 838:59:59. This is useful for storing the duration of some activity. The values that can be stored are outside the range of the 24-hour clock to allow large differences between time values (up to 34 days, 22 hours, 59 minutes, and 59 seconds) to be computed and stored. *fraction* in TIME and other related data types specifies the fractional seconds precision in the range 0 to 6. The default value is 0, meaning that no fractional seconds are preserved.

Times must always be input in the order *days*, *hours*, *minutes*, *seconds*, using the following formats:

DD HH:MM:SS[.fraction], HH:MM:SS[.fraction], DD HH:MM, HH:MM, DD HH, or SS[.fraction]

DD represents a one-digit or two-digit value of days in the range 0 to 34. The DD value is separated from the hour value, *HH*, by a space, while the other components are separated by a colon. Note that *MM:SS* is not a valid combination, since it cannot be disambiguated from *HH:MM*. If the TIME definition doesn't specify *fraction* or sets it to 0, inserting fractional seconds will result in values being rounded to the nearest second.

For example, if you insert 2 13:25:58.999999 into a TIME column with a *fraction* of 0, the value 61:25:59 is stored, since the sum of 2 days (48 hours) and 13 hours is 61 hours. Starting with MySQL 5.7, the default SQL mode set prohibits insertion of incorrect values. However, it is possible to enable the older behavior. Then, if you try inserting a value that's out of bounds, a warning is generated, and the value is limited to the maximum time available. Similarly, if you try inserting an invalid value, a warning is generated and the value is set to zero. You can use the SHOW WARNINGS command to report the details of the warning generated by the previous SQL statement. Our recommendation is to stick to the default strict SQL mode. Unlike with the DATE type, there's seemingly no benefit to allowing incorrect TIME entries, apart from easier error management on the application side and maintaining legacy behaviors.

Let's try all these out in practice:

```
mysql> CREATE TABLE test_time(id SMALLINT, mytime TIME);
Query OK, 0 rows affected (0.00 sec)

mysql> INSERT INTO test_time VALUES(1, "2 13:25:59");
Query OK, 1 row affected (0.00 sec)

mysql> INSERT INTO test_time VALUES(2, "35 13:25:59");
ERROR 1292 (22007): Incorrect time value: '35 13:25:59'
for column 'mytime' at row 1

mysql> INSERT INTO test_time VALUES(3, "900.32");
Query OK, 1 row affected (0.00 sec)

mysql> SELECT * FROM test_time;
+------+----------+
| id   | mytime   |
+------+----------+
|    1 | 61:25:59 |
|    3 | 00:09:00 |
+------+----------+
2 rows in set (0.00 sec)
```

H:M:S, and single-, double-, and triple-digit combinations

You can use different combinations of digits when inserting or updating data; MySQL converts them into the internal time format and displays them consistently. For example, 1:1:3 is equivalent to 01:01:03. Different numbers of digits can be mixed; for example, `1:12:3` is equivalent to `01:12:03`. Consider these examples:

```
mysql> CREATE TABLE mytime (testtime TIME);

Query OK, 0 rows affected (0.12 sec)

mysql> INSERT INTO mytime VALUES
    -> ('-1:1:1'), ('1:1:1'),
    -> ('1:23:45'), ('123:4:5'),
    -> ('123:45:6'), ('-123:45:6');

Query OK, 4 rows affected (0.00 sec)
Records: 4  Duplicates: 0  Warnings: 0

mysql> SELECT * FROM mytime;
+------------+
| testtime   |
+------------+
|  -01:01:01 |
|   01:01:01 |
|   01:23:45 |
|  123:04:05 |
|  123:45:06 |
| -123:45:06 |
+------------+
5 rows in set (0.01 sec)
```

Note that hours are shown with two digits for values within the range –99 to 99.

HHMMSS, MMSS, and SS

Punctuation can be omitted, but the digit sequences must be two, four, or six digits in length. Note that the rightmost pair of digits is always interpreted as a *SS* (seconds) value, the second rightmost pair (if present) as *MM* (minutes), and the third rightmost pair (if present) as *HH* (hours). The result is that a value such as 1222 is interpreted as 12 minutes and 22 seconds, not 12 hours and 22 minutes.

You can also input a time by providing both a date and time in the formats described for DATETIME and TIMESTAMP, but only the time component is stored in a TIME column. Regardless of the input type, the storage and display type is always *HH:MM:SS*. The *zero time* `00:00:00` can be used to represent an unknown or dummy value.

TIMESTAMP[(*fraction*)]

Stores and displays a date and time pair in the format *YYYY-MM-DD HH:MM:SS[.fraction][time zone offset]* for the range `1970-01-01 00:00:01.000000` to `2038-01-19 03:14:07.999999`. This type is very similar to the DATETIME type, but there are a few differences. Both types accept a time zone modifier to the input value MySQL 8.0, and both types will store and present the data in the same way to any client in the same time zone. However, the values in TIMESTAMP columns are internally always stored in the UTC time zone, making it possible to get a local time zone automatically for clients in different time zones. That on its own is a very important distinction to remember. Arguably, TIME STAMP is more convenient to use when dealing with different time zones.

Prior to MySQL 5.6, only the TIMESTAMP type supported automatic initialization and update. Moreover, only a single such column per a given table could do that. However, starting with 5.6, both TIMESTAMP and DATETIME support the behaviors, and any number of columns can do so.

Values stored in a TIMESTAMP column always match the template *YYYY-MM-DD HH:MM:SS[.fraction][time zone offset]*, but the values can be provided in a wide range of formats:

YYYY-MM-DD HH:MM:SS or YY-MM-DD HH:MM:SS
> The date and time components follow the same relaxed restrictions as the DATE and TIME components described previously. This includes allowance for any punctuation characters, including (unlike for TIME) flexibility in the punctuation used in the time component. For example, 0 is valid.

YYYYMMDDHHMMSS or YYMMDDHHMMSS
> Punctuation can be omitted, but the string should be either 12 or 14 digits in length. We recommend using only the unambiguous 14-digit version, for the reasons discussed for the DATE type. You can specify values with other lengths without providing separators, but we don't recommend doing so.

Let's look at the automatic-update feature in more detail. You control this by adding the following attributes to the column definition when creating a table, or later, as we'll explain in "Altering Structures" on page 170:

1. If you want the timestamp to be set only when a new row is inserted into the table, add DEFAULT CURRENT_TIMESTAMP to the end of the column declaration.

2. If you don't want a default timestamp but would like the current time to be used whenever the data in a row is updated, add ON UPDATE CURRENT_TIME STAMP to the end of the column declaration.

3. If you want both of the above—that is, you want the timestamp set to the current time in each new row and whenever an existing row is modified— add DEFAULT CURRENT_TIMESTAMP ON UPDATE CURRENT_TIMESTAMP to the end of the column declaration.

If you do not specify `DEFAULT NULL` or `NULL` for a `TIMESTAMP` column, it will have 0 as the default value.

`YEAR[(4)]`

Stores a four-digit year in the range 1901 to 2155, as well as the *zero year*, 0000. Illegal values are converted to the zero year. You can input year values as either strings (such as `'2005'`) or integers (such as 2005). The `YEAR` type requires 1 byte of storage space.

In earlier versions of MySQL, it was possible to specify the *digits* parameter, passing either 2 or 4. The two-digit version stored values from 70 to 69, representing 1970 to 2069. MySQL 8.0 doesn't support the two-digit `YEAR` type, and specifying the *digits* parameter for display purposes is deprecated.

`DATETIME[(fraction)]`

Stores and displays a date and time pair in the format *YYYY-MM-DD HH:MM:SS[.fraction][time zone offset]* for the range `1000-01-01 00:00:00` to `9999-12-31 23:59:59`. As for `TIMESTAMP`, the value stored always matches the template *YYYY-MM-DD HH:MM:SS*, but the value can be input in the same formats listed in the `TIMESTAMP` description. If you assign only a date to a `DATETIME` column, the zero time `00:00:00` is assumed. If you assign only a time to a `DATETIME` column, the zero date `0000-00-00` is assumed. This type has the same automatic update features as `TIMESTAMP`. Unless the `NOT NULL` attribute is specified for a `DATETIME` column, a `NULL` value is the default; otherwise, the default is 0. Unlike for `TIMESTAMP`, `DATETIME` values aren't converted to the UTC time zone for storage.

Other types

Currently, as of MySQL 8.0, the spatial and `JSON` data types fall under this broad category. Using these is a quite advanced topic, and we won't cover them in depth.

Spatial data types are concerned with storing geometrical objects, and MySQL has types corresponding to OpenGIS classes. Working with these types is a topic worth a book on its own.

The `JSON` data type allows native storage of valid JSON documents. Before MySQL 5.7, JSON was usually stored in a `TEXT` or a similar column. However, that has a lot of disadvantages: for example, documents aren't validated, and no storage optimization is performed (all JSON is just stored in its text form). With the native `JSON` type, it's stored in binary format. If we were to summarize in one sentence: use the `JSON` data type for JSON, dear reader.

Keys and Indexes

You'll find that almost all tables you use will have a PRIMARY KEY clause declared in their CREATE TABLE statement, and sometimes multiple KEY clauses. The reasons why you need a primary key and secondary keys were discussed in Chapter 2. This section discusses how primary keys are declared, what happens behind the scenes when you do so, and why you might want to also create other keys and indexes on your data.

A *primary key* uniquely identifies each row in a table. Even more importantly, for the default InnoDB storage engine, a primary key is also used as a *clustered index*. That means that all of the actual table data is stored in an index structure. That is different from MyISAM, which stores data and indexes separately. When a table is using a clustered index, it's called a clustered table. As we said, in a clustered table each row is stored within an index, compared to being stored in what's usually called a *heap*. Clustering a table results in its rows being sorted according to the clustered index ordering and actually physically stored within the leaf pages of that index. There can't be more than one clustered index per table. For such tables, secondary indexes refer to records in the clustered index instead of the actual table rows. That generally results in improved query performance, though it can be detrimental to writes. InnoDB does not allow you to choose between clustered and nonclustered tables; this is a design decision that you cannot change.

Primary keys are generally a recommended part of any database design, but for InnoDB they are necessary. In fact, if you do not specify a PRIMARY KEY clause when creating an InnoDB table, MySQL will use the first UNIQUE NOT NULL column as a base for the clustered index. If no such column is available, a hidden clustered index is created, based on ID values assigned by InnoDB to each row.

Given that InnoDB is MySQL's default storage engine and a de facto standard nowadays, we will concentrate on its behavior in this chapter. Alternative storage engines like MyISAM, MEMORY, or MyRocks will be discussed in "Alternative Storage Engines" on page 297.

As mentioned previously, when a primary key is defined, it becomes a clustered index, and all data in the table is stored in the leaf blocks of that index. InnoDB uses B-tree indexes (more specifically, the B+tree variant), with the exception of indexes on spatial data types, which use the R-tree structure. Other storage engines might implement different index types, but when a table's storage engine is not specified, you can assume that all indexes are B-trees.

Having a clustered index, or in other words having index-organized tables, speeds up queries and sorts involving the primary key columns. However, a downside is that modifying columns in a primary key is expensive. Thus, a good design will require a primary key based on columns that are frequently used for filtering in queries but are rarely modified. Remember that having no primary key at all will result in InnoDB using an implicit cluster index; thus, if you're not sure what columns to pick for a primary key, consider using a synthetic id-like column. For example, the SERIAL data type might fit well in that case.

Stepping away from InnoDB's internal details, when you declare a primary key for a table in MySQL, it creates a structure that stores information about where the data from each row in the table is stored. This information is called an *index*, and its purpose is to speed up searches that use the primary key. For example, when you declare PRIMARY KEY (actor_id) in the actor table in the sakila database, MySQL creates a structure that allows it to find rows that match a specific actor_id (or a range of identifiers) extremely quickly.

This is useful to match actors to films or films to categories, for example. You can display the indexes available on a table using the SHOW INDEX (or SHOW INDEXES) command:

```
mysql> SHOW INDEX FROM category\G
*************************** 1. row ***************************
        Table: category
   Non_unique: 0
     Key_name: PRIMARY
 Seq_in_index: 1
  Column_name: category_id
    Collation: A
  Cardinality: 16
     Sub_part: NULL
       Packed: NULL
         Null:
   Index_type: BTREE
      Comment:
Index_comment:
      Visible: YES
   Expression: NULL
1 row in set (0.00 sec)
```

The *cardinality* is the number of unique values in the index; for an index on a primary key, this is the same as the number of rows in the table.

Note that all columns that are part of a primary key must be declared as NOT NULL, since they must have a value for the row to be valid. Without the index, the only way to find rows in the table is to read each one from disk and check whether it matches the category_id you're searching for. For tables with many rows, this exhaustive, sequential searching is extremely slow. However, you can't just index everything; we'll come back to this point at the end of this section.

You can create other indexes on the data in a table. You do this so that other searches (whether on other columns or combinations of columns) are fast, and to avoid sequential scans. For example, take the actor table again. Apart from having a primary key on `actor_id`, it also has a secondary key on `last_name` to improve searching by an actor's last name:

```
mysql> SHOW CREATE TABLE actor\G
*************************** 1. row ***************************
        Table: actor
Create Table: CREATE TABLE `actor` (
  `actor_id` smallint unsigned NOT NULL AUTO_INCREMENT,
  ...
  `last_name` varchar(45) NOT NULL,
  ...
  PRIMARY KEY (`actor_id`),
  KEY `idx_actor_last_name` (`last_name`)
) ...
1 row in set (0.00 sec)
```

You can see the keyword KEY is used to tell MySQL that an extra index is needed. Alternatively, you can use the word INDEX in place of KEY. Following that keyword is an index name, and then the column to index is included in parentheses. You can also add indexes after tables are created—in fact, you can pretty much change anything about a table after its creation. This is discussed in "Altering Structures" on page 170.

You can build an index on more than one column. For example, consider the following table, which is a modified table from `sakila`:

```
mysql> CREATE TABLE customer_mod (
    -> customer_id smallint unsigned NOT NULL AUTO_INCREMENT,
    -> first_name varchar(45) NOT NULL,
    -> last_name varchar(45) NOT NULL,
    -> email varchar(50) DEFAULT NULL,
    -> PRIMARY KEY (customer_id),
    -> KEY idx_names_email (first_name, last_name, email));

Query OK, 0 rows affected (0.06 sec)
```

You can see that we've added a primary key index on the `customer_id` identifier column, and we've also added another index—called `idx_names_email`—that includes the `first_name`, `last_name`, and `email` columns in this order. Let's now consider how you can use that extra index.

You can use the `idx_names_email` index for fast searching by combinations of the three name columns. For example, it's useful in the following query:

```
mysql> SELECT * FROM customer_mod WHERE
    -> first_name = 'Rose' AND
    -> last_name = 'Williams' AND
    -> email = 'rose.w@nonexistent.edu';
```

We know it helps the search, because all the columns listed in the index are used in the query. You can use the EXPLAIN statement to check whether what you think should happen is in fact happening:

```
mysql> EXPLAIN SELECT * FROM customer_mod WHERE
    -> first_name = 'Rose' AND
    -> last_name = 'Williams' AND
    -> email = 'rose.w@nonexistent.edu'\G

*************************** 1. row ***************************
           id: 1
  select_type: SIMPLE
        table: customer_mod
   partitions: NULL
         type: ref
possible_keys: idx_names_email
          key: idx_names_email
      key_len: 567
          ref: const,const,const
         rows: 1
     filtered: 100.00
        Extra: Using index
1 row in set, 1 warning (0.00 sec)
```

You can see that MySQL reports that the possible_keys are idx_names_email (meaning that the index could be used for this query) and that the key that it's decided to use is idx_names_email. So, what you expect and what is happening are the same, and that's good news! You'll find out more about the EXPLAIN statement in Chapter 7.

The index we've created is also useful for queries on only the first_name column. For example, it can be used by the following query:

```
mysql> SELECT * FROM customer_mod WHERE
    -> first_name = 'Rose';
```

You can use EXPLAIN again to check whether the index is being used. The reason it can be used is because the first_name column is the first one listed in the index. In practice, this means that the index *clusters*, or stores together, information about rows for all people with the same first name, and so the index can be used to find anyone with a matching first name.

The index can also be used for searches involving combinations of first name and last name, for exactly the same reasons we've just discussed. The index clusters together people with the same first name, and it clusters people with identical first names by last name. So, it can be used for this query:

```
mysql> SELECT * FROM customer_mod WHERE
    -> first_name = 'Rose' AND
    -> last_name = 'Williams';
```

However, the index can't be used for this query because the leftmost column in the index, first_name, does not appear in the query:

```
mysql> SELECT * FROM customer_mod WHERE
    -> last_name = 'Williams' AND
    -> email = 'rose.w@nonexistent.edu';
```

The index should help narrow down the set of rows to a smaller set of possible answers. For MySQL to be able to use an index, the query needs to meet both the following conditions:

1. The leftmost column listed in the KEY (or PRIMARY KEY) clause must be in the query.

2. The query must contain no OR clauses for columns that aren't indexed.

Again, you can always use the EXPLAIN statement to check whether an index can be used for a particular query.

Before we finish this section, here are a few ideas on how to choose and design indexes. When you're considering adding an index, think about the following:

- Indexes cost space on disk, and they need to be updated whenever data changes. If your data changes frequently, or lots of data changes when you do make a change, indexes will slow the process down. However, in practice, since SELECT statements (data reads) are usually much more common than other statements (data modifications), indexes are usually beneficial.

- Only add an index that'll be used frequently. Don't bother indexing columns before you see what queries your users and your applications need. You can always add indexes afterward.

- If all columns in an index are used in all queries, list the column with the highest number of duplicates at the left of the KEY clause. This minimizes index size.

- The smaller the index, the faster it'll be. If you index large columns, you'll get a larger index. This is a good reason to ensure your columns are as small as possible when you design your tables.

- For long columns, you can use only a prefix of the values from a column to create the index. You can do this by adding a value in parentheses after the column definition, such as KEY idx_names_email (first_name(3), last_name(2), email(10)). This means that only the first 3 characters of first_name are indexed, then the first 2 characters of last_name, and then 10 characters from email. This is a significant savings over indexing 140 characters from the three columns! When you do this, your index will be less able to uniquely identify rows, but it'll be much smaller and still reasonably good at finding matching rows. Using a prefix is mandatory for long types like TEXT.

To wrap up this section, we need to discuss some peculiarities regarding secondary keys in InnoDB. Remember that all the table data is stored in the leaves of the clustered index. That means, using the `actor` example, that if we need to get the `first_name` data when filtering by `last_name`, even though we can use `idx_actor_last_name` for quick filtering, we will need to access the data by the primary key. As a consequence, each secondary key in InnoDB has all of the primary key columns appended to its definition implicitly. Having unnecessarily long primary keys in InnoDB thus results in significantly bloated secondary keys.

This can also be seen in the EXPLAIN output (note the `Extra: Using index` in the first output of the first command):

```
mysql> EXPLAIN SELECT actor_id, last_name FROM actor WHERE last_name = 'Smith'\G

*************************** 1. row ***************************
           id: 1
  select_type: SIMPLE
        table: actor
   partitions: NULL
         type: ref
possible_keys: idx_actor_last_name
          key: idx_actor_last_name
      key_len: 182
          ref: const
         rows: 1
     filtered: 100.00
        Extra: Using index
1 row in set, 1 warning (0.00 sec)

mysql> EXPLAIN SELECT first_name FROM actor WHERE last_name = 'Smith'\G

*************************** 1. row ***************************
           id: 1
  select_type: SIMPLE
        table: actor
   partitions: NULL
         type: ref
possible_keys: idx_actor_last_name
          key: idx_actor_last_name
      key_len: 182
          ref: const
         rows: 1
     filtered: 100.00
        Extra: NULL
1 row in set, 1 warning (0.00 sec)
```

Effectively, `idx_actor_last_name` is a *covering index* for the first query, meaning that InnoDB can extract all the required data from that index alone. However, for the second query, InnoDB will have to do an additional lookup of a clustered index to get the value for the `first_name` column.

The AUTO_INCREMENT Feature

MySQL's proprietary AUTO_INCREMENT feature allows you to create a unique identifier for a row without running a SELECT query. Here's how it works. Let's take the simplified actor table again:

```
mysql> CREATE TABLE actor (
    -> actor_id smallint unsigned NOT NULL AUTO_INCREMENT,
    -> first_name varchar(45) NOT NULL,
    -> last_name varchar(45) NOT NULL,
    -> PRIMARY KEY (actor_id)
    -> );
Query OK, 0 rows affected (0.03 sec)
```

It's possible to insert rows into that table without specifying the actor_id:

```
mysql> INSERT INTO actor VALUES (NULL, 'Alexander', 'Kaidanovsky');
Query OK, 1 row affected (0.01 sec)

mysql> INSERT INTO actor VALUES (NULL, 'Anatoly', 'Solonitsyn');
Query OK, 1 row affected (0.01 sec)

mysql> INSERT INTO actor VALUES (NULL, 'Nikolai', 'Grinko');
Query OK, 1 row affected (0.00 sec)
```

When you view the data in this table, you can see that each row has a value assigned for the actor_id column:

```
mysql> SELECT * FROM actor;
+----------+------------+-------------+
| actor_id | first_name | last_name   |
+----------+------------+-------------+
|        1 | Alexander  | Kaidanovsky |
|        2 | Anatoly    | Solonitsyn  |
|        3 | Nikolai    | Grinko      |
+----------+------------+-------------+
3 rows in set (0.00 sec)
```

Each time a new row is inserted, a unique value for the actor_id column is created for that new row.

Consider how this feature works. You can see that the actor_id column is declared as an integer with the clauses NOT NULL AUTO_INCREMENT. AUTO_INCREMENT tells MySQL that when a value isn't provided for this column, the value allocated should be one more than the maximum currently stored in the table. The AUTO_INCREMENT sequence begins at 1 for an empty table.

The NOT NULL clause is required for AUTO_INCREMENT columns; when you insert NULL (or 0, though this isn't recommended), the MySQL server automatically finds the next available identifier and assigns it to the new row. You can manually insert negative values if the column was not defined as UNSIGNED; however, for the next automatic increment, MySQL will simply use the largest (positive) value in the column, or start from 1 if there are no positive values.

The AUTO_INCREMENT feature has the following requirements:

- The column it is used on must be indexed.

- The column it is used on cannot have a DEFAULT value.

- There can be only one AUTO_INCREMENT column per table.

MySQL supports different storage engines; we'll talk more about these in "Alternative Storage Engines" on page 297. When using the nondefault MyISAM table type, you can use the AUTO_INCREMENT feature on keys that comprise multiple columns. In effect, you can have multiple independent counters within a single AUTO_INCREMENT column. However, this is not possible with InnoDB.

While the AUTO_INCREMENT feature is useful, it isn't portable to other database environments, and it hides the logical steps for creating new identifiers. It can also lead to ambiguity; for example, dropping or truncating a table will reset the counter, but deleting selected rows (with a WHERE clause) doesn't reset the counter. Moreover, if a row is inserted inside a transaction but then that transaction is rolled back, an identifier will be used up anyway. As an example, let's create the table count that contains an auto-incrementing field counter:

```
mysql> CREATE TABLE count (counter INT AUTO_INCREMENT KEY);

Query OK, 0 rows affected (0.13 sec)

mysql> INSERT INTO count VALUES (),(),(),(),(),();

Query OK, 6 rows affected (0.01 sec)
Records: 6  Duplicates: 0  Warnings: 0

mysql> SELECT * FROM count;

+---------+
| counter |
+---------+
| 1       |
| 2       |
| 3       |
| 4       |
| 5       |
| 6       |
+---------+
6 rows in set (0.00 sec)
```

Inserting several values works as expected. Now, let's delete a few rows and then add six new rows:

```
mysql> DELETE FROM count WHERE counter > 4;

Query OK, 2 rows affected (0.00 sec)

mysql> INSERT INTO count VALUES (),(),(),(),(),();

Query OK, 6 rows affected (0.00 sec)
Records: 6  Duplicates: 0  Warnings: 0

mysql> SELECT * FROM count;

+---------+
| counter |
+---------+
| 1       |
| 2       |
| 3       |
| 4       |
| 7       |
| 8       |
| 9       |
| 10      |
| 11      |
| 12      |
+---------+
10 rows in set (0.00 sec)
```

Here, we see that the counter is not reset and continues from 7. If, however, we truncate the table, thus removing all of the data, the counter is reset to 1:

```
mysql> TRUNCATE TABLE count;

Query OK, 0 rows affected (0.00 sec)

mysql> INSERT INTO count VALUES (),(),(),(),(),();

Query OK, 6 rows affected (0.01 sec)
Records: 6  Duplicates: 0  Warnings: 0

mysql> SELECT * FROM count;

+---------+
| counter |
+---------+
| 1       |
| 2       |
| 3       |
| 4       |
| 5       |
| 6       |
+---------+
6 rows in set (0.00 sec)
```

To summarize: `AUTO_INCREMENT` guarantees a sequence of transactional and monotonically increasing values. However, it does not in any way guarantee that each individual identifier provided will exactly follow the previous one. Usually, this behavior of `AUTO_INCREMENT` is clear enough and should not be a problem. However, if your particular use case requires a counter that guarantees no gaps, you should consider using some kind of workaround. Unfortunately, it'll likely be implemented on the application side.

Altering Structures

We've shown you all the basics you need for creating databases, tables, indexes, and columns. In this section, you'll learn how to add, remove, and change columns, databases, tables, and indexes in structures that already exist.

Adding, Removing, and Changing Columns

You can use the `ALTER TABLE` statement to add new columns to a table, remove existing columns, and change column names, types, and lengths.

Let's begin by considering how you modify existing columns. Consider an example in which we rename a table column. The `language` table has a column called `last_update` that contains the time the record was modified. To change the name of this column to `last_updated_time`, you would write:

```
mysql> ALTER TABLE language RENAME COLUMN last_update TO last_updated_time;

Query OK, 0 rows affected (0.03 sec)
Records: 0  Duplicates: 0  Warnings: 0
```

This particular example utilizes the *online DDL* feature of MySQL. What actually happens behind the scenes is that MySQL only modifies metadata and doesn't need to actually rewrite the table in any way. You can see that by the lack of affected rows. Not all DDL statements can be performed online, so this won't be the case with many of the changes you make.

DDL stands for data definition language, and in the context of SQL it's a subset of syntax and statements used to create, modify, and delete schema objects such as databases, tables, indexes, and columns. `CREATE TABLE` and `ALTER TABLE` are both DDL operations, for example.

Executing DDL statements requires special internal mechanisms, including special locking—this is a good thing, as you probably wouldn't like tables changing while your queries are running! These special locks are called metadata locks in MySQL, and we give a detailed overview of how they work in "Metadata Locks" on page 249.

Note that all DDL statements, including those that execute through online DDL, require metadata locks to be obtained. In that sense, online DDL statements are not so "online," but they won't lock the target table entirely while they are running. Executing DDL statements on a running system under load is a risky venture: even a statement that should execute almost instantaneously may wreak havoc. We recommend that you read carefully about metadata locking in Chapter 6 and in the link to MySQL documentation (*https://oreil.ly/xNZYg*), and experiment with running different DDL statements with and without concurrent load. That may not be too important while you're learning MySQL, but we think it's worth cautioning you up front. With that covered, let's get back to our ALTER of the language table.

You can check the result with the SHOW COLUMNS statement:

```
mysql> SHOW COLUMNS FROM language;
+-------------------+-------------------+------+-----+-------------------+...
| Field             | Type              | Null | Key | Default           |...
+-------------------+-------------------+------+-----+-------------------+...
| language_id       | tinyint unsigned  | NO   | PRI | NULL              |...
| name              | char(20)          | NO   |     | NULL              |...
| last_updated_time | timestamp         | NO   |     | CURRENT_TIMESTAMP |...
+-------------------+-------------------+------+-----+-------------------+...
3 rows in set (0.01 sec)
```

In the previous example we used the ALTER TABLE statement with the RENAME COLUMN keyword. That is a MySQL 8.0 feature. We could alternatively use ALTER TABLE with the CHANGE keyword for compatibility:

```
mysql> ALTER TABLE language CHANGE last_update last_updated_time TIMESTAMP
    -> NOT NULL DEFAULT CURRENT_TIMESTAMP ON UPDATE CURRENT_TIMESTAMP;
Query OK, 0 rows affected (0.04 sec)
Records: 0  Duplicates: 0  Warnings: 0
```

In this example, you can see that we provided four parameters to the ALTER TABLE statement with the CHANGE keyword:

1. The table name, language

2. The original column name, last_update

3. The new column name, last_updated_time

4. The column type, TIMESTAMP, with a lot of extra attributes, which are necessary to avoid changing the original definition

You must provide all four; that means you need to respecify the type and any clauses that go with it. In this example, as we're using MySQL 8.0 with the default settings, TIMESTAMP no longer has explicit defaults. As you can see, using RENAME COLUMN is much easier than CHANGE.

If you want to modify the type and clauses of a column, but not its name, you can use the MODIFY keyword:

```
mysql> ALTER TABLE language MODIFY name CHAR(20) DEFAULT 'n/a';

Query OK, 0 rows affected (0.14 sec)
Records: 0  Duplicates: 0  Warnings: 0
```

You can also do this with the CHANGE keyword, but by specifying the same column name twice:

```
mysql> ALTER TABLE language CHANGE name name CHAR(20) DEFAULT 'n/a';

Query OK, 0 rows affected (0.03 sec)
Records: 0  Duplicates: 0  Warnings: 0
```

Be careful when you're modifying types:

- Don't use incompatible types, since you're relying on MySQL to successfully convert data from one format to another (for example, converting an INT column to a DATETIME column isn't likely to do what you hoped).

- Don't truncate the data unless that's what you want. If you reduce the size of a type, the values will be edited to match the new width, and you can lose data.

Suppose you want to add an extra column to an existing table. Here's how to do it with the ALTER TABLE statement:

```
mysql> ALTER TABLE language ADD native_name CHAR(20);

Query OK, 0 rows affected (0.04 sec)
Records: 0  Duplicates: 0  Warnings: 0
```

You must supply the ADD keyword, the new column name, and the column type and clauses. This example adds the new column, native_name, as the last column in the table, as shown with the SHOW COLUMNS statement:

```
mysql> SHOW COLUMNS FROM artist;
+-------------------+------------------+------+-----+-------------------+...
| Field             | Type             | Null | Key | Default           |...
+-------------------+------------------+------+-----+-------------------+...
| language_id       | tinyint unsigned | NO   | PRI | NULL              |...
| name              | char(20)         | YES  |     | n/a               |...
| last_updated_time | timestamp        | NO   |     | CURRENT_TIMESTAMP |...
| native_name       | char(20)         | YES  |     | NULL              |...
+-------------------+------------------+------+-----+-------------------+...
4 rows in set (0.00 sec)
```

If you want it to instead be the first column, use the FIRST keyword as follows:

```
mysql> ALTER TABLE language ADD native_name CHAR(20) FIRST;
```

```
Query OK, 0 rows affected (0.08 sec)
Records: 0  Duplicates: 0  Warnings: 0

mysql> SHOW COLUMNS FROM language;

+-------------------+------------------+------+-----+-------------------+...
| Field             | Type             | Null | Key | Default           |...
+-------------------+------------------+------+-----+-------------------+...
| native_name       | char(20)         | YES  |     | NULL              |...
| language_id       | tinyint unsigned | NO   | PRI | NULL              |...
| name              | char(20)         | YES  |     | n/a               |...
| last_updated_time | timestamp        | NO   |     | CURRENT_TIMESTAMP |...
+-------------------+------------------+------+-----+-------------------+...
4 rows in set (0.01 sec)
```

If you want it added in a specific position, use the AFTER keyword:

```
mysql> ALTER TABLE language ADD native_name CHAR(20) AFTER name;

Query OK, 0 rows affected (0.08 sec)
Records: 0  Duplicates: 0  Warnings: 0

mysql> SHOW COLUMNS FROM language;

+-------------------+------------------+------+-----+-------------------+...
| Field             | Type             | Null | Key | Default           |...
+-------------------+------------------+------+-----+-------------------+...
| language_id       | tinyint unsigned | NO   | PRI | NULL              |...
| name              | char(20)         | YES  |     | n/a               |...
| native_name       | char(20)         | YES  |     | NULL              |...
| last_updated_time | timestamp        | NO   |     | CURRENT_TIMESTAMP |...
+-------------------+------------------+------+-----+-------------------+...
4 rows in set (0.00 sec)
```

To remove a column, use the DROP keyword followed by the column name. Here's how to get rid of the newly added native_name column:

```
mysql> ALTER TABLE language DROP native_name;

Query OK, 0 rows affected (0.07 sec)
Records: 0  Duplicates: 0  Warnings: 0
```

This removes both the column structure and any data contained in that column. It also removes the column from any indexes it was in; if it's the only column in the index, the index is dropped, too. You can't remove a column if it's the only one in a table; to do this, you drop the table instead, as explained in "Deleting Structures" on page 177. Be careful when dropping columns, because when the structure of a table changes, you will generally have to modify any INSERT statements that you use to insert values in a particular order. For more on this, see "The INSERT Statement" on page 111.

MySQL allows you to specify multiple alterations in a single ALTER TABLE statement by separating them with commas. Here's an example that adds a new column and adjusts another:

```
mysql> ALTER TABLE language ADD native_name CHAR(255), MODIFY name CHAR(255);
Query OK, 6 rows affected (0.06 sec)
Records: 6  Duplicates: 0  Warnings: 0
```

Note that this time, you can see that six records were changed. In the previous ALTER TABLE commands, MySQL reported that no rows were affected. The difference is that this time, we're not performing an online DDL operation, because changing any column's type will always result in a table being rebuilt. We recommend reading about online DDL operations (*https://oreil.ly/EEOw0*) in the Reference Manual when planning your changes. Combining online and offline operations will result in an offline operation.

When not using online DDL or when any of the modifications is "offline," it's very efficient to join multiple modifications in a single operation. That potentially saves the cost of creating a new table, copying data from the old table to the new table, dropping the old table, and renaming the new table with the name of the old table for each modification individually.

Adding, Removing, and Changing Indexes

As we discussed previously, it's often hard to know what indexes are useful before the application you're building is used. You might find that a particular feature of the application is much more popular than you expected, causing you to evaluate how to improve performance for the associated queries. You'll therefore find it useful to be able to add, alter, and remove indexes on the fly after your application is deployed. This section shows you how. Note that modifying indexes does not affect the data stored in a table.

We'll start with adding a new index. Imagine that the language table is frequently queried using a WHERE clause that specifies the name. To speed up these queries, you've decided to add a new index, which you've named idx_name. Here's how you add it after the table is created:

```
mysql> ALTER TABLE language ADD INDEX idx_name (name);
Query OK, 0 rows affected (0.05 sec)
Records: 0  Duplicates: 0  Warnings: 0
```

Again, you can use the terms KEY and INDEX interchangeably. You can check the results with the SHOW CREATE TABLE statement:

```
mysql> SHOW CREATE TABLE language\G
*************************** 1. row ***************************
       Table: language
Create Table: CREATE TABLE `language` (
  `language_id` tinyint unsigned NOT NULL AUTO_INCREMENT,
  `name` char(255) DEFAULT NULL,
  `last_updated_time` timestamp NOT NULL
```

```
        DEFAULT CURRENT_TIMESTAMP ON UPDATE CURRENT_TIMESTAMP,
      PRIMARY KEY (`language_id`),
      KEY `idx_name` (`name`)
    ) ENGINE=InnoDB AUTO_INCREMENT=8
        DEFAULT CHARSET=utf8mb4 COLLATE=utf8mb4_0900_ai_ci
```

As expected, the new index forms part of the table structure. You can also specify a primary key for a table after it's created:

```
mysql> CREATE TABLE no_pk (id INT);

Query OK, 0 rows affected (0.02 sec)

mysql> INSERT INTO no_pk VALUES (1),(2),(3);

Query OK, 3 rows affected (0.01 sec)
Records: 3  Duplicates: 0  Warnings: 0

mysql> ALTER TABLE no_pk ADD PRIMARY KEY (id);

Query OK, 0 rows affected (0.13 sec)
Records: 0  Duplicates: 0  Warnings: 0
```

Now let's consider how to remove an index. To remove a non-primary key index, you do the following:

```
mysql> ALTER TABLE language DROP INDEX idx_name;

Query OK, 0 rows affected (0.08 sec)
Records: 0  Duplicates: 0  Warnings: 0
```

You can drop a primary key index as follows:

```
mysql> ALTER TABLE no_pk DROP PRIMARY KEY;

Query OK, 3 rows affected (0.07 sec)
Records: 3  Duplicates: 0  Warnings: 0
```

MySQL won't allow you to have multiple primary keys in a table. If you want to change the primary key, you'll have to remove the existing index before adding the new one. However, we know that it's possible to group DDL operations. Consider this example:

```
mysql> ALTER TABLE language DROP PRIMARY KEY,
    -> ADD PRIMARY KEY (language_id, name);

Query OK, 0 rows affected (0.09 sec)
Records: 0  Duplicates: 0  Warnings: 0
```

You can't modify an index once it's been created. However, sometimes you'll want to; for example, you might want to reduce the number of characters indexed from a column or add another column to the index. The best method to do this is to drop the index and then create it again with the new specification. For example, suppose you decide that you want the idx_name index to include only the first 10 characters of the artist_name. Simply do the following:

```
mysql> ALTER TABLE language DROP INDEX idx_name,
    -> ADD INDEX idx_name (name(10));

Query OK, 0 rows affected (0.05 sec)
Records: 0  Duplicates: 0  Warnings: 0
```

Renaming Tables and Altering Other Structures

We've seen how to modify columns and indexes in a table; now let's see how to modify tables themselves. It's easy to rename a table. Suppose that you want to rename language to languages. Use the following command:

```
mysql> ALTER TABLE language RENAME TO languages;

Query OK, 0 rows affected (0.04 sec)
```

The TO keyword is optional.

There are several other things you can do with ALTER statements, including:

- Change the default character set and collation order for a database, a table, or a column.

- Manage and change constraints. For example, you can add and remove foreign keys.

- Add partitioning to a table, or alter the current partitioning definition.

- Change the storage engine of a table.

You can find more about these operations in the MySQL Reference Manual, in the sections on the ALTER DATABASE (*https://oreil.ly/2FpoZ*) and ALTER TABLE (*https://oreil.ly/68PA3*) statements. An alternative shorter notation for the same statement is RENAME TABLE:

```
mysql> RENAME TABLE languages TO language;

Query OK, 0 rows affected (0.04 sec)
```

One thing that it's not possible to alter is a name of a particular database. However, if you're using the InnoDB engine, you can use RENAME to move tables between databases:

```
mysql> CREATE DATABASE sakila_new;

Query OK, 1 row affected (0.05 sec)

mysql> RENAME TABLE sakila.language TO sakila_new.language;

Query OK, 0 rows affected (0.05 sec)

mysql> USE sakila;

Database changed

mysql> SHOW TABLES LIKE 'lang%';
```

```
Empty set (0.00 sec)

mysql> USE sakila_new;

Database changed

mysql> SHOW TABLES LIKE 'lang%';

+-----------------------------+
| Tables_in_sakila_new (lang%) |
+-----------------------------+
| language                    |
+-----------------------------+
1 row in set (0.00 sec)
```

Deleting Structures

In the previous section, we showed how you can delete columns and rows from a database; now we'll describe how to remove databases and tables.

Dropping Databases

Removing, or *dropping*, a database is straightforward. Here's how you drop the sakila database:

```
mysql> DROP DATABASE sakila;

Query OK, 25 rows affected (0.16 sec)
```

The number of rows returned in the response is the number of tables removed. You should take care when dropping a database, since all its tables, indexes, and columns are deleted, as are all the associated disk-based files and directories that MySQL uses to maintain them.

If a database doesn't exist, trying to drop it causes MySQL to report an error. Let's try dropping the sakila database again:

```
mysql> DROP DATABASE sakila;

ERROR 1008 (HY000): Can't drop database 'sakila'; database doesn't exist
```

You can avoid the error, which is useful when including the statement in a script, by using the IF EXISTS phrase:

```
mysql> DROP DATABASE IF EXISTS sakila;

Query OK, 0 rows affected, 1 warning (0.00 sec)
```

You can see that a warning is reported since the sakila database has already been dropped.

Removing Tables

Removing tables is as easy as removing a database. Let's create and remove a table from the sakila database:

```
mysql> CREATE TABLE temp (id SERIAL PRIMARY KEY);
Query OK, 0 rows affected (0.05 sec)

mysql> DROP TABLE temp;
Query OK, 0 rows affected (0.03 sec)
```

Don't worry: the 0 rows affected message is misleading. You'll find the table is definitely gone.

You can use the IF EXISTS phrase to prevent errors. Let's try dropping the temp table again:

```
mysql> DROP TABLE IF EXISTS temp;
Query OK, 0 rows affected, 1 warning (0.01 sec)
```

As usual, you can investigate the warning with the SHOW WARNINGS statement:

```
mysql> SHOW WARNINGS;
+-------+------+-----------------------------+
| Level | Code | Message                     |
+-------+------+-----------------------------+
| Note  | 1051 | Unknown table 'sakila.temp' |
+-------+------+-----------------------------+
1 row in set (0.00 sec)
```

You can drop more than one table in a single statement by the separating table names with commas:

```
mysql> DROP TABLE IF EXISTS temp, temp1, temp2;
Query OK, 0 rows affected, 3 warnings (0.00 sec)
```

In this case there are three warnings because none of these tables existed.

## CHAPTER 5

Advanced Querying

Over the previous two chapters, you've completed an introduction to the basic features of querying and modifying databases with SQL. You should now be able to create, modify, and remove database structures, as well as work with data as you read, insert, delete, and update entries. Over this and the next two chapters, we'll look at more advanced concepts and then will proceed to more administrative and operations-oriented content. You can skim these chapters and return to read them thoroughly when you're comfortable using MySQL.

This chapter teaches you more about querying, giving you skills to answer complex information needs. You'll learn how to do the following:

- Use nicknames, or *aliases*, in queries to save typing and allow a table to be used more than once in a query.
- Aggregate data into groups so you can discover sums, averages, and counts.
- Join tables in different ways.
- Use nested queries.
- Save query results in variables so they can be reused in other queries.

Aliases

Aliases are nicknames. They give you a shorthand way of expressing a column, table, or function name, allowing you to:

- Write shorter queries.
- Express your queries more clearly.
- Use one table in two or more ways in a single query.

- Access data more easily from programs.
- Use special types of nested queries, discussed in "Nested Queries" on page 215.

Column Aliases

Column aliases are useful for improving the expression of your queries, reducing the number of characters you need to type, and making it easier to work with programming languages such as Python or PHP. Consider a simple, not-very-useful example:

```
mysql> SELECT first_name AS 'First Name', last_name AS 'Last Name'
    -> FROM actor LIMIT 5;

+------------+-------------+
| First Name | Last Name   |
+------------+-------------+
| PENELOPE   | GUINESS     |
| NICK       | WAHLBERG    |
| ED         | CHASE       |
| JENNIFER   | DAVIS       |
| JOHNNY     | LOLLOBRIGIDA |
+------------+-------------+
5 rows in set (0.00 sec)
```

The column first_name is aliased as First Name, and column last_name as Last Name. You can see that in the output, the usual column headings, first_name and last_name, are replaced by the aliases First Name and Last Name. The advantage is that the aliases might be more meaningful to users. In this case, at the very least, they are more human-readable. Other than that, it's not very useful, but it does illustrate the idea that for a column, you add the keyword AS and then a string that represents what you'd like the column to be known as. Specifying the AS keyword is not required but makes things much clearer.

 We'll be using the LIMIT clause extensively throughout this chapter, as otherwise almost every output would be unwieldy and long. Sometimes we'll mention that explicitly, sometimes not. You can experiment on your own by removing LIMIT from the queries we give. More information about the LIMIT clause can be found in "The LIMIT Clause" on page 107.

Now let's see column aliases doing something useful. Here's an example that uses a MySQL function and an ORDER BY clause:

```
mysql> SELECT CONCAT(first_name, ' ', last_name, ' played in ', title) AS movie
    -> FROM actor JOIN film_actor USING (actor_id)
    -> JOIN film USING (film_id)
    -> ORDER BY movie LIMIT 20;
```

```
+-----------------------------------------------+
| movie                                         |
+-----------------------------------------------+
| ADAM GRANT played in ANNIE IDENTITY           |
| ADAM GRANT played in BALLROOM MOCKINGBIRD     |
| ...                                           |
| ADAM GRANT played in TWISTED PIRATES          |
| ADAM GRANT played in WANDA CHAMBER            |
| ADAM HOPPER played in BLINDNESS GUN           |
| ADAM HOPPER played in BLOOD ARGONAUTS         |
+-----------------------------------------------+
20 rows in set (0.03 sec)
```

The MySQL function CONCAT() *concatenates* the strings that are parameters—in this case, the first_name, a constant string with a space, the last_name, the constant string played in, and the title—to give output such as ZERO CAGE played in CAN YON STOCK. We've added an alias to the function, AS movie, so that we can refer to it easily as movie throughout the query. You can see that we do this in the ORDER BY clause, where we ask MySQL to sort the output by ascending movie value. This is much better than the unaliased alternative, which requires you to write out the CON CAT() function again:

```
mysql> SELECT CONCAT(first_name, ' ', last_name, ' played in ', title) AS movie
    -> FROM actor JOIN film_actor USING (actor_id)
    -> JOIN film USING (film_id)
    -> ORDER BY CONCAT(first_name, ' ', last_name, ' played in ', title)
    -> LIMIT 20;
+-----------------------------------------------+
| movie                                         |
+-----------------------------------------------+
| ADAM GRANT played in ANNIE IDENTITY           |
| ADAM GRANT played in BALLROOM MOCKINGBIRD     |
| ...                                           |
| ADAM GRANT played in TWISTED PIRATES          |
| ADAM GRANT played in WANDA CHAMBER            |
| ADAM HOPPER played in BLINDNESS GUN           |
| ADAM HOPPER played in BLOOD ARGONAUTS         |
+-----------------------------------------------+
20 rows in set (0.03 sec)
```

The alternative is unwieldy, and worse, you risk mistyping some part of the ORDER BY clause and getting a result different from what you expect. (Note that we've used AS movie on the first line so that the displayed column has the label movie.)

There are restrictions on where you can use column aliases. You can't use them in a WHERE clause, or in the USING and ON clauses that we discuss later in this chapter. This means you can't write a query like this:

```
mysql> SELECT first_name AS name FROM actor WHERE name = 'ZERO CAGE';

ERROR 1054 (42S22): Unknown column 'name' in 'where clause'
```

You can't do that because MySQL doesn't always know the column values before it executes the WHERE clause. However, you can use column aliases in the ORDER BY clause, and in the GROUP BY and HAVING clauses discussed later in this chapter.

The AS keyword is optional, as we've mentioned. Because of this, the following two queries are equivalent:

```
mysql> SELECT actor_id AS id FROM actor WHERE first_name = 'ZERO';

+----+
| id |
+----+
| 11 |
+----+
1 row in set (0.00 sec)

mysql> SELECT actor_id id FROM actor WHERE first_name = 'ZERO';

+----+
| id |
+----+
| 11 |
+----+
1 row in set (0.00 sec)
```

We recommend using the AS keyword, since it helps to clearly distinguish an aliased column, especially where you're selecting multiple columns from a list of columns separated by commas.

Alias names have a few restrictions. They can be at most 255 characters in length and can contain any character. Aliases don't always need to be quoted, and they follow the same rules as table and column names do, which we described in Chapter 4. If an alias is a single word and doesn't include special symbols—like a dash, a plus sign, or a space, for example—and is not a keyword, like USE, then you don't need to put quotes around it. Otherwise, you need to quote the alias, which you can do using double quotes, single quotes, or backticks. We recommend using lowercase alphanumeric strings for alias names and using a consistent character choice—such as an underscore—to separate words. Aliases are case-insensitive on all platforms.

Table Aliases

Table aliases are useful for the same reasons as column aliases, but they are also sometimes the only way to express a query. This section shows you how to use table aliases, and "Nested Queries" on page 215 shows you some other sample queries where table aliases are essential.

Here's a basic table alias example that shows you how to save some typing:

```
mysql> SELECT ac.actor_id, ac.first_name, ac.last_name, fl.title FROM
    -> actor AS ac INNER JOIN film_actor AS fla USING (actor_id)
    -> INNER JOIN film AS fl USING (film_id)
    -> WHERE fl.title = 'AFFAIR PREJUDICE';
+----------+------------+-----------+------------------+
| actor_id | first_name | last_name | title            |
+----------+------------+-----------+------------------+
|       41 | JODIE      | DEGENERES | AFFAIR PREJUDICE |
|       81 | SCARLETT   | DAMON     | AFFAIR PREJUDICE |
|       88 | KENNETH    | PESCI     | AFFAIR PREJUDICE |
|      147 | FAY        | WINSLET   | AFFAIR PREJUDICE |
|      162 | OPRAH      | KILMER    | AFFAIR PREJUDICE |
+----------+------------+-----------+------------------+
5 rows in set (0.00 sec)
```

You can see that the film and actor tables are aliased as fl and ac, respectively, using the AS keyword. This allows you to express column names more compactly, such as fl.title. Notice also that you can use table aliases in the WHERE clause; unlike column aliases, there are no restrictions on where table aliases can be used in queries. From our example, you can see that we're referring to the table aliases in SELECT before they have been defined in FROM. There is, however, a catch with table aliases: if an alias has been used for a table, it's impossible to refer to that table without using its new alias. For example, the following statement will error out, as it would if we'd mentioned film in the SELECT clause:

```
mysql> SELECT ac.actor_id, ac.first_name, ac.last_name, fl.title FROM
    -> actor AS ac INNER JOIN film_actor AS fla USING (actor_id)
    -> INNER JOIN film AS fl USING (film_id)
    -> WHERE film.title = 'AFFAIR PREJUDICE';
ERROR 1054 (42S22): Unknown column 'film.title' in 'where clause'
```

As with column aliases, the AS keyword is optional. This means that:

```
actor AS ac INNER JOIN film_actor AS fla
```

is the same as

```
actor ac INNER JOIN film_actor fla
```

Again, we prefer the AS style because it's clearer to anyone looking at your queries than the alternative. The length and content restrictions on table aliases names are the same as for column aliases, and our recommendations on choosing them are the same, too.

As discussed in the introduction to this section, table aliases allow you to write queries that you can't otherwise easily express. Consider an example: suppose you want to know whether two or more films in our collection have the same title, and if so, what those films are. Let's think about the basic requirement: you want to know if two movies have the same name. To do get that, you might try a query like this:

```
mysql> SELECT * FROM film WHERE title = title;
```

But that doesn't make sense—every film has the same title as itself, so the query just produces all films as output:

```
+----------+--------------------...
| film_id  | title          ...
+----------+--------------------...
|        1 | ACADEMY DINOSAUR ...
|        2 | ACE GOLDFINGER   ...
|        3 | ADAPTATION HOLES ...
|      ... |                  ...
|     1000 | ZORRO ARK        ...
+----------+--------------------...
1000 rows in set (0.01 sec)
```

What you really want is to know whether two different films from the film table have the same name. But how can you do that in a single query? The answer is to give the table two different aliases; you then check to see whether one row in the first aliased table matches a row in the second:

```
mysql> SELECT m1.film_id, m2.title
    -> FROM film AS m1, film AS m2
    -> WHERE m1.title = m2.title;
+----------+-------------------+
| film_id  | title             |
+----------+-------------------+
|        1 | ACADEMY DINOSAUR  |
|        2 | ACE GOLDFINGER    |
|        3 | ADAPTATION HOLES  |
|      ... |                   |
|     1000 | ZORRO ARK         |
+----------+-------------------+
1000 rows in set (0.02 sec)
```

But it still doesn't work! We get all 1,000 movies as answers. The reason is that again, each film matches itself because it occurs in both aliased tables.

To get the query to work, we need to make sure a movie from one aliased table doesn't match itself in the other aliased table. The way to do that is to specify that the movies in each table shouldn't have the same ID:

```
mysql> SELECT m1.film_id, m2.title
    -> FROM film AS m1, film AS m2
    -> WHERE m1.title = m2.title
    -> AND m1.film_id <> m2.film_id;
Empty set (0.00 sec)
```

You can now see that there aren't two films in the database with the same name. The additional AND m1.film_id != m2.film_id stops answers from being reported where the movie ID is the same in both tables.

Table aliases are also useful in nested queries that use the EXISTS and ON clauses. We'll show you examples later in this chapter when we introduce nested queries.

Aggregating Data

Aggregate functions allow you to discover the properties of a group of rows. You use them for purposes such as finding out how many rows there are in a table, how many rows in a table share a property (such as having the same name or date of birth), finding averages (such as the average temperature in November), or finding the maximum or minimum values of rows that meet some condition (such as finding the coldest day in August).

This section explains the GROUP BY and HAVING clauses, the two most commonly used SQL statements for aggregation. But first it explains the DISTINCT clause, which is used to report unique results for the output of a query. When neither the DISTINCT nor the GROUP BY clause is specified, the returned raw data can still be processed using the aggregate functions that we describe in this section.

The DISTINCT Clause

To begin our discussion of aggregate functions, we'll focus on the DISTINCT clause. This isn't really an aggregate function, but more of a post-processing filter that allows you to remove duplicates. We've added it into this section because, like aggregate functions, it's concerned with picking examples from the output of a query, rather than processing individual rows.

An example is the best way to understand DISTINCT. Consider this query:

```
mysql> SELECT DISTINCT first_name
    -> FROM actor JOIN film_actor USING (actor_id);
+------------+
| first_name |
+------------+
| PENELOPE   |
| NICK       |
| ...        |
| GREGORY    |
| JOHN       |
| BELA       |
| THORA      |
+------------+
128 rows in set (0.00 sec)
```

The query finds all first names of all the actors listed in our database that have participated in a film and reports one example of each name. If you remove the DISTINCT clause, you get one row of output for each role in every film we have in our database, or 5,462 rows. That's a lot of output, so we're limiting it to five rows, but you can spot the difference immediately with names being repeated:

```
mysql> SELECT first_name
    -> FROM actor JOIN film_actor USING (actor_id)
    -> LIMIT 5;
+------------+
| first_name |
+------------+
| PENELOPE   |
| PENELOPE   |
| PENELOPE   |
| PENELOPE   |
| PENELOPE   |
+------------+
5 rows in set (0.00 sec)
```

So, the DISTINCT clause helps you get a summary.

The DISTINCT clause applies to the query output and removes rows that have identical values in the columns selected for output in the query. If you rephrase the previous query to output both first_name and last_name (but otherwise don't change the JOIN clause and still use DISTINCT), you'll get 199 rows in the output (that's why we use last names):

```
mysql> SELECT DISTINCT first_name, last_name
    -> FROM actor JOIN film_actor USING (actor_id);
+------------+-----------+
| first_name | last_name |
+------------+-----------+
| PENELOPE   | GUINESS   |
| NICK       | WAHLBERG  |
| ...        |           |
| JULIA      | FAWCETT   |
| THORA      | TEMPLE    |
+------------+-----------+
199 rows in set (0.00 sec)
```

Unfortunately, people's names even when last names are added still make for a bad unique key. There are 200 rows in the actor table in the sakila database, and we're missing one of them. You should remember this issue, as using DISTINCT indiscriminately may result in incorrect query results.

To remove duplicates, MySQL needs to sort the output. If indexes are available that are in the same order as required for the sort, or the data itself is in an order that's useful, this process has very little overhead. However, for large tables and without an easy way of accessing the data in the right order, sorting can be very slow. You should use DISTINCT (and other aggregate functions) with caution on large datasets. If you do use it, you can check its behavior using the EXPLAIN statement discussed in Chapter 7.

The GROUP BY Clause

The GROUP BY clause groups output data for the purpose of aggregation. Particularly, that allows us to use aggregate functions (covered in "Aggregate functions" on page 193) on our data when our projection (that is, the contents of the SELECT clause) contains columns other than those within an aggregate function. GROUP BY is similar to ORDER BY in that it takes a list of columns as an argument. However, these clauses are evaluated at different times and are only similar in how they look, not how they operate.

Let's take a look at a few GROUP BY examples that will demonstrate what it can be used for. In its most basic form, when we list every column we SELECT in GROUP BY, we end up with a DISTINCT equivalent. We've already established that a first name is not a unique identifier for an actor:

```
mysql> SELECT first_name FROM actor
    -> WHERE first_name IN ('GENE', 'MERYL');

+------------+
| first_name |
+------------+
| GENE       |
| GENE       |
| MERYL      |
| GENE       |
| MERYL      |
+------------+
5 rows in set (0.00 sec)
```

We can tell MySQL to group the output by a given column to get rid of duplicates. In this case, we've selected only one column, so let's use that:

```
mysql> SELECT first_name FROM actor
    -> WHERE first_name IN ('GENE', 'MERYL')
    -> GROUP BY first_name;

+------------+
| first_name |
+------------+
| GENE       |
| MERYL      |
+------------+
2 rows in set (0.00 sec)
```

You can see that the original five rows were folded—or, more accurately, grouped—into just two resulting rows. That's not very helpful, as DISTINCT could do the same. It's worth mentioning, however, that this is not always going to be the case. DISTINCT and GROUP BY are evaluated and executed at different stages of query execution, so you should not confuse them, even if sometimes the effects are similar.

According to the SQL standard, every column projected in the SELECT clause that is not part of an aggregate function should be listed in the GROUP BY clause. The only time this rule may be violated is when the resulting groups have only one row each. If you think about it, that's logical: if you select first_name and last_name from the actor table and group only by first_name, how should the database behave? It cannot output more than one row with the same first name, as that goes against the grouping rules, but there may be more than one last name for a given first name.

For a long time, MySQL extended the standard by allowing you to GROUP BY based on fewer columns than defined in SELECT. What did it do with the extra columns? Well, it output some value in a nondeterministic way. For example, when you grouped by first name but not by the last name, you could get either of the two rows GENE, WIL LIS and GENE, HOPKINS. That's a nonstandard and dangerous behavior. Imagine that for a year you got Hopkins, as if the results were ordered alphabetically, and came to rely on that—but then the table was reorganized, and the order changed. We firmly believe that the SQL standard is correct to limit such behaviors, to avoid unpredictability.

Note also that while every column in the SELECT must be used either in GROUP BY or in an aggregate function, you can GROUP BY columns that are not part of the SELECT. You'll see some examples of that later.

Now let's construct a more useful example. An actor usually takes part in many films throughout their career. We may want to find out just how many films a particular actor has played in, or do a calculation for each actor we know of and get a rating by productivity. To start, we can use the techniques we've learned so far and perform an INNER JOIN between the actor and film_actor tables. We don't need the film table as we're not looking for any details on the films themselves. We can then order the output by actor's name, making it easier to count what we want:

```
mysql> SELECT first_name, last_name, film_id
    -> FROM actor INNER JOIN film_actor USING (actor_id)
    -> ORDER BY first_name, last_name LIMIT 20;
+------------+-----------+---------+
| first_name | last_name | film_id |
+------------+-----------+---------+
| ADAM       | GRANT     |      26 |
| ADAM       | GRANT     |      52 |
| ADAM       | GRANT     |     233 |
| ADAM       | GRANT     |     317 |
```

```
| ADAM       | GRANT      |     359 |
| ADAM       | GRANT      |     362 |
| ADAM       | GRANT      |     385 |
| ADAM       | GRANT      |     399 |
| ADAM       | GRANT      |     450 |
| ADAM       | GRANT      |     532 |
| ADAM       | GRANT      |     560 |
| ADAM       | GRANT      |     574 |
| ADAM       | GRANT      |     638 |
| ADAM       | GRANT      |     773 |
| ADAM       | GRANT      |     833 |
| ADAM       | GRANT      |     874 |
| ADAM       | GRANT      |     918 |
| ADAM       | GRANT      |     956 |
| ADAM       | HOPPER     |      81 |
| ADAM       | HOPPER     |      82 |
+------------+------------+---------+
20 rows in set (0.01 sec)
```

By running down the list, it's easy to count off how many films we've got for each actor, or at least for Adam Grant. Without a LIMIT, however, the query would return 5,462 distinct rows, and calculating our counts manually would take a lot of time. The GROUP BY clause can help automate this process by grouping the movies by actor; we can then use the COUNT() function to count off the number of films in each group. Finally, we can use ORDER BY and LIMIT to get the top 10 actors by the number of films they've appeared in. Here's the query that does what we want:

```
mysql> SELECT first_name, last_name, COUNT(film_id) AS num_films FROM
    -> actor INNER JOIN film_actor USING (actor_id)
    -> GROUP BY first_name, last_name
    -> ORDER BY num_films DESC LIMIT 5;
+------------+-------------+-----------+
| first_name | last_name   | num_films |
+------------+-------------+-----------+
| SUSAN      | DAVIS       |        54 |
| GINA       | DEGENERES   |        42 |
| WALTER     | TORN        |        41 |
| MARY       | KEITEL      |        40 |
| MATTHEW    | CARREY      |        39 |
| SANDRA     | KILMER      |        37 |
| SCARLETT   | DAMON       |        36 |
| VAL        | BOLGER      |        35 |
| ANGELA     | WITHERSPOON |        35 |
| UMA        | WOOD        |        35 |
+------------+-------------+-----------+
10 rows in set (0.01 sec)
```

You can see that the output we've asked for is first_name, last_name, COUNT(film_id) as num_films, and this tells us exactly what we wanted to know. We group our data by the first_name and last_name columns, running the COUNT()

aggregate function in the process. For each "bucket" of rows we got in the previous query, we now get only a single row, albeit giving the information we want. Notice how we've combined GROUP BY and ORDER BY to get the ordering we wanted: by the number of films, from more to fewer. GROUP BY doesn't guarantee ordering, only grouping. Finally, we LIMIT the output to 10 rows representing our most productive actors, as otherwise we'd get 199 rows of output.

Let's consider the query further. We'll start with the GROUP BY clause. This tells us how to put rows together into groups: in this example, we're telling MySQL that the way to group rows is by first_name, last_name. The result is that rows for actors with the same name form a cluster, or bucket—that is, each distinct name becomes one group. Once the rows are grouped, they're treated in the rest of the query as if they're one row. So, for example, when we write SELECT first_name, last_name, we get just one row for each group. This is exactly the same as DISTINCT, as we've already discussed. The COUNT() function tells us about the properties of the group. More specifically, it tells us the number of rows that form each group; you can count any column in a group and you'll get the same answer, so COUNT(film_id) is almost always the same as COUNT(*) or COUNT(first_name). (See "Aggregate functions" on page 193 for more details on why we say *almost*.) We could also just do COUNT(1), or in fact specify any literal. Think of this as doing SELECT 1 from a table and then counting the results. A value of 1 will be output for each row in the table, and COUNT() does the counting. One exception is NULL: while it's perfectly acceptable and legal to specify COUNT(NULL), the result will always be zero, as COUNT() discards NULL values. Of course, you can use a column alias for the COUNT() column.

Let's try another example. Suppose you want to know how many different actors played in each movie, along with the film name and its category, and get the five films with the largest crews. Here's the query:

```
mysql> SELECT title, name AS category_name, COUNT(*) AS cnt
    -> FROM film INNER JOIN film_actor USING (film_id)
    -> INNER JOIN film_category USING (film_id)
    -> INNER JOIN category USING (category_id)
    -> GROUP BY film_id, category_id
    -> ORDER BY cnt DESC LIMIT 5;
+------------------+---------------+-----+
| title            | category_name | cnt |
+------------------+---------------+-----+
| LAMBS CINCINATTI | Games         |  15 |
| CRAZY HOME       | Comedy        |  13 |
| CHITTY LOCK      | Drama         |  13 |
| RANDOM GO        | Sci-Fi        |  13 |
| DRACULA CRYSTAL  | Classics      |  13 |
+------------------+---------------+-----+
5 rows in set (0.03 sec)
```

Before we discuss what's new, think about the general function of the query. We join four tables together with INNER JOIN using their identifier columns: film, film_actor, film_category, and category. Forgetting the aggregation for a moment, the output of this query is one row per combination of movie and actor.

The GROUP BY clause puts the rows together into clusters. In this query, we want the films grouped together with their categories. The GROUP BY clause uses film_id and category_id to do that. You can use the film_id column from any of the three tables; film.film_id, film_actor.film_id, and film_category.film_id are the same for this purpose. It doesn't matter which one you use; the INNER JOIN makes sure they match anyway. The same applies to category_id.

As mentioned earlier, even though it's required to list every non-aggregated column in GROUP BY, you can GROUP BY on columns outside of the SELECT. In the previous example query, we're using the COUNT() function to tell us how many rows are in each group. For example, you can see that COUNT(*) tells us that there are 13 actors in the comedy *CRAZY HOME*. Again, it doesn't matter what column or columns you count in the query: for example, COUNT(*) has the same effect as COUNT(film.film_id) or COUNT(category.name).

We're then ordering the output by the COUNT(*) column aliased cnt in descending order and picking the first five rows. Note how there are multiple rows with cnt equal to 13. In fact, there are even more of those—six in all—in the database, making this ordering a bit unfair, as movies having the same number of actors will be sorted randomly. You can add another column to the ORDER BY clause, like title, to make sorting more predictable.

Let's try another example. The sakila database isn't only about movies and actors: it's based on movie rentals, after all. We have, among other things, customer information, including data on what films they rented. Say we want to know which customers tend to rent movies from the same category. For example, we might want to adjust our ads based on whether a person likes different film categories or sticks to a single one most of the time. We need to carefully think about our grouping: we don't want to group by movie, as that would just give us the number of times a customer rented it. The resulting query is quite complex, although it's still based around INNER JOIN and GROUP BY:

```
mysql> SELECT email, name AS category_name, COUNT(category_id) AS cnt
    -> FROM customer cs INNER JOIN rental USING (customer_id)
    -> INNER JOIN inventory USING (inventory_id)
    -> INNER JOIN film_category USING (film_id)
    -> INNER JOIN category cat USING (category_id)
    -> GROUP BY 1, 2
    -> ORDER BY 3 DESC LIMIT 5;
```

```
+--------------------------------------+---------------+-----+
| email                                | category_name | cnt |
+--------------------------------------+---------------+-----+
| WESLEY.BULL@sakilacustomer.org       | Games         |   9 |
| ALMA.AUSTIN@sakilacustomer.org       | Animation     |   8 |
| KARL.SEAL@sakilacustomer.org         | Animation     |   8 |
| LYDIA.BURKE@sakilacustomer.org       | Documentary   |   8 |
| NATHAN.RUNYON@sakilacustomer.org     | Animation     |   7 |
+--------------------------------------+---------------+-----+
5 rows in set (0.08 sec)
```

These customers repeatedly rent films from the same category. What we don't know is if any of them have rented the same movie multiple times, or if those were all different movies within a category. The GROUP BY clause hides the details. Again, we use COUNT(*) to do the counting of rows in the groups, and you can see the INNER JOIN spread over lines 2 to 5 in the query.

The interesting thing about this query is that we didn't explicitly specify column names for the GROUP BY or ORDER BY clauses. Instead, we used the columns' position numbers (counted from 1) as they appear in the SELECT clause. This technique saves on typing but can be problematic if you later decide to add another column in the SELECT, which would break the ordering.

As with DISTINCT, there's a danger with GROUP BY that we should mention. Consider the following query:

```
mysql> SELECT COUNT(*) FROM actor GROUP BY first_name, last_name;
+----------+
| COUNT(*) |
+----------+
|        1 |
|        1 |
|      ... |
|        1 |
|        1 |
+----------+
199 rows in set (0.00 sec)
```

It looks simple enough, and it produces the number of times a combination of a given first name and last name was found in the actor table. You might assume that it just outputs 199 rows of the digit 1. However, if we do a COUNT(*) on the actor table, we get 200 rows. What's the catch? Apparently, two actors have the same first name and last name. These things happen, and you have to be mindful of them. When you group based on columns that do not form a unique identifier, you may accidentally group together unrelated rows, resulting in misleading data. To find the duplicates, we can modify a query that we constructed in "Table Aliases" on page 182 to look for films with the same name:

```
mysql> SELECT a1.actor_id, a1.first_name, a1.last_name
    -> FROM actor AS a1, actor AS a2
    -> WHERE a1.first_name = a2.first_name
    -> AND a1.last_name = a2.last_name
    -> AND a1.actor_id <> a2.actor_id;
+----------+------------+-----------+
| actor_id | first_name | last_name |
+----------+------------+-----------+
|      101 | SUSAN      | DAVIS     |
|      110 | SUSAN      | DAVIS     |
+----------+------------+-----------+
2 rows in set (0.00 sec)
```

Before we end this section, let's again touch on how MySQL extends the SQL standard around the GROUP BY clause. Before MySQL 5.7, it was possible by default to specify an incomplete column list in the GROUP BY clause, and, as we've explained, that resulted in a random rows being output within groups for non-grouped dependent columns. For reasons of supporting legacy software, both MySQL 5.7 and My SQL 8.0 continue providing this behavior, though it has to be explicitly enabled. The behavior is controlled by the ONLY_FULL_GROUP_BY SQL mode, which is set by default. If you find yourself in a situation where you need to port a program that relies on the legacy GROUP BY behavior, we recommend that you do not resort to changing the SQL mode. There are generally two ways to handle this problem. The first is to understand whether the query logic requires incomplete grouping at all—that is rarely the case. The second is to support the random data behavior for non-grouped columns by using either an aggregate function like MIN() or MAX() or the special ANY_VALUE() aggregate function, which, unsurprisingly, just produces a random value from within a group. We'll look more closely at aggregate functions next.

Aggregate functions

We've seen examples of how the COUNT() function can be used to tell how many rows are in a group. Here we will cover some other functions commonly used to explore the properties of aggregated rows. We'll also expand a bit on COUNT() as it's used frequently:

COUNT()
> Returns the number of rows *or* the number of values in a column. Remember we mentioned that COUNT(*) is *almost* always the equivalent of COUNT(<column>). The problem is NULL. COUNT(*) will do a count of rows returned, regardless of whether the column in those rows is NULL or not. However, when you do a COUNT(<column>), only non-NULL values will be counted. For example, in the sakila database, a customer's email address may be NULL, and we can observe the impact:

> ```
> mysql> SELECT COUNT(*) FROM customer;
> ```

```
+----------+
| count(*) |
+----------+
|      599 |
+----------+
1 row in set (0.00 sec)

mysql> SELECT COUNT(email) FROM customer;

+--------------+
| count(email) |
+--------------+
|          598 |
+--------------+
1 row in set (0.00 sec)
```

We should also add that COUNT() can be run with an internal DISTINCT clause, as in COUNT(DISTINCT <column>), and will return the number of distinct values instead of all values in this case.

AVG()

Returns the average (mean) of the values in the specified column for all rows in a group. For example, you could use it to find the average cost of a house in a city, when the houses are grouped by city:

```
SELECT AVG(cost) FROM house_prices GROUP BY city;
```

MAX()

Returns the maximum value from rows in a group. For example, you could use it to find the warmest day in a month, when the rows are grouped by month.

MIN()

Returns the minimum value from rows in a group. For example, you could use it to find the youngest student in a class, when the rows are grouped by class.

STD(), STDDEV(), and STDDEV_POP()

Return the standard deviation of values from rows in a group. For example, you could use these to understand the spread of test scores, when rows are grouped by university course. All three of these are synonyms. STD() is a MySQL extension, STDDEV() is added for compatibility with Oracle, and STDDEV_POP() is a SQL standard function.

SUM()

Returns the sum of values from rows in a group. For example, you could use it to compute the dollar amount of sales in a given month, when rows are grouped by month.

There are other functions available for use with GROUP BY, but they're less frequently used than the ones we've introduced here. You can find more details on them in the section on aggregate function descriptions (*https://oreil.ly/QSZst*) in the MySQL Reference Manual.

The HAVING Clause

You're now familiar with the GROUP BY clause, which allows you to sort and cluster data. You should be able to use it to find counts, averages, minimums, and maximums. This section shows how you can use the HAVING clause to gain additional control over the aggregation of rows in a GROUP BY operation.

Suppose you want to know how many popular actors there are in our database. You've decided to define an actor as popular if they've taken part in at least 40 movies. In the previous section, we tried an almost identical query but without the popularity limitation. We also found that when we grouped the actors by first and last name, we lost one record, so we'll add grouping on the actor_id column, which we know to be unique. Here's the new query, with an additional HAVING clause that adds the constraint:

```
mysql> SELECT first_name, last_name, COUNT(film_id)
    -> FROM actor INNER JOIN film_actor USING (actor_id)
    -> GROUP BY actor_id, first_name, last_name
    -> HAVING COUNT(film_id) > 40
    -> ORDER BY COUNT(film_id) DESC;

+------------+-----------+----------------+
| first_name | last_name | COUNT(film_id) |
+------------+-----------+----------------+
| GINA       | DEGENERES |             42 |
| WALTER     | TORN      |             41 |
+------------+-----------+----------------+
2 rows in set (0.01 sec)
```

You can see there are only two actors that meet the new criteria.

The HAVING clause must contain an expression or column that's listed in the SELECT clause. In this example, we've used HAVING COUNT(film_id) >= 40, and you can see that COUNT(film_id) is part of the SELECT clause. Typically, the expression in the HAVING clause uses an aggregate function such as COUNT(), SUM(), MIN(), or MAX(). If you find yourself wanting to write a HAVING clause that uses a column or expression that isn't in the SELECT clause, chances are you should be using a WHERE clause instead. The HAVING clause is only for deciding how to form each group or cluster, not for choosing rows in the output. We'll show you an example later that illustrates when not to use HAVING.

Let's try another example. Suppose you want a list of the top 5 movies that were rented more than 30 times, together with the number of times they were rented, ordered by popularity in reverse. Here's the query you'd use:

```
mysql> SELECT title, COUNT(rental_id) AS num_rented FROM
    -> film INNER JOIN inventory USING (film_id)
    -> INNER JOIN rental USING (inventory_id)
    -> GROUP BY title
    -> HAVING num_rented > 30
    -> ORDER BY num_rented DESC LIMIT 5;

+---------------------+------------+
| title               | num_rented |
+---------------------+------------+
| BUCKET BROTHERHOOD  |         34 |
| ROCKETEER MOTHER    |         33 |
| FORWARD TEMPLE      |         32 |
| GRIT CLOCKWORK      |         32 |
| JUGGLER HARDLY      |         32 |
+---------------------+------------+
5 rows in set (0.04 sec)
```

You can again see that the expression COUNT() is used in both the SELECT and HAVING clauses. This time, though, we aliased the COUNT(rental_id) function to num_rented and used the alias in both the HAVING and ORDER BY clauses.

Now let's consider an example where you shouldn't use HAVING. You want to know how many films a particular actor played in. Here's the query you shouldn't use:

```
mysql> SELECT first_name, last_name, COUNT(film_id) AS film_cnt FROM
    -> actor INNER JOIN film_actor USING (actor_id)
    -> GROUP BY actor_id, first_name, last_name
    -> HAVING first_name = 'EMILY' AND last_name = 'DEE';

+------------+-----------+----------+
| first_name | last_name | film_cnt |
+------------+-----------+----------+
| EMILY      | DEE       |       14 |
+------------+-----------+----------+
1 row in set (0.02 sec)
```

It gets the right answer, but in the wrong—and, for large amounts of data, a much slower—way. It's not the correct way to write the query because the HAVING clause isn't being used to decide what rows should form each group but is instead being incorrectly used to filter the answers to display. For this query, we should really use a WHERE clause, as follows:

```
mysql> SELECT first_name, last_name, COUNT(film_id) AS film_cnt FROM
    -> actor INNER JOIN film_actor USING (actor_id)
    -> WHERE first_name = 'EMILY' AND last_name = 'DEE'
    -> GROUP BY actor_id, first_name, last_name;
```

```
+------------+-----------+----------+
| first_name | last_name | film_cnt |
+------------+-----------+----------+
| EMILY      | DEE       |       14 |
+------------+-----------+----------+
1 row in set (0.00 sec)
```

This correct query forms the groups and then picks which groups to display based on the WHERE clause.

Advanced Joins

So far in the book, we've used the INNER JOIN clause to bring together rows from two or more tables. We'll explain the inner join in more detail in this section, contrasting it with the other join types we discuss: the union, left and right joins, and natural joins. At the conclusion of this section, you'll be able to answer difficult information needs and be familiar with the correct choice of join for the task at hand.

The Inner Join

The INNER JOIN clause matches rows between two tables based on the criteria you provide in the USING clause. For example, you're very familiar now with an inner join of the actor and film_actor tables:

```
mysql> SELECT first_name, last_name, film_id FROM
    -> actor INNER JOIN film_actor USING (actor_id)
    -> LIMIT 20;
+------------+-----------+---------+
| first_name | last_name | film_id |
+------------+-----------+---------+
| PENELOPE   | GUINESS   |       1 |
| PENELOPE   | GUINESS   |      23 |
| ...        |           |         |
| PENELOPE   | GUINESS   |     980 |
| NICK       | WAHLBERG  |       3 |
+------------+-----------+---------+
20 rows in set (0.00 sec)
```

Let's review the key features of an INNER JOIN:

- Two tables (or results of a previous join) are listed on either side of the INNER JOIN keyphrase.

- The USING clause defines one or more columns that are in both tables or results and are used to join or match rows.

- Rows that don't match aren't returned. For example, if you have a row in the actor table that doesn't have any matching films in the film_actor table, it won't be included in the output.

You can actually write inner-join queries with the WHERE clause without using the INNER JOIN keyphrase. Here's a rewritten version of the previous query that produces the same result:

```
mysql> SELECT first_name, last_name, film_id
    -> FROM actor, film_actor
    -> WHERE actor.actor_id = film_actor.actor_id
    -> LIMIT 20;
+------------+-----------+---------+
| first_name | last_name | film_id |
+------------+-----------+---------+
| PENELOPE   | GUINESS   |       1 |
| PENELOPE   | GUINESS   |      23 |
| ...        |           |         |
| PENELOPE   | GUINESS   |     980 |
| NICK       | WAHLBERG  |       3 |
+------------+-----------+---------+
20 rows in set (0.00 sec)
```

You can see that we didn't spell out the inner join: we're selecting from the actor and film_actor tables the rows where the identifiers match between the tables.

You can modify the INNER JOIN syntax to express the join criteria in a way that's similar to using a WHERE clause. This is useful if the names of the identifiers don't match between the tables, although that's not the case in this example. Here's the previous query, rewritten in this style:

```
mysql> SELECT first_name, last_name, film_id FROM
    -> actor INNER JOIN film_actor
    -> ON actor.actor_id = film_actor.actor_id
    -> LIMIT 20;
+------------+-----------+---------+
| first_name | last_name | film_id |
+------------+-----------+---------+
| PENELOPE   | GUINESS   |       1 |
| PENELOPE   | GUINESS   |      23 |
| ...        |           |         |
| PENELOPE   | GUINESS   |     980 |
| NICK       | WAHLBERG  |       3 |
+------------+-----------+---------+
20 rows in set (0.00 sec)
```

You can see that the ON clause replaces the USING clause and that the columns that follow are fully specified to include the table and column names. If the columns were named differently and uniquely between the two tables, you could omit the table names. There's no real advantage or disadvantage to using ON or a WHERE clause; it's just a matter of taste. Typically, these days, you'll find most SQL professionals use the INNER JOIN with an ON clause in preference to WHERE, but it's not universal.

Before we move on, let's consider what purpose the WHERE, ON, and USING clauses serve. If you omit the WHERE clause from the query we just showed you, you get a very different result. Here's the query and the first few lines of output:

```
mysql> SELECT first_name, last_name, film_id
    -> FROM actor, film_actor LIMIT 20;
+------------+------------+---------+
| first_name | last_name  | film_id |
+------------+------------+---------+
| THORA      | TEMPLE     |       1 |
| JULIA      | FAWCETT    |       1 |
| ...        |            |         |
| DEBBIE     | AKROYD     |       1 |
| MATTHEW    | CARREY     |       1 |
+------------+------------+---------+
20 rows in set (0.00 sec)
```

The output is nonsensical: what's happened is that each row from the actor table has been output alongside each row from the film_actor table, for all possible combinations. Since there are 200 actors and 5,462 records in the film_actor table, there are 200 × 5,462 = 1,092,400 rows of output, and we know that only 5,462 of those combinations actually make sense (there are only 5,462 records for actors who played in films). We can see the number of rows we'd get without a LIMIT with the following query:

```
mysql> SELECT COUNT(*) FROM actor, film_actor;
+----------+
| COUNT(*) |
+----------+
|  1092400 |
+----------+
1 row in set (0.00 sec)
```

This type of query, without a clause that matches rows, is known as a *Cartesian product*. Incidentally, you also get the Cartesian product if you perform an inner join without specifying a column with a USING or ON clause, as in this query:

```
SELECT first_name, last_name, film_id
FROM actor INNER JOIN film_actor;
```

In "The Natural Join" on page 211 we'll introduce the natural join, which is an inner join on identically named columns. While the natural join doesn't use explicitly specified columns, it still produces an inner join, rather than a Cartesian product.

The keyphrase INNER JOIN can be replaced with JOIN or STRAIGHT JOIN; they all do the same thing. However, STRAIGHT JOIN forces MySQL to always read the table on the left before it reads the table on the right. We'll have a look at how MySQL processes queries behind the scenes in Chapter 7. The keyphrase JOIN is the one you'll see most commonly used: it's a standard shorthand for INNER JOIN used by many other database systems besides MySQL, and we will use it in most of our inner-join examples.

The Union

The UNION statement isn't really a join operator. Rather, it allows you to combine the output of more than one SELECT statement to give a consolidated result set. It's useful in cases where you want to produce a single list from more than one source, or you want to create lists from a single source that are difficult to express in a single query.

Let's look at an example. If you wanted to output all actor *and* movie *and* customer names in the sakila database, you could do this with a UNION statement. It's a contrived example, but you might want to do this just to list all of the text fragments, rather than to meaningfully present the relationships in the data. There's text in the actor.first_name, film.title, and customer.first_name columns. Here's how to display it:

```
mysql> SELECT first_name FROM actor
    -> UNION
    -> SELECT first_name FROM customer
    -> UNION
    -> SELECT title FROM film;

+----------------------------+
| first_name                 |
+----------------------------+
| PENELOPE                   |
| NICK                       |
| ED                         |
| ...                        |
| ZHIVAGO CORE               |
| ZOOLANDER FICTION          |
| ZORRO ARK                  |
+----------------------------+
1647 rows in set (0.00 sec)
```

We've shown only a few of the 1,647 rows. The UNION statement outputs the results from all the queries together, under a heading appropriate to the first query.

A slightly less contrived example is to create a list of the five most- and least-rented movies in our database. You can do this easily with the UNION operator:

```
mysql> (SELECT title, COUNT(rental_id) AS num_rented
    -> FROM film JOIN inventory USING (film_id)
```

```
    -> JOIN rental USING (inventory_id)
    -> GROUP BY title ORDER BY num_rented DESC LIMIT 5)
    -> UNION
    -> (SELECT title, COUNT(rental_id) AS num_rented
    -> FROM film JOIN inventory USING (film_id)
    -> JOIN rental USING (inventory_id)
    -> GROUP BY title ORDER BY num_rented ASC LIMIT 5);
```

```
+--------------------+------------+
| title              | num_rented |
+--------------------+------------+
| BUCKET BROTHERHOOD |         34 |
| ROCKETEER MOTHER   |         33 |
| FORWARD TEMPLE     |         32 |
| GRIT CLOCKWORK     |         32 |
| JUGGLER HARDLY     |         32 |
| TRAIN BUNCH        |          4 |
| HARDLY ROBBERS     |          4 |
| MIXED DOORS        |          4 |
| BUNCH MINDS        |          5 |
| BRAVEHEART HUMAN   |          5 |
+--------------------+------------+
10 rows in set (0.04 sec)
```

The first query uses ORDER BY with the DESC (descending) modifier and a LIMIT 5 clause to find the top five most-rented movies. The second query uses ORDER BY with the ASC (ascending) modifier and a LIMIT 5 clause to find the five least-rented movies. The UNION combines the result sets. Note that there are multiple titles with the same num_rented value, and the ordering of titles with the same value is not guaranteed to be determined. You may see different titles listed for num_rented values of 32 and 5 on your end.

The UNION operator has several limitations:

- The output is labeled with the names of the columns or expressions from the first query. Use column aliases to change this behavior.

- The queries must output the same number of columns. If you try using different numbers of columns, MySQL will report an error.

- All matching columns must have the same type. So, for example, if the first column output from the first query is a date, the first column output from any other query must also be a date.

- The results returned are unique, as if you'd applied a DISTINCT to the overall result set. To see this in action, let's try a simple example. Remember we had issues with actors' names—the first name is a bad unique identifier. If we select two actors with the same first name and UNION the two queries, we will end up with just one row. The implicit DISTINCT operation hides the duplicate (for UNION) rows:

```
mysql> SELECT first_name FROM actor WHERE actor_id = 88
    -> UNION
    -> SELECT first_name FROM actor WHERE actor_id = 169;
+------------+
| first_name |
+------------+
| KENNETH    |
+------------+
1 row in set (0.01 sec)
```

If you want to show any duplicates, replace UNION with UNION ALL:

```
mysql> SELECT first_name FROM actor WHERE actor_id = 88
    -> UNION ALL
    -> SELECT first_name FROM actor WHERE actor_id = 169;
+------------+
| first_name |
+------------+
| KENNETH    |
| KENNETH    |
+------------+
2 rows in set (0.00 sec)
```

Here, the first name KENNETH appears twice.

The implicit DISTINCT that UNION performs has a nonzero cost on the performance side of things. Whenever you use UNION, see whether UNION ALL fits logically, and if it can improve query performance.

- If you want to apply LIMIT or ORDER BY to an individual query that is part of a UNION statement, enclose that query in parentheses (as shown in the previous example). It's useful to use parentheses anyway to keep the query easy to understand.

The UNION operation simply concatenates the results of the component queries with no attention to order, so there's not much point in using ORDER BY within one of the subqueries. The only time that it makes sense to order a subquery in a UNION operation is when you want to select a subset of the results. In our example, we've ordered the movies by the number of times they were rented and then selected only the top five (in the first subquery) and the bottom five (in the second subquery).

For efficiency, MySQL will actually ignore an ORDER BY clause within a subquery if it's used without LIMIT. Let's look at some examples to see exactly how this works.

First, let's run a simple query to list the rental information for a particular movie, along with the time at which the rental happened. We've enclosed the query in parentheses for consistency with our other examples—the parentheses don't actually have any effect here—and haven't used an ORDER BY or LIMIT clause:

```
mysql> (SELECT title, rental_date, return_date
    -> FROM film JOIN inventory USING (film_id)
    -> JOIN rental USING (inventory_id)
    -> WHERE film_id = 998);
+--------------+---------------------+---------------------+
| title        | rental_date         | return_date         |
+--------------+---------------------+---------------------+
| ZHIVAGO CORE | 2005-06-17 03:19:20 | 2005-06-21 00:19:20 |
| ZHIVAGO CORE | 2005-07-07 12:18:57 | 2005-07-12 09:47:57 |
| ZHIVAGO CORE | 2005-07-27 14:53:55 | 2005-07-31 19:48:55 |
| ZHIVAGO CORE | 2005-08-20 17:18:48 | 2005-08-26 15:31:48 |
| ZHIVAGO CORE | 2005-05-30 05:15:20 | 2005-06-07 00:49:20 |
| ZHIVAGO CORE | 2005-06-18 06:46:54 | 2005-06-26 09:48:54 |
| ZHIVAGO CORE | 2005-07-12 05:24:02 | 2005-07-16 03:43:02 |
| ZHIVAGO CORE | 2005-08-02 02:05:04 | 2005-08-10 21:58:04 |
| ZHIVAGO CORE | 2006-02-14 15:16:03 | NULL                |
+--------------+---------------------+---------------------+
9 rows in set (0.00 sec)
```

The query returns all the times the movie was rented, in no particular order (see the fourth and fifth entries).

Now, let's add an ORDER BY clause to this query:

```
mysql> (SELECT title, rental_date, return_date
    -> FROM film JOIN inventory USING (film_id)
    -> JOIN rental USING (inventory_id)
    -> WHERE film_id = 998
    -> ORDER BY rental_date ASC);
+--------------+---------------------+---------------------+
| title        | rental_date         | return_date         |
+--------------+---------------------+---------------------+
| ZHIVAGO CORE | 2005-05-30 05:15:20 | 2005-06-07 00:49:20 |
| ZHIVAGO CORE | 2005-06-17 03:19:20 | 2005-06-21 00:19:20 |
| ZHIVAGO CORE | 2005-06-18 06:46:54 | 2005-06-26 09:48:54 |
| ZHIVAGO CORE | 2005-07-07 12:18:57 | 2005-07-12 09:47:57 |
| ZHIVAGO CORE | 2005-07-12 05:24:02 | 2005-07-16 03:43:02 |
| ZHIVAGO CORE | 2005-07-27 14:53:55 | 2005-07-31 19:48:55 |
| ZHIVAGO CORE | 2005-08-02 02:05:04 | 2005-08-10 21:58:04 |
| ZHIVAGO CORE | 2005-08-20 17:18:48 | 2005-08-26 15:31:48 |
| ZHIVAGO CORE | 2006-02-14 15:16:03 | NULL                |
+--------------+---------------------+---------------------+
9 rows in set (0.00 sec)
```

As expected, we get all the times the movie was rented, in the order of the rental date.

Adding a LIMIT clause to the previous query selects the first five rentals, in chronological order—no surprises here:

```
mysql> (SELECT title, rental_date, return_date
    -> FROM film JOIN inventory USING (film_id)
    -> JOIN rental USING (inventory_id)
    -> WHERE film_id = 998
    -> ORDER BY rental_date ASC LIMIT 5);
```

```
+--------------+---------------------+---------------------+
| title        | rental_date         | return_date         |
+--------------+---------------------+---------------------+
| ZHIVAGO CORE | 2005-05-30 05:15:20 | 2005-06-07 00:49:20 |
| ZHIVAGO CORE | 2005-06-17 03:19:20 | 2005-06-21 00:19:20 |
| ZHIVAGO CORE | 2005-06-18 06:46:54 | 2005-06-26 09:48:54 |
| ZHIVAGO CORE | 2005-07-07 12:18:57 | 2005-07-12 09:47:57 |
| ZHIVAGO CORE | 2005-07-12 05:24:02 | 2005-07-16 03:43:02 |
+--------------+---------------------+---------------------+
5 rows in set (0.01 sec)
```

Now, let's see what happens when we perform a UNION operation. In this example, we're using two subqueries, each with an ORDER BY clause. We've used a LIMIT clause for the second subquery, but not for the first:

```
mysql> (SELECT title, rental_date, return_date
    -> FROM film JOIN inventory USING (film_id)
    -> JOIN rental USING (inventory_id)
    -> WHERE film_id = 998
    -> ORDER BY rental_date ASC)
    -> UNION ALL
    -> (SELECT title, rental_date, return_date
    -> FROM film JOIN inventory USING (film_id)
    -> JOIN rental USING (inventory_id)
    -> WHERE film_id = 998
    -> ORDER BY rental_date ASC LIMIT 5);
```

```
+--------------+---------------------+---------------------+
| title        | rental_date         | return_date         |
+--------------+---------------------+---------------------+
| ZHIVAGO CORE | 2005-06-17 03:19:20 | 2005-06-21 00:19:20 |
| ZHIVAGO CORE | 2005-07-07 12:18:57 | 2005-07-12 09:47:57 |
| ZHIVAGO CORE | 2005-07-27 14:53:55 | 2005-07-31 19:48:55 |
| ZHIVAGO CORE | 2005-08-20 17:18:48 | 2005-08-26 15:31:48 |
| ZHIVAGO CORE | 2005-05-30 05:15:20 | 2005-06-07 00:49:20 |
| ZHIVAGO CORE | 2005-06-18 06:46:54 | 2005-06-26 09:48:54 |
| ZHIVAGO CORE | 2005-07-12 05:24:02 | 2005-07-16 03:43:02 |
| ZHIVAGO CORE | 2005-08-02 02:05:04 | 2005-08-10 21:58:04 |
| ZHIVAGO CORE | 2006-02-14 15:16:03 | NULL                |
| ZHIVAGO CORE | 2005-05-30 05:15:20 | 2005-06-07 00:49:20 |
| ZHIVAGO CORE | 2005-06-17 03:19:20 | 2005-06-21 00:19:20 |
| ZHIVAGO CORE | 2005-06-18 06:46:54 | 2005-06-26 09:48:54 |
```

```
| ZHIVAGO CORE | 2005-07-07 12:18:57 | 2005-07-12 09:47:57 |
| ZHIVAGO CORE | 2005-07-12 05:24:02 | 2005-07-16 03:43:02 |
+--------------+---------------------+---------------------+
14 rows in set (0.01 sec)
```

As expected, the first subquery returns all the times the movie was rented (the first nine rows of this output), and the second subquery returns the first five rentals (the last five rows of this output). Notice how the first nine rows are not in order (see the fourth and fifth rows), even though the first subquery does have an ORDER BY clause. Since we're performing a UNION operation, the MySQL server has decided that there's no point sorting the results of the subquery. The second subquery includes a LIMIT operation, so the results of that subquery are sorted.

The output of a UNION operation isn't guaranteed to be ordered even if the subqueries are ordered, so if you want the final output to be ordered, you should add an ORDER BY clause at the end of the whole query. Note that it can be in another order from the subqueries. See the following:

```
mysql> (SELECT title, rental_date, return_date
    -> FROM film JOIN inventory USING (film_id)
    -> JOIN rental USING (inventory_id)
    -> WHERE film_id = 998
    -> ORDER BY rental_date ASC)
    -> UNION ALL
    -> (SELECT title, rental_date, return_date
    -> FROM film JOIN inventory USING (film_id)
    -> JOIN rental USING (inventory_id)
    -> WHERE film_id = 998
    -> ORDER BY rental_date ASC LIMIT 5)
    -> ORDER BY rental_date DESC;
+--------------+---------------------+---------------------+
| title        | rental_date         | return_date         |
+--------------+---------------------+---------------------+
| ZHIVAGO CORE | 2006-02-14 15:16:03 | NULL                |
| ZHIVAGO CORE | 2005-08-20 17:18:48 | 2005-08-26 15:31:48 |
| ZHIVAGO CORE | 2005-08-02 02:05:04 | 2005-08-10 21:58:04 |
| ZHIVAGO CORE | 2005-07-27 14:53:55 | 2005-07-31 19:48:55 |
| ZHIVAGO CORE | 2005-07-12 05:24:02 | 2005-07-16 03:43:02 |
| ZHIVAGO CORE | 2005-07-12 05:24:02 | 2005-07-16 03:43:02 |
| ZHIVAGO CORE | 2005-07-07 12:18:57 | 2005-07-12 09:47:57 |
| ZHIVAGO CORE | 2005-07-07 12:18:57 | 2005-07-12 09:47:57 |
| ZHIVAGO CORE | 2005-06-18 06:46:54 | 2005-06-26 09:48:54 |
| ZHIVAGO CORE | 2005-06-18 06:46:54 | 2005-06-26 09:48:54 |
| ZHIVAGO CORE | 2005-06-17 03:19:20 | 2005-06-21 00:19:20 |
| ZHIVAGO CORE | 2005-06-17 03:19:20 | 2005-06-21 00:19:20 |
| ZHIVAGO CORE | 2005-05-30 05:15:20 | 2005-06-07 00:49:20 |
| ZHIVAGO CORE | 2005-05-30 05:15:20 | 2005-06-07 00:49:20 |
+--------------+---------------------+---------------------+
14 rows in set (0.00 sec)
```

Here's another example of sorting the final results, including a limit on the number of returned results:

```
mysql> (SELECT first_name, last_name FROM actor WHERE actor_id < 5)
    -> UNION
    -> (SELECT first_name, last_name FROM actor WHERE actor_id > 190)
    -> ORDER BY first_name LIMIT 4;
```

```
+------------+-----------+
| first_name | last_name |
+------------+-----------+
| BELA       | WALKEN    |
| BURT       | TEMPLE    |
| ED         | CHASE     |
| GREGORY    | GOODING   |
+------------+-----------+
4 rows in set (0.00 sec)
```

The UNION operation is somewhat unwieldy, and there are generally alternative ways of getting the same result. For example, the previous query could have been written more simply like this:

```
mysql> SELECT first_name, last_name FROM actor
    -> WHERE actor_id < 5 OR actor_id > 190
    -> ORDER BY first_name LIMIT 4;
```

```
+------------+-----------+
| first_name | last_name |
+------------+-----------+
| BELA       | WALKEN    |
| BURT       | TEMPLE    |
| ED         | CHASE     |
| GREGORY    | GOODING   |
+------------+-----------+
4 rows in set (0.00 sec)
```

The Left and Right Joins

The joins we've discussed so far output only rows that match between tables. For example, when you join the film and rental tables through the inventory table, you see only the films that were rented. Rows for films that haven't been rented are ignored. This makes sense in many cases, but it isn't the only way to join data. This section explains other options you have.

Suppose you do want a comprehensive list of all films and the number of times they've been rented. Unlike in the example earlier in this chapter, included in the list you want to see a zero next to movies that haven't been rented. You can do this with a *left join*, a different type of join that's driven by one of the two tables participating in the join. In a left join, each row in the left table—the one that's doing the driving—is processed and output, with the matching data from the second table if it exists and

NULL values if there is no matching data in the second table. We'll show you how to write this type of query later in this section, but we'll start with a simpler example.

Here's a simple LEFT JOIN example. You want to list all movies, and next to each movie you want to show when it was rented. If a movie has never been rented, you want to see that. If it's been rented many times, you want to see that too. Here's the query:

```
mysql> SELECT title, rental_date
    -> FROM film LEFT JOIN inventory USING (film_id)
    -> LEFT JOIN rental USING (inventory_id);

+----------------------------+---------------------+
| title                      | rental_date         |
+----------------------------+---------------------+
| ACADEMY DINOSAUR           | 2005-07-08 19:03:15 |
| ACADEMY DINOSAUR           | 2005-08-02 20:13:10 |
| ACADEMY DINOSAUR           | 2005-08-21 21:27:43 |
| ...                        |                     |
| WAKE JAWS                  | NULL                |
| WALLS ARTIST               | NULL                |
| ...                        |                     |
| ZORRO ARK                  | 2005-07-31 07:32:21 |
| ZORRO ARK                  | 2005-08-19 03:49:28 |
+----------------------------+---------------------+
16087 rows in set (0.06 sec)
```

You can see what happens: movies that have been rented have dates and times, and those that haven't don't (the rental_date value is NULL). Note also that we LEFT JOIN twice in this example. First we join film and inventory, and we want to make sure that even if a movie is not in our inventory (and thus cannot be rented by definition), we still output it. Then we join the rental table with the dataset resulting from the previous join. We use a LEFT JOIN again, as we may have films that are not in our inventory, and those won't have any rows in the rental table. However, we may also have films listed in our inventory that just haven't been rented. That's why we need to LEFT JOIN both tables here.

The order of the tables in the LEFT JOIN is important. If you reverse the order in the previous query, you get very different output:

```
mysql> SELECT title, rental_date
    -> FROM rental LEFT JOIN inventory USING (inventory_id)
    -> LEFT JOIN film USING (film_id)
    -> ORDER BY rental_date DESC;

+----------------------------+---------------------+
| title                      | rental_date         |
+----------------------------+---------------------+
| ...                        |                     |
| LOVE SUICIDES              | 2005-05-24 23:04:41 |
| GRADUATE LORD              | 2005-05-24 23:03:39 |
```

```
| FREAKY POCUS                    | 2005-05-24 22:54:33 |
| BLANKET BEVERLY                 | 2005-05-24 22:53:30 |
+--------------------------------+---------------------+
16044 rows in set (0.06 sec)
```

In this version, the query is driven by the `rental` table, so all rows from it are matched against the `inventory` table and then against `film`. Since all the rows in the `rental` table by definition are based on the `inventory` table, which is linked to the `film` table, we have no NULL values in the output. There can be no rental for a film that doesn't exist. We adjusted the query with ORDER BY `rental_date` DESC to show that we really didn't get any NULL values (these would have been last).

By now you can see that left joins are useful when we're sure that our *left* table has some important data, but we're not sure whether the *right* table does. We want to get the rows from the left one with or without the corresponding rows from the right one. Let's try to apply this to a query we wrote in "The GROUP BY Clause" on page 187, which showed customers renting a lot from the same category. Here's the query, as a reminder:

```
mysql> SELECT email, name AS category_name, COUNT(cat.category_id) AS cnt
    -> FROM customer cs INNER JOIN rental USING (customer_id)
    -> INNER JOIN inventory USING (inventory_id)
    -> INNER JOIN film_category USING (film_id)
    -> INNER JOIN category cat USING (category_id)
    -> GROUP BY email, category_name
    -> ORDER BY cnt DESC LIMIT 5;

+--------------------------------+---------------+-----+
| email                          | category_name | cnt |
+--------------------------------+---------------+-----+
| WESLEY.BULL@sakilacustomer.org | Games         |   9 |
| ALMA.AUSTIN@sakilacustomer.org | Animation     |   8 |
| KARL.SEAL@sakilacustomer.org   | Animation     |   8 |
| LYDIA.BURKE@sakilacustomer.org | Documentary   |   8 |
| NATHAN.RUNYON@sakilacustomer.org | Animation   |   7 |
+--------------------------------+---------------+-----+
5 rows in set (0.06 sec)
```

What if we now want to see whether a customer we found this way rents films from anything but their favorite category? It turns out that's actually pretty difficult!

Let's consider this task. We need to start with the `category` table, as that will have all the categories we have for our films. We then need to start constructing a whole chain of left joins. First we left join `category` to `film_category`, as we may have categories with no films. Then we left join the result to the `inventory` table, as some movies we know about may not be in our catalog. We then left join that result to the `rental` table, as customers may not have rented some of the films in a category. Finally, we need to left join that result to our `customer` table. Even though there can be no associated customer record without a rental, omitting the left join here will cause MySQL to discard rows for categories that end up with no customer records.

Now, after this whole long explanation, can we finally go ahead and filter by email address and get our data? No! Unfortunately, by adding a WHERE condition on the table that is not *left* in our left-join relationship, we break the idea of this join. See what happens:

```
mysql> SELECT COUNT(*) FROM category;

+----------+
| COUNT(*) |
+----------+
|       16 |
+----------+
1 row in set (0.00 sec)

mysql> SELECT email, name AS category_name, COUNT(category_id) AS cnt
    -> FROM category cat LEFT JOIN film_category USING (category_id)
    -> LEFT JOIN inventory USING (film_id)
    -> LEFT JOIN rental USING (inventory_id)
    -> JOIN customer cs ON rental.customer_id = cs.customer_id
    -> WHERE cs.email = 'WESLEY.BULL@sakilacustomer.org'
    -> GROUP BY email, category_name
    -> ORDER BY cnt DESC;

+--------------------------------+---------------+-----+
| email                          | category_name | cnt |
+--------------------------------+---------------+-----+
| WESLEY.BULL@sakilacustomer.org | Games         |   9 |
| WESLEY.BULL@sakilacustomer.org | Foreign       |   6 |
| ...                            |               |     |
| WESLEY.BULL@sakilacustomer.org | Comedy        |   1 |
| WESLEY.BULL@sakilacustomer.org | Sports        |   1 |
+--------------------------------+---------------+-----+
14 rows in set (0.00 sec)
```

We got 14 categories for our customer, while there are 16 in total. In fact, MySQL will optimize away all the left joins in this query, as it understands they are meaningless when put like this. There's no easy way to answer the question we have with just joins—we'll get back to this example in "Nested Queries in JOINs" on page 233.

The query that we've written is still useful, though. While by default sakila does not have a film category in which no films have been rented, if we expand our database slightly, we can see the effectiveness of left joins:

```
mysql> INSERT INTO category(name) VALUES ('Thriller');

Query OK, 1 row affected (0.01 sec)

mysql> SELECT cat.name, COUNT(rental_id) cnt
    -> FROM category cat LEFT JOIN film_category USING (category_id)
    -> LEFT JOIN inventory USING (film_id)
```

```
    -> LEFT JOIN rental USING (inventory_id)
    -> LEFT JOIN customer cs ON rental.customer_id = cs.customer_id
    -> GROUP BY 1
    -> ORDER BY 2 DESC;
+---------------+------+
| category_name | cnt  |
+---------------+------+
| Sports        | 1179 |
| Animation     | 1166 |
| ...           |      |
| Music         |  830 |
| Thriller      |    0 |
+---------------+------+
17 rows in set (0.07 sec)
```

If we were to use a regular INNER JOIN (or just JOIN, its synonym) here, we wouldn't get information for the Thriller category, and we might get different counts for other categories. As category is our leftmost table, it drives the process of the query, and every row from that table is present in the output.

We've shown you that it matters what comes before and after the LEFT JOIN key-phrase. Whatever is on the left drives the process, hence the name "left join." If you really don't want to reorganize your query so it matches that template, you can use RIGHT JOIN. It's exactly the same, except whatever is on the right drives the process.

Earlier we showed the importance of the order of the tables in a left join using two queries for film rental information. Let's rewrite the second of them (which showed incorrect data) using a right join:

```
mysql> SELECT title, rental_date
    -> FROM rental RIGHT JOIN inventory USING (inventory_id)
    -> RIGHT JOIN film USING (film_id)
    -> ORDER BY rental_date DESC;
...
| SUICIDES SILENCE        | NULL              |
| TADPOLE PARK            | NULL              |
| TREASURE COMMAND        | NULL              |
| VILLAIN DESPERATE       | NULL              |
| VOLUME HOUSE            | NULL              |
| WAKE JAWS               | NULL              |
| WALLS ARTIST            | NULL              |
+-------------------------+-------------------+
16087 rows in set (0.06 sec)
```

We got the same number of rows, and we can see that the NULL values are the same as those the "correct" query gave us. The right join is useful sometimes because it allows you to write a query more naturally, expressing it in a way that's more intuitive. However, you won't often see it used, and we'd recommend avoiding it where possible.

Both left and right joins can use the USING and ON clauses discussed in "The Inner Join" on page 197. You should use one or the other: without them you'll get the Cartesian product, as discussed in that section.

There's also an extra OUTER keyword that you can optionally use in left and right joins to make them read as LEFT OUTER JOIN and RIGHT OUTER JOIN. It's just an alternative syntax that doesn't do anything different, and you won't often see it used. We stick to the basic versions in this book.

The Natural Join

We're not big fans of the natural join that we describe in this section. It's included here only for completeness, and because you'll see it used sometimes in SQL statements you'll encounter. Our advice is to avoid using it where possible.

A natural join is, well, supposed to be magically natural. This means that you tell MySQL what tables you want to join, and it figures out how to do it and gives you an INNER JOIN result set. Here's an example for the actor_info and film_actor tables:

```
mysql> SELECT first_name, last_name, film_id
    -> FROM actor_info NATURAL JOIN film_actor
    -> LIMIT 20;
+------------+-----------+---------+
| first_name | last_name | film_id |
+------------+-----------+---------+
| PENELOPE   | GUINESS   |       1 |
| PENELOPE   | GUINESS   |      23 |
| ...        |           |         |
| PENELOPE   | GUINESS   |     980 |
| NICK       | WAHLBERG  |       3 |
+------------+-----------+---------+
20 rows in set (0.28 sec)
```

In reality, it's not quite magical: all MySQL does is look for columns with the same names and, behind the scenes, add these silently into an inner join with join conditions written into the WHERE clause. So, the previous query is actually translated into something like this:

```
mysql> SELECT first_name, last_name, film_id FROM
    -> actor_info JOIN film_actor
    -> WHERE (actor_info.actor_id = film_actor.actor_id)
    -> LIMIT 20;
```

If the identifier columns don't share the same name, natural joins won't work. Also, more dangerously, if columns that do share the same names aren't identifiers, they'll get thrown into the behind-the-scenes USING clause anyway. You can very easily see this in the sakila database. In fact, that's why we resorted to showing the preceding example with `actor_info`, which isn't even a table: it's a view. Let's see what would have happened if we used the regular `actor` and `film_actor` tables:

```
mysql> SELECT first_name, last_name, film_id FROM actor NATURAL JOIN film_actor;
Empty set (0.01 sec)
```

But how? The problem is: NATURAL JOIN really does take *all* of the columns into consideration. With the `sakila` database, that's a huge roadblock, as every table has a `last_update` column. If you were to run an EXPLAIN statement on the previous query and then execute SHOW WARNINGS, you'd see that the resulting query is meaningless:

```
mysql> SHOW WARNINGS\G
*************************** 1. row ***************************
  Level: Note
   Code: 1003
Message: /* select#1 */ select `sakila`.`customer`.`email` AS `email`,
 `sakila`.`rental`.`rental_date` AS `rental_date`
from `sakila`.`customer` join `sakila`.`rental`
where ((`sakila`.`rental`.`last_update` = `sakila`.`customer`.`last_update`)
and (`sakila`.`rental`.`customer_id` = `sakila`.`customer`.`customer_id`))
1 row in set (0.00 sec)
```

You'll sometimes see the natural join mixed with left and right joins. The following are valid join syntaxes: NATURAL LEFT JOIN, NATURAL LEFT OUTER JOIN, NATURAL RIGHT JOIN, and NATURAL RIGHT OUTER JOIN. The former two are left joins without ON or USING clauses, and the latter two are right joins. Again, avoid writing them when you can, but you should understand what they mean if you see them used.

Constant Expressions in Joins

In all of the examples of joins we've given you so far, we've used column identifiers to define the join condition. When you're using the USING clause, that's the only possible way to go. When you're defining the join conditions in a WHERE clause, that's also the only thing that will work. However, when you're using the ON clause, you can actually add constant expressions.

Let's consider an example, listing all films for a particular actor:

```
mysql> SELECT first_name, last_name, title
    -> FROM actor JOIN film_actor USING (actor_id)
    -> JOIN film USING (film_id)
    -> WHERE actor_id = 11;
+------------+-----------+--------------------+
| first_name | last_name | title              |
+------------+-----------+--------------------+
| ZERO       | CAGE      | CANYON STOCK       |
| ZERO       | CAGE      | DANCES NONE        |
| ...        |           |                    |
```

```
| ZERO        | CAGE       | WEST LION           |
| ZERO        | CAGE       | WORKER TARZAN       |
+-------------+------------+---------------------+
25 rows in set (0.00 sec)
```

We can move the `actor_id` clause into the join like this:

```
mysql> SELECT first_name, last_name, title
    -> FROM actor JOIN film_actor
    ->   ON actor.actor_id = film_actor.actor_id
    ->   AND actor.actor_id = 11
    -> JOIN film USING (film_id);

+-------------+------------+---------------------+
| first_name  | last_name  | title               |
+-------------+------------+---------------------+
| ZERO        | CAGE       | CANYON STOCK        |
| ZERO        | CAGE       | DANCES NONE         |
| ...         |            |                     |
| ZERO        | CAGE       | WEST LION           |
| ZERO        | CAGE       | WORKER TARZAN       |
+-------------+------------+---------------------+
25 rows in set (0.00 sec)
```

Well, that's neat, of course, but why? Is this any more expressive than having the proper WHERE clause? The answer to both questions is that constant conditions in joins are evaluated and resolved differently than the conditions in the WHERE clause are. It's easier to show this with an example, but the preceding query is a poor one. The impact of constant conditions in joins is best shown with a left join.

Remember this query from the section on left joins:

```
mysql> SELECT email, name AS category_name, COUNT(rental_id) AS cnt
    -> FROM category cat LEFT JOIN film_category USING (category_id)
    -> LEFT JOIN inventory USING (film_id)
    -> LEFT JOIN rental USING (inventory_id)
    -> LEFT JOIN customer cs USING (customer_id)
    -> WHERE cs.email = 'WESLEY.BULL@sakilacustomer.org'
    -> GROUP BY email, category_name
    -> ORDER BY cnt DESC;

+--------------------------------+---------------+-----+
| email                          | category_name | cnt |
+--------------------------------+---------------+-----+
| WESLEY.BULL@sakilacustomer.org | Games         |   9 |
| WESLEY.BULL@sakilacustomer.org | Foreign       |   6 |
| ...                            |               |     |
| WESLEY.BULL@sakilacustomer.org | Comedy        |   1 |
| WESLEY.BULL@sakilacustomer.org | Sports        |   1 |
+--------------------------------+---------------+-----+
14 rows in set (0.01 sec)
```

If we go ahead and move the `cs.email` clause to the `LEFT JOIN customer cs` part, we'll see completely different results:

```
mysql> SELECT email, name AS category_name, COUNT(rental_id) AS cnt
    -> FROM category cat LEFT JOIN film_category USING (category_id)
    -> LEFT JOIN inventory USING (film_id)
    -> LEFT JOIN rental USING (inventory_id)
    -> LEFT JOIN customer cs ON rental.customer_id = cs.customer_id
    -> AND cs.email = 'WESLEY.BULL@sakilacustomer.org'
    -> GROUP BY email, category_name
    -> ORDER BY cnt DESC;
```

```
+--------------------------------+------------+------+
| email                          | name       | cnt  |
+--------------------------------+------------+------+
| NULL                           | Sports     | 1178 |
| NULL                           | Animation  | 1164 |
| ...                            |            |      |
| NULL                           | Travel     | 834  |
| NULL                           | Music      | 829  |
| WESLEY.BULL@sakilacustomer.org | Games      | 9    |
| WESLEY.BULL@sakilacustomer.org | Foreign    | 6    |
| ...                            |            |      |
| WESLEY.BULL@sakilacustomer.org | Comedy     | 1    |
| NULL                           | Thriller   | 0    |
+--------------------------------+------------+------+
31 rows in set (0.07 sec)
```

That's interesting! Instead of getting only Wesley's rental counts per category, we also get rental counts for everyone else broken down by category. That even includes our new and so far empty Thriller category. Let's try to understand what happens here.

The `WHERE` clause's contents are applied logically after the joins are resolved and executed. We tell MySQL we only need rows from whatever we join where the `cs.email` column equals `'WESLEY.BULL@sakilacustomer.org'`. In reality, MySQL is smart enough to optimize this situation and will actually start the plan execution as if regular inner joins were used. When we have the `cs.email` condition within the `LEFT JOIN customer` clause, we tell MySQL that we want to add columns from the `customer` table to our result set so far (which includes the `category`, `inventory`, and `rental` tables), but only when the certain value is present in the `email` column. Since this is a `LEFT JOIN`, we get `NULL` in every column of `customer` in rows that didn't match.

It's important to be aware of this behavior.

Nested Queries

Nested queries, supported by MySQL since version 4.1, are the most difficult to learn. However, they provide a powerful, useful, and concise way of expressing difficult information needs in short SQL statements. This section explains them, beginning with simple examples and leading to the more complex features of the EXISTS and IN statements. At the conclusion of this section, you'll have completed everything this book contains about querying data, and you should understand almost any SQL query you encounter.

Nested Query Basics

You know how to find the names of all the actors who played in a particular movie using an INNER JOIN:

```
mysql> SELECT first_name, last_name FROM
    -> actor JOIN film_actor USING (actor_id)
    -> JOIN film USING (film_id)
    -> WHERE title = 'ZHIVAGO CORE';
+------------+-----------+
| first_name | last_name |
+------------+-----------+
| UMA        | WOOD      |
| NICK       | STALLONE  |
| GARY       | PENN      |
| SALMA      | NOLTE     |
| KENNETH    | HOFFMAN   |
| WILLIAM    | HACKMAN   |
+------------+-----------+
6 rows in set (0.00 sec)
```

But there's another way, using a *nested query*:

```
mysql> SELECT first_name, last_name FROM
    -> actor JOIN film_actor USING (actor_id)
    -> WHERE film_id = (SELECT film_id FROM film
    -> WHERE title = 'ZHIVAGO CORE');
+------------+-----------+
| first_name | last_name |
+------------+-----------+
| UMA        | WOOD      |
| NICK       | STALLONE  |
| GARY       | PENN      |
| SALMA      | NOLTE     |
| KENNETH    | HOFFMAN   |
| WILLIAM    | HACKMAN   |
+------------+-----------+
6 rows in set (0.00 sec)
```

It's called a nested query because one query is inside another. The *inner query*, or *subquery*—the one that is nested—is written in parentheses, and you can see that it determines the film_id for the film with the title ZHIVAGO CORE. The parentheses are required for inner queries. The *outer query* is the one that's listed first and isn't parenthesized here: you can see that it finds the first_name and last_name of the actors from a JOIN with film_actor with a film_id that matches the result of the subquery. So, overall, the inner query finds the film_id, and the outer query uses it to find actors' names. Whenever nested queries are used, it's possible to rewrite them as a few separate queries. Let's do that with the previous example, as it may help you understand what is going on:

```
mysql> SELECT film_id FROM film WHERE title = 'ZHIVAGO CORE';

+---------+
| film_id |
+---------+
|     998 |
+---------+
1 row in set (0.03 sec)

mysql> SELECT first_name, last_name
    -> FROM actor JOIN film_actor USING (actor_id)
    -> WHERE film_id = 998;

+------------+-----------+
| first_name | last_name |
+------------+-----------+
| UMA        | WOOD      |
| NICK       | STALLONE  |
| GARY       | PENN      |
| SALMA      | NOLTE     |
| KENNETH    | HOFFMAN   |
| WILLIAM    | HACKMAN   |
+------------+-----------+
6 rows in set (0.00 sec)
```

So, which approach is preferable: nested or not nested? The answer isn't easy. In terms of performance, the answer is usually *not*: nested queries are hard to optimize, so they're almost always slower to run than the unnested alternative.

Does this mean you should avoid nesting? The answer is no: sometimes it's your only choice if you want to write a single query, and sometimes nested queries can answer information needs that can't be easily solved otherwise. What's more, nested queries are expressive. Once you're comfortable with the idea, they're a very readable way to show how a query is evaluated. In fact, many SQL designers advocate teaching nested queries before the join-based alternatives we've shown you in the past few sections. We'll show you examples where nesting is readable and powerful throughout this section.

Before we begin to cover the keywords that can be used in nested queries, let's take a look at an example that can't be done easily in a single query—at least, not without MySQL's nonstandard, although ubiquitous, LIMIT clause! Suppose you want to know what movie a customer rented most recently. To do this, following the methods we've learned previously, you could find the date and time of the most recently stored row in the rental table for that customer:

```
mysql> SELECT MAX(rental_date) FROM rental
    -> JOIN customer USING (customer_id)
    -> WHERE email = 'WESLEY.BULL@sakilacustomer.org';

+---------------------+
| MAX(rental_date)    |
+---------------------+
| 2005-08-23 15:46:33 |
+---------------------+
1 row in set (0.01 sec)
```

You can then use the output as input to another query to find the film title:

```
mysql> SELECT title FROM film
    -> JOIN inventory USING (film_id)
    -> JOIN rental USING (inventory_id)
    -> JOIN customer USING (customer_id)
    -> WHERE email = 'WESLEY.BULL@sakilacustomer.org'
    -> AND rental_date = '2005-08-23 15:46:33';

+-------------+
| title       |
+-------------+
| KARATE MOON |
+-------------+
1 row in set (0.00 sec)
```

 In "User Variables" on page 234 we'll show you how you can use variables to avoid having to type in the value in the second query.

With a nested query, you can do both steps in one shot:

```
mysql> SELECT title FROM film JOIN inventory USING (film_id)
    -> JOIN rental USING (inventory_id)
    -> WHERE rental_date = (SELECT MAX(rental_date) FROM rental
    -> JOIN customer USING (customer_id)
    -> WHERE email = 'WESLEY.BULL@sakilacustomer.org');
```

```
+-------------+
| title       |
+-------------+
| KARATE MOON |
+-------------+
1 row in set (0.01 sec)
```

You can see the nested query combines the two previous queries. Rather than using the constant date and time value discovered from a previous query, it executes the query directly as a subquery. This is the simplest type of nested query, one that returns a *scalar operand*--that is, a single value.

 The previous example used the equality operator (=). You can use all types of comparison operators: < (less than), <= (less than or equal to), > (greater than), >= (greater than or equal to), and != (not equals) or <> (not equals).

The ANY, SOME, ALL, IN, and NOT IN Clauses

Before we start to show some more advanced features of nested queries, we need to switch to a new database in our examples. Unfortunately, the sakila database is a little too well normalized to effectively demonstrate the full power of nested querying. So, let's add a new database to give us something to play with.

The database we'll install is the employees sample database. You can find instructions for installation in the MySQL documentation (*https://oreil.ly/vODJG*) or in the database's GitHub repo. Either clone the repository using git or download the latest release (1.0.7 (*https://oreil.ly/zW0E1*) at the time of writing). Once you have the necessary files ready, you need to run two commands.

The first command creates the necessary structures and loads the data:

```
$ mysql -uroot -p < employees.sql
INFO
CREATING DATABASE STRUCTURE
INFO
storage engine: InnoDB
INFO
LOADING departments
INFO
LOADING employees
INFO
LOADING dept_emp
INFO
LOADING dept_manager
INFO
LOADING titles
INFO
LOADING salaries
```

```
data_load_time_diff
00:00:28
```

The second command verifies the installation:

```
$ mysql -uroot -p < test_employees_md5.sql
INFO
TESTING INSTALLATION
table_name      expected_records        expected_crc
departments     9       d1af5e170d2d1591d776d5638d71fc5f
dept_emp        331603  ccf6fe516f990bdaa49713fc478701b7
dept_manager    24      8720e2f0853ac9096b689c14664f847e
employees       300024  4ec56ab5ba37218d187cf6ab09ce1aa1
salaries        2844047 fd220654e95aea1b169624ffe3fca934
titles  443308  bfa016c472df68e70a03facafa1bc0a8
table_name      found_records   found_crc
departments     9       d1af5e170d2d1591d776d5638d71fc5f
dept_emp        331603  ccf6fe516f990bdaa49713fc478701b7
dept_manager    24      8720e2f0853ac9096b689c14664f847e
employees       300024  4ec56ab5ba37218d187cf6ab09ce1aa1
salaries        2844047 fd220654e95aea1b169624ffe3fca934
titles  443308  bfa016c472df68e70a03facafa1bc0a8
table_name      records_match   crc_match
departments     OK      ok
dept_emp        OK      ok
dept_manager    OK      ok
employees       OK      ok
salaries        OK      ok
titles  OK      ok
computation_time
00:00:25
summary result
CRC     OK
count   OK
```

Once this is done, you can proceed to work through the examples we'll be providing next.

To connect to the new database, either run mysql from the command line like this (or specify employees as a target for your MySQL client of choice):

```
$ mysql employees
```

Or execute the following at a mysql prompt to change the default database:

```
mysql> USE employees
```

Now you're ready to move forward.

Using ANY and IN

Now that you've created the sample tables, you can try an example using ANY. Suppose you're looking to find assistant engineers who've been working longer than the least experienced manager. You can express this information need as follows:

```
mysql> SELECT emp_no, first_name, last_name, hire_date
    -> FROM employees JOIN titles USING (emp_no)
    -> WHERE title = 'Assistant Engineer'
    -> AND hire_date < ANY (SELECT hire_date FROM
    -> employees JOIN titles USING (emp_no)
    -> WHERE title = 'Manager');
+--------+------------+------------------+------------+
| emp_no | first_name | last_name        | hire_date  |
+--------+------------+------------------+------------+
|  10009 | Sumant     | Peac             | 1985-02-18 |
|  10066 | Kwee       | Schusler         | 1986-02-26 |
| ...                                                 |
| ...                                                 |
| 499958 | Srinidhi   | Theuretzbacher   | 1989-12-17 |
| 499974 | Shuichi    | Piazza           | 1989-09-16 |
+--------+------------+------------------+------------+
10747 rows in set (0.20 sec)
```

Turns out there are a lot of people who meet these criteria! The subquery finds the dates on which managers were hired:

```
mysql> SELECT hire_date FROM
    -> employees JOIN titles USING (emp_no)
    -> WHERE title = 'Manager';
+------------+
| hire_date  |
+------------+
| 1985-01-01 |
| 1986-04-12 |
| ...        |
| 1991-08-17 |
| 1989-07-10 |
+------------+
24 rows in set (0.10 sec)
```

The outer query goes through each employee with the title Associate Engineer, returning the engineer if their hire date is lower (older) than any of the values in the set returned by the subquery. So, for example, Sumant Peac is output because 1985-02-18 is older than at least one value in the set (as you can see, the second hire date returned for managers is 1986-04-12). The ANY keyword means just that: it's true if the column or expression preceding it is true for *any* of the values in the set returned by the subquery. Used in this way, ANY has the alias SOME, which was included so that some queries can be read more clearly as English expressions; it doesn't do anything different, and you'll rarely see it used.

The ANY keyword gives you more power in expressing nested queries. Indeed, the previous query is the first nested query in this section with a *column subquery*—that is, the results returned by the subquery are one or more values from a column, instead of a single scalar value as in the previous section. With this, you can now compare a column value from an outer query to a set of values returned from a subquery.

Consider another example using ANY. Suppose you want to know the managers who also have some other title. You can do this with the following nested query:

```
mysql> SELECT emp_no, first_name, last_name
    -> FROM employees JOIN titles USING (emp_no)
    -> WHERE title = 'Manager'
    -> AND emp_no = ANY (SELECT emp_no FROM employees
    -> JOIN titles USING (emp_no) WHERE
    -> title <> 'Manager');
+--------+------------+------------+
| emp_no | first_name | last_name  |
+--------+------------+------------+
| 110022 | Margareta  | Markovitch |
| 110039 | Vishwani   | Minakawa   |
| ...    |            |            |
| 111877 | Xiaobin    | Spinelli   |
| 111939 | Yuchang    | Weedman    |
+--------+------------+------------+
24 rows in set (0.11 sec)
```

The = ANY causes the outer query to return a manager when the emp_no is equal to any of the engineer employee numbers returned by the subquery. The = ANY keyphrase has the alias IN, which you'll see commonly used in nested queries. Using IN, the previous example can be rewritten as:

```
mysql> SELECT emp_no, first_name, last_name
    -> FROM employees JOIN titles USING (emp_no)
    -> WHERE title = 'Manager'
    -> AND emp_no IN (SELECT emp_no FROM employees
    -> JOIN titles USING (emp_no) WHERE
    -> title <> 'Manager');
+--------+------------+------------+
| emp_no | first_name | last_name  |
+--------+------------+------------+
| 110022 | Margareta  | Markovitch |
| 110039 | Vishwani   | Minakawa   |
| ...    |            |            |
| 111877 | Xiaobin    | Spinelli   |
| 111939 | Yuchang    | Weedman    |
+--------+------------+------------+
24 rows in set (0.11 sec)
```

Of course, for this particular example, you could also have used a join query. Note that we have to use DISTINCT here, because otherwise we get 30 rows returned. Some people hold more than one non-engineer title:

```
mysql> SELECT DISTINCT emp_no, first_name, last_name
    -> FROM employees JOIN titles mgr USING (emp_no)
    -> JOIN titles nonmgr USING (emp_no)
    -> WHERE mgr.title = 'Manager'
    -> AND nonmgr.title <> 'Manager';

+--------+------------+--------------+
| emp_no | first_name | last_name    |
+--------+------------+--------------+
| 110022 | Margareta  | Markovitch   |
| 110039 | Vishwani   | Minakawa     |
| ...    |            |              |
| 111877 | Xiaobin    | Spinelli     |
| 111939 | Yuchang    | Weedman      |
+--------+------------+--------------+
24 rows in set (0.11 sec)
```

Again, nested queries are expressive but typically slow in MySQL, so use a join where you can.

Using ALL

Suppose you want to find assistant engineers who are more experienced than all of the managers—that is, more experienced than the most experienced manager. You can do this with the ALL keyword in place of ANY:

```
mysql> SELECT emp_no, first_name, last_name, hire_date
    -> FROM employees JOIN titles USING (emp_no)
    -> WHERE title = 'Assistant Engineer'
    -> AND hire_date < ALL (SELECT hire_date FROM
    -> employees JOIN titles USING (emp_no)
    -> WHERE title = 'Manager');

Empty set (0.18 sec)
```

You can see that there are no answers. We can inspect the data further to check what is the oldest hire date of a manager and of an assistant engineer:

```
mysql> (SELECT 'Assistant Engineer' AS title,
    -> MIN(hire_date) AS mhd FROM employees
    -> JOIN titles USING (emp_no)
    -> WHERE title = 'Assistant Engineer')
    -> UNION
    -> (SELECT 'Manager' title, MIN(hire_date) mhd FROM employees
    -> JOIN titles USING (emp_no)
    -> WHERE title = 'Manager');
```

```
+---------------------+------------+
| title               | mhd        |
+---------------------+------------+
| Assistant Engineer  | 1985-02-01 |
| Manager             | 1985-01-01 |
+---------------------+------------+
2 rows in set (0.26 sec)
```

Looking at the data, we see that the first manager was hired on January 1, 1985, and the first assistant engineer only on February 1 of the same year. While the ANY keyword returns values that satisfy at least one condition (Boolean OR), the ALL keyword returns values only where all the conditions are satisfied (Boolean AND).

We can use the alias NOT IN in place of <> ANY or != ANY. Let's find all the managers who aren't senior staff:

```
mysql> SELECT emp_no, first_name, last_name
    -> FROM employees JOIN titles USING (emp_no)
    -> WHERE title = 'Manager' AND emp_no NOT IN
    -> (SELECT emp_no FROM titles
    -> WHERE title = 'Senior Staff');

+--------+-------------+--------------+
| emp_no | first_name  | last_name    |
+--------+-------------+--------------+
| 110183 | Shirish     | Ossenbruggen |
| 110303 | Krassimir   | Wegerle      |
| ...    |             |              |
| 111400 | Arie        | Staelin      |
| 111692 | Tonny       | Butterworth  |
+--------+-------------+--------------+
15 rows in set (0.09 sec)
```

As an exercise, try writing this query using the ANY syntax and as a join query.

The ALL keyword has a few tricks and traps:

- If it's false for any value, it's false. Suppose that table a contains a row with the value 14, and table b contains the values 16, 1, and NULL. If you check whether the value in a is greater than ALL values in b, you'll get false, since 14 isn't greater than 16. It doesn't matter that the other values are 1 and NULL.

- If it isn't false for any value, it isn't true unless it's true for all values. Suppose that table a again contains 14, and b contains 1 and NULL. If you check whether the value in a is greater than ALL values in b, you'll get UNKNOWN (neither true nor false) because it can't be determined whether NULL is greater than or less than 14.

- If the table in the subquery is empty, the result is always true. Hence, if a contains 14 and b is empty, you'll get true when you check if the value in a is greater than ALL values in b.

When using the ALL keyword, be very careful with tables that can have NULL values in columns; consider disallowing NULL values in such cases. Also, be careful with empty tables.

Writing row subqueries

In the previous examples, the subquery returned a single scalar value (such as an actor_id) or a set of values from one column (such as all of the emp_no values). This section describes another type of subquery, the *row subquery*, that works with multiple columns from multiple rows.

Suppose you're interested in whether a manager had another position within the same calendar year. To answer this need, you must match both the employee number and the title assignment date, or, more precisely, year. You can write this as a join:

```
mysql> SELECT mgr.emp_no, YEAR(mgr.from_date) AS fd
    -> FROM titles AS mgr, titles AS other
    -> WHERE mgr.emp_no = other.emp_no
    -> AND mgr.title = 'Manager'
    -> AND mgr.title <> other.title
    -> AND YEAR(mgr.from_date) = YEAR(other.from_date);

+--------+------+
| emp_no | fd   |
+--------+------+
| 110765 | 1989 |
| 111784 | 1988 |
+--------+------+
2 rows in set (0.11 sec)
```

But you can also write it as a nested query:

```
mysql> SELECT emp_no, YEAR(from_date) AS fd
    -> FROM titles WHERE title = 'Manager' AND
    -> (emp_no, YEAR(from_date)) IN
    -> (SELECT emp_no, YEAR(from_date)
    -> FROM titles WHERE title <> 'Manager');

+--------+------+
| emp_no | fd   |
+--------+------+
| 110765 | 1989 |
| 111784 | 1988 |
+--------+------+
2 rows in set (0.12 sec)
```

You can see there's a different syntax being used in this nested query: a list of two column names in parentheses follows the WHERE statement, and the inner query returns two columns. We'll explain this syntax next.

The row subquery syntax allows you to compare multiple values per row. The expression (emp_no, YEAR(from_date)) means two values per row are compared to the output of the subquery. You can see following the IN keyword that the subquery returns two values, emp_no and YEAR(from_date). So, the fragment:

```
(emp_no, YEAR(from_date)) IN (SELECT emp_no, YEAR(from_date)
FROM titles WHERE title <> 'Manager')
```

matches manager numbers and starting years to nonmanager numbers and starting years, and returns a true value when a match is found. The result is that if a matching pair is found, the overall query outputs a result. This is a typical row subquery: it finds rows that exist in two tables.

To explain the syntax further, let's consider another example. Suppose you want to see if a particular employee is a senior staff member. You can do this with the following query:

```
mysql> SELECT first_name, last_name
    -> FROM employees, titles
    -> WHERE (employees.emp_no, first_name, last_name, title) =
    -> (titles.emp_no, 'Marjo', 'Giarratana', 'Senior Staff');
+------------+------------+
| first_name | last_name  |
+------------+------------+
| Marjo      | Giarratana |
+------------+------------+
1 row in set (0.09 sec)
```

It's not a nested query, but it shows you how the new row subquery syntax works. You can see that the query matches the list of columns before the equals sign, (employees.emp_no, first_name, last_name, title), to the list of columns and values after the equals sign, (titles.emp_no, 'Marjo', 'Giarratana', 'Senior Staff'). So, when the emp_no values match, the employee's full name is Marjo Giarratana, and the title is Senior Staff, we get output from the query. We don't recommend writing queries like this—use a regular WHERE clause with multiple AND conditions instead—but it does illustrate exactly what's going on. For an exercise, try writing this query using a join.

Row subqueries require that the number, order, and type of values in the columns match. So, for example, our previous example matches an INT to an INT, and two character strings to two character strings.

The EXISTS and NOT EXISTS Clauses

You've now seen three types of subquery: scalar subqueries, column subqueries, and row subqueries. In this section, you'll learn about a fourth type, the *correlated subquery*, where a table used in the outer query is referenced in the subquery. Correlated subqueries are often used with the IN statement we've already discussed and almost always used with the EXISTS and NOT EXISTS clauses that are the focus of this section.

EXISTS and NOT EXISTS basics

Before we start on our discussion of correlated subqueries, let's investigate what the EXISTS clause does. We'll need a simple but strange example to introduce the clause, since we're not discussing correlated subqueries just yet. So, here goes: suppose you want to find a count of all films in the database, but only if the database is active, which you've defined to mean only if at least one movie from any branch has been rented. Here's the query that does it (don't forget to connect to the sakila database again before running this query—hint: use the use <db> command):

```
mysql> SELECT COUNT(*) FROM film
    -> WHERE EXISTS (SELECT * FROM rental);

+----------+
| COUNT(*) |
+----------+
|     1000 |
+----------+
1 row in set (0.01 sec)
```

The subquery returns all rows from the rental table. However, what's important is that it returns at least one row; it doesn't matter what's in the row, how many rows there are, or whether the row contains only NULL values. So, you can think of the subquery as being true or false, and in this case it's true because it produces some output. When the subquery is true, the outer query that uses the EXISTS clause returns a row. The overall result is that all rows in the film table are counted because, for each one, the subquery is true.

Let's try a query where the subquery isn't true. Again, let's contrive a query: this time, we'll output the names of all films in the database, but only if a particular film exists. Here's the query:

```
mysql> SELECT title FROM film
    -> WHERE EXISTS (SELECT * FROM film
    -> WHERE title = 'IS THIS A MOVIE?');

Empty set (0.00 sec)
```

Since the subquery isn't true—no rows are returned because IS THIS A MOVIE? isn't in our database—no results are returned by the outer query.

The NOT EXISTS clause does the opposite. Imagine you want a list of all actors if you *don't* have a particular movie in the database. Here it is:

```
mysql> SELECT * FROM actor WHERE NOT EXISTS
    -> (SELECT * FROM film WHERE title = 'ZHIVAGO CORE');

Empty set (0.00 sec)
```

This time, the inner query is true, but the NOT EXISTS clause negates it to give false. Since it's false, the outer query doesn't produce results.

You'll notice that the subquery begins with `SELECT * FROM film`. It doesn't actually matter what you select in an inner query when you're using the EXISTS clause, since it's not used by the outer query anyway. You can select one column, everything, or even a constant (as in `SELECT 'cat' from film`), and it'll have the same effect. Traditionally, though, you'll see most SQL authors write `SELECT *` by convention.

Correlated subqueries

So far, it's probably difficult to imagine what you'd do with the EXISTS and NOT EXISTS clauses. This section shows you how they're really used, illustrating the most advanced type of nested query that you'll typically see in action.

Let's think about the realistic kinds of information you might want from the `sakila` database. Suppose you want a list of all employees who've rented something from our company, or are just customers. You can do this easily with a join query, which we recommend you try to think about before you continue. You can also do it with the following nested query that uses a correlated subquery:

```
mysql> SELECT first_name, last_name FROM staff
    -> WHERE EXISTS (SELECT * FROM customer
    -> WHERE customer.first_name = staff.first_name
    -> AND customer.last_name = staff.last_name);

Empty set (0.01 sec)
```

There's no output because nobody from the staff is also a customer (or that's forbidden, but we'll bend the rules). Let's add a customer with the same details as one of the staff members:

```
mysql> INSERT INTO customer(store_id, first_name, last_name,
    -> email, address_id, create_date)
    -> VALUES (1, 'Mike', 'Hillyer',
    -> 'Mike.Hillyer@sakilastaff.com', 3, NOW());

Query OK, 1 row affected (0.02 sec)
```

And try the query again:

```
mysql> SELECT first_name, last_name FROM staff
    -> WHERE EXISTS (SELECT * FROM customer
    -> WHERE customer.first_name = staff.first_name
    -> AND customer.last_name = staff.last_name);

+------------+-----------+
| first_name | last_name |
+------------+-----------+
| Mike       | Hillyer   |
+------------+-----------+
1 row in set (0.00 sec)
```

So, the query works; now, we just need to understand how!

Let's examine the subquery in our previous example. You can see that it lists only the customer table in the FROM clause, but it uses a column from the staff table in the WHERE clause. If you run it in isolation, you'll see this isn't allowed:

```
mysql> SELECT * FROM customer WHERE customer.first_name = staff.first_name;
ERROR 1054 (42S22): Unknown column 'staff.first_name' in 'where clause'
```

However, it's legal when executed as a subquery because tables listed in the outer query are allowed to be accessed in the subquery. So, in this example, the current value of staff.first_name and staff.last_name in the outer query is supplied to the subquery as a constant, scalar value and compared to the customer's first and last names. If the customer's name matches the staff member's name, the subquery is true, and so the outer query outputs a row. Consider two cases that illustrate this more clearly:

- When the first_name and last_name being processed by the outer query are Jon and Stephens, the subquery is false because SELECT * FROM customer WHERE first_name = 'Jon' and last_name = 'Stephens'; doesn't return any rows, and so the staff row for Jon Stephens isn't output as an answer.

- When the first_name and last_name being processed by the outer query are Mike and Hillyer, the subquery is true because SELECT * FROM customer WHERE first_name = 'Mike' and last_name = 'Hillyer'; returns at least one row. Overall, the staff row for Mike Hillyer is returned.

Can you see the power of correlated subqueries? You can use values from the outer query in the inner query to evaluate complex information needs.

We'll now explore another example using EXISTS. Let's try to find a count of all films of which we own at least two copies. To do this with EXISTS, we need to think through what the inner and outer queries should do. The inner query should produce a result only when the condition we're checking is true; in this case, it should produce output when there are at least two rows in the inventory for the same film. The outer query should increment the counter whenever the inner query is true. Here's the query:

```
mysql> SELECT COUNT(*) FROM film WHERE EXISTS
    -> (SELECT film_id FROM inventory
    -> WHERE inventory.film_id = film.film_id
    -> GROUP BY film_id HAVING COUNT(*) >= 2);
+----------+
| COUNT(*) |
+----------+
|      958 |
+----------+
1 row in set (0.00 sec)
```

This is yet another query where nesting isn't necessary and a join would suffice, but let's stick with this version for the purpose of explanation. Have a look at the inner query: you can see that the WHERE clause ensures that films match by the unique film_id, and only matching rows for the current film are considered by the subquery. The GROUP BY clause clusters the rows for that film, but only if there are at least two entries in the inventory. Therefore, the inner query produces output only when there are at least two rows for the current film in our inventory. The outer query is straightforward: it can be thought of as incrementing a counter when the subquery produces output.

Here's one more example before we move on and discuss other issues. This example will be in the employees database, so switch your client. We've already shown you a query that uses IN and finds managers who also had some other position:

```
mysql> SELECT emp_no, first_name, last_name
    -> FROM employees JOIN titles USING (emp_no)
    -> WHERE title = 'Manager'
    -> AND emp_no IN (SELECT emp_no FROM employees
    -> JOIN titles USING (emp_no) WHERE
    -> title <> 'Manager');
+--------+------------+------------+
| emp_no | first_name | last_name  |
+--------+------------+------------+
| 110022 | Margareta  | Markovitch |
| 110039 | Vishwani   | Minakawa   |
| ...    |            |            |
| 111877 | Xiaobin    | Spinelli   |
| 111939 | Yuchang    | Weedman    |
+--------+------------+------------+
24 rows in set (0.11 sec)
```

Let's rewrite the query to use EXISTS. First, think about the subquery: it should produce output when there's a title record for an employee with the same name as a manager.

Second, think about the outer query: it should return the employee's name when the inner query produces output. Here's the rewritten query:

```
mysql> SELECT emp_no, first_name, last_name
    -> FROM employees JOIN titles USING (emp_no)
    -> WHERE title = 'Manager'
    -> AND EXISTS (SELECT emp_no FROM titles
    -> WHERE titles.emp_no = employees.emp_no
    -> AND title <> 'Manager');
+--------+------------+------------+
| emp_no | first_name | last_name  |
+--------+------------+------------+
| 110022 | Margareta  | Markovitch |
| 110039 | Vishwani   | Minakawa   |
```

```
| ...                                        |
| 111877 | Xiaobin      | Spinelli     |
| 111939 | Yuchang      | Weedman      |
+--------+--------------+--------------+
24 rows in set (0.09 sec)
```

Again, you can see that the subquery references the emp_no column, which comes from the outer query.

Correlated subqueries can be used with any nested query type. Here's the previous IN query rewritten with an outer reference:

```
mysql> SELECT emp_no, first_name, last_name
    -> FROM employees JOIN titles USING (emp_no)
    -> WHERE title = 'Manager'
    -> AND emp_no IN (SELECT emp_no FROM titles
    -> WHERE titles.emp_no = employees.emp_no
    -> AND title <> 'Manager');
+--------+--------------+--------------+
| emp_no | first_name   | last_name    |
+--------+--------------+--------------+
| 110022 | Margareta    | Markovitch   |
| 110039 | Vishwani     | Minakawa     |
| ...                                   |
| 111877 | Xiaobin      | Spinelli     |
| 111939 | Yuchang      | Weedman      |
+--------+--------------+--------------+
24 rows in set (0.09 sec)
```

The query is more convoluted than it needs to be, but it illustrates the idea. You can see that the emp_no in the subquery references the employees table from the outer query.

If the query would return a single row, it can also be rewritten to use an equals instead of IN:

```
mysql> SELECT emp_no, first_name, last_name
    -> FROM employees JOIN titles USING (emp_no)
    -> WHERE title = 'Manager'
    -> AND emp_no = (SELECT emp_no FROM titles
    -> WHERE titles.emp_no = employees.emp_no
    -> AND title <> 'Manager');
ERROR 1242 (21000): Subquery returns more than 1 row
```

This doesn't work in this case because the subquery returns more than one scalar value. Let's narrow it down:

```
mysql> SELECT emp_no, first_name, last_name
    -> FROM employees JOIN titles USING (emp_no)
    -> WHERE title = 'Manager'
    -> AND emp_no = (SELECT emp_no FROM titles
```

```
    -> WHERE titles.emp_no = employees.emp_no
    -> AND title = 'Senior Engineer');
+--------+------------+-----------+
| emp_no | first_name | last_name |
+--------+------------+-----------+
| 110344 | Rosine     | Cools     |
| 110420 | Oscar      | Ghazalie  |
| 110800 | Sanjoy     | Quadeer   |
+--------+------------+-----------+
3 rows in set (0.10 sec)
```

It works now—there's only one manager and senior engineer title with each name—so the column subquery operator IN isn't necessary. Of course, if titles are duplicated (for example, if a person switches back and forth between positions), you'd need to use IN, ANY, or ALL instead.

Nested Queries in the FROM Clause

The techniques we've shown all use nested queries in the WHERE clause. This section shows you how they can alternatively be used in the FROM clause. This is useful when you want to manipulate the source of the data you're using in a query.

In the employees database, the salaries table stores the annual wage alongside the employee ID. If you want to find the monthly rate, for example, you can do some math in the query. One option in this case is to do it with a subquery:

```
mysql> SELECT emp_no, monthly_salary FROM
    -> (SELECT emp_no, salary/12 AS monthly_salary FROM salaries) AS ms
    -> LIMIT 5;
+--------+----------------+
| emp_no | monthly_salary |
+--------+----------------+
|  10001 |      5009.7500 |
|  10001 |      5175.1667 |
|  10001 |      5506.1667 |
|  10001 |      5549.6667 |
|  10001 |      5580.0833 |
+--------+----------------+
5 rows in set (0.00 sec)
```

Focus on what follows the FROM clause. The subquery uses the salaries table and returns two columns: the first column is the emp_no; the second column is aliased as monthly_salary and is the salary value divided by 12. The outer query is straightforward: it just returns the emp_no and the monthly_salary value created through the subquery. Note that we've added the table alias ms for the subquery. When we use a subquery as a table—that is, we use a SELECT FROM operation on it—this "derived table" must have an alias, even if we don't use the alias in our query. MySQL complains if we omit the alias:

```
mysql> SELECT emp_no, monthly_salary FROM
    -> (SELECT emp_no, salary/12 AS monthly_salary FROM salaries)
    -> LIMIT 5;

ERROR 1248 (42000): Every derived table must have its own alias
```

Here's another example, now in the sakila database. Suppose we want to find out the average sum a film brings us through rentals, or the average gross, as we'll call it. Let's begin by thinking through the subquery. It should return the sum of payments that we have for each film. Then, the outer query should average the values to give the answer. Here's the query:

```
mysql> SELECT AVG(gross) FROM
    -> (SELECT SUM(amount) AS gross
    -> FROM payment JOIN rental USING (rental_id)
    -> JOIN inventory USING (inventory_id)
    -> JOIN film USING (film_id)
    -> GROUP BY film_id) AS gross_amount;

+------------+
| AVG(gross) |
+------------+
|  70.361754 |
+------------+
1 row in set (0.05 sec)
```

You can see that the inner query joins together payment, rental, inventory, and film, and groups the sales together by film so you can get a sum for each film. If you run it in isolation, here's what happens:

```
mysql> SELECT SUM(amount) AS gross
    -> FROM payment JOIN rental USING (rental_id)
    -> JOIN inventory USING (inventory_id)
    -> JOIN film USING (film_id)
    -> GROUP BY film_id;

+--------+
| gross  |
+--------+
|  36.77 |
|  52.93 |
|  37.88 |
|   ...  |
|  14.91 |
|  73.83 |
| 214.69 |
+--------+
958 rows in set (0.08 sec)
```

Now, the outer query takes these sums—which are aliased as gross--and averages them to give the final result. This query is the typical way that you apply two aggregate functions to one set of data. You can't apply aggregate functions in a cascade, as in AVG(SUM(amount)):

```
mysql> SELECT AVG(SUM(amount)) AS avg_gross
    -> FROM payment JOIN rental USING (rental_id)
    -> JOIN inventory USING (inventory_id)
    -> JOIN film USING (film_id) GROUP BY film_id;
ERROR 1111 (HY000): Invalid use of group function
```

With subqueries in FROM clauses, you can return a scalar value, a set of column values, more than one row, or even a whole table. However, you can't use correlated subqueries, meaning that you can't reference tables or columns from tables that aren't explicitly listed in the subquery. Note also that you must alias the whole subquery using the AS keyword and give it a name, even if you don't use that name anywhere in the query.

Nested Queries in JOINs

The last use of nested queries we'll show, but not the least useful, is using them in joins. In this use case, the results of the subquery basically form a new table and can be used in any of the join types we have discussed.

For an example of this, let's go back to the query that listed the number of films from each of the categories a particular customer has rented. Remember, we had an issue writing that query using just joins: we didn't get a zero count for categories from which our customer didn't rent. This was the query:

```
mysql> SELECT cat.name AS category_name, COUNT(cat.category_id) AS cnt
    -> FROM category AS cat LEFT JOIN film_category USING (category_id)
    -> LEFT JOIN inventory USING (film_id)
    -> LEFT JOIN rental USING (inventory_id)
    -> JOIN customer AS cs ON rental.customer_id = cs.customer_id
    -> WHERE cs.email = 'WESLEY.BULL@sakilacustomer.org'
    -> GROUP BY category_name ORDER BY cnt DESC;
+---------------+-----+
| name          | cnt |
+---------------+-----+
| Games         |   9 |
| Foreign       |   6 |
| ...           |     |
| ...           |     |
| Comedy        |   1 |
| Sports        |   1 |
+---------------+-----+
14 rows in set (0.00 sec)
```

Now that we know about subqueries and joins and that subqueries can be used in joins, we can easily finish the task. This is our new query:

```
mysql> SELECT cat.name AS category_name, cnt
    -> FROM category AS cat
    -> LEFT JOIN (SELECT cat.name, COUNT(cat.category_id) AS cnt
```

```
    ->      FROM category AS cat
    ->      LEFT JOIN film_category USING (category_id)
    ->      LEFT JOIN inventory USING (film_id)
    ->      LEFT JOIN rental USING (inventory_id)
    ->      JOIN customer cs ON rental.customer_id = cs.customer_id
    ->      WHERE cs.email = 'WESLEY.BULL@sakilacustomer.org'
    ->      GROUP BY cat.name) customer_cat USING (name)
    -> ORDER BY cnt DESC;
+-------------+------+
| name        | cnt  |
+-------------+------+
| Games       |    9 |
| Foreign     |    6 |
| ...         |      |
| Children    |    1 |
| Sports      |    1 |
| Sci-Fi      | NULL |
| Action      | NULL |
| Thriller    | NULL |
+-------------+------+
17 rows in set (0.01 sec)
```

Finally, we get all the categories displayed, and we get NULL values for those where no rentals were made. Let's review what's going on in our new query. The subquery, which we aliased as customer_cat, is our previous query without the ORDER BY clause. Thus, we know what it will return: 14 rows for categories in which Wesley rented something, and the number of rentals in each. Next, use LEFT JOIN to concatenate that information to the full list of categories from the category table. The category table is driving the join, so it'll have every row selected. We join the subquery using the name column that matches between the subquery's output and the category table's column.

The technique we showed here is a very powerful one; however, as always with subqueries, it comes at a cost. MySQL cannot optimize the whole query as efficiently when a subquery is present in the join clause.

User Variables

Often you'll want to save values that are returned from queries. You might want to do this so that you can easily use a value in a later query. You might also simply want to save a result for later display. In both cases, user variables solve the problem: they allow you to store a result and use it later.

Let's illustrate user variables with a simple example. The following query finds the title of a film and saves the result in a user variable:

```
mysql> SELECT @film:=title FROM film WHERE film_id = 1;
```

```
+------------------+
| @film:=title     |
+------------------+
| ACADEMY DINOSAUR |
+------------------+
1 row in set, 1 warning (0.00 sec)
```

The user variable is named film, and it's denoted as a user variable by the @ character that precedes it. The value is assigned using the := operator. You can print out the contents of the user variable with the following very short query:

```
mysql> SELECT @film;

+------------------+
| @film            |
+------------------+
| ACADEMY DINOSAUR |
+------------------+
1 row in set (0.00 sec)
```

You may have noticed the warning—what was that about?

```
mysql> SELECT @film:=title FROM film WHERE film_id = 1;
mysql> SHOW WARNINGS\G

*************************** 1. row ***************************
  Level: Warning
   Code: 1287
Message: Setting user variables within expressions is deprecated
and will be removed in a future release. Consider alternatives:
'SET variable=expression, ...', or
'SELECT expression(s) INTO variables(s)'.
1 row in set (0.00 sec)
```

Let's cover the two alternatives proposed. First, we can still execute a nested query within a SET statement:

```
mysql> SET @film := (SELECT title FROM film WHERE film_id = 1);

Query OK, 0 rows affected (0.00 sec)

mysql> SELECT @film;

+------------------+
| @film            |
+------------------+
| ACADEMY DINOSAUR |
+------------------+
1 row in set (0.00 sec)
```

Second, we can use the SELECT INTO statement:

```
mysql> SELECT title INTO @film FROM film WHERE film_id = 1;

Query OK, 1 row affected (0.00 sec)

mysql> SELECT @film;
```

```
+------------------+
| @film            |
+------------------+
| ACADEMY DINOSAUR |
+------------------+
1 row in set (0.00 sec)
```

You can explicitly set a variable using the SET statement without a SELECT. Suppose you want to initialize a counter to zero:

```
mysql> SET @counter := 0;

Query OK, 0 rows affected (0.00 sec)
```

The := is optional, and you can write = instead and mix them up. You should separate several assignments with a comma or put each in a statement of its own:

```
mysql> SET @counter = 0, @age := 23;

Query OK, 0 rows affected (0.00 sec)
```

The alternative syntax for SET is SELECT INTO. You can initialize a single variable:

```
mysql> SELECT 0 INTO @counter;

Query OK, 1 row affected (0.00 sec)
```

Or multiple variables at once:

```
mysql> SELECT 0, 23 INTO @counter, @age;

Query OK, 1 row affected (0.00 sec)
```

The most common use of user variables is to save a result and use it later. You'll recall the following example from earlier in the chapter, which we used to motivate nested queries (which are certainly a better solution for this problem). Here, we want to find the name of the film that a particular customer rented most recently:

```
mysql> SELECT MAX(rental_date) FROM rental
    -> JOIN customer USING (customer_id)
    -> WHERE email = 'WESLEY.BULL@sakilacustomer.org';

+---------------------+
| MAX(rental_date)    |
+---------------------+
| 2005-08-23 15:46:33 |
+---------------------+
1 row in set (0.01 sec)

mysql> SELECT title FROM film
    -> JOIN inventory USING (film_id)
    -> JOIN rental USING (inventory_id)
    -> JOIN customer USING (customer_id)
    -> WHERE email = 'WESLEY.BULL@sakilacustomer.org'
    -> AND rental_date = '2005-08-23 15:46:33';
```

```
+-------------+
| title       |
+-------------+
| KARATE MOON |
+-------------+
1 row in set (0.00 sec)
```

You can use a user variable to save the result for input into the following query. Here's the same query pair rewritten using this approach:

```
mysql> SELECT MAX(rental_date) INTO @recent FROM rental
    -> JOIN customer USING (customer_id)
    -> WHERE email = 'WESLEY.BULL@sakilacustomer.org';

1 row in set (0.01 sec)

mysql> SELECT title FROM film
    -> JOIN inventory USING (film_id)
    -> JOIN rental USING (inventory_id)
    -> JOIN customer USING (customer_id)
    -> WHERE email = 'WESLEY.BULL@sakilacustomer.org'
    -> AND rental_date = @recent;

+-------------+
| title       |
+-------------+
| KARATE MOON |
+-------------+
1 row in set (0.00 sec)
```

This can save you cutting and pasting, and it certainly helps you avoid typing errors.

Here are some guidelines on using user variables:

- User variables are unique to a connection: variables that you create can't be seen by anyone else, and two different connections can have two different variables with the same name.

- The variable names can be alphanumeric strings and can also include the period (.), underscore (_), and dollar sign ($) characters.

- Variable names are case-sensitive in MySQL versions earlier than version 5, and case-insensitive from version 5 onward.

- Any variable that isn't initialized has the value NULL; you can also manually set a variable to be NULL.

- Variables are destroyed when a connection closes.

- You should avoid trying to both assign a value to a variable and use the variable as part of a SELECT query. Two reasons for this are that the new value may not be available for use immediately in the same statement, and a variable's type is set when it's first assigned in a query; trying to use it later as a different type in the same SQL statement can lead to unexpected results.

Let's look at the first issue in more detail using the new variable @fid. Since we haven't used this variable before, it's empty. Now, let's show the film_id for movies that have an entry in the inventory table. Instead of showing it directly, we'll assign the film_id to the @fid variable. Our query will show the variable three times—once before the assignment operation, once as part of the assignment operation, and once afterward:

```
mysql> SELECT @fid, @fid:=film.film_id, @fid FROM film, inventory
    -> WHERE inventory.film_id = @fid;

Empty set, 1 warning (0.16 sec)
```

This returns nothing apart from a deprecation warning; since there's nothing in the variable to start with, the WHERE clause tries to look for empty inventory.film_id values. If we modify the query to use film.film_id as part of the WHERE clause, things work as expected:

```
mysql> SELECT @fid, @fid:=film.film_id, @fid FROM film, inventory
    -> WHERE inventory.film_id = film.film_id LIMIT 20;

+------+--------------------+------+
| @fid | @fid:=film.film_id | @fid |
+------+--------------------+------+
| NULL |                  1 | 1    |
| 1    |                  1 | 1    |
| 1    |                  1 | 1    |
| ...  |                    |      |
| 4    |                  4 | 4    |
| 4    |                  4 | 4    |
+------+--------------------+------+
20 rows in set, 1 warning (0.00 sec)
```

Now that if @fid isn't empty, the initial query will produce some results:

```
mysql> SELECT @fid, @fid:=film.film_id, @fid FROM film, inventory
    -> WHERE inventory.film_id = film.film_id LIMIT 20;

+------+--------------------+------+
| @fid | @fid:=film.film_id | @fid |
+------+--------------------+------+
|    4 |                  1 |    1 |
|    1 |                  1 |    1 |
| ...  |                    |      |
|    4 |                  4 |    4 |
|    4 |                  4 |    4 |
+------+--------------------+------+
20 rows in set, 1 warning (0.00 sec)
```

It's best to avoid such circumstances where the behavior is not guaranteed and is hence unpredictable.

## CHAPTER 6

Transactions and Locking

Using locks for transaction isolation is a pillar of SQL databases—but this is also an area that can cause a lot of confusion, especially for newcomers. Developers often think that locking is a database issue and belongs to the DBA realm. The DBAs, in turn, believe this is an application issue and consequently the responsibility of the developers. This chapter will clarify what happens in situations where different processes are trying to write in the same row at the same time. It will also shed light on the behavior of read queries inside a transaction with the different types of isolation levels available in MySQL.

First, let's define the key concepts. A *transaction* is an operation performed (using one or more SQL statements) on a database as a single logical unit of work. All the SQL statements' modifications in a transaction are either committed (applied to the database) or rolled back (undone from the database) as a unit, never only partially. A database transaction must be atomic, consistent, isolated, and durable (the famous acronym *ACID*).

Locks are mechanisms used to ensure the integrity of the data stored in the database while applications and users are interacting with it. We will see that there are different types of lock, and some are more restrictive than others.

Databases would not need transactions and locks if requests were issued serially and processed in order, one at a time (a SELECT, then an INSERT, then an UPDATE, and so on). We illustrate this behavior in Figure 6-1.

However, the reality (fortunately!) is that MySQL can handle thousands of requests per second and process them in parallel, rather than serially. This chapter discusses what MySQL does to achieve this parallelism, for example, when requests to SELECT and UPDATE in the same row arrive simultaneously, or one arrives while the other is still executing. Figure 6-2 shows what this looks like.

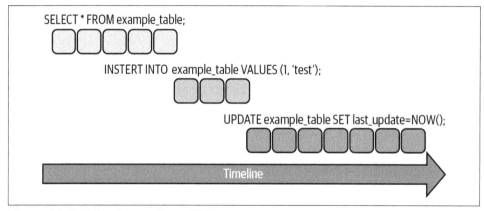

Figure 6-1. Serialized execution of SQL statements

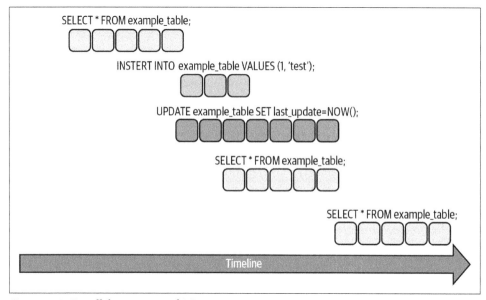

Figure 6-2. Parallel execution of SQL statements

For this chapter, we are particularly interested in how MySQL *isolates* the transactions (the *I* of ACID). We will show you common situations where locking occurs, investigate them, and discuss the MySQL parameters that control how much time a transaction can wait for a lock to be granted.

Isolation Levels

The *isolation level* is the setting that balances performance, reliability, consistency, and reproducibility of results when multiple transactions are making changes and performing queries simultaneously.

The SQL:1992 standard defines four classic isolation levels, and MySQL supports all of them. InnoDB supports each of the transaction isolation levels described here using different locking strategies. A user can also change the isolation level for a single session or all subsequent connections with the statement SET [GLOBAL/SESSION] TRANSACTION.

We can enforce a high degree of consistency with the default REPEATABLE READ isolation level for operations on data where ACID compliance is essential, and we can relax the consistency rules with READ COMMITTED or even READ UNCOMMITTED isolation in situations such as bulk reporting where precise consistency and repeatable results are less important than minimizing the amount of overhead for locking. SERIALIZABLE isolation enforces even stricter rules than REPEATABLE READ and is used mainly for special situations such as troubleshooting. Before diving into the details, let's take a look at some more terminology:

Dirty reads
> These occur when a transaction is able to read data from a row that has been modified by another transaction that has not executed a COMMIT yet. If the transaction that made the modifications gets rolled back, the other one will have seen incorrect results that do not reflect the state of the database. Data integrity is compromised.

Non-repeatable reads
> These occur when two queries in a transaction execute a SELECT and the values returned differ between the readings because of changes made by another transaction in the interim (if you read a row at time T1 and then try to read it again at time T2, the row may have been updated). The difference from a dirty read is that in this case there is a COMMIT. The initial SELECT query is not repeatable because it returns different values when issued the second time.

Phantom reads
> These occur when a transaction is running, and another transaction adds rows to or deletes them from the records being read (again, in this case there is a COMMIT by the transaction modifying the data). This means that if the same query is executed again in the same transaction, it will return a different number of rows. Phantom reads can occur when there are no range locks guaranteeing the consistency of the data.

With those concepts in mind, let's take a closer look at the different isolation levels in MySQL.

REPEATABLE READ

REPEATABLE READ is the default isolation level for InnoDB. It ensures consistent reads within the same transaction—that is, that all queries within the transaction will see the same snapshot of the data, established by the first read. In this mode, InnoDB locks the index range scanned, using gap locks or next-key locks (described in "Locking" on page 248) to block insertions by other sessions into any gaps within that range.

For example, suppose that in one session (session 1), we execute the following SELECT:

```
session1 > SELECT * FROM person WHERE i BETWEEN 1 AND 4;

+---+----------+
| i | name     |
+---+----------+
| 1 | Vinicius |
| 2 | Sergey   |
| 3 | Iwo      |
| 4 | Peter    |
+---+----------+
4 rows in set (0.00 sec)
```

And in another session (session 2), we update the name in the second row:

```
session2 > UPDATE person SET name = 'Kuzmichev' WHERE i=2;

Query OK, 1 row affected (0.00 sec)
Rows matched: 1  Changed: 1  Warnings: 0

session2> COMMIT;

Query OK, 0 rows affected (0.00 sec)
```

We can confirm the change in session 2:

```
session2 > SELECT * FROM person WHERE i BETWEEN 1 AND 4;

+---+-----------+
| i | name      |
+---+-----------+
| 1 | Vinicius  |
| 2 | Kuzmichev |
| 3 | Iwo       |
| 4 | Peter     |
+---+-----------+
4 rows in set (0.00 sec)
```

But session 1 still shows the old value from its original snapshot of the data:

```
session1> SELECT * FROM person WHERE i BETWEEN 1 AND 4;

+---+----------+
| i | name     |
+---+----------+
| 1 | Vinicius |
| 2 | Sergey   |
| 3 | Iwo      |
| 4 | Peter    |
+---+----------+
```

With the REPEATABLE READ isolation level, there are thus no dirty reads and or non-repeatable reads. Each transaction reads the snapshot established by the first read.

READ COMMITTED

As a curiosity, the READ COMMITTED isolation level is the default for many databases, like Postgres, Oracle, and SQL Server, but not MySQL. So, those who are migrating to MySQL must be aware of this difference in the default behavior.

The main difference between READ COMMITTED and REPEATABLE READ is that with READ COMMITTED each consistent read, even within the same transaction, creates and reads its own fresh snapshot. This behavior can lead to *phantom reads* when executing multiple queries inside a transaction. Let's take a look at an example. In session 1, row 1 looks like this:

```
session1 > SELECT * FROM person WHERE i = 1;

+---+----------+
| i | name     |
+---+----------+
| 1 | Vinicius |
+---+----------+
1 row in set (0.00 sec)
```

Now suppose that in session 2 we update the first row of the person table and commit the transaction:

```
session2 > UPDATE person SET name = 'Grippa' WHERE i = 1;

Query OK, 1 row affected (0.00 sec)
Rows matched: 1  Changed: 1  Warnings: 0

session2 > COMMIT;

Query OK, 0 rows affected (0.00 sec)
```

If we check session 1 again, we'll see that the value of the first row has changed:

```
session1 > SELECT * FROM person WHERE i = 1;
```

```
+---+--------+
| i | name   |
+---+--------+
| 1 | Grippa |
+---+--------+
```

The significant advantage of READ COMMITTED is that there are no gap locks, allowing the free insertion of new records next to locked records.

READ UNCOMMITTED

With the READ UNCOMMITTED isolation level MySQL performs SELECT statements in a non-locking fashion, which means two SELECT statements within the same transaction might not read the same version of a row. As we saw earlier, this phenomenon is called a dirty read. Consider how the previous example would play out using READ UNCOMMITTED. The main difference is that session 1 can see the results of session 2's update *before* the commit. Let's walk through another example. Suppose that in session 1 we execute the following SELECT statement:

```
session1 > SELECT * FROM person WHERE i = 5;

+---+---------+
| i | name    |
+---+---------+
| 5 | Marcelo |
+---+---------+
1 row in set (0.00 sec)
```

And in session 2, we perform this update *without* committing:

```
session2 > UPDATE person SET name = 'Altmann' WHERE i = 5;

Query OK, 1 row affected (0.00 sec)
Rows matched: 1  Changed: 1  Warnings: 0
```

If we now perform the SELECT again in session 1, here's what we'll see:

```
session1 > SELECT * FROM person WHERE i = 5;

+---+---------+
| i | name    |
+---+---------+
| 5 | Altmann |
+---+---------+
1 row in set (0.00 sec)
```

We can see that session 1 can read the modified data even though it is in a transient state, and this change may end up being rolled back and not committed.

SERIALIZABLE

The most restricted isolation level available in MySQL is `SERIALIZABLE`. This is similar to `REPEATABLE READ`, but has an additional restriction of not allowing one transaction to interfere with another. So, with this locking mechanism, the inconsistent data scenario is no longer possible.

 For applications using `SERIALIZABLE`, it is important to have a retry strategy.

To make this clearer, imagine a finance database where we register customers' account balances in an `accounts` table. What will happen if two transactions try to update a customer's account balance at the same time? The following example illustrates this scenario. Assume that we have started two sessions using the default isolation level, `REPEATABLE READ`, and explicitly opened a transaction in each with `BEGIN`. In session 1, we select all the accounts in the `accounts` table:

```
session1> SELECT * FROM accounts;

+----+--------+---------+----------+---------------------+
| id | owner  | balance | currency | created_at          |
+----+--------+---------+----------+---------------------+
|  1 | Vinnie |      80 | USD      | 2021-07-13 20:39:27 |
|  2 | Sergey |     100 | USD      | 2021-07-13 20:39:32 |
|  3 | Markus |     100 | USD      | 2021-07-13 20:39:39 |
+----+--------+---------+----------+---------------------+
3 rows in set (0.00 sec)
```

Then, in session 2, we select all accounts with balance of at least 80 USD:

```
session2> SELECT * FROM accounts WHERE balance >= 80;

+----+--------+---------+----------+---------------------+
| id | owner  | balance | currency | created_at          |
+----+--------+---------+----------+---------------------+
|  1 | Vinnie |      80 | USD      | 2021-07-13 20:39:27 |
|  2 | Sergey |     100 | USD      | 2021-07-13 20:39:32 |
|  3 | Markus |     100 | USD      | 2021-07-13 20:39:39 |
+----+--------+---------+----------+---------------------+
3 rows in set (0.00 sec)
```

Now, in session 1, we subtract 10 USD from account 1 and check the result:

```
session1> UPDATE accounts SET balance = balance - 10 WHERE id = 1;
Query OK, 1 row affected (0.00 sec)
Rows matched: 1  Changed: 1  Warnings: 0

session1> SELECT * FROM accounts;
```

```
+----+--------+---------+----------+---------------------+
| id | owner  | balance | currency | created_at          |
+----+--------+---------+----------+---------------------+
|  1 | Vinnie |      70 | USD      | 2021-07-13 20:39:27 |
|  2 | Sergey |     100 | USD      | 2021-07-13 20:39:32 |
|  3 | Markus |     100 | USD      | 2021-07-13 20:39:39 |
+----+--------+---------+----------+---------------------+
3 rows in set (0.00 sec)
```

We can see that the balance of account 1 has decreased to 70 USD. So, we commit session 1 and then move to session 2 to see if it can read the new changes made by session 1:

```
session1> COMMIT;

Query OK, 0 rows affected (0.01 sec)

session2> SELECT * FROM accounts WHERE id = 1;

+----+--------+---------+----------+---------------------+
| id | owner  | balance | currency | created_at          |
+----+--------+---------+----------+---------------------+
|  1 | Vinnie |      80 | USD      | 2021-07-13 20:39:27 |
+----+--------+---------+----------+---------------------+
1 row in set (0.01 sec)
```

This SELECT query still returns the old data for account 1, with a balance of 80 USD, even though transaction 1 changed it to 70 USD and was committed successfully. That's because the REPEATABLE READ isolation level ensures that all read queries in a transaction are repeatable, which means they always return the same result, even if changes have been made by other committed transactions.

But what will happen if we also run the UPDATE query to subtract 10 USD from account 1's balance in session 2? Will it change the balance to 70 USD, or 60 USD, or throw an error? Let's see:

```
session2> UPDATE accounts SET balance = balance - 10 WHERE id = 1;

Query OK, 1 row affected (0.00 sec)
Rows matched: 1  Changed: 1  Warnings: 0

session2> SELECT * FROM accounts WHERE id = 1;

+----+--------+---------+----------+---------------------+
| id | owner  | balance | currency | created_at          |
+----+--------+---------+----------+---------------------+
|  1 | Vinnie |      60 | USD      | 2021-07-13 20:39:27 |
+----+--------+---------+----------+---------------------+
1 row in set (0.01 sec)
```

There's no error, and the account balance is now 60 USD, which is the correct value because transaction 1 has already committed the change that modified the balance to 70 USD.

However, from transaction 2's point of view, this doesn't make sense: in the last SELECT query it saw a balance of 80 USD, but after subtracting 10 USD from the account, now it sees a balance of 60 USD. The math doesn't work here because this transaction is still being affected by concurrent updates from other transactions.

This is the scenario where using SERIALIZABLE can help. Let's rewind to before we made any changes. This time we'll explicitly set the isolation level of both sessions to SERIALIZABLE with SET SESSION TRANSACTION ISOLATION LEVEL SERIALIZABLE before starting the transactions with BEGIN. Again, in session 1 we select all the accounts:

```
session1> SELECT * FROM accounts;
```

```
+----+--------+---------+----------+---------------------+
| id | owner  | balance | currency | created_at          |
+----+--------+---------+----------+---------------------+
|  1 | Vinnie |      80 | USD      | 2021-07-13 20:39:27 |
|  2 | Sergey |     100 | USD      | 2021-07-13 20:39:32 |
|  3 | Markus |     100 | USD      | 2021-07-13 20:39:39 |
+----+--------+---------+----------+---------------------+
3 rows in set (0.00 sec)
```

And in session 2 we select all the accounts with a balance greater than 80 USD:

```
session2> SELECT * FROM accounts WHERE balance >= 80;
```

```
+----+--------+---------+----------+---------------------+
| id | owner  | balance | currency | created_at          |
+----+--------+---------+----------+---------------------+
|  1 | Vinnie |      80 | USD      | 2021-07-13 20:39:27 |
|  2 | Sergey |     100 | USD      | 2021-07-13 20:39:32 |
|  3 | Markus |     100 | USD      | 2021-07-13 20:39:39 |
+----+--------+---------+----------+---------------------+
3 rows in set (0.00 sec)
```

Now, in session 1 we subtract 10 USD from account 1:

```
session1> UPDATE accounts SET balance = balance - 10 WHERE id = 1;
```

And…nothing happens. This time the UPDATE query is blocked—the SELECT query in session 1 has locked those rows and prevents the UPDATE in session 2 from succeeding. Because we explicitly started our transactions with BEGIN (which has the same effect as disabling autocommit), InnoDB implicitly converts all plain SELECT statements in each transaction to SELECT ... FOR SHARE. It does not know ahead of time if the transaction will perform only reads or will modify rows, so InnoDB needs to place a lock on it to avoid the issue we demonstrated in the previous example. In this example, if autocommit were enabled, the SELECT query in session 2 would not block the update that we are trying to perform in session 1: MySQL would recognize that the query is a plain SELECT and does not need to block other queries because it is not going to modify any rows.

However, the update in session 2 will not hang forever; this lock has a timeout duration that is controlled by the innodb_lock_wait_timeout parameter (*https://oreil.ly/rfrv0*). So, if session 1 doesn't commit or roll back its transaction to release the lock, once the session timeout is reached, MySQL will throw the following error:

```
ERROR 1205 (HY000): Lock wait timeout exceeded; try restarting transaction
```

Locking

Now that we've seen how each isolation level works, let's look at the different locking strategies InnoDB employs to implement them.

Locks are used in databases to protect shared resources or objects. They can act at different levels, such as:

- Table locking
- Metadata locking
- Row locking
- Application-level locking

MySQL uses metadata locking to manage concurrent access to database objects and to ensure data consistency. When there is an active transaction (explicit or implicit) on the table, MySQL does not allow writing of metadata (DDL statements, for example, update the metadata of the table). It does this to maintain metadata consistency in a concurrent environment.

If there is an active transaction (running, uncommitted, or rolled back) when a session performs one of the operations mentioned in the following list, the session requesting the data write will be held in the Waiting for table metadata lock status. A metadata lock wait may occur in any of the following scenarios:

- When you create or delete an index
- When you modify the table structure
- When you perform table maintenance operations (OPTIMIZE TABLE REPAIR TABLE, etc.)
- When you delete a table
- When you try to obtain a table-level write lock on the table (LOCK TABLE table_name WRITE)

To enable simultaneous write access by multiple sessions, InnoDB supports row-level locking.

Application-level or user-level locks, such as those provided by GET_LOCK(), can be used to simulate database locks such as record locks.

This book focuses on metadata and the row locks since they are the ones that affect the majority of users and are the most common.

Metadata Locks

The MySQL documentation (*https://oreil.ly/zjDjG*) provides the best definition of metadata locks:

> To ensure transaction serializability, the server must not permit one session to perform a data definition language (DDL) statement on a table that is used in an uncompleted explicitly or implicitly started transaction in another session. The server achieves this by acquiring metadata locks on tables used within a transaction and deferring the locks' release until the transaction ends. A metadata lock on a table prevents changes to the table's structure. This locking approach has the implication that a table that is being used by a transaction within one session cannot be used in DDL statements by other sessions until the transaction ends.

With this definition in mind, let's take a look at metadata locking in action. First, we will create a dummy table and load some rows into it:

```
USE test;

DROP TABLE IF EXISTS `joinit`;

CREATE TABLE `joinit` (
  `i` int(11) NOT NULL AUTO_INCREMENT,
  `s` varchar(64) DEFAULT NULL,
  `t` time NOT NULL,
  `g` int(11) NOT NULL,
  PRIMARY KEY (`i`)
) ENGINE=InnoDB  DEFAULT CHARSET=latin1;

INSERT INTO joinit VALUES (NULL, uuid(), time(now()),  (FLOOR( 1 +
RAND( ) *60 )));
INSERT INTO joinit SELECT NULL, uuid(), time(now()),  (FLOOR( 1 + RAND( ) *60 ))
FROM joinit;
INSERT INTO joinit SELECT NULL, uuid(), time(now()),  (FLOOR( 1 + RAND( ) *60 ))
FROM joinit;
INSERT INTO joinit SELECT NULL, uuid(), time(now()),  (FLOOR( 1 + RAND( ) *60 ))
FROM joinit;
INSERT INTO joinit SELECT NULL, uuid(), time(now()),  (FLOOR( 1 + RAND( ) *60 ))
FROM joinit;
INSERT INTO joinit SELECT NULL, uuid(), time(now()),  (FLOOR( 1 + RAND( ) *60 ))
FROM joinit;
INSERT INTO joinit SELECT NULL, uuid(), time(now()),  (FLOOR( 1 + RAND( ) *60 ))
FROM joinit;
INSERT INTO joinit SELECT NULL, uuid(), time(now()),  (FLOOR( 1 + RAND( ) *60 ))
FROM joinit;
```

```
INSERT INTO joinit SELECT NULL, uuid(), time(now()),  (FLOOR( 1 + RAND( ) *60 ))
FROM joinit;
```

Now that we have some dummy data, we will open one session (session 1) and execute an UPDATE:

```
session1> UPDATE joinit SET t=now();
```

Then, in a second session, we will try to add a new column to this table while the UPDATE is still running:

```
session2> ALTER TABLE joinit ADD COLUMN b INT;
```

And in a third session, we can execute the SHOW PROCESSLIST command to visualize the metadata lock:

```
session3> SHOW PROCESSLIST;
+----+----------+-----------+------+---------+------+...
| Id | User     | Host      | db   | Command | Time |...
+----+----------+-----------+------+---------+------+...
| 10 | msandbox | localhost | test | Query   |    3 |...
| 11 | msandbox | localhost | test | Query   |    1 |...
| 12 | msandbox | localhost | NULL | Query   |    0 |...
+----+----------+-----------+------+---------+------+...

...+------------------------------------+------------------------------------------+...
...| State                              | Info                                     |...
...+------------------------------------+------------------------------------------+...
...| updating                           | UPDATE joinit SET t=now()                |...
...| Waiting for table metadata lock    | ALTER TABLE joinit ADD COLUMN b INT      |...
...| starting                           | SHOW PROCESSLIST                         |...
...+------------------------------------+------------------------------------------+...

...+-----------+---------------+
...| Rows_sent | Rows_examined |
...+-----------+---------------+
...|         0 |        179987 |
...|         0 |             0 |
...|         0 |             0 |
...+-----------+---------------+
```

Note that a long-running query or a query that is not using autocommit will have the same effect. For example, suppose we have an UPDATE running in session 1:

```
mysql > SET SESSION autocommit=0;

Query OK, 0 rows affected (0.00 sec)

mysql > UPDATE joinit SET t=NOW() LIMIT 1;

Query OK, 1 row affected (0.00 sec)
Rows matched: 1  Changed: 1  Warnings: 0
```

And we execute a DML statement in session 2:

```
mysql > ALTER TABLE joinit ADD COLUMN b INT;
```

If we check the process list in session 3, we can see the DDL waiting on the metadata lock (thread 11), while thread 10 has been sleeping since it executed the UPDATE (still not committed):

```
mysql > SHOW PROCESSLIST;
```

 MySQL is multithreaded, so there may be many clients issuing queries for a given table simultaneously. To minimize the problem with multiple client sessions having different states for the same table, each concurrent session opens the table independently. This uses additional memory but typically increases performance.

Before we start using the sys schema, it is necessary to enable MySQL instrumentation to monitor these locks. To do this, run the following command:

```
mysql> UPDATE performance_schema.setup_instruments SET enabled = 'YES'
    -> WHERE NAME = 'wait/lock/metadata/sql/mdl';
Query OK, 0 rows affected (0.00 sec)
Rows matched: 1 Changed: 0 Warnings: 0
```

The following query uses the schema_table_lock_waits view from the sys schema to illustrate how to observe metadata locks in the MySQL database:

```
mysql> SELECT * FROM sys.schema_table_lock_waits;
```

This view displays which sessions are blocked waiting on metadata locks and what is blocking them. Rather than selecting all fields, the following example shows a more compact view:

```
mysql> SELECT object_name, waiting_thread_id, waiting_lock_type,
    -> waiting_query, sql_kill_blocking_query, blocking_thread_id
    -> FROM sys.schema_table_lock_waits;
+-------------+-------------------+-------------------+...
| object_name | waiting_thread_id | waiting_lock_type |...
+-------------+-------------------+-------------------+...
| joinit      |                29 | EXCLUSIVE         |...
| joinit      |                29 | EXCLUSIVE         |...
+-------------+-------------------+-------------------+...
...+----------------------------------------------------------------+...
...| waiting_query                                                  |...
...+----------------------------------------------------------------+...
...| ALTER TABLE joinit ADD COLUMN  ...  CHAR(32) DEFAULT 'dummy_text' |...
...| ALTER TABLE joinit ADD COLUMN  ...  CHAR(32) DEFAULT 'dummy_text' |...
...|-----------------------------------------------------------------+...
```

```
...+-----------------------------+-------------------+
...| sql_kill_blocking_query     | blocking_thread_id |
...+-----------------------------+-------------------+
...| KILL QUERY 3                |                29 |
...| KILL QUERY 5                |                31 |
...+-----------------------------+-------------------+
2 rows in set (0.00 sec)
```

 The MySQL sys schema is a set of objects that helps DBAs and developers interpret data collected by the Performance Schema, a feature for monitoring MySQL Server execution at a low level. It is available for MySQL 5.7 and MySQL 8.0. If you want to use the sys schema in MySQL 5.6, it is possible to install it using the sys project available on GitHub:

```
# git clone https://github.com/mysql/mysql-sys.git
# cd mysql-sys/
# mysql -u root -p < ./sys_56.sql
```

Let's see what happens when we query the metadata_locks table:

```
mysql> SELECT * FROM performance_schema.metadata_locks\G

*************************** 1. row ***************************
            OBJECT_TYPE: GLOBAL
          OBJECT_SCHEMA: NULL
            OBJECT_NAME: NULL
  OBJECT_INSTANCE_BEGIN: 140089691017472
              LOCK_TYPE: INTENTION_EXCLUSIVE
          LOCK_DURATION: STATEMENT
            LOCK_STATUS: GRANTED
                 SOURCE:
        OWNER_THREAD_ID: 97
         OWNER_EVENT_ID: 34
...
*************************** 6. row ***************************
            OBJECT_TYPE: TABLE
          OBJECT_SCHEMA: performance_schema
            OBJECT_NAME: metadata_locks
  OBJECT_INSTANCE_BEGIN: 140089640911984
              LOCK_TYPE: SHARED_READ
          LOCK_DURATION: TRANSACTION
            LOCK_STATUS: GRANTED
                 SOURCE:
        OWNER_THREAD_ID: 98
         OWNER_EVENT_ID: 10
6 rows in set (0.00 sec)
```

Note that a SHARED_UPGRADABLE lock is set on the joinit table, and an EXCLUSIVE lock is pending on the same table.

We can get a nice view of all metadata locks from other sessions, excluding our current one, with the following query:

```
mysql> SELECT object_type, object_schema, object_name, lock_type,
    -> lock_status, thread_id, processlist_id, processlist_info FROM
    -> performance_schema.metadata_locks INNER JOIN performance_schema.threads
    -> ON thread_id = owner_thread_id WHERE processlist_id <> connection_id();
```

OBJECT_TYPE	OBJECT_SCHEMA	OBJECT_NAME	LOCK_TYPE	...
GLOBAL	NULL	NULL	INTENTION_EXCLUSIVE	...
SCHEMA	test	NULL	INTENTION_EXCLUSIVE	...
TABLE	test	joinit	SHARED_UPGRADABLE	...
BACKUP	NULL	NULL	INTENTION_EXCLUSIVE	...
TABLE	test	joinit	EXCLUSIVE	...

...	LOCK_STATUS	THREAD_ID	PROCESSLIST_ID	...
...	GRANTED	97	71	...
...	GRANTED	97	71	...
...	GRANTED	97	71	...
...	GRANTED	97	71	...
...	PENDING	97	71	...

...	PROCESSLIST_INFO
...	alter table joinit add column b int
...	alter table joinit add column b int
...	alter table joinit add column b int
...	alter table joinit add column b int
...	alter table joinit add column b int

```
5 rows in set (0.00 sec)
```

If we look carefully, a DDL statement waiting for a query on its own is not a problem: it will have to wait until it can acquire the metadata lock, which is expected. The problem is that while waiting, it blocks every other query from accessing the resource.

We recommend the following actions to avoid long metadata locks:

- Perform DDL operations in non-busy times. This way you reduce the concurrency in the database between the regular application workload and the extra workload that the operation carries.

- Always use autocommit. MySQL has autocommit enabled by default. This will avoid transactions with pending commits.

- When performing a DDL operation, set a low value for `lock_wait_timeout` at the session level. Then, if the metadata lock can't be acquired, it won't block for a long time waiting. For example:

```
mysql> SET lock_wait_timeout = 3;
mysql> CREATE INDEX idx_1 ON example (col1);
```

You might also want to consider using the `pt-kill` tool (*https://oreil.ly/C4rMb*) to kill queries that have been running for a long time. For example, to kill queries that have been running for more than 60 seconds, issue this command:

```
$ pt-kill --busy-time 60 --kill
```

Row Locks

InnoDB implements standard row-level locking. This means that, in general terms, there are two types of locks:

- A *shared* (S) lock permits the transaction that holds the lock to read a row.
- An *exclusive* (X) lock permits the transaction that holds the lock to update or delete a row.

The names are self-explanatory: exclusive locks don't allow multiple transactions to acquire an exclusive lock in the same row while sharing a shared lock. That is why it is possible to have parallel reads for the same row, while parallel writes are not allowed.

InnoDB also supports multiple granularity locking, which permits the coexistence of row locks and table locks. Granular locking is possible due to the existence of *intention locks*, which are table-level locks that indicate which type of lock (shared or exclusive) a transaction requires later for a row in a table. There are two types of intention locks:

- An *intention shared* (IS) lock indicates that a transaction intends to set a shared lock on individual rows in a table.
- An *intention exclusive* (IX) lock indicates that a transaction intends to set an exclusive lock on individual rows in a table.

Before a transaction can acquire a shared or an exclusive lock, it is necessary to obtain the respective intention lock (IS or IX).

To make things a bit easier to understand, take a look at Table 6-1.

Table 6-1. Lock type compatibility matrix

	X	IX	S	IS
X	Conflict	Conflict	Conflict	Conflict
IX	Conflict	Compatible	Conflict	Compatible
S	Conflict	Conflict	Compatible	Compatible
IS	Conflict	Compatible	Compatible	Compatible

Another important concept is the *gap lock*, which is a lock on the gap between index records. Gap locks ensure that no new rows are added in the interval specified by the query; this means that when you run the same query twice, you get the same number of rows, regardless of other sessions' modifications to that table. They make the reads consistent and therefore make the replication between servers consistent. If you execute SELECT * FROM example_table WHERE id > 1000 FOR UPDATE twice, you expect to get the same result twice. To accomplish that, InnoDB locks all index records found by the WHERE clause with an exclusive lock and the gaps between them with a shared gap lock.

Let's see an example of a gap lock in action. First, we will execute a SELECT statement on the person table:

```
mysql> SELECT * FROM PERSON;

+----+-----------+
| i  | name      |
+----+-----------+
|  1 | Vinicius  |
|  2 | Kuzmichev |
|  3 | Iwo       |
|  4 | Peter     |
|  5 | Marcelo   |
|  6 | Guli      |
|  7 | Nando     |
| 10 | Jobin     |
| 15 | Rafa      |
| 18 | Leo       |
+----+-----------+
10 rows in set (0.00 sec)
```

Now, in session 1, we will perform a delete operation, but we will *not* commit:

```
session1> DELETE FROM person WHERE name LIKE 'Jobin';

Query OK, 1 row affected (0.00 sec)
```

And if we check in session 2, we can still see the row with Jobin:

```
session2> SELECT * FROM person;

+----+-----------+
| i  | name      |
+----+-----------+
|  1 | Vinicius  |
|  2 | Kuzmichev |
|  3 | Iwo       |
|  4 | Peter     |
|  5 | Marcelo   |
|  6 | Guli      |
|  7 | Nando     |
| 10 | Jobin     |
| 15 | Rafa      |
| 18 | Leo       |
+----+-----------+
10 rows in set (0.00 sec)
```

The results show that there are gaps in the values of the primary key column that in theory are available to be used to insert new records. So what happens if we try to insert a new row with a value of 11? The insert will be locked and will fail:

```
transaction2 > INSERT INTO person VALUES (11, 'Bennie');

ERROR 1205 (HY000): Lockwait timeout exceeded; try restarting transaction
```

If we run SHOW ENGINE INNODB STATUS, we will see the locked transaction in the TRANSACTIONS section:

```
------- TRX HAS BEEN WAITING 17 SEC FOR THIS LOCK TO BE GRANTED:
RECORD LOCKS space id 28 page no 3 n bits 80 index PRIMARY of table
`test`.`person` trx id 4773 lock_mode X locks gap before rec insert
intention waiting
```

Note that MySQL does not need gap locking for statements that lock rows using a unique index to search for a unique row. (This does not include the case where the search condition includes only some columns of a multiple-column unique index; in that case, gap locking does occur.) For example, if the name column has a unique index, the following DELETE statement uses only an index-record lock:

```
mysql> CREATE UNIQUE INDEX idx ON PERSON (name);

Query OK, 0 rows affected (0.01 sec)
Records: 0  Duplicates: 0  Warnings: 0

mysql> DELETE FROM person WHERE name LIKE 'Jobin';

Query OK, 1 row affected (0.00 sec)
```

Deadlocks

A *deadlock* is a situation where two (or more) competing actions are waiting for the other to finish. As a consequence, neither ever does. In computer science, the term refers to a specific condition where two or more processes are each waiting for another to release a resource. In this section, we will talk specifically about transaction deadlocks and how InnoDB solves this issue.

For a deadlock to happen, four conditions (known as the *Coffman conditions*) must exist:

1. *Mutual exclusion.* The process must hold at least one resource in a non-shareable mode. Otherwise, MySQL would not prevent the process from using the resource when necessary. Only one process can use the resource at any given moment in time.
2. *Hold and wait or resource holding.* A process is currently holding at least one resource and requesting additional resources held by other processes.
3. *No preemption.* A resource can be released only voluntarily by the process holding it.
4. *Circular wait.* Each process must be waiting for a resource held by another process, which in turn is waiting for the first process to release the resource.

Before moving on to an example, there are some misconceptions that you might hear and that it is essential to clarify. They are:

Transaction isolation levels are responsible for deadlocks.
The possibility of deadlocks is not affected by the isolation level. The READ COM MITTED isolation level sets fewer locks, and hence it can help you avoid certain lock types (e.g., gap locking), but it won't prevent deadlocks entirely.

Small transactions are not affected by deadlocks.
Small transactions are less prone to deadlocks because they run fast, so the chance of a conflict occurring is smaller than with more prolonged operations. However, it can still happen if transactions do not use the same order of operations.

Deadlocks are terrible things.
It's problematic to have deadlocks in a database, but InnoDB can resolve them automatically, unless deadlock detection is disabled (by changing the value of innodb_deadlock_detect). A deadlock is a a bad situation, but resolution through the termination of one of the transactions ensures that processes cannot hold onto the resources for a long time, slowing or stalling the database completely until the offending query gets canceled by the innodb_lock_wait_time out setting.

To illustrate deadlocks, we'll use the `world` database. If you need to import it, you can do so now by following the instructions in "Entity Relationship Modeling Examples" on page 77.

Let's start by getting a list of Italian cities in the province of Toscana:

```
mysql> SELECT * FROM city WHERE CountryCode = 'ITA' AND District='Toscana';

+------+---------+-------------+----------+------------+
| ID   | Name    | CountryCode | District | Population |
+------+---------+-------------+----------+------------+
| 1471 | Firenze | ITA         | Toscana  |     376662 |
| 1483 | Prato   | ITA         | Toscana  |     172473 |
| 1486 | Livorno | ITA         | Toscana  |     161673 |
| 1516 | Pisa    | ITA         | Toscana  |      92379 |
| 1518 | Arezzo  | ITA         | Toscana  |      91729 |
+------+---------+-------------+----------+------------+
5 rows in set (0.00 sec)
```

Now let's say we have two transactions trying to update the populations of the same two cities in Toscana at the same time, but in different orders:

```
session1> UPDATE city SET Population=Population + 1 WHERE ID = 1471;

Query OK, 1 row affected (0.00 sec)
Rows matched: 1  Changed: 1  Warnings: 0

session2> UPDATE city SET Population=Population + 1 WHERE ID =1516;

Query OK, 1 row affected (0.00 sec)
Rows matched: 1  Changed: 1  Warnings: 0

session1> UPDATE city SET Population=Population + 1 WHERE ID =1516;

ERROR 1213 (40001): Deadlock found when trying to get lock; try restarting transaction

session2> UPDATE city SET Population=Population + 1 WHERE ID = 1471;

Query OK, 1 row affected (5.15 sec)
Rows matched: 1  Changed: 1  Warnings: 0
```

And we had a deadlock in session 1. It is important to note that it is not always the second transaction that will fail. In this example, session 1 was the one that MySQL aborted. We can get information on the latest deadlock that happened in the MySQL database by running SHOW ENGINE INNODB STATUS:

```
mysql> SHOW ENGINE INNODB STATUS\G

------------------------
LATEST DETECTED DEADLOCK
------------------------
2020-12-05 16:08:19 0x7f6949359700
*** (1) TRANSACTION:
TRANSACTION 10502342, ACTIVE 34 sec starting index read
mysql tables in use 1, locked 1
LOCK WAIT 3 lock struct(s), heap size 1136, 2 row lock(s), undo log
```

```
entries 1
MySQL thread id 71, OS thread handle 140090386671360, query id 5979282
localhost msandbox updating
update city set Population=Population + 1 where ID = 1471
*** (1) WAITING FOR THIS LOCK TO BE GRANTED:
RECORD LOCKS space id 6041 page no 15 n bits 248 index PRIMARY of table
`world`.`city` trx id 10502342 lock_mode X locks rec but not gap waiting
*** (2) TRANSACTION:
TRANSACTION 10502341, ACTIVE 62 sec starting index read
mysql tables in use 1, locked 1
3 lock struct(s), heap size 1136, 2 row lock(s), undo log entries 1
MySQL thread id 75, OS thread handle 140090176542464, query id 5979283
localhost msandbox updating
update city set Population=Population + 1 where ID =1516
*** (2) HOLDS THE LOCK(S):
RECORD LOCKS space id 6041 page no 15 n bits 248 index PRIMARY of table
`world`.`city` trx id 10502341 lock_mode X locks rec but not gap
*** (2) WAITING FOR THIS LOCK TO BE GRANTED:
RECORD LOCKS space id 6041 page no 16 n bits 248 index PRIMARY of table
`world`.`city` trx id 10502341 lock_mode X locks rec but not gap waiting
*** WE ROLL BACK TRANSACTION (2)
...
```

If you want, you can log all the deadlocks that happen in MySQL in the MySQL error log. Using the `innodb_print_all_deadlocks` parameter, MySQL records all information about deadlocks from InnoDB user transactions in the error log. Otherwise, you see information about only the last deadlock using the `SHOW ENGINE INNODB STATUS` command.

MySQL Parameters Related to Isolation and Locks

To round out this chapter, let's take a look at a few MySQL parameters that are related to isolation behavior and lock duration:

`transaction_isolation`
Sets the transaction isolation level. This parameter can change the behavior at the `GLOBAL`, `SESSION`, or `NEXT_TRANSACTION` level:

```
mysql> SET SESSION transaction_isolation='READ-COMMITTED';

Query OK, 0 rows affected (0.00 sec)

mysql> SHOW SESSION VARIABLES LIKE '%isol%';

+-----------------------+----------------+
| Variable_name         | Value          |
+-----------------------+----------------+
| transaction_isolation | READ-COMMITTED |
| tx_isolation          | READ-COMMITTED |
+-----------------------+----------------+
```

transaction_isolation was added in MySQL 5.7.20 as a synonym for tx_isolation, which is now deprecated and has been removed in MySQL 8.0. Applications should be adjusted to use transaction_isolation in preference to tx_isolation.

innodb_lock_wait_timeout

Specifies the amount of time in seconds an InnoDB transaction waits for a row lock before giving up. The default value is 50 seconds. The transaction raises the following error if the time waiting for the lock exceeds the innodb_lock_wait_timeout value:

```
ERROR 1205 (HY000): Lock wait timeout exceeded; try restarting transaction
```

innodb_print_all_deadlocks

Causes MySQL to record information about all deadlocks resulting from InnoDB user transactions in the MySQL error log. We can enable this dynamically with the following command:

```
mysql> SET GLOBAL innodb_print_all_deadlocks = 1;
```

lock_wait_timeout

Specifies the timeout in seconds for attempts to acquire metadata locks. To avoid long metadata locks stalling the database, we can set lock_wait_timeout=1 at the session level before executing the DDL statement. In this case, if the operation can't acquire the lock, it will give up and let other requests execute. For example:

```
mysql> SET SESSION lock_wait_timeout=1;
mysql> CREATE TABLE t1(i INT NOT NULL AUTO_INCREMENT PRIMARY KEY)
    -> ENGINE=InnoDB;
```

innodb_deadlock_detect

Disables deadlock monitoring. Note that this only means that MySQL will not kill a query to undo the deadlock knot. Disabling deadlock detection will *not* prevent deadlocks from happening, but it will make MySQL rely on the innodb_lock_wait_timeout setting for transaction rollback when a deadlock occurs.

## CHAPTER 7

Doing More with MySQL

MySQL is feature-rich. Over the past three chapters, you've seen the wide variety of techniques that can be used to query, modify, and manage data. However, there's still much more that MySQL can do, and some of those additional features are the subject of this chapter.

In this chapter, you'll learn how to:

- Insert data into a database from other sources, including with queries and from text files.
- Perform updates and deletes using multiple tables in a single statement.
- Replace data.
- Use MySQL functions in queries to meet more complex information needs.
- Analyze queries using the EXPLAIN statement and then improve their performance with simple optimization techniques.
- Use alternative storage engines to change table properties.

Inserting Data Using Queries

Much of the time, you'll create tables using data from another source. The examples you saw in Chapter 3 therefore illustrate only part of the problem: they show you how to insert data that's already in the form you want (that is, formatted as a SQL INSERT statement). The other ways to insert data include using SQL SELECT statements on other tables or databases and reading in files from other sources. This section shows you how to tackle the former method of inserting data; you'll learn how to insert data from a file of comma-separated values in the next section, "Loading Data from Comma-Delimited Files" on page 267.

Suppose we've decided to create a new table in the sakila database. It's going to store a random list of movies that we want to advertise more heavily. In the real world, you'd probably want to use some data science to find out what movies to highlight, but we're going to stick to the basics. This list of films will be a way for customers to check out different parts of the catalog, rediscover some old favorites, and learn about hidden treasures they haven't yet explored. We've decided to structure the table as follows:

```
mysql> CREATE TABLE recommend
    ->     film_id SMALLINT UNSIGNED,
    ->     language_id TINYINT UNSIGNED,
    ->     release_year YEAR,
    ->     title VARCHAR(128),
    ->     length SMALLINT UNSIGNED,
    ->     sequence_id SMALLINT AUTO_INCREMENT,
    ->     PRIMARY KEY (sequence_id)
    -> );
Query OK, 0 rows affected (0.05 sec)
```

This table stores a few details about each film, allowing you to find the actor, category, and other information using simple queries on the other tables. It also stores a sequence_id, which is a unique number that enumerates where the film is in our short list. When you start using the recommendation feature, you'll first see the movie with a sequence_id of 1, then 2, and so on. You can see that we're using the MySQL AUTO_INCREMENT feature to allocate the sequence_id values.

Now we need to fill up our new recommend table with a random selection of films. Importantly, we're going to do the SELECT and INSERT together in one statement. Here we go:

```
mysql> INSERT INTO recommend (film_id, language_id, release_year, title, length)
    -> SELECT film_id, language_id, release_year, title, length
    -> FROM film ORDER BY RAND() LIMIT 10;
Query OK, 10 rows affected (0.02 sec)
Records: 10  Duplicates: 0  Warnings: 0
```

Now, let's investigate what happened before we explain how this command works:

```
mysql> SELECT * FROM recommend;
+---------+-----+--------------------+--------+-------------+
| film_id | ... | title              | length | sequence_id |
+---------+-----+--------------------+--------+-------------+
|     542 | ... | LUST LOCK          |     52 |           1 |
|     661 | ... | PAST SUICIDES      |    157 |           2 |
|     613 | ... | MYSTIC TRUMAN      |     92 |           3 |
|     757 | ... | SAGEBRUSH CLUELESS |    106 |           4 |
|     940 | ... | VICTORY ACADEMY    |     64 |           5 |
|     917 | ... | TUXEDO MILE        |    152 |           6 |
|     709 | ... | RACER EGG          |    147 |           7 |
```

```
|     524 | ... | LION UNCUT        |    50 |           8 |
|      30 | ... | ANYTHING SAVANNAH |    82 |           9 |
|     602 | ... | MOURNING PURPLE   |   146 |          10 |
+---------+-----+-------------------+-------+-------------+
10 rows in set (0.00 sec)
```

You can see that we have 10 films in our recommendation list, numbered with sequence_id values from 1 to 10. We're ready to start recommending the random movie selection. Don't worry if your results differ; it's a consequence of how the RAND() function works.

There are two parts to the SQL statement we used to populate the table: an INSERT INTO and a SELECT. The INSERT INTO statement lists the destination table into which the data will be stored, followed by an optional list of column names in parentheses; if you omit the column names, all columns in the destination table are assumed in the order they appear in the output of a DESCRIBE TABLE or SHOW CREATE TABLE statement. The SELECT statement outputs columns that must match the type and order of the list provided for the INSERT INTO statement (or the implicit complete list if one isn't provided). The overall effect is that the rows output from the SELECT statement is inserted into the destination table by the INSERT INTO statement. In our example, film_id, language_id, release_year, title, and length values from the film table are inserted into the five columns with the same names and types in the recommend table; the sequence_id is automatically created using MySQL's AUTO_INCREMENT feature, so it isn't specified in the statements.

Our example includes the clause ORDER BY RAND(); this orders the results according to the MySQL function RAND(). The RAND() function returns a pseudorandom number in the range 0 to 1:

```
mysql> SELECT RAND();

+--------------------+
| RAND()             |
+--------------------+
| 0.4593397513584604 |
+--------------------+
1 row in set (0.00 sec)
```

A pseudorandom number generator doesn't generate truly random numbers, but rather generates numbers based on some property of the system, such as the time of day. This is sufficiently random for most applications; a notable exception is cryptography applications that depend on the true randomness of numbers for security.

If you ask for the RAND() value in a SELECT operation, you'll get a random value for each returned row:

```
mysql> SELECT title, RAND() FROM film LIMIT 5;
```

```
+------------------+----------------------+
| title            | RAND()               |
+------------------+----------------------+
| ACADEMY DINOSAUR |   0.5514843506286706 |
| ACE GOLDFINGER   |  0.37940252980161693 |
| ADAPTATION HOLES |   0.2425596278557178 |
| AFFAIR PREJUDICE |  0.07459058060738312 |
| AFRICAN EGG      |   0.6452740502034072 |
+------------------+----------------------+
5 rows in set (0.00 sec)
```

Since the values are effectively random, you'll almost certainly see different results than we've shown here. Moreover, if you repeat the statement, you'll also see different values returned. It is possible to pass RAND() an integer argument called *seed*. That will result in the RAND() function generating the same values for the same inputs each time that seed is used—it's not really useful for what we're trying to achieve here, but a possibility nonetheless. You can try running the following statement as many times as you want, and the results won't change:

```
SELECT title, RAND(1) FROM film LIMIT 5;
```

Let's return to the INSERT operation. When we ask that the results be ordered by RAND(), the results of the SELECT statement are sorted in a pseudorandom order. The LIMIT 10 is there to limit the number of rows returned by the SELECT; we've limited in this example simply for readability.

The SELECT statement in an INSERT INTO statement can use all of the usual features of SELECT statements. You can use joins, aggregation, functions, and any other features you choose. You can also query data from one database in another, by prefacing the table names with the database name followed by a period (.) character. For example, if you wanted to insert the actor table from the film database into a new art database, you could do the following:

```
mysql> CREATE DATABASE art;

Query OK, 1 row affected (0.01 sec)

mysql> USE art;

Database changed

mysql> CREATE TABLE people
    ->    person_id SMALLINT UNSIGNED,
    ->    first_name VARCHAR(45),
    ->    last_name VARCHAR(45),
    ->    PRIMARY KEY (person_id)
    -> );

Query OK, 0 rows affected (0.03 sec)

mysql> INSERT INTO art.people (person_id, first_name, last_name)
    -> SELECT actor_id, first_name, last_name FROM sakila.actor;
```

```
Query OK, 200 rows affected (0.01 sec)
Records: 200  Duplicates: 0  Warnings: 0
```

You can see that the new `people` table is referred to as `art.people` (though it doesn't need to be, since `art` is the database that's currently in use), and the `actor` table is referred to as `sakila.actor` (which it needs to be, since that isn't the database being used). Note also that the column names don't need to be the same for the `SELECT` and the `INSERT`.

Sometimes, you'll encounter duplication issues when inserting with a `SELECT` statement. If you try to insert the same primary key value twice, MySQL will abort. This won't happen in the `recommend` table, as long as you automatically allocate a new `sequence_id` using the `AUTO_INCREMENT` feature. However, we can force a duplicate into the table to show the behavior:

```
mysql> USE sakila;

Database changed

mysql> INSERT INTO recommend (film_id, language_id, release_year,
    -> title, length, sequence_id )
    -> SELECT film_id, language_id, release_year, title, length, 1
    -> FROM film LIMIT 1;

ERROR 1062 (23000): Duplicate entry '1' for key 'recommend.PRIMARY'
```

If you want MySQL to ignore this and keep going, add the `IGNORE` keyword after `INSERT`:

```
mysql> INSERT IGNORE INTO recommend (film_id, language_id, release_year,
    -> title, length, sequence_id )
    -> SELECT film_id, language_id, release_year, title, length, 1
    -> FROM film LIMIT 1;

Query OK, 0 rows affected, 1 warning (0.00 sec)
Records: 1  Duplicates: 1  Warnings: 1
```

MySQL doesn't complain, but it does report that it encountered a duplicate. Note that the data is not changed; all we did was ignore the error. This is useful in bulk load operations where you don't want to fail halfway through running a script that inserts a million rows. We can inspect the warning to see the *Duplicate entry* error as a warning now:

```
mysql> SHOW WARNINGS;

+---------+------+--------------------------------------------------+
| Level   | Code | Message                                          |
+---------+------+--------------------------------------------------+
| Warning | 1062 | Duplicate entry '1' for key 'recommend.PRIMARY'  |
+---------+------+--------------------------------------------------+
1 row in set (0.00 sec)
```

Finally, note that it is possible to insert into a table that's listed in the SELECT statement, but you still need to avoid duplicate primary keys:

```
mysql> INSERT INTO actor SELECT
    -> actor_id, first_name, last_name, NOW() FROM actor;

ERROR 1062 (23000): Duplicate entry '1' for key 'actor.PRIMARY'
```

There are two ways to avoid getting the error. First, the actor table has AUTO_INCRE MENT enabled for actor_id, so if you omit this column in the INSERT completely, you won't get an error, as the new values will be generated automatically. (INSERT statement syntax is explained in "Alternative Syntaxes" on page 114.) Here's an example that would only one record (due to the LIMIT clause):

```
INSERT INTO actor(first_name, last_name, last_update)
SELECT first_name, last_name, NOW() FROM actor LIMIT 1;
```

The second way is to modify actor_id in the SELECT query in a way that prevents collisions. Let's try that:

```
mysql> INSERT INTO actor SELECT
    -> actor_id+200, first_name, last_name, NOW() FROM actor;

Query OK, 200 rows affected (0.01 sec)
Records: 200  Duplicates: 0  Warnings: 0
```

Here, we're copying the rows but increasing their actor_id values by 200 before we insert them, because we remember that there are 200 rows initially. This is the result:

```
mysql> SELECT * FROM actor;

+----------+------------+-------------+---------------------+
| actor_id | first_name | last_name   | last_update         |
+----------+------------+-------------+---------------------+
|        1 | PENELOPE   | GUINESS     | 2006-02-15 04:34:33 |
|        2 | NICK       | WAHLBERG    | 2006-02-15 04:34:33 |
|      ... |            |             |                     |
|      198 | MARY       | KEITEL      | 2006-02-15 04:34:33 |
|      199 | JULIA      | FAWCETT     | 2006-02-15 04:34:33 |
|      200 | THORA      | TEMPLE      | 2006-02-15 04:34:33 |
|      201 | PENELOPE   | GUINESS     | 2021-02-28 10:24:49 |
|      202 | NICK       | WAHLBERG    | 2021-02-28 10:24:49 |
|      ... |            |             |                     |
|      398 | MARY       | KEITEL      | 2021-02-28 10:24:49 |
|      399 | JULIA      | FAWCETT     | 2021-02-28 10:24:49 |
|      400 | THORA      | TEMPLE      | 2021-02-28 10:24:49 |
+----------+------------+-------------+---------------------+
400 rows in set (0.00 sec)
```

You can see how first names, last names, and `last_update` values start repeating from the `actor_id` 201.

It's also possible to use subqueries in the `INSERT SELECT` statements. For example, the next statement is valid:

```
*INSERT INTO actor SELECT * FROM*
*(SELECT actor_id+400, first_name, last_name, NOW() FROM actor) foo;*
```

Loading Data from Comma-Delimited Files

These days, databases are usually not an afterthought. They are ubiquitous and easier than ever to use, and most IT professionals know about them. Nevertheless, end users find them difficult, and unless specialized UIs are created, a lot of data entry and analysis is instead done in various spreadsheet programs. These programs typically have unique file formats, open or closed, but most of them will allow you to export data as rows of comma-separated values (CSVs), also called a *comma-delimited format*. You can then import the data with a little effort into MySQL.

Another common task that can be accomplished by working with CSVs is transferring data in a heterogeneous environment. If you have various database software running in your setup, and especially if you're using a DBaaS in the cloud, moving data between these systems can be daunting. However, the basic CSV data can be a lowest common denominator for them. Note that in the case of any data transfer you should always remember that CSV does not have the notions of schemas, data types, or constraints. But as a flat data file format, it works well.

If you're not using a spreadsheet program, you can still often use command-line tools such as sed and awk—very old and powerful Unix utilities—to convert text data into a CSV format suitable for import by MySQL. Some cloud databases allow export of their data directly into CSV. In some other cases, small programs have to be written that read data and produce a CSV file. This section shows you the basics of how to import CSV data into MySQL.

Let's work through an example. We have a list of NASA facilities with their addresses and contact information that we want to store in a database. At present, it's stored in a CSV file named *NASA_Facilities.csv* and has the format shown in Figure 7-1.

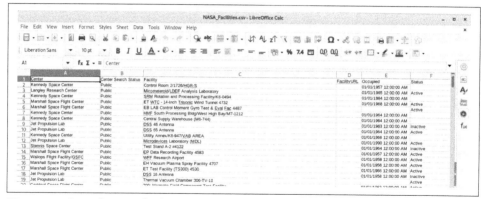

Figure 7-1. List of NASA facilities stored in a spreadsheet file

You can see that each facility is associated with a center, and may list the date it was occupied and optionally its status. The full column list is as follows:

- Center
- Center Search Status
- Facility
- FacilityURL
- Occupied
- Status
- URL Link
- Record Date
- Last Update
- Country
- Contact
- Phone
- Location
- City
- State
- Zipcode

This example comes directly from NASA's publicly available Open Data Portal (*https://oreil.ly/xIm3A*), and the file is available in the book's GitHub repository (*https://oreil.ly/ayDai*). Since this is already a CSV file, we don't need to convert it from another file format (like XLS). However, if you do need to do that in your own project, it's usually as easy as using the Save As command in the spreadsheet program; just don't forget to pick CSV as the output format.

If you open the *NASA_facilities.csv* file using a text editor, you'll see that it has one line per spreadsheet row, with the values for each column separated by commas. If you're on a non-Windows platform, you may find that in some CSV files each line is terminated with a ^M, but don't worry about this; it's an artifact of the origins of Windows. Data in this format is often referred to as *DOS format*, and most software applications can handle it without problem. In our case, the data is in *Unix format*, and thus on Windows you may see that all the lines are concatenated. You can try to use another text editor if that's the case. Here are a few width-truncated lines selected from *NASA_Facilities.csv*:

```
Center,Center Search Status,Facility,FacilityURL,Occupied,Status,...
Kennedy Space Center,Public,Control Room 2/1726/HGR-S ,,...
Langley Research Center,Public,Micometeroid/LDEF Analysis Laboratory,,,...
Kennedy Space Center,Public,SRM Rotation and Processing Facility/K6-0494 ,...
Marshall Space Flight Center,..."35812(34.729538, -86.585283)",Huntsville,...
```

If there are commas or other special symbols within values, the whole value is enclosed in quotes, as in the last line shown here.

Let's import this data into MySQL. First, create the new nasa database:

```
mysql> CREATE DATABASE nasa;
Query OK, 1 row affected (0.01 sec)
```

Choose this as the active database:

```
mysql> USE nasa;
Database changed
```

Now, create the facilities table to store the data. This needs to handle all of the fields that we see in the CSV file, which conveniently has a header:

```
mysql> CREATE TABLE facilities (
    ->     center TEXT,
    ->     center_search_status TEXT,
    ->     facility TEXT,
    ->     facility_url TEXT,
    ->     occupied TEXT,
    ->     status TEXT,
    ->     url_link TEXT,
    ->     record_date DATETIME,
    ->     last_update TIMESTAMP NULL,
    ->     country TEXT,
    ->     contact TEXT,
    ->     phone TEXT,
    ->     location TEXT,
    ->     city TEXT,
    ->     state TEXT,
```

```
    ->   zipcode TEXT
    -> );

Query OK, 0 rows affected (0.03 sec)
```

We're cheating here somewhat with the data types. NASA provides the schema of the dataset, but for most of the fields the type is given as the "Plain Text," and we can't really store a "Website URL" as anything but text, either. We don't, however, know how much data each column will hold. Thus, we default to using the TEXT type, which is similar to defining a column as VARCHAR(65535). There are some differences between the two types, as you can probably remember from "String types" on page 144, but they are not important in this example. We don't define any indexes and don't put any constraints on our table. If you're loading a completely new dataset that's quite small, it can be beneficial to load it first and then analyze it. For larger datasets, make sure the table is structured as well as possible, or you'll spend a considerable amount of time changing it later.

Now that we've set up the database table, we can import the data from the file using the LOAD DATA INFILE command:

```
mysql> LOAD DATA INFILE 'NASA_Facilities.csv' INTO TABLE facilities
    -> FIELDS TERMINATED BY ',';

ERROR 1290 (HY000): The MySQL server is running with
the --secure-file-priv option so it cannot execute this statement
```

Oh, no! We got an error. By default, MySQL doesn't let you load *any* data using the LOAD DATA INFILE command. The behavior is controlled by the secure_file_priv system variable. If the variable is set to a path, the file to be loaded should reside in that particular path and be readable by the MySQL server. If the variable isn't set, which is considered insecure, then the file to be loaded should be readable only by the MySQL server. By default, MySQL 8.0 on Linux sets this variable as follows:

```
mysql> SELECT @@secure_file_priv;

+-----------------------+
| @@secure_file_priv    |
+-----------------------+
| /var/lib/mysql-files/ |
+-----------------------+
1 row in set (0.00 sec)
```

And on Windows:

```
mysql> SELECT @@secure_file_priv;

+-------------------------------------------------+
| @@secure_file_priv                              |
+-------------------------------------------------+
| C:\ProgramData\MySQL\MySQL Server 8.0\Uploads\ |
+-------------------------------------------------+
1 row in set (0.00 sec)
```

The value of the `secure_file_priv` system variable may be different in your installation of MySQL, or it may even be empty. A NULL value for `secure_file_priv` means that MySQL will allow loading a file in any location as long as that file is accessible to the MySQL server. On Linux, that means that the file has to be readable by the `mysqld` process, which usually runs under the `mysql` user. You can change `secure_file_priv` variable's value by updating your MySQL configuration and restarting the server. You can find information on how to configure MySQL in Chapter 9.

On Linux or other Unix-like systems, you need to copy the file into that directory, possibly using `sudo` to allow the operation, and then change its permissions so that the `mysqld` program can access the file. On Windows, you only need to copy the file to the correct destination.

Let's do this. On Linux or similar systems, you can run commands like this:

```
$ ls -lh $HOME/Downloads/NASA_Facilities.csv
-rw-r--r--. 1 skuzmichev skuzmichev 114K
    Feb 28 14:19 /home/skuzmichev/Downloads/NASA_Facilities.csv
$ sudo cp -vip ~/Downloads/NASA_Facilities.csv /var/lib/mysql-files
[sudo] password for skuzmichev:
'/home/skuzmichev/Downloads/NASA_Facilities.csv'
    -> '/var/lib/mysql-files/NASA_Facilities.csv'
$ sudo chown mysql:mysql /var/lib/mysql-files/NASA_Facilities.csv
$ sudo ls -lh /var/lib/mysql-files/NASA_Facilities.csv
-rw-r--r--. 1 mysql mysql 114K
    Feb 28 14:19 /var/lib/mysql-files/NASA_Facilities.csv
```

On Windows, you can use the File Manager to copy or move the file.

Now we're ready to try the loading again. When our target file is not in the current directory, we need to pass the full path to the command:

```
mysql> LOAD DATA INFILE '/var/lib/mysql-files/NASA_Facilities.csv'
    -> INTO TABLE facilities FIELDS TERMINATED BY ',';

ERROR 1292 (22007): Incorrect datetime value:
'Record Date' for column 'record_date' at row 1
```

Well, that doesn't look correct: Record Date is indeed not a date, but a column name. We've made a silly but common mistake, loading the CSV file with the header. We need to tell MySQL to omit it:

```
mysql> LOAD DATA INFILE '/var/lib/mysql-files/NASA_Facilities.csv'
    -> INTO TABLE facilities FIELDS TERMINATED BY ','
    -> IGNORE 1 LINES;

ERROR 1292 (22007): Incorrect datetime value:
'03/01/1996 12:00:00 AM' for column 'record_date' at row 1
```

Turns out, that date format we have is not something MySQL expects. That's an extremely common issue. There are a couple of ways out. First, we can just change our record_date column to the TEXT type. We'll lose the niceties of a proper date-time data type, but we'll be able to get the data into our database. Second, we can convert the data ingested from the file on the fly. To demonstrate the difference in the results, we specified the occupied column (which is a date field) to be TEXT. Before we jump into the conversion complexities, though, let's try running the same command on Windows:

```
mysql> LOAD DATA INFILE
    -> 'C:\ProgramData\MySQL\MySQL Server 8.0\Uploads\NASA_Facilities.csv'
    -> INTO TABLE facilities FIELDS TERMINATED BY ',';

ERROR 1290 (HY000): The MySQL server is running with
the --secure-file-priv option so it cannot execute this statement
```

Even though the file is present in that directory, LOAD DATA INFILE errors out. The reason for that is how MySQL works with paths on Windows. We can't just use regular Windows-style paths with this or other MySQL commands. We need to escape each backslash (\) with another backslash, or change our path to use forward slashes (/). Both will work…or rather, in this case, both will error out due to the expected record_date conversion issue:

```
mysql> LOAD DATA INFILE
    -> 'C:\\ProgramData\\MySQL\\MySQL Server 8.0\\Uploads\\NASA_Facilities.csv'
    -> INTO TABLE facilities FIELDS TERMINATED BY ',';

ERROR 1292 (22007): Incorrect datetime value:
'Record Date' for column 'record_date' at row 1

mysql> LOAD DATA INFILE
    -> 'C:/ProgramData/MySQL/MySQL Server 8.0/Uploads/NASA_Facilities.csv'
    -> INTO TABLE facilities FIELDS TERMINATED BY ',';

ERROR 1292 (22007): Incorrect datetime value:
'Record Date' for column 'record_date' at row 1
```

With that covered, let's get back to our date conversion issue. As we mentioned, this is an extremely common issue. You will inevitably face type conversion problems, because CSV is typeless, and different databases have different expectations about various types. In this case, the open dataset that we obtained has dates in the following format: 03/01/1996 12:00:00 AM. While this will make our operation more complex, we believe converting the date values from our CSV file is a good exercise. To convert an arbitrary string to a date, or at least to attempt such a conversion, we can use the STR_TO_DATE() function. After reviewing the documentation, we came up with the following cast:

```
mysql> SELECT STR_TO_DATE('03/01/1996 12:00:00 AM',
    -> '%m/%d/%Y %h:%i:%s %p') converted;
```

```
+--------------------+
| converted          |
+--------------------+
| 1996-03-01 00:00:00 |
+--------------------+
1 row in set (0.01 sec)
```

Since the function returns NULL when the cast is unsuccessful, we know we have managed to find a correct invocation. Now we need to find out how to use the function in the LOAD DATA INFILE command. The much longer version using the function looks like this:

```
mysql> LOAD DATA INFILE '/var/lib/mysql-files/NASA_Facilities.csv'
    -> INTO TABLE facilities FIELDS TERMINATED BY ','
    -> OPTIONALLY ENCLOSED BY '"'
    -> IGNORE 1 LINES
    -> (center, center_search_status, facility, facility_url,
    -> occupied, status, url_link, @var_record_date, @var_last_update,
    -> country, contact, phone, location, city, state, zipcode)
    -> SET record_date = IF(
    ->    CHAR_LENGTH(@var_record_date)=0, NULL,
    ->      STR_TO_DATE(@var_record_date, '%m/%d/%Y %h:%i:%s %p')
    -> ),
    -> last_update = IF(
    ->    CHAR_LENGTH(@var_last_update)=0, NULL,
    ->      STR_TO_DATE(@var_last_update, '%m/%d/%Y %h:%i:%s %p')
    -> );
Query OK, 485 rows affected (0.05 sec)
Records: 485  Deleted: 0  Skipped: 0  Warnings: 0
```

That's a lot of command! Let's break it down. The first line specifies our LOAD DATA INFILE command and the path to a file. The second line specifies the target table and begins the FIELDS specification, starting with TERMINATED BY ',', which means our fields are delimited by commas, as expected for CSV. The third line adds another parameter to the FIELDS specification and tells MySQL that some fields (but not all) are enclosed by the " symbol. That's important, because our dataset has some entries with commas within "..." fields. On line four we specify that we skip the first line of the file, where we know the header resides.

Lines 5 through 7 have the column list specification. We need to convert two date-time columns, and for that we need to read their values into variables, which are then set to the nasa.facilities table's column values. However, we can't tell that to MySQL without also specifying all the other columns. If we were to omit some columns from the list or specify them in the wrong order, MySQL would not assign the values correctly. CSV is inherently a position-based format. By default, when the FIELDS specification is not given, MySQL will read each CSV line and will expect each field in all lines to map to a column in the target table (in the order of columns that the DESCRIBE or SHOW CREATE TABLE command gives). By changing the order of columns in this specification, we can populate a table from a CSV file that has fields misplaced. By specifying fewer columns, we can populate a table from a file that is missing some of the fields.

Lines 8 through 15 are our function calls to convert the date-time values. In the preceding column spec, we defined that field 8 is read into the @var_record_date variable, and field 9 into @var_last_update. We know that fields 8 and 9 are our problematic date-time fields. With the variables populated, we can define the SET parameter, which allows modification of the target table column values based on fields read from the CSV file. In this very basic example, you could multiply a specific value by two. In our case, we cast two functions: first we check that a variable is not empty (, , in CSV) by assessing the number of characters read from the file, and second we call the actual conversion if the previous check doesn't return zero. If we found the length to be zero, we set the value to NULL.

Finally, when the command has been executed, it's possible to check the results:

```
mysql> SELECT facility, occupied, last_update
    -> FROM facilities
    -> ORDER BY last_update DESC LIMIT 5;
+----------------------...+------------------------+---------------------+
| facility           ...| occupied               | last_update         |
+----------------------...+------------------------+---------------------+
| Turn Basin/K7-1005  ...| 01/01/1963 12:00:00 AM | 2015-06-22 00:00:00 |
| RPSF Surge Building ...| 01/01/1984 12:00:00 AM | 2015-06-22 00:00:00 |
| Thermal Protection S...| 01/01/1988 12:00:00 AM | 2015-06-22 00:00:00 |
| Intermediate Bay/M7-...| 01/01/1995 12:00:00 AM | 2015-06-22 00:00:00 |
| Orbiter Processing F...| 01/01/1987 12:00:00 AM | 2015-06-22 00:00:00 |
+----------------------...+------------------------+---------------------+
5 rows in set (0.00 sec)
```

Remember we mentioned that occupied will remain TEXT. You can see that here. While it can be used for sorting, no date functions will work on values in this column unless they are explicitly cast to DATETIME.

This was a complex example, but it shows the unexpected complexity of loading data and the power of the LOAD DATA INFILE command.

Writing Data into Comma-Delimited Files

You can use the SELECT INTO OUTFILE statement to write out the result of a query into a CSV file that can be opened by a spreadsheet or other program.

Let's export the list of current managers from our employees database into a CSV file. The query used to list all the current managers is shown here:

```
mysql> USE employees;
```

Database changed

```
mysql> SELECT emp_no, first_name, last_name, title, from_date
    -> FROM employees JOIN titles USING (emp_no)
    -> WHERE title = 'Manager' AND to_date = '9999-01-01';

+--------+------------+------------+---------+------------+
| emp_no | first_name | last_name  | title   | from_date  |
+--------+------------+------------+---------+------------+
| 110039 | Vishwani   | Minakawa   | Manager | 1991-10-01 |
| 110114 | Isamu      | Legleitner | Manager | 1989-12-17 |
| 110228 | Karsten    | Sigstam    | Manager | 1992-03-21 |
| 110420 | Oscar      | Ghazalie   | Manager | 1996-08-30 |
| 110567 | Leon       | DasSarma   | Manager | 1992-04-25 |
| 110854 | Dung       | Pesch      | Manager | 1994-06-28 |
| 111133 | Hauke      | Zhang      | Manager | 1991-03-07 |
| 111534 | Hilary     | Kambil     | Manager | 1991-04-08 |
| 111939 | Yuchang    | Weedman    | Manager | 1996-01-03 |
+--------+------------+------------+---------+------------+
9 rows in set (0.13 sec)
```

We can change this SELECT query slightly to write this data into an output file as comma-separated values. INTO OUTFILE is subject to the same --secure-file-priv option rules as LOAD DATA INFILE. The file path by default is limited, and we listed the default options in "Loading Data from Comma-Delimited Files" on page 267:

```
mysql> SELECT emp_no, first_name, last_name, title, from_date
    -> FROM employees JOIN titles USING (emp_no)
    -> WHERE title = 'Manager' AND to_date = '9999-01-01'
    -> INTO OUTFILE '/var/lib/mysql-files/managers.csv'
    -> FIELDS TERMINATED BY ',';

Query OK, 9 rows affected (0.14 sec)
```

Here, we've saved the results into the file *managers.csv* in the */var/lib/mysql-files* directory; the MySQL server must be able to write to the directory that you specify, and it should be one listed in the secure_file_priv system variable (if set). On a Windows system, specify a path such as *C:\ProgramData\MySQL\MySQL Server 8.0\Uploads\managers.csv* instead. If you omit the FIELDS TERMINATED BY clause, the server will use tabs as the default separator between the data values.

You can view the contents of the file *managers.csv* in a text editor, or import it into a spreadsheet program:

```
110039,Vishwani,Minakawa,Manager,1991-10-01
110114,Isamu,Legleitner,Manager,1989-12-17
110228,Karsten,Sigstam,Manager,1992-03-21
110420,Oscar,Ghazalie,Manager,1996-08-30
110567,Leon,DasSarma,Manager,1992-04-25
110854,Dung,Pesch,Manager,1994-06-28
111133,Hauke,Zhang,Manager,1991-03-07
111534,Hilary,Kambil,Manager,1991-04-08
111939,Yuchang,Weedman,Manager,1996-01-03
```

When our data fields contain commas or another delimiter of our choice, MySQL by default will escape the delimiters within fields. Let's switch to the `sakila` database and test this:

```
mysql> USE sakila;

Database changed

mysql> SELECT title, special_features FROM film LIMIT 10
    -> INTO OUTFILE '/var/lib/mysql-files/film.csv'
    -> FIELDS TERMINATED BY ',';

Query OK, 10 rows affected (0.00 sec)
```

If you take a look at the data in the *film.csv* file now (again, feel free to use a text editor, a spreadsheet program, or a command-line utility like head on Linux), here's what you'll see:

```
ACADEMY DINOSAUR,Deleted Scenes\,Behind the Scenes
ACE GOLDFINGER,Trailers\,Deleted Scenes
ADAPTATION HOLES,Trailers\,Deleted Scenes
AFFAIR PREJUDICE,Commentaries\,Behind the Scenes
AFRICAN EGG,Deleted Scenes
AGENT TRUMAN,Deleted Scenes
AIRPLANE SIERRA,Trailers\,Deleted Scenes
AIRPORT POLLOCK,Trailers
ALABAMA DEVIL,Trailers\,Deleted Scenes
ALADDIN CALENDAR,Trailers\,Deleted Scenes
```

Notice how in rows where the second field contains a comma, it has been automatically escaped with a backslash to distinguish it from the separator. Some spreadsheet programs may understand this and remove the backslashes when importing the file, and some may not. MySQL will respect the escaping and not treat such commas as separators. Note that if we specified FIELDS TERMINATED BY '^', all ^ symbols within fields would get escaped; this is not specific to commas.

Since not all programs may deal with escapes gracefully, we can ask MySQL to explicitly define fields by using the ENCLOSED option:

```
mysql> SELECT title, special_features FROM film LIMIT 10
    -> INTO OUTFILE '/var/lib/mysql-files/film_quoted.csv'
    -> FIELDS TERMINATED BY ',' ENCLOSED BY '"';

Query OK, 10 rows affected (0.00 sec)
```

We used this option before when loading data. Take a look at the results in the file *film_quoted.csv*:

```
"ACADEMY DINOSAUR","Deleted Scenes,Behind the Scenes"
"ACE GOLDFINGER","Trailers,Deleted Scenes"
"ADAPTATION HOLES","Trailers,Deleted Scenes"
"AFFAIR PREJUDICE","Commentaries,Behind the Scenes"
"AFRICAN EGG","Deleted Scenes"
```

```
"AGENT TRUMAN","Deleted Scenes"
"AIRPLANE SIERRA","Trailers,Deleted Scenes"
"AIRPORT POLLOCK","Trailers"
"ALABAMA DEVIL","Trailers,Deleted Scenes"
"ALADDIN CALENDAR","Trailers,Deleted Scenes"
```

Our delimiters—commas—are now not escaped, which may work better with modern spreadsheet programs. You may wonder what will happen if there are double quotes within exported fields: MySQL will escape those instead of the commas, which again may cause problems. When doing data export, do not forget to make sure that the resulting output will work for your consumers.

Creating Tables with Queries

You can create a table or easily create a copy of a table using a query. This is useful when you want to build a new database using existing data—for example, you might want to copy across a list of countries—or when you want to reorganize data for some reason. Data reorganization is common when producing reports, merging data from two or more tables, and redesigning on the fly. This short section shows you how it's done.

We base all the examples here on the unmodified sakila database. You should repeat the steps given in "Entity Relationship Modeling Examples" on page 77 to get the database back to its clean state before proceeding.

In MySQL, you can easily duplicate the structure of a table using a variant of the CREATE TABLE syntax:

```
mysql> USE sakila;

Database changed

mysql> CREATE TABLE actor_2 LIKE actor;

Query OK, 0 rows affected (0.24 sec)

mysql> DESCRIBE actor_2;

+-------------+-------------------+------+-----+...
| Field       | Type              | Null | Key |...
+-------------+-------------------+------+-----+...
| actor_id    | smallint unsigned | NO   | PRI |...
| first_name  | varchar(45)       | NO   |     |...
| last_name   | varchar(45)       | NO   | MUL |...
| last_update | timestamp         | NO   |     |...
+-------------+-------------------+------+-----+...
```

```
...+-----------------+----------------------------------------------+
...| Default         | Extra                                        |
...+-----------------+----------------------------------------------+
...| NULL            | auto_increment                               |
...| NULL            |                                              |
...| NULL            |                                              |
...| CURRENT_TIMESTAMP | DEFAULT_GENERATED on update CURRENT_TIMESTAMP |
...+-----------------+----------------------------------------------+
4 rows in set (0.01 sec)

mysql> SELECT * FROM actor_2;

Empty set (0.00 sec)
```

The LIKE syntax allows you to create a new table with exactly the same structure as another, including keys. You can see that it doesn't copy the data across. You can also use the IF NOT EXISTS and TEMPORARY features with this syntax.

If you want to create a table and copy some data, you can do that with a combination of the CREATE TABLE and SELECT statements. Let's remove the actor_2 table and re-create it using this new approach:

```
mysql> DROP TABLE actor_2;

Query OK, 0 rows affected (0.08 sec)

mysql> CREATE TABLE actor_2 AS SELECT * from actor;

Query OK, 200 rows affected (0.03 sec)
Records: 200  Duplicates: 0  Warnings: 0

mysql> SELECT * FROM actor_2 LIMIT 5;

+----------+------------+-------------+---------------------+
| actor_id | first_name | last_name   | last_update         |
+----------+------------+-------------+---------------------+
|        1 | PENELOPE   | GUINESS     | 2006-02-15 04:34:33 |
|        2 | NICK       | WAHLBERG    | 2006-02-15 04:34:33 |
|        3 | ED         | CHASE       | 2006-02-15 04:34:33 |
|        4 | JENNIFER   | DAVIS       | 2006-02-15 04:34:33 |
|        5 | JOHNNY     | LOLLOBRIGIDA | 2006-02-15 04:34:33 |
+----------+------------+-------------+---------------------+
5 rows in set (0.01 sec)
```

An identical table, actor_2, is created, and all the data is copied across by the SELECT statement. CREATE TABLE AS SELECT, or CTAS, is a common name for this action, but it's actually not mandatory to specify the AS part, and we'll omit that later.

This technique is powerful. You can create new tables with new structures and use powerful queries to populate them with data. For example, here's a report table that's created to contain the names of the films in our database and their categories:

```
mysql> CREATE TABLE report (title VARCHAR(128), category VARCHAR(25))
    -> SELECT title, name AS category FROM
```

```
 -> film JOIN film_category USING (film_id)
 -> JOIN category USING (category_id);
Query OK, 1000 rows affected (0.06 sec)
Records: 1000  Duplicates: 0  Warnings: 0
```

You can see that the syntax is a little different from the previous example. In this example, the new table name, report, is followed by a list of column names and types in parentheses; this is necessary because we're not duplicating the structure of an existing table. Moreover, we actually change name to category. Then, the SELECT statement follows, with its output matching the new columns in the new table. You can check the contents of the new table to see the result:

```
mysql> SELECT * FROM report LIMIT 5;

+----------------------+----------+
| title                | category |
+----------------------+----------+
| AMADEUS HOLY         | Action   |
| AMERICAN CIRCUS      | Action   |
| ANTITRUST TOMATOES   | Action   |
| ARK RIDGEMONT        | Action   |
| BAREFOOT MANCHURIAN  | Action   |
+----------------------+----------+
5 rows in set (0.00 sec)
```

So, in this example, the title and name values from the SELECT statement are used to populate the new title and category columns in the report table.

Creating tables with a query has a major caveat that you need to be careful about: it doesn't copy the indexes (or foreign keys, if you use them). This is a feature, since it gives you a lot of flexibility, but it can be a catch if you forget. Have a look at our actor_2 example:

```
mysql> DESCRIBE actor_2;

+-------------+-------------------+------+-----+...
| Field       | Type              | Null | Key |...
+-------------+-------------------+------+-----+...
| actor_id    | smallint unsigned | NO   |     |...
| first_name  | varchar(45)       | NO   |     |...
| last_name   | varchar(45)       | NO   |     |...
| last_update | timestamp         | NO   |     |...
+-------------+-------------------+------+-----+...
...+-------------------+------------------------------------------------------+
...| Default           | Extra                                                |
...+-------------------+------------------------------------------------------+
...| 0                 |                                                      |
...| NULL              |                                                      |
...| NULL              |                                                      |
...| CURRENT_TIMESTAMP | DEFAULT_GENERATED on update CURRENT_TIMESTAMP        |
...+-------------------+------------------------------------------------------+
4 rows in set (0.00 sec)
```

```
mysql> SHOW CREATE TABLE actor_2\G
*************************** 1. row ***************************
       Table: actor_2
Create Table: CREATE TABLE `actor_2` (
  `actor_id` smallint unsigned NOT NULL DEFAULT '0',
  `first_name` varchar(45) NOT NULL,
  `last_name` varchar(45) NOT NULL,
  `last_update` timestamp NOT NULL
    DEFAULT CURRENT_TIMESTAMP
    ON UPDATE CURRENT_TIMESTAMP
) ENGINE=InnoDB DEFAULT CHARSET=utf8mb4
    COLLATE=utf8mb4_0900_ai_ci
1 row in set (0.00 sec)
```

You can see that there's no primary key; the idx_actor_last_name key is missing as well, as is the AUTO_INCREMENT property of the actor_id column.

To copy indexes across to the new table, there are at least three things you can do. The first is to use the LIKE statement to create the empty table with the indexes, as described earlier, and then copy the data across using an INSERT with a SELECT statement, as described in "Inserting Data Using Queries" on page 261.

The second thing you can do is to use CREATE TABLE with a SELECT statement and then add indexes using ALTER TABLE as described in Chapter 4.

The third option is to use the UNIQUE (or PRIMARY KEY or KEY) keyword in combination with CREATE TABLE and SELECT to add a primary key index. Here's an example of this approach:

```
mysql> DROP TABLE actor_2;

Query OK, 0 rows affected (0.04 sec)

mysql> CREATE TABLE actor_2 (UNIQUE(actor_id))
    -> AS SELECT * from actor;

Query OK, 200 rows affected (0.05 sec)
Records: 200  Duplicates: 0  Warnings: 0

mysql> DESCRIBE actor_2;
```

```
+-------------+------------------+------+-----+...
| Field       | Type             | Null | Key |...
+-------------+------------------+------+-----+...
| actor_id    | smallint unsigned | NO   | PRI |...
| first_name  | varchar(45)      | NO   |     |...
| last_name   | varchar(45)      | NO   |     |...
| last_update | timestamp        | NO   |     |...
+-------------+------------------+------+-----+...
```

```
...+-----------------+-------------------------------------------------+
...| Default         | Extra                                           |
...+-----------------+-------------------------------------------------+
...| 0               |                                                 |
...| NULL            |                                                 |
...| NULL            |                                                 |
...| CURRENT_TIMESTAMP | DEFAULT_GENERATED on update CURRENT_TIMESTAMP |
...+-----------------+-------------------------------------------------+
4 rows in set (0.01 sec)
```

The UNIQUE keyword is applied to the `actor_id` column, making it the primary key in the newly created table. The keywords UNIQUE and PRIMARY KEY can be interchanged.

You can use different modifiers when you're creating tables using these techniques. For example, here's a table created with defaults and other settings:

```
mysql> CREATE TABLE actor_3 (
    ->   actor_id SMALLINT UNSIGNED NOT NULL AUTO_INCREMENT,
    ->   first_name VARCHAR(45) NOT NULL,
    ->   last_name VARCHAR(45) NOT NULL,
    ->   last_update TIMESTAMP NOT NULL
    ->     DEFAULT CURRENT_TIMESTAMP ON UPDATE CURRENT_TIMESTAMP,
    ->   PRIMARY KEY (actor_id),
    ->   KEY idx_actor_last_name (last_name)
    -> ) SELECT * FROM actor;
Query OK, 200 rows affected (0.05 sec)
Records: 200  Duplicates: 0  Warnings: 0
```

Here, we've set NOT NULL for the new columns, used the AUTO_INCREMENT feature on `actor_id`, and created two keys. Anything you can do in a regular CREATE TABLE statement can be done in this variant; just remember to add those indexes explicitly!

Performing Updates and Deletes with Multiple Tables

In Chapter 3, we showed you how to update and delete data. In the examples there, each update and delete affected one table and used properties of that table to decide what to modify. This section shows you more complex updates and deletes. As you'll see, you can delete or update rows from more than one table in one statement, and you can use those or other tables to decide what rows to change.

Deletion

Imagine you're cleaning up a database, perhaps because you're running out of space. One way to solve this problem is to remove some data. For example, in the sakila database, it might make sense to remove films that are present in our inventory, but have never been rented. Unfortunately, this means you need to remove data from the inventory table using information from the rental table.

With the techniques we've described so far in the book, there's no way of doing this without creating a table that combines the two tables (perhaps using INSERT with SELECT), removing unwanted rows, and copying the data back to its source. This section shows you how you can perform this procedure and other more advanced types of deletion more elegantly.

Consider the query you need to write to find films in the inventory table that have never been rented. One way to do it is to use a nested query, employing the techniques we showed you in Chapter 5, with the NOT EXISTS clause. Here's the query:

```
mysql> SELECT * FROM inventory WHERE NOT EXISTS
    -> (SELECT 1 FROM rental WHERE
    -> rental.inventory_id = inventory.inventory_id);

+--------------+---------+----------+---------------------+
| inventory_id | film_id | store_id | last_update         |
+--------------+---------+----------+---------------------+
|            5 |       1 |        2 | 2006-02-15 05:09:17 |
+--------------+---------+----------+---------------------+
1 row in set (0.01 sec)
```

You can probably see how it works, but let's briefly discuss it anyway before we move on. You can see that this query uses a correlated subquery, where the current row being processed in the outer query is referenced by the subquery; you can tell this because the inventory_id column from inventory is referenced, but the inventory table isn't listed in the FROM clause of the subquery. The subquery produces output when there's a row in the rental table that matches the current row in the outer query (and so an inventory entry was rented). However, since the query uses NOT EXISTS, the outer query doesn't produce output when this is the case, and so the overall result is that rows are output for inventory records of movies that haven't been rented.

Now let's take our query and turn it into a DELETE statement. Here it is:

```
mysql> DELETE FROM inventory WHERE NOT EXISTS
    -> (SELECT 1 FROM rental WHERE
    -> rental.inventory_id = inventory.inventory_id);

Query OK, 1 row affected (0.04 sec)
```

You can see that the subquery remains the same, but the outer SELECT query is replaced by a DELETE statement. Here, we're following the standard DELETE syntax: the keyword DELETE is followed by FROM and a specification of the table or tables from which rows should be removed, then a WHERE clause (and any other query clauses, such as GROUP BY or HAVING). In this query, rows are deleted from the inventory table, but in the WHERE clause a subquery is specified within a NOT EXISTS statement.

While this statement does indeed delete rows from one table based on data from another table, it's basically a variation of a regular DELETE. To convert this particular statement into a multitable DELETE, we should switch from a nested subquery to a LEFT JOIN, like so:

```
DELETE inventory FROM inventory LEFT JOIN rental
USING (inventory_id) WHERE rental.inventory_id IS NULL;
```

Note how the syntax changes to include the specific table (or tables) where we want to delete the rows we find. These tables are specified after DELETE but before the FROM and query specification. There's another way to write this query, however, and it's the one we prefer:

```
DELETE FROM inventory USING inventory
LEFT JOIN rental USING (inventory_id)
WHERE rental.inventory_id IS NULL;
```

This query is a mix of the previous two. We do not specify the deletion targets between DELETE and FROM, and write them down as if this were a regular deletion. Instead, we use a special USING clause, which indicates that a filter query (a join or otherwise) is going to follow. This is slightly clearer in our opinion than the previous example of DELETE *table* FROM *table*. One downside of using the USING keyword is that it can be mixed up with the USING keyword of a JOIN statement. With some practice, you'll never make that mistake, though.

Now that we know both multitable syntax variants, we can construct a query that actually requires a multitable delete. One example of a situation that could require such a statement is deleting records from tables that are involved in foreign key relationships. In the sakila database, there are records for films in the film table that have no associated records in the inventory table. That is, there are films that there's information on, but that cannot be rented. Suppose that as part of the database cleanup operation, we're tasked with removing such dangling data. Initially this seems easy enough:

```
mysql> DELETE FROM film WHERE NOT EXISTS
    -> (SELECT 1 FROM inventory WHERE
    -> film.film_id = inventory.film_id);
ERROR 1451 (23000): Cannot delete or update a parent row:
a foreign key constraint fails (
`sakila`.`film_actor`, CONSTRAINT `fk_film_actor_film`
FOREIGN KEY (`film_id`) REFERENCES `film` (`film_id`)
ON DELETE RESTRICT ON UPDATE CASCADE)
```

Alas, the integrity constraint prevents this deletion. We will have to remove not only the films, but also relationships between those films and actors. That may generate orphan actors, which can be deleted next. We could try to delete films and references to actors in one go, like this:

```
DELETE FROM film_actor, film USING
film JOIN film_actor USING (film_id)
LEFT JOIN inventory USING (film_id)
WHERE inventory.film_id IS NULL;
```

Unfortunately, even though the film_actor table is listed before the film table, the deletion from film still fails. It's not possible to tell the optimizer to process tables in a particular order. Even if this example were to have executed successfully, it's not a good practice to rely on such behavior as the optimizer may later change the table order unpredictably, causing failures. This example highlights a difference between MySQL and the SQL standard: the standard specifies that the foreign keys are checked at transaction commit, whereas MySQL checks them immediately, preventing this statement from succeeding. Even if we were able to resolve this problem, films are also related to categories, so that will have to be taken care of too.

MySQL allows a few ways out of this situation. The first one is to execute a series of DELETE statements within one transaction (we talked more about transactions in Chapter 6):

```
mysql> BEGIN;

Query OK, 0 rows affected (0.00 sec)

mysql> DELETE FROM film_actor USING
    -> film JOIN film_actor USING (film_id)
    -> LEFT JOIN inventory USING (film_id)
    -> WHERE inventory.film_id IS NULL;

Query OK, 216 rows affected (0.01 sec)

mysql> DELETE FROM film_category USING
    -> film JOIN film_category USING (film_id)
    -> LEFT JOIN inventory USING (film_id)
    -> WHERE inventory.film_id IS NULL;

Query OK, 42 rows affected (0.00 sec)

mysql> DELETE FROM film USING
    -> film LEFT JOIN inventory USING (film_id)
    -> WHERE inventory.film_id IS NULL;

Query OK, 42 rows affected (0.00 sec)

mysql> ROLLBACK;

Query OK, 0 rows affected (0.02 sec)
```

You can see that we executed ROLLBACK instead of COMMIT to preserve the rows. In reality, you would of course use COMMIT to "save" the results of your operation.

The second option is dangerous. It is possible to suspend foreign key constraints by temporarily setting the foreign_key_checks system variable to 0 on the session level. We recommend against this practice, but it's the only way to delete from all three tables at the same time:

```
mysql> SET foreign_key_checks=0;

Query OK, 0 rows affected (0.00 sec)

mysql> BEGIN;

Query OK, 0 rows affected (0.00 sec)

mysql> DELETE FROM film, film_actor, film_category
    -> USING film JOIN film_actor USING (film_id)
    -> JOIN film_category USING (film_id)
    -> LEFT JOIN inventory USING (film_id)
    -> WHERE inventory.film_id IS NULL;

Query OK, 300 rows affected (0.03 sec)

mysql> ROLLBACK;

Query OK, 0 rows affected (0.00 sec)

mysql> SET foreign_key_checks=1;

Query OK, 0 rows affected (0.00 sec)
```

While we don't recommend disabling foreign key checks, doing so allows us to show the power of multitable deletes. Here, with one query it was possible to achieve what took three queries in the previous example.

Let's break down this query. The tables from which rows will be deleted (if matched) are film, film_actor, and film_category. We specified them between the DELETE FROM and USING terms for clarity. USING starts our query, the filtering part of the DELETE statement. In this example, we have constructed a four-table join. We have joined film, film_actor, and film_category using INNER JOIN, as we need only matching rows. To the result of those joins, we LEFT JOIN the inventory table. In this context, using a left join is extremely important, because we are actually interested only in rows where inventory will have no records. We express that with WHERE inventory.film_id IS NULL. The result of this query is that we get all films not in inventory, then all film-actor relationships for those films, along with all category relationships for the films.

Is it possible to make this query safe to use with foreign keys? Not without breaking it down, unfortunately, but we can do better than having to run three queries:

```
mysql> BEGIN;

Query OK, 0 rows affected (0.00 sec)

mysql> DELETE FROM film_actor, film_category USING
    -> film JOIN film_actor USING (film_id)
    -> JOIN film_category USING (film_id)
    -> LEFT JOIN inventory USING (film_id)
    -> WHERE inventory.film_id IS NULL;

Query OK, 258 rows affected (0.02 sec)
```

```
mysql> DELETE FROM film USING
    -> film LEFT JOIN inventory USING (film_id)
    -> WHERE inventory.film_id IS NULL;

Query OK, 42 rows affected (0.01 sec)

mysql> ROLLBACK;

Query OK, 0 rows affected (0.01 sec)
```

What we've done here is combined deletion from the `film_actor` and `film_category` tables into a single DELETE statement, thus allowing deletion from `film` without any error. The difference from the previous example is that we DELETE FROM two tables instead of three.

Let's talk about the number of rows affected. In the first example, we deleted 42 rows from `film`, 42 rows from `film_category`, and 216 rows from the `film_actor` table. In the second example, our single DELETE query removed 300 rows. In the final example, we removed 258 rows combined from the `film_category` and `film_actor` tables, and 42 rows from the `film` table. You can probably guess by now that for a multitable delete MySQL will output the total number of rows deleted, without a breakdown into individual tables. This makes it harder to keep track of exactly how many rows were touched in each table.

Also, in multitable deletes you can't use the ORDER BY or LIMIT clauses.

Updates

Now we'll contrive an example using the `sakila` database to illustrate multiple-table updates. We've decided to change the ratings of all horror films to R, regardless of the original rating. To begin, let's display the horror films and their ratings:

```
mysql> SELECT name category, title, rating
    -> FROM film JOIN film_category USING (film_id)
    -> JOIN category USING (category_id)
    -> WHERE name = 'Horror';
+----------+----------------------------+--------+
| category | title                      | rating |
+----------+----------------------------+--------+
| Horror   | ACE GOLDFINGER             | G      |
| Horror   | AFFAIR PREJUDICE           | G      |
| Horror   | AIRPORT POLLOCK            | R      |
| Horror   | ALABAMA DEVIL              | PG-13  |
| ...      |                            |        |
| Horror   | ZHIVAGO CORE               | NC-17  |
+----------+----------------------------+--------+
56 rows in set (0.00 sec)
```

```
mysql> SELECT COUNT(title)
    -> FROM film JOIN film_category USING (film_id)
    -> JOIN category USING (category_id)
    -> WHERE name = 'Horror' AND rating <> 'R';
+--------------+
| COUNT(title) |
+--------------+
|           42 |
+--------------+
1 row in set (0.00 sec)
```

We don't know about you, but we'd love to see a G-rated horror film! Now, let's put that query into an UPDATE statement:

```
mysql> UPDATE film JOIN film_category USING (film_id)
    -> JOIN category USING (category_id)
    -> SET rating = 'R' WHERE category.name = 'Horror';
Query OK, 42 rows affected (0.01 sec)
Rows matched: 56  Changed: 42  Warnings: 0
```

Let's look at the syntax. A multiple-table update looks similar to a SELECT query. The UPDATE statement is followed by a list of tables that incorporates whatever join clauses you need or prefer; in this example, we've used JOIN (remember, that's INNER JOIN) to bring together the film and film_category tables. This is followed by the keyword SET, with assignments to individual columns. Here you can see that only one column is modified (to change the ratings to R), so columns in all other tables besides film aren't modified. The following WHERE is optional, but is necessary in this example to only touch rows with the category name Horror.

Note how MySQL reports that 56 rows were matched, but only 42 updated. If you look at the results of the previous SELECT queries, you'll see that they show the counts of films in the Horror category (56), and films in that category with a rating other than R (42). Only 42 rows were updated because the other films already had that rating.

As with multitable deletes, there are some limitations on multitable updates:

- You can't use ORDER BY.
- You can't use LIMIT.
- You can't update a table that's read from in a nested subquery.

Other than that, multitable updates are much the same as single-table ones.

Replacing Data

You'll sometimes want to overwrite data. You can do this in two ways using the techniques we've shown previously:

- Delete an existing row using its primary key and then insert a replacement with the same primary key.
- Update a row using its primary key, replacing some or all of the values (except the primary key).

The REPLACE statement gives you a third, convenient way to change data. This section explains how it works.

The REPLACE statement is just like INSERT, but with one difference. You can't INSERT a new row if there is an existing row in the table with the same primary key. You can get around this problem with a REPLACE query, which first removes any existing row with the same primary key and then inserts the new one.

Let's try an example, where we'll replace the row for the actress PENELOPE GUINESS in the sakila database:

```
mysql> REPLACE INTO actor VALUES (1, 'Penelope', 'Guiness', NOW());
ERROR 1451 (23000): Cannot delete or update a parent row:
a foreign key constraint fails (`sakila`.`film_actor`,
CONSTRAINT `fk_film_actor_actor` FOREIGN KEY (`actor_id`)
REFERENCES `actor` (`actor_id`) ON DELETE RESTRICT ON UPDATE CASCADE)
```

Unfortunately, as you'll have guessed after reading the previous paragraph, REPLACE actually has to perform a DELETE. If your database is highly constrained referentially, like the sakila database is, the REPLACE will often not work. Let's not fight against the database here and instead use the actor_2 table we created in "Creating Tables with Queries" on page 277:

```
mysql> REPLACE actor_2 VALUES (1, 'Penelope', 'Guiness', NOW());
Query OK, 2 rows affected (0.00 sec)
```

You can see that MySQL reports that two rows were affected: first the old row was deleted, and then the new row was inserted. You can see that the change we made was minor—we just changed the case of the name—and therefore it could easily have been accomplished with an UPDATE. Because the tables in the sakila database are relatively small, it's difficult to construct an example in which REPLACE looks simpler than UPDATE.

You can use the different INSERT syntaxes with REPLACE, including using SELECT queries. Here are some examples:

```
mysql> REPLACE INTO actor_2 VALUES (1, 'Penelope', 'Guiness', NOW());
Query OK, 2 rows affected (0.00 sec)

mysql> REPLACE INTO actor_2 (actor_id, first_name, last_name)
    -> VALUES (1, 'Penelope', 'Guiness');
Query OK, 2 rows affected (0.00 sec)

mysql> REPLACE actor_2 (actor_id, first_name, last_name)
    -> VALUES (1, 'Penelope', 'Guiness');
Query OK, 2 rows affected (0.00 sec)

mysql> REPLACE actor_2 SET actor_id = 1,
    -> first_name = 'Penelope', last_name = 'Guiness';
Query OK, 2 rows affected (0.00 sec)
```

The first variant is almost identical to our previous example, except it includes the optional INTO keyword (which, arguably, improves the readability of the statement). The second variant explicitly lists the column names that the matching values should be inserted into. The third variant is the same as the second, without the optional INTO keyword. The final variant uses the SET syntax; you can add the optional keyword INTO to this variant if you want. Note that if you don't specify a value for a column, it's set to its default value, just like for INSERT.

You can also bulk-replace into a table, removing and inserting more than one row. Here's an example:

```
mysql> REPLACE actor_2 (actor_id, first_name, last_name)
    -> VALUES (2, 'Nick', 'Wahlberg'),
    -> (3, 'Ed', 'Chase');
Query OK, 4 rows affected (0.00 sec)
Records: 2  Duplicates: 2  Warnings: 0
```

Note that four rows are affected: two deletions and two insertions. You can also see that two duplicates were found, meaning the replacement of existing rows succeeded. In contrast, if there isn't a matching row in a REPLACE statement, it acts just like an INSERT:

```
mysql> REPLACE actor_2 (actor_id, first_name, last_name)
    -> VALUES (1000, 'William', 'Dyer');
Query OK, 1 row affected (0.00 sec)
```

You can tell that only the insert occurred, since only one row was affected.

Replacing also works with a SELECT statement. Recall the recommend table from "Inserting Data Using Queries" on page 261, at the beginning of this chapter. Suppose you've added 10 films to it, but you don't like the choice of the seventh film in the list. Here's how you can replace it with a random choice of another film:

```
mysql> REPLACE INTO recommend SELECT film_id, language_id,
    -> release_year, title, length, 7 FROM film
    -> ORDER BY RAND() LIMIT 1;

Query OK, 2 rows affected (0.00 sec)
Records: 1  Duplicates: 1  Warnings: 0
```

Again, the syntax is the same as with INSERT, but a deletion is attempted (and succeeds!) before the insertion. Note that we keep the value of the sequence_id as 7.

If a table doesn't have a primary key or another unique key, replacing doesn't make sense. This is because there's no way of uniquely identifying a matching row in order to delete it. When you use REPLACE on such a table, its behavior is identical to INSERT. Also, as with INSERT, you can't replace rows in a table that's used in a subquery. Finally, note the difference between INSERT IGNORE and REPLACE: the first keeps the existing data with the duplicate key and does not insert the new row, while the second deletes the existing row and replaces it with the new one.

When specifying a list of columns for REPLACE, you have to list every column that does not have a default value. In our examples, we had to specify actor_id, first_name, and last_name, but we omitted the last_update column, which has a default value of CURRENT_TIMESTAMP.

 REPLACE is a powerful statement, but be careful when using it, as the results can be unexpected. Pay special attention when you have auto-increment columns and multiple unique keys defined.

MySQL provides another nonstandard extension of SQL: INSERT ... ON DUPLICATE KEY UPDATE. It is similar to REPLACE, but instead of DELETE followed by INSERT, it executes an UPDATE whenever a duplicate key is found. At the beginning of this section, we had an issue replacing a row in the actor table. MySQL refused to run a REPLACE, because deleting a row from the actor table would violate a foreign key constraint. It is, however, easily possible to achieve the desired result with the following statement:

```
mysql> INSERT INTO actor_3 (actor_id, first_name, last_name)
    -> VALUES (1, 'Penelope', 'Guiness')
    -> ON DUPLICATE KEY UPDATE first_name = 'Penelope', last_name = 'Guiness';

Query OK, 2 rows affected (0.00 sec)
```

Note that we're using the `actor_3` table created in "Creating Tables with Queries" on page 277, as it has all the same constraints as the original `actor` table. The statement that we've just shown is very similar to REPLACE semantically, but has a few key differences. When you do not specify a value for a field in a REPLACE command, that field must have a DEFAULT value, and that default value will be set. That naturally follows from the fact that a completely new row is inserted. In the case of INSERT ... ON DUPLICATE KEY UPDATE, we are updating an existing row, so it's not necessary to list every column. We can do that if we want, though:

```
mysql> INSERT INTO actor_3 VALUES (1, 'Penelope', 'Guiness', NOW())
    -> ON DUPLICATE KEY UPDATE
    -> actor_id = 1, first_name = 'Penelope',
    -> last_name = 'Guiness', last_update = NOW();
Query OK, 2 rows affected (0.01 sec)
```

To minimize the amount of typing necessary for this command and to allow inserting multiple rows, we can refer to the new field values in the UPDATE clause. Here's an example with multiple rows, one of which is new:

```
mysql> INSERT INTO actor_3 (actor_id, first_name, last_name) VALUES
    -> (1, 'Penelope', 'Guiness'), (2, 'Nick', 'Wahlberg'),
    -> (3, 'Ed', 'Chase'), (1001, 'William', 'Dyer')
    -> ON DUPLICATE KEY UPDATE first_name = VALUES(first_name),
    -> last_name = VALUES(last_name);
Query OK, 5 rows affected (0.01 sec)
Records: 4  Duplicates: 2
```

Let's review this query in more detail. We're inserting four rows into the `actor_3` table, and by using ON DUPLICATE KEY UPDATE we're telling MySQL to run an update on any duplicate rows it finds. Unlike in our previous example, however, this time we don't set updated column values explicitly. Instead, we use the special VALUES() function to obtain the value of each column in the rows we passed to the INSERT. For example, for the second row, 2, Nick, Walhberg, VALUES(first_name) will return Nick. Notice that MySQL reports we've updated an odd number of rows: five. Whenever a new row is inserted, the number of affected rows is incremented by one. Whenever an old row is updated, the number of affected rows is incremented by two. Since we've already updated the record for Penelope by running the previous query, our new insert doesn't add anything new, and MySQL will skip the update as well. We are left with two updates for duplicate rows, and insertion of a completely new row, or five rows affected in total.

> In most situations, we recommend that you default to using INSERT ... ON DUPLICATE KEY UPDATE instead of REPLACE.

The EXPLAIN Statement

You'll sometimes find that MySQL doesn't run queries as quickly as you expect. For example, you'll often notice that a nested query runs slowly. You might also find—or, at least, suspect—that MySQL isn't doing what you hoped, because you know an index exists but the query still seems slow. You can diagnose and solve query optimization problems using the EXPLAIN statement.

Analyzing query plans, understanding optimizer decisions, and tuning query performance are advanced topics, and more art than science: there's no one way to do it. We are adding this section so that you know this capability exists, but we won't get too deep into this topic.

The EXPLAIN statement helps you learn about a SELECT or any other query. Specifically, it tells you how MySQL is going to do the job in terms of the indexes, keys, and steps it'll take if you ask it to resolve a query. EXPLAIN does not actually execute a query (unless you ask it to) and in general doesn't take a lot of time to run.

Let's try a simple example that illustrates the idea:

```
mysql> EXPLAIN SELECT * FROM actor\G
*************************** 1. row ***************************
           id: 1
  select_type: SIMPLE
        table: actor
   partitions: NULL
         type: ALL
possible_keys: NULL
          key: NULL
      key_len: NULL
          ref: NULL
         rows: 200
     filtered: 100.00
        Extra: NULL
1 row in set, 1 warning (0.00 sec)
```

The statement gives you lots of information. It tells you that:

- The id is 1, meaning this row in the output refers to the first (and only!) SELECT statement in this query. If we utilize a subquery, each SELECT statement will have a different id in the EXPLAIN output (although some subqueries will not result in multiple ids being reported, as MySQL might rewrite the query). We'll show an example with a subquery and different id values later.

- The select_type is SIMPLE, meaning it doesn't use a UNION or subqueries.

- The table that this row is referring to is actor.

- The partitions column is empty, because no tables are partitioned.

- The `type` of join is `ALL`, meaning all rows in the table are processed by this `SELECT` statement. This is often bad, but not in this case; we'll explain why later.
- The `possible_keys` that could be used are listed. In this case, no index will help find all rows in a table, so `NULL` is reported.
- The `key` that is actually used is listed, taken from the list of `possible_keys`. In this case, since no key is available, none is used.
- The `key_len` (key length) of the key MySQL plans to use is listed. Again, no key means a `NULL` `key_len` is reported.
- The `ref` (reference) columns or constants that are used with the key are listed. Again, there are none in this example.
- The `rows` that MySQL thinks it needs to process to get an answer are listed.
- The `filtered` column tells us the percentage of rows from the table that this stage will return: 100 means all rows will be returned. This is expected as we're asking for all rows.
- Any `Extra` information about the query resolution is listed. Here, there's none.

In summary, the output of `EXPLAIN SELECT * FROM actor` tells you that all rows from the `actor` table will be processed (there are 200 of them), and no indexes will be used to resolve the query. This makes sense and is probably exactly what you expected would happen.

Note that every EXPLAIN statement reports a warning. Each query we send to MySQL gets rewritten before execution, and the warning message will contain the rewritten query. For example, * may be expanded to an explicit list of columns, or a subquery may be optimized implicitly into a `JOIN`. Here's an example:

```
mysql> EXPLAIN SELECT * FROM actor WHERE actor_id IN
    -> (SELECT actor_id FROM film_actor
    -> WHERE film_id = 11);

+----+-------------+------------+------------+--------+...
| id | select_type | table      | partitions | type   |...
+----+-------------+------------+------------+--------+...
|  1 | SIMPLE      | film_actor | NULL       | ref    |...
|  1 | SIMPLE      | actor      | NULL       | eq_ref |...
+----+-------------+------------+------------+--------+...
...+----------------------+---------------+---------+...
...| possible_keys        | key           | key_len |...
...+----------------------+---------------+---------+...
...| PRIMARY,idx_fk_film_id | idx_fk_film_id | 2      |...
...| PRIMARY              | PRIMARY       | 2       |...
...+----------------------+---------------+---------+...
```

```
...+-----------------------------+------+----------+-------------+
...| ref                         | rows | filtered | Extra       |
...+-----------------------------+------+----------+-------------+
...| const                       |    4 |   100.00 | Using index |
...| sakila.film_actor.actor_id  |    1 |   100.00 | NULL        |
...+-----------------------------+------+----------+-------------+
2 rows in set, 1 warning (0.00 sec)

mysql> SHOW WARNINGS\G

*************************** 1. row ***************************

  Level: Note
   Code: 1003
Message: /* select#1 */ select
`sakila`.`actor`.`actor_id` AS `actor_id`,
`sakila`.`actor`.`first_name` AS `first_name`,
`sakila`.`actor`.`last_name` AS `last_name`,
`sakila`.`actor`.`last_update` AS `last_update`
from `sakila`.`film_actor` join `sakila`.`actor` where
((`sakila`.`actor`.`actor_id` = `sakila`.`film_actor`.`actor_id`)
and (`sakila`.`film_actor`.`film_id` = 11))
1 row in set (0.00 sec)
```

We mentioned that we would show an example with different `id` values and a sub-query. Here's the query:

```
mysql> EXPLAIN SELECT * FROM actor WHERE actor_id IN
    -> (SELECT actor_id FROM film_actor JOIN
    -> film USING (film_id)
    -> WHERE title = 'ZHIVAGO CORE');
```

```
+----+--------------+-------------+------------+------+...
| id | select_type  | table       | partitions | type |...
+----+--------------+-------------+------------+------+...
|  1 | SIMPLE       | <subquery2> | NULL       | ALL  |...
|  1 | SIMPLE       | actor       | NULL       | ALL  |...
|  2 | MATERIALIZED | film        | NULL       | ref  |...
|  2 | MATERIALIZED | film_actor  | NULL       | ref  |...
+----+--------------+-------------+------------+------+...

...+----------------------+---------------+---------+----------------------+...
...| possible_keys        | key           | key_len | ref                  |...
...+----------------------+---------------+---------+----------------------+...
...| NULL                 | NULL          | NULL    | NULL                 |...
...| PRIMARY              | NULL          | NULL    | NULL                 |...
...| PRIMARY,idx_title    | idx_title     | 514     | const                |...
...| PRIMARY,idx_fk_film_id | idx_fk_film_id | 2     | sakila.film.film_id  |...
...+----------------------+---------------+---------+----------------------+...
```

```
...+------+----------+-----------------------------------------------+
...| rows | filtered | Extra                                         |
...+------+----------+-----------------------------------------------+
...| NULL |   100.00 | NULL                                          |
...|  200 |     0.50 | Using where; Using join buffer (hash join)    |
...|    1 |   100.00 | Using index                                   |
...|    5 |   100.00 | Using index                                   |
...+------+----------+-----------------------------------------------+
4 rows in set, 1 warning (0.01 sec)
```

In this example, you can see that id 1 is used for the actor and <subquery2> tables, and id 2 is used for film and film_actor. But what is <subquery2>? That's a virtual table name used here because the optimizer materialized the results of the subquery, or in other words stored them in a temporary table in memory. You can see that the query with an id of 2 has a select_type of MATERIALIZED. The outside query (id 1) will look up the results of the inner query (id 2) from this temporary table. This is just one of many optimizations that MySQL can perform while executing complex queries.

Next, we'll give the EXPLAIN statement some real work to do. Let's ask it to explain an INNER JOIN between actor, film_actor, film, film_category, and category:

```
mysql> EXPLAIN SELECT first_name, last_name FROM actor
    -> JOIN film_actor USING (actor_id)
    -> JOIN film USING (film_id)
    -> JOIN film_category USING (film_id)
    -> JOIN category USING (category_id)
    -> WHERE category.name = 'Horror';
```

id	select_type	table	partitions	type |...
1	SIMPLE	category	NULL	ALL |...
1	SIMPLE	film_category	NULL	ref |...
1	SIMPLE	film	NULL	eq_ref |...
1	SIMPLE	film_actor	NULL	ref |...
1	SIMPLE	actor	NULL	eq_ref |...

possible_keys	key	key_len |...
PRIMARY	NULL	NULL |...
PRIMARY,fk_film_category_category	fk_film_category_category	1 |...
PRIMARY	PRIMARY	2 |...
PRIMARY,idx_fk_film_id	idx_fk_film_id	2 |...
PRIMARY	PRIMARY	2 |...

```
...+---------------------------------+------+----------+------------+
...| ref                             | rows | filtered | Extra      |
...+---------------------------------+------+----------+------------+
...| NULL                            |  16  |   10.00  | Using where |
...| sakila.category.category_id     |  62  |  100.00  | Using index |
...| sakila.film_category.film_id    |   1  |  100.00  | Using index |
...| sakila.film_category.film_id    |   5  |  100.00  | Using index |
...| sakila.film_actor.actor_id      |   1  |  100.00  | NULL       |
...+---------------------------------+------+----------+------------+
5 rows in set, 1 warning (0.00 sec)
```

Before we discuss the output, think about how the query could be evaluated. MySQL could go through each row in the actor table, then match that with film_actor, then with film, film_category, and finally category. We have a filter on the category table, so in this imaginary case MySQL would only be able to match fewer rows once it gets to that table. That is a poor execution strategy. Can you think of a better one?

Let's now look at what MySQL actually decided to do. This time, there are five rows because there are five tables in the join. Let's run through this, focusing on those things that are different from the previous examples:

- The first row is similar to what we saw before. MySQL will read all 16 rows from the category table. This time, the value in the Extra column is Using where. That means a filter based on a WHERE clause is going to be applied. In this example, the filtered column shows 10, meaning that roughly 10% of the table rows will be produced by this stage for further operations. The MySQL optimizer expects 16 rows in the table and expects that one to two rows will be returned here.

- Now let's look at row 2. The join type for the film_category table is ref, meaning that all rows in the film_category table that match rows in the category table will be read. In practice, this means one or more rows from the film_category table will be read for each category_id from the category table. The possible_keys column shows both PRIMARY and fk_film_category_category, and the latter is chosen as the index. The primary key of the film_category table has two columns, and the first one of them is film_id, making that index less optimal for filtering on category_id. The key used to search film_category has a key_len of 1 and is searched using the sakila.category.category_id value from the category table.

- Moving to the next row, we can see that the join type for the film table is eq_ref. This means that for each row we got from the previous stage (scanning film_category), we'll read exactly one row in this stage. MySQL can guarantee that because the index used to access the film table is PRIMARY. In general, if a UNIQUE NOT NULL index is used, eq_ref is possible. This is one of the best join strategies.

The two nested rows in the output do not show us anything new. In the end, we see that MySQL selected an optimal execution plan. Usually, the fewer rows that are read during the first step of the execution, the faster the query will be.

MySQL 8.0 introduced a new format of EXPLAIN PLAN output, which is available through the EXPLAIN ANALYZE statement. While it may be somewhat easier to read, the caveat here is that the statement actually has to be executed, unlike with the regular EXPLAIN. We won't go into the details of this new format, but we'll show an example here:

```
mysql> EXPLAIN ANALYZE SELECT first_name, last_name
    -> FROM actor JOIN film_actor USING (actor_id)
    -> JOIN film USING (film_id)
    -> WHERE title = 'ZHIVAGO CORE'\G

*************************** 1. row ***************************
EXPLAIN:
-> Nested loop inner join
   (cost=3.07 rows=5)
   (actual time=0.036..0.055 rows=6 loops=1)
  -> Nested loop inner join
     (cost=1.15 rows=5)
     (actual time=0.028..0.034 rows=6 loops=1)
    -> Index lookup on film
       using idx_title (title='ZHIVAGO CORE')
       (cost=0.35 rows=1)
       (actual time=0.017..0.018 rows=1 loops=1)
    -> Index lookup on film_actor
       using idx_fk_film_id (film_id=film.film_id)
       (cost=0.80 rows=5)
       (actual time=0.010..0.015 rows=6 loops=1)
  -> Single-row index lookup on actor
     using PRIMARY (actor_id=film_actor.actor_id)
     (cost=0.27 rows=1)
     (actual time=0.003..0.003 rows=1 loops=6)

1 row in set (0.00 sec)
```

This output is even more advanced than the regular EXPLAIN output, as it gives more data. We'll leave analyzing it as an exercise for the reader. You should be able to figure it out based on our explanation for the regular EXPLAIN output.

Alternative Storage Engines

One of the features of MySQL that distinguishes it from many other RDBMSs is its support for different storage engines. The mechanism of MySQL's support of multiple engines is complicated, and to explain it properly we'd need to go into more depth on its architecture and implementation than we have space for here. We can, however, try to give you a bird's-eye overview of what engines are available, why you might want to use a nondefault engine, and why having this choice is important.

Instead of saying *storage engine*, which sounds complicated, we could say *table type*. In very simplified terms, MySQL allows you to create tables of different types, with each type giving those tables distinct properties. There's no universally good table type, as each storage engine has pros and cons.

In the book so far, we've used only the default InnoDB table type. The reason is simple: almost everything you're likely to want from a modern database can be achieved using InnoDB. It's generally fast, reliable, and a proven and well-supported engine, and is widely considered (including by us) to provide the best balance of pros and cons. We've seen this engine used successfully by applications requiring very high throughput of short queries, and also by data warehouse applications that run few but "large" queries.

At the time of writing, the official MySQL documentation documents 8 additional storage engines, and 18 additional engines are documented for MariaDB. In reality, there are even more storage engines available, but not all of them make it into a major MySQL flavor's documentation. Here we'll only describe those engines we find useful and that are at least somewhat commonly used. It may well be that the storage engine that best fits your use case is not one we describe. Take no offense; there are just too many of them to cover them all fairly.

Before we dive into our overview of different engines, let's briefly look at why this matters. The pluggable nature of storage engines in MySQL and the ability to create tables with different types is important because it allows you to unify your database access layer. Instead of using multiple database products, each with its own driver, query language, configuration, management, backups, and so on, you can just use MySQL and achieve different behaviors by changing table types. Your apps may not even need to know what types tables have. That said, it's not all that simple and rosy. You may not be able to use all of the backup solutions we'll explain in Chapter 10. You will also need to understand the trade-offs each engine provides. However, we still think that it's better to have this ability to change table types than not.

We'll start our review by defining broad categories based on important properties of the different storage engines. One of the most important divisions is the ability of the engine to support transactions (you can read more about transactions, locking, and why all of this is important in Chapter 6).

Currently available transactional engines include the default InnoDB, the actively developed MyRocks, and the deprecated TokuDB. All of the different engines available across major MySQL flavors; only these three support transactions. Every other engine is nontransactional.

The next broad division we can perform is based on crash safety, or the ability of the engine to guarantee the durability property of the ACID set of properties. If a table uses a crash-safe engine, then we can expect every bit of data a committed transaction has written to be available after an unclean instance restart. Crash-safe engines include the already mentioned InnoDB, MyRocks, and TokuDB, as well as the Aria engine. None of the other available engines guarantees crash safety.

We could come up with more examples of how to group the table types, but let's get to actually describing some of the engines and their properties. First things first, let's see how to actually view the list of engines available. To achieve that, we use the special SHOW ENGINES command. Here's its output on a default MySQL 8.0.23 Linux installation:

```
mysql> SHOW ENGINES;
+--------------------+----------+...
| Engine             | Support  |...
+--------------------+----------+...
| ARCHIVE            | YES      |...
| BLACKHOLE          | YES      |...
| MRG_MYISAM         | YES      |...
| FEDERATED          | NO       |...
| MyISAM             | YES      |...
| PERFORMANCE_SCHEMA | YES      |...
| InnoDB             | DEFAULT  |...
| MEMORY             | YES      |...
| CSV                | YES      |...
+--------------------+----------+...
   ...+-----------------------------------------------------------------+...
   ...| Comment                                                         |...
   ...+-----------------------------------------------------------------+...
   ...| Archive storage engine                                          |...
   ...| /dev/null storage engine (anything you write to it disappears)  |...
   ...| Collection of identical MyISAM tables                           |...
   ...| Federated MySQL storage engine                                  |...
   ...| MyISAM storage engine                                           |...
   ...| Performance Schema                                              |...
   ...| Supports transactions, row-level locking, and foreign keys      |...
   ...| Hash based, stored in memory, useful for temporary tables       |...
   ...| CSV storage engine                                              |...
   ...+-----------------------------------------------------------------+...
   ...+--------------+------+------------+
   ...| Transactions | XA   | Savepoints |
   ...+--------------+------+------------+
   ...| NO           | NO   | NO         |
   ...| NO           | NO   | NO         |
   ...| NO           | NO   | NO         |
   ...| NULL         | NULL | NULL       |
   ...| NO           | NO   | NO         |
   ...| NO           | NO   | NO         |
   ...| YES          | YES  | YES        |
```

```
...| NO            | NO  | NO         |
...| NO            | NO  | NO         |
...+--------------+------+-----------+
9 rows in set (0.00 sec)
```

You can see that MySQL conveniently tells us whether an engine supports transactions. The XA column is for distributed transactions—we won't be covering these in this book. Savepoints are basically the ability to create mini-transactions within transactions, another advanced topic. As an exercise, consider executing SHOW ENGINES; in MariaDB and Percona Server installations.

InnoDB

Before we move on to "alternative" storage engines, let's discuss the default one: InnoDB. InnoDB is reliable, performant, and full-featured. Pretty much everything you'd expect from a modern RDBMS is achievable in some way with InnoDB. In this book, we never change the engine of a table, so every example uses InnoDB. While you are learning MySQL, we recommend that you stick with this engine. It's important to understand its downsides, but unless they become problematic for you, there's almost no reason not to use it all the time.

The InnoDB table type includes the following features:

Support for transactions
  This is discussed in detail in Chapter 6.

Advanced crash recovery features
  The InnoDB table type uses logs, which are files that contain a record of the actions that MySQL has taken to change the database. Logs enable MySQL to recover effectively from power losses, crashes, and other basic database failures. Of course, nothing can help you recover from the loss of a machine, failure of a disk drive, or other catastrophic failures. For these, you need offsite backups and new hardware. Every backup tool we explore in Chapter 10 works with InnoDB.

Row-level locking
  Unlike the previous default engine, MyISAM (which we'll explore in the following section), InnoDB provides fine-grained locking infrastructure. The lowest level of locking is row-level, meaning that an individual row can be locked by a running query or transaction. This is important for most write-heavy online transaction processing (OLTP) applications; if you're locking at a higher level, like the table level, you can end up with too many concurrency issues.

Foreign key support
  InnoDB is currently the only MySQL table type that supports foreign keys. If you are building a system that requires a high level of data safety enforced by referential constraints, InnoDB is your only choice.

Encryption support

InnoDB tables can be encrypted transparently by MySQL.

Partitioning support

InnoDB supports *partitioning*; that is, spreading of data physically between multiple data files based on some rules. This allows InnoDB to work with tables of tremendous size efficiently.

That's a lot of pros, but there are also a few cons:

Complexity

InnoDB is relatively complex. This means that there's a lot to configure and understand. Out of almost a thousand server options in MySQL, more than two hundred are specific to InnoDB. This downside is, however, far outweighed by the benefits this engine provides.

Data footprint

InnoDB is a relatively disk-hungry storage engine, making it less appealing for storing extremely large datasets.

Scaling with database size

InnoDB shines when the so-called "hot" dataset, or frequently accessed data, is present in its buffer pool. This limits its scalability.

MyISAM and Aria

MyISAM was the default storage engine in MySQL for a long time, and a staple of this database. It is simple in use and design, is quite performant, and has low overhead. So why did it stop being the default? There are actually several good reasons for this, as you'll see when we discuss its limitations.

Nowadays, we do not recommend using MyISAM unless it's required for legacy reasons. You may read on the internet that its performance is better than InnoDB's. Unfortunately, most of that information is very old and hasn't aged well—today, that's simply not the case in the vast majority of cases. One reason for this is the changes to the Linux kernel necessitated by the Spectre and Meltdown security vulnerabilities in January 2018, which resulted in a performance decrease of up to 90% for MyISAM.

Until MySQL 8.0, MyISAM was used in MySQL for all data dictionary objects. Starting with that version, the data dictionary is now fully InnoDB, to support advanced features like atomic DDL.

Aria is a reworked MyISAM provided in MariaDB. Apart from promising better performance and being improved and worked on continuously, the most important feature of Aria is its crash safety. MyISAM, unlike InnoDB, does not guarantee data safety when your write succeeds, which is a major drawback of this storage engine. Aria, on the other hand, allows the creation of durable tables, supported by a global transaction log. In the future Aria may also support full-fledged transactions, but this is not the case at the time of writing.

The MyISAM table type includes the following features:

Table-level locking
Unlike InnoDB, MyISAM only supports locks at the high level of whole tables. This is much simpler and less nuanced than row-level locking and has lower overhead and memory requirements. However, a major drawback becomes apparent with highly concurrent, write-heavy workloads: even if each session would update or insert a separate row, they will each execute in turn. Reads in MyISAM can coexist simultaneously, but they will block concurrent writes. Writes also block reads.

Partitioning support
Until MySQL 8.0, MyISAM supported partitioning. In MySQL 8.0 this is no longer the case, and to achieve this one must resort to using different storage engines (Merge or MRG_MyISAM).

Compression
It's possible to create read-only compressed tables with the `myisampack` utility, which are quite a bit smaller than the equivalent InnoDB tables without compression. Since InnoDB supports compression, however, we recommend you first check whether this option will give you better results.

The MyISAM type has the following limitations:

Crash safety and recovery
MyISAM tables are not crash-safe. MySQL does not guarantee that when a write succeeds, the data actually reaches files on the disk. If MySQL doesn't exit cleanly, MyISAM tables may get corrupted, require repairs, and lose data.

Transactions
MyISAM does not support transactions. Thus, MyISAM only provides atomicity for each individual statement, which may not be enough in your case.

Encryption
MyISAM tables do not support encryption.

MyRocks and TokuDB

One of the most significant problems with InnoDB is its relative difficulty in dealing with large datasets. We've mentioned that it is desirable to have your frequently accessed data in memory, but that is not always possible to achieve. Moreover, when data sizes go into multiterabyte territory, InnoDB's on-disk performance suffers, too. The objects in InnoDB also have quite a large overhead in terms of size. In recent years, a few different projects have appeared that attempt to fix issues inherent to InnoDB's basic data structure the B-tree by basing the storage engine on a different data structure. These include MyRocks, based on the LSM-tree, and TokuDB, based on a proprietary fractal tree data structure.

 We wanted to mention TokuDB in this section for completeness, but its developer, Percona, has deprecated this storage engine, and its future is unclear. TokuDB has similar properties to MyRocks, and in fact MyRocks is the preferable migration path off of TokuDB.

How data structures affect the properties of storage engines is a complex topic, arguably falling outside the scope of database administration and operation. We try to keep things reasonably simple in this book, so we won't go into that particular topic. You should also remember what we wrote earlier about InnoDB: that default is not unreasonable, and more often than not, just using InnoDB is going to give you the best set of trade-offs. It continues to be our recommendation that you use InnoDB while learning MySQL, and beyond that, but we also feel that we should cover the alternatives.

The MyRocks table type includes the following features:

Support for transactions
MyRocks is a transactional storage engine, supporting regular transactions and distributed transactions. Savepoints are not fully supported.

Advanced crash recovery features
MyRocks relies on internal log files called WAL files (for "write-ahead log") to provide crash recovery guarantees. You can expect everything that was committed to be present once the database is restarted after a crash.

Encryption support
MyRocks tables can be encrypted.

Partitioning support
MyRocks tables can be partitioned.

Data compression and compactness
The storage footprint of MyRocks tables is usually lower than that of InnoDB tables. There are two properties leading to that: it uses a more compact storage structure and data within that storage structure can be compressed. While compression is not unique to MyRocks, and InnoDB in fact provides compression options, MyRocks consistently shows better results.

Consistent write performance at scale

This one is difficult to properly explain without going deep into the weeds. However, the minimal version is that the write performance of MyRocks is almost unaffected by the volume of the data. In the real world, this means that MyRocks tables show worse performance than InnoDB tables until the size of the data becomes much larger than memory. What happens then is that InnoDB's performance decreases faster than MyRocks', eventually falling behind.

The MyRocks table type has the following limitations:

Transactions and locking

MyRocks doesn't support the `SERIALIZABLE` isolation level or gap locking, described in Chapter 6.

Foreign keys

Only InnoDB supports foreign key constraints.

Performance tradeoffs

MyRocks does not cope well with read-heavy and analytical workloads. InnoDB provides better generalized performance.

Complexity

We mentioned that InnoDB is more complex than MyISAM. However, in some respects MyRocks is more complex than InnoDB. It is not well documented, is being actively developed (so is less stable), and can be difficult to operate.

General availability

MyRocks is not available in Community or Enterprise MySQL; to use it, you need to use another version of MySQL, like MariaDB or Percona Server. That may result in operational difficulties. Packaged versions lag behind development, and to use all of the current features, a dedicated MySQL server has to be built with MyRocks sources.

Other Table Types

We've covered all the major table types, but there are a few more that we will summarize briefly. Some of these storage engines are rarely used, and they may have documentation issues and bugs.

Memory

Tables of this type are stored entirely in memory and are never persisted on disk. The obvious advantage is performance: memory is many times faster than disk and will probably always be. The disadvantage is that the data is lost as soon as MySQL is restarted or crashes. Memory tables are usually used as temporary tables. Apart from that, memory tables can be used to hold small-sized, frequently accessed hot data, such as a dictionary of sorts.

Archive

This type provides a way to store data in a highly compressed and append-only manner. You cannot modify or delete data in tables using the Archive storage engine. As its name suggests, it's mostly useful for long-term storage of data. In reality, it's rarely used, and it has a few issues with primary key and auto-increment handling. InnoDB with compressed tables and MyRocks may provide better alternatives.

CSV

This storage engine stores tables on disk in CSV format. That allows you to view and manipulate such tables with spreadsheet applications or just text editors. It's not often used, but can be an alternative approach to what we explained in "Loading Data from Comma-Delimited Files" on page 267, and also can be used for data export.

Federated

This type provides a way to query data in remote MySQL systems. Federated tables do not contain any data, only some metadata related to connection details. This is an interesting way of getting or modifying remote data without setting up replication. Compared to just connecting to remote MySQL, it has the benefit of simultaneously providing access to local and remote tables.

Blackhole

This storage engine discards every bit of data that would be stored within its tables. In other words, whatever is written into a Blackhole table is immediately lost. That doesn't sound terribly useful, but there are use cases for this engine. Usually it's used to filter replication through an intermediate server, where unneeded tables are blackholed. Another potential use case is to get rid of a table in a closed-source application: you can't just drop the table, as that'll break the app, but by making it Blackhole you remove any processing and storage over-head.

These storage engines are pretty exotic and are rarely seen in the wild. However, you should know they exist, as you may never know when something might become useful.

## CHAPTER 8

Managing Users and Privileges

The simplest database system is just a bunch of files lying around, with some data in them, and no unified access process. With any RDBMS, we come to expect a significantly higher level of sophistication and abstraction. For one, we want to be able to access the database from multiple clients simultaneously. However, not all of the clients are similar, and not every one of them necessarily needs access to all of the data in the database. It's possible to imagine a database where every user is a superuser, but that would mean you'd have to install a dedicated database for every app and dataset: wasteful. Instead, databases have evolved to support multiple users and roles and provide a means to control privileges and access on a very fine-grained level to guarantee secure shared environments.

Understanding users and privileges is an important part of working efficiently with a database system. Well-planned and managed roles result in a secure system that is easy to manage and work with. In this chapter, we will review most of the things one needs to know about user and privilege management, starting from the basics and moving toward new features like roles. After finishing this chapter, you should have all the basics required to manage access within a MySQL database.

Understanding Users and Privileges

The first building block in the foundation of a shared system is the concept of a *user*. Most modern operating systems have user-based access, so it's highly likely that you already know what that means. Users in MySQL are special objects used for the purpose of:

- Authentication (making sure that a user can access the MySQL server)
- Authorization (making sure that a user can interact with objects in the database)

One thing that makes MySQL distinct from other DBMSs is that users do not *own* schema objects.

Let's consider these points in a little more detail. Every time you access the MySQL server, you must specify a user to be used during authentication. Once you've been authenticated and your identity has been confirmed, you have access to the database. Usually, the user you will be acting as when interacting with schema objects will be the same as the one you used for authentication, but that's not strictly necessary, and that's why we separate the second point. A proxy user is a user that is used for the purpose of checking privileges and actually acting within the database, when another user is used during authentication. That's a rather complex topic and requires nondefault configuration, but it's still possible.

This is an important distinction to remember between authentication and authorization. While you can authenticate with one user, you can be authorized as another and have or not have various permissions.

With these two covered, let's discuss the last point. Some DBMSs support the concept of object ownership. That is, when the user creates a database object—a database or schema, a table, or a stored procedure—that user automatically becomes the new object's owner. The owner usually has the ability to modify objects it owns and grant other users access to them. The important thing here is that MySQL does not in any way have a concept of object ownership.

This lack of ownership makes it even more important to have flexible rules so that users can create objects and then potentially share access to those objects with other users. That is achieved using *privileges*. Privileges can be thought of as sets of rules controlling what actions users are allowed to perform and what data they can access. It's important to understand that by default in MySQL a database user has no privileges at all. Granting a privilege means allowing some action that by default is forbidden.

Users in MySQL are also a bit different than in other databases, because the user object includes a network access control list (ACL). Usually, a MySQL user is represented not just by its name, like bob, but with an appended network address, like bob@localhost. This particular example defines a user that can be accessed only locally through the loopback interface or a Unix socket connection. We will touch on this topic later, when we discuss the SQL syntax for creating and manipulating existing users.

MySQL stores all information related to users and privileges in special tables in the mysql system database called *grant tables*. We'll talk about this concept in a bit more depth in "Grant Tables" on page 317.

This short theoretical foundation should be sufficient to form a basic understanding of MySQL's system of users and privileges. Let's get practical and review the commands and capabilities that the database provides for managing users and privileges.

The root User

Every MySQL installation comes with a few users installed by default. Most of them you don't ever need to touch, but there's one that's extremely frequently used. Some might even say that it's overused, but that's not the discussion we want to have here. The user we're talking about is the ubiquitous and all-powerful root user. With the same name as the default Unix and Linux superuser, this user is just that in MySQL: a user that can do anything by default.

To be more specific, the user is root@localhost, sometimes called the *initial user*. The localhost part of the username, as you now know, limits its use to only local connections. When you install MySQL, depending on the specific MySQL flavor and the OS, you might be able to access root@localhost from the OS root account by just executing the mysql command. In some other cases, a temporary password will be generated for this user.

The initial user is not the only superuser you can create, as you'll see in "The SUPER Privilege" on page 331. While you can create a root@<ip> user, or even a root@% user, we strongly discourage you from doing so, as it is a security hole waiting to be exploited. Not every MySQL server even needs to listen on an interface apart from loopback (that is, localhost), let alone have a superuser with a default name available for login. Of course, you can set secure passwords for all users and should probably set one for root, but it is arguably that little bit safer to not allow remote superuser access, if that is possible.

For all intents and purposes, root@localhost is just a regular user with all privileges granted. You can even drop it, which can happen by mistake. Losing access to the root@localhost user is a fairly common problem when running MySQL. You may have set a password and forgotten it or you inherited a server and were not given the password or something else might have happened. We cover the procedure to recover a forgotten password for the root@localhost initial user in "Changing root's Password and Insecure Startup" on page 347. If you dropped your last available superuser, you will have to follow the same procedure but create a new user instead of changing an existing one.

Creating and Using New Users

The first task we'll cover is creating a new user. Let's start with a rather simple example and review each part:

```
CREATE USER ❶
'bob'@'10.0.2.%' ❷
IDENTIFIED BY 'password'; ❸
```

❶   SQL statement to create a user

❷   User and host definition

❸   Password specification

Here's a more complex example:

```
CREATE USER ❶
'bob'@'10.0.2.%' ❷
IDENTIFIED WITH mysql_native_password ❸
BY 'password' ❹
DEFAULT ROLE 'user_role' ❺
REQUIRE SSL ❻
AND CIPHER 'EDH-RSA-DES-CBC3-SHA' ❼
WITH MAX_USER_CONNECTIONS 10 ❽
PASSWORD EXPIRE NEVER; ❾
```

❶   SQL statement to create a user

❷   User and host definition

❸   Authentication plugin specification

❹   Authentication string/password

❺   Default role set once user is authenticated and connected

❻   Require SSL for connections for this user

❼   Require specific ciphers

❽   Limit maximum number of connections from this user

❾   Override global password expiration settings

This is just scratching the surface, but should give an idea of the parameters that can be changed for a user during its creation. There are quite a lot of them. Let's review the specific parts of that statement in a little more detail:

User and host definition

We mentioned in "Understanding Users and Privileges" on page 307 that users in MySQL are defined not only by their name, but also by hostname. In the previous example, the user is `'bob'@'10.0.2.%'`, where *bob* is the username and *10.0.2.%* is a hostname specification. In fact, it's a hostname specification with a wildcard. Each time someone connects with the username *bob* using TCP, MySQL will do a few things:

1. Get the IP address of the connecting client.

2. Perform a reverse DNS lookup of the IP address to a hostname.

3. Perform a DNS lookup for that hostname (to make sure the reverse lookup wasn't compromised).

4. Check the hostname or IP address with the user's hostname specification.

Only if the hostnames match is access granted. For our user *bob*, a connection from IP address `10.0.2.121` would be allowed, while a connection from `10.0.3.22` would be denied. In fact, to allow connections from another hostname, a new user should be created. Internally, `'bob'@'10.0.2.%'` is a completely different user from `'bob'@'10.0.3.%'`. It's also possible to use fully qualified domain names (FQDNs) in the hostname specification, as in `'bob'@'acme.com'`, but DNS lookups take time, and it's a common optimization to disable them completely.

Specifying all possible hostnames for all users to connect from might be tedious, but it's a useful security feature. However, sometimes a database is set up behind a firewall, or it's simply impractical to specify hostnames. To completely subvert this system, a single wildcard can be used in the host specification, as in `'bob'@'10.0.2%'`. The `'%'` wildcard is also used when you do not specify the host at all (`'bob'@'%'`).

 When proxying connections to MySQL, pay attention to what IP address MySQL "sees" for incoming connections. For example, when HAProxy is used, by default all connections will come from the IP addresses of machines where HAProxy is running. This fact should be taken into consideration when configuring users. We cover HAProxy configuration for MySQL in Chapter 15.

You'll notice that we've enclosed both the username and the host specification in single quotes (`''`). That is not mandatory, and username and host specification follow a similar set of rules to those that were outlined for table and column names and aliases in "Creating and Using Databases" on page 127 and "Aliases" on page 179. For example, when creating or altering the user bob@localhost or bob@172.17.0.2, there's no need to use any quoting. You can't, though, create this user without using quotes: `'username with a space'@'172.%'`. Double quotes, single quotes, or backticks can be used to enclose usernames and hostnames with special symbols.

Authentication plugins specification

MySQL supports a wide variety of ways to authenticate users through its system of authentication plugins. These plugins also provide a way for developers to implement new means of authentication without changing MySQL itself. You can set a particular plugin for a user in the creation phase or later.

You might never need to change the plugin for a user, but it's still worth knowing about this subsystem. In particular, LDAP authentication with MySQL can be achieved by using a special authentication plugin. MySQL Enterprise Edition supports a first-class LDAP plugin, and other MySQL versions and flavors can use PAM as a middleman.

 PAM stands for Pluggable Authentication Modules. It's a standard interface on Unix-like systems that, in very simple terms, allows MySQL to provide authentication by various methods, such as OS passwords, or LDAP. PAM hides the complexity of those authentication methods, and programs like MySQL only need to interface with PAM itself.

MySQL 8.0 uses the `caching_sha2_password` plugin by default, which provides superior security and performance compared to the legacy `mysql_native_pass word` but is not compatible with every client library. To change the default plugin you can configure the `default_authentication_plugin` variable, which will cause new users to be created with the specified plugin instead.

Authentication string/password

Some authentication plugins, including the default one, require you to set a password for the user. Other plugins, like the PAM one, require you to define a mapping from OS users to MySQL users. `auth_string` will be used in both cases. Let's take a look at an example mapping with PAM:

```
mysql> CREATE USER ''@'' IDENTIFIED WITH auth_pam
    -> AS 'mysqld, dba=dbausr, dev=devusr';

Query OK, 0 row affected (0.01 sec)
```

What's defined here is a mapping that can be read as follows: the PAM configuration file *mysqld* will be used (usually located at */etc/pam.d/mysqld*); OS users with group `dba` will be mapped to MySQL user `dbausr`, and OS users with group `dev` to devusr. The mapping alone is not enough, however, as the necessary permissions have to be assigned.

Note that either the Percona PAM plugin or MySQL Enterprise Edition is required for this to work. This example creates a proxy user, which we briefly discussed in "Understanding Users and Privileges" on page 307.

Using nondefault authentication plugins is a relatively advanced topic, so we're only bringing up PAM here to show you that the authentication string is not always a password.

 You can consult the documentation for details on installing the Percona plugin (*https://oreil.ly/A5rbp*) and the MySQL Enterprise Edition plugin (*https://oreil.ly/oihnX*).

Default role set

Roles are a fairly recent addition to MySQL. You may think of a role as a collection of privileges. We discuss them in "Roles" on page 341.

SSL configuration

You can force connections from particular users to use SSL by passing `REQUIRE SSL` to the `CREATE USER` or `ALTER USER` command. Unencrypted connections to the user will be forbidden. Additionally, you can, as shown in the example we gave, specify a particular cipher suite or a number of suites that can be used for this user. Ideally, you should set the acceptable cipher suites on the system level, but setting this on the user level is useful to allow some less safe suites for specific connections. You don't need to specify `REQUIRE SSL` to specify `REQUIRE CIPHER`, and in that case unencrypted connections can be established. However, if an encrypted connection is established, it will use only the particular set of ciphers you supply:

```
mysql> CREATE USER 'john'@'192.168.%' IDENTIFIED BY 'P@ssw0rd#'
    -> REQUIRE CIPHER 'EDH-RSA-DES-CBC3-SHA';
Query OK, 0 row affected (0.02 sec)
```

Additional configurable options that are available include the following:

`X509`

Forcing a client to present a valid certificate. This, as well as the following options, implies the use of SSL.

`ISSUER issuer`

Forcing a client to present a valid certificate issued by a particular CA, specified in `issuer`.

SUBJECT *subject*

Forcing a client to present a valid certificate with a particular subject.

These options can be combined to specify a very particular certificate and encryption requirement:

```
mysql> CREATE USER 'john'@'192.168.%'
    -> REQUIRE SUBJECT '/C=US/ST=NC/L=Durham/
    -> O=BI Dept certificate/
    -> CN=client/emailAddress=john@nonexistent.com'
    -> AND ISSUER '/C=US/ST=NC/L=Durham/
    -> O=MySQL/CN=CA/emailAddress=ca@nonexistent.com'
    -> AND CIPHER 'EDH-RSA-DES-CBC3-SHA';
```

Resource consumption limits

You can define resource consumption limits. In our example we are limiting the maximum number of concurrent connections by this user to 10. This and other resource options default to 0, meaning unlimited. The other possible constraints are `MAX_CONNECTIONS_PER_HOUR`, `MAX_QUERIES_PER_HOUR`, and `MAX_UPDATES_PER_HOUR`. All of these options are part of the `WITH` specification.

Let's create a fairly restricted user, which can run only 10 queries during each given hour, can have only a single concurrent connection, and may not connect more than twice per hour:

```
mysql> CREATE USER 'john'@'192.168.%'
    -> WITH MAX_QUERIES_PER_HOUR 10
    -> MAX_CONNECTIONS_PER_HOUR 2
    -> MAX_USER_CONNECTIONS 1;
```

Note that the number of `MAX_QUERIES_PER_HOUR` is inclusive of `MAX_UPDATES_PER_HOUR` and will limit updates as well. The number of queries also includes everything that the MySQL CLI executes, so setting a really low value is not recommended.

Password management options override

For authentication plugins that deal with passwords, which are stored in grant tables (covered in "Grant Tables" on page 317), you can specify a variety of options related to passwords. In our example, we're setting up a user that has the `PASSWORD EXPIRE NEVER` policy, meaning that its password will never expire based on time. You could also create a user that would have a password expiring every other day, or each week.

MySQL 8.0 extends control capabilities to include tracking of failed authentication attempts and the ability to lock an account temporarily. Let's consider an important user with strict control:

```
mysql> CREATE USER 'app_admin'@'192.168.%'
    -> IDENTIFY BY '...'
    -> WITH PASSWORD EXPIRE INTERVAL 30 DAY
    -> PASSWORD REUSE INTERVAL 180 DAY
    -> PASSWORD REQUIRE CURRENT
    -> FAILED_LOGIN_ATTEMPTS 3
    -> PASSWORD_LOCK_TIME 1;
```

This user's password will need to be changed every 30 days, and previous passwords will not be eligible for reuse for 180 days. When changing the password, the current password must be presented. For good measure, we also only allow three consecutive failed login attempts and will block this user for one day if those are made.

Note that these are overrides on the default system options. It's impractical to set up each individual user manually, so we instead recommend that you set up the defaults and only use overrides for particular users. For example, you can have your DBA users' passwords expire more frequently.

There are some other options available for user creation, which we won't cover here. As MySQL evolves, more options become available, but we believe the ones we've covered so far should be enough while learning your way around MySQL.

Since this section is about not only creating but also using new users, let's talk about these uses. They typically fall into a few categories:

Connecting and authenticating

This is the default and most widespread use of any user entity. You specify the user and password, and MySQL authenticates you with that user and your origin host. Then that pair forms a user as defined within grant tables, which will be used for authorization when you access database objects. This is the default situation. You can run the following query to see the currently authenticated user as well as the user provided by the client:

```
mysql> SELECT CURRENT_USER(), USER();
+----------------+----------------+
| CURRENT_USER() | USER()         |
+----------------+----------------+
| root@localhost | root@localhost |
+----------------+----------------+
1 row in set (0.00 sec)
```

Quite unsurprisingly, the records match. This is the most common occurrence, but as you'll see next, it's not the only possibility.

Providing security for stored objects

When a stored object (like a stored procedure or a view) is created, any user can be specified within the DEFINER clause of that object. That allows you to execute an object from the standpoint of another user: definer, instead of invoker. This can be a useful way to provide elevated privileges for some specific operation, but it can also be a security hole in your system.

When a MySQL account is specified in the `DEFINER` clause of an object, such as a stored procedure, that account will be used for authorization when the stored procedure is executed or when a view is queried. In other words, the current user of a session changes temporarily. As we mentioned, this can be used to elevate privileges in a controlled manner. For example, instead of granting a user permission to read from some tables, you can create a view with a `DEFINER`: the account you specify will be allowed to access the tables when the view is being queried, but not under any other circumstances. Also, the view itself can further restrict what data is returned. The same is true for stored procedures. To interact with an object that has a `DEFINER`, a caller must have the necessary permissions.

Let's take a look at an example. Here's a simple stored procedure that returns the current user used for authorization, as well as the authenticated user. The `DEFINER` is set to `'bob'@'localhost'`:

```
DELIMITER ;;
CREATE DEFINER = 'bob'@'localhost' PROCEDURE test_proc()
BEGIN
    SELECT CURRENT_USER(), USER();
END;
;;
DELIMITER ;
```

If this procedure is executed by the user john from the previous examples, output similar to the following will be printed:

```
mysql> CALL test_proc();

+----------------+---------------------+
| CURRENT_USER() | USER()              |
+----------------+---------------------+
| bob@localhost  | john@192.168.1.174  |
+----------------+---------------------+
1 row in set (0.00 sec)
```

It's important to keep this in mind. Sometimes users are not who they appear to be, and to keep your database safe that has to be noted.

Proxying

Some authentication methods, like PAM and LDAP, do not operate with a one-to-one mapping from authenticating users to database ones. We showed before how to create a PAM-authenticated user—let's see what such a user would see if they queried the authenticating and provided users:

```
mysql> SELECT CURRENT_USER(), USER();
```

```
+------------------+-------------------------+
| CURRENT_USER()   | USER()                  |
+------------------+-------------------------+
| dbausr@localhost | localdbauser@localhost  |
+------------------+-------------------------+
1 row in set (0.00 sec)
```

Before we close this section, we should bring up a couple of important points related to the CREATE USER statement. First, it is possible to create multiple user accounts with a single command, instead of executing multiple CREATE USER statements individually. Second, if the user already exists, CREATE USER doesn't fail, but will change that user in subtle ways. This can be dangerous. To avoid this, you can specify an IF NOT EXISTS option to the command. By doing so, you tell MySQL to create the user only if no such user already exists, and do nothing if it does.

At this point, you should have a good understanding of what a MySQL user is and how it can be used. Next we'll show you how users can be modified, but first you need to understand how user-related information is stored internally.

Grant Tables

MySQL stores both user information and privileges as records in *grant tables*. These are special internal tables in the mysql database, which should ideally never be modified manually and instead are implicitly modified when statements like CREATE USER or GRANT are run. For example, here is the slightly truncated output of a SELECT query on the mysql.user table, which contains user records, including their passwords (in hashed form):

```
mysql> SELECT * FROM user WHERE user = 'root'\G

*************************** 1. row ***************************
                  Host: localhost
                  User: root
           Select_priv: Y
           Insert_priv: Y
           Update_priv: Y
           Delete_priv: Y
...
    Create_routine_priv: Y
     Alter_routine_priv: Y
       Create_user_priv: Y
             Event_priv: Y
           Trigger_priv: Y
 Create_tablespace_priv: Y
              ssl_type:
            ssl_cipher: 0x
           x509_issuer: 0x
          x509_subject: 0x
         max_questions: 0
```

```
          max_updates: 0
      max_connections: 0
 max_user_connections: 0
               plugin: mysql_native_password
 authentication_string: *E1206987C3E6057289D6C3208EACFC1FA0F2FA56
     password_expired: N
password_last_changed: 2020-09-06 17:20:57
     password_lifetime: NULL
        account_locked: N
      Create_role_priv: Y
        Drop_role_priv: Y
 Password_reuse_history: NULL
    Password_reuse_time: NULL
Password_require_current: NULL
       User_attributes: NULL
1 row in set (0.00 sec)
```

You can immediately see that a lot of the fields directly correspond to specific invocations of the CREATE USER or ALTER USER statements. For example, you can see that this root user doesn't have any specific rules set regarding its password's lifecycle. You can also see quite a lot of privileges, though we have omitted some for brevity. These are privileges that don't require a target, like a table. Such privileges are called *global*. We'll show you how to view targeted privileges later.

As of MySQL 8.0, the other grant tables are:

mysql.user
: User accounts, static global privileges, and other nonprivilege columns

mysql.global_grants
: Dynamic global privileges

mysql.db
: Database-level privileges

mysql.tables_priv
: Table-level privileges

mysql.columns_priv
: Column-level privileges

mysql.procs_priv
: Stored procedure and function privileges

mysql.proxies_priv
: Proxy-user privileges

mysql.default_roles
: Default user roles

`mysql.role_edges`
   Edges for role subgraphs

`mysql.password_history`
   Password change history

You don't need to remember all of these tables, let alone their structure and contents, but you should remember that they exist. When necessary, you can easily look up the necessary structure information in the docs or in the database itself.

Internally, MySQL caches grant tables in memory and refreshes this cached representation every time an account management statement is run and thus modifies grant tables. Cache invalidation happens only for the specific user affected. Ideally, you should never modify these grant tables directly, and there's rarely a use case for that. However, in the unfortunate event that you do need to modify a grant table, you can tell MySQL to reread them by running the `FLUSH PRIVILEGES` command. Failure to do so will mean that the in-memory cache won't get updated until either the database is restarted, an account management statement is run against the same user that was updated directly in the grant tables, or `FLUSH PRIVILEGES` is executed for some other purpose. Even though the command's name suggests it only affects privileges, MySQL will reread information from all of the tables and refresh its cache in memory.

User Management Commands and Logging

There are some direct consequences of the fact that all the commands we're discussing in this chapter are, under the hood, modifying the grant tables. They are close to DML operations in some regards. They are atomic: any `CREATE USER`, `ALTER USER`, `GRANT`, or other such operation either succeeds or fails without actually changing its target. They are logged: all of the changes done to grant tables either manually or through the relevant commands are logged to the binary log. Thus, they are replicated (see Chapter 13) and will also be available for point-in-time recovery (see Chapter 10).

Application of these statements on the source can break replication if the targeted user doesn't exist on the replica. We therefore recommend that you keep your replicas consistent with their sources not only in data, but also in users and other metadata. Of course, it's only "meta" in the sense that it exists outside of your real application data; users are records in the `mysql.user` table, and that should be remembered when setting up replication.

Mostly, replicas are full copies of their sources. In more complex topologies, like fan-in, that may not be true, but even in such cases we recommend keeping users consistent across the topology. In general, it is easier and safer than fixing broken replicas or remembering whether you need to disable binary logging before altering a user.

While we say that execution of CREATE USER is similar to an INSERT to the mysql.user table, the CREATE USER statement itself is not changed in any way before being logged. That is true for the binary log, the slow query log (with a caveat), the general query log, and audit logs. The same is true for every other operation discussed in this chapter. The caveat for the slow query log is that an extra server option, log_slow_admin_statements, has to be enabled for administrative statements to be logged here.

 You can find the locations of the logs we've mentioned under the following system variable names: log_bin_basename, slow_query_log_file, and general_log_file. Their values can include the full path to the file or just the filename. In the latter case, that file will be in the MySQL server's data directory. Binary logs always have a numeric suffix: for example, *binlog.000271*. We do not cover audit log configuration in this book.

Consider the following example:

```
mysql> CREATE USER 'vinicius' IDENTIFIED BY '...';
Query OK, 0 rows affected (0.02 sec)
```

Here's an example of how the same CREATE USER command is reflected in the general, slow query, and binary logs:

General log
```
2020-11-22T15:53:17.354270Z        29 Query
    CREATE USER 'vinicius'@'%' IDENTIFIED BY <secret>
```

Slow query log
```
# Time: 2020-11-22T15:53:17.368010Z
# User@Host: root[root] @ localhost [] Id:     29
# Query_time: 0.013772  Lock_time: 0.000161 Rows_sent: 0   Rows_examined: 0
SET timestamp=1606060397;
CREATE USER 'vinicius'@'%' IDENTIFIED BY <secret>;
```

Binary log
```
#201122 18:53:17 server id 1  end_log_pos 4113 CRC32 0xa12ac622
    Query    thread_id=29    exec_time=0    error_code=0    Xid = 243
SET TIMESTAMP=1606060397.354238/*!*/;
CREATE USER 'vinicius'@'%' IDENTIFIED WITH 'caching_sha2_password'
    AS '$A$005$|v>\ZKe^R...'
/*!*/;
```

Don't worry if the binary log output is intimidating. It's not intended for easy human consumption. However, you can see that the actual hash of the password, as it would appear in mysql.user, gets written to the binary log. We'll talk more about this log in Chapter 10.

Modifying and Dropping Users

Creating a user usually isn't the end of your interaction with it. You may later need to change its properties, perhaps to require an encrypted connection. It also happens that users need to be dropped. Neither of these operations is too different from user creation, but you need to know how to perform them in order to fully grasp user management.

Modifying a User

Any parameter that it's possible to set during user creation can also be altered at a later time. This is generally achieved using the ALTER USER command. MySQL 5.7 and before also have RENAME USER and SET PASSWORD shortcuts, while version 8.0 expanded that list to include SET DEFAULT ROLE (we'll cover the role system in "Roles" on page 341). Note that ALTER USER can be used to change everything about the user, and the other commands are just convenient ways to run common maintenance operations.

> We called RENAME USER a shortcut, but it's special in that it doesn't have a "full" ALTER USER alternative. As you'll see, the privileges required to run the RENAME USER command are also different, and are the same as for user creation (we'll talk more about privileges soon).

We will start with the regular ALTER USER command. In the first example, we're going to modify the authentication plugin used. A lot of older programs do not support the new and standard in MySQL 8.0 caching_sha2_password plugin and require you to either create the users using the older mysql_native_password plugin or alter them after creation to use that plugin. We can check the current plugin in use by querying one of the grant tables (see "Grant Tables" on page 317 for more information on these):

```
mysql> SELECT plugin FROM mysql.user WHERE
    -> user = 'bob' AND host = 'localhost';

+----------------------+
| plugin               |
+----------------------+
| caching_sha2_password |
+----------------------+
1 row in set (0.00 sec)
```

And now we can alter the plugin for this user and make sure the change is reflected:

```
mysql> ALTER USER 'bob'@'localhost' IDENTIFIED WITH mysql_native_password;

Query OK, 0 rows affected (0.01 sec)

mysql> SELECT plugin FROM mysql.user WHERE
    -> user = 'bob' AND host = 'localhost';

+-----------------------+
| plugin                |
+-----------------------+
| mysql_native_password |
+-----------------------+
1 row in set (0.00 sec)
```

Since the change was made via an ALTER command, there's no need to run FLUSH PRIVILEGES. Once this command executes successfully, each new authentication attempt will use the new plugin. You could modify the user record directly to make this change, but again, we recommend against that.

The properties that ALTER USER can modify are pretty numerous and were explained or at least outlined in "Creating and Using New Users" on page 310. There are, however, some frequently required operations that you should know a bit more about:

Changing a user's password

This is probably the single most frequent operation that's ever done on a user. Changing a user's password can be done by another user that has the necessary privileges, or by anyone authorized as that user, using a command like the following:

```
mysql> ALTER USER 'bob'@'localhost' IDENTIFIED by 'new password';

Query OK, 0 rows affected (0.01 sec)
```

This change takes effect immediately, so the next time this user authenticates they'll need to use the updated password. There's also a SET PASSWORD shortcut for this command. It can be executed by the authenticated user without any target specification like this:

```
mysql> SET PASSWORD = 'new password';

Query OK, 0 rows affected (0.01 sec)
```

Or it can be executed by another user, with the target specification.

```
mysql> SET PASSWORD FOR 'bob'@'localhost' = 'new password';

Query OK, 0 rows affected (0.01 sec)
```

Locking and unlocking a user

If you need to temporarily (or permanently) block access to a specific user, you can do that using the ACCOUNT LOCK option of ALTER USER. The user in this case is only blocked for authentication. While nobody will be able to connect to MySQL as the blocked user, it can still be used both as a proxy and in a DEFINER clause. That makes such users slightly more secure and easier to manage. The ACCOUNT LOCK can also be used to, for example, block traffic from an application connecting as a specific user that is generating excessive load.

We can block bob from authenticating using the following command:

```
mysql> ALTER USER 'bob'@'localhost' ACCOUNT LOCK;

Query OK, 0 rows affected (0.00 sec)
```

Only new connections will be affected. The message that MySQL produces in this case is clear:

```
$ mysql -ubob -p
Enter password:
ERROR 3118 (HY000): Access denied for user 'bob'@'localhost'.
Account is locked.
```

The counterpart to ACCOUNT LOCK is ACCOUNT UNLOCK. This option to ALTER USER does exactly what it says. Let's allow access to bob again:

```
mysql> ALTER USER 'bob'@'localhost' ACCOUNT UNLOCK;

Query OK, 0 rows affected (0.01 sec)
```

Now the connection attempt will succeed:

```
$ mysql -ubob -p
Enter password:

mysql>
```

Expiring a user's password

Instead of blocking a user's access completely or changing the password for them, you may instead want to force them to change their password. That is possible in MySQL with the PASSWORD EXPIRE option of the ALTER USER command. After this command is executed, the user will still be able to connect to the server using the previous password. However, as soon as they run a query from the new connection—that is, as soon as their privileges are checked—the user will be presented with an error and forced to change the password. Existing connections are not affected.

Let's see what this looks like for the user. First, the actual alter:

```
mysql> ALTER USER 'bob'@'localhost' PASSWORD EXPIRE;

Query OK, 0 rows affected (0.01 sec)
```

Now, what the user gets. Note the successful authentication:

```
$ mysql -ubob -p
Enter password:
mysql> SELECT id, data FROM bobs_db.bobs_private_table;
ERROR 1820 (HY000): You must reset your password using ALTER USER
statement before executing this statement.
```

Even though the error states you have to run ALTER USER, you now know that you can use SET PASSWORD instead. It also doesn't matter who changes the password: the user in question or another user. The PASSWORD EXPIRE option just forces the password change. If another user changes the password, then sessions authenticated with the old password after the password has been expired will need to be reopened. As we saw earlier, the authenticated user can change the password without a target specification, and they'll be able to continue with their session as normal (new connections, however, will need to be authenticated with the new password):

```
mysql> SET PASSWORD = 'new password';
Query OK, 0 rows affected (0.06 sec)
mysql> SELECT id, data FROM bobs_db.bobs_private_table;
Empty set (0.00 sec)
```

In this case, you should also be aware that without password reuse and history controls in place, the user could just reset the password to the original one.

Renaming a user

Changing a username is a relatively rare operation, but it is sometimes necessary. This operation has a special command: RENAME USER. It requires the CREATE USER privilege, or the UPDATE privilege on the mysql database or just the grant tables. There's no ALTER USER alternative for this command.

You can change both the "name" part of the username and the "host" part. Since, as you know by now, the "host" part acts as a firewall, be cautious when changing it, as you may cause outages (actually, the same is true of the "name" part as well). Let's rename our bob user to something more formal:

```
mysql> RENAME USER 'bob'@'localhost' TO 'robert'@'172.%';
Query OK, 0 rows affected, 1 warning (0.01 sec)
```

When the username changes, MySQL automatically scans through its internal tables to see whether that user has been named in the DEFINER clause of a view or a stored object. Whenever that is the case, a warning is produced. Since we did get a warning when we renamed bob, let's check it out:

```
mysql> SHOW WARNINGS\G
*************************** 1. row ***************************
  Level: Warning
   Code: 4005
Message: User 'bob'@'localhost' is referenced as a definer
   account in a stored routine.
1 row in set (0.00 sec)
```

Failure to address this issue can potentially result in orphaned objects that will error out when accessed or executed. We discuss this in detail in the next section.

Dropping a User

The final part of the lifecycle of a database user is its end of life. Like any database object, users can be deleted. In MySQL, the DROP USER command is used to achieve that. This is one of the simplest commands discussed in this chapter, and potentially in the whole book. DROP USER takes a user or, optionally, a list of users as an argument, and has a single modifier: IF NOT EXISTS. Successful execution of the command irrevocably deletes the user-related information from the grant tables (with a caveat we'll discuss later) and thus prevents further logins.

When you drop a user that has made one or more connections to the database that are still open, even though the drop succeeds, the associated records will be removed only when the last of those connections ends. The next attempt to connect with the given user will result in the ERROR 1045 (28000): Access denied message.

The IF NOT EXISTS modifier works similarly to with CREATE USER: if the user you target with DROP USER does not exist, no error will be returned. This is useful in unattended scripts. If the host part of the username is not specified, the wildcard % is used by default.

In its most basic form, the DROP USER command looks like this:

```
mysql> DROP USER 'jeff'@'localhost';
Query OK, 0 rows affected (0.02 sec)
```

Executing the same command again will result in an error:

```
mysql> DROP USER 'jeff'@'localhost';
ERROR 1396 (HY000): Operation DROP USER failed for 'jeff'@'localhost'
```

If you want to construct an idempotent command that won't fail, then use the following construct instead:

```
mysql> DROP USER IF EXISTS 'jeff'@'localhost';
Query OK, 0 rows affected, 1 warning (0.01 sec)

mysql> SHOW WARNINGS;
```

```
+-------+------+-------------------------------------------------------+
| Level | Code | Message                                               |
+-------+------+-------------------------------------------------------+
| Note  | 3162 | Authorization ID 'jeff'@'localhost' does not exist.   |
+-------+------+-------------------------------------------------------+
1 row in set (0.01 sec)
```

Again, if you do not specify the host part of the username, MySQL will assume the default %. It's also possible to drop multiple users at once:

```
mysql> DROP USER 'jeff', 'bob'@'192.168.%';

Query OK, 0 rows affected (0.01 sec)
```

In MySQL, as users do not own objects, they can be dropped quite easily and without much preparation. However, as we have already discussed, users can fulfill extra roles. If the dropped user is used as a proxy user or is part of the DEFINER clause of some object, then dropping it can create an orphaned record. Whenever the user you drop is part of such a relationship, MySQL emits a warning. Note that the DROP USER command will still succeed, so it's up to you to resolve the resulting inconsistencies and fix any orphaned records:

```
mysql> DROP USER 'bob'@'localhost';

Query OK, 0 rows affected, 1 warning (0.01 sec)

mysql> SHOW WARNINGS\G

*************************** 1. row ***************************
   Level: Warning
    Code: 4005
Message: User 'bob'@'localhost' is referenced as a definer
   account in a stored routine.
1 row in set (0.00 sec)
```

We recommend that you check this before actually dropping the user. If you fail to notice the warning and take action, the objects are left orphaned. Orphaned objects will produce errors when used:

```
mysql> CALL test.test_proc();

ERROR 1449 (HY000): The user specified as a definer ('bob'@'localhost')
   does not exist
```

For users in a proxy relationship, no warning is produced. However, a subsequent attempt to use the proxied user will result in an error. As proxy users are used in authentication, the end result will be the inability to log into MySQL with users dependent on the dropped one. This arguably can be more impactful than temporarily losing the ability to call a procedure or query a view, but still, no warning will be emitted. If you are using pluggable authentication relying on proxy users, remember this.

If you find yourself in a situation where you dropped a user and unexpectedly got a warning, you can easily create the user again to avoid the errors. Note how the following CREATE USER statement results in the now-familiar warning:

```
mysql> CREATE USER 'bob'@'localhost' IDENTIFIED BY 'new password';

Query OK, 0 rows affected, 1 warning (0.01 sec)

mysql> SHOW WARNINGS\G

*************************** 1. row ***************************
  Level: Warning
   Code: 4005
Message: User 'bob'@'localhost' is referenced as a definer
  account in a stored routine.
1 row in set (0.00 sec)
```

However, the problem here is that if you don't know or remember the initial privileges of the account, the new one can become a security issue.

To identify orphaned records, you need to manually review MySQL's catalog tables. Specifically, you're going to need to look at the DEFINER column of the following tables:

```
mysql> SELECT table_schema, table_name FROM information_schema.columns
    -> WHERE column_name = 'DEFINER';

+--------------------+------------+
| TABLE_SCHEMA       | TABLE_NAME |
+--------------------+------------+
| information_schema | EVENTS     |
| information_schema | ROUTINES   |
| information_schema | TRIGGERS   |
| information_schema | VIEWS      |
+--------------------+------------+
```

Now that you know that, you can easily construct a query to check if a user you're going to drop or have already dropped is specified within any DEFINER clauses:

```
SELECT EVENT_SCHEMA AS obj_schema
     , EVENT_NAME obj_name
     , 'EVENT' AS obj_type
FROM INFORMATION_SCHEMA.EVENTS
WHERE DEFINER = 'bob@localhost'
UNION
SELECT ROUTINE_SCHEMA AS obj_schema
     , ROUTINE_NAME AS obj_name
     , ROUTINE_TYPE AS obj_type
FROM INFORMATION_SCHEMA.ROUTINES
WHERE DEFINER = 'bob@localhost'
UNION
SELECT TRIGGER_SCHEMA AS obj_schema
     , TRIGGER_NAME AS obj_name
     , 'TRIGGER' AS obj_type
```

```
FROM INFORMATION_SCHEMA.TRIGGERS
WHERE DEFINER = 'bob@localhost'
UNION
SELECT TABLE_SCHEMA AS obj_scmea
    , TABLE_NAME AS obj_name
    , 'VIEW' AS obj_type
FROM INFORMATION_SCHEMA.VIEWS
WHERE DEFINER = 'bob@localhost';
```

That query might look intimidating, but by now you should've seen UNION used in "The Union" on page 200, and the query is just a union of four simple queries. Each individual query looks for an object with a DEFINER value of bob@localhost in one of the following tables: EVENTS, ROUTINES, TRIGGERS, and VIEWS.

In our example, the query returns a single record for bob@localhost:

```
+------------+-----------+-----------+
| obj_schema | obj_name  | obj_type  |
+------------+-----------+-----------+
| test       | test_proc | PROCEDURE |
+------------+-----------+-----------+
```

It's similarly easy to check if the proxy privilege was granted for this user:

```
mysql> SELECT user, host FROM mysql.proxies_priv
    -> WHERE proxied_user = 'bob'
    -> AND proxied_host = 'localhost';

+------+------+
| user | host |
+------+------+
| jeff | %    |
+------+------+
```

We recommend that you always check for possible orphaned objects and proxy privileges before you drop a particular user. Such gaps left in the database will not only cause obvious issues (errors) but are, in fact, a security risk.

Privileges

When a user connects to a MySQL server, authentication is performed using the username and host information, as explained before. However, the permissions the user has to perform different actions aren't checked before any commands are executed. MySQL grants privileges according to the identity of the connected user and the actions it performs. As discussed at the beginning of this chapter, privileges are sets of permissions to perform actions on various objects. By default, a user is not entitled to any permissions, and thus it has no privileges assigned after CREATE USER is executed.

There are a lot of privileges that you can grant to a user and later revoke. For example, you can allow a user to read from a table or modify data in it. You can grant a privilege to create tables and databases, and another to create stored procedures. The list is vast. Curiously, you will not find a connection privilege anywhere: it's impossible to disallow a user from connecting to MySQL, assuming the host part of username matches. That's a direct consequence of what was outlined in the previous paragraph: privileges are checked only when an action is performed, so by nature they will apply only once a user is authenticated.

To get a full list of privileges supported and provided by your MySQL installation, we always recommend checking the manual. However, we'll cover the few broad categories of privileges here. We'll also talk about levels of privileges, as the same privileges can be allowed on multiple levels. Actually, that's what we'll start with. There are four levels of privileges in MySQL:

Global privileges

These privileges allow the *grantee* (the user who is granted the privilege—we cover the GRANT command in "Privilege Management Commands" on page 332) to either act on every object in every database or act on the cluster as a whole. The latter applies to commands that are usually considered administrative. For example, you can allow a user to shut down the cluster.

Privileges in this category are stored within the tables `mysql.user` and `mysql.global_grants`. The first one stores conventional static privileges, and the second one stores dynamic privileges. The difference is explained in the following section. MySQL versions prior to 8.0 store all global privileges in `mysql.user`.

Database privileges

Privileges granted on a database level will allow the user to act upon objects within that database. As you can imagine, the list of privileges is narrower at this level, since there's little sense in breaking down the SHUTDOWN privilege below the global level, for example. Records for these privileges are stored within the `mysql.db` table and include the ability to run DDL and DML queries within the target database.

Object privileges

A logical continuation of database-level privileges, these target a particular object. Tracked in `mysql.tables_priv`, `mysql.procs_priv`, and `mysql.prox ies_priv`, they respectively cover tables and views, all types of stored routines, and finally the proxy user permissions. Proxy privileges are special, but the other privileges in this category are again regular DDL and DML permissions.

Column privileges

Stored in `mysql.columns_priv`, these are an interesting set of privileges. You can separate permissions within a particular table by column. For example, a reporting user may not have the need to read the `password` column of a particular table.

This is a powerful tool, but column privileges can be difficult to manage and maintain.

The complete list of privileges, frankly, is very long. It is always advisable to consult the MySQL documentation for your particular version for the complete details. You should remember that any action a user can perform either will have a dedicated privilege assigned or will be covered by a privilege controlling a wider range of behaviors. In general, database- and object-level privileges will have a dedicated privilege name that you can grant (UPDATE, SELECT, and so on), and global privileges will be quite broadly grouped together, allowing multiple actions at once. For example, the GROUP_REPLICATION_ADMIN privilege allows five different actions at once. Global privileges will also usually be granted on a system level (the . object).

You can always access the list of privileges available in your MySQL instance by running the SHOW PRIVILEGES command:

```
mysql> SHOW PRIVILEGES;
+----------------------------+----------------------+--------------------+
| Privilege                  | Context              | Comment            |
+----------------------------+----------------------+--------------------+
| Alter                      | Tables               | To alter the table |
| Alter routine              | Functions,Procedures | ...                |
| ...                        |                      |                    |
| REPLICATION_SLAVE_ADMIN    | Server Admin         |                    |
| AUDIT_ADMIN                | Server Admin         |                    |
+----------------------------+----------------------+--------------------+
58 rows in set (0.00 sec)
```

Static Versus Dynamic Privileges

Before we go on to review the commands used to manage privileges in MySQL, we must pause and talk about an important distinction. There are two types of privileges in MySQL, starting with version 8.0: static and dynamic. The *static* privileges are built into the server, and every installation will have them available and usable. The *dynamic* privileges are, on the other hand, "volatile": they are not guaranteed to be present all the time.

What are these dynamic privileges? They are privileges that are registered within the server at runtime. Only registered privileges can be granted, so it is possible that some privileges will never be registered and will never be grantable. All of that is a fancy way of saying that it's now possible to extend privileges via plugins and components. However, most of the dynamic privileges currently available are registered by default in a regular Community Server installation.

The important role of the dynamic privileges provided with MySQL 8.0 is that they are aimed at reducing the necessity of using the SUPER privilege, which was previously abused (we'll talk about this privilege in the next section). The other distinction of dynamic privileges is that they usually control a set of activities users can perform. For example, unlike a direct SELECT privilege on a table, which just allows querying the data, the CONNECTION_ADMIN privilege allows a whole list of actions. In this particular example, that includes killing other accounts' connections, updating data in a read-only server, connecting through an extra connection when the limit is reached, and more. You can easily spot the difference.

The SUPER Privilege

This section is not long, but it is important. We mentioned in "The root User" on page 309 that there's a superuser created by default with every MySQL installation: root@localhost. Sometimes you might want to provide the same capabilities to another user, for example one used by a DBA. The convenient built-in way of doing so is by using the special SUPER privilege.

SUPER is basically a catchall privilege that turns a user to which it is assigned into a superuser. As with any privilege, it can be assigned via a GRANT statement, which we'll review in the following section.

There are two huge problems with the SUPER privilege, however. First, starting with MySQL 8.0 it is deprecated, and it is going to be removed in a future release of MySQL. Second, it is a security and operational nightmare. The first point is clear, so let's talk about the second one, and about the alternatives we have.

Using the SUPER privilege poses the same risks and results in the same issues as using the default root@localhost user. Instead of carefully inspecting the scope of privileges required, we're resorting to using an all-purpose hammer to solve all problems. The main problem with SUPER is its all-encompassing scope. When you create a superuser, you create a liability: the user must be restricted and ideally audited, and operators and programs authenticating as the user must be extremely precise and careful in their actions. With great power comes great responsibility—and, among other things, the ability to just outright shut down the MySQL instance. Imagine executing that by mistake.

In MySQL versions before 8.0, it's not feasible to avoid using the SUPER privilege, as there are no alternatives provided for some of the permissions. Starting with version 8.0, which deprecates SUPER, MySQL provides a whole set of dynamic privileges that are aimed at removing the need for the single catchall privilege. You should try to avoid using the SUPER privilege, if possible.

Consider the example of a user that needs to control group replication. In MySQL 5.7, you would need to grant the SUPER privilege to that user. Starting with version 8.0, however, you can instead grant the special GROUP_REPLICATION_ADMIN privilege, which only allows users to perform a very small subset of actions related to group replication.

Sometimes, you will still need a full-on DBA user that can do anything. Instead of granting SUPER, consider looking at the root@localhost privileges and copying them instead. We show you how to do that in "Checking Privileges" on page 335. Taking this further, you can skip granting some of the privileges, such as the INNODB_REDO_LOG_ENABLE privilege, which authorizes a user to basically enable a crash-unsafe mode. It is much safer to not have that privilege granted at all, and to be able to grant it to yourself when absolutely required, than to open up the risk of someone running that statement by mistake.

Privilege Management Commands

Now that you know a bit about privileges, we can proceed to the basic commands that allow you to control them. You can never ALTER a privilege itself, though, so by controlling privileges here we mean giving them to and removing them from users. These actions are achieved with the GRANT and REVOKE statements.

GRANT

The GRANT statement is used to grant users (or roles) permissions to perform activities, either in general or on specific objects. The same statement can also be used to assign roles to users, but you cannot at the same time alter permissions and assign roles. To be able to grant a permission (privilege), you need to have that privilege assigned yourself and have the special GRANT OPTION privilege (we'll review that later). Users with the SUPER (or newer CONNECTION_ADMIN) privilege can grant anything, and there's a special condition related to grant tables, which we'll discuss shortly.

For now, let's check out the basic structure of a GRANT statement:

```
mysql> GRANT SELECT ON app_db.* TO 'john'@'192.168.%';
Query OK, 0 row affected (0.01 sec)
```

That statement, once executed, tells MySQL that user 'john'@'192.168.%' is allowed to perform read-only queries (SELECT) on any table in the app_db database. Note that we have used a wildcard in the object specification. We could allow a particular user access to every table of every database by specifying a wildcard for the database as well:

```
mysql> GRANT SELECT ON *.* TO 'john';
Query OK, 0 row affected (0.01 sec)
```

The preceding invocation notably lacks the host specification for the user 'john'. This shortcut translates to 'john'@'%'; thus, it will not be the same user as the 'john'@'192.168.%' we used before. Speaking of wildcards and users, it is not possible to specify a wildcard for the username portion of the user. Instead, you can specify multiple users or roles in one go like this:

```
mysql> GRANT SELECT ON app_db.* TO 'john'@'192.168.%',
    -> 'kate'@'192.168.%';

Query OK, 0 row affected (0.06 sec)
```

We cautioned you about granting too many privileges in the previous section, but it can be useful to remember that there's an ALL shortcut that allows you to grant every possible privilege on an object or set of objects. That can come handy when you define permissions for the "owner" user—for example, a read/write application user:

```
mysql> GRANT ALL ON app_db.* TO 'app_db_user';

Query OK, 0 row affected (0.06 sec)
```

You cannot chain object specifications, so you won't be able to grant the SELECT privilege on two tables at once, unless that statement can be expressed using wildcards. As you'll see in the next section, you can combine wildcard grants and specific revokes for extra flexibility.

An interesting property of the GRANT command is that it doesn't check for the presence of the objects that you allow. That is, a wildcard is not expanded, but stays a wildcard forever. No matter how many new tables are added to the app_db database, both john and kate will be able to issue SELECT statements on them. Earlier versions of MySQL also would create a user to whom privileges were granted if it wasn't found in the mysql.user table, but that behavior is deprecated starting with MySQL 8.0.

As we discussed in depth in "Grant Tables" on page 317 the GRANT statement updates grant tables. One thing that follows from the fact that there's an update on grant tables is that if a user has the UPDATE privilege on those tables, that user can grant any account any privilege. Be extremely careful with permissions on objects in the mysql database: there's little benefit to granting users any privileges there. Note also that when the read_only system variable is enabled, any grant requires super user privileges (SUPER or CONNECTION_ADMIN).

There are a few other points we'd like to make about GRANT before moving on. In the introduction to this section, we mentioned column privileges. This set of privileges controls whether a user can read and update data in a particular column of a table. Like all other privileges, they can be permitted using the GRANT command:

```
mysql> GRANT SELECT(id), INSERT(id, data)
    -> ON bobs_db.bobs_private_table TO 'kate'@'192.168.%';

Query OK, 0 rows affected (0.01 sec)
```

The user kate will now be able to issue the statement SELECT id FROM bobs_db.bobs_private_table, but not SELECT * or SELECT data.

Finally, you can grant every static privilege on a particular object, or globally, by running GRANT ALL PRIVILEGES instead of specifying each privilege in turn. ALL PRIVILEGES is just a shorthand and is not itself a special privilege, unlike SUPER, for example.

REVOKE

The REVOKE statement is the opposite of the GRANT statement: you can use it to revoke privileges and roles assigned using GRANT. Unless otherwise specified, every property of GRANT applies to REVOKE. For example, to revoke privileges you need to have the GRANT OPTION privilege and the particular privileges that you are revoking.

Starting with MySQL version 8.0.16, it's possible to revoke privileges for particular schemas from users that have privileges granted globally. That makes it possible to easily restrict access to some databases while allowing access to all others, including ones that are newly created. For example, consider a database system where you have a single restricted schema. You need to create a user for your BI application. You start by running the usual command:

```
mysql> GRANT SELECT ON *.* TO 'bi_app_user';
Query OK, 0 rows affected (0.03 sec)
```

However, this user has to be forbidden from querying any data in the restricted database. This is extremely easy to set up using partial revokes:

```
mysql> REVOKE SELECT ON restricted_database.* FROM 'bi_app_user';
Query OK, 0 rows affected (0.03 sec)
```

Before version 8.0.16 to achieve this you would need to fall back to explicitly running GRANT SELECT for each individual allowed schema.

Just as you can grant all privileges, a special invocation of REVOKE exists that allows the removal of all privileges from a particular user. Remember that you need to have all the privileges you are revoking, and thus this option is likely to be used only by an administrative user. The following statement will strip a user of their privileges, including the ability to assign any privileges:

```
mysql> REVOKE ALL PRIVILEGES, GRANT OPTION FROM 'john'@'192.168.%';
Query OK, 0 rows affected (0.03 sec)
```

The REVOKE statement doesn't under any circumstances remove the user itself. You can use the DROP USER statement for that, as described earlier in this chapter.

Checking Privileges

An important part of managing privileges is reviewing them—but it would be impossible to remember every privilege granted to every user. You can query the grant tables to see what users have what privileges, but that's not always convenient. (It is still an option, however, and it can be a good way to find, for example, every user that has write privileges on a certain table.) The more straightforward option for viewing the privileges granted to a particular user is to use the built-in SHOW GRANTS command. Let's take a look at it:

```
mysql> SHOW GRANTS FOR 'john'@'192.168.%';
+---------------------------------------------------+
| Grants for john@192.168.%                         |
+---------------------------------------------------+
| GRANT UPDATE ON *.* TO `john`@`192.168.%`         |
| GRANT SELECT ON `sakila`.* TO `john`@`192.168.%`  |
+---------------------------------------------------+
2 rows in set (0.00 sec)
```

In general, you can expect to see every privilege in this output, but there's a special case. When a user has every static privilege granted for a particular object, instead of listing each and every one of them, MySQL will output ALL PRIVILEGES instead. This is not a special privilege itself, but rather a shorthand for every possible privilege. Internally, ALL PRIVILEGES just translates to Y set for every privilege in the respective grant table:

```
mysql> SHOW GRANTS FOR 'bob'@'localhost';
+------------------------------------------------------------+
| Grants for bob@localhost                                   |
+------------------------------------------------------------+
...
| GRANT ALL PRIVILEGES ON `bobs_db`.* TO `bob`@`localhost`   |
...
```

You can also view the permissions granted to roles using the SHOW GRANTS command, but we'll talk about that in more detail in "Roles" on page 341. To review the permissions of the currently authenticated and authorized user, you can use any of the following statements, which are synonymous:

```
SHOW GRANTS;
SHOW GRANTS FOR CURRENT_USER;
SHOW GRANTS FOR CURRENT_USER();
```

Whenever you do not remember what a specific privilege means, you can either consult the documentation or run the SHOW PRIVILEGES command, which will list every privilege currently available. That covers both static object privileges and dynamic server privileges.

Sometimes you might need to review privileges related to all accounts or transfer those privileges to another system. One option that you have is to use the mysqldump command provided with MySQL Server for all supported platforms. We will be reviewing that command in detail in Chapter 10. In short, you'll need to dump all of the grant tables, as otherwise you might miss some of the permissions. The safest way to go is to dump all of the data in the mysql database:

```
$ mysqldump -uroot -p mysql
Enter password:
```

The output will include all the table definitions, along with a lot of INSERT statements. This output can be redirected to a file and then used to seed a new database. We talk more about that in Chapter 10. If your server versions don't match or the target server already has some users and privileges stored, it might be best to avoid dropping the existing objects. Add the --no-create-info option to the mysqldump invocation to only receive the INSERT statements.

By using mysqldump you get a portable list of users and privileges, but it's not exactly easily readable. Here is an example of some of the rows in the output:

```
--
-- Dumping data for table `tables_priv`
--

LOCK TABLES `tables_priv` WRITE;
/*!40000 ALTER TABLE `tables_priv` DISABLE KEYS */;
INSERT INTO `tables_priv` VALUES ('172.%','sakila','robert'...
'Select,Insert,Update,Delete,Create,Drop,Grant,References,...
('localhost','sys','mysql.sys','sys_config','root@localhost'
    '2020-07-13 07:14:57','Select','');
/*!40000 ALTER TABLE `tables_priv` ENABLE KEYS */;
UNLOCK TABLES;
```

Another option to review the privileges would be to write custom queries over grant tables, as already mentioned. We won't give any guidelines on that, as there's no one-size-fits-all solution.

Yet another way is by running SHOW GRANTS for every user in the database. By combining that with the SHOW CREATE USER statement, you can generate the list of privileges, which can also be used to re-create the users and their privileges in another database:

```
mysql> SELECT CONCAT("SHOW GRANTS FOR `", user, "`@`", host,
    -> "`; SHOW CREATE USER `", user, "`@`", host, "`;") grants
    -> FROM mysql.user WHERE user = "bob";

+------------------------------------------------------------------+
| grants                                                           |
+------------------------------------------------------------------+
| SHOW GRANTS FOR bob@%; SHOW CREATE USER bob@%;                   |
| SHOW GRANTS FOR bob@localhost; SHOW CREATE USER bob@localhost;   |
+------------------------------------------------------------------+
2 rows in set (0.00 sec)
```

As you can imagine, the idea of automating this procedure is not new. In fact, there's a tool in Percona Toolkit—pt-show-grants—that does exactly that, and more. Unfortunately, the tool can be used only on Linux officially and might not work at all on any other platform:

```
$ pt-show-grants

-- Grants dumped by pt-show-grants
-- Dumped from server Localhost via Unix socket,
    MySQL 8.0.22 at 2020-12-12 14:32:33
-- Roles
CREATE ROLE IF NOT EXISTS `application_ro`;
-- End of roles listing
...
-- Grants for 'robert'@'172.%'
CREATE USER IF NOT EXISTS 'robert'@'172.%';
ALTER USER 'robert'@'172.%' IDENTIFIED WITH 'mysql_native_password'
AS '*E1206987C3E6057289D6C3208EACFC1FA0F2FA56' REQUIRE NONE
PASSWORD EXPIRE DEFAULT ACCOUNT UNLOCK PASSWORD HISTORY DEFAULT
PASSWORD REUSE INTERVAL DEFAULT PASSWORD REQUIRE CURRENT DEFAULT;
GRANT ALL PRIVILEGES ON `bobs_db`.* TO `robert`@`172.%`;
GRANT ALL PRIVILEGES ON `sakila`.`actor` TO `robert`@`172.%` WITH GRANT OPTION;
GRANT SELECT ON `sakila`.* TO `robert`@`172.%` WITH GRANT OPTION;
GRANT SELECT ON `test`.* TO `robert`@`172.%` WITH GRANT OPTION;
GRANT USAGE ON *.* TO `robert`@`172.%`;
...
```

The GRANT OPTION Privilege

As discussed at the beginning of this chapter, MySQL does not have a concept of object ownership. Thus, unlike in some other systems, the fact that some user created a table does not automatically mean that the same user can allow another user to do anything with that table. To make this slightly less convoluted, let's review an example.

Suppose the user bob has permissions to create tables in a database called bobs_db:

```
mysql> CREATE TABLE bobs_db.bobs_private_table
    -> (id SERIAL PRIMARY KEY, data TEXT);

Query OK, 0 rows affected (0.04 sec)
```

An operator using the bob user wants to allow the john user to read data in the newly created table—but, alas, that is not possible:

```
mysql> GRANT SELECT ON bobs_db.bobs_private_table TO 'john'@'192.168.%';

ERROR 1142 (42000): SELECT, GRANT command denied
to user 'bob'@'localhost' for table 'bobs_private_table'
```

Let's check what privileges bob actually has:

```
mysql> SHOW GRANTS FOR 'bob'@'localhost';

+----------------------------------------------------------+
| Grants for bob@localhost                                 |
+----------------------------------------------------------+
| GRANT USAGE ON *.* TO `bob`@`localhost`                  |
| GRANT SELECT ON `sakila`.* TO `bob`@`localhost`          |
| GRANT ALL PRIVILEGES ON `bobs_db`.* TO `bob`@`localhost` |
+----------------------------------------------------------+
3 rows in set (0.00 sec)
```

The missing piece here is a privilege that would allow a user to grant other users privileges it has been granted. If a DBA wants to allow bob to grant other users access to tables in the bobs_db database, an extra privilege needs to be granted. bob can't grant that to itself, so a user with administrative privileges is required:

```
mysql> GRANT SELECT ON bobs_db.* TO 'bob'@'localhost'
    -> WITH GRANT OPTION;

Query OK, 0 rows affected (0.01 sec)
```

Note the WITH GRANT OPTION addition. That's exactly the privilege that we were looking for. This option will allow the bob user to pass its privileges to other users. Let's confirm that by running the GRANT SELECT statement as bob again:

```
mysql> GRANT SELECT ON bobs_db.bobs_private_table TO 'john'@'192.168.%';

Query OK, 0 rows affected (0.02 sec)
```

As expected, the statement was accepted and executed. There are still few clarifications to make, however. First, we may want to know how granular the GRANT OPTION privilege is. That is, what exactly (apart from SELECT on bobs_private_table) can bob grant to other users? SHOW GRANTS can answer that question for us neatly:

```
mysql> SHOW GRANTS FOR 'bob'@'localhost';
```

```
+-----------------------------------------------------------------------+
| Grants for bob@localhost                                              |
+-----------------------------------------------------------------------+
| GRANT USAGE ON *.* TO `bob`@`localhost`                               |
| GRANT SELECT ON `sakila`.* TO `bob`@`localhost`                       |
| GRANT ALL PRIVILEGES ON `bobs_db`.* TO `bob`@`localhost` WITH GRANT OPTION |
+-----------------------------------------------------------------------+
3 rows in set (0.00 sec)
```

That's much clearer. We can see that WITH GRANT OPTION is applied to privileges that bob has on a particular database. That's important to remember. Even though we executed GRANT SELECT ... WITH GRANT OPTION, bob got the ability to grant every privilege it has in the bobs_db database.

Second, we may want to know if it is possible to revoke just the GRANT OPTION privilege:

```
mysql> REVOKE GRANT OPTION ON bobs_db.* FROM 'bob'@'localhost';

Query OK, 0 rows affected (0.01 sec)

mysql> SHOW GRANTS FOR 'bob'@'localhost';
```

```
+----------------------------------------------------------+
| Grants for bob@localhost                                 |
+----------------------------------------------------------+
| GRANT USAGE ON *.* TO `bob`@`localhost`                  |
| GRANT SELECT ON `sakila`.* TO `bob`@`localhost`          |
| GRANT ALL PRIVILEGES ON `bobs_db`.* TO `bob`@`localhost` |
+----------------------------------------------------------+
3 rows in set (0.00 sec)
```

Finally, looking at how GRANT OPTION can be revoked, we may want to know whether it can be granted alone. The answer is yes, with a caveat that we'll show. Let's grant the GRANT OPTION privilege to bob on the sakila and test databases. As you can see from the preceding output, bob currently has the SELECT privilege on sakila, but no privileges on the test database:

```
mysql> GRANT GRANT OPTION ON sakila.* TO 'bob'@'localhost';

Query OK, 0 rows affected (0.00 sec)

mysql> GRANT GRANT OPTION ON test.* TO 'bob'@'localhost';

Query OK, 0 rows affected (0.01 sec)
```

Both statements succeeded. It's pretty clear what exactly bob can grant on sakila: the SELECT privilege. However, it's less clear what happened with test. Let's check it out:

```
mysql> SHOW GRANTS FOR 'bob'@'localhost';
```

```
+-------------------------------------------------------------------+
| Grants for bob@localhost                                          |
+-------------------------------------------------------------------+
| GRANT USAGE ON *.* TO `bob`@`localhost`                           |
| GRANT SELECT ON `sakila`.* TO `bob`@`localhost` WITH GRANT OPTION |
| GRANT USAGE ON `test`.* TO `bob`@`localhost` WITH GRANT OPTION    |
| GRANT ALL PRIVILEGES ON `bobs_db`.* TO `bob`@`localhost`          |
+-------------------------------------------------------------------+
4 rows in set (0.00 sec)
```

Okay, so GRANT OPTION alone only gives the user a USAGE privilege, which is the "no privileges" specifier. However, the GRANT OPTION privilege can be seen as a switch, and when "turned on," it'll apply for privileges bob is granted in the test database:

```
mysql> GRANT SELECT ON test.* TO 'bob'@'localhost';

Query OK, 0 rows affected (0.00 sec)

mysql> SHOW GRANTS FOR 'bob'@'localhost';

+------------------------------------------------------------------+
| Grants for bob@localhost                                         |
+------------------------------------------------------------------+
...
| GRANT SELECT ON `test`.* TO `bob`@`localhost` WITH GRANT OPTION  |
...
+------------------------------------------------------------------+
4 rows in set (0.00 sec)
```

So far we've been using wildcard privileges, but it is possible to enable GRANT OPTION for a specific table:

```
mysql> GRANT INSERT ON sakila.actor
    -> TO 'bob'@'localhost' WITH GRANT OPTION;

Query OK, 0 rows affected (0.01 sec)

mysql> SHOW GRANTS FOR 'bob'@'localhost';

+---------------------------------------------------------------------+
| Grants for bob@localhost                                            |
+---------------------------------------------------------------------+
...
| GRANT INSERT ON `sakila`.`actor` TO `bob`@`localhost` WITH GRANT OPTION |
+---------------------------------------------------------------------+
5 rows in set (0.00 sec)
```

By now, it should be clear that GRANT OPTION is a powerful addition to the privileges system. Given that MySQL lacks the concept of ownership, it's the only way to make sure users that aren't superusers can grant each other permissions. However, it is also important, as always, to remember that GRANT OPTION applies to every permission the user has.

Roles

Roles, introduced in MySQL 8.0, are collections of privileges. They simplify user and privilege management by grouping and "containerizing" necessary permissions. You may have a few different DBA users that all need the same permissions. Instead of granting privileges individually to each of the users, you can create a role, grant permissions to that role, and assign users that role. In doing so, you also simplify management in that you won't need to update each user individually. Should your DBAs need their privileges adjusted, you can simply adjust the role.

Roles are quite similar to users in how they are created, stored, and managed. To create a role, you need to execute a CREATE ROLE [IF NOT EXISTS] *role1*[, *role2*[, *role3* ...]] statement. To remove a role, you execute a DROP ROLE [IF EXISTS] *role1*[, *role2*[, *role3* ...]] statement. When you drop a role, the assignments of that role to all users is removed. Privileges required to create a role are CREATE ROLE or CREATE USER. To drop a role, the DROP ROLE or DROP USER privilege is required. As with the user management commands, if read_only is set, an admin privilege is additionally required to create and drop roles. Direct modification privileges on grant tables allow a user to modify anything, as we've also discussed.

Just like usernames, role names consist of two parts: the name itself and the host specification. When host is not specified, the % wildcard is assumed. The host specification for a role does not limit its use in any way. The reason it's there is because roles are stored just like users in the mysql.user grant table. As a consequence, you cannot have the same *rolename@host* as an existing user. To have a role with the same name as an existing user, specify a different hostname for the role.

Unlike privileges, roles are not active all the time. When a user is granted a role, they're authorized to use that role but not obliged to do so. In fact, a user can have multiple roles and can "enable" one or more of them within the same connection.

One or more roles can be assigned as defaults to a user during the user's creation or at a later time through the ALTER USER command. Such roles will be active as soon as the user is authenticated.

Let's review the commands, settings, and terminology related to role management:

GRANT PRIVILEGE *and* REVOKE PRIVILEGE *commands*
> We covered these commands in "Privilege Management Commands" on page 332. For all intents and purposes, roles can be used just the same as users with the GRANT and REVOKE PRIVILEGE commands. That is, you can assign all the same privileges to a role as you can to a user, and revoke them, too.

GRANT *role [, role ...] TO user`* command

> The basic command related to role management. By running this command, you authorize a user to assume a particular role. As mentioned previously, the user is not obliged to use the role. Let's create a couple of roles that will be able to operate on the `sakila` database:

```
mysql> CREATE ROLE 'application_rw';
Query OK, 0 rows affected (0.01 sec)

mysql> CREATE ROLE 'application_ro';
Query OK, 0 rows affected (0.00 sec)

mysql> GRANT ALL ON sakila.* TO 'application_rw';
Query OK, 0 rows affected (0.06 sec)

mysql> GRANT SELECT ON sakila.* TO 'application_ro';
Query OK, 0 rows affected (0.00 sec)
```

Now you can assign these roles to an arbitrary number of users and change the roles only when needed. Here, we allow our bob user read-only access to the `sakila` database:

```
mysql> GRANT 'application_ro' TO 'bob'@'localhost';
Query OK, 0 rows affected (0.00 sec)
```

You can also grant more than one role in a single statement.

WITH ADMIN OPTION *modifier*

> When you grant a role to a user, that user is allowed only to activate the role, but not to alter it in any way. That user may not grant the role to any other user. If you wish to allow both modification of the role and the ability to grant it to other users, you can specify WITH ADMIN OPTION in the GRANT ROLE command. The result will be reflected in grant tables and will be visible in the SHOW GRANTS command's output:

```
mysql> SHOW GRANTS FOR 'bob'@'localhost';
+-------------------------------------------------------------------+
| Grants for bob@localhost                                          |
+-------------------------------------------------------------------+
| GRANT USAGE ON *.* TO `bob`@`localhost`                           |
| GRANT `application_ro`@`%` TO `bob`@`localhost` WITH ADMIN OPTION |
+-------------------------------------------------------------------+
2 rows in set (0.00 sec)
```

SHOW GRANTS *and roles*

> The SHOW GRANTS command, which we introduced in "Checking Privileges" on page 335, is capable of showing you both assigned roles and the effective permis-

sions with one or more roles activated. This is possible by adding an optional USING *role* modifier. Here, we show the effective privileges that bob will have as soon as the application_ro role is activated:

```
mysql> SHOW GRANTS FOR 'bob'@'localhost' USING 'application_ro';
+------------------------------------------------------------------+
| Grants for bob@localhost                                         |
+------------------------------------------------------------------+
| GRANT USAGE ON *.* TO `bob`@`localhost`                          |
| GRANT SELECT ON `sakila`.* TO `bob`@`localhost`                  |
| GRANT `application_ro`@`%` TO `bob`@`localhost` WITH ADMIN OPTION |
+------------------------------------------------------------------+
3 rows in set (0.00 sec)
```

SET ROLE DEFAULT | NONE | ALL | ALL EXCEPT *role [, role1 ...]* | *role [, role1 ...] command*

The SET ROLE role management command is invoked by an authenticated user to assign a particular role or roles to itself. Once the role is set, its permissions apply to the user. Let's continue with our example for bob:

```
$ mysql -ubob
mysql> SELECT staff_id, first_name FROM sakila.staff;
ERROR 1142 (42000): SELECT command denied to user 'bob'@'localhost' for
table 'staff'
mysql> SET ROLE 'application_rw';
ERROR 3530 (HY000): `application_rw`@`%` is not granted to
`bob`@`localhost`
mysql> SET ROLE 'application_ro';
Query OK, 0 rows affected (0.00 sec)
mysql> SELECT staff_id, first_name FROM sakila.staff;
+----------+------------+
| staff_id | first_name |
+----------+------------+
|        1 | Mike       |
|        2 | Jon        |
+----------+------------+
2 rows in set (0.00 sec)
```

Only when the role is assigned can bob use its privileges. Note that you cannot use SET ROLE to assign yourself a role you aren't authorized (through GRANT ROLE) to use.

There's no UNSET ROLE command, but there are few other extensions to SET ROLE that allow this behavior. To unset every role, run SET ROLE NONE. A user can also go back to its default set of roles by executing SET ROLE DEFAULT, or activate all the roles it has access to by running SET ROLE ALL. If you need to set a subset of roles which is neither default nor all, you can construct a SET ROLE ALL EXCEPT *role* [, *role1* ...] statement and explicitly avoid setting one or more roles.

DEFAULT ROLE *user option*

When you run CREATE USER, or later through ALTER USER, you can set one or more roles to be the default for a particular user. These roles will be implicitly set once the user is authenticated, saving you a SET ROLE statement. This is convenient, for example, for application users that use a single role or a known set of roles most of the time. Let's set application_ro as a default role for bob:

```
$ mysql -uroot

mysql> ALTER USER 'bob'@'localhost' DEFAULT ROLE 'application_ro';

Query OK, 0 rows affected (0.02 sec)

$ mysql -ubob

mysql> SELECT CURRENT_ROLE();

+----------------------+
| CURRENT_ROLE()       |
+----------------------+
| `application_ro`@`%` |
+----------------------+
1 row in set (0.00 sec)
```

As soon as bob@localhost is logged in, the CURRENT_ROLE() function returns the desired application_ro.

Mandatory roles

It is possible to grant one or more roles to every user in the database implicitly. This is achieved by setting the mandatory_roles system parameter (global in scope, and dynamic) to a list of roles. Roles granted this way are not activated until SET ROLE is run. It's impossible to revoke roles assigned this way, but you can grant them explicitly to a user. Roles listed in mandatory_roles cannot be dropped until removed from the setting.

Automatically activating roles

By default, roles are not active until SET ROLE is executed. However, it is possible to override that behavior and automatically activate every role available to a user upon authentication. This is analogous to running SET ROLE ALL upon login. This behavior can be enabled or disabled (which is the default) by changing the activate_all_roles_on_login system parameter (global in scope, and dynamic). When activate_all_roles_on_login is set to ON, both explicitly and implicitly (through `mandatory_roles`) granted roles will be activated for every user.

Cascading role permissions

Roles can be granted to roles. What happens then is that all permissions of the granted role are inherited by the grantee role. Once the grantee role is activated by a user, you can think of that user as having activated a granted role. Let's make our example slightly more complex. We will have an `application` role that is granted the `application_ro` and `application_rw` roles. The `application` role itself has no direct permissions assign. We will assigned the `application` role to our bob user and examine the result:

```
mysql> CREATE ROLE 'application';
Query OK, 0 rows affected (0.01 sec)
mysql> GRANT 'application_rw', 'application_ro' TO 'application';
Query OK, 0 rows affected (0.01 sec)
mysql> REVOKE 'application_ro' FROM 'bob'@'localhost';
Query OK, 0 rows affected (0.02 sec)
mysql> GRANT 'application' TO 'bob'@'localhost';
Query OK, 0 rows affected (0.00 sec)
```

What happens now is that when bob activates the `application` role, it will have the permissions of both the `rw` and `ro` roles. We can easily verify this. Note that bob cannot activate any of the roles it was granted indirectly:

```
$ mysql -ubob
mysql> SET ROLE 'application';
Query OK, 0 rows affected (0.00 sec)
mysql> SELECT staff_id, first_name FROM sakila.staff;
+----------+------------+
| staff_id | first_name |
+----------+------------+
|        1 | Mike       |
|        2 | Jon        |
+----------+------------+
2 rows in set (0.00 sec)
```

Roles graph

Since roles can be granted to roles, the resulting hierarchy can be pretty hard to follow. You can review it by examining the `mysql.role_edges` grant table:

```
mysql> SELECT * FROM mysql.role_edges;
```

```
+-----------+----------------+-----------+-------------+----------------+
| FROM_HOST | FROM_USER      | TO_HOST   | TO_USER     | WITH_ADMIN_... |
+-----------+----------------+-----------+-------------+----------------+
| %         | application    | localhost | bob         | N              |
| %         | application_ro | %         | application | N              |
| %         | application_rw | %         | application | N              |
| %         | developer      | 192.168.% | john        | N              |
| %         | developer      | localhost | bob         | N              |
| 192.168.% | john           | %         | developer   | N              |
+-----------+----------------+-----------+-------------+----------------+
6 rows in set (0.00 sec)
```

For more complex hierarchies, MySQL conveniently includes a built-in function that allows you to generate an XML document in a valid GraphML format. You can use any capable software to visualize the output. Here's the function call, and the resulting heavily formatted output (XML doesn't work well in books):

```
mysql> SELECT * FROM mysql.roles_graphml()\G

*************************** 1. row ***************************
roles_graphml(): <?xml version="1.0" encoding="UTF-8"?>
<graphml xmlns="...
...
    <node id="n0">
      <data key="key1">`application`@`%`</data>
    </node>
    <node id="n1">
      <data key="key1">`application_ro`@`%`</data>
    </node>
...
```

Ideally, you should use SELECT ... INTO OUTFILE (see "Writing Data into Comma-Delimited Files" on page 274). Then you can use a tool such as the yEd graph editor (*https://oreil.ly/VpIYA*), which is a powerful, cross-platform, free desktop application, to visualize that output. You can see a zoomed-in section of the complete graph, concentrating on our bob user and surrounding roles, in Figure 8-1. The privilege required to run this function is ROLE_ADMIN.

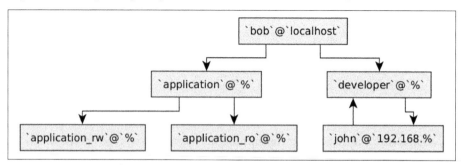

Figure 8-1. Section of a visualized MySQL roles graph

Differences between roles and users

Earlier we mentioned that the CREATE USER and DROP USER privileges allow modification of roles. Given that roles are stored along with users in mysql.user, you might also guess that the regular user management commands will work for roles. That's easy to test and confirm: just run RENAME USER or a DROP USER on a role. Another thing to note is how the GRANT and REVOKE PRIVILEGE commands target roles as if they were users.

Roles are, at their core, just regular users. In fact, it is possible to use GRANT ROLE to grant an unlocked user to another unlocked user or to a role:

```
mysql> CREATE ROLE 'developer';
Query OK, 0 rows affected (0.02 sec)

mysql> GRANT 'john'@'192.168.%' TO 'developer';
Query OK, 0 rows affected (0.01 sec)

mysql> SELECT from_user, to_user FROM mysql.role_edges;
+-----------+-----------+
| from_user | to_user   |
+-----------+-----------+
| john      | developer |
+-----------+-----------+
1 row in set (0.00 sec)
```

Roles are a powerful and flexible addition to MySQL's user and privilege system. As with almost any feature, they can be overused, resulting in unnecessarily complex hierarchies that will be hard to follow. However, if you keep things simple, roles can save you a lot of work.

Changing root's Password and Insecure Startup

Sometimes, it can become necessary to gain access to a MySQL instance without knowing any user's password. Or you could accidentally drop every user in the database, effectively locking you out. MySQL provides a workaround in such situations, but requires you to be able to change its configuration and restart the instance in question. You might think this is shady or dangerous, but actually it's just a protection from one of the simplest problems DBAs run up against: forgotten passwords. Just imagine having a production instance running that has no superuser access available: that's obviously not something desirable. Luckily, it's possible to bypass authorization when necessary.

To perform the authentication and privileges bypass, you have to restart a MySQL instance with the `--skip-grant-tables` option specified. Since most installations use service scripts to start the instance, you can specify `skip-grant-tables` in the *my.cnf* configuration file under the `[mysqld]` section. When `mysqld` is started in this mode, it (pretty obviously) skips reading grant tables, which has the following effects:

- No authentication is performed; thus, there's no need to know any usernames or passwords.
- No privileges are loaded, and no permissions are checked.
- MySQL will implicitly set `--skip-networking` to prevent any but local access while it's running in the unsafe configuration.

When you connect to a MySQL instance running with `--skip-grant-tables`, you'll be authorized as a special user. This user has access to every table and can alter any user. Before altering, for example, the `root` user's lost password, you need to run `FLUSH PRIVILEGES`; otherwise, the `ALTER` will fail:

```
mysql> SELECT current_user();

+-----------------------------------+
| current_user()                    |
+-----------------------------------+
| skip-grants user@skip-grants host |
+-----------------------------------+
1 row in set (0.00 sec)

mysql> ALTER USER 'root'@'localhost' IDENTIFIED BY 'P@ssw0rd!';

ERROR 1290 (HY000): The MySQL server is running with the --skip-grant-tables
option so it cannot execute this statement

mysql> FLUSH PRIVILEGES;

Query OK, 0 rows affected (0.02 sec)

mysql> ALTER USER 'root'@'localhost' IDENTIFIED BY 'P@ssw0rd!';

Query OK, 0 rows affected (0.01 sec)
```

Once the password is reset, it's recommended to restart the MySQL instance in a normal mode.

There's also another way to recover `root`'s password, which is arguably more secure. One of the numerous command-line arguments that `mysqld` takes is `--init-file` (or `init_file` if used through *my.cnf*). This argument specifies a path to a file containing some SQL statements that will be executed during MySQL startup. No privilege checks are done at that time, so it's possible to put an `ALTER USER root` statement there. It's recommended to delete the file and unset the option once you've regained access or created a new `root` user.

Both of the options presented here can potentially lead to security issues. Please use them carefully!

Some Ideas for Secure Setup

During the course of this chapter, we outlined a few practices related to user and privilege management that can help make your server more secure and safe. Here we will provide a short summary of those techniques and our recommendations for using them.

From the administrative side, we have the following recommendations:

- Avoid overusing the built-in superuser root@localhost. Imagine five people having access to this user. Even if you have auditing enabled in MySQL, you won't be able to effectively discern which particular person accessed the user and when. This user will also be the first one that potential attackers will try to exploit.

- Starting with MySQL 8.0, avoid creating new superusers through the SUPER privilege. Instead, you can create a special DBA role that has either all dynamic privileges assigned individually or just some of them that are frequently required.

- Consider organizing privileges for DBA functions into separate roles. For example, the INNODB_REDO_LOG_ARCHIVE and INNODB_REDO_LOG_ENABLE privileges could be a part of the innodb_redo_admin role. Since roles are not by default automatically activated, one would first need to SET ROLE explicitly before running potentially dangerous administrative commands.

For regular users, the recommendations are pretty similar:

- Try to minimize the scope of permissions. Always ask if this user needs access to every database in the cluster, or even every table in a particular database.

- With MySQL 8.0, using roles is a convenient and arguably safer way to group and manage privileges. If you have three users that need the same or similar privileges, they could share a single role.

- Never allow any non-superuser modification permissions on tables in the mysql database. This is a simple mistake that follows from the first recommendation in this list. Granting UPDATE on *.* will allow the grantee to grant itself any permissions.

- To make things even more secure and visible, you can consider periodically saving all of the privileges currently assigned to users and comparing the result with the previously saved sample. You can easily diff the `pt-show-grants` output, or even the `mysqldump` output.

With this chapter done, you should be comfortable administering users and privileges in MySQL.

Using Option Files

Almost every piece of software is capable of being configured, or even must be configured. MySQL is not much different in this regard. While the default configuration will probably suit an astonishing number of installations, more likely than not, you will end up needing to configure the server, or a client. MySQL provides two ways to configure itself: through command-line argument options, and through the configuration file. Since this file contains only the options that could be specified on the command line, it's also called the *option* file.

The option file is not exclusive to MySQL Server. It's also not strictly correct to talk about the option *file*, as pretty much every installation of MySQL will have multiple option files. Most MySQL software supports inclusion in the option files, and we'll cover that, too.

Knowing your way around an option file—understanding its sections and option precedence—is an important part of efficiently working with MySQL Server and related software. After going through this chapter, you should feel comfortable configuring MySQL Server and other programs that use option files. This chapter will focus on the files themselves. The configuration of the server itself and some tuning ideas are discussed in depth in Chapter 11.

Structure of the Option File

Configuration files in MySQL follow the ubiquitous INI file scheme. In short, they are regular text files that are intended to be edited manually. Of course, you can automate the editing process, but the structure of these files is purposefully very simple. Almost every MySQL configuration file can be created and modified with any text editor. There are just two exceptions to this rule, reviewed in "Special Option Files" on page 360.

To give you an idea of the file structure, let's take a look at a configuration file shipped with MySQL 8 on Fedora Linux (note that the exact contents of the option files on your system may be different). We've redacted a few lines for brevity:

```
$ cat /etc/my.cnf
...
[mysqld]
#
# Remove leading # and set to the amount of RAM for the most important data
# cache in MySQL. Start at 70% of total RAM for dedicated server, else 10%.
# innodb_buffer_pool_size = 128M
...
datadir=/var/lib/mysql
socket=/var/lib/mysql/mysql.sock

log-error=/var/log/mysqld.log
pid-file=/run/mysqld/mysqld.pid
```

 On some Linux distributions, such as Ubuntu, the */etc/my.cnf* configuration file doesn't exist in a default MySQL installation. Look for */etc/mysql/my.cnf* on those systems, or refer to "Search Order for Option Files" on page 359 for a way to get a full list of option files mysqld reads.

There are a few main parts to the file structure:

Section (group) headers

These are the values in square brackets preceding the configuration parameters. All programs using option files look for parameters in one or more named sections. For example, [mysqld] is a section used by the MySQL server, and [mysql] is used by the mysql CLI program. The name of the sections are, strictly speaking, arbitrary, and you can put anything there. However, if you change [mysqld] to [section], your MySQL server will ignore all the options following that header.

MySQL documentation calls sections *groups*, but both terms can be used interchangeably.

Headers control how the files are parsed, and by which programs. Each option after a section header and before the next section header will be attributed to the first header. An example will make this clearer:

```
[mysqld]
datadir=/var/lib/mysql
socket=/var/lib/mysql/mysql.sock
[mysql]
default-character-set=latin1
```

Here, the `datadir` and `socket` options are under (and will be attributed to) the `[mysqld]` section, whereas the `default-character-set` option is under `[mysql]`. Note that some MySQL programs read multiple sections; but we'll talk about that later.

Section headers can be intertwined. The following example is completely valid:

```
[mysqld]
datadir=/var/lib/mysql
[mysql]
default-character-set=latin1
[mysqld]
socket=/var/lib/mysql/mysql.sock
[mysqld_safe]
core-file-size=unlimited
[mysqld]
core-file
```

Such a configuration might be difficult for a person to read, but programs that parse the file will not care about the order. Still, it's probably best to keep the configuration files as human-readable as possible.

Option-value pairs

This is the main part of the option file, consisting of the configuration variables themselves and their values. Each of these pairs is defined on a new line and follows one of two general patterns. In addition to the *option=value* pattern shown in the previous example, there's also just the *option* pattern. For example, the same standard MySQL 8 configuration file has the following lines:

```
# Remove the leading "# " to disable binary logging
# Binary logging captures changes between backups and is enabled by
# default. Its default setting is log_bin=binlog
# disable_log_bin
```

`disable_log_bin` is an option without a value. If we uncomment it, MySQL Server will apply the option.

With the *option=value* pattern, you can add spaces around the equals sign for readability if you prefer. Any whitespace preceding and following the option name and value will be truncated automatically.

Option values can also be enclosed in single or double quote characters. That is useful if you're not sure whether the value is going to be interpreted correctly. For example, on Windows, paths contain the \ symbol, which is treated like an escape symbol. Thus, you should put paths on Windows in double quotes (although you could also escape each \ by doubling it as \\). Quoting the option values is required when the value includes the # symbol, which would otherwise be treated as indicating the start of a comment.

The rule of thumb that we recommend is to use quotes when you're not sure. Here are some valid option/value pairs that illustrate the previous points:

```
slow_query_log_file = "C:\mysqldata\query.log"
slow_query_log_file=C:\\mysqldata\\query.log
innodb_temp_tablespaces_dir="./#innodb_temp/"
```

When setting values for numerical options, like the sizes of different buffers and files, working with bytes can get tedious. To make life easier, MySQL understands a variety of suffixes standing in for different units. For example, the following are all equivalent and define a buffer pool of the same size (268,435,456 bytes):

```
innodb_buffer_pool_size = 268435456
innodb_buffer_pool_size = 256M
innodb_buffer_pool_size = 256MB
innodb_buffer_pool_size = 256MiB
```

You can also specify G, GB, and GiB for gigabytes and T, TB, and TiB for terabytes if you have a server large enough. Of course, K and other forms are also accepted. MySQL always uses base-2 units: 1 GB is 1,024 MB, not 1,000 MB.

You cannot specify fractional values for options. So, for example, 0.25G is an incorrect value for the innodb_buffer_pool_size variable. Also, unlike when setting values from the mysql CLI or another client connection, you cannot use mathematical notation for option values. You can run SET GLOBAL max_heap_table_size=16*1024*1024;, but you cannot put the same value in the option file.

You can even configure the same option multiple times, as we did with innodb_buffer_pool_size. The last setting will take precedence over the previous ones, and the files are scanned from top to bottom. Option files have a global order of precedence as well; we'll talk about that in "Search Order for Option Files" on page 359.

A very important thing to remember is that setting an incorrect option name will lead to programs not starting. Of course, if the incorrect option is under a section that particular program doesn't read, it's fine. But mysqld will fail if it finds an option it doesn't know under [mysqld]. In MySQL 8.0 you can validate some of the changes you make in option files by using the --validate-config command-line argument with mysqld. However, that validation will cover only core server functionality and won't verify storage engine options.

Sometimes you'll need to set an option that MySQL doesn't know at startup time. For example, this can be useful when configuring plugins that may be loaded after startup. You can prepend such options with the loose- prefix (or --loose- on the command line), and MySQL will only output a warning when it sees these but not fail to start. Here's an example with an unknown option:

```
# mysqld --validate-config
2021-02-11T08:02:58.741347Z 0 [ERROR] [MY-000067] [Server] ...
    ... unknown variable audit_log_format=JSON.
2021-02-11T08:02:58.741470Z 0 [ERROR] [MY-010119] [Server] Aborting
```

After the option is changed to `loose-audit_log_format`, we see the following instead. No output means that all the options were successfully validated:

```
# mysqld --validate-config
#
```

Comments

An often overlooked but important feature of MySQL option files is the ability to add comments. Comments allow you to include arbitrary text, usually a description of why the setting is here, that will not be parsed by any MySQL programs. As you saw in the `disable_log_bin` example, comments are lines starting with #. You can also create comments that start with semicolon (;); either is accepted. You don't necessarily need to have a whole line dedicated to a comment: they can also appear at the end of a line, although in this case they must start with a #, not a ;. Once MySQL finds a # on a line (unless it's escaped), everything beyond that point is treated as a comment. The following line is a valid configuration:

```
innodb_buffer_pool_size = 268435456 # 256M
```

Inclusion directives

Configuration files (and whole directories) can be included within other config files. This can make it easier to manage complex configurations, but it also makes reading the options more difficult, because humans, unlike programs, can't really merge the files together easily. Still, it's useful to be able to separate the configurations of different MySQL programs. The `xtrabackup` utility (see Chapter 10), for example, doesn't have any special config file and reads standard system option files. With inclusion, you can have `xtrabackup`'s configs neatly organized in a dedicated file and declutter your main MySQL option file. You can then include it as follows:

```
$ cat /etc/my.cnf
!include /etc/mysql.d/xtrabackup.cnf
...
```

You can see that *etc/my.cnf* includes the */etc/mysql.d/xtrabackup.cnf* file, which in turn has a few configuration options listed in the [`xtrabackup`] section.

It is not necessary to have different sections in different files, though. For example, Percona XtraDB Cluster has `wsrep` library configuration options under the [`mysqld`] section. There are plenty of such configurations, and they aren't necessarily useful to have in your *my.cnf*. You could create a separate file—for example, */etc/mysql.d/wsrep.conf*—and list the `wsrep` variables under the [`mysqld`] section there. Any program reading the main *my.cnf* file will also read all of the included files and only then parse the variables under the different sections.

When a lot of such extra configuration files are created, you may want to just go ahead and include the whole directory or directories that contain them instead of including each individual option file. That's done with another directive, `include dir`, that expects a directory path as an argument:

```
!includedir /etc/mysql.d
```

MySQL programs will understand that path as a directory and try to include every option file in that directory's tree. On Unix-like systems, *.cnf* files are included; on Windows, both *.cnf* and *.ini* files are included.

Usually, inclusions are defined at the beginning of a particular config file, but that isn't mandatory. You can think of the inclusion as appending the contents of the included file or files to the parent file; wherever an inclusion is defined in the file, the included file's contents will be placed right under that inclusion. In reality, things are a bit more complicated, but this mental model works when, for example, thinking about option precedence, which we cover in "Search Order for Option Files" on page 359.

Each included file must have at least one configuration section defined. For example, it may have [`mysqld`] at the beginning.

Empty lines

There's no meaning to empty lines in the option files. You can use them to separate the sections or individual options visually to make the file easier to read.

Scope of Options

We can talk about option scope in MySQL from two perspectives. First, each individual option can have global scope, session scope, or both, and can be set dynamically or statically. Second, we can talk about how options set in option files are scoped through sections and what the scope and order of precedence of the option files themselves is.

We mentioned that section headers define which particular program (or programs, as nothing prevents one from reading multiple sections) is intended to be reading the options under a particular header. Some configuration options do not make sense outside of their sections, but some can be defined under multiple sections and do not necessarily need to be set equally.

Let's consider an example where we have a MySQL server configured with the `latin1` character set for legacy reasons. However, there are now newer tables with the `utf8mb4` charset. We want our `mysqldump` logical dumps to just be in UTF-8, so we want to override the charset for this program. Conveniently, `mysqldump` reads its own configuration section, so we can write an option file like this:

```
[mysqld]
character_set_server=latin1
[mysqldump]
default_character_set=utf8mb4
```

This small example shows how options can be set on different levels. In this particular case we used different options, but it could be the same one in different scopes. For example, suppose we want to limit the future size of BLOB and TEXT values (see "String types" on page 144) to 32 MiB, but we already have rows of up to 256 MiB in size. We can add an artificial barrier for local clients using a configuration like this:

```
[mysqld]
max_allowed_packet=256M
[client]
max_allowed_packet=32M
```

The MySQL server's `max_allowed_packet` value will be set on a global scope and will act as a hard limit on the maximum query size (and also on BLOB or TEXT field size). The client's value will be set on a session scope and will act as a soft limit. If a particular client requires a larger value (to read an old row, for example), it can use the SET statement to go up to the server's limit.

The option files themselves also have different scopes. MySQL option files can be divided by scope into a few groups: global, client, server, and extra. Global option files are read by all or most MySQL programs, whereas client and server files are only read by client programs and `mysqld`, respectively. Since it's possible to specify an extra configuration file to be read by a program, we're also listing the "extra" category.

Let's outline the option files installed and read on Linux and Windows by a regular MySQL 8.0 installation. We'll start with Windows, in Table 9-1.

Table 9-1. MySQL option files on Windows

Filename	Scope and purpose
%WINDIR%\my.ini, %WINDIR%\my.cnf	Global options read by all programs
C:\my.ini, C:\my.cnf	Global options read by all programs
BASEDIR\my.ini, BASEDIR\my.cnf	Global options read by all programs
Extra config file	File optionally specified with `--defaults-extra-file`
%APPDATA%\MySQL\.mylogin.cnf	Login path config file
DATADIR\mysqld-auto.cnf	Option file for persisted variables

Table 9-2 breaks down the option files for a typical installation on Fedora Linux.

Table 9-2. *MySQL option files on Fedora Linux*

Filename	Scope and purpose
/etc/my.cnf, /etc/mysql/my.cnf, /usr/etc/my.cnf	Global options read by all programs
$MYSQL_HOME/my.cnf	Server options, only read if the variable is set
~/.my.cnf	Global options read by all programs run by a particular OS user
Extra config file	File optionally specified with --defaults-extra-file
~/.mylogin.cnf	Login path config file under a particular OS user
DATADIR/mysqld-auto.cnf	Option file for persisted variables

With Linux, it's difficult to identify a universal, complete list of configuration files, as MySQL packages for different Linux distributions may read slightly different files or locations. As a rule of thumb, */etc/my.cnf* is a good starting point on Linux, and either *%WINDIR%\my.cnf* or *BASEDIR\my.cnf* on Windows.

A couple of the configuration files we've listed may differ in their paths between different systems. */usr/etc/my.cnf* can be also written as *SYSCONFIGDIR/my.cnf*, and the path is defined at compilation time. *$MYSQL_HOME/my.cnf* is only read if the variable is set. The default packaged mysqld_safe program (used to start the mysqld daemon) will set $MYSQL_HOME to *BASEDIR* before running mysqld. You won't find $MYSQL_HOME set for any of the OS users, and setting that variable is relevant only if you're starting mysqld manually—in other words, not using the service or sys temctl commands.

There's one peculiar difference between Windows and Linux. On Linux, MySQL programs read some configuration files located under the given OS user's home directory. In Table 9-2, the home directory is represented by ~. MySQL on Windows lacks this ability. One frequent use case for such config files is controlling options for clients based on their OS user. Usually, they will contain credentials. However, the login path facility described in "Special Option Files" on page 360 makes this redundant.

An extra config file, specified on the command line with --defaults-extra-file, will be read after every other global file is read, according to its position in the table. This is a useful option when you want to do a one-off run of a program to test new variables, for example. Overusing this option, though, can lead to trouble in understanding the current set of options in effect (see "Determining the Options in Effect" on page 364). The --defaults-extra-file option is not the only one that alters option file handling. --no-defaults prevents the program from reading *any* configuration files at all. --defaults-file forces the program to read a single file, which can be useful if you have your custom configuration all in one place.

By now you should have a firm grasp on what option files most installations of MySQL use. The next section talks more about how different programs read different files, in which order, and what specific group or groups they read from those files.

Search Order for Option Files

At this point you should know the structure of an option file and where to find them. Most MySQL programs read one or more option files, and it's important to know in which specific order a program searches for these files and reads them. This section covers the topics of search order and options precedence and discusses their importance.

If a MySQL program reads any option files, you can find the specific files it reads, as well as the order in which it reads them. The general order of the configuration files read will be either exactly the same or very similar to that outlined in Tables 9-1 and 9-2. You can use the following command to see the exact order:

```
$ mysqld --verbose --help | grep "Default options" -A2
Default options are read from the following files in the given order:
/etc/my.cnf /etc/mysql/my.cnf /usr/etc/my.cnf ~/.my.cnf
The following groups are read: mysqld server mysqld-8.0
```

On Windows you need to run `mysqld.exe` instead of `mysqld`, but the output will stay the same. That output includes the list of configuration files read, and their order. You can also see the list of option groups read by `mysqld`: [`mysqld`], [`server`], and [`mysqld-8.0`]. Note that you can alter the list of option groups that any program reads by adding the `--defaults-group-suffix` option:

```
$ mysqld --defaults-group-suffix=-test --verbose --help | grep "groups are read"
The following groups are read: mysqld server mysqld-8.0 ...
... mysqld-test server-test mysqld-8.0-test
```

You know at this point what option files and option groups are read. However, it's also important to know the order of precedence for those option files. Nothing prevents you from setting one or more options in multiple configuration files, after all. In the case of MySQL programs, the order of precedence for config files is simple: options from files read later take precedence over options in previously read files. Options passed to commands directly as command-line arguments take precedence over any configuration options in any config files.

In Tables 9-1 and 9-2, the files are read in order from top to bottom. The lower the config file in the list, the higher the "weight" of options there. For example, for any programs that are not `mysqld`, values in *.mylogin.cnf* take precedence over those in any other config files, and only have lower precedence than values set through command-line arguments. For `mysqld`, the same is true for persisted variables set in *DATADIR /mysqld-auto.cnf*.

The ability to include configuration files in other files through inclusion directives makes things slightly more complicated, but you always include extras within one or more of the option files listed in Tables 9-1 and 9-2. You can think of this as MySQL appending the included files to the parent config file just before reading it, inserting each one into the file just after its inclusion directive. Thus, the precedence of the options globally is that of the parent configuration file. Within the resulting file itself (with all the included files added in order), options defined later take precedence over ones defined earlier.

Special Option Files

There are two special configuration files used by MySQL, which are exceptions to the structure outlined in "Structure of the Option File" on page 351.

Login Path Configuration File

First, there's a *.mylogin.cnf* file, which is used as part of the *login path* system. Even though you can think of its structure as similar to that of a regular option file, this particular file is not a regular text file. In fact, it's an encrypted text file. This file is intended to be created and modified through use of the special `mysql_config_editor` program, which is supplied with MySQL, usually in the client package. It is encrypted because the purpose of *.mylogin.cnf* (and the whole login path system) is to store MySQL connection options, including passwords, in a convenient and secure manner.

By default, `mysql_config_editor` and other MySQL programs will look for *.mylogin.cnf* in the *$HOME* of the current user on Linux and various Unix flavors, and in *%APPDATA%\MySQL* on Windows. It is possible to change the location and name of the file by setting the `MYSQL_TEST_LOGIN_FILE` environment variable.

You can create this file, if it doesn't already exist, by storing a password for the `root` user in it:

```
$ mysql_config_editor set --user=root --password
Enter password:
```

After entering the password and confirming the input, we can take a look at the file's contents:

```
$ ls -la ~/.mylogin.cnf
-rw-------. 1 skuzmichev skuzmichev 100 Jan 18 18:03 .mylogin.cnf
$ cat ~/.mylogin.cnf


>pZ
   prI
         R86w">#  &.h.m:4+|DDKnl_K3>73x$
$ file ~/.mylogin.cnf
.mylogin.cnf: data
$ file ~/.my.cnf
.my.cnf: ASCII text
```

As you can see, on the surface at least, *.mylogin.cnf* is for sure not a regular configuration file. As such, it requires special treatment. In addition to creating the file, you can view and modify *.mylogin.cnf* with the `mysql_config_editor`. Let's start with how to actually see what's inside. The option for that is `print`:

```
$ mysql_config_editor print
[client]
user = "root"
password = *****
```

`client` is a default login path. All operations done with `mysql_config_editor` without an explicit login path specification affect the `client` login path. We didn't specify any login path when running `set` earlier, so root's credentials were written under the `client` path. It's possible to specify a specific login path for any operation, though. Let's put root's credentials under a login path named `root`:

```
$ mysql_config_editor set --login-path=root --user=root --password
Enter password:
```

To specify the login path, use the `--login-path` or `-G` option, and to view all the paths when using `print`, add the `--all` option:

```
$ mysql_config_editor print --login-path=root
[root]
user = root
password = *****
$ mysql_config_editor print --all
[client]
user = root
password = *****
[root]
user = root
password = *****
```

You can see that the output resembles an option file, so you can think of *.mylogin.cnf* as an option file with some special treatment. Just don't edit it manually. Speaking of editing, let's add a few more options to the `set` command as `mysql_config_editor` calls it. We'll create a new login path in the process.

`mysql_config_editor` supports the `--help` (or `-?`) argument, which can be combined with other options to get help specifically on `print` or `set`, for example. Let's start by looking at a slightly truncated help output for `set`:

```
$ mysql_config_editor set --help
...
MySQL Configuration Utility.

Description: Write a login path to the login file.
Usage: mysql_config_editor [program options] [set [command options]]
  -?, --help        Display this help and exit.
  -h, --host=name   Host name to be entered into the login file.
```

```
-G, --login-path=name
                        Name of the login path to use in the login file. (Default
                        : client)
-p, --password          Prompt for password to be entered into the login file.
-u, --user=name         User name to be entered into the login file.
-S, --socket=name       Socket path to be entered into login file.
-P, --port=name         Port number to be entered into login file.
-w, --warn              Warn and ask for confirmation if set command attempts to
                        overwrite an existing login path (enabled by default).
                        (Defaults to on; use --skip-warn to disable.)
...
```

You can see here another interesting property of *.mylogin.cnf*: you can't put arbitrary parameters into it. Now we know that we can basically set only a few options related to logging into a MySQL instance or instances—which is, of course, to be expected of the "login path" file. Now, let's get back to editing the file:

```
$ mysql_config_editor set --login-path=scott --user=scott
$ mysql_config_editor set --login-path=scott --user=scott
WARNING : scott path already exists and will be overwritten.
  Continue? (Press y|Y for Yes, any other key for No) : y
$ mysql_config_editor set --login-path=scott --user=scott --skip-warn
```

Here we've shown all the behaviors that mysql_config_editor can exhibit when modifying or creating a login path. If the login path doesn't yet exist, no warning is produced. If there's already such a path, a warning and confirmation will be printed, but only if --skip-warn is not specified. Note that we're talking here in terms of the whole login path! It is not possible to modify a single property of the path: the whole login path is written out every time. If you want to change a single property, you'll need to specify all the other properties that you need too.

Let's add some more details and view the result:

```
$ mysql_config_editor set --login-path=scott \
--user=scott --port=3306 --host=192.168.122.1 \
--password --skip-warn
Enter password:
$ mysql_config_editor print --login-path=scott
[scott]
user = scott
password = *****
host = 192.168.122.1
port = 3306
```

Persistent System Variables Configuration File

The second special file is *mysqld-auto.cnf*, which has resided in the data directory since MySQL 8.0. It is a part of the new persisted system variables feature, which allows you to update MySQL options on disk using regular SET statements. Before, you could not change MySQL's configuration from within a database connection. The usual flow was to change the option files on disk and then run a SET GLOBAL statement to change the configuration variables online. As you can imagine, this can lead to mistakes and to changes only being made online, for example. The new SET PERSIST statement takes care of both tasks: variables updated online are also updated on disk. It's also possible to update a variable on disk only.

The file itself is, surprisingly, not like any other configuration file in MySQL at all. Whereas *.mylogin.cnf* was an encrypted but still regular option file, *mysqld-auto.cnf* uses a common but completely different format: JSON.

Before you persist anything, *mysqld-auto.cnf* doesn't exist. So, we'll start by changing a system variable:

```
mysql> SELECT @@GLOBAL.max_connections;
+--------------------------+
| @@GLOBAL.max_connections |
+--------------------------+
|                      100 |
+--------------------------+
1 row in set (0.00 sec)

mysql> SET PERSIST max_connections = 256;
Query OK, 0 rows affected (0.01 sec)

mysql> SELECT @@GLOBAL.max_connections;
+--------------------------+
| @@GLOBAL.max_connections |
+--------------------------+
|                      256 |
+--------------------------+
1 row in set (0.00 sec)
```

As expected, the variable was updated on a global scope online. Let's now explore the resulting config file. Since we know that the contents are in JSON format, we'll use the jq utility to format it nicely. That's not necessary, but makes the file easier to read:

```
$ cat /var/lib/mysql/mysqld-auto.cnf | jq .
{
  "Version": 1,
  "mysql_server": {
    "max_connections": {
      "Value": "256",
      "Metadata": {
        "Timestamp": 1611728445802834,
        "User": "root",
        "Host": "localhost"
      }
    }
  }
}
```

Just by looking at this file containing a single variable value, you can see why plain *.ini* is used for config files that are intended to be edited by humans. This is verbose! However, JSON is excellent for reading by computers, so it's a good match for a configuration written and read by MySQL itself. As an added benefit, you get auditing of the changes: as you can see, the `max_connection` property has metadata containing the time when the change occurred and the author of the change.

Since this is a text file, unlike the login path config file, which is binary, it's possible to edit *mysqld-auto.cnf* manually. However, it's unlikely that there will be many cases where that's needed.

Determining the Options in Effect

The last routine task that pretty much anyone working with MySQL will face is finding out values for the variables, and in what option files they are set (and why, but no amount of technology can help with human reasoning sometimes!).

At this point, we know what files MySQL programs read, in what order, and their precedence. We also know that command-line arguments override any other settings. Still, understanding where exactly some variable is set can be a daunting task. Multiple files scanned, potentially with nested inclusions, can make for a long investigation.

Let's start by looking at how to determine the options currently used by a program. For some, like MySQL Server (`mysqld`), that is easy. You can get the list of current values used by `mysqld` by running `SHOW GLOBAL VARIABLES`. It's impossible to change an option value that `mysqld` uses and not see the effect reflected in the global variables' state. For other programs, things get more complicated. To understand what options are used by `mysql`, you'd have to run it and then check the outputs of `SHOW VARIABLES` and `SHOW GLOBAL VARIABLES` to see which options are overridden on the session level. But even before a successful connection to the server is established, `mysql` must read or receive connection information.

There are two easy ways to determine the list of options in effect when the program starts: by passing the `--print-defaults` argument to that program or by using the special `my_print_defaults` program. Let's take a look at the former option as executed on Linux. You can ignore the `sed` part, but it makes the output slightly nicer for human eyes:

```
$ mysql --print-defaults
mysql would have been started with the following arguments:
--user=root --password=*****
$ mysqld --print-defaults | sed 's/--/\n--/g'
/usr/sbin/mysqld would have been started with the following arguments:
```

```
--datadir=/var/lib/mysql
--socket=/var/lib/mysql/mysql.sock
--log-error=/var/log/mysqld.log
--pid-file=/run/mysqld/mysqld.pid
--max_connections=100000
--core-file
--innodb_buffer_pool_in_core_file=OFF
--innodb_buffer_pool_size=256MiB
```

The variables picked up here come from all the option files we discussed before. If a variable value was set multiple times, the last occurrence will take precedence. However, --print-defaults will actually output every option set. For example, the output could look like this—even though innodb_buffer_pool_size is set five times, the value in effect will be 384 M:

```
$ mysqld --print-defaults | sed 's/--/\n--/g'
/usr/sbin/mysqld would have been started with the following arguments:

--datadir=/var/lib/mysql
--socket=/var/lib/mysql/mysql.sock
--log-error=/var/log/mysqld.log
--pid-file=/run/mysqld/mysqld.pid
--max_connections=100000
--core-file
--innodb_buffer_pool_in_core_file=OFF
--innodb_buffer_pool_size=268435456
--innodb_buffer_pool_size=256M
--innodb_buffer_pool_size=256MB
--innodb_buffer_pool_size=256MiB
--large-pages
--innodb_buffer_pool_size=384M
```

You can also combine --print-defaults with other command-line arguments. For example, if you intend to run a program with command-line arguments, you can see whether they will override or repeat already set values for configuration options for a particular session:

```
$ mysql --print-defaults --host=192.168.4.23 --user=bob | sed 's/--/\n--/g'
mysql would have been started with the following arguments:

--user=root
--password=*****
--host=192.168.4.23
--user=bob
```

The other way to print variables is using the my_print_defaults program. It takes one or more section headers as arguments and will print all options it finds in scanned files that fall into the requested groups. That can be better than using --print-defaults when you just need to review one option group. In MySQL 8.0, the [mysqld] program reads the following groups: [mysqld], [server], and [mysqld-8.0]. The combined output of options may be lengthy, but what if we only need to view options specifically set for 8.0? For this example, we've added the [mysqld-8.0] option group to the option file and put a couple of configuration parameter values there:

```
$ my_print_defaults mysqld-8.0
--character_set_server=latin1
--collation_server=latin1_swedish_ci
```

That can also help with other software, like PXC, or with the MariaDB flavor of MySQL, both of which include multiple configuration groups. In particular, you would likely want to review the [wsrep] section without any other options. my_print_defaults can, of course, be used to output a complete set of options too; it just needs to be passed all the section headers a program reads. For example, the [mysql] program reads the [mysql] and [client] option groups, so we could use:

```
$ my_print_defaults mysql client
--user=root
--password=*****
--default-character-set=latin1
```

The user and password definitions come from the client group in the login path config we set before, and the charset from the [mysql] option group in the regular *.my.cnf*. Note that we added that group and charset config manually; by default that option is not set.

You can see that while both ways to read options talk of *defaults*, they actually output the options that we have explicitly set, making them nondefault. This is an interesting tidbit, but it doesn't change anything in the grand scheme of things.

Unfortunately, neither of these ways of reviewing options is perfect at determining the complete set of options in effect. The problem is they only read the configuration files listed in Tables 9-1 and 9-2, but it's possible for MySQL programs to read other config files or to be started with command-line arguments. Additionally, the variables persisted in *DATADIR* /mysqld-auto.cnf through SET PERSIST are not provided by defaults-printing routines.

We mentioned that MySQL programs do not read options from any other files than the ones that were listed in Tables 9-1 and 9-2. However, those lists do include the "extra config file," which can be in an arbitrary location. Unless you specify the same extra file when invoking my_print_defaults or another program with --print-defaults, options from that extra file won't be read. The extra file is specified with the command-line argument, --defaults-extra-file, and can be specified for most if not all MySQL programs. The two defaults-printing routines only read predefined config files and will miss that file. You can, however, specify --defaults-extra-file both for my_print_defaults and for the program invoked with --print-defaults, and both will read the extra file then. The same applies to the --defaults-file option we mentioned earlier, which basically forces the MySQL program to only read the single file passed as a value for this option.

Both `--defaults-extra-file` and `--defaults-file` share a thing in common: they are command-line arguments. Command-line arguments passed to a MySQL program override any options read from configuration files, but at the same time you can miss them when you do `--print-defaults` or `my_print_defaults`, as they are coming from outside of any config files. To put it more concisely: a particular MySQL program, such as `mysqld`, can be started by someone with unknown and arbitrary command-line arguments. Thus, when we're talking about options, in effect we must also consider the presence of such arguments.

On Linux and Unix-like systems, you can use the `ps` utility (or an equivalent) to view information on currently running processes, including their full command lines. Let's see an example on Linux where `mysqld` was started with `--no-defaults` and with all config options passed as arguments:

```
$ ps auxf | grep mysqld | grep -v grep
root      397830  ... \_ sudo -u mysql bash -c mysqld ...
mysql     397832  ...   \_ mysqld --datadir=/var/lib/mysql ...
```

Or, if we print just the command line for the `mysqld` process and make it cleaner with sed:

```
$ ps -p 397832 -ocommand ww | sed 's/--/\n--/g'
COMMAND
mysqld
--datadir=/var/lib/mysql
--socket=/var/lib/mysql/mysql.sock
--log-error=/var/log/mysqld.log
--pid-file=/run/mysqld/mysqld.pid
...
--character_set_server=latin1
--collation_server=latin1_swedish_ci
```

Note that for this example we started `mysqld` without using any of the provided scripts. You won't often see this way of starting the MySQL server, but it's possible.

You can pass any configuration option as an argument, so the output can be quite lengthy. However, when you're not sure how exactly `mysqld` or another program was executed, that's an important thing to check. On Windows, you can view the command-line arguments of a running program either by opening the Task Manager and adding a Command Line column to the Processes tab (through the View menu) or by using the Process Explorer tool from the `sysinternals` package.

If your MySQL program is started from within a script, you should inspect that script to find all the arguments used. While this is probably going to be a rare occasion for mysqld, it's a common practice to run mysql, mysqldump, and xtrabackup from custom scripts.

Understanding the currently used options can be a daunting task, but it's extremely important at times. Hopefully, these guidelines and hints will help you.

## CHAPTER 10

Backups and Recovery

The most important task for any DBA is backing up the data. Correct and tested backup and recovery procedures can save a company and thus a job. Mistakes happen, disasters happen, and errors happen. MySQL is a robust piece of software, but it's not completely free of bugs or crashes. Thus, it is crucial to understand why and how to perform backups.

Apart from preserving database contents, most backup methods can also be used for another important purpose: copying the contents of the database between separate systems. Though probably not as important as saving the day when corruption happens, this copying is a routine operation for the vast majority of database operators. Developers will often need to use downstream environments, which should be similar to production. QA staff may need a volatile environment with a lifespan of an hour. Analytics may be run on a dedicated host. Some of these tasks can be solved by replication, but any replica starts from a restored backup.

This chapter first briefly reviews two major types of backups and discusses their fundamental properties. It then looks at some of the tools available in the MySQL world for the purpose of backup and recovery. Covering each and every tool and their parameters would be beyond the scope of this book, but by the end of the chapter you should know your way around backing up and recovering MySQL data. We'll also explore some basic data transfer scenarios. Finally, the chapter outlines a robust backup architecture that you can use as a foundation for your work.

An overview of what we think is a good backup strategy is given in "Database Backup Strategy Primer" on page 409. We believe it's important to understand the tools and moving parts before deciding on the strategy, and therefore that section comes last.

Physical and Logical Backups

Broadly speaking, most if not all of the backup tools fit into just two wide categories: logical and physical. *Logical* backups operate on the internal structures: databases (schemas), tables, views, users, and other objects. *Physical* backups are concerned with the OS-side representation of the database structures: data files, transaction journals, and so on.

It might be easier to explain with an example. Imagine backing up a single MyISAM table in MySQL database. As you will see later in this chapter, the InnoDB storage engine is more complex to back up correctly. Knowing that MyISAM is not transactional and that there are no ongoing writes to this table, we may go ahead and copy the files related to it. In doing so, we create a physical backup of the table. We could instead go ahead and run `SELECT *` and `SHOW CREATE TABLE` statements against this table and preserve the outputs of those statements somewhere. That's a very basic form of a logical backup. Of course, these are just simple examples, and in reality the process of obtaining both types of backup will be more complex and nuanced. The conceptual differences between these imaginary backups can, however, be transferred and applied to any logical and physical backups.

Logical Backups

Logical backups are concerned with the *actual data*, and not its *physical representation*. As you've already seen, such backups don't copy any existing database files and instead rely on queries or other means to obtain needed database contents. The result is usually some textual representation, though that's not granted, and a logical backup's output may well be binary-encoded. Let's see some more examples of how such backups might look and then discuss their properties.

Here are some examples of logical backups:

- Table data queried and saved into an external *.csv* file using the `SELECT ... INTO OUTFILE` statement that we cover in "Writing Data into Comma-Delimited Files" on page 274.

- A table or any other object's definition saved as a SQL statement.

- One or more `INSERT` SQL statements that, run against a database and an empty table, would populate that table up to a preserved state.

- A recording of all statements ever run that touched a particular table or database and modified data or schema objects. By this we mean DML and DDL commands; you should be familiar with both types, covered in Chapters 3 and 4

That last example actually represents how both replication and point-in-time recovery work in MySQL. We tackle those topics later, and you'll see that the term *logical* doesn't just apply to backups.

Recovery of a logical backup is usually done by executing one or more SQL statements. Continuing with our earlier examples, let's review the options for recovery:

- Data from a *.csv* file can be loaded into a table using the `LOAD DATA INFILE` command.
- The table can be created or re-created by running a DDL SQL statement.
- `INSERT` SQL statements can be executed using the `mysql` CLI or any other client.
- A replay of all the statements run in a database will restore it to its state after the last statement.

Logical backups have some interesting properties that make them extremely useful in some situations. More often than not, a logical backup is some form of text file, consisting mostly of SQL statements. That is not necessary, however, and is not a defining property (albeit useful one). The process of creating logical backups also usually involves the execution of some queries. These are important features because they allow for a great degree of flexibility and portability.

Logical backups are flexible because they make it very easy to back up a part of a database. For example, you can back up schema objects without their contents or easily back up only a few of the database's tables. You can even back up part of a table's data, which is usually impossible with physical backups. Once the backup file is ready, there are tools you can use to review and modify it either manually or automatically, which is something not easily done with copies of database files.

Portability comes from the fact that logical backups can be loaded easily into different versions of MySQL running on different operating systems and architectures. With some modification, you can actually load logical backups taken from one RDBMS into an absolutely different one. Most database migration tools use logical replication internally due to this fact. This property also makes this backup type suitable for backing up cloud-managed databases off-site, and for migrations between them.

Another interesting property of logical backups is that they are effective in combating *corruption*—that is, physical corruption of a physical data file. Errors in data can still be introduced, for example, by bugs in software or by gradual degradation of storage media. The topic of corruption and its counterpart, integrity, is very wide, but this brief explanation should suffice for now.

Once a data file becomes corrupted, a database might not be able to read data from it and serve the queries. Since corruption tends to happen silently, you might not know when it occurred. However, if a logical backup was generated without error, that means it's sound and has good data. Corruption could happen in a *secondary index* (any non-primary index; see Chapter 4, *Working with Database Structures* for more details), so a logical backup doing a full table scan might generate normally and not face an error. In short, a logical backup can both help you detect corruption early (as it scans all tables) and help you save the data (as the last successful logical backup will have a sound copy).

The inherent problem with all logical backups comes from the fact that they are created and restored by executing SQL statements against a running database system. While that allows for flexibility and portability, it also means that these backups result in load on the database and are generally quite slow. DBAs always frown when someone runs a query that reads all the data from a table indiscriminately, and that's exactly what logical backup tools usually do. Similarly, the restore operation for a logical backup usually results in the interpreting and running of each statement as if it came from a regular client. This doesn't mean that logical backups are bad or shouldn't be used, but it's a trade-off that must be remembered.

Physical Backups

Whereas logical backups are all about data as in database contents, physical backups are all about data as in operating system files and internal RDBMS workings. Remember, in the example with a MyISAM table being backed up, a physical backup was a copy of the files representing that table. Most of the backups and tools of this type are concerned with copying and transferring all or parts of database files.

Some examples of physical backups include the following:

- A *cold* database directory copy, meaning it's done when the database is shut down (as opposed to a *hot* copy, done while the database is running).
- A storage snapshot of volumes and filesystems used by database.
- A copy of table data files.
- A stream of changes to database data files of some form. Most RDBMSs use a stream like this for crash recovery, and sometimes for replication; InnoDB's redo log is a similar concept.

Recovery of a physical backup is usually done by copying back the files and making them consistent. Let's review the recovery options for the previous examples:

- A cold copy can be moved to a desired location or server and then used as a data directory by a MySQL instance, old or new.
- A snapshot can be restored in place or on another volume and then used by MySQL.
- Table files can be put in place of existing ones.
- A replay of the changes stream against the data files will recover their state to the last point in time.

Of these, the simplest physical backup that can be performed is a cold database directory backup. Yes, it's simple and basic, but it's a very powerful tool.

Physical backups, unlike logical ones, are very rigid, giving little leeway in terms of control over what can be backed up and where the backup can be used. Generally speaking, most physical backups can only be used to restore the exact same state of a database or a table. Usually, these backups also put constraints on the target database software version and operating system. With some work, you can restore a logical backup from MySQL to PostgreSQL. However, a cold copy of the MySQL data directory done on Linux may not work if restored on Windows. Also, you cannot take a physical backup if you don't have physical access to the database server. This means that performing such a backup on a managed database in the cloud is impossible: the vendor might be performing physical backups in the background, but you may not have a way to get them out.

Since a physical backup is by nature a copy of all or a subset of the original backup pages, any corruption present in the original will be included in the backup. It's important to remember that, because this property makes physical backups ill-suited for combating corruption.

You may wonder why you would use such a seemingly inconvenient way of backing up. The reason is that physical backups are fast. Operating on the OS or even storage level, physical backup methods are sometimes the only possible way to actually back up a database. By way of example, a storage snapshot of a multiterabyte volume might take a few seconds or minutes, whereas querying and streaming that data for a logical backup might take hours or days. The same goes for recovery.

Overview of Logical and Physical Backups

We've now covered the two categories of backups and are ready to start exploring the actual tools used for these backups in the MySQL world. Before we do that, though, let's summarize the differences between logical and physical backups and take a quick look at the properties of the tools used to create them.

Properties of logical backups:

- Contain a description and the contents of the logical structures
- Are human-readable and editable
- Are relatively slow to take and restore

Logical backup tools are:

- Very flexible, allowing you to rename objects, combine separate sources, perform partial restores, and more
- Not usually bound to a specific database version or platform
- Able to extract data from corrupted tables and safeguard from corruption
- Suitable for backing up remote databases (for example, in the cloud)

Properties of physical backups:

- Are byte-by-byte copies of parts of data files, or entire filesystems/volumes
- Are fast to take and restore
- Offer little flexibility and will always result in the same structure upon restore
- Can include corrupted pages

Physical backup tools are:

- Cumbersome to operate
- Usually don't allow for an easy cross-platform or even cross-version portability
- Cannot back up remote databases without OS access

 These are not conflicting approaches. In fact, a generally good idea is to perform both types of backups on a regular basis. They serve different purposes and satisfy different requirements.

Replication as a Backup Tool

Replication is a very wide topic that upcoming chapters cover in detail. In this section, we briefly discuss how replication relates to the concept of backing up and recovering a database.

In brief, replication is not a substitute for taking backups. The specifics of replications are such that they result in a full or partial copy of a target database. This lets you use replication in a lot of, but not all, possible failure scenarios involving MySQL. Let's review two examples. They will be helpful later in the chapter as well.

 In the MySQL world, replication is a type of logical backup. That's because it's based on transferring logical SQL statements.

Infrastructure Failure

Infrastructure is prone to failure: drives go bad, power goes out, fires happen. Almost no system can provide 100% uptime, and only vastly distributed ones can even get close. What that means is that eventually *any* database will crash due to its host server failing. In a good case, a restart might be enough to recover. In a bad case, part or all of the data may be gone.

Restoring and recovering a backup is by no means an instantaneous operation. In a replicated environment, a special operation called *switchover* can be performed to put a replica in place of the failed database. In many cases, switchover saves a lot of time and allows for work on a failed system to proceed without too much rush.

Imagine a setup with two identical servers running MySQL. One is a dedicated primary, which receives all the connections and serves all the queries. The other one is a replica. There's a mechanism to redirect connections to the replica, with switchover resulting in 5 minutes of downtime.

One day, a hard disk drive goes bad in the primary server. It's a simple server, so that alone results in a crash and downtime. Monitoring catches the issue, and the DBA immediately understands that to restore the database on that server, they'll need to install a new disk and then restore and recover the recent backup. The whole operation will take a couple of hours.

Switching over to a replica is a good idea in this case, because it saves a lot of valuable uptime.

Deployment Bug

Software bugs are a fact of life that has to be accepted. The more complex the system, the higher the possible incidence of logical errors. While we all strive to limit and reduce bugs, we must understand that they will happen and plan accordingly.

Imagine that a new version of an application is released that includes a database migration script. Even though both the new version and the script were tested in downstream environments, there's a bug. Migration irrecoverably corrupts all customers' last names that have "special" non-ASCII symbols. The corruption is silent, since the script finishes successfully, and the issue is noticed only a week later by an angry customer, whose name is now incorrect.

Even though there's a replica of the production database, it has the same data and the same logical corruption. Switching over to the replica *won't* help in this case, and a backup taken prior to the migration must be restored to obtain a list of correct last names.

 Delayed replicas can protect you in such situations, but the longer the delay, the less practical it is to operate such a replica. You can create a replica with a delay of a week, but you may need data from an hour ago. Usually, replica delays are measured in minutes and hours.

The two failure scenarios just discussed cover two distinct domains: physical and logical. Replication is a good fit for protection in case of physical issues, whereas it provides no (or little) protection from logical issues. Replication is a useful tool, but it's no substitute for backups.

The mysqldump Program

Possibly the simplest way to back up a database online is to dump its contents as SQL statements. This is the paramount logical backup type. *Dumping* in computing usually means outputting the contents of some system or its parts, and the result is a *dump*. In the database world, a dump is usually a logical backup, and dumping is the action of obtaining such a backup. Restoring the backup involves applying the statements to the database. You can generate dumps manually using, for example, SHOW CREATE TABLE and some CONCAT operations to get INSERT statements from data rows in the tables, like this:

```
mysql> SHOW CREATE TABLE sakila.actor\G
*************************** 1. row ***************************
       Table: actor
Create Table: CREATE TABLE `actor` (
  `actor_id` smallint unsigned NOT NULL AUTO_INCREMENT,
  `first_name` varchar(45) NOT NULL,
  `last_name` varchar(45) NOT NULL,
  `last_update` timestamp NOT NULL DEFAULT CURRENT_TIMESTAMP
       ON UPDATE CURRENT_TIMESTAMP,
  PRIMARY KEY (`actor_id`),
  KEY `idx_actor_last_name` (`last_name`)
) ENGINE=InnoDB AUTO_INCREMENT=201 DEFAULT CHARSET=utf8mb4
       COLLATE=utf8mb4_0900_ai_ci
1 row in set (0.00 sec)
```

```
mysql> SELECT CONCAT("INSERT INTO actor VALUES",
    -> "(",actor_id,",'",first_name,"','",
    -> last_name,"','",last_update,"');")
    -> AS insert_statement FROM actor LIMIT 1\G

*************************** 1. row ***************************
insert_statement: INSERT INTO actor VALUES
(1,'PENELOPE','GUINESS','2006-02-15 04:34:33');
1 row in set (0.00 sec)
```

That, however, becomes extremely impractical very fast. Moreover, there are more things to consider: *order of statements*, so that upon restore an INSERT doesn't run before the table is created, and *ownership* and *consistency*. Even though generating logical backups manually is good for understanding, it is tedious and error-prone. Fortunately, MySQL is bundled with a powerful logical backup tool called mysqldump that hides most of the complexity.

The mysqldump program bundled with MySQL allows you to produce dumps from running database instances. The output of mysqldump is a number of SQL statements that can later be applied to the same or another instance of MySQL. mysqldump is a cross-platform tool, available on all the operating systems on which the MySQL server itself is available. As the resulting backup file is just a lot of text, it's also platform-independent.

The command-line arguments to mysqldump are numerous, so it is wise to review the MySQL Reference Manual (*https://oreil.ly/7T8dD*) before jumping into using the tool. However, the most basic scenario requires just one argument: the target database name.

We recommend that you set up a client login path following the instructions in "Login Path Configuration File" on page 360 to the root user and password. You then won't need to specify an account and give its credentials to any of the commands we show in this chapter.

In the following example, mysqldump is invoked without output redirection, and the tool will print all the statements to standard output:

```
$ mysqldump sakila

...
--
-- Table structure for table `actor`
--

DROP TABLE IF EXISTS `actor`;
/*!40101 SET @saved_cs_client     = @@character_set_client */;
/*!50503 SET character_set_client = utf8mb4 */;
```

```
CREATE TABLE `actor` (
  `actor_id` smallint unsigned NOT NULL AUTO_INCREMENT,
  `first_name` varchar(45) NOT NULL,
  `last_name` varchar(45) NOT NULL,
  `last_update` timestamp NOT NULL DEFAULT CURRENT_TIMESTAMP
        ON UPDATE CURRENT_TIMESTAMP,
  PRIMARY KEY (`actor_id`),
  KEY `idx_actor_last_name` (`last_name`)
) ENGINE=InnoDB AUTO_INCREMENT=201 DEFAULT CHARSET=utf8mb4
        COLLATE=utf8mb4_0900_ai_ci;
/*!40101 SET character_set_client = @saved_cs_client */;

--
-- Dumping data for table `actor`
--

LOCK TABLES `actor` WRITE;
/*!40000 ALTER TABLE `actor` DISABLE KEYS */;
INSERT INTO `actor` VALUES
(1,'PENELOPE','GUINESS','2006-02-15 01:34:33'),
(2,'NICK','WAHLBERG','2006-02-15 01:34:33'),
...
(200,'THORA','TEMPLE','2006-02-15 01:34:33');
/*!40000 ALTER TABLE `actor` ENABLE KEYS */;
UNLOCK TABLES;
...
```

The outputs of mysqldump are lengthy and ill-suited for printing in books. Here and elsewhere, the outputs are truncated to include only the lines we're interested in.

You may notice that this output is more nuanced than you might expect. For example, there's a DROP TABLE IF EXISTS statement, which prevents an error for the following CREATE TABLE command when the table already exists on the target. The LOCK and UNLOCK TABLES statements will improve data insertion performance, and so on.

Speaking of schema structure, it is possible to generate a dump that has no data. This can be useful to create a logical clone of the database, for example, for a development environment. Flexibility like this is one of the key features of logical backups and mysqldump:

```
$ mysqldump --no-data sakila

...
--
-- Table structure for table `actor`
--

DROP TABLE IF EXISTS `actor`;
```

```
/*!40101 SET @saved_cs_client      = @@character_set_client */;
/*!50503 SET character_set_client = utf8mb4 */;
CREATE TABLE `actor` (
  `actor_id` smallint unsigned NOT NULL AUTO_INCREMENT,
  `first_name` varchar(45) NOT NULL,
  `last_name` varchar(45) NOT NULL,
  `last_update` timestamp NOT NULL DEFAULT CURRENT_TIMESTAMP
        ON UPDATE CURRENT_TIMESTAMP,
  PRIMARY KEY (`actor_id`),
  KEY `idx_actor_last_name` (`last_name`)
) ENGINE=InnoDB AUTO_INCREMENT=201 DEFAULT CHARSET=utf8mb4
        COLLATE=utf8mb4_0900_ai_ci;
/*!40101 SET character_set_client = @saved_cs_client */;

--
-- Temporary view structure for view `actor_info`
--
...
```

It's also possible to create a dump of a single table in a database. In the next example, sakila is the database and category is the target table:

```
$ mysqldump sakila category
```

Turning the flexibility up a notch, you can dump just a few rows from a table by specifying the --where or -w argument. As the name suggests, the syntax is the same as for the WHERE clause in a SQL statement:

```
$ mysqldump sakila actor --where="actor_id > 195"

...
--
-- Table structure for table `actor`
--

DROP TABLE IF EXISTS `actor`;
CREATE TABLE `actor` (
...

--
-- Dumping data for table `actor`
--
-- WHERE:  actor_id > 195

LOCK TABLES `actor` WRITE;
/*!40000 ALTER TABLE `actor` DISABLE KEYS */;
INSERT INTO `actor` VALUES
(196,'BELA','WALKEN','2006-02-15 09:34:33'),
(197,'REESE','WEST','2006-02-15 09:34:33'),
(198,'MARY','KEITEL','2006-02-15 09:34:33'),
(199,'JULIA','FAWCETT','2006-02-15 09:34:33'),
(200,'THORA','TEMPLE','2006-02-15 09:34:33');
/*!40000 ALTER TABLE `actor` ENABLE KEYS */;
```

```
UNLOCK TABLES;
/*!40103 SET TIME_ZONE=@OLD_TIME_ZONE */;
```

The examples covered so far have only covered dumping all or part of a single database: `sakila`. Sometimes it's necessary to output every database, every object, and even every user. `mysqldump` is capable of that. The following command will effectively create a full and complete logical backup of a database instance:

```
$ mysqldump --all-databases --triggers --routines --events > dump.sql
```

Triggers are dumped by default, so this option won't appear in future command outputs. In the event you don't want to dump triggers, you can use `--no-triggers`.

There are a couple of problems with this command, however. First, even though we have redirected the output of the command to a file, the resulting file can be huge. Fortunately, its contents are likely going to be well suited for compression, though this depends on the actual data. Regardless, it's a good idea to compress the output:

```
$ mysqldump --all-databases \
--routines --events | gzip > dump.sql.gz
```

On Windows, compressing output through a pipe is difficult, so just compress the *dump.sql* file produced by running the previous command. On a system that is CPU-choked, like the little VM we're using here, compression might add significant time to the backup process. That's a trade-off that will have to be weighted for your particular system:

```
$ time mysqldump --all-databases \
--routines --events > dump.sql

real    0m24.608s
user    0m15.201s
sys     0m2.691s

$ time mysqldump --all-databases \
--routines --events | gzip > dump.sql.gz

real    2m2.769s
user    2m4.400s
sys     0m3.115s

$ ls -lh dump.sql

-rw... 2.0G ... dump.sql
-rw... 794M ... dump.sql.gz
```

The second problem is that to ensure consistency, locks will be placed on tables, preventing writes while a database is being dumped (writes to other databases can continue). This is bad both for performance and backup consistency. The resulting dump is consistent only within the database, not across the whole instance. This default behavior is necessary because some of the storage engines that MySQL uses are non-transactional (mainly the older MyISAM). The default InnoDB storage engine, on the other hand, has a multiversion concurrency control (MVCC) model that allows maintenance of a *read snapshot*. We covered different storage engines in more depth in "Alternative Storage Engines" on page 297, and locking in Chapter 6.

Utilizing InnoDB's transaction capabilities is possible by passing the `--single-transaction` command-line argument to `mysqldump`. However, that removes table locking, thus making nontransactional tables prone to inconsistencies during the dump. If your system uses, for example, both InnoDB and MyISAM tables, it may be necessary to dump them separately, if no interruption of writes and consistency are required.

> Although `--single-transaction` ensures that writes can continue while `mysqldump` is running, there are still some caveats: DDL statements that are run concurrently might cause inconsistencies, and long-running transactions, such as one initiated by `mysqldump`, can have a negative impact on the overall instance performance (*https://oreil.ly/pH2pJ*).

The basic command to make a dump of a system using mainly InnoDB tables, which guarantees limited impact on concurrent writes, is as follows:

```
$ mysqldump --single-transaction --all-databases \
  --routines --events | gzip > dump.sql.gz
```

In the real world, you will probably have some more arguments to specify connection options. You might also script around the `mysqldump` statement to catch any issues and notify you if anything went wrong.

Dumping with `--all-databases` includes internal MySQL databases such as `mysql`, `sys`, and `information_schema`. That information is not always needed to restore your data and might cause problems when restoring into an instance that already has some databases. However, you should remember that MySQL user details will only be dumped as part of the `mysql` database.

In general, using `mysqldump` and the logical backups it produces allows for the following:

- Easy transfer of the data between environments.
- Editing of the data in place both by humans and programs. For example, you can delete personal or unnecessary data from the dump.
- Finding certain data file corruptions.
- Transfer of the data between major database versions, different platforms, and even databases.

Bootstrapping Replication with mysqldump

The `mysqldump` program can be used to create a replica instance either empty or with data. To facilitate that, multiple command-line arguments are available. For example, when `--master-data` is specified, the resulting output will contain a SQL statement (`CHANGE MASTER TO`) that will set replication coordinates correctly on the target instance. When replication is later started using these coordinates on the target instance, there will be no gaps in data. In a GTID-based replication topology, `--set-gtid-purged` can be used to achieve the same result. However, `mysqldump` will detect that `gtid_mode=ON` and include the necessary output even without any additional command-line argument.

An example of setting up replication with `mysqldump` is provided in "Creating a Replica Using mysqldump" on page 498.

Loading Data from a SQL Dump File

When performing a backup, it's always important to keep in mind that you're doing that to be able to later restore the data. With logical backups, the restoration process is as simple as *piping* contents of the backup file to the `mysql` CLI. As discussed earlier, the fact that MySQL has to be up for a logical backup restore makes for both good and bad consequences:

- You can restore a single object while other parts of your system are working normally, which is a plus.
- The process of restoration is inefficient and will load a system just like any regular client would if it decided to insert a large amount of data. That's a minus.

Let's take a look at a simple example with a single database backup and restore. As we've seen before, `mysqldump` will include the necessary `DROP` statements into the dump, so even if the objects are present, they will be successfully restored:

```
$ mysqldump sakila > /tmp/sakila.sql
$ mysql -e "CREATE DATABASE sakila_mod"
$ mysql sakila_mod < /tmp/sakila.sql
$ mysql sakila_mod -e "SHOW TABLES"

+---------------------------+
| Tables_in_sakila_mod      |
+---------------------------+
| actor                     |
| actor_info                |
| ...                       |
| store                     |
+---------------------------+
```

Restoring SQL dumps like the one produced by mysqldump or mysqlpump (discussed in the next section) is a resource-heavy operation. By default, it's also a serial process, which might take a significant amount of time. There are a couple of tricks you can use to make this process faster, but keep in mind that mistakes can lead to missing or incorrectly restored data. Options include:

- Parallel restore per-schema/per-database
- Parallel restore of objects within a schema

The first one is easily done if the dumping with mysqldump is done on a per-database basis. The backup process can also be parallelized if consistency across databases isn't required (it won't be guaranteed). The following example uses the & modifier, which instructs the shell to execute the preceding command in the background:

```
$ mysqldump sakila > /tmp/sakila.sql &
$ mysqldump nasa > /tmp/nasa.sql &
```

The resulting dumps are independent. mysqldump doesn't process users and grants unless the mysql database is dumped, so you need to take care of that. Restoration is just as straightforward:

```
$ mysql sakila < /tmp/sakila.sql &
$ mysql nasa < /tmp/nasa.sql &
```

On Windows, it's also possible to send command execution to the background using the PowerShell command Start-Process or, in later versions, the same &.

The second option is a bit more involved. Either you need to dump on a per-table basis (e.g., mysqldump sakila artists > sakila.artists.sql), which results in a straightforward restore, or you need to go ahead and edit the dump file to split it into multiple ones. Taken to the extreme, you can even parallelize data insertion on the table level, although that's probably not going to be practical.

Although this is doable, it's preferable to use tools that are purpose-built for this task.

mysqlpump

mysqlpump is a utility program bundled with MySQL versions 5.7 and later that improves mysqldump in several areas, mainly around performance and usability. The key differentiators are as follows:

- Parallel dump capability
- Built-in dump compression
- Improved restore performance though delayed creation of secondary indexes

- Easier control over what objects are dumped
- Modified behavior of dumping user accounts

Using the program is very similar to using mysqldump. The main immediate difference is that when no arguments are passed, mysqlpump will default to dumping all of the databases (excluding INFORMATION_SCHEMA, performance_schema, ndbinfo, and the sys schema). The other notable things are that there's a progress indicator and that mysqlpump defaults to parallel dump with two threads:

```
$ mysqlpump > pump.out

Dump progress: 1/2 tables, 0/530419 rows
Dump progress: 80/184 tables, 2574413/646260694 rows
...
Dump progress: 183/184 tables, 16297773/646260694 rows
Dump completed in 10680
```

The concept of parallelism in mysqlpump is somewhat complicated. You can use concurrency between different databases and between different objects within a given database. By default, when no other parallel options are specified, mysqlpump will use a single queue with two parallel threads to process all databases and user definitions (if requested). You can control the level of parallelism of the default queue using the --default-parallelism argument. To further fine-tune concurrency, you can set up multiple parallel queues to process separate databases. Take care when choosing your desired concurrency level, since you could end up using most of the database resources for the backup run.

An important distinction from mysqldump when using mysqlpump lies in how the latter handles user accounts. mysqldump managed users by dumping mysql.user and other relevant tables. If the mysql database wasn't included in the dump, no user information will be preserved. mysqlpump improves on that by introducing the command-line arguments --users and --include-users. The first one tells the utility to add user-related commands to the dump for all users, and the second accepts a list of usernames. This is a great improvement on the old way of doing things.

Let's combine all the new features to produce a compressed dump of non-system databases and user definitions, and use concurrency in the process:

```
$ mysqlpump --compress-output=zlib --include-users=bob,kate \
--include-databases=sakila,nasa,employees \
--parallel-schemas=2:employees \
--parallel-schemas=sakila,nasa > pump.out

Dump progress: 1/2 tables, 0/331579 rows
Dump progress: 19/23 tables, 357923/3959313 rows
...
Dump progress: 22/23 tables, 3755358/3959313 rows
Dump completed in 10098
```

mysqlpump output can be compressed with the ZLIB or LZ4 algorithms. When the OS-level commands `lz` and `openssl zlib` aren't available, you can use the `lz4_decompress` and `zlib_decompress` utilities included in your MySQL distribution.

A dump resulting from a `mysqlpump` run is not suitable for parallel restore because the data inside it is interleaved. For example, the following is the result of a `mysqlpump` execution showing table creation amidst inserts to tables in different databases:

```
...,(294975,"1955-07-31","Lucian","Rosis","M","1986-12-08");
CREATE TABLE `sakila`.`store` (
`store_id` tinyint unsigned NOT NULL AUTO_INCREMENT,
`manager_staff_id` tinyint unsigned NOT NULL,
`address_id` smallint unsigned NOT NULL,
`last_update` timestamp NOT NULL DEFAULT
CURRENT_TIMESTAMP ON UPDATE CURRENT_TIMESTAMP,
PRIMARY KEY (`store_id`)
) ENGINE=InnoDB AUTO_INCREMENT=3 DEFAULT
CHARSET=utf8mb4 COLLATE=utf8mb4_0900_ai_ci
;
INSERT INTO `employees`.`employees` VALUES
(294976,"1961-03-19","Rayond","Khalid","F","1989-11-03"),...
```

mysqlpump is an improvement over `mysqldump` and adds important concurrency, compression, and object control features. However, the tool doesn't allow parallel restore of the dump and in fact makes it impossible. The only improvement to the restore performance is that secondary indexes are added after the main load is complete.

mydumper and myloader

mydumper and `myloader` are both part of the open source project `mydumper` (*https://oreil.ly/oOo8F*). This set of tools attempts to make logical backups more performant, easier to manage, and more human-friendly. We won't go into too much depth here, as we could easily run out of space in the book covering every possible MySQL backup variety.

These programs can be installed either by taking the freshest release from the project's GitHub page or by compiling the source. At the time of writing, the latest release is somewhat behind the main branch. Step-by-step installation instructions are available in "Setting up the mydumper and myloader utilities" on page 499.

We previously showed how `mysqlpump` improves dumping performance but mentioned that its intertwined outputs don't help with restoration. mydumper combines the parallel dumping approach with preparing ground for parallel restore with `myloader`. That's achieved by dumping every table into a separate file.

The default invocation of mydumper is very simple. The tool tries to connect to the database, initiates a consistent dump, and creates a directory under the current one for the export files. Note that each table has its own file. By default, mydumper will also dump the mysql and sys databases. The default parallelism setting for the dump operation is 4, meaning four separate tables will be read simultaneously. myloader invoked on this directory will be able to restore the tables in parallel.

To create the dump and explore it, execute the following commands:

```
$ mydumper -u root -a
Enter the MySQL password:
$ ls -ld export
drwx... export-20210613-204512
$ ls -la export-20210613-204512
...
-rw... sakila.actor.sql
-rw... sakila.address-schema.sql
-rw... sakila.address.sql
-rw... sakila.category-schema.sql
-rw... sakila.category.sql
-rw... sakila.city-schema.sql
-rw... sakila.city.sql
...
```

Apart from parallel dumping and restore capabilities, mydumper has some more advanced features:

- Lightweight backup locks support. Percona Server for MySQL implements some additional lightweight locking that's used by Percona XtraBackup. mydumper utilizes these locks by default when possible. These locks do not block concurrent reads and writes to InnoDB tables, but will block any DDL statements, which could otherwise render the backup invalid.

- Use of savepoints. mydumper uses a trick with transaction savepoints to minimize metadata locking.

- Limits on duration of metadata locking. To work around prolonged metadata locking, a problem we described in "Metadata Locks" on page 249, mydumper allows two options: failing quickly or killing long-running queries that prevent mydumper from succeeding.

mydumper and myloader are advanced tools taking logical backup capabilities to the maximum. However, as part of a community project, they lack the documentation and polish that other tools provide. Another major downside is the lack of any support or guarantees. Still, they can be a useful addition to a database operator's toolbelt.

Cold Backup and Filesystem Snapshots

The cornerstone of physical backups, a *cold backup* is really just a copy of the data directory and other necessary files, done while the database instance is down. This technique isn't frequently used, but it can save the day when you need to create a consistent backup quickly. With databases now regularly approaching the multiterabyte size range, just copying the files can take a very long time. However, the cold backup still has its good points:

- Very fast (arguably the fastest backup method apart from snapshots)
- Straightforward
- Easy to use, hard to do wrong

Modern storage systems and some filesystems have readily available snapshot capabilities. They allow you to create near-instantaneous copies of volumes of arbitrary size by utilizing internal mechanisms. The properties of different snapshot-capable systems vary widely, making it impossible for us to cover all of them. However, we can still talk a bit about them from the database perspective.

Most snapshots will be *copy-on-write* (COW) and internally consistent to some point in time. However, we already know that database files aren't consistent on disk, especially with transactional storage engines like InnoDB. This makes it somewhat difficult to get the snapshot backup right. There are two options:

Cold backup snapshot
When the database is shut down, its data files may still not be perfectly consistent. But if you do a snapshot of all of the database files (including InnoDB redo logs, for example), together they will allow for the database to start. That's only natural, because otherwise the database would lose data on every restart. Don't forget that you may have database files split among many volumes. You will need to have all of them. This method will work for all storage engines.

Hot backup snapshot
With a running database, taking a snapshot correctly is a greater challenge than when the database is down. If your database files are located over multiple volumes, you cannot guarantee that snapshots, even initiated simultaneously, will be consistent to the same point in time, which can lead to disastrous results. Moreover, nontransactional storage engines like MyISAM don't guarantee consistency for files on disk while the database is running. That's actually true for InnoDB as

well, but InnoDB's redo logs are always consistent (unless safeguards are disabled), and MyISAM lacks this functionality.

The recommended way to do a hot backup snapshot would therefore be to utilize some amount of locking. Since the snapshot-taking process is usually a quick one, the resulting downtime shouldn't be significant. Here's the process:

1. Create a new session, and lock all of the tables with the FLUSH TABLES WITH READ LOCK command. This session cannot be closed, or else locks will be released.

2. Optionally, record the current binlog position by running the SHOW MASTER STATUS command.

3. Create snapshots of all volumes where MySQL's database files are located according to the storage system's manual.

4. Unlock the tables with the UNLOCK TABLES command in the session opened initially.

This general approach should be suitable for most if not all of the current storage system and filesystems capable of doing snapshots. Note that they all differ subtly in the actual procedure and requirements. Some cloud vendors require you to additionally perform an fsfreeze on the filesystems.

Always test your backups thoroughly before implementing them in production and trusting them with your data. You can only trust a solution that you've tested and are comfortable using. Copying arbitrary backup strategy suggestions is not a very good idea.

Percona XtraBackup

The logical step forward in physical backups is implementing so-called *hot backups*—that is, making a copy of database files while the database is running. We've already mentioned that MyISAM tables can be copied, but that doesn't work for InnoDB and other transactional storage engines like MyRocks. The problem therefore is that you can't just copy the files because the database is constantly undergoing changes. For example, InnoDB might be flushing some dirty pages in the background even if no writes are hitting the database right now. You can try your luck and copy the database directory under a running system and then try to restore that directory and start a MySQL server using it. Chances are, it won't work. And while it may work sometimes, we strongly recommend against taking chances with database backups.

The capability to perform hot backups is built into three main MySQL backup tools: Percona XtraBackup (*https://oreil.ly/yMK8t*), MySQL Enterprise Backup (*https://oreil.ly/rkSrr*), and mariabackup (*https://oreil.ly/DJvoa*). We'll briefly talk about all of them, but will mainly concentrate on the XtraBackup utility. It's important to understand that all the tools share properties, so knowing how to use one will help you use the others.

Percona XtraBackup is a free and open source tool maintained by Percona and the wider MySQL community. It's capable of performing online backups of MySQL instances with InnoDB, MyISAM, and MyRocks tables. The program is available only on Linux. Note that it's impossible to use XtraBackup with recent versions of MariaDB: only MySQL and Percona Server are supported. For MariaDB, use the utility we cover in "mariabackup" on page 396.

Here is an overview of how XtraBackup operates:

1. Records the current log sequence number (LSN), an internal version number for the operation
2. Starts accumulating InnoDB *redo data* (the type of data InnoDB stores for crash recovery)
3. Locks tables in the least intrusive way possible
4. Copies InnoDB tables
5. Locks nontransactional tables completely
6. Copies MyISAM tables
7. Unlocks all tables
8. Processes MyRocks tables, if present
9. Puts accumulated redo data alongside the copied database files

The main idea behind XtraBackup and hot backups in general is combining the no-downtime nature of logical backups with the performance and relative lack of performance impact of cold backups. XtraBackup doesn't guarantee no disruption of service, but it's a great step forward compared with a regular cold backup. The lack of performance impact means that XtraBackup will use some CPU and I/O, but only that needed to copy the database files. Logical backups, on the other hand, must pass each row through all of the database internals, making them inherently slow.

XtraBackup requires physical access to the database files and cannot be run remotely. This makes it unsuitable for doing offsite backups of managed databases (DBaaS), for example. Some cloud vendors, however, allow you to import databases using backups made by this tool.

The XtraBackup utility is widely available in various Linux distributions' repositories and thus can easily be installed using a package manager. Alternatively, you can download packages and binary distributions directly from the XtraBackup Downloads page (*https://oreil.ly/XjN4C*) on Percona's website.

 To back up MySQL 8.0, you must use XtraBackup 8.0. The minor versions of XtraBackup and MySQL ideally should also match: XtraBackup 8.0.25 is guaranteed to work with MySQL 8.0.25. For MySQL 5.7 and older releases, use XtraBackup 2.4.

Backing Up and Recovering

Unlike other tools we've mentioned previously, XtraBackup, by nature of it being a physical backup tool, requires not only access to the MySQL server but also read access to the database files. On most MySQL installations, that usually means that the xtrabackup program should be run by the root user, or sudo must be used. We'll be using the root user throughout this section, and we set up a login path using the steps from "Login Path Configuration File" on page 360.

First, we need to run the basic xtrabackup command:

```
# xtrabackup --host=127.0.0.1 --target-dir=/tmp/backup --backup

...
Using server version 8.0.25
210613 22:23:06 Executing LOCK INSTANCE FOR BACKUP...
...
210613 22:23:07 [01] Copying ./sakila/film.ibd
    to /tmp/backup/sakila/film.ibd
210613 22:23:07 [01]        ...done
...
210613 22:23:10 [00] Writing /tmp/backup/xtrabackup_info
210613 22:23:10 [00]        ...done
xtrabackup: Transaction log of lsn (6438976119)
    to (6438976129) was copied.
210613 22:23:11 completed OK!
```

If the login path doesn't work, you can pass root user's credentials to xtrabackup using the --user and --password command-line arguments. XtraBackup will usually be able to identify the target server's data directory by reading the default option files, but if that doesn't work or you have multiple installations of MySQL, you may need to specify the --datadir option, too. Even though xtrabackup only works locally, it still needs to connect to a local running MySQL instance and thus has --host, --port, and --socket arguments. You may need to specify some of them according to your particular setup.

While we use */tmp/backup* as the backup's destination path for our example, you should avoid storing important files under */tmp*. That's especially true for backups.

The result of that `xtrabackup --backup` invocation is a bunch of database files, which are actually not consistent to any point in time, and a chunk of redo data that InnoDB won't be able to apply:

```
# ls -l /tmp/backup/

...
drwxr-x---. 2 root root       160 Jun 13 22:23 mysql
-rw-r-----. 1 root root  46137344 Jun 13 22:23 mysql.ibd
drwxr-x---. 2 root root        60 Jun 13 22:23 nasa
drwxr-x---. 2 root root       580 Jun 13 22:23 sakila
drwxr-x---. 2 root root       580 Jun 13 22:23 sakila_mod
drwxr-x---. 2 root root        80 Jun 13 22:23 sakila_new
drwxr-x---. 2 root root        60 Jun 13 22:23 sys
...
```

To make the backup ready for future restore, another phase must be performed— preparation. There's no need to connect to a MySQL server for that:

```
# xtrabackup --target-dir=/tmp/backup --prepare

...
xtrabackup: cd to /tmp/backup/
xtrabackup: This target seems to be not prepared yet.
...
Shutdown completed; log sequence number 6438976524
210613 22:32:23 completed OK!
```

The resulting data directory is actually perfectly ready to be used. You can start up a MySQL instance pointing directly to this directory, and it will work. A very common mistake here is trying to start MySQL Server under the `mysql` user while the restored and prepared backup is owned by `root` or another OS user. Make sure to incorporate `chown` and `chmod` as required into your backup recovery procedure. However, there's a useful user experience feature of `--copy-back` available. `xtrabackup` preserves the original database file layout locations, and invoked with `--copy-back` will restore all files to their original locations:

```
# xtrabackup --target-dir=/tmp/backup --copy-back

...
Original data directory /var/lib/mysql is not empty!
```

That didn't work, because our original MySQL Server is still running, and its data directory is not empty. XtraBackup will refuse to restore a backup unless the target data directory is empty. That should protect you from accidentally restoring a backup. Let's shut down the running MySQL Server, remove or move its data directory, and restore the backup:

```
# systemctl stop mysqld
# mv /var/lib/mysql /var/lib/mysql_old
# xtrabackup --target-dir=/tmp/backup --copy-back

...
210613 22:39:01 [01] Copying ./sakila/actor.ibd
    to /var/lib/mysql/sakila/actor.ibd
210613 22:39:01 [01]          ...done
...
210613 22:39:01 completed OK!
```

After that, the files are in their correct locations, but owned by root:

```
# ls -l /var/lib/mysql/

drwxr-x---. 2 root root        4096 Jun 13 22:39 sakila
drwxr-x---. 2 root root        4096 Jun 13 22:38 sakila_mod
drwxr-x---. 2 root root        4096 Jun 13 22:39 sakila_new
```

You'll need to change the owner of the files back to mysql (or the user used in your system) and fix the directory permissions. Once that's done, you can start MySQL and verify the data:

```
# chown -R mysql:mysql /var/lib/mysql/
# chmod o+rx /var/lib/mysql/
# systemctl start mysqld
# mysql sakila -e "SHOW TABLES;"

+---------------------------+
| Tables_in_sakila          |
+---------------------------+
| actor                     |
...
| store                     |
+---------------------------+
```

The best practice is to do both the backup and prepare work during the backup phase, minimizing the number of possible surprises later. Imagine having the prepare phase fail while you're trying to recover some data! However, note that incremental backups that we cover later have special handling procedures contradicting this tip.

Advanced Features

In this section we discuss some of XtraBackup's more advanced features. They are not required to use the tool, and we give them just as a brief overview:

Database file verification
> While performing the backup, XtraBackup will verify the checksums of all of the pages of the data files it's processing. This is an attempt to alleviate the inherent problem of physical backups, which is that they will contain any corruptions in the source database. We recommend augmenting this check with other steps listed in "Testing and Verifying Your Backups" on page 407.

Compression
> Even though copying physical files is much faster than querying the database, the backup process can be limited by disk performance. You cannot decrease the amount of data you read, but you can utilize compression to make the backup itself smaller, decreasing the amount of data that has to be written. That's especially important when a backup destination is a network location. In addition, you will just use less space for storing backups. Note that, as we showed in "The mysqldump Program" on page 376, on a CPU-choked system compression may actually increase the time it takes to create a backup. XtraBackup uses the `qpress` tool for compression. This tool is available in the `percona-release` package:

```
# xtrabackup --host=127.0.0.1 \
--target-dir=/tmp/backup_compressed/ \
--backup --compress
```

Parallelism
> It's possible to run the backup and copy-back processes in parallel by using the `--parallel` command-line argument.

Encryption
> In addition to being able to work with encrypted databases, it's also possible for XtraBackup to create encrypted backups.

Streaming
> Instead of creating a directory full of backed-up files, XtraBackup can stream the resulting backup in an `xbstream` format. This results in more portable backups and allows integration with `xbcloud`. You can stream backups over SSH, for example.

Cloud upload
> Backups taken with XtraBackup can be uploaded to any S3-compatible storage using `xbcloud`. S3 is Amazon's object storage facility and an API that is widely adopted by many companies. This tool only works with backups streamed through the `xbstream`.

Incremental Backups with XtraBackup

As described earlier, a hot backup is a copy of every byte of information in the database. This is how XtraBackup works by default. But in a lot of cases, databases undergo change at an *irregular* rate—new data is added frequently, while old data doesn't change that much (or at all). For example, new financial records may be added every day, and accounts get modified, but in a given week only a small percentage of accounts are changed. Thus, the next logical step in improving hot backups is adding the ability to perform so-called *incremental backups*, or backups of only the changed data. That will allow you to perform backups more frequently by decreasing the need for space.

For incremental backups to work, you need first to have a full backup of the database, called a *base backup*—otherwise there's nothing to increment from. Once your base backup is ready, you can perform any number of incremental backups, each consisting of the changes made since the previous one (or from the base backup in the case of the first incremental backup). Taken to the extreme, you could create an incremental backup every minute, achieving something called *point-in-time recovery* (PITR), but this is not very practical, and as you will soon learn there are better ways to do that.

Here's an example of the XtraBackup commands you could use to create a base backup and then an incremental backup. Notice how the incremental backup points to the base backup via the --incremental-basedir argument:

```
# xtrabackup --host=127.0.0.1 \
--target-dir=/tmp/base_backup --backup
# xtrabackup --host=127.0.0.1 --backup \
--incremental-basedir=/tmp/base_backup \
--target-dir=/tmp/inc_backup1
```

If you check the backup sizes, you'll see that the incremental backup is very small compared to the base backup:

```
# du -sh /tmp/base_backup

2.2G    /tmp/base_backup
6.0M    /tmp/inc_backup1
```

Let's create another incremental backup. In this case, we'll pass the previous incremental backup's directory as the base directory:

```
# xtrabackup --host=127.0.0.1 --backup \
--incremental-basedir=/tmp/inc_backup1 \
--target-dir=/tmp/inc_backup2

210613 23:32:20 completed OK!
```

You may be wondering whether it's possible to specify the original base backup's directory as the --incremental-basedir for each new incremental backup. In fact,

---

that results in a completely valid backup, which is a variation of an incremental backup (or the other way around). Such incremental backups that contain changes made not just since the previous incremental backup but since the base backup are usually called *cumulative* backups. Incremental backups targeting any previous backup are called *differential* backups. Cumulative incremental backups usually consume more space, but can considerably decrease the time needed for the prepare phase when a backup is restored.

Importantly, the prepare process for incremental backups (*https://oreil.ly/2c4LM*) differs from that for regular backups. Let's prepare the backups we've just taken, starting with the base backup:

```
# xtrabackup --prepare --apply-log-only \
--target-dir=/tmp/base_backup
```

The `--apply-log-only` argument tells `xtrabackup` to not finalize the prepare process, as we still need to apply changes from the incremental backups. Let's do that:

```
# xtrabackup --prepare --apply-log-only \
--target-dir=/tmp/base_backup \
--incremental-dir=/tmp/inc_backup1
# xtrabackup --prepare --apply-log-only \
--target-dir=/tmp/base_backup \
--incremental-dir=/tmp/inc_backup2
```

All commands should report `completed` `OK!` at the end. Once the `--prepare` `--apply-log-only` operation is run, the base backup advances to the point of the incremental backup, making PITR to an earlier time impossible. So, it's not a good idea to prepare immediately when performing incremental backups. To finalize the prepare process, the base backup with the changes applied from incremental backups must be prepared normally:

```
# xtrabackup --prepare --target-dir=/tmp/base_backup
```

Once the base backup is "fully" prepared, attempts to apply incremental backups will fail with the following message:

```
xtrabackup: This target seems to be already prepared.
xtrabackup: error: applying incremental backup needs
    target prepared with --apply-log-only.
```

Incremental backups are inefficient when the relative amount of changes in the database is high. In the worst case, where every row in the database was changed between full a backup and an incremental backup, the latter will actually just be a full backup, storing 100% of the data. Incremental backups are most efficient when most of the data is appended and the relative amount of old data being changed is low. There are no rules regarding this, but if 50% of your data changes between your base backup and an incremental backup, consider not using incremental backups.

Other Physical Backup Tools

XtraBackup isn't the only tool available that's capable of performing hot MySQL physical backups. Our decision to explain the concepts using that particular tool was driven by our experience with it. However, that doesn't mean that other tools are worse in any way. They may well be better suited to your needs. However, we have limited space, and the topic of backing up is very wide. We could write a *Backing Up MySQL* book of considerable volume!

That said, to give you an idea of some of the other options, let's take a look at two other readily available physical backup tools.

MySQL Enterprise Backup

Called MEB for short, this tool is available as part of Oracle's MySQL Enterprise Edition. It's a closed-source proprietary tool that is similar in functionality to XtraBackup. You'll find comprehensive documentation for it on the MYSQL website (*https://oreil.ly/nj7xI*). The two tools are currently at feature parity, so almost everything that was covered for XtraBackup will be true for MEB as well.

MEB's standout property is that it's truly a cross-platform solution. XtraBackup works only on Linux, whereas MEB also works on Solaris, Windows, macOS, and FreeBSD. MEB doesn't support flavors of MySQL other than Oracle's standard one.

Some additional features that MEB has, which are not available in XtraBackup, include the following:

- Backup progress reporting
- Offline backups
- Tape backups through Oracle Secure Backups
- Binary and relay log backups
- Table rename at restore time

mariabackup

mariabackup is a tool by MariaDB for backing up MySQL databases. Originally forked from XtraBackup, this is a free open source tool that is available on Linux and Windows. The standout property of mariabackup is its seamless work with the MariaDB fork of MySQL, which continues to diverge significantly from both the mainstream MySQL and Percona Server. Since this is a direct fork of XtraBackup, you'll find many similarities in how the tools are used and in their properties. Some of XtraBackup's newer features, like backup encryption and secondary index omission, are not present in `mariabackup`. However, using XtraBackup to back up MariaDB is currently impossible.

Point-in-Time Recovery

Now that you're familiar with the concept of hot backups, you have almost everything you need to complete your backup toolkit. So far all the backup types that we've discussed share a similar trait—a deficiency. They allow restore only at the point in time when they were taken. If you have two backups, one done at 23:00 on Monday and the second at 23:00 on Tuesday, you cannot restore to 17:00 on Tuesday.

Remember the infrastructure failure example given at the beginning of the chapter? Now, let's make it worse and say that the data is gone, all the drives failed, and there's no replication. The event happened on Wednesday at 21:00. Without PITR and with daily backups taken at 23:00, this means that you've just lost a full day's worth of data irrevocably. Arguably, incremental backups done with XtraBackup allow you to make that problem somewhat less pronounced, but they still leave some room for data loss, and it's less than practical to be running them very often.

MySQL maintains a journal of transactions called the *binary log*. By combining any of the backup methods we've discussed so far with binary logs, we get the ability to restore to a transaction at an arbitrary point in time. It's very important to understand that you need both a backup *and* binary logs from after the backup for this to work. You also cannot go back in time, so you cannot recover the data to a point in time before your oldest base backup or dump was created.

Binary logs contain both transaction timestamps and their identifiers. You can rely on either for recovery, and it is possible to tell MySQL to recover to a certain timestamp. This is not a problem when you want to recover to the latest point in time, but can be extremely important and helpful when trying to perform a restore to fix a logical inconsistency, like the one described in "Deployment Bug" on page 375. However, in most situations, you will need to identify a specific problematic transaction, and we'll show you how to do that.

One interesting peculiarity of MySQL is that it allows for PITR for logical backups. "Loading Data from a SQL Dump File" on page 382 discusses storing the binlog position for replica provisioning using `mysqldump`. The same binlog position can be used as a starting point for PITR. Every backup type in MySQL is suitable for PITR, unlike in other databases. To facilitate this property, make sure to note the binlog position when taking your backup. Some backup tools do that for you. When using those that don't, you can run SHOW MASTER STATUS to get that data.

Technical Background on Binary Logs

MySQL differs from a lot of other mainstream RDBMS in that it supports multiple storage engines, as discussed in "Alternative Storage Engines" on page 297. Not only that, but it supports multiple storage engines for tables inside a single database. As a result, some concepts in MySQL are different from in other systems.

Binary logs in MySQL are essentially transaction logs. When binary logging is enabled, every transaction (excluding read-only transactions) will be reflected in the binary logs. There are three ways to write transactions to binary logs:

Statement

   In this mode, statements are logged to the binary logs as they were written, which might cause indeterministic execution in replication scenarios.

Row

   In this mode, statements are broken down into minimal DML operations, each modifying a single specific row. Although it guarantees deterministic execution, this mode is the most verbose and results in the largest files and thus the greatest I/O overhead.

Mixed

   In this mode, "safe" statements are logged as is, while others are broken down.

Usually, in database management systems, the transaction log is used for crash recovery, replication, and PITR. However, because MySQL supports multiple storage engines, its binary logs can't be used for crash recovery. Instead, each engine maintains its own crash recovery mechanism. For example, MyISAM is not crash-safe, whereas InnoDB has its own redo logs. Every transaction in MySQL is a distributed transaction with two-phase commit, to allow for this multiengined nature. Each committed transaction is guaranteed to be reflected in the storage engine's redo logs, if the engine is transactional, as well as in MySQL's own transaction log (the binary logs).

Binary logging has to be enabled in your MySQL instance for PITR to be possible. You should also default to having sync_binlog=1, which guarantees the durability of each write. Refer to the MySQL documentation (*https://oreil.ly/ygjVz*) to understand the trade-offs of disabling binlog syncing.

We'll talk more about how binary logs work in Chapter 13.

Preserving Binary Logs

To allow PITR, you must preserve the binary logs starting from the binlog position of the oldest backup. There are few ways to do this:

- Copy or sync binary logs "manually" using some readily available tool like rsync. Remember that MySQL continues to write to the current binary log file. If you're copying files instead of continuously syncing them, do not copy the current binary log file. Continuously syncing files will take care of this problem by over-writing the partial file once it becomes non-current.

- Use mysqlbinlog to copy individual files or stream binlogs continuously. Instructions are available in the documentation (*https://oreil.ly/GAsjw*).

- Use MySQL Enterprise Backup, which has a built-in binlog copy feature. Note that it's not a continuous copying, but relies on incremental backups to have binlog copies. This allows for PITR between two backups.

- Allow MySQL Server to store all the needed binary logs in its data directory by setting a high value for the binlog_expire_logs_seconds or expire_logs_days variables. This option should ideally not be used on its own, but can be used in addition to any of the others. If anything happens to the data directory, like file-system corruption, binary logs stored there may also get lost.

Identifying a PITR Target

You may use the PITR technique to achieve two objectives:

1. Recover to the latest point in time.
2. Recover to an arbitrary point in time.

The first one, as discussed earlier, is useful to recover a completely lost database to the latest available state. The second is useful to get data as it was before. An example of a case when this can be useful was given in "Deployment Bug" on page 375. To recover lost or incorrectly modified data, you can restore a backup and then recover it to a point in time just before the deployment was executed.

Identifying the actual specific time when an issue happened can be a challenge. More often than not, the only way for you to find the desired point in time is by inspecting binary logs written around the time when the issue occurred. For example, if you suspect that a table was dropped, you may look for the table name, then for any DDL statements issued on that table, or specifically for a DROP TABLE statement.

Let's illustrate that example. First, we need to actually drop a table, so we'll drop the `facilities` table we created in "Loading Data from Comma-Delimited Files" on page 267. However, before that we'll insert a record that's for sure missing in the original backup:

```
mysql> INSERT INTO facilities(center)
    -> VALUES ('this row was not here before');
Query OK, 1 row affected (0.01 sec)

mysql> DROP TABLE nasa.facilities;
Query OK, 0 rows affected (0.02 sec)
```

We could now go back and restore one of the backups we've taken throughout this chapter, but then we would lose any changes made to the database between that point and the DROP. Instead, we'll use `mysqlbinlog` to inspect the content of the binary logs and find the recovery target just before the DROP statement was run. To find the list of binary logs available in the data directory, you can run the following command:

```
mysql> SHOW BINARY LOGS;

+----------------+-----------+-----------+
| Log_name       | File_size | Encrypted |
+----------------+-----------+-----------+
| binlog.000291  |       156 | No        |
| binlog.000292  |       711 | No        |
+----------------+-----------+-----------+
2 rows in set (0.00 sec)
```

MySQL won't keep binary logs in its data directory forever. They're removed automatically when they are older than the duration specified under `binlog_expire_logs_seconds` or `expire_log_days`, and also can be removed manually by running PURGE BINARY LOGS. If you want to make sure binary logs are available, you should preserve them outside of the data directory as described in the previous section.

Now that the list of binary logs is available, you can either try to search in them, from the newest one to the oldest one, or you can just dump all their contents together. In our example, the files are small, so we can use the latter approach. In any case, the `mysqlbinlog` command is used:

```
# cd /var/lib/mysql
# mysqlbinlog binlog.000291 binlog.000292 \
-vvv --base64-output='decode-rows' > /tmp/mybinlog.sql
```

Inspecting the output file, we can find the problematic statement:

```
...
#210613 23:32:19 server id 1  end_log_pos 200 ... Rotate to binlog.000291
```

```
...
# at 499
#210614  0:46:08 server id 1  end_log_pos 576 ...
# original_commit_timestamp=1623620769019544 (2021-06-14 00:46:09.019544 MSK)
# immediate_commit_timestamp=1623620769019544 (2021-06-14 00:46:09.019544 MSK)
/*!80001 SET @@session.original_commit_timestamp=1623620769019544*//*!*/;
/*!80014 SET @@session.original_server_version=80025*//*!*/;
/*!80014 SET @@session.immediate_server_version=80025*//*!*/;
SET @@SESSION.GTID_NEXT= 'ANONYMOUS'/*!*/;
# at 576
#210614  0:46:08 server id 1  end_log_pos 711 ... Xid = 25
use `nasa`/*!*/;
SET TIMESTAMP=1623620768/*!*/;
DROP TABLE `facilities` /* generated by server */
/*!*/;
SET @@SESSION.GTID_NEXT= 'AUTOMATIC' /* added by mysqlbinlog */ /*!*/;
DELIMITER ;
...
```

We should stop our recovery before 2021-06-14 00:46:08, or at binary log position 499. We'll also need all binary logs from the latest backup, up to and including *binlog. 00291*. Using this information, we can proceed to backup restoration and recovery.

Point-in-Time-Recovery Example: XtraBackup

On its own, XtraBackup doesn't provide PITR capabilities. You need to add the additional step of running `mysqlbinlog` to replay the binlog contents on the restored database:

1. Restore the backup. See "Backing Up and Recovering" on page 390 for the exact steps.

2. Start MySQL Server. If you are restoring on the source instance directly, it is recommended to use the `--skip-networking` option to prevent nonlocal clients from accessing the database. Otherwise, some clients may change the database before you've actually finished the recovery.

3. Locate the backup's binary log position. It's available in the *xtrabackup_binlog_info* file in the backup directory:

    ```
    # cat /tmp/base_backup/xtrabackup_binlog_info

    binlog.000291   156
    ```

4. Find the timestamp or binlog position to which you want to recover—for example, immediately before a `DROP TABLE` was executed, as discussed earlier.

5. Replay the binlogs up to the desired point. For this example, we've preserved binary log *binlog.000291* separately, but you would use your centralized binlog storage for the source of the binary logs. You use the `mysqlbinlog` command for this:

```
# mysqlbinlog /opt/mysql/binlog.000291 \
/opt/mysql/binlog.000292 --start-position=156 \
--stop-datetime="2021-06-14 00:46:00" | mysql
```

6. Make sure the recovery was successful and that no data is missing. In our case, we'll look for the record we added to the `facilities` table before dropping it:

```
mysql> SELECT center FROM facilities
    -> WHERE center LIKE '%before%';

+-----------------------------+
| center                      |
+-----------------------------+
| this row was not here before |
+-----------------------------+
1 row in set (0.00 sec)
```

Point-in-Time-Recovery Example: mysqldump

The steps necessary for PITR with `mysqldump` are analogous to the steps taken earlier with XtraBackup. We're only showing this for completeness and so that you can see that PITR is similar with each and every backup type in MySQL. Here's the process:

1. Restore the SQL dump. Again, if your recovery target server is the backup source, you probably want to make it inaccessible to clients.

2. Locate the binary log position in the `mysqldump` backup file:

```
CHANGE MASTER TO MASTER_LOG_FILE='binlog.000010',
MASTER_LOG_POS=191098797;
```

3. Find the timestamp or binlog position to which you want to recover (for example, immediately before a `DROP TABLE` was executed, as discussed before).

4. Replay the binlogs up to the desired point:

```
# mysqlbinlog /path/to/datadir/mysql-bin.000010 \
/path/to/datadir/mysql-bin.000011 \
--start-position=191098797 \
--stop-datetime="20-05-25 13:00:00" | mysql
```

Exporting and Importing InnoDB Tablespaces

One of the major downsides of physical backups is that they usually require a significant portion of your database files to be copied at the same time. Although a storage engine like MyISAM allows for the copying of idle tables' data files, you cannot guarantee consistency of InnoDB files. There are situations, though, where you need to transfer only a few tables, or just one table. So far the only option we've seen for that would be to utilize logical backups, which can be unacceptably slow. The export and import tablespaces feature of InnoDB, officially called *Transportable Tablespace*, is a way to get the best of both worlds. We will also call this feature *export/import* for brevity.

The Transportable Tablespaces feature lets you combine the performance of an online physical backup with the granularity of a logical one. In essence, it offers the ability to do an online copy of an InnoDB table's data files to be used for import into the same or a different table. Such a copy can serve as a backup, or as a way to transfer data between separate MySQL installations.

Why use export/import when a logical dump achieves the same thing? Export/import is much faster and, apart from the table being locked, doesn't impact the server significantly. This is especially true for import. With table sizes in the multigigabyte range, this is one of the few feasible options for data transfer.

Technical Background

To help you understand how this feature works, we'll briefly review two concepts: physical backups and tablespaces.

As we've seen, for a physical backup to be consistent, we can generally take two routes. The first is to shut down the instance, or otherwise make the data read-only in a guaranteed manner. The second is to make the data files consistent to point in time and then accumulate all changes between that point in time and the end of the backup. The Transportable Tablespaces feature works in the first way, requiring the table to be made read-only for a short while.

A tablespace is a file that stores a table's data and its indexes. By default, InnoDB uses the `innodb_file_per_table` option, which forces the creation of a dedicated tablespace file for each table. It's possible to create a tablespace that will contain data for multiple tables, and you can use the "old" behavior of having all tables reside in a single *ibdata* tablespace. However, export is supported only for the default configuration, where there's a dedicated tablespace for each table. Tablespaces exist separately for each partition in a partitioned table, which allows for an interesting ability to transfer partitions between separate tables or create a table from a partition.

Exporting a Tablespace

Now that those concepts have been covered, you know what needs to be done for the export. However, one thing that's still missing is the table definition. Even though most InnoDB tablespace files actually contain a redundant copy of the data dictionary records for their tables, the current implementation of Transportable Tablespaces requires a table to be present on the target before import.

The steps for exporting a tablespace are:

1. Get the table definition.

2. Stop all writes to the table (or tables) and make it consistent.

3. Prepare the extra files necessary for import of the tablespace later:

   - The *.cfg* file stores metadata used for schema verification.

   - The *.cfp* file is generated only when encryption is used and contains the transition key that the target server needs to decrypt the tablespace.

To get the table definition, you can use the SHOW CREATE TABLE command that we've shown quite a few times throughout this book. All the other steps are done automatically by MySQL with a single command: FLUSH TABLE ... FOR EXPORT. That command locks the table and generates the additional required file (or files, if encryption is used) near the regular *.ibd* file of the target table. Let's export the actor table from the sakila database:

```
mysql> USE sakila
mysql> FLUSH TABLE actor FOR EXPORT;

Query OK, 0 rows affected (0.00 sec)
```

The session where FLUSH TABLE was executed should remain open, because the actor table will be released as soon as the session is terminated. A new file, *actor.cfg*, should appear near the regular *actor.ibd* file in the MySQL data directory. Let's verify:

```
# ls -1 /var/lib/mysql/sakila/actor.

/var/lib/mysql/sakila/actor.cfg
/var/lib/mysql/sakila/actor.ibd
```

This pair of *.ibd* and *.cfg* files can now be copied somewhere and used later. Once you've copied the files, it's generally advisable to release the locks on the table by running the UNLOCK TABLES statement, or closing the session where FLUSH TABLE was called. Once all that is done, you have a tablespace ready for import.

Partitioned tables have multiple *.ibd* files, and each of them gets a dedicated *.cfg* file. For example:

- *learning_mysql_partitioned#p#p0.cfg*

- *learning_mysql_partitioned#p#p0.ibd*

- *learning_mysql_partitioned#p#p1.cfg*

- *learning_mysql_partitioned#p#p1.ibd*

Importing a Tablespace

Importing a tablespace is quite straightforward. It consists of the following steps:

1. Create a table using the preserved definition. It is not possible to change the table's definition in any way.

2. Discard the table's tablespace.

3. Copy over the *.ibd* and *.cfg* files.

4. Alter the table to import the tablespace.

If the table exists on the target server and has the same definition, then there's no need to perform step 1.

Let's restore the `actor` table in another database on the same server. The table needs to exist, so we'll create it:

```
mysql> USE nasa
mysql> CREATE TABLE `actor` (
    -> `actor_id` smallint unsigned NOT NULL AUTO_INCREMENT,
    -> `first_name` varchar(45) NOT NULL,
    -> `last_name` varchar(45) NOT NULL,
    -> `last_update` timestamp NOT NULL DEFAULT CURRENT_TIMESTAMP
    ->   ON UPDATE CURRENT_TIMESTAMP,
    -> PRIMARY KEY (`actor_id`),
    -> KEY `idx_actor_last_name` (`last_name`)
    -> ) ENGINE=InnoDB AUTO_INCREMENT=201 DEFAULT
    ->   CHARSET=utf8mb4 COLLATE=utf8mb4_0900_ai_ci;
Query OK, 0 rows affected (0.04 sec)
```

As soon as the actor table is created, MySQL creates an *.ibd* file for it:

```
# ls /var/lib/mysql/nasa/
actor.ibd  facilities.ibd
```

This brings us to the next step: discarding this new table's tablespace. That's done by running a special ALTER TABLE:

```
mysql> ALTER TABLE actor DISCARD TABLESPACE;
Query OK, 0 rows affected (0.02 sec)
```

Now the *.ibd* file will be gone:

```
# ls /var/lib/mysql/nasa/
facilities.ibd
```

Discarding the tablespace leads to total deletion of the associated tablespace files and is not a recoverable operation. You will need to recover from a backup if you run ALTER TABLE ... DISCARD TABLESPACE accidentally.

We can now copy the exported tablespace of the original actor table along with the *.cfg* file:

```
# cp -vip /opt/mysql/actor.* /var/lib/mysql/nasa/

'/opt/mysql/actor.cfg' -> '/var/lib/mysql/nasa/actor.cfg'
'/opt/mysql/actor.ibd' -> '/var/lib/mysql/nasa/actor.ibd'
```

With all the steps done, it's now possible to import the tablespace and verify the data:

```
mysql> ALTER TABLE actor IMPORT TABLESPACE;

Query OK, 0 rows affected (0.02 sec)

mysql> SELECT * FROM nasa.actor LIMIT 5;

+----------+------------+-------------+---------------------+
| actor_id | first_name | last_name   | last_update         |
+----------+------------+-------------+---------------------+
|        1 | PENELOPE   | GUINESS     | 2006-02-15 04:34:33 |
|        2 | NICK       | WAHLBERG    | 2006-02-15 04:34:33 |
|        3 | ED         | CHASE       | 2006-02-15 04:34:33 |
|        4 | JENNIFER   | DAVIS       | 2006-02-15 04:34:33 |
|        5 | JOHNNY     | LOLLOBRIGIDA | 2006-02-15 04:34:33 |
+----------+------------+-------------+---------------------+
5 rows in set (0.00 sec)
```

You can see that we have the data from sakila.actor in nasa.actor.

The best thing about Transportable Tablespaces is probably the efficiency. You can move very large tables between databases easily using this feature.

XtraBackup Single-Table Restore

Perhaps surprisingly, we're going to mention XtraBackup once again in the context of Transportable Tablespaces. That's because XtraBackup allows for the export of the tables from any existing backup. In fact, that's the most convenient way to restore an individual table, and it's also a first building block for a single-table or partial-database PITR.

This is one of the most advanced backup and recovery techniques, and it's completely based on the Transportable Tablespaces feature. It also carries over all of the limitations: for example, it won't work on non-file-per-table tablespaces. We won't give the exact steps here, and only cover this technique so that you know it's possible.

To perform a single-table restore, you should first run `xtrabackup` with the `--export` command-line argument to prepare the table for export. You may notice that the table's name isn't specified in this command, and in reality each table will be exported. Let's run the command on one of the backups we took earlier:

```
# xtrabackup --prepare --export --target-dir=/tmp/base_backup
# ls -1 /tmp/base_backup/sakila/

actor.cfg
actor.ibd
address.cfg
address.ibd
category.cfg
category.ibd
...
```

You can see that we have a *.cfg* file for each table: every tablespace is now ready to be exported and imported in another database. From here, you can repeat the steps from the previous section to restore the data from one of the tables.

Single-table or partial-database PITR is tricky, and that's true for most of the database management systems out there. As you saw in "Point-in-Time Recovery" on page 397, PITR in MySQL is based on binlogs. What that means for partial recovery is that transactions concerning all tables in all databases are recorded, but binlogs can be filtered when applied through replication. Very briefly, therefore, the partial recovery procedure is this: you export the required tables, build a completely separate instance, and feed it with binlogs through a replication channel.

You can find more information in community blogs and articles like "MySQL Single Table PITR" (*https://oreil.ly/jjdfT*), "Filtering Binary Logs with MySQL" (*https://oreil.ly/YWWpY*), and "How to Make MySQL PITR Faster" (*https://oreil.ly/zoWpw*).

The export/import feature is a powerful technique when used correctly and under certain circumstances.

Testing and Verifying Your Backups

Backups are good only when you're sure you can trust them. There are numerous examples of people having backup systems that failed when most needed. It's entirely possible to be taking backups frequently and still lose the data.

There are multiple ways in which backups can be unhelpful or can fail:

Inconsistent backups

The simplest example of this is a snapshot backup incorrectly taken from multiple volumes when the database is running. The resulting backup may be broken or missing data. Unfortunately, some of the backups you take may be consistent, and others may not be broken or inconsistent enough for you to notice until it's too late.

Corruption of the source database

Physical backups, as we covered extensively, will have copies of all of the database pages, corrupted or not. Some tools try to verify the data as they go, but this is not completely error-free. Your successful backups may contain bad data that cannot be read later.

Corruption of the backups

Backups are just data on their own and as such are susceptible to the same issues as the original data. Your successful backup might end up being completely useless if its data gets corrupted while it's being stored.

Bugs

Things happen. A backup tool you've been using for a dozen years might have a bug that you, of all people, will discover. In the best case, your backup will fail; in the worst case, it might fail to restore.

Operational errors

We're all human, and we make mistakes. If you automate everything, the risk here changes from human errors to bugs.

That's not a comprehensive list of the issues that you might face, but it gives you some insight into the problems you might encounter even when your backup strategy is sound. Let's review some steps you can take to make you sleep better:

- When implementing a backup system, test it thoroughly, and test it in various modes. Make sure you can back up your system, and use the backup for recovery. Test with and without load. Your backups can be consistent when no connection is modifying the data, and fail when that's not true.

- Use both physical and logical backups. They have different properties and failure modes, especially around source data corruption.

- Back up your backups, or just make sure that they are at least as durable as the database.

- Periodically perform backup restoration tests.

The last point is especially interesting. No backup should be considered safe until it's been restored and tested. That means that in a perfect world, your automation will actually try to use the backup to build a database server and report back success only when that goes well. Additionally, that new database can be attached to the source as a replica, and a data verification tool like `pt-table-checksum` from Percona Toolkit (*https://oreil.ly/YgfuM*) can be used to check the data consistency.

Here are some possible steps for backup data verification for physical backups:

1. Prepare the backup.

2. Restore the backup.

3. Run `innochecksum` on all of the *.ibd* files.

   The following command will run four `innochecksum` processes in parallel on Linux:

   ```
   $ find . -type f -name "*.ibd" -print0 |\
   xargs -t -0r -n1 --max-procs=4 innochecksum
   ```

4. Start a new MySQL instance using the restored backup. Use a spare server, or just a dedicated *.cnf* file, and don't forget to use nondefault ports and paths.

5. Use `mysqldump` or any alternative to dump all of the data, making sure it's readable and providing another copy of the backup.

6. Attach the new MySQL instance as a replica to the original source database, and use `pt-table-checksum` or any alternative to verify that the data matches. The procedure is nicely explained in the `xtrabackup` documentation (*https://oreil.ly/fHruN*), among other sources.

These steps are complex and might take a long time, so you should decide whether it's appropriate for your business and environment to utilize all of them.

Database Backup Strategy Primer

Now that we've covered many of the bits and pieces related to backups and recovery, we can piece together a robust backup strategy. Here are the elements we'll need to consider:

Point-in-time recovery
We need to decide whether we'll need PITR capabilities, as that'll drive our decisions regarding the backup strategy. You have to make the call for your specific case, but our suggestion is to default to having PITR available. It can be a lifesaver. If we decide that we're going to need this capability, we need to set up binary logging and binlog copying.

Logical backups
We will likely need logical backups, either for their portability or for the corruption safeguard. Since logical backups load the source database significantly, schedule them for a time when there's the least load. In some circumstances it won't be possible to do logical backups of your production database, either due to time or load constraints, or both. Since we still want to have the ability to run logical backups, we can use following techniques:

- Run logical backups on a replicated database. It can be problematic to track binlog position in this case, so it's recommended to use GTID-based replication in this case.

- Incorporate creation of logical backups into the physical backup's verification process. A prepared backup is a data directory that can by used by a MySQL server right away. If you run a server targeting the backup, you will spoil that backup, so you need to copy that prepared backup somewhere first.

Physical backups

Based on the OS, MySQL flavor, system properties, and careful review of documentation, we need to choose the tool we'll be using for physical backups. For the sake of simplicity, we're choosing XtraBackup here.

The first decision to make is how important the mean time to recovery (MTTR) target is for us. For example, if we only do weekly base backups, we might end up needing to apply almost a week's worth of transactions to recover the backup. To decrease the MTTR, implement incremental backups on a daily or perhaps even hourly basis.

Taking a step back, your system might be so large that even a hot backup with one of the physical backup tools is not viable for you. In that case, you need to go for snapshots of the volumes, if that's possible.

Backup storage

We need to make sure our backups are safely, and ideally redundantly, stored. We might accomplish this with a hardware storage setup utilizing a less-performant but redundant RAID array of level 5 or 6, or with a less reliable storage setup if we also continuously stream our backups to a cloud storage like Amazon's S3. Or we might just default to using S3 if that's possible for us with the backup tools of choice.

Backup testing and verification

Finally, once we have backups in place, we need to implement a backup testing process. Depending on the budget available for implementation and maintenance of this exercise, we should decide how many steps will be run each time and which steps will be run only periodically.

With all of this done, we can say that we have our bases covered and our database safely backed up. It may seem like a lot of effort, considering how infrequently backups are used, but you have to remember that you will eventually face a disaster—it's just a question of time.

## CHAPTER 11

Configuring and Tuning the Server

The MySQL installation process (see Chapter 1) provides everything necessary to install the MySQL process and start using it. However, it is required for production systems to do some fine-tuning, adjusting MySQL parameters and the operating system to optimize MySQL Server's performance. This chapter will cover the recommended best practices for different installations and show you the parameters that need to be adjusted based on the expected or current workload. As you'll see, it is not necessary to memorize all the MySQL parameters. Based on the *Pareto principle* (*https://oreil.ly/1d58s*), which states that, for many events, roughly 80% of the effects come from 20% of the causes, we will concentrate on the MySQL and operating system parameters that are responsible for most of the performance issues. There are some advanced topics in this chapter related to computer architecture (such as NUMA); the intent here is to introduce you to a few components that can affect MySQL performance that you will need to interact with sooner or later in your career.

The MySQL Server Daemon

Since 2015, the majority of Linux distributions have adopted systemd. Because of that, Linux operating systems do not use the mysqld_safe process to start MySQL anymore. mysqld_safe is called an *angel process*, because it adds some safety features, such as restarting the server when an error occurs and logging runtime information to the MySQL error log. For operating systems that use systemd (controlled and configured with the systemctl command), these functionalities have been incorporated into systemd and the mysqld process.

mysqld is the core process of MySQL Server. It is a single multithreaded program that does most of the work in the server. It does not spawn additional processes—we're talking about a single process with multiple threads, making MySQL a *multithreaded process*.

Let's take a closer look at some of those terms. A *program* is code that is designed to accomplish a specific objective. There are many types of programs, including ones to assist parts of the operating system and others that are designed for user needs, such as web browsing.

A *process* is what we call a program that has been loaded into memory along with all the resources it needs to operate. The operating system allocates memory and other resources for it.

A *thread* is the unit of execution within a process. A process can have just one thread or many threads. In single-threaded processes, the process contains one thread, so only one command is executed at a time.

Because modern CPUs have multiple cores, they can execute multiple threads at the same time, so multithreaded processes are widespread nowadays. It's important to be aware of this concept to understand some of the proposed settings in the following sections.

To conclude, MySQL is single-process software that spawns multiple threads for various purposes, such as serving user activities and executing background tasks.

MySQL Server Variables

MySQL Server has many variables that allow tuning its operation. For example, MySQL Server 8.0.25 has an impressive *588* server variables!

Each system variable has a default value. Also, we can adjust most system variables dynamically (or "on the fly"); however, a few of them are static, which means that we need to change the *my.cnf* file and restart the MySQL process so they can take effect (as discussed in Chapter 9).

The system variables can have two different scopes: SESSION and GLOBAL. That is, a system variable can have a global value that affects server operation as a whole, like the innodb_log_file_size, or a session value that affects only a specific session, like the sql_mode.

Checking Server Settings

Databases are not static entities; on the contrary, their workload is dynamic and changes over time, with a tendency to growth. This organic behavior requires constant monitoring, analysis, and adjustment. The command to show the MySQL settings is:

```
SHOW [GLOBAL|SESSION] VARIABLES;
```

When you use the GLOBAL modifier, the statement displays global system variable values. When you use SESSION, it displays the system variable values that affect the current connection. Observe that different connections can have different values.

If no modifier is present, the default is SESSION.

Best Practices

There are many aspects to optimize in a database. If the database runs on *bare metal* (a physical host), we can control hardware and operating system resources. When we move to virtualized machines, we have reduced control over these resources because we can't control what happens with the underlying host. The last option is managed databases in the cloud, like those provided by Amazon Relational Database Service (RDS), where only a few database settings are available. There's a trade-off between being able to perform fine-grained tuning to extract the most performance and the comfort of having most of the tasks automated (at the cost of a few extra dollars).

Let's start by reviewing some settings at the operating system level. After that, we will check out the MySQL parameters.

Operating system best practices

There are several operating system settings that can affect the performance of MySQL. We'll run through some of the most important ones here.

The swappiness setting and swap usage. The swappiness parameter controls the behavior of the Linux operating system in the swap area. Swapping is the process of transferring data between memory and the disk. This can have a significant effect on performance, because disk access (even with NVMe disks) is at least an order of magnitude slower than memory access.

The default setting (60) encourages the server to swap. You will want your MySQL server to keep swapping to a minimum for performance reasons. The recommended value is 1, which means do not swap until it is absolutely necessary for the OS to be functional. To adjust this parameter, execute the following command as root:

```
# echo 1 > /proc/sys/vm/swappiness
```

Note that this is a nonpersistent change; the setting will revert to its original value when you reboot the OS. To make this change persistent after an operating system reboot, adjust the setting in *sysctl.conf*:

```
# sudo sysctl -w vm.swappiness=1
```

You can get information on swap space usage using the following command:

```
# free -m
```

Or, if you want more detailed information, you can run the following snippet in the shell:

```
#!/bin/bash
SUM=0
OVERALL=0
for DIR in `find /proc/ -maxdepth 1 -type d | egrep "^/proc/[0-9]"` ; do
        PID=`echo $DIR | cut -d / -f 3`
        PROGNAME=`ps -p $PID -o comm --no-headers`
        for SWAP in `grep Swap $DIR/smaps 2>/dev/null| awk '{ print $2 }'`
        do
                let SUM=$SUM+$SWAP
        done
        echo "PID=$PID - Swap used: $SUM - ($PROGNAME )"
        let OVERALL=$OVERALL+$SUM
        SUM=0
done
echo "Overall swap used: $OVERALL"
```

 The difference between setting vm.swappiness to 1 and 0 is negligible. We chose the value of 1 because in some kernels there is a bug that can lead the Out of Memory (OOM) Killer to terminate MySQL when it's set to 0.

I/O scheduler. The I/O scheduler is an algorithm the kernel uses to commit reads and writes to disk. By default, most Linux installs use the Completely Fair Queuing (cfq) scheduler. This works well for many general use cases, but offers few latency guarantees. Two other schedulers are deadline and noop. The deadline scheduler excels at latency-sensitive use cases (like databases), and noop is closer to no scheduling at all. For bare-metal installations, either deadline or noop (the performance difference between them is imperceptible) will be better than cfq.

If you are running MySQL in a VM (which has its own I/O scheduler), it is best to use noop and let the virtualization layer take care of the I/O scheduling itself.

First, verify which algorithm is currently in use by Linux:

```
# cat /sys/block/xvda/queue/scheduler
```
```
noop [deadline] cfq
```

To change it dynamically, run this command as root:

```
# echo "noop" > /sys/block/xvda/queue/scheduler
```

In order to make this change persistent, you need to edit the GRUB configuration file (usually */etc/sysconfig/grub*) and add the `elevator` option to `GRUB_CMDLINE_LINUX_DEFAULT`. For example, you would replace this line:

```
GRUB_CMDLINE_LINUX="console=tty0 crashkernel=auto console=ttyS0,115200
```

with this line:

```
GRUB_CMDLINE_LINUX="console=tty0 crashkernel=auto console=ttyS0,115200
    elevator=noop"
```

It is essential to take extra care when editing the GRUB config. Errors or incorrect settings can make the server unusable and require installing the operating system again.

There are cases where the I/O scheduler has a value of none—most notably in AWS VM instance types where EBS volumes are exposed as NVMe block devices. This is because the setting has no use in modern PCIe/NVMe devices, which have a substantial internal queue and bypass the I/O scheduler altogether. The none setting is optimal in such disks.

Filesystems and mount options. Choosing the filesystem appropriate for your database is an important decision due to the many options available and the trade-offs involved. It is worth mentioning two important ones that are frequently used: *XFS* and *ext4*.

XFS is a high-performance journaling filesystem designed for high scalability. It provides near-native I/O performance even when the filesystem spans multiple storage devices. XFS has features that make it suitable for very large filesystems, supporting files up to 8 EiB in size. Other features include fast recovery, fast transactions, delayed allocation for reduced fragmentation, and near-raw I/O performance with direct I/O.

The make filesystem XFS command (*https://oreil.ly/IJ9em*) (`mkfs.xfs`) has several options to configure the filesystem. However, the default options for `mkfs.xfs` are good for optimal speed, so the default command to create the filesystem will provide good performance while ensuring data integrity:

```
# mkfs.xfs /dev/target_volume
```

Regarding the filesystem mount options, the defaults again should fit most cases. You may see a performance increase on some filesystems by adding the `noatime` mount option to the */etc/fstab* file. For XFS filesystems, the default `atime` behavior is `relatime`, which has almost no overhead compared to `noatime` and still maintains sane `atime` values. If you create an XFS filesystem on a logical unit number (LUN) that has a battery-backed, nonvolatile cache, you can further increase the filesystem's performance by disabling the write barrier with the mount option nobarrier. These settings help you avoid flushing data more often than necessary. If a backup battery unit (BBU) is not present, however, or you are unsure about it, leave barriers on; otherwise, you may jeopardize data consistency. The example below shows two imaginary mountpoints with these options:

```
/dev/sda2              /datastore         xfs     noatime,nobarrier
/dev/sdb2              /binlog            xfs     noatime,nobarrier
```

The other popular option is ext4, developed as the successor to ext3 with added performance improvements. It is a solid option that will fit most workloads. We should note here that it supports files up to 16 TB in size, a smaller limit than XFS. This is something you should consider if excessive tablespace size/growth is a requirement. Regarding mount options, the same considerations apply. We recommend the defaults for a robust filesystem without risks to data consistency. However, if an enterprise storage controller with a BBU cache is present, the following mount options will provide the best performance:

```
/dev/sda2              /datastore              ext4
noatime,data=writeback,barrier=0,nobh,errors=remount-ro
/dev/sdb2              /binlog                 ext4
noatime,data=writeback,barrier=0,nobh,errors=remount-ro
```

Transparent Huge Pages. The operating system manages memory in blocks known as *pages*. A page has a size of 4,096 bytes (or 4 KB); 1 MB of memory is equal to 256 pages, 1 GB of memory is equivalent to 256,000 pages, etc. CPUs have a built-in memory management unit that contains a list of these pages, with each page referenced through a *page table entry*. It is common to see servers nowadays with hundreds or terabytes of memory. There are two ways to enable the system to manage large amounts of memory:

- Increase the number of page table entries in the hardware memory management unit.

- Increase the page size.

The first method is expensive since the hardware memory management unit in a modern processor only supports hundreds or thousands of page table entries. Besides, hardware and memory management algorithms that work well with thousands of pages (megabytes of memory) may have problems performing well with millions (or even billions) of pages. To address the scalability issue, operating systems started using huge pages. Simply put, huge pages are blocks of memory that can come in sizes of 2 MB, 4 MB, 1 GB size, etc. Using huge page memory increases the CPU cache hits against the transaction lookaside buffer (TLB).

You can run cpuid to verify the processor cache and TLB:

```
# cpuid | grep "cache and TLB information" -A 5
    cache and TLB information (2):
        0x5a: data TLB: 2M/4M pages, 4-way, 32 entries
        0x03: data TLB: 4K pages, 4-way, 64 entries
        0x76: instruction TLB: 2M/4M pages, fully, 8 entries
        0xff: cache data is in CPUID 4
        0xb2: instruction TLB: 4K, 4-way, 64 entries
```

Transparent Huge Pages (THP), as the name suggests, is intended to bring huge page support automatically to applications without requiring custom configuration.

For MySQL in particular, using THP is not recommended, for a couple of reasons. First, MySQL databases use small memory pages (16 KB), and using THP can cause excessive I/O because MySQL believes it is accessing 16 KB while THP is scanning a page larger than that. Also, the huge pages tend to become fragmented and impact performance. There have also been some cases reported over the years where using THP can result in memory leaking, eventually crashing MySQL.

To disable THP for RHEL/CentOS 6 and RHEL/CentOS 7, execute the following commands:

```
# echo "never" > /sys/kernel/mm/transparent_hugepage/enabled
# echo "never" > /sys/kernel/mm/transparent_hugepage/defrag
```

To ensure that this change will survive a server restart, you'll have to add the flag transparent_hugepage=never to your kernel options (*/etc/sysconfig/grub*):

```
GRUB_CMDLINE_LINUX="console=tty0 crashkernel=auto console=ttyS0,115200
elevator=noop transparent_hugepage=never"
```

Back up the existing GRUB2 configuration file (*/boot/grub2/grub.cfg*), and then rebuild it. On BIOS-based machines, you can do this with the following command:

```
# grub2-mkconfig -o /boot/grub2/grub.cfg
```

If THP is still not disabled, it may be necessary to disable the tuned services:

```
# systemctl stop tuned
# systemctl disable tuned
```

To disable THP for Ubuntu 20.04 (Focal Fossa), we recommend you use the sysfsu tils package. To install it, execute the following command:

```
# apt install sysfsutils
```

Then append the following lines to the */etc/sysfs.conf* file:

```
kernel/mm/transparent_hugepage/enabled = never
kernel/mm/transparent_hugepage/defrag = never
```

Reboot the server and check if the settings are in place:

```
# cat /sys/kernel/mm/transparent_hugepage/enabled
always madvise [never]
# cat /sys/kernel/mm/transparent_hugepage/defrag
always defer defer+madvise madvise [never]
```

jemalloc. MySQL Server uses dynamic memory allocation, so a good memory allocator is important for proper CPU and RAM resource utilization. An efficient memory allocator should improve scalability, increase throughput, and keep the memory footprint under control.

It is important to mention a characteristic of InnoDB here. InnoDB creates a read view for every transaction and allocates memory for this structure from the heap area. The problem is that MySQL deallocates the heap on each commit, and thus the read view memory is reallocated on the next transaction, leading to memory fragmentation.

jemalloc is a memory allocator that emphasizes fragmentation avoidance and scalable concurrency support.

Using jemalloc (with THP disabled), you have less memory fragmentation and more efficient resource management of the available server memory. You can install the jemalloc package from the jemalloc repository (*https://oreil.ly/NZMtb*) or the Percona *yum* or *apt* repository. We prefer to use the Percona repository because we consider it simpler to install and manage. We describe the steps to install the *yum* repository in "Installing Percona Server 8.0" on page 10 and the *apt* repository in "Installing Percona Server 8" on page 21.

Once you have the repo, you run the install command for your operating system.

 In CentOS, if the server has the Extra Packages for Enterprise Linux (EPEL) repository installed, it is possible to install jemalloc from this repo with yum. To install the EPEL package, use:

```
# yum install epel-release -y
```

If you are using Ubuntu 20.04, then you need to execute the following steps to enable jemalloc:

1. Install jemalloc:

   ```
   # apt-get install libjemalloc2
   # dpkg -L libjemalloc2
   ```

2. The dpkg command will show the location of the jemalloc library:

   ```
   # dpkg -L libjemalloc2
   /.
   ```

```
/usr
/usr/lib
/usr/lib/x86_64-linux-gnu
/usr/lib/x86_64-linux-gnu/libjemalloc.so.2
/usr/share
/usr/share/doc
/usr/share/doc/libjemalloc2
/usr/share/doc/libjemalloc2/README
/usr/share/doc/libjemalloc2/changelog.Debian.gz
/usr/share/doc/libjemalloc2/copyright
```

3. Override the default configuration of the service with the command:

```
# systemctl edit mysql
```

which will create the */etc/systemd/system/mysql.service.d/override.conf* file.

4. Add the following configuration to the file:

```
[Service]
Environment="LD_PRELOAD=/usr/lib/x86_64-linux-gnu/libjemalloc.so.2"
```

5. Restart the MySQL service to enable the jemalloc library:

```
# systemctl restart mysql
```

6. To verify if it worked, with the mysqld process running, execute the following command:

```
# lsof -Pn -p $(pidof mysqld) | grep "jemalloc"
```

You should see similar output to the following:

```
mysqld  3844 mysql  mem      REG          253,0   744776  36550
/usr/lib/x86_64-linux-gnu/libjemalloc.so.2
```

If you are using CentOS/RHEL, you need to execute the following steps:

1. Install the jemalloc package:

```
# yum install jemalloc
# rpm -ql jemalloc
```

2. The rpm -ql command will show the library location:

```
/usr/bin/jemalloc.sh
/usr/lib64/libjemalloc.so.1
/usr/share/doc/jemalloc-3.6.0
/usr/share/doc/jemalloc-3.6.0/COPYING
/usr/share/doc/jemalloc-3.6.0/README
/usr/share/doc/jemalloc-3.6.0/VERSION
/usr/share/doc/jemalloc-3.6.0/jemalloc.html
```

3. Override the default configuration of the service with the command:

```
# systemctl edit mysqld
```

which will create the */etc/systemd/system/mysqld.service.d/override.conf* file.

4. Add the following configuration to the file:

```
[Service]
Environment="LD_PRELOAD=/usr/lib64/libjemalloc.so.1"
```

5. Restart the MySQL service to enable the jemalloc library:

```
# systemctl restart mysqld
```

6. To verify if it worked, with the mysqld process running, execute the following command:

```
# lsof -Pn -p $(pidof mysqld) |  grep "jemalloc"
```

You should see similar output to the following:

```
mysqld  4784 mysql  mem        REG              253,0    212096  33985101
/usr/lib64/libjemalloc.so.1
```

CPU governor. One of the most effective ways to reduce the power consumption and heat output on your system is to use CPUfreq. CPUfreq, also referred to as CPU frequency scaling or CPU speed scaling, allows the processor's clock speed to be adjusted on the fly. This feature enables the system to run at a reduced clock speed to save power. The rules for shifting frequencies—whether and when to shift to a faster or slower clock speed—are defined by the CPUfreq *governor*. The governor defines the power characteristics of the system CPU, which in turn affects CPU performance. Each governor has its own unique behavior, purpose, and suitability in terms of workload. However, for MySQL databases, we recommend using the maximum performance setting to achieve the best throughput.

For CentOS, you can view which CPU governor is currently being used by executing:

```
# cat /sys/devices/system/cpu/cpu/cpufreq/scaling_governor
```

You can enable performance mode by running:

```
# cpupower frequency-set --governor performance
```

For Ubuntu, we recommend installing the linux-tools-common package so you have access to the cpupower utility:

```
# apt install linux-tools-common
```

Once you've installed it, you can change the governor to performance mode with the following command:

```
# cpupower frequency-set --governor performance
```

MySQL best practices

Now let's look at MySQL Server settings. This section proposes recommended values for the main MySQL parameters that have a direct impact on performance. You'll see that it's not necessary to change the default values for the majority of the parameters.

Buffer pool size. The `innodb_buffer_pool_size` parameter controls the size in bytes of the InnoDB buffer pool, the memory area where InnoDB caches table and index data. There's no question that for tuning InnoDB, this is the most important parameter. The typical rule of thumb is to set it to around 70% of the total available RAM for a MySQL dedicated server.

However, the larger the server is, the more likely it is that this will end up wasting RAM. For a server with 512 GB of RAM, for example, this would leave 153 GB of RAM for the operating system, which is more than it needs.

So what's a better rule of thumb? Set the `innodb_buffer_pool_size` as large as possible, without causing swapping when the system is running the production workload. This will require some tuning.

In MySQL 5.7 and later this is a dynamic parameter, so you can change it on the fly without the need to restart the database. For example, to set it to 1 GB, use this command:

```
mysql> SET global innodb_buffer_pool_size = 1024*1024*1024;
Query OK, 0 rows affected (0.00 sec)
```

To make the change persistent across restarts, you'll need to add this parameter to *my.cnf*, under the `[mysqld]` section:

```
[mysqld]
innodb_buffer_pool_size = 1G
```

The innodb_buffer_pool_instances parameter. One of the more obscure MySQL parameters is `innodb_buffer_pool_instances`. This parameter defines the number of instances that InnoDB will split the buffer pool into. For systems with buffer pools in the multigigabyte range, dividing the buffer pool into separate instances can improve concurrency by reducing contention as different threads read and write to cached pages.

However, in our experience, setting a high value for this parameter may also introduce additional overhead. The reason is that each buffer pool instance manages its own free list, flush list, LRU list, and all other data structures connected to a buffer pool, and is protected by its own buffer pool mutex.

Unless you run benchmarks that prove performance gains, we suggest using the default value (8).

The innodb_buffer_pool_instances parameter was deprecated in MariaDB 10.5.1 and removed in MariaDB 10.6. According to MariaDB architect Marko Makela, this is because the original reasons for splitting the buffer pool have mostly gone away nowadays. You can find more details in the MariaDB Jira ticket (*https://oreil.ly/HOCNA*).

Redo log size. The redo log is a structure used during crash recovery to correct data written by incomplete transactions. The main goal is to guarantee the durability (D) property of ACID transactions by providing redo recovery for committed transactions. Because the redo file logs all data written to MySQL even before the commit, having the right redo log size is fundamental for MySQL to run smoothly without struggling. An undersized redo log can even lead to errors in operations!

Here's an example of the kind of error you might see if using a small redo log file:

```
[ERROR] InnoDB: The total blob data length (12299456) is greater than 10%
of the total redo log size (100663296). Please increase total redo log size.
```

In this case MySQL was using the default value for the innodb_log_file_size parameter, which is 48 MB. To estimate the optimal redo log size, there is a formula that we can use in the majority of cases. Take a look at the following commands:

```
mysql> pager grep sequence
PAGER set to 'grep sequence'
mysql> show engine innodb status\G select sleep(60);
    -> show engine innodb status\G
Log sequence number 3836410803
1 row in set (0.06 sec)

1 row in set (1 min 0.00 sec)

Log sequence number 3838334638
1 row in set (0.05 sec)
```

The log sequence number is the total number of bytes written to the redo log. Using the SLEEP() command, we can calculate the delta for that period. Then, using the following formula, we can reach an estimated value for the amount of space needed to hold an hour or so of logs (a good rule of thumb):

```
mysql> SELECT (((3838334638 - 3836410803)/1024/1024)*60)/2
    -> AS Estimated_innodb_log_file_size;
+-------------------------------+
| Estimated_innodb_log_file_size |
+-------------------------------+
|                55.041360855088 |
+-------------------------------+
1 row in set (0.00 sec)
```

We usually round up, so the final number will be 56 MB. This is the value that needs to be added to *my.cnf* under the [mysqld] section:

```
[mysqld]
innodb_log_file_size=56M
```

The sync_binlog parameter. The binary log is a set of log files that contain information about data modifications made to a MySQL server instance. They are different from the redo files and have other uses. For example, they are used to create replicas and InnoDB Clusters, and are helpful for performing PITR.

By default, the MySQL server synchronizes its binary log to disk (using fdatasync()) before transactions are committed. The advantage is that in the event of a power failure or operating system crash, transactions that are missing from the binary log are only in a prepared state; this allows the automatic recovery routine to roll back the transactions, guaranteeing that no transaction is lost from the binary log. However, the default value (sync_binlog = 1) brings a penalty in performance. As this is a dynamic option, you can change it while the server is running with the following command:

```
mysql> SET GLOBAL sync_binlog = 0;
```

For the change to persist after a restart, add the parameter to your *my.cnf* file under the [mysqld] section:

```
[mysqld]
sync_binlog=0
```

 Most of the time, using sync_binlog=0 will provide good performance (when binary logs are enabled). However, the performance variance can be significant because MySQL will rely on the OS flushing to flush the binary logs. Depending on the workload, using sync_binlog=1000 or higher will provide better performance than sync_binlog=1 and less variance than sync_binlog=0.

The binlog_expire_logs_seconds and expire_logs_days parameters. To avoid MySQL filling the entire disk with binary logs, you can adjust the settings of the parameters binlog_expire_logs_seconds and expire_logs_days. expire_logs_days specifies the number of days before automatic removal of binary log files. However, this parameter is deprecated in MySQL 8.0, and you should expect it to be removed in a future release.

Consequently, a better option is to use binlog_expire_logs_seconds, which sets the binary log expiration period in seconds. The default value for this parameter is 2592000 (30 days). MySQL can automatically remove the binary log files after this expiration period ends, either at startup or the next time the binary log is flushed.

If you want to flush the binary log manually, you can execute the following command:

```
mysql> FLUSH BINARY LOGS;
```

The innodb_flush_log_at_trx_commit parameter. `innodb_flush_log_at_trx_commit` controls the balance between strict ACID compliance for commit operations and the higher performance possible when commit-related I/O operations are rearranged and done in batches. It is a delicate option, and many prefer to use the default value (`innodb_flush_log_at_trx_commit=1`) in the source servers, while for replicas they use a value of 0 or 2. The value 2 instructs InnoDB to write to the log files after each transaction commit, but to flush them to disk only once per second. This means you can lose up to a second of updates if the OS crashes, which, with modern hardware that supports up to one million inserts per second, is not negligible. The value 0 is even worse: logs are written and flushed to disk just once per second, so you may lose up to a second's worth of transactions even if the `mysqld` process crashes.

Many operating systems, and some disk hardware, "fool" the flush-to-disk operation. They may tell `mysqld` that the flush has taken place, even though it has not. In this case, the durability of transactions is not guaranteed even with the recommended settings, and in the worst case, a power outage can corrupt InnoDB data. Using a battery-backed disk cache in the SCSI disk controller or in the disk itself speeds up file flushes and makes the operation safer. You can also disable the caching of disk writes in hardware caches if the battery is not working correctly.

The innodb_thread_concurrency parameter. `innodb_thread_concurrency` is set to 0 by default, which means that an infinite number (up to the hardware limit) of threads can be opened and executed inside MySQL. The usual recommendation is to leave this parameter with its default value and only change it to solve contention problems.

If your workload is consistently heavy or has occasional spikes, you can set the value of `innodb_thread_concurrency` using the following formula:

```
innodb_thread_concurrency = Number of Cores * 2
```

Because MySQL does not use multiple cores to execute a single query (it is a 1:1 relation), each core will run one query per single unit of time. Based on our experience, because modern CPUs are fast in general, setting the maximum number of executing threads to double the CPUs available is a good start.

Once the number of executing threads reaches this limit, additional threads sleep for a number of microseconds, set by the configuration parameter innodb_thread_sleep_delay, before being placed into the queue.

innodb_thread_concurrency is a dynamic variable, and we can change it at runtime:

```
mysql> SET GLOBAL innodb_thread_concurrency = 0;
```

To make the change persistent, you'll also need to add this to *my.cnf*, under the [mysqld] section:

```
[mysqld]
innodb-thread-concurrency=0
```

You can validate that MySQL applied the setting with this command:

```
mysql> SHOW GLOBAL VARIABLES LIKE '%innodb_thread_concurrency%';
```

> The MySQL 8.0.14 release notes (*https://oreil.ly/EqPrG*) state: "As of MySQL 8.0.14, InnoDB supports parallel clustered index reads, which can improve CHECK TABLE performance." Parallel clustered index reads also work for a simple COUNT(*) (without a WHERE condition). You can control the number of parallel threads with the innodb_parallel_read_threads parameter.
>
> This feature is currently limited and available only for queries without a WHERE condition (full scans). However, it is a great start for MySQL and opens the road to real parallel query execution.

NUMA architecture. Non-uniform memory access (NUMA) is a shared memory architecture that describes the placement of main memory modules relative to processors in a multiprocessor system. In the NUMA shared memory architecture, each processor has its own local memory module, leading to a distinct performance advantage because the memory and the processor are physically closer. At the same time, it can also access any memory module belonging to another processor using a shared bus (or some other type of interconnect), as shown in Figure 11-1.

> A nice alternative that can show memory usage across NUMA nodes is the numastat command. You can get a more detailed memory usage per node by executing:
>
> ```
> # numastat -m
> ```
>
> Another way to visualize this is by specific process. For example, to check the memory usage in NUMA nodes of the mysqld process:
>
> ```
> # numastat -p $(pidof mysqld)
> ```

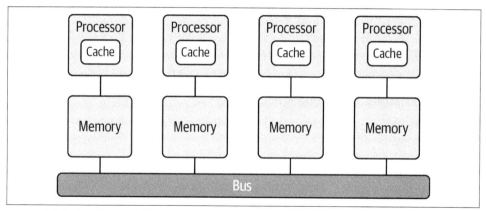

Figure 11-1. NUMA architecture overview

The following command shows an example of the available nodes on a server that has NUMA enabled:

```
shell> numactl --hardware

available: 2 nodes (0-1)
node 0 cpus: 0 1 2 3 4 5 6 7 8 9 10 11 24 25 26 27 28 29 30 31 32 33 34 35
node 0 size: 130669 MB
node 0 free: 828 MB
node 1 cpus: 12 13 14 15 16 17 18 19 20 21 22 23 36 37 38 39 40 41 42 43 44 45 46
node 1 size: 131072 MB
node 1 free: 60 MB
node distances:
node    0    1
  0:   10   21
  1:   21   10
```

As we can see, node 0 has more free memory than node 1. There is an issue with this that causes the OS to swap even with memory available, as explained in the excellent article "The MySQL *Swap Insanity* Problem and the Effects of the NUMA Architecture" (*https://oreil.ly/lBRSk*) by Jeremy Cole.

In MySQL 5.7 the `innodb_buffer_pool_populate` and `numa_interleave` parameters were removed, and their functions are now controlled by the `innodb_numa_inter leave` parameter. When we enable it, we balance memory allocation across nodes in a NUMA system, avoiding the swap insanity problem.

This parameter is not dynamic, so to enable it we need to add it to the *my.cnf* file, under the [`mysqld`] section, and restart MySQL:

```
[mysqld]
innodb_numa_interleave = 1
```

## CHAPTER 12

Monitoring MySQL Servers

Monitoring can be defined as observing or checking the quality or progress of something over a period of time. Applying that definition to MySQL, what we observe and check are the server's "health" and performance. Quality, then, would be maintaining uptime and having performance meet desired levels. So really, monitoring is a continuous effort to keep things under observation and control. Usually it's thought of as something optional, which may not be needed unless there's a particularly high load or high stakes. However, just like backups, monitoring benefits almost every installation of any database.

We think that having monitoring in place and understanding the metrics you're getting from it is one of the most important tasks for anyone operating a database system—probably just after setting up proper verified backups. Like operating a database without backups, failing to monitor your database is dangerous: what use is a system that provides unpredictable performance and may be "down" randomly? The data may be safe, but it might not be usable.

In this chapter, we'll try to give you a foundation for understanding how to monitor MySQL efficiently. This book is not called *High Performance MySQL*, and we won't be going into depth on the specifics of exactly what different metrics mean or how to perform a complex analysis of a system. But we will talk about few basic metrics that should be checked regularly in every MySQL installation, and we'll discuss important OS-level metrics and tools. We'll then briefly touch on a few widely used methodologies for assessing system performance. After that, we will review a few popular open source monitoring solutions, and finally we'll show you how to gather data for investigation and monitoring purposes manually.

After completing this chapter, you should feel comfortable picking a monitoring tool and be able to understand some of the most important metrics it shows.

Operating System Metrics

An operating system is a complex computer program: an interface between applications, mainly MySQL in our case, and hardware. In the early days, OSs were simple; now they are arguably quite complex, but the idea behind them never really changed. An OS tries to hide, or abstract away, the complexity of dealing with the underlying hardware. It's possible to imagine some special-purpose RDBMS running directly on hardware, being its own operating system, but realistically you'll likely never see that. Apart from providing a convenient and powerful interface, operating systems also expose a lot of performance metrics. You don't need to know each and every one of them, but it's important to have a basic understanding of how to assess the performance of the layer underneath your database.

Usually, when we talk about operating system performance and metrics, what's really being discussed is hardware performance assessed at the operating system level. There's nothing wrong in saying "OS metrics," but remember that at the end of the day they are mostly showing hardware performance.

Let's take a look at the most important OS metrics that you'll want to monitor and in general have a feel for. We will be covering two major OSs in this section: Linux and Windows. Unix-like systems, like macOS and others, will have either the same tools as Linux or at least tools showing the same or similar outputs.

CPU

The *central processing unit* (CPU) is the heart of any computer. Nowadays, CPUs are so complex they can be considered separate computers within computers. Luckily, the basic metrics we think you should understand are universal. In this section, we'll take a look at CPU utilization as reported by Linux and Windows and see what contributes to the overall load.

Before we get into measuring CPU utilization, let's do a quick recap of what a CPU is and what characteristics of it are most important for database operators. We called it the "heart of a computer," but that's oversimplified. In fact, a CPU is a device that can do a few basic (and not so basic) operations, on top of which we build layers and layers of complexity from machine code up to the high-level programming languages running operating systems and ultimately (for us) database systems.

Every operation a computer does is done by a CPU. As Kevin Closson (*https://oreil.ly/8uwkg*) has said, "Everything is a CPU problem." When a program is actively being executed—for example, MySQL parsing a query—the CPU is doing all the work. When a program is waiting for a resource—MySQL waiting for a data read from disk—the CPU is involved in "telling" the program when the data is available. Such a list could go on forever.

Here are a few of the most important metrics of a CPU for a server (or any computer in general):

CPU frequency
CPU frequency is the number of times per second a CPU core can "wake up" to execute a piece of work. This is basically the "speed" of the CPU. The more the merrier, but surprisingly often frequency is not the most important metric.

Cache memory
The size of the cache defines the amount of memory located directly within the CPU, making it extremely fast. Again, the more the better, and there are no downsides to having more.

Number of cores
This is the number of execution units within a single CPU "package" (a physical item), and the sum of those units across all CPUs we can fit into a server. Nowadays, it's increasingly difficult to find a CPU that has a single core: most CPUs are multicore systems. Some even have "virtual" cores, making the difference between the "actual" number of CPUs and the total number of cores even higher.

Usually, having more cores is a good thing, but there are caveats to that. In general, the more cores are available, the more processes can be scheduled by the OS to be executed simultaneously. For MySQL, that means more queries executed in parallel, and less impact from background operations.

But if half of the available cores are "virtual," you don't get the 2x performance increase you might expect. Rather, you *may* get a 2x increase, or you may get anywhere between a 1x and a 2x increase: not every workload (even within MySQL) benefits from virtual cores.

Also, having multiple CPUs in different sockets makes interfacing with memory (RAM) and other onboard devices (like network cards) more complicated. Usually, regular servers are physically laid out in such a way that some CPUs (and their cores) will access parts of RAM quicker than other parts—this is the NUMA architecture we talked about in the previous chapter. For MySQL, this means that memory allocation and memory-related issues can become a pain point. We covered the necessary configuration on NUMA systems in "NUMA architecture" on page 425.

The basic measurement of CPU is its load in percent. When someone tells you "CPU 20," you can be *pretty* sure that they mean "the CPU is 20% busy at the moment." You can never be totally sure, though, so you'd better double-check. For example, 20% of one core on a multicore system may be just 1% of the overall load. Let's try to visualize this load.

On Linux, the basic command to get the CPU load is `vmstat`. If run without arguments, it will output current average values and then exit. If we run it with a digit argument (we'll call it X here), it'll print values every X seconds. We recommend that you run `vmstat` with a digit argument—for example, `vmstat 1`—for a few seconds. If you run just `vmstat`, you get averages since boot, which are usually misleading. `vmstat 1` will execute forever until interrupted (pressing Ctrl+C is the easiest way out).

The `vmstat` program prints information not only on CPU load, but also memory and disk-related metrics, as well as advanced system metrics. We will be exploring some other sections of the `vmstat` output soon, but here we'll concentrate on CPU and process metrics.

To start, let's see the `vmstat` output on an idle system. The CPU section is truncated; we'll review it in detail later:

```
$ vmstat 1
procs -----------memory---------- ---swap-- -----io---- -system-- ------cpu-----
 r  b   swpd   free    buff  cache   si   so    bi    bo   in   cs us sy id …
 2  0      0 1229924 1856608 6968268    0    0    39   125   61  144 18  7 75…
 1  0      0 1228028 1856608 6969384    0    0     0    84 2489 3047  2  1 97…
 0  0      0 1220972 1856620 6977688    0    0     0    84 2828 4712  3  1 96…
 0  0      0 1217420 1856644 6976796    0    0     0   164 2405 3164  2  2 96…
 0  0      0 1223768 1856648 6968352    0    0     0    84 2109 2762  2  1 97…
```

The first line of the output after the header is an average since boot, and later lines represent current values when printed. The output can be hard to read at first, but you get used to it rather quickly. For clarity, in the rest of this section we will provide a truncated output with only the information we want, in the `procs` and `cpu` sections:

```
procs ------cpu-----
 r  b us sy id wa st
 2  0 18  7 75  0  0
 1  0  2  1 97  0  0
 0  0  3  1 96  0  0
 0  0  2  2 96  0  0
 0  0  2  1 97  0  0
```

`r` and `b` are process metrics: the number of processes actively running and the number of processes blocked (usually waiting for I/O). The other columns represent a breakdown of CPU utilization in percentage points (from 0% to 100%, even on a multicore system). Together, the values in these columns will always add up to 100. Here's what the `cpu` columns indicate:

us *(user)*

Time spent running user programs (or, the load put on a system by these programs). MySQL Server is a user program, as is every piece of code that exists outside of the kernel. Importantly, this metric shows time spent purely inside the program itself. For example, when MySQL is doing some computation, or parsing a complex query, this value will go up. When MySQL wants to perform a disk or network operation, this value will also go up, but so will two other values, as you'll soon see.

sy *(system)*

Time spent running kernel code. Due to the way Linux and other Unix-like systems are organized, user programs increase this counter. For example, whenever MySQL needs to do a disk read, some work will have to be done by the OS kernel. Time spent doing that work will be included in the sy value.

id *(idle)*

Time spent doing nothing; idle time. On a perfectly idle server, this metric will be 100.

wa *(I/O wait)*

Time spent waiting for I/O. This is an important metric for MySQL, as reading and writing to various files are a relatively large part of MySQL operation. When MySQL does a disk read, some time will be spent in MySQL's internal functions and reflected in us. Then some time will be spent inside the kernel and reflected in sy. Finally, once the kernel has sent a read request to the underlying storage device (which could be a local or network device) and is waiting for the response and data, all the time spent is accumulated in wa. If our program and kernel are very slow and all we do is I/O, in theory this metric could be close to 100. In reality, double-digit values are rare and usually indicate some I/O issues. We'll talk about I/O in depth in "Disk" on page 436.

st *(steal)*

This is a difficult metric to explain without getting deep into the weeds. It's defined by the MySQL Reference Manual as "time stolen from a virtual machine." You can think of this as the time during which the VM wanted to execute its instructions but had to wait for the host server to allocate CPU time. There are multiple reasons for this behavior, a couple of which are notable. The first is host overprovisioning: running too many large VMs, resulting in a situation where the sum of resources the VMs require is more than the host's capacity. The second is the "noisy neighbor" situation, where one or more VMs suffer from a particularly loaded VM.

Other commands, like top (which we'll show in a bit), will have finer CPU load breakdowns. However, the columns just listed are a good starting point and cover most of what you need to know about a running system.

Now let's get back to our `vmstat 1` output on an idle system:

```
procs ------cpu-----
 r  b us sy id wa st
 2  0 18  7 75  0  0
 1  0  2  1 97  0  0
 0  0  3  1 96  0  0
 0  0  2  2 96  0  0
 0  0  2  1 97  0  0
```

What can we tell from this output? As mentioned previously, the first line is an average since boot. On average, there are two processes running (`r`) on this system, with 0 blocked (`b`); user CPU utilization is 18% (`us`), system CPU utilization is 7% (`sy`), and overall the CPU is 75% idle (`id`). I/O wait (`wa`) and steal time (`st`) are 0.

After the first one, each line of the output printed is an average over a sampling interval, which is 1 second in our example. This is pretty close to what we could call "current" values. As this is an idle machine, we see that overall the values are below average. Only one or no processes are running or blocked, user CPU time is 2–3%, system CPU time is 1–2%, and the system is idle 96–97% of the time.

For good measure, let's look at the `vmstat 1` output on the same system doing a CPU-intensive computation in a single process:

```
procs ------cpu-----
 r  b us sy id wa st
 2  0 18  7 75  0  0
 1  0 13  0 87  0  0
 1  0 13  0 86  0  0
 1  0 14  0 86  0  0
 1  0 15  0 84  0  0
```

The averages since boot are the same, but we have a single process running in every sample, and it drives the user CPU time to 13–15%. The problem with `vmstat` is that we can't learn from its output which process specifically is burning the CPU. Of course, if this is a dedicated database server, you can suppose that most if not all user CPU time is going to be accounted for by MySQL and its threads, but things happen. The other problem is that on machines with a high CPU core count, you can mistakenly take low readings in `vmstat` output for a fact—but `vmstat` gives a reading from 0% to 100% even on a 256-core machine. If 8 cores of such a machine are 100% loaded, the user time shown by `vmstat` will be 3%, but in reality some workload may be throttled.

Before we talk about a solution to those problems, let's talk Windows a little bit. A lot of what we've said in general about CPU utilization and especially about CPUs will translate to Windows, with some notable differences:

- There's no I/O wait accounting in Windows, as the I/O subsystem is fundamentally different. Time spent by threads waiting for I/O is going into the idle counter.
- The system CPU time counterpart is, roughly, the privileged CPU time.
- Steal information is not available.

The user and idle counters remain unchanged, so you can base your CPU monitoring on user, privileged, and idle CPU time as it is exposed by Windows. There are other counters and metrics available, but this should have you covered quite well. Getting the current CPU utilization on Windows can be done using many different tools. The simplest one, and probably the closest one to vmstat in spirit, is the good old Task Manager, a staple of looking at Windows performance metrics. It's readily available, it's simple, and you've probably used it before. The Task Manager can show you CPU utilization in percentage points broken down by CPU cores and also split between user and kernel time.

Figure 12-1 shows the Task Manager running on an idle system.

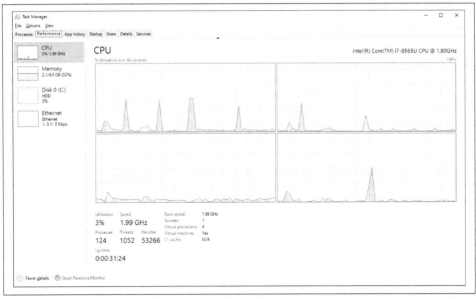

Figure 12-1. Task Manager showing an idle CPU

Figure 12-2 shows the Task Manager running on a busy system.

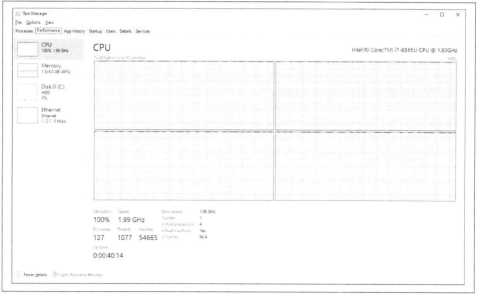

Figure 12-2. Task Manager showing a busy CPU

As we said earlier, vmstat has a couple of problems: it doesn't break down load per process or per CPU core. Solving both problems requires running other tools. Why not just run them right away? vmstat is universal, gives more than just CPU readings, and is very concise. It's a good way to quickly see if there's anything very wrong with a given system. The same goes for the Task Manager, although it is actually more capable than vmstat.

On Linux, the next-simplest tool to use after vmstat is top, another basic element in the toolbox of anyone dealing with a Linux server. It expands on the basic CPU metrics we have discussed, and adds both per-core load breakdown and per-process load accounting. When you execute top without any arguments, it starts in a terminal UI, or TUI, mode. Press ? to see the help menu. To display the per-core load breakdown, press 1. Figure 12-3 shows what the output of top looks like.

You can see here that each process gets its own overall CPU utilization shown under the %CPU column. For example, mysqld is using 104.7% of the overall CPU time. Now we can also see how that load is distributed among the many cores the server has. In this particular case, one core (Cpu0) is slightly more loaded than the other one. There are cases when MySQL hits a limit of single-CPU throughput, and thus having per-core load breakdown is important. Having a view on how load is distributed between processes is important if you suspect some rogue process is eating into the server's capacity.

```
top - 06:27:27 up 2 min,  2 users,  load average: 0.90, 0.22, 0.07
Tasks: 120 total,   1 running, 119 sleeping,   0 stopped,   0 zombie
%Cpu0  : 27.0 us, 39.8 sy,  0.0 ni, 29.0 id,  1.2 wa,  0.0 hi,  2.9 si,  0.0 st
%Cpu1  : 21.2 us, 32.4 sy,  0.0 ni, 42.0 id,  3.8 wa,  0.0 hi,  0.7 si,  0.0 st
KiB Mem :  1014596 total,    67232 free,   397304 used,   550060 buff/cache
KiB Swap:  1572860 total,  1572596 free,      264 used.   447692 avail Mem

  PID USER      PR  NI    VIRT    RES    SHR S  %CPU %MEM     TIME+ COMMAND
 6186 mysql     20   0  942688 331964  51760 S 104.7 32.7   0:21.13 mysqld
   30 root      20   0       0      0      0 S   7.6  0.0   0:01.50 kworker/0:1
  334 root       0 -20       0      0      0 S   5.0  0.0   0:00.98 kworker/0:1H
 6232 root      20   0  275916   3468   2556 S   4.7  0.3   0:00.97 mysqlslap
    6 root      20   0       0      0      0 S   2.7  0.0   0:00.50 ksoftirqd/0
   38 root      20   0       0      0      0 S   0.3  0.0   0:00.02 kswapd0
  233 root      20   0       0      0      0 S   0.3  0.0   0:00.07 kworker/1:2
    1 root      20   0  128016   5212   2684 S   0.0  0.5   0:00.95 systemd
    2 root      20   0       0      0      0 S   0.0  0.0   0:00.00 kthreadd
    3 root      20   0       0      0      0 S   0.0  0.0   0:00.00 kworker/0:0
```

Figure 12-3. top in TUI mode

There are many more tools that can show you even more data. We can't talk in detail about all of them, but we'll name a few. mpstat can give very in-depth CPU statistics. pidstat is a universal tool that provides stats on CPU, memory, disk, and network utilization for each individual process running. atop is an advanced version of top. There are more, and everyone has their favorite set of tools. We firmly believe that what really matters is not the tools themselves, though they help, but an understanding of the core metrics and stats that they provide.

On Windows, the Task Manager program is actually much closer to top than it is to vmstat, although we've done just that comparison. The Task Manager's ability to show per-core load and per-process load makes it quite a useful first step in any investigation. We recommend diving into the Resource Monitor right away, as it provides more details. The easiest way to access it is to click the Open Resource Monitor link in the Task Manager.

Figure 12-4 shows a Resource Monitor window with CPU load details.

The Task Manager and Resource Monitor are not the only tools on Windows capable of showing performance metrics. Here are a couple other tools that you may want to get comfortable using. They are more advanced, so we won't go into detail here:

Performance Monitor
    This built-in tool is a GUI for the performance counter subsystem in Windows. In short, you can view and plot any (or all) of the various performance metrics Windows measures, not only those related to the CPU.

Process Explorer
    This tool is a part of a suite of advanced system utilities called Windows Sysinternals (*https://oreil.ly/mKGKF*). It's more powerful and more advanced than the other tools listed here and can be useful to learn. Unlike the other tools, you'll

have to install Process Explorer separately from its home page on the Sysinternals site (*https://oreil.ly/C2tGo*).

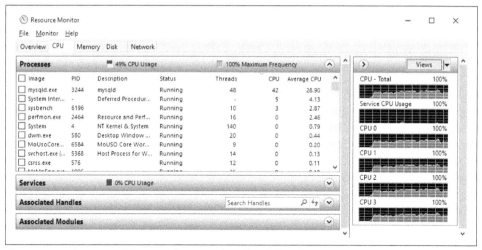

Figure 12-4. Resource Monitor showing CPU load details

Disk

The disk or I/O subsystem is crucial for database performance. Although the CPU underpins every operation done on any given system, for databases in particular, the disk is likely to be the most problematic bottleneck. That's only logical—after all, databases store data on disk and then serve that data from disk. There are many layers of caches on top of slow and durable long-term storage, but they cannot always be utilized and are not infinitely large. Thus, understanding basic disk performance is extremely important when dealing with database systems. The other important and frequently underestimated property of any storage system is not related to performance at all—it's the capacity. We'll start with that.

Disk capacity and utilization refer to the total amount of data that can be stored on a given disk (or a lot of disks together in a storage system) and how much of that data is already stored. These are boring but important metrics. While it's not really necessary to monitor the disk capacity, as it's unlikely to change without you noticing, you absolutely must keep an eye on the disk utilization and available space.

Most databases only grow in size over time. MySQL in particular requires a healthy amount of available disk space headroom to accommodate table changes, long-running transactions, and spikes in write load. When there's no more disk space available for use by a MySQL database instance, it may crash or stop working and is unlikely to start working again until some space is freed up or more disk capacity is added. Depending on your circumstances, adding more capacity may take from minutes to days. That's something you probably want to plan for ahead of time.

Luckily, monitoring disk space usage is very easy. On Linux, it can be done using the simple `df` command. Without arguments, it will show capacity and usage in 1 KB blocks for every filesystem. You can add the `-h` argument to get human-readable measurements, and specify a mountpoint (or just a path) to limit the check. Here's an example:

```
$ df -h /var/lib/mysql
Filesystem      Size  Used Avail Use% Mounted on
/dev/sda1        40G   18G   23G  45% /
```

`df`'s output is self-explanatory, and it's one of the easiest tools to work with. We recommend that you try to keep your database mountpoints at 90% capacity unless you run multiterabyte systems. In that case, go higher. A trick that you can use is to put some large dummy files on the same filesystem as your database. Should you start running out of space, you can remove one or more of these files to give yourself some more time to react. Instead of relying on this trick, though, we recommend that you have some disk space monitoring in place.

On Windows, the trusty File Explorer can provide disk space utilization and capacity information, as shown in Figure 12-5.

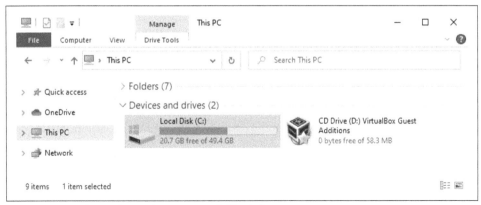

Figure 12-5. File Explorer showing available disk space

With disk space covered, we will now explore the key performance properties of any I/O subsystem:

Bandwidth
> How many bytes of data can be pushed to (or pulled from) storage per unit of time

I/O operations per second (IOPS)
> The number of operations a disk (or other storage system) is capable of serving per unit of time

Latency

How long it takes for a read or a write to be served by the storage system

These three properties are enough to describe any storage system and start forming an understanding of whether it's good, bad, or ugly. As we did in the CPU section, we'll show you a couple of tools to inspect disk performance and use their output to explain the specific metrics. We're again focusing on Linux and Windows; other systems will have something similar, so the knowledge is portable.

The I/O load analog to vmstat on Linux is the iostat program. The pattern of interaction should be familiar: invoke the command without arguments, and you get average values since boot; pass a number as an argument, and you get averages for the sampling period. We also prefer running the tool with the -x argument, which adds a lot of useful details. Unlike vmstat, iostat gives metrics broken down by a block device, similar to the mpstat command we mentioned earlier.

 iostat is usually installed as part of the sysstat package. Use apt on Ubuntu/Debian or yum on RHEL-based operating systems to install the package. You should be comfortable using these tools after following the instructions in Chapter 1.

Let's take a look at an example output. We'll use a iostat -dxyt 5 command, which translates to: print the device utilization report, display extended statistics, omit the first report with averages since boot, add the timestamp for each report, and report the average values over every 5-second period some sample output on a loaded system:

```
05/09/2021 04:45:09 PM
Device:        rrqm/s   wrqm/s   r/s        w/s     rkB/s       wkB/s...
sda              0.00     0.00   0.00    1599.00     0.00   204672.00...
...avgrq-sz avgqu-sz   await r_await  w_await  svctm    %util
...  256.00   141.67   88.63    0.00    88.63   0.63   100.00
```

There's quite a lot to unpack here. We won't cover every column, but we'll highlight the ones that correspond to properties we mentioned before:

Bandwidth

In iostat output, the columns rkB/s and wkB/s correspond to bandwidth utilization (read and write, respectively). If you know the characteristics of the underlying storage (for example, you may know it promises 200 MiB/s of combined read and write bandwidth), you can tell if you're pushing the limits. Here you can see a respectable figure of just over 200,000 KB per second being written to the /dev/sda device and no reads taking place.

IOPS

This metric is represented by the r/s and w/s columns, giving the number of read and write operations per second, respectively. Our example shows 1,599 write operation per second happening. As expected, no read operations are registered.

Latency

Shown in a slightly more complex manner, latency is broken down into four columns (or more, in newer iostat versions): await, r_await, w_await, and svctm. For a basic analysis you should be looking at the await value, which is the average latency for serving any request. r_await and w_await break await down by reads and writes. svctime is a deprecated metric, which attempts to show the pure device latency without any queueing.

Having these basic metric readings and knowing some basic facts about the storage used, it is possible to tell what's going on. Our example is running on a modern consumer-grade NVMe SSD in one of the author's laptops. While the bandwidth is pretty good, each request averages 88 ms, which is a lot. You can also do some simple math to get an I/O load pattern from these metrics. For example, if we divide bandwidth by IOPS, we get a figure of 128 KB per request. iostat does, actually, include that metric in the avgrq-sz column, which shows the average request size in a historical unit of *sectors* (512 bytes). You can go forward and measure that 1,599 writes per second can be served only at ~40 ms/request, meaning that there's parallel write load (and also that our device is capable of serving parallel requests).

I/O patterns—size of requests, degree of parallelism, random versus sequential—can shift the upper limits of the underlying storage. Most devices will advertise maximum bandwidth, maximum IOPS, and minimal latency at specific conditions, but these conditions may vary for maximum IOPS and maximum bandwidth measurements, as well as for optimal latency. It is rather difficult to definitely answer the question of whether metric readings are good or bad. Without knowing anything about the underlying storage, one way to look at utilization is to try to assess saturation. Saturation, which we'll touch on in "The USE Method" on page 474, is a measure of how overloaded a resource is. This becomes increasingly complicated with modern storage, capable of servicing long queues efficiently in parallel, but in general, queueing on a storage device is a sign of saturation. In the iostat output, that is the avgqu-sz column (or aqu-sz in newer versions of iostat), and values larger than 1 usually mean that a device is saturated. Our example shows a queue of 146 requests, which is a lot, likely telling us that I/O is highly utilized and may be a bottleneck.

Unfortunately, as you might've noticed, there's no simple straight measure of I/O utilization: there seems to be a caveat for every metric. Measuring storage performance is a difficult task!

The same metrics define storage devices on Linux, Windows, and any other OS.

Let's now take a look at basic Windows tools for assessing I/O performance. Their readings should be familiar by now. We recommend using the Resource Monitor, which we showed in the CPU section, but this time navigate to the Disk tab. Figure 12-6 shows that view with MySQL under heavy write load.

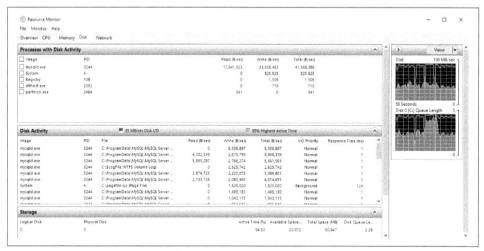

Figure 12-6. Resource Monitor showing IO load details

The metrics presented by the Resource Monitor are similar to those of `iostat`. You can see bandwidth, latency, and length of the request queue. One metric that's missing is IOPS. To get that information, you'll need to use the Performance Monitor (`perfmon`), but we'll leave that as an exercise.

The Resource Monitor actually shows a slightly more detailed view than `iostat`. There's a breakdown of I/O load per process, and a further breakdown of that load per file. We don't know of a single tool on Linux that is capable of showing load broken down like that simultaneously. To get the load breakdown per program, you can use the `pidstat` tool on Linux, which we mentioned before. Here's some example output:

```
# pidstat -d 5
...
10:50:01 AM   UID       PID   kB_rd/s   kB_wr/s kB_ccwr/s  Command
10:50:06 AM    27      4725      0.00  30235.06      0.00  mysqld

10:50:06 AM   UID       PID   kB_rd/s   kB_wr/s kB_ccwr/s  Command
10:50:11 AM    27      4725      0.00  23379.20      0.00  mysqld
...
```

Getting a breakdown per file on Linux is quite easily achieved using the BCC Toolkit, specifically the `filetop` tool. There are many more tools to explore in the toolkit, but most are quite advanced. The tools we've shown here should be enough to cover basic investigation and monitoring needs.

Memory

Memory, or RAM, is another important resource for any database. Memory offers vastly superior performance to disk for reading and writing data, and thus databases strive to operate "in memory" as much as possible. Unfortunately, memory is not persistent, so eventually every operation must be reflected on the disk. (For more on disk performance, refer to the previous section.)

In contrast to the CPU and disk sections, we won't actually be talking about memory performance. Even though it's important, it's also a very advanced and deep topic. Instead, we will be focusing on memory utilization. That can also get quite complex quite quickly, so we'll try to stay focused.

Let's start with some basic premises. Every program needs some memory to operate. Database systems, including MySQL, usually need a *lot* of memory. When you run out of it, applications start having performance issues and may even fail, as you'll see at the end of the section. Monitoring memory utilization therefore is crucial to any system's stability, but especially to a database system's.

In this case, we'll actually start with Windows, since on the surface it has slightly less convoluted memory accounting mechanism than Linux. To get the overall OS memory utilization on Windows, all you need to do is start the Task Manager, as described in "CPU" on page 428, navigate to the Performance tab, and pick Memory. You can see the Task Manager's memory usage display in Figure 12-7.

This machine has 4 GB of memory in total, with 2.4 GB being currently used and 1.6 GB available, making overall utilization 60%. This is a safe amount, and we may even want to allocate more memory to MySQL to minimize "wasted" free memory. Some ideas on MySQL's InnoDB buffer pool sizing can be found in "Buffer pool size" on page 421.

On Linux, the simplest tool to get memory utilization details is the `free` command. We recommend using it with the `-h` argument, which converts all fields to a human-readable format. Here's some sample output on a machine running CentOS 7:

```
$ free -h
              total        used        free      shared  buff/cache   available
Mem:           3.7G        2.7G        155M        8.5M        905M        787M
Swap:          2.0G         13M        2.0G
```

Figure 12-7. Task Manager showing memory utilization details

Now, that's more data than we saw on Windows. In reality, Windows has most of these counters; they are just not as visible.

Let's go through the output. For now, we'll be covering the Mem row, and we'll talk about Swap later.

The two key metrics here are used and available, which translate to the Task Manager's *In use* and *Available*. A frequent mistake, and one your authors used to make, is to look at the free metric instead of available. That's not correct! Linux (and, in fact, Windows) doesn't like to keep memory free. After all, free memory is a wasted resource. When there's memory available that's not needed by applications directly, Linux will use that memory to keep a cache of data being read and written from and to the disk. We'll show later that Windows does the same, but you cannot see that from the Task Manager. For more on why it's a mistake to focus on the free metric, see the site "Linux ate my ram" (*https://oreil.ly/qa88s*).

Let's further break down the output of this command. The columns are:

total
    Total amount of memory available on the machine

used
    Amount of memory currently used by applications

free
    Actual free memory not used by the OS at all

shared
    A special type of memory that needs to be specifically requested and allocated and that multiple processes can access together; because it's not used by MySQL, we're skipping the details here

buff/cache
    Amount of memory the OS is currently using as a cache to improve I/O

available
    Amount of memory that applications could use if they needed it; usually the sum of free and buff/cache

In general, for basic but robust monitoring, you only need to look at the total, used, and available amounts. Linux should be capable of handling the cached memory on its own. We're deliberately not covering the page cache here, as that's an advanced topic. By default, MySQL on Linux will utilize the page cache, so you should size your instance to accommodate for that. An often recommended change, however, is to tell MySQL to avoid the page cache (look for the documentation on innodb_flush_method), which will allow more memory to be used by MySQL itself.

We've mentioned that Windows has mostly the same metrics; they're just hidden. To see that, open the Resource Monitor and navigate to the Memory tab. Figure 12-8 shows the contents of this tab.

You'll immediately notice that the amount of free memory is just 52 MB, and there's a hefty chunk of standby memory, with a little bit of modified memory. The Cached value in the list below is the sum of the modified and standby amounts. When the screenshot was taken, 1,593 MB of memory was being used by cache, with 33 MB of that being dirty (or modified). Windows, like Linux, caches filesystem pages in an attempt to minimize and smooth I/O and utilize the memory to its fullest capacity.

Another thing you can see is a breakdown of memory utilization per process, with mysqld.exe holding just under 500 MB of memory. On Linux, a similar output can be obtained with the top command, which we first used in "CPU" on page 428. Once top is running, press Shift+M to sort the output by memory usage and get human-readable figures. top output showing memory usage details is in Figure 12-9.

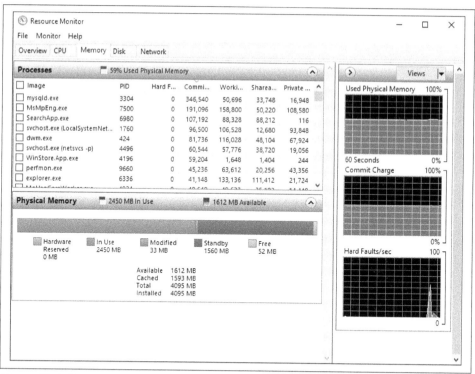

Figure 12-8. Resource Monitor showing memory utilization details

```
top - 19:59:54 up  1:37,  2 users,  load average: 0.02, 0.02, 0.05
Tasks: 113 total,   1 running, 112 sleeping,   0 stopped,   0 zombie
%Cpu(s):  0.0 us,  0.1 sy,  0.0 ni, 99.9 id,  0.0 wa,  0.0 hi,  0.0 si,  0.0 st
KiB Mem :  3880160 total,   144280 free,  2805208 used,   930672 buff/cache
KiB Swap:  2097148 total,  2083060 free,    14088 used.   794528 avail Mem

  PID USER      PR  NI    VIRT    RES    SHR S  %CPU %MEM     TIME+ COMMAND
 5576 mysql     20   0 4330756   2.5g  16468 S   0.3 66.7   0:27.77 mysqld
 5309 root      20   0  741500  80444  29052 S   0.0  2.1   0:02.14 dockerd
 5296 root      20   0  536684  45276  15272 S   0.0  1.2   0:01.60 containerd
 2722 root      20   0  574032  17244   6104 S   0.0  0.4   0:01.38 tuned
 2340 polkitd   20   0  613016  13300   5072 S   0.0  0.3   0:00.21 polkitd
 3832 root      20   0  625648   9000   6696 S   0.0  0.2   0:00.36 NetworkManager
    1 root      20   0  193696   6744   4192 S   0.0  0.2   0:02.19 systemd
 2724 root      20   0  216416   5772   2740 S   0.0  0.1   0:00.70 rsyslogd
 4552 root      20   0  154664   5528   4212 S   0.0  0.1   0:00.35 sshd
 6294 root      20   0  154664   5524   4212 S   0.0  0.1   0:00.17 sshd
 3857 root      20   0  107472   5436   3444 S   0.0  0.1   0:00.01 dhclient
 1215 root      20   0   47580   5056   2884 S   0.0  0.1   0:00.24 systemd-udevd
 6250 root      20   0  241280   4604   3440 S   0.0  0.1   0:00.03 sudo
 2721 root      20   0  112872   4340   3312 S   0.0  0.1   0:00.02 sshd
 2954 postfix   20   0   89832   4072   3068 S   0.0  0.1   0:00.02 qmgr
```

Figure 12-9. `top` showing memory utilization details

On this system the output is not very interesting, but you can quickly see that it's MySQL that consumes the most memory with its `mysqld` process.

Before finishing this section, we want to talk about what happens when you run out of memory. Before that, though, let's discuss swapping, or paging. We should mention here that most modern OSs implement memory management in such a way that individual applications each have their own view of the system's memory (hence you may see application memory being called *virtual* memory) and that the sum total of the virtual memory that applications can use exceeds the total actual memory capacity of the system. Discussion of the former point is better suited for a university course on operating system design, but the latter point is very important when running database systems.

The implications of this design are important, because an OS can't just magically extend the capacity of the system's memory. In fact, what happens is the OS uses disk storage to extend the amount of memory, and as we've mentioned, RAM is usually far more performant than even the fastest disk. Thus, as you can imagine, there's a price to pay for this memory extension. *Paging* can occur in a few different ways and for different reasons. Most important for MySQL is the type of paging called *swapping*—writing out parts of memory into a dedicated place on disk. On Linux, that place can be a separate partition, or a file. On Windows, there's a special file called *pagefile.sys* that has mostly the same use.

Swapping is not bad per se, but it's problematic for MySQL. The problem is that our database thinks it's reading something from memory, whereas in reality the OS has paged out some of that data into the swap file and will actually read it from disk. MySQL cannot predict when this situation will happen and can do nothing to prevent it or optimize the access. For the end user, this can mean a sudden unexplained drop in query response times. Having *some* swap space, though, is an important protective measure, as we'll show.

Let's move on to answer the question of what really happens when you run out of memory. In short: nothing good. There are only a couple of general outcomes for MySQL when the system is running out of memory, so let's talk through them:

- MySQL requests more memory from the OS, but there's none available—everything that could be paged out is not in memory, and the swap file is absent or already full. Usually, this situation results in a crash. That's a really bad outcome.
- On Linux, a variation of the preceding point is that the OS detects a situation where the system is close to running out of memory and forcefully terminates—in other words, kills one or more processes. Usually, the processes terminated will be the ones holding the most memory, and usually on a database server, MySQL will be the top memory consumer. This usually happens before the situation explained in the previous point.
- MySQL, or some other program, fills up memory to a point where the OS has to start swapping. This assumes the swap space (or pagefile in Windows) is set up.

As explained a few paragraphs back, MySQL's performance will degrade unexpectedly and unpredictably when its memory is swapped out. This arguably is a better outcome than just a crash or MySQL being terminated, but nevertheless it's something to avoid.

So, MySQL will either get slower, crash, or get killed, as simple as that. You now should see clearly why monitoring available and used memory is *very* important. We also recommend leaving some memory headroom on your servers and having a swap/pagefile set up. For some advice on Linux swap setup, see "Operating system best practices" on page 413.

Network

Of all the OS resources, the network is probably the one most frequently blamed for random unexplained issues. There's a good reason for that: monitoring the network is difficult. Understanding issues with the network sometimes requires a detailed analysis of the whole network stream. It's a peculiar resource because, unlike CPU, disk, and memory, it is not contained within a single server. At the very least, you need two machines communicating with each other for "network" to even be a factor. Of course, there are local connections, but they are usually stable. And granted, disk storage may be shared, and CPU and memory in case of virtual machines can be shared, too, but networking is *always* about multiple machines.

Since this chapter is about monitoring, we're not going to cover connectivity issues here—yet a surprising number of issues with networking boil down to the simple problem of one computer not being able to talk to another. Do not take connectivity for granted. Network topologies are usually complex, with each packet following a complicated route through multiple machines. In cloud environments, the routes can be even more complex and less obvious. If you think you have some network issues, it's wise to check that connections can be established at all.

We'll be touching on the following properties of any network:

Bandwidth and its utilization (throughput)
> This is similar to the same concept defined in "Disk" on page 436. Every network connection has a maximum bandwidth capacity, usually expressed as some unit of volume of data per second. Internet connections usually use Mbps or megabits per second, but MBps, or megabytes per second, can also be used. Network links and equipment put a hard cap on maximum bandwidth. For example, currently, common household network equipment rarely exceeds 1 Gbps bandwidth. More advanced data center equipment regularly supports 10 Gbps. Special equipment exists that can drive bandwidth to hundreds of Gbps, but such connections are usually unrouted direct connections between two servers.

Errors—their number and sources

Network errors are unavoidable. In fact, the Transmission Control Protocol (TCP), a backbone of the internet and a protocol used by MySQL, is built around the premise that packets will be lost. You'll undoubtedly see errors from time to time, but having a high rate of errors will cause connections to be slow, as communicating parties will need to resend packets over and over.

Continuing the analogy with the disk, we could also include latency and number of packets sent and received (loosely resembling IOPS). However, packet transmission latency can be measured only by the application that's doing the actual transmission. The OS can't measure and show some average latency for a network. And the number of packets is usually redundant, as it follows the bandwidth and throughput figures.

One particular metric that is useful to add when looking at networks is the number of *retransmitted* packets. Retransmission happens when a packet is lost or damaged. It is not an error, but is usually a result of some issues with the connection. Just like running out of bandwidth, an increased number of retransmissions will lead to choppy network performance.

On Linux, we can start by looking at the network interface statistics. The easiest way to do this is to run the `ifconfig` command. Its output by default will include every network interface on a particular host. Since we know in this case all load comes through `eth1`, we can show only stats for that:

```
$ ifconfig eth1
...
eth1: flags=4163<UP,BROADCAST,RUNNING,MULTICAST>  mtu 1500
        inet 192.168.10.11  netmask 255.255.255.0  broadcast 192.168.10.255
        inet6 fe80::a00:27ff:fef6:b4f  prefixlen 64  scopeid 0x20<link>
        ether 08:00:27:f6:0b:4f  txqueuelen 1000  (Ethernet)
        RX packets 6217203  bytes 735108061 (701.0 MiB)
        RX errors 0  dropped 0  overruns 0  frame 0
        TX packets 11381894  bytes 18025086781 (16.7 GiB)
        TX errors 0  dropped 0 overruns 0  carrier 0  collisions 0
...
```

We can immediately see that the network is pretty healthy just by the fact that there are no errors receiving (RX) or sending (TX) packets. The RX and TX total data stats (701.0 MiB and 16.7 GiB, respectively) will grow each time you run `ifconfig`, so you can easily measure bandwidth utilization by running it over time. That's not terribly convenient, and there are programs that show transmission rates in real time, but none of those ships by default in common Linux distributions. To see a history of the transmission rate and errors, you can use the `sar -n DEV` or `sar -n EDEV` command, respectively (`sar` is a part of the `sysstat` package we mentioned when talking about `iostat`):

```
$ sar -n DEV
                IFACE   rxpck/s   txpck/s    rxkB/s    txkB/s...
06:30:01 PM     eth0       0.16      0.08      0.01      0.01...
06:30:01 PM     eth1    7269.55  13473.28    843.84  21618.70...
06:30:01 PM       lo       0.00      0.00      0.00      0.00...
06:40:01 PM     eth0       0.48      0.28      0.03      0.05...
06:40:01 PM     eth1    7844.90  13941.09    893.95  19204.10...
06:40:01 PM       lo       0.00      0.00      0.00      0.00...
...rxcmp/s   txcmp/s  rxmcst/s
...   0.00      0.00      0.00
...   0.00      0.00      0.00
...   0.00      0.00      0.00
...   0.00      0.00      0.00
...   0.00      0.00      0.00
...   0.00      0.00      0.00

$ sar -n EDEV
04:30:01 PM     IFACE    rxerr/s   txerr/s    coll/s  rxdrop/s...
06:40:01 PM     eth0       0.00      0.00      0.00      0.00...
06:40:01 PM     eth1       0.00      0.00      0.00      0.00...
06:40:01 PM       lo       0.00      0.00      0.00      0.00...
...txdrop/s  txcarr/s  rxfram/s  rxfifo/s  txfifo/s
...   0.00      0.00      0.00      0.00      0.00
...   0.00      0.00      0.00      0.00      0.00
...   0.00      0.00      0.00      0.00      0.00
```

Again, we see that in our example interface eth1 is quite loaded, but there are no errors being reported. If we stay within bandwidth limits, network performance should be normal.

To get a full detailed view of the various errors and issues that have happened within the network, you can use the netstat command. With the -s flag, it will report a lot of counters. To keep things basic, we will show just the Tcp section of the output, with a number of retransmits. For a more detailed overview, check the TcpExt section of the output:

```
$ netstat -s
...
Tcp:
    55 active connections openings
    39 passive connection openings
    0 failed connection attempts
    3 connection resets received
    9 connections established
    14449654 segments received
    25994151 segments send out
    54 segments retransmitted
    0 bad segments received.
    19 resets sent
...
```

Considering the sheer number of segments sent out, the retransmission rate is excellent. This network seems to be fine.

On Windows, we again resort to checking the Resource Monitor, which provides most of the metrics we want, and more. Figure 12-10 shows network-related views the Resource Monitor has to offer on a host running a synthetic load against MySQL.

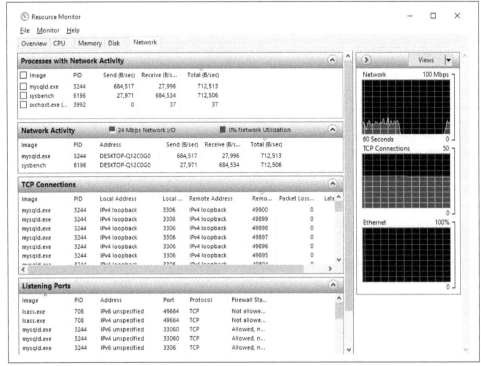

Figure 12-10. Resource Monitor showing network utilization details

To get a reading on the number of errors on Windows, you can use the `netstat` command. Note that even though it has the same name as the Linux tool we used previously, they are slightly different. In this case, we have no errors:

```
C:\Users\someuser> netstat -e
Interface Statistics

                        Received            Sent
Bytes                   58544920            7904968
Unicast packets         62504               32308
Non-unicast packets     0                   364
Discards                0                   0
Errors                  0                   0
Unknown protocols       0
```

The `-s` modifier for `netstat` exists on Windows, too. Again, we're only showing a part of the output here:

```
C:\Users\someuser> netstat -s
...
TCP Statistics for IPv4

    Active Opens                      = 457
    Passive Opens                     = 30
    Failed Connection Attempts        = 3
    Reset Connections                 = 121
    Current Connections               = 11
    Segments Received                 = 61237201
    Segments Sent                     = 30866526
    Segments Retransmitted            = 0
...
```

Judging by the metrics we highlighted for monitoring—bandwidth utilization and errors—this system's network is operating perfectly fine. We understand this is barely scratching the surface when it comes to the complexity of networking. However, this minimal set of tools can help you out immensely in understanding whether you should be blaming your network at all.

That finishes a pretty lengthy overview of OS monitoring basics. We could probably have kept it shorter, and you may ask why we put all this in a book about MySQL. The answer is pretty simple: because it is important. Any program interacts with an OS and requires some of the system's resources. MySQL, by nature, is usually going to be a very demanding program, which you expect to be performing well. For that, however, you need to make sure that you have the necessary resources and you're not running out of a performance capacity for disk, CPU, or network, or just out of capacity for disk and memory. Sometimes, an issue with system resources caused by MySQL can also lead you to uncover issues within MySQL itself. For example, a badly written query may put a lot of load on the CPU and disk while causing a spike in memory usage. The next section shows some basic ways to monitor and diagnose a running MySQL server.

MySQL Server Observability

Monitoring MySQL is simultaneously easy and difficult. It's easy, because MySQL exposes almost 500 status variables, which allow you to see almost exactly what is going on inside your database. In addition to that, InnoDB has its own diagnostic output. Monitoring is hard, though, because it may be tricky to make sense of the data you have.

In this section, we're going to explain the basics of MySQL monitoring, starting with going over what the status variables are and how to get them, and moving on to InnoDB's diagnostics. Once that's covered, we'll show a few basic recipes we believe should be a part of every MySQL database monitoring suite. With these recipes and what you learned about OS monitoring in the previous section, you should be able to understand what's going on with your system.

Status Variables

We'll start with MySQL's *server status variables*. These variables, unlike configuration options, are read-only, and they show you information about the current state of the MySQL server. They vary in nature: most of them are either ever-increasing counters, or gauges with values moving up and down. Some, though, are static text fields, which are helpful to understand the current server configuration. All status variables can be accessed at the global server level and at the current session level. But not every variable makes sense on a session level, and some will show the same values on both levels.

SHOW STATUS is used to get the current status variable values. It has two optional modifiers, GLOBAL and SESSION, and defaults to SESSION. You can also specify the name of a variable, or a pattern, but that's not mandatory. The command in the following example shows all the status variable values for the current session:

```
mysql> SHOW STATUS;
+-------------------------------------------+---------------------+
| Variable_name                             | Value               |
+-------------------------------------------+---------------------+
| Aborted_clients                           | 0                   |
| Aborted_connects                          | 0                   |
| Acl_cache_items_count                     | 0                   |
| ...                                       |                     |
| Threads_connected                         | 2                   |
| Threads_created                           | 2                   |
| Threads_running                           | 2                   |
| Uptime                                    | 305662              |
| Uptime_since_flush_status                 | 305662              |
| validate_password.dictionary_file_last_parsed | 2021-05-22 20:53:08 |
| validate_password.dictionary_file_words_count | 0                   |
+-------------------------------------------+---------------------+
482 rows in set (0.01 sec)
```

Scrolling through hundreds of rows of output is suboptimal, so let's instead use a wildcard to limit the number of variables we request. LIKE in SHOW STATUS works the same as it does for regular SELECT statements, as explained in Chapter 3:

```
mysql> SHOW STATUS LIKE 'Created%';
```

```
+-------------------------+-------+
| Variable_name           | Value |
+-------------------------+-------+
| Created_tmp_disk_tables | 0     |
| Created_tmp_files        | 7     |
| Created_tmp_tables       | 0     |
+-------------------------+-------+
3 rows in set (0.01 sec)
```

Now the output is much easier to read. To read the value of a single variable, just specify its full name within quotes without the wildcard, like so:

```
mysql> SHOW STATUS LIKE 'Com_show_status';

+-----------------+-------+
| Variable_name   | Value |
+-----------------+-------+
| Com_show_status | 11    |
+-----------------+-------+
1 row in set (0.00 sec)
```

You might notice in the output for the Created% status variables that MySQL showed a value of 7 for Created_tmp_files. Does that mean this session created seven temporary files, while creating zero temporary tables? No—in fact, the Cre ated_tmp_files status variable has only a global scope. This is a known issue with MySQL at the moment: you always see all status variables, regardless of the requested scope, but their values will be properly scoped. The MySQL documentation includes a helpful "Server Status Variable Reference" (*https://oreil.ly/kgYBx*) that can help you understand the scope of the different variables.

Unlike Created_tmp_files, the Com_show_status variable has scope "both," meaning that you can get a global counter as well as a per-session value. Let's see that in practice:

```
mysql> SHOW STATUS LIKE 'Com_show_status';

+-----------------+-------+
| Variable_name   | Value |
+-----------------+-------+
| Com_show_status | 13    |
+-----------------+-------+
1 row in set (0.00 sec)

mysql> SHOW GLOBAL STATUS LIKE 'Com_show_status';

+-----------------+-------+
| Variable_name   | Value |
+-----------------+-------+
| Com_show_status | 45    |
+-----------------+-------+
1 row in set (0.00 sec)
```

Another important thing to note when looking at the status variables is that it's possible to reset most of them back to zero on a session level. That is achieved by running the FLUSH STATUS command. This command resets status variables within all connected sessions to zero, after adding their current values to the global counters. Thus, FLUSH STATUS operates on a session level, but for all sessions. To illustrate this, we'll reset the status variable values in the session we used before:

```
mysql> FLUSH STATUS;

Query OK, 0 rows affected (0.00 sec)

mysql> SHOW STATUS LIKE 'Com_show_status';

+-----------------+-------+
| Variable_name   | Value |
+-----------------+-------+
| Com_show_status | 1     |
+-----------------+-------+
1 row in set (0.00 sec)

mysql> SHOW GLOBAL STATUS LIKE 'Com_show_status';

+-----------------+-------+
| Variable_name   | Value |
+-----------------+-------+
| Com_show_status | 49    |
+-----------------+-------+
1 row in set (0.00 sec)
```

Even though the global counter keeps on increasing, the session counter was reset to 0 and incremented to only 1 when we ran the SHOW STATUS command. This can be useful to see in isolation how, for example, running a single query changes the status variable values (in particular, the Handler_* family of status variables).

Note that it's impossible to reset global counters without a restart.

Basic Monitoring Recipes

You could monitor numerous metrics, in different combinations. We believe, however, that there are a few that must be in the toolbox of every database operator. While you are learning MySQL, these should be enough to give you a reasonable sense of how your database is doing. Most of the existing monitoring systems should have these covered and usually include many more metrics. You may never set up collection yourself, but our explanation should also allow you to get a better understanding of just what your monitoring system tells you.

We're going to give few broad categories of metrics in the following subsections, within which we'll detail what we think are some of the more important counters.

MySQL server availability

This is the most important thing you should monitor. If MySQL Server is not accepting connections or is not running, all the other metrics don't matter at all.

MySQL Server is a robust piece of software that's capable of running with an uptime of months or years. Yet, there are situations that can lead to a premature unplanned shutdown (or, more plainly, a crash). For example, in "Memory" on page 441 we discussed that out-of-memory conditions may lead to MySQL crashing or being killed. Other incidents happen, too. There are crashing bugs in MySQL, however rare they are nowadays. There are also operational mistakes: who hasn't forgotten to bring up a database after planned maintenance? Hardware fails, servers restart—many things may compromise the availability of MySQL.

There are a few approaches to monitoring MySQL availability, and there's no single best one; it's better to combine a few. A very simple basic approach is to check that the mysqld (or mysqld.exe) process is actually running and visible from the OS level. On Linux and Unix-like systems you can use the ps command for this, and on Windows, you can check the Task Manager or run the Get-Service PowerShell command. This is not a useless check, but it has its issues. For one, the fact that MySQL is running does not guarantee that it's actually doing what it should be—that is, processing clients' queries. MySQL could be swamped by load or suffering from a disk failure and running unbearably slowly. From the OS's perspective, the process is running, but from the client's perspective it's as good as shut down anyway.

The second approach is to check MySQL's availability from the application's point of view. Usually, that's achieved by running the MySQL monitor and executing some simple, short query. Unlike the previous check, this one makes sure that a new connection to MySQL can be established and that the database is processing queries. You can locate these checks on the application side to make them even closer to how apps see the database. Instead of setting up such checks as independent entities, applications can be adjusted to probe MySQL and report clear errors either to operators or to the monitoring system.

The third approach lies between the previous two and is concentrated on the DB side. While monitoring MySQL, you will at least need to execute simple queries against the database to check status variables. If those queries fail, your monitoring system should alert, as potentially MySQL is starting to have issues. A variation would be to check whether any data from the target instance has been received by your monitoring system in the last few minutes.

What ideally should come out of these checks is not only the alert "MySQL is down" at the appropriate time but also some clue as to why it is down. For example, if the second type of check cannot initiate a new connection because MySQL has run out of connections, then that should be a part of the alert. If the third type of check is failing, but the first type is okay, then it's a different situation than a crash.

Client connections

MySQL Server is a multithreaded program, as was laid out in depth in "The MySQL Server Daemon" on page 411. Every client connecting to a database causes a new thread to be spawned within the process of the MySQL server (mysqld or mysqld.exe). That thread will be responsible for executing statements sent by a client, and in theory there can be as many concurrent queries executing as there are client threads.

Each connection and its thread put some low overhead on the MySQL server, even when they are idle. Apart from that, from the database's point of view, each connection is a liability: the database cannot know when a connection will send a statement. *Concurrency*, or the number of simultaneously running transactions and queries, usually increases with an increase in the number of established connections. Concurrency is not bad in itself, but each system will have a limit of scalability. As you'll remember from "Operating System Metrics" on page 428, CPU and disk resources have performance limits, and it's impossible to push past them. And even with an infinite amount of OS resources, MySQL itself has internal scalability limits.

To put it simply: the number of connections, especially active connections, should ideally be kept minimal. From the MySQL side, no connections is the perfect situation, but from the application side that's unacceptable. Some applications, though, make no attempt at limiting the number of connections they make and queries they send, assuming that the database will take care of the load. This can create a dangerous situation known as a *thundering herd*: for some reason, queries run longer, and the app reacts by sending more and more queries, overloading the database.

Finally, MySQL has an upper limit on the number of client connections, controlled by the system variable max_connections. Once the number of existing connections hits the value of that variable, MySQL will refuse to create new connections. That's a bad thing. max_connections should be used as a protection from complete server meltdown if clients establish thousands of connections. But ideally, you should monitor the number of connections and work with the app teams to keep that number low.

Let's review the specific connection and thread counters that MySQL exposes:

Threads_connected
: Number of currently connected client threads, or in other words number of established client connections. We've been explaining the importance of this one for the last few paragraphs, so you should know why you have to check it.

Threads_running

Number of client threads that are currently executing a statement. Whereas Threads_connected indicates a potential for high concurrency, Threads_running actually shows the current measure of that concurrency. Spikes in this counter indicate either an increased load from the application or a slowness in the database leading to queries stacking up.

Max_used_connections

Maximum number of connections established that was recorded since the last MySQL server restart. If you suspect that a connection flood happened, but don't have a recorded history of changes in Threads_connected, you can check this status variable to see the highest peak recorded.

Max_used_connections_time

Date and time when MySQL Server saw the maximum number of connections since the last restart to date.

Another important metric to monitor about connections is their rate of failure. An increased rate of errors may indicate that your applications are having trouble communicating with your database. MySQL distinguishes between connections that clients failed to establish and existing connections that failed due to a timeout, for example:

Aborted_clients

Number of already established connections that were aborted. The MySQL documentation mentions "the client died without closing the connection properly," but this can also happen if there's a network issue between the server and client. Frequent sources of increases in this counter are max_allowed_packet violations (see "Scope of Options" on page 356) and session timeouts (see the wait_timeout and interactive_timeout system variables). Some errors are to be expected, but sharp spikes should be checked.

Aborted_connects

Number of new connections that failed to be established. Causes include incorrect passwords, connecting to a database for which the user has no permission, protocol mismatches, connect_timeout violations, and reaching max_connec tions, among other things. They also include various network-related issues. There's a family of status variables under the Connection_errors_% wildcard that look in more depth into some of the specific issues. An increase in Aborted_con nects should be checked, as it can indicate an application configuration issue (wrong user/password) or a database issue (running out of connections).

MySQL Enterprise Edition, Percona Server, and MariaDB offer a thread pool functionality. This changes the connection and thread accounting. With a thread pool, the number of connections stays the same, but the number of threads running within MySQL is limited by the size of the pool. When a connection needs to execute a statement, it will have to get an available thread from the pool and wait if such a thread is not available. Using a thread pool improves MySQL performance with hundreds or thousands of connections. Since this feature is not available in regular MySQL and we believe it's an advanced one, we're not covering it in this book.

Query counts

The next broad category of metrics is query-related metrics. Where `Threads_running` shows how many sessions are active at once, metrics in this category will show the quality of the load those sessions produce. Here, we'll start by looking at the overall amount of queries, then move on to breaking down queries by type, and last but not least we'll look into how the queries execute.

It's important to monitor query counts. Thirty running threads may each be executing a single hour-long query, or a few dozen queries per second. The conclusions you make will be completely different in each case, and the load profile will likely change, too. These are the important metrics showing the number of queries executed:

Queries

This global status variable, simply put, gives the number of statements executed by the server (excluding COM_PING and COM_STATISTICS). If you run SHOW GLOBAL STATUS LIKE 'Queries' on an idle server, you will see the counter value increasing with each execution of the SHOW STATUS command.

Questions

Almost the same as Queries, but excludes statements executed within stored procedures, and also the following types of queries: COM_PING, COM_STATISTICS, COM_STMT_PREPARE, COM_STMT_CLOSE, or COM_STMT_RESET. Unless your database clients use stored procedures extensively, the Questions metric is closer to the amount of actual queries being executed by the server, compared to the amount of statements in Queries. In addition to that, Questions is both a session-level and a global status variable.

 Both Queries and Questions are incremented when the query starts executing, so it's necessary to also look at the Threads_running value to see how many queries are actually being executed right now.

QPS

Queries per second. This is a synthetic metric that you can arrive at by looking at how the `Queries` variable changes over time. QPS based on `Queries` will include almost any statement that the server executes.

The QPS metric does not tell us about the quality of queries executed—that is, the extent of their impact on the server—but it's a useful gauge nevertheless. Usually, the load on a database from applications is regular. It may move in waves (more during the day, fewer at night), but over a week or a month a pattern of number of queries over time will show. When you get a report about a database being slow, looking at QPS may give you a quick indication of whether there's been a sudden unexpected growth in application load. A drop in QPS, on the other hand, may indicate that issues are on the database side, as it cannot process as many queries as usual in the same time.

Query types and quality

The next logical step from knowing the QPS is understanding what types of queries are being executed by the clients, and the impact of those queries on the server. All queries are not equal, and some, you may say, are *bad*, or produce unnecessary load on the system. Looking for and catching such queries is an important part of monitoring. In this section we're trying to answer the question "are there a lot of bad queries?" and in "The Slow Query Log" on page 467 we'll show you how to catch the specific offenders.

Types of queries.   Each query MySQL executes has a type. What's more, any *command* that you can execute has a type. MySQL keeps track of the different types of commands and queries executed with the `Com_%` family of status variables. There are 172 of these variables in MySQL 8.0.25, accounting for almost a third of all status variables. As you can guess from this number, MySQL counts a lot of commands that you perhaps wouldn't even think of: for example, `Com_uninstall_plugin` counts the number of times UNINSTALL PLUGIN was called, and `Com_help` counts uses of the HELP statment.

Every `Com_%` status variable is available on both the global and session levels, as was shown with `Com_show_status` in "Status Variables" on page 451. However, MySQL doesn't expose other threads' counters for `Com_%` variables, so for monitoring purposes, global status variables are assumed here. It's possible to get other sessions' statement counters, but that's achieved through the Performance Schema family of events, called `statement/sql/%`. That can be useful to attempt to find a thread that's sending a disproportional amount of some type of statement, but it's a bit advanced and falls under investigation rather than monitoring. You can find more details in the "Performance Schema Status Variable Tables" section (*https://oreil.ly/6wif5*) of the MySQL documentation.

Since there are so many Com_% status variables, monitoring every type of command would be both too noisy and unnecessary. You should, however, try to store the values of all of them. You can go two ways with looking at these counters.

The first option is to pick the command types that are relevant for your database load profile, and monitor those. For example, if your database clients do not use stored procedures, then looking at Com_call_procedure is a waste of time. A good starting selection is to cover SELECT and basic DML statements, which usually comprise the bulk of any database system's load—for example, Com_select, Com_insert, Com_update, and Com_delete (the status variables' names are self-explanatory here). One interesting thing MySQL does is account for multitable updates and deletes (see "Performing Updates and Deletes with Multiple Tables" on page 281) separately, under Com_update_multi and Com_delete_multi; these should also be monitored, unless you're sure such statements are never run in your system.

You can then look at all of the Com_% status variables, see which ones are growing, and add those to your selection of monitored variables. Unfortunately, the flaw with this approach is that you can miss some unexpected spikes.

Another way of looking at these counters could be to look at the top 5 or 10 of them over time. This way, a sudden change of load pattern can be more difficult to miss.

Knowing what types of queries are running is important in shaping an overall understanding of the load on a given database. Moreover, it changes how you approach tuning the database, because, for example, an insert-heavy workload may require a different setup compared to a read-only or mostly-read workload. Changes in query load profile, like a sudden appearance of thousands of UPDATE statements executed per second, can indicate changes on the application side.

Query quality.   The next step after knowing what queries are running is to understand their quality, or their impact on the system. We mentioned this, but it's worth reiterating: all queries are not equal. Some will put more burden on the system than others. Looking at the overall query-related metrics may give you advance warning of problems growing in the database. You will learn that it's possible to notice problematic behaviors by monitoring just a few counters.

Select_scan counts the number of queries that caused a full table scan, or in other words forced MySQL to read the whole table to form the result. Now, we should immediately acknowledge that full table scans are not always a problem. After all, sometimes just reading all of the data in a table is a viable query execution strategy, especially when the number of rows is low. You can also expect to always see some amount of full table scans happening, as a lot of MySQL catalog tables are read that way. For example, just running a SHOW GLOBAL STATUS query will cause Select_scan to increase by two. Often, however, full table scans imply that there are queries hitting the database that are performing suboptimally: either they are improperly written and don't filter out data efficiently, or there are simply no indexes that the queries can use. We give more information about query execution details and plans in "The EXPLAIN Statement" on page 292.

Select_full_join is similar to Select_scan, but counts the number of queries that caused a full table scan on a referenced table within a JOIN query. The referenced table is the rightmost table in the JOIN condition—see "Joining Two Tables" on page 109 for more information. Again, as with Select_scan, it's hard to say that a high Select_full_join count is always bad. It's common in large data warehouse systems, for example, to have compact dictionary tables, and reading those fully may not be a problem. Still, usually a high value for this status variable indicates the presence of badly behaving queries.

Select_range counts the number of queries that scanned data with some range condition (covered in "Selecting Rows with the WHERE Clause" on page 96). Usually this is not a problem at all. If the range condition is not possible to satisfy using an index, then the value of Select_scan or Select_full_join will grow alongside this status variable. Probably the only time when this counter's value may indicate an issue is when you see it growing even though you know that most of the queries running in the database in fact do not utilize ranges. As long as the associated table scan counters aren't growing as well, the issue is likely still benign.

Select_full_range_join combines Select_range and Select_full_join. This variable holds a counter for queries that caused a range scan on referenced tables in JOIN queries.

So far, we've been counting individual queries, but MySQL also does a similar accounting for *every row* it reads from the storage engines! The family of status variables showing those counters are the Handler_% variables. Simply put, every row MySQL reads increments some Handler_% variable. Combining this information with the query type and query quality counters you've seen so far can tell you, for example, if full table scans that run in your database are a problem at all.

The first handler we'll look at is Handler_read_rnd_next, which counts the number of rows read when a full or partial table scan is performed. Unlike the Select_% status variables, the Handler_% variables do not have nice, easy-to-remember names, so some memorization is necessary. High values in the Handler_read_rnd_next status variable in general indicate that either a lot of tables are not indexed properly or many queries do not utilize the existing indexes. Remember we mentioned when explaining Select_scan that some full table scans are not problematic. To see whether that's true or not in your case, look at the ratio of Handler_read_rnd_next to other handlers. You want to see a low value for that counter. If your database returns on average a million rows per minute, then you probably want the number of rows returned by full scans to be in the thousands, not tens or hundreds of thousands.

Handler_read_rnd counts the number of rows usually read when the sorting of a result set is performed. High values may indicate the presence of many full table scans and joins not using indexes. However, unlike with Handler_read_rnd_next, this is not a sure sign of problems.

Handler_read_first counts how many times the first index entry was read. A high value for this counter indicates that a lot of full index scans are occurring. This is better than full table scans, but still a problematic behavior. Likely, some of the queries are missing filters in their WHERE clauses. The value of this status variable should again be viewed in relation to the other handlers, as some full index scans are unavoidable.

Handler_read_key counts the number of rows read by an index. You want this handler's value to be high compared to other read-related handlers. In general, a high number here means your queries are using indexes properly.

Note that handlers still can hide some issues. If a query only reads rows using indexes, but does so inefficiently, then Select_scan will not be increased, and Handler_read_key—our good read handler—will grow, but the end result will still be a slow query. We explain how to find specific slow queries in "The Slow Query Log" on page 467, but there's also a special counter for them: Slow_queries. This status variable counts the queries that took longer than the value of Long_query_time to execute, regardless of whether the slow query log is enabled. You can gradually drop the value of Long_query_time and see when Slow_queries starts to approach the total number of queries executed by your server. This is a good way to assess how many queries in your system take, for example, longer than a second without actually turning on the slow query log, which has an overhead.

Not every query executed is read-only, and MySQL also counts the number of rows inserted, updated, or deleted under, respectively, the Handler_insert, Handler_update, and Handler_delete status variables. Unlike with SELECT queries, it's hard to make conclusions about the quality of your write statements based on the status variables alone. However, you can monitor these to see if, for example, your database clients start updating more rows. Without a change in the number of UPDATE statements (the Com_update and Com_update_multi status variables), that may indicate a change in the parameters passed to the same queries: wider ranges, more items in the IN clauses, and so on. This may not indicate a problem on its own, but it may be used during investigation of slowness to see whether more strain is being put on the database.

Apart from INSERT statements, UPDATE, DELETE, and even INSERT SELECT statements have to look for rows to change. Thus, for example, a DELETE statement will increase read-related counters and may result in an unexpected situation: no Select_scan growth, but an increasing `Handler_read_rnd_next` value. Do not forget about this peculiarity if you see a discrepancy between status variables. The slow query log will include `SELECT` as well as DML statements.

Temporary objects. Sometimes, when queries execute, MySQL needs to create and use temporary objects, which may reside in memory or on disk. Examples of reasons for temporary object creation include use of the `UNION` clause, derived tables, common table expressions, and some variations of `ORDER BY` and `GROUP BY` clauses, among other things. We've been saying this about almost everything in this chapter, but temporary objects are not a problem: some number of them is unavoidable and actually desired. Yet they do eat into your server's resources: if temporary tables are small enough, they'll be kept in memory and use it up, and if they grow large, MySQL will start offloading them to disk, using up both the disk space and affecting performance.

MySQL maintains three status variables related to temporary objects created during query execution. Note that this doesn't include temporary tables created explicitly through the `CREATE TEMPORARY TABLE` statement; look for those under the `Com_cre ate_table` counter.

`Created_tmp_tables` counts the number of temporary tables created implicitly by MySQL server while executing various queries. You cannot know why or for which queries these were created, but every table will be accounted for here. Under a stable workload, you should see a uniform number of temporary tables created, as roughly the same queries run the same amount of times. Growth of this counter is usually associated with changing queries or their plans, for example due to growth of the database, and may be problematic. Although useful, creating temporary tables, even in memory, takes resources. You cannot completely avoid temporary tables, but you should check why their number is growing by performing a query audit with the slow query log, for example.

`Created_tmp_disk_tables` counts the number of temporary tables that "spilled," or were written to disk after their size surpassed the configured upper limits for in-memory temporary tables. With the older Memory engine, the limit was controlled by `tmp_table_size` or `max_heap_table_size`. MySQL 8.0 moved by default to a new TempTable engine for the temporary tables, which, by default, does not spill to disk in the same way Memory tables did. If the `temptable_use_mmap` variable is set to its default of `ON`, then TempTable temporary tables do not increase this variable even if they are written to disk.

`Created_tmp_files` counts the number of temporary files created by MySQL. This is different from Memory engine temporary tables spilling to disk, but will account for TempTable tables being written out to disk. We understand that this may seem complicated, and it truly is, but major changes don't usually come without some downsides.

Whatever configuration you're using, sizing the temporary tables is important, as is monitoring the rate of their creation and spillage. If a workload creates a lot of temporary tables of roughly 32 MB in size, but the upper limit for in-memory tables is 16 MB, then the server will see an increased rate of I/O due to those tables being written out to and read back from the disk. That's fine for a server strapped for memory, but it's a waste if you have memory available. Conversely, setting the upper limit too high may result in the server swapping or outright crashing, as explained in "Memory" on page 441.

We've seen servers brought down by memory spikes when lots of simultaneously open connections all ran queries requiring temporary tables. We've also seen servers where the bulk of I/O load was produced by temporary tables spilling to disk. As with most things related to operating databases, the table sizing decision is a balancing act. The three counters we've shown can help you make an informed choice.

InnoDB I/O and transaction metrics

So far, we've been mostly talking about overall MySQL metrics and ignoring the fact that there are things like transactions and locking. In this subsection we'll take a look at some of the useful metrics the InnoDB storage engine exposes. Some of those metrics relate to how much data InnoDB reads and writes, and why. Some, however, can show important information on locking, which can be combined with MySQL-wide counters to get a solid grasp on the current locking situation in a database.

The InnoDB storage engine provides 61 status variables showing various information about its internal state. By looking at their change over time you can see how loaded InnoDB is and how much load on the OS it produces. Given that InnoDB is the default storage engine, that will likely be most of the load MySQL produces.

We perhaps should've put these in the section about query quality, but InnoDB maintains its own counters for the number of rows it has read, inserted, updated, or deleted. The variables are, respectfully, `Inndb_rows_read`, `Inndb_rows_inserted`, `Inndb_rows_updated`, and `Inndb_rows_deleted`. Usually their values correspond pretty well to the values of the related `Handler_%` variables. If you primarily use InnoDB tables, it may be simpler to use the `Innodb_rows_%` counters instead of the `Handler_%` ones to monitor relative load from queries expressed in the number of rows processed.

Other important and useful status variables InnoDB provides show the amount of data that the storage engine reads and writes. In "Disk" on page 436 we saw how to check and monitor overall and per-process I/O utilization. InnoDB allows you to see exactly why it's reading and writing data, and how much of it:

Innodb_data_read

> The amount of data expressed in bytes read from disk since server startup. If you take measurements of this variable's value over time, you can translate it into bandwidth utilization in bytes/second. This metric is tightly related to InnoDB buffer pool sizing and its effectiveness, and we'll get to that in a bit. All of this data can be assumed to be read from the data files to satisfy queries.

Innodb_data_written

> The amount of data expressed in bytes written to disk since server startup. This is the same as Innodb_data_read, but in the other direction. Usually, this value will account for a large portion of the overall amount of write bandwidth MySQL will generate. Unlike with reading data, InnoDB writes data out in a variety of situations; thus, there are additional variables specifying parts of this I/O, as well as other sources of I/O.

Innodb_os_log_written

> The amount of data expressed in bytes written by InnoDB into its redo logs. This amount is also included in Innodb_data_written, but it's worth monitoring individually to see if your redo logs may need a size change. See "Redo log size" on page 422 for more details.

Innodb_pages_written

> The amount of data expressed in pages (16 KiB by default) written by InnoDB during its operation. This is the second half of the Innodb_data_written status variable. It's useful to see the amount of non-redo I/O that InnoDB generates.

Innodb_buffer_pool_pages_flushed

> The amount of data expressed in pages written by InnoDB due to flushing. Unlike the writes covered by two previous counters, writes caused by flushing do not happen immediately after an actual write is performed. Flushing is a complex background operation, the details of which are beyond the scope of our book. However, you should at least know that flushing exists and that it generates I/O independent of other counters.

By combining Innodb_data_written and Innodb_buffer_pool_pages_flushed, you should be able to come up with a pretty accurate figure for the disk bandwidth utilized by InnoDB and MySQL Server. Adding Innodb_data_read completes the I/O profile of InnoDB. MySQL doesn't only use InnoDB, and there can be I/O from other parts of the system, like temporary tables spilling to disk, as we discussed earlier. Yet often InnoDB I/O matches that of MySQL Server observed from the OS.

One use of this information is to see how close your MySQL Server is to hitting the limits of your storage system's performance capacity. This is especially important in the cloud where storage often has strict limits. During incidents related to database performance, you can check the I/O-related counters to see if MySQL is writing or reading more, perhaps indicating increased load, or instead doing fewer actual I/O operations. The latter may mean that MySQL is currently limited by some other resource, like CPU, or suffers from other issues, like locking. Unfortunately, decreased I/O may also mean that the storage is having issues.

There are some status variables in InnoDB that may help to find issues with storage or its performance: `Innodb_data_pending_fsyncs`, `Innodb_data_pending_reads`, `Innodb_data_pending_writes`, `Innodb_os_log_pending_fsyncs`, and `Innodb_os_log_pending_writes`. You can expect to see some amount of pending data reads and writes, though as always it's helpful to look at the trends and previous data. The most important of all of these is `Innodb_os_log_pending_fsyncs`. Redo logs are synced often, and the performance of the syncing operation is extremely important for the overall performance and transaction throughput of InnoDB.

Unlike many other status variables, all of these are gauges, meaning that their values go up and down and don't just increase. You should sample these variables and look at how often there are pending operations, in particular for the redo log sync. Even small increases in `Innodb_os_log_pending_fsyncs` may indicate serious issues with storage: either you're running out of performance capacity or there are hardware issues.

While writing about the `Innodb_data_read` variable, we mentioned that the amount of data that InnoDB reads is related to its buffer pool size and usage. Let's elaborate on that. InnoDB caches pages it reads from disk inside its buffer pool. The larger the buffer pool is, the more pages will be stored there, and the less frequently pages will have to be read from disk. We talk about that in "Buffer pool size" on page 421. Here, while discussing monitoring, let's see how to monitor the effectiveness of the buffer pool. That's easily done with just two status variables:

`Innodb_buffer_pool_read_requests`
   The MySQL documentation defines this as "the number of logical read requests." Put simply, this is the number of pages that various operations within InnoDB wanted to read from the buffer pool. Usually most of the pages are read due to query activity.

`Innodb_buffer_pool_reads`
   This is the number of pages that InnoDB had to read from disk to satisfy the read requests by queries or other operations. The value of this counter is usually smaller than or equal to `Innodb_buffer_pool_read_requests` even in the very worst case with a completely empty (or "cold") buffer pool, because reads from disk are performed to satisfy the read requests.

Under normal conditions, even with a small buffer pool, you won't get a 1:1 ratio between these variables. That is, it will be possible to satisfy at least some reads from the buffer pool. Ideally, you should try keep the number of disk reads to a minimum.

That may not always be possible, especially if the database size is much larger than server memory.

You may attempt estimating a buffer pool hit ratio, and there are formulas available online. However, comparing the two variables' values is not exactly correct, like comparing apples and oranges. If you think that your `Innodb_buffer_pool_reads` is too high, it may be worth going through queries running on the system (for example, using slow query log) instead of trying to increase the buffer pool size. Of course, you should try to keep buffer pool as large as possible to cover most or all of the hot data in the database. However, there will still be queries that may cause high read I/O through getting pages from disk (and increasing `Innodb_buffer_pool_reads` while doing so), and attempting to fix them by increasing the buffer pool size even more will provide diminishing returns.

Finally, to close our discussion of InnoDB, we'll move on to transaction and locking. A lot of information on both topics was given in Chapter 6, so here we'll do a brief overview of the related status variables:

Transaction-related command counters

> `BEGIN`, `COMMIT`, and `ROLLBACK` are all special MySQL commands. Thus, MySQL will count the number of times they were executed with `Com_%` status variables: `Com_begin`, `Com_commit`, and `Com_rollback`. By looking at these counters you can see how many transactions are started explicitly and either committed or rolled back.

Locking-related status variables

> You know by now that InnoDB provides locking with row-level granularity. This is a huge improvement over MyISAM's table-level locking, as the impact of each individual lock is minimized. Still, there can be an impact if transactions are waiting for each other even for a short time.
>
> InnoDB provides status variables that let you see just how many locks are being created and give you details on the lock waits that are happening:
>
> `Innodb_row_lock_current_waits` shows how many transactions operating on InnoDB tables are currently waiting for a lock to be released by some other transactions. The value of this variable will go up from zero when there are blocked sessions then go back to zero as soon as locking is resolved.
>
> `Innodb_row_lock_waits` shows how many times since server startup transactions on InnoDB tables have waited for row-level locks. This variable is a counter and will continually increase until MySQL Server is restarted.
>
> `Innodb_row_lock_time` shows the total time in milliseconds spent by sessions trying to acquire locks on InnoDB tables.

`Innodb_row_lock_time_avg` shows an average time in milliseconds that it takes for a session to acquire a row-level lock on an InnoDB table. You can arrive at the same value by dividing `Innodb_row_lock_time` by `Innodb_row_lock_waits`. This value may go up and down depending on how many lock waits are encountered and how much accumulated lock time grows.

`Innodb_row_lock_time_max` shows the maximum time in milliseconds it took to obtain a lock on an InnoDB table. This value will go up only if the record is broken by some other unfortunate transaction.

Here's an example from a MySQL server running a moderate read/write load:

```
mysql> SHOW GLOBAL STATUS LIKE 'Innodb_row_lock%';
+-------------------------------+--------+
| Variable_name                 | Value  |
+-------------------------------+--------+
| Innodb_row_lock_current_waits | 0      |
| Innodb_row_lock_time          | 367465 |
| Innodb_row_lock_time_avg      | 165    |
| Innodb_row_lock_time_max      | 51056  |
| Innodb_row_lock_waits         | 2226   |
+-------------------------------+--------+
5 rows in set (0.00 sec)
```

There were 2,226 individual transactions waiting for locks, and it took 367,465 milliseconds to obtain all of those locks, with an average lock acquisition duration of 165 milliseconds and a maximum duration of just over 51 seconds. There are currently no sessions waiting for locks. On its own this information doesn't tell us much: it's neither a lot nor a little. However, we know that at the same time more than 100,000 transactions were executed by this MySQL server. The resulting locking metric values are more than reasonable for the level of concurrency.

Locking issues are a frequent source of headache for database administrators and application developers alike. While these metrics, like everything we've discussed so far, are aggregated across every session running, deviation from the normal values may help you in pinning down some of the issues. To find and investigate individual locking situations, you may use the InnoDB status report; see "InnoDB Engine Status Report" on page 471 for more details.

The Slow Query Log

In "Query types and quality" on page 458 we showed how to look for tell-tale signs of unoptimized queries in MySQL. However, that's not enough to start optimizing those queries. We need specific examples. There are few ways to do that, but probably the most robust one is using the slow query log facility. The slow query log is exactly what it sounds like: a special text log where MySQL puts information about *slow* queries. Just how slow those queries should be is controllable, and you can go as far as logging every query.

To enable the slow query log, you must change the setting of the `slow_query_log` system variable to `ON` from its default of `OFF`. By default, when the slow query log is enabled, MySQL will log queries taking longer than 10 seconds. That's configurable by changing the `long_query_time` variable, which has a minimum value of 0, meaning every query executed by the server will be logged. The log location is controlled by the `slow_query_log_file` variable, which defaults to a value of *hostname*-`slow.log`. When the path to the slow query log is relative, meaning it doesn't start from / on Linux or, for example, *C:* on Windows, then this file will be located in the MySQL data directory.

You can also tell MySQL to log queries not using indexes regardless of the time they take to execute. To do so, the `log_queries_not_using_indexes` variable has to be set to `ON`. By default, DDL and administrative statements are not logged, but this behavior can be changed by setting `log_slow_admin_statements` to `ON`.

MariaDB and Percona Server expand the functionality of the slow query log by adding filtering capabilities, rate limiting, and enhanced verbosity. If you're using those products, it's worth reading their documentation on the subject to see if you can utilize the enhanced slow query log.

Here's an example from a record in the slow query log showing a `SELECT` statement taking longer than the configured `long_query_time` value of 1 second:

```
# Time: 2021-05-29T17:21:12.433992Z
# User@Host: root[root] @ localhost [] Id:    11
# Query_time: 1.877495  Lock_time: 0.000823 Rows_sent: 9  Rows_examined: 3473725
use employees;
SET timestamp=1622308870;
SELECT
        dpt.dept_name
    , emp.emp_no
    , emp.first_name
    , emp.last_name
    , sal.salary
FROM
        departments dpt
    JOIN dept_emp ON dpt.dept_no = dept_emp.dept_no
    JOIN employees emp ON dept_emp.emp_no = emp.emp_no
    JOIN salaries sal ON emp.emp_no = sal.emp_no
    JOIN (SELECT dept_emp.dept_no, MAX(sal.salary) maxsal
        FROM dept_emp JOIN salaries sal
            ON dept_emp.emp_no = sal.emp_no
        WHERE
                sal.from_date < now()
            AND sal.to_date > now()
        GROUP BY dept_no
```

```
      ) largest_sal_by_dept ON dept_emp.dept_no = largest_sal_by_dept.dept_no
        AND sal.salary = largest_sal_by_dept.maxsal;
```

By analyzing this output you can immediately start making conclusions about this query. This is much more descriptive than looking at server-wide metrics. For example, we can see that this query was executed at 17:21:12 UTC by user root@localhost in the employees database, took 1.88 seconds to run, and produced 9 rows but had to scan 3,473,725 rows to produce that result. That information on its own can tell you a whole lot about the query, especially once you've gained more experience with MySQL. You now also have the complete query text, which you can turn into execution plan information to see exactly how MySQL is executing this query. You can find more details on that process in "The EXPLAIN Statement" on page 292.

If the long_query_time is set low, the slow query log may grow large. Sometimes this may be reasonable, but reading through the resulting log may be nearly impossible if the number of queries is high. There's a tool called mysqldumpslow that solves this problem. It takes the path to the slow query log file as an argument and will summarize queries from that file and sort them (by default by time). In the following example, the command is run such that it will show the two top queries sorted by the number of rows returned:

```
$ mysqldumpslow -s r -t 2 /var/lib/mysql/mysqldb1-slow.log

Reading mysql slow query log from /var/lib/mysql/mysqldb1-slow.log
Count: 2805  Time=0.00s (0s)  Lock=0.00s (0s)  Rows=100.0 (280500), sbuser[
sbuser]@localhost
  SELECT c FROM sbtest1 WHERE id BETWEEN N AND N

Count: 2760  Time=0.00s (0s)  Lock=0.00s (0s)  Rows=100.0 (276000), sbuser[
sbuser]@localhost
  SELECT c FROM sbtest1 WHERE id BETWEEN N AND N ORDER BY c
```

You can see that these two queries alone were recorded in the slow query log 5,565 times. Imagine trying to get that information without help! Another tool that can help with summarizing the information in the slow query log is pt-query-digest from Percona Toolkit. The tool is a bit more advanced and more difficult to use than mysqldumpslow, but gives a lot of information and has many features. The report it produces starts with a summary:

```
$ pt-query-digest /var/lib/mysql/mysqldb1-slow.log

# 7.4s user time, 60ms system time, 41.96M rss, 258.35M vsz
# Current date: Sat May 29 22:36:47 2021
# Hostname: mysqldb1
# Files: /var/lib/mysql/mysqldb1-slow.log
# Overall: 109.42k total, 15 unique, 7.29k QPS, 1.18x concurrency _____
# Time range: 2021-05-29T19:28:57 to 2021-05-29T19:29:12
# Attribute          total     min     max     avg     95%  stddev  median
# ============     ======= ======= ======= ======= ======= ======= =======
# Exec time            18s     1us    10ms   161us     1ms   462us    36us
```

```
# Lock time           2s       0     7ms    16us    14us    106us      5us
# Rows sent        1.62M       0     100   15.54   97.36    34.53     0.99
# Rows examine     3.20M       0     200   30.63  192.76    61.50     0.99
# Query size       5.84M       5     245   55.93  151.03    50.37    36.69

# Profile
# Rank Query ID                                    Response time  Calls R/Call V/M
# ==== ===================================== ============= ===== ====== ====
#    1 0xFFFCA4D67EA0A78...  11.1853 63.1%    5467 0.0020   0.00 COMMIT
#    2 0xB2249CB854EE3C2...   1.5985  9.0%    5467 0.0003   0.00 UPDATE sbtest?
#    3 0xE81D0B3DB4FB31B...   1.5600  8.8%   54670 0.0000   0.00 SELECT sbtest?
#    4 0xF0C5AE75A52E847...   0.8853  5.0%    5467 0.0002   0.00 SELECT sbtest?
#    5 0x9934EF6887CC7A6...   0.5959  3.4%    5467 0.0001   0.00 SELECT sbtest?
#    6 0xA729E7889F57828...   0.4748  2.7%    5467 0.0001   0.00 SELECT sbtest?
#    7 0xFF7C69F51BBD3A7...   0.4511  2.5%    5467 0.0001   0.00 SELECT sbtest?
#    8 0x6C545CFB5536512...   0.3092  1.7%    5467 0.0001   0.00 INSERT sbtest?
# MISC 0xMISC                 0.6629  3.7%   16482 0.0000    0.0 <7 ITEMS>
```

And each query is then summarized as follows:

```
# Query 2: 546.70 QPS, 0.16x concurrency, ID 0xB2249CB854E... at byte 1436377
# Scores: V/M = 0.00
# Time range: 2021-05-29T19:29:02 to 2021-05-29T19:29:12
# Attribute    pct   total    min     max     avg     95% stddev  median
# ============ === ======= ======= ======= ======= ======= ======= =======
# Count          4    5467
# Exec time      9      2s    54us     7ms   292us     1ms   446us    93us
# Lock time     61      1s     7us     7ms   203us     1ms   437us     9us
# Rows sent      0       0       0       0       0       0       0       0
# Rows examine   0   5.34k       1       1       1       1       0       1
# Query size     3 213.55k      40      40      40      40       0      40
# String:
# Databases    sysbench
# Hosts        localhost
# Users        sbuser
# Query_time distribution
#   1us
#  10us  ##################################################################
# 100us  ##############################################
#   1ms  ############
#  10ms
# 100ms
#    1s
#  10s+
# Tables
#    SHOW TABLE STATUS FROM `sysbench` LIKE 'sbtest2'\G
#    SHOW CREATE TABLE `sysbench`.`sbtest2`\G
UPDATE sbtest2 SET k=k+1 WHERE id=497658\G
# Converted for EXPLAIN
# EXPLAIN /*!50100 PARTITIONS*/
select  k=k+1 from sbtest2 where  id=497658\G
```

That's a lot of valuable information in a dense format. One of the distinguishing features of this output is the query duration distribution visualization, which allows you to quickly see whether a query has parameter-dependent performance issues. Explaining every feature of pt-query-digest would take another chapter, and it's an advanced tool, so we leave this for you to try once you're done learning MySQL.

The slow query log is a powerful tool that allows you to get a very detailed view of the queries executed by MySQL Server. We recommend using the slow query log like this:

- Set long_query_time to a value large enough that it covers most of the queries normally running in your system, but small enough that you catch outliers. For example, in an OLTP system, where most of the queries are expected to complete in milliseconds, a value of 0.5 may be reasonable, only catching relatively slow queries. On the other hand, if your system has queries running in minutes, then long_query_time should be set accordingly.

- Logging to the slow query log has some performance cost, and you should avoid logging more queries than you need. If you have the slow query log enabled, make sure you adjust the long_query_time setting if you find the log too noisy.

- Sometimes you may want to perform a "query audit," where you temporarily (for a few minutes) set long_query_time to 0 to catch every query. This is a good way to get a snapshot of your database load. Such snapshots may be saved and compared later. However, we recommend strongly against setting long_query_time too low.

- If you have the slow query log set up, we recommend running mysqldumpslow, pt-query-digest, or a similar tool on it periodically to see if there are new queries appearing or if existing ones start behaving worse than usual.

InnoDB Engine Status Report

The InnoDB storage engine has a built-in report that exposes deep technical details on the current state of the engine. A lot can be said about InnoDB load and performance from reading just this one report, ideally sampled over time. Reading the InnoDB status report is an advanced topic that requires more instruction than we can convey in our book, and also a lot of practice. Still, we believe you should know that this report exists, and we'll give you some hints as to what to look for there.

To view the report, you need to run only a single command. We recommend using the vertical result display:

```
mysql> SHOW ENGINE INNODB STATUS\G

*************************** 1. row ***************************
  Type: InnoDB
  Name:
Status:
```

```
========================================
2021-05-31 12:21:05 139908633830976 INNODB MONITOR OUTPUT
========================================
Per second averages calculated from the last 35 seconds
-----------------
BACKGROUND THREAD
-----------------
srv_master_thread loops: 121 srv_active, 0 srv_shutdown, 69961 srv_idle
...
--------------
ROW OPERATIONS
--------------
0 queries inside InnoDB, 0 queries in queue
2 read views open inside InnoDB
Process ID=55171, Main thread ID=139908126139968 , state=sleeping
Number of rows inserted 2946375, updated 87845, deleted 46063, read 88688110
572.50 inserts/s, 1145.00 updates/s, 572.50 deletes/s, 236429.64 reads/s
Number of system rows inserted 109, updated 367, deleted 60, read 13218
0.00 inserts/s, 0.00 updates/s, 0.00 deletes/s, 0.00 reads/s
----------------------------
END OF INNODB MONITOR OUTPUT
============================
```

The output, which we've truncated here, is presented broken down in sections. At first, it may seem intimidating, but over time you will come to appreciate the details. For now, we'll walk through a few sections that we believe provide information that will benefit operators of any experience level:

Transactions

This section provides information about the transactions of every session, including duration, current query, number of locks held, and information on lock waits. You can also find some data here on transaction visibility, but that's rarely required. Usually, you want to look at the transactions section to see the current state of transactions active within InnoDB. A sample record from this section looks like this:

```
---TRANSACTION 252288, ACTIVE (PREPARED) 0 sec
5 lock struct(s), heap size 1136, 3 row lock(s), undo log entries 4
MySQL thread id 82, OS thread handle 139908634125888,...
...query id 925076 localhost sbuser waiting for handler commit
COMMIT
Trx read view will not see trx with id >= 252287, sees < 252285
```

This tells us that the transaction is currently waiting for a COMMIT to finish it holds three row locks, and it's pretty fast, likely to finish in under a second. Sometimes, you will see long transactions here: you should try to avoid those. InnoDB does not handle long transactions well, and even an idle transaction staying open for too long can cause a performance impact.

This section will also show you information on the current locking behavior if there are transactions waiting to obtain locks. Here's an example:

```
---TRANSACTION 414311, ACTIVE 4 sec starting index read
mysql tables in use 1, locked 1
LOCK WAIT 2 lock struct(s), heap size 1136, 1 row lock(s)
MySQL thread id 84, OS thread handle 139908634125888,...
...query id 2545483 localhost sbuser updating
UPDATE sbtest1 SET k=k+1 WHERE id=347110
Trx read view will not see trx with id >= 414310, sees < 413897
------- TRX HAS BEEN WAITING 4 SEC FOR THIS LOCK TO BE GRANTED:
RECORD LOCKS space id 333 page no 4787 n bits 144 index PRIMARY of...
...table `sysbench`.`sbtest1` trx id 414311 lock_mode X locks...
...rec but not gap waiting
Record lock, heap no 33
-----------------
```

Unfortunately, the status report doesn't point at the lock holder directly, so you'll need to look for blocking transactions separately. Some information on that is available in Chapter 6. Usually, if you see one transaction active while others are waiting, it's a good indication that it's that active transaction that's holding the locks.

File I/O

This section contains information on the current I/O operations, as well as aggregated summaries over time. We discussed this in more detail in "InnoDB I/O and transaction metrics" on page 463, but this is an additional way of checking whether InnoDB has pending data and log operations.

Buffer pool and memory

In this section InnoDB prints information about its buffer pool and memory usage. If you have multiple buffer pool instances configured, then this section will show both totals and per-instance breakdowns. There's a lot of information, including on the buffer pool size and the internal state of the buffer pool:

```
Total large memory allocated 274071552
Dictionary memory allocated 1377188
Buffer pool size   16384
Free buffers       1027
Database pages     14657
Old database pages 5390
Modified db pages  4168
```

These are also exposed as `Innodb_buffer_pool_%` variables.

Semaphores

This section includes information on internal InnoDB semaphores, or synchronization primitives. In basic terms, *semaphores* are special internal in-memory structures that allow multiple threads to operate without interfering with each other. You will rarely see anything of value in this section unless there's semaphore contention on your system. Usually that happens when InnoDB is put under extreme load, so every operation takes longer, and there are more chances to see active semaphore waits in the status output.

Investigation Methods

Having so many available metrics that need to be monitored, checked, and understood may cause your head to spin. You may notice that we haven't defined a single metric that has a definite range from good to bad. Is the locking bad? Could be, but it's also expected and normal. The same can be said about almost every aspect of MySQL, with the exception of server availability.

This problem is not unique to MySQL server monitoring, and in fact it's common for any complex system. There are a lot of metrics, complicated dependencies, and almost no strictly definable rules for whether something is good or bad. To solve this problem, we need some approach, some methodology that we can apply to abundant data to quickly and easily come to conclusions about current system performance.

Luckily, such methodologies already exist. In this section, we will briefly describe two of them and give ideas on how to apply them to monitoring MySQL and OS metrics.

The USE Method

The Utilization, Saturation, and Errors (USE) method, popularized by Brendan Gregg, is a general-purpose methodology that can be applied to any system. Though better suited for resources with well-defined performance characteristics like CPU or disk, it can also be applied to some parts of MySQL.

The USE method is best used by creating a checklist for each individual part of the system. First, we need to define what metrics to use to measure utilization, saturation, and errors. Some example checklists for Linux can be found on the USE homepage: Gregg's website (*https://oreil.ly/MeF2B*).

Let's look at the three different categories for the example of disk I/O:

Utilization
For a disk subsystem, as we've laid out in "Disk" on page 436, we might look at metrics for any:

- Overall storage bandwidth utilization
- Per-process storage bandwidth utilization
- Current IOPS (where the upper IOPS limit for the device is known)

Saturation

We mentioned saturation when talking about the `iostat` output and disk metrics. It's a measure of work that the resource cannot process and that is usually queued. For disk, this is expressed as the I/O request queue size (`avgqu-sz` in `iostat` output). On most systems, values >1 mean the disk is saturated, and thus some requests will be queued and waste time doing nothing.

Errors

For disk devices, this may mean I/O errors due to hardware degradation.

The problem with the USE method is that it's difficult to apply to a complex system as a whole. Take MySQL, for example: what metrics could we use to measure overall utilization, saturation, and errors? Some attempts can be made to apply USE to MySQL as a whole, but it's much better suited to use on some isolated parts of the system.

Let's take a look at some possible MySQL applications:

USE method for client connections

A good fit for the USE method is making sense of the client connection metrics we discussed in "Basic Monitoring Recipes" on page 453.

Utilization metrics include the `Threads_connected` and `Threads_running`.

Saturation can be defined arbitrarily based on `Threads_running`. For example, in an OLTP system that is read-heavy and doesn't generate a lot of I/O, a saturation point for `Threads_running` will likely be around the number of available CPU cores. In a system that is mostly I/O-bound, a starting point could be twice the available CPU cores, but it's much better to find what number of concurrently running threads start to saturate the storage subsystem.

Errors are measured by the `Aborted_clients` and `Aborted_connects` metrics. Once the value of the `Threads_connected` status variable becomes equal to that of the `max_connections` system variable, requests to create new connections will be declined, and clients will get errors. Connections can also fail for other reasons, and existing clients may be terminating their connections uncleanly without waiting for MySQL to respond.

USE method for transactions and locking

Another example of how USE can be applied is to look at the InnoDB locking-related metrics relative to the number of queries processed by the system.

Utilization can be measured using the synthetic QPS metric we defined earlier.

Saturation can be the fact that there's some number of lock waits occurring. Remember, by the USE definition, saturation is a measure of work that cannot be performed and has to wait in the queue. There's no queue here, but transactions are waiting for locks to be acquired. Alternatively, the regular amount of lock waits can be multiplied twofold to construct an arbitrary threshold, or better yet, some experiments can be performed to find a number of lock waits relative to QPS that result in lock timeouts occurring.

Errors can be measured as the number of times sessions timed out waiting for locks or were terminated to resolve a deadlock situation. Unlike the previously mentioned metrics, these two are not exposed as global status variables, but can instead be found in the `information_schema.innodb_metrics` table under `lock_deadlocks` (number of deadlocks registered) and `lock_timeouts` (number of times lock waits timed out).

Determining the rate of errors from monitoring metrics alone can be difficult, so frequently just the US part of USE is used. As you can see, this method allows us to look at the system from a predefined point of view. Instead of analyzing every possible metric when there's an incident, an existing checklist can be reviewed, saving time and effort.

RED Method

The Rate, Errors, and Duration (RED) method was created to address the shortcomings of USE. The methodology is similar, but it's is easier to apply to complex systems and services.

The logical application of RED to MySQL is done by looking at query performance:

Rate
QPS of the database

Errors
Number or rate of errors and failing queries

Duration
Average query latency

One problem with RED in the context of this book and learning MySQL in general is that applying this method requires monitoring data that can't be obtained just by reading status variables. Not every existing monitoring solution for MySQL can provide the necessary data, either, though you can see an example of how it's done in the blog post "RED Method for MySQL Performance Analyses" (*https://oreil.ly/TVT2x*) by Peter Zaitsev. One way to apply RED to MySQL or any other database system is by looking at the metrics from the application side instead of from the database side. Multiple monitoring solutions allow you to instrument (manually or automatically) your applications to capture data such as number of queries, rate of failures, and query latency. Just what's needed for RED!

You can, and should, use RED and USE together. In the article explaining RED, The RED Method: How to Instrument Your Services (*https://oreil.ly/dHHMS*), its author Tom Wilkie mentions that "It's really just two different views on the same system."

One perhaps unexpected benefit of applying RED, USE, or any other method is that you do so before an incident happens. Thus, you are forced to understand what it is you monitor and measure and how that relates to what actually matters for your system and its users.

MySQL Monitoring Tools

Throughout this chapter we've been talking about metrics and monitoring methodologies, but we haven't mentioned a single actual tool that can turn those metrics into dashboards or alerts. In other words, we haven't talked about the actual monitoring tools and systems. The first reason for that is simple enough: we believe that in the beginning it's much more important for you to know *what* to monitor and *why*, rather than *how*. If we'd concentrated on the *how*, we could have spent this whole chapter talking about the peculiarities and differences of various monitoring tools. The second reason is that MySQL and OS metrics don't change often, but if you're reading this book in 2025, our choice of monitoring tools may already seem antiquated.

Nevertheless, as a starting point we've put together a list of notable popular open source monitoring tools that can be used to monitor MySQL availability and performance. We're not going to go too deep into the specifics of their setup or configuration, or into comparing them. We cannot also list every possible monitoring solution available: brief research shows us that almost anything that is a "monitoring tool" or "monitoring system" can monitor MySQL in some way. We're also not covering non–open source and non-free monitoring solutions, with the one exception of the Oracle Enterprise Monitor. We hold nothing against such systems in general, and a lot of them are great. Most of them, though, have excellent documentation and support available, so you should be able to get familiar with them quickly.

The following monitoring systems will be mentioned here:

- Prometheus
- InfluxDB and TICK stack
- Zabbix
- Nagios Core
- Percona Monitoring and Management
- Oracle Enterprise Monitor

We'll start with Prometheus and InfluxDB and its TICK stack. Both of these systems are a modern take on monitoring, well suited to monitoring microservices and vast cloud deployments, but are also widely used as general-purpose monitoring solutions:

Prometheus

Born out of Google's internal monitoring system Borgmon, Prometheus (*https:// oreil.ly/em47V*) is an extremely popular general-purpose monitoring and alerting system. At its core is a time-series database and a data-gathering engine based around a pull model. What that means is that it's the Prometheus server that actively gathers data from its monitoring targets.

Actual data gathering from Prometheus targets is performed by special programs called *exporters*. Exporters are purpose-built: there's a dedicated MySQL exporter, a PostgreSQL exporter, a basic OS metrics/node exporter, and many more. What these programs do is collect metrics from the system they are written to monitor and present those metrics in a format suitable for the Prometheus server to consume.

MySQL monitoring with Prometheus is done by running the `mysqld_exporter` program (*https://oreil.ly/tvltY*). Like most parts of Prometheus ecosystem, it's written in Go and is available for Linux, Windows, and many other operating systems, making it a good choice for a heterogeneous environment.

The MySQL exporter gathers all the metrics we've covered in this chapter (and many more!), and since it actively tries to get information from MySQL, it can also report on the MySQL server's availability. In addition to standard metrics, it is possible to supply custom queries that exporter will execute, turning their results into additional metrics.

Prometheus offers only very basic visualization capabilities, so the Grafana analytics and data visualization web application (*https://oreil.ly/YAIpl*) is usually added to the setup.

InfluxDB and the TICK stack

Built around the InfluxDB time-series database (*https://oreil.ly/jv0ZC*), TICK, standing for Telegraf, InfluxDB, Chronograf, and Kapacitor, is a complete time-series and monitoring platform. Comparing this to Prometheus, Telegraf takes the place of the exporters; it's a unified program that is capable of monitoring a multitude of targets. Unlike exporters, Telegraf actively pushes data to InfluxDB instead of data being pulled by the server. Chronograf is an administrative and data interface. Kapacitor is a data processing and alerting engine.

Where you had to install a dedicated exporter for MySQL, Telegraf is extended using plugins. The MySQL plugin (*https://oreil.ly/ciQVF*) is part of a standard bundle and provides a detailed overview of MySQL database metrics.

Unfortunately, it is not capable of running arbitrary queries, so extensibility is limited. As a workaround, the exec plugin (*https://oreil.ly/83QgS*) can be used. Telegraf is also a multiplatform program, and it does support Windows among other OSs.

The TICK stack is frequently used in part, with Grafana added to InfluxDB and Telegraf.

A common thread between Prometheus and TICK is that they are collections of building blocks allowing you to build your own monitoring solution. Neither of them offers any out-of-the-box recipes for dashboards, alerting, and so forth. They are powerful, but they may require some getting used to. Apart from that, they are very automation- and infrastructure-as-code-oriented. Prometheus especially, but TICK as well, provides a minimal GUI and was not initially conceived for data exploration and visualization. It's monitoring as in reacting to metric value changes by alerting, not by visually inspecting various metrics. Adding Grafana to the equation, especially with either home-brewed or community dashboards for MySQL, makes visual inspection possible. Still, most of the configuration and setup will not be done in a GUI.

Both of these systems saw an influx in popularity in the mid- and late-2010s, with the shift to running a multitude of small servers compared to running a few large servers. That shift required some changes in monitoring approaches, and these systems became almost the de facto standard monitoring solutions for a lot of companies.

Next in our review are a couple of more "old-school" monitoring solutions:

Zabbix
> A completely free and open source monitoring system first released in 2001, Zabbix (*https://oreil.ly/ZLi1Q*) is proven and powerful. It supports a wide range of monitored targets and advanced auto-discovery and alerting capabilities.
>
> MySQL monitoring with Zabbix can be done by using plugins or with the official MySQL templates (*https://oreil.ly/GMgSo*). Metrics coverage is quite good, with every recipe we defined available. However, both mysqld_exporter and Telegraf offer more data. The standard MySQL metrics Zabbix collects are sufficient to set up basic MySQL monitoring, but for deeper insight you will need to go custom or use some of the community templates and plugins.
>
> The Zabbix agent is cross-platform, so you can monitor MySQL running on almost any OS.
>
> While Zabbix offers quite powerful alerting, its visualization capabilities may feel slightly dated. It is possible to set up custom dashboards based on MySQL data, and it's also possible to use Zabbix as a data source for Grafana.

Zabbix is fully configurable through its GUI. The commercial offering includes various levels of support and consulting.

Nagios Core

Like Zabbix, Nagios (*https://oreil.ly/jwE5S*) is a veteran monitoring system, with its first release seeing light in 2002. Unlike other systems we've seen so far, Nagios is an "open core" system. The Nagios Core distribution is free and open source, but there's also a commercial Nagios system.

Monitoring of MySQL is set up by use of plugins. They should provide enough data to set up basic monitoring similar to that of the official Zabbix templates. It is possible to extend the collected metrics if needed.

Alerting, visualizations, and configuration are similar to Zabbix. One notable feature of Nagios is that at its peak of popularity it was forked multiple times. Some of the most popular Nagios forks are Icinga and Shinken. Check_MK was also initially a Nagios extension that eventually moved on to become its own commercial product.

Both Nagios and its forks and Zabbix can and are successfully used by many companies to monitor MySQL. Even though they may feel outdated in their architecture and data representation, they can get the job done. Their biggest problem is that the standard data they collect may feel limited compared with alternatives, and you'll need to use community plugins and extensions. Percona used to maintain a set of monitoring plugins for Nagios (*https://oreil.ly/bocia*), as well as for Zabbix, but has deprecated them and now concentrates on its own monitoring offering, Percona Monitoring and Management (PMM), which we'll discuss shortly.

All the systems we've covered so far have one thing in common: they are general-purpose monitoring solutions, not tailor-made for database monitoring. It's their power, and also their weakness. When it comes to monitoring and investigating deep database internals, you'll often be forced to manually extend those systems' capabilities. One feature, for example, that none of them have is storing individual query execution statistics. Technically, it's possible to add that feature, but it may be cumbersome and problematic.

We will finish this section by looking at two database-oriented monitoring solutions, MySQL Enterprise Monitor from Oracle and Percona Monitoring and Management. As you'll see, they are similar in the functionality they provide, and both are big improvements over nonspecialized monitoring systems:

MySQL Enterprise Monitor

Part of MySQL Enterprise Edition, Enterprise Monitor (*https://oreil.ly/cQ8tQ*) is a complete monitoring and management platform for MySQL databases.

In terms of monitoring, MySQL Enterprise Monitor extends the usual metrics gathered by monitoring systems by adding details on MySQL memory utilization, per-file I/O details, and a wide variety of dashboards based on InnoDB's status variables. The data is taken from MySQL itself without any agents involved. Theoretically, all the same data can be gathered and visualized by any other monitoring system, but here it's tightly packed with well-thought-out dashboards and categories.

Enterprise Monitor includes the Events subsystem, which is a set of predefined alerts. Adding to the database-specific features, the Enterprise Monitor includes a replication topology overview for regular and multisource replication, Group Replication, and NDB Cluster. Another feature is monitoring of backup execution status (for backups done with MySQL Enterprise Backup).

We mentioned that individual query execution statistics and query history are usually missing in the general-purpose monitoring systems. MySQL Enterprise Monitor includes a Query Analyzer that provides insight into the history of queries executed over time, as well as statistics gathered about the queries. It's possible to view information like the average numbers of rows read and returned and a duration distribution, and even see the execution plans of the queries.

Enterprise Monitor is a good database monitoring system. Its biggest downside, really, is that it's only available in the Enterprise Edition of MySQL. Unfortunately, most MySQL installations cannot benefit from the Enterprise Monitor and the level of insight it provides into the database and OS metrics. It's also not suitable for monitoring anything apart from MySQL, the queries it's executing, and the OS it's running on, and MySQL monitoring is limited in scope to Oracle's products.

There's a 30-day trial of MySQL Enterprise Edition available, which includes the Enterprise Monitor, and Oracle also maintains a list of visual demos of the system (*https://oreil.ly/AC58l*).

Percona Monitoring and Management

Percona's monitoring solution, PMM (*https://oreil.ly/3cu2k*), is similar in functionality to Oracle's Enterprise Monitor, but is fully free and open source. Intended to be a "single pane of glass," it tries to provide deep insight into MySQL and OS performance and can also be used to monitor MongoDB and PostgreSQL databases.

PMM is built on top of existing open source components like the already reviewed Prometheus and its exporters, and Grafana. Percona maintains forks of the database exporters it uses, including the one for MySQL, and adds functionality and metrics that were lacking in the original versions. In addition to that,

PMM hides complexity usually associated with deploying and configuring those tools and instead provides its own bundled package and configuration interface.

Like Enterprise Monitor, PMM offers a selection of dashboards visualizing pretty much every aspect of MySQL's and InnoDB's operation, as well as giving a lot of details on the underlying OS state. This has been extended to include technologies like PXC/Galera, discussed in Chapter 13, and ProxySQL, discussed in Chapter 15. As PMM uses Prometheus and exporters, it's possible to extend the range of monitored databases by adding external exporters. In addition to that, PMM supports DBaaS systems like RDS and CloudSQL.

PMM ships with a custom application called Query Analytics (QAN), which is a query monitoring and metrics system. Like the Enterprise Monitor's Query Analyzer, QAN shows the overall history of queries executed in a given system, as well as information about the individual queries. That includes a history of the number of executions of the query over time, rows read and sent, locking, and temporary tables created, among other things. QAN allows you to view the query plan and structures of the involved tables.

The *Management* part of PMM for now exists only in its name, as at the time of writing it is purely a monitoring system. PMM supports alerting through Prometheus's standard AlertManager or through the use of internal templates.

One significant problem with PMM is that out of the box it only supports targets running on Linux. Since Prometheus exporters are cross-platform, you can add Windows (or other OS) targets to PMM, but you won't be able to utilize some of the benefits of the tool, like simplified exporter configuration and bundled installation of the client software.

Both authors of this book are currently employed by Percona, so you may be tempted to dismiss our description of PMM as an advertisement. However, we've tried to give a fair overview of a few monitoring systems, and we don't claim that PMM is perfect. If your company is already using the Enterprise version of MySQL, then you should absolutely first see what MySQL Enterprise Monitor has to offer.

Before we close this section, we want to note that in many cases the actual monitoring system you use doesn't matter much. Every system we've mentioned provides MySQL availability monitoring, as well as some level of insight into the internal metrics—enough for the selection of recipes we gave earlier. Especially while you're learning your way around MySQL, and perhaps starting to operate its installations in production, you should try to leverage existing monitoring infrastructure. Rushing to change everything to the best often leads to unsatisfactory results. As you get more experienced, you will see more and more data missing in the tools you have and will be able to make an informed decision on which new tool to choose.

Incident/Diagnostic and Manual Data Collection

Sometimes, you may not have a monitoring system set up for a database, or you may not trust it to contain all the information you might need to investigate some issue. Or you may have a DBaaS instance running and want to get more data than your cloud provider gives you. In such situations, manual data collection can be a viable option in the short term to quickly get some data out of the system. We will show you few tools you can use to do just that: quickly gather a lot of diagnostic information from any MySQL instance.

The following sections are short, useful recipes that you can take away and use in your day-to-day work with MySQL databases.

Gathering System Status Variable Values Periodically

In "Status Variables" on page 451 and "Basic Monitoring Recipes" on page 453 we talked a lot about looking at how different status variables' values change over time. Every monitoring tool mentioned in the previous section does that to accumulate data, which is then used for plots and alerting. The same sampling of status variables can be performed manually if you want to look at raw data or simply sample at an interval lower than your monitoring system uses.

You could write a simple script that runs the MySQL monitor in a loop, but the better approach is to use the built-in `mysqladmin` utility. This program can be used to perform a wide range of administrative operations on a running MySQL server, though we should note that every one of those can also be done through the regular `mysql`. `mysqladmin` can, however, be used to sample global status variables easily, which is exactly how we're going to use it here.

`mysqladmin` includes two status outputs: regular and extended. The regular one is less informative:

```
$ mysqladmin status
Uptime: 176190  Threads: 5  Questions: 5287160 ...
... Slow queries: 5114814  Opens: 761  Flush tables: 3 ...
... Open tables: 671  Queries per second avg: 30.008
```

The extended output will be familiar to you at this point. It's the same as the output of SHOW GLOBAL STATUS:

```
$ mysqladmin extended-status
+---------------------------------------+---------------------+
| Variable_name                         | Value               |
+---------------------------------------+---------------------+
| Aborted_clients                       | 2                   |
| Aborted_connects                      | 30                  |
| ...                                   |                     |
```

```
| Uptime                                    | 176307              |
| Uptime_since_flush_status                 | 32141               |
| validate_password.dictionary_file_last_parsed | 2021-05-29 21:50:38 |
| validate_password.dictionary_file_words_count | 0               |
+-------------------------------------------+---------------------+
```

Conveniently, `mysqladmin` is capable of repeating the commands it runs at a given interval a given number of times. For example, the following command will cause `mysqladmin` to print status variable values every second for a minute (ext is a shorthand for *extended-status*):

```
$ mysqladmin -i1 -c60 ext
```

By redirecting its output to a file, you can get a minute-long sample of database metric changes. Text files are not as nice to work with as proper monitoring systems, but again, this is usually done under special circumstances. For a long time, gathering information about MySQL like this with `mysqladmin` was standard practice, so there's a tool called `pt-mext` (*https://oreil.ly/6MnC5*) that can turn plain SHOW GLOBAL STATUS outputs into a format better suited for consumption by humans. Unfortunately, the tool is available only on Linux. Here's an example of its output:

```
$ pt-mext -r -- cat mysqladmin.output | grep Bytes_sent
Bytes_sent 10836285314 15120 15120 31080 15120 15120 31080 15120 15120
```

The initial large number is the status variable value at the first sample, and values after that represent the change to the initial number. If the value were to decrease, a negative number would be shown.

Using pt-stalk to Collect MySQL and OS Metrics

`pt-stalk` (*https://oreil.ly/SU9bG*) is a part of Percona Toolkit and is normally run alongside MySQL and used to continuously check for some specified condition. Once that condition is met—for example, the value of `Threads_running` is larger than 15—`pt-stalk` triggers a data collection routine gathering extensive information on MySQL and the operating system. However, it is possible to utilize the data collection part without actually stalking the MySQL server. Although it's not a correct way to use `pt-stalk`, it's a useful method to quickly glance at an unknown server or try to gather as much information as possible on a misbehaving server.

`pt-stalk`, like other tools in the Percona Toolkit, is available only for Linux, even though the target MySQL server can run on any OS. The basic invocation of `pt-stalk` to achieve that is simple:

```
$ sudo pt-stalk --no-stalk --iterations=2 --sleep=30 \
--dest="/tmp/collected_data" \
-- --user=root --password=<root password>;
```

The utility will run two data collection rounds, each of which will span a minute, and will sleep for 30 seconds between them. In case you don't need OS information, or can't get it because your target is a DBaaS instance, you can use the `--mysql-only` flag:

```
$ sudo pt-stalk --no-stalk --iterations=2 --sleep=30 \
--mysql-only --dest="/tmp/collected_data" \
-- --user=root --password=<root password> \
--host=<mysql host> --port=<mysql port>;
```

Here is the list of files created by a single collection round. We've omitted the OS-related files deliberately, but there are quite a lot of them:

```
2021_04_15_04_33_44-innodbstatus1
2021_04_15_04_33_44-innodbstatus2
2021_04_15_04_33_44-log_error
2021_04_15_04_33_44-mutex-status1
2021_04_15_04_33_44-mutex-status2
2021_04_15_04_33_44-mysqladmin
2021_04_15_04_33_44-opentables1
2021_04_15_04_33_44-opentables2
2021_04_15_04_33_44-processlist
2021_04_15_04_33_44-slave-status
2021_04_15_04_33_44-transactions
2021_04_15_04_33_44-trigger
2021_04_15_04_33_44-variables
```

Extended Manual Data Collection

`pt-stalk` is not always available, and it doesn't run on all platforms. Sometimes, you may also want to add to (or remove some of) the data it gathers. You can use the `mysqladmin` command introduced earlier to gather a bit more data and wrap it all up in a simple script. A version of this script is frequently used by authors of this book in their daily work.

This script, which should run on any Linux or Unix-like system, will execute continuously either until terminated or until the */tmp/exit-flag* file is found to be present. You can run `touch /tmp/exit-flag` to gracefully finish the execution of this script. We recommend putting it into a file and running it through `nohup ... &` or executing it within a `screen` or `tmux` session. If you're unfamiliar with the terms we've just mentioned, they are all ways to make sure a script continues to execute when your session disconnects. Here's the script:

```
DATADEST="/tmp/collected_data";
MYSQL="mysql --host=127.0.0.1  -uroot -proot";
MYSQLADMIN="mysqladmin  --host=127.0.0.1 -uroot -proot";
[ -d "$DATADEST" ] || mkdir $DATADEST;
while true; do {
  [ -f /tmp/exit-flag ] \
    && echo "exiting loop (/tmp/exit-flag found)" \
```

```
      && break;
    d=$(date +%F_%T |tr ":" "-");
    $MYSQL -e "SHOW ENGINE INNODB STATUS\G" > $DATADEST/$d-innodbstatus &
    $MYSQL -e "SHOW ENGINE INNODB MUTEX;" > $DATADEST/$d-innodbmutex &
    $MYSQL -e "SHOW FULL PROCESSLIST\G" > $DATADEST/$d-processlist &
    $MYSQLADMIN -i1 -c15 ext > $DATADEST/$d-mysqladmin ;
} done;
$MYSQL -e "SHOW GLOBAL VARIABLES;" > $DATADEST/$d-variables;
```

 Do not forget to adjust user credentials in these scripts before executing. Note that output files scripts produce may take a substantial
amount of disk space. Always test any scripts in a safe environment
before executing on critical servers.

We've also created a Windows version of the same script written in PowerShell. It
behaves exactly in the same way as the previous script and will terminate on its own
as soon as the file *C:\tmp\exit-flag* is found:

```
$mysqlbin='C:\Program Files\MySQL\MySQL Server 8.0\bin\mysql.exe'
$mysqladminbin='C:\Program Files\MySQL\MySQL Server 8.0\bin\mysqladmin.exe'

$user='root'
$password='root'
$mysqlhost='127.0.0.1'

$destination='C:\tmp\collected_data'
$stopfile='C:\tmp\exit-flag'

if (-Not (Test-Path -Path '$destination')) {
  mkdir -p '$destination'
}

Start-Process -NoNewWindow $mysqlbin -ArgumentList `
  '-h$mysqlhost','-u$user','-p$password','-e 'SHOW GLOBAL VARIABLES;' `
  -RedirectStandardOutput '$destination\variables'

while(1) {
  if (Test-Path -Path '$stopfile') {
    echo 'Found exit monitor file, aborting'
    break;
  }
  $d=(Get-Date -Format 'yyyy-MM-d_HHmmss')
  Start-Process -NoNewWindow $mysqlbin -ArgumentList `
    '-h$mysqlhost','-u$user','-p$password','-e 'SHOW ENGINE INNODB STATUS\G'' `
    -RedirectStandardOutput '$destination\$d-innodbstatus'
  Start-Process -NoNewWindow $mysqlbin -ArgumentList `
    '-h$mysqlhost','-u$user','-p$password','-e 'SHOW ENGINE INNODB MUTEX;'' `
    -RedirectStandardOutput '$destination\$d-innodbmutex'
  Start-Process -NoNewWindow $mysqlbin -ArgumentList `
    '-h$mysqlhost','-u$user','-p$password','-e 'SHOW FULL PROCESSLIST\G'' `
```

```
        -RedirectStandardOutput '$destination\$d-processlist'
    & $mysqladminbin '-h$mysqlhost' -u'$user' -p'$password' `
        -i1 -c15 ext > '$destination\$d-mysqladmin';
}
```

You should remember that script-based data collection is not a substitute for proper monitoring. It has its uses, which we described at the start of this section, but it should always be an addition to what you already have, not the only way to look at MySQL metrics.

By now, after reading through this chapter, you should have a pretty good idea of how to approach MySQL monitoring. Remember that issues, incidents, and outages will happen—they are unavoidable. With proper monitoring, however, you can make sure that the same issue doesn't happen twice, as you'll be able to find the root cause after the first occurrence. Of course, you'll also be able to avoid some issues by changing your system to fix the problems revealed by your MySQL monitoring efforts.

We'll leave you with a closing thought: perfect monitoring is unattainable, but even pretty basic monitoring is better than no monitoring at all.

## CHAPTER 13

High Availability

In the IT context, the term *high availability* defines a state of continuous operation for a specified length of time. The goal is not eliminating the risk of failure—that would be impossible. Rather, we are trying to guarantee that in a failure situation, the system remains available so that operation can continue. We often measure availability against a 100% operational or never-fails standard. A common standard of availability is known as *five 9s*, or 99.999% availability. Two 9s would be a system that guarantees 99% availability, allowing up to 1% downtime. Over the course of a year, this would translate to 3.65 days of unavailability.

Reliability engineering uses three principles of systems design to help achieve high availability: elimination of single points of failure (SPOFs), reliable crossover or failover points, and failure detection capabilities (including monitoring, discussed in Chapter 12).

Redundancy is required for many components to achieve high availability. A simple example is an airplane with two engines. If one engine fails while flying, the aircraft can still land at an airport. A more complex example is a nuclear power plant, where there are numerous redundant protocols and components to avoid catastrophic failures. Similarly, to achieve high availability of a database we need network redundancy, disk redundancy, different power supplies, multiple application and database servers, and much more.

This chapter will focus on the options to achieve high availability that MySQL databases offer.

Asynchronous Replication

Replication enables data from one MySQL database server (known as a *source*) to be copied to one or more other MySQL database servers (known as *replicas*). MySQL replication by default is asynchronous. With asynchronous replication, the source writes events to its binary log, and replicas request them when ready. There is no guarantee that any event will ever reach any replica. It's a loosely coupled source/replica relationship, where the following are true:

- The source does not wait for the replica to catch up.
- The replica determines how much to read and from which point in the binary log.
- The replica can be arbitrarily far behind the source in reading or applying changes. This issue is known as *replication lag*, and we will look at ways of minimizing it.

Asynchronous replication provides lower write latency since a write is acknowledged locally by a source before being written to the replicas.

MySQL implements its replication capabilities using three main threads, one on the source server and two on the replicas:

Binary log dump thread
> The source creates a thread to send the binary log contents to a replica when the replica connects. We can identify this thread in the output of SHOW PROCESSLIST on the source as the Binlog Dump thread.
>
> The binary log dump thread acquires a lock on the source's binary log for reading each event sent to the replica. When the source reads the event, the lock is released, even before the source sends the event to the replica.

Replication I/O thread
> When we execute the START SLAVE statement on a replica server, the replica creates an I/O thread connected to the source and asks it to send the updates recorded in its binary logs.
>
> The replication I/O thread reads the updates that the source's Binlog Dump thread sends (see the previous item) and copies them to local files that comprise the replica's relay log.
>
> MySQL shows the state of this thread as Slave_IO_running in the output of SHOW SLAVE STATUS.

Replication SQL thread

The replica creates a SQL thread to read the relay log written by the replication I/O thread and execute the transactions contained in it.

 As mentioned in Chapter 1, Oracle, Percona, and Maria DB are working to remove legacy terminology with negative connotations from their products. The documentation already uses the terms *source* and *replica*, as we do in this book, but because of the need to maintain backward compatibility and support for older versions, it would be impossible to completely change the terminology in one release. This is an ongoing effort.

There are ways to improve replication parallelization, as you'll see later in this chapter.

Figure 13-1 shows what the MySQL replication architecture looks like.

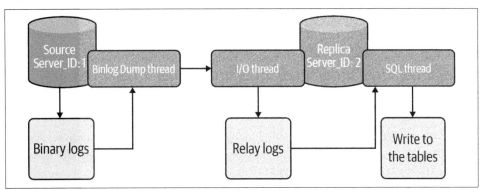

Figure 13-1. Asynchronous replication architecture flow

Replication works because events written to the binary log are read from the source and then processed on the replica, as shown in Figure 13-1. The events are recorded within the binary log in different formats according to the type of event. MySQL replication has three kinds of binary logging formats:

Row-based replication (RBR)

The source writes events to the binary log that indicate how individual table rows are changed. Replication of the source to the replica works by copying the events representing the replica's table rows' changes. For MySQL 5.7 and 8.0, this is the default replication format.

Statement-based replication (SBR)

The source writes SQL statements to the binary log. Replication of the source to the replica works by executing the SQL statements on the replica.

Mixed replication

You can also configure MySQL to use a mix of both statement-based and row-based logging, depending on which one is most appropriate to log the changes. With mixed-format logging, MySQL uses a statement-based log by default but switches to a row-based log for certain unsafe statements that have a nondeterministic behavior. For example, suppose we have the following statement:

```
mysql> UPDATE customer SET last_update=NOW() WHERE customer_id=1;
```

We know that the function NOW() returns the current date and time. Imagine that the source replicates the statement with 1 second of delay (there could be various reasons for this, such as the replica being on a different continent than the source). When the replica receives the statement and executes it, there will be a 1-second difference in the date and time returned by the function, leading to data inconsistency between the source and replica. When the mixed replication format is used, whenever MySQL parses a nondeterministic function like this, it will convert the statement to row-based replication. You can find a list of other functions that MySQL considers unsafe in the documentation (*https://oreil.ly/RGyxB*).

Basic Parameters to Set on the Source and the Replica

There are some basic settings that we need to set on both the source server and the replica server in order to make replication work. They are required for all methods explained in this section.

On the source server, you must enable binary logging and define a unique server ID. You'll need to restart the server after making these changes (if you haven't already) because these parameters are not dynamic.

> The server ID does not need to be incremental or be in any order, like having the source server ID be smaller than the replica server ID. The only requirement is that it be unique in each server that is part of the replication topology.

Here's what this will look like in the *my.cnf* file:

```
[mysqld]
log-bin=mysql-bin
server-id=1
```

You also need to establish a unique server ID for each replica. Like with the source, if you haven't done this yet, you'll need to restart the replica server after assigning it its ID. It is not mandatory to enable the binary log in the replica server, although it is a recommended practice:

```
[mysqld]
log-bin=mysql-replica-bin
server-id=1617565330
binlog_format = ROW
log_slave_updates
```

Using the `log_slave_updates` option tells the replica server that commands from a source server should be logged to the replica's own binary log. Again, this is not mandatory, but it is recommended as a good practice.

Each replica connects to the source using a MySQL username and password, so you'll also need to create a user account on the source server that the replica can use to connect (for a refresher on this, see "Creating and Using New Users" on page 317). Any account can be used for this operation, provided it has been granted the REPLICATION SLAVE privilege. Here's an example of how to create the user on the source server:

```
mysql> CREATE USER 'repl'@'%' IDENTIFIED BY 'P@ssw0rd!';
mysql> GRANT REPLICATION SLAVE ON *.* TO 'repl'@'%';
```

 If you are using an automation tool like Ansible to deploy MySQL, you can use the following bash command to create server IDs:

```
# date '+%s'
1617565330
```

The command converts the current date and time to an integer value, so it increases monotonically. Note that the date command does not guarantee the values' uniqueness, but you may find it convenient to use as it provides a relatively good uniqueness level.

In the next sections, you will see different options to create a replica server.

Creating a Replica Using PerconaXtraBackup

As we saw in Chapter 10, the Percona XtraBackup tool provides a method of performing a hot backup of your MySQL data while the system is running. It also offers advanced capabilities like parallelization, compression, and encryption.

The first step is taking a copy of the current source so we can start our replica. The XtraBackup tool performs a physical backup of the source (see "Physical and Logical Backups" on page 376). We will use the commands provided in "Percona Xtra-Backup" on page 388:

```
# xtrabackup --defaults-file=my.cnf -uroot -p_<password>_ \
    -H <host> -P 3306 --backup --parallel=4 \
    --datadir=./data/ --target-dir=./backup/
```

Alternatively, you can use rsync, NFS, or any other method that you feel comfortable with.

Once XtraBackup finishes the backup, we will send the files to a backup directory on the replica server. In this example, we will send the files using the scp command:

```
# scp -r ./backup/* <user>@<host>:/backup
```

At this point we're finished with the source. The following steps will run only on the replica server. The next step is to prepare our backup:

```
# xtrabackup --prepare --apply-log --target-dir=./
```

With everything set, we are going to move the backup to the data directory:

```
# xtrabackup --defaults-file=/etc/my.cnf --copy-back --target-dir=./backup
```

 Before proceeding, verify that your replica server does not have the same server_id as your source. If you followed the steps outlined in the previous section, you should have taken care of this already; if not, do so now.

On the replica, the content of the file *xtrabackup_binlog_info* will look something like this:

```
$ cat /backup/xtrabackup_binlog_info
mysql-bin.000003    156
```

This information is essential because it tells us where to start replicating. Remember that the source was still receiving operations when we took the backup, so we need to know what position MySQL was at in the binary log file when the backup finished.

With that information, we can run the command to start the replication. It will look something like this:

```
mysql> CHANGE MASTER TO MASTER_HOST='192.168.1.2', MASTER_USER='repl',
    -> MASTER_PASSWORD='P@ssw0rd!',
    -> MASTER_LOG_FILE='mysql-bin.000003', MASTER_LOG_POS=156;
mysql> START SLAVE;
```

Once you've started, you can run the SHOW SLAVE STATUS command to check if the replication is working:

```
mysql> SHOW SLAVE STATUS\G
            Slave_IO_Running: Yes
           Slave_SQL_Running: Yes
                  Last_Errno: 0
                  Last_Error:
                Skip_Counter: 0
          Exec_Master_Log_Pos: 8332
             Relay_Log_Space: 8752
```

```
         Until_Condition: None
     Seconds_Behind_Master: 0
Master_SSL_Verify_Server_Cert: No
            Last_IO_Errno: 0
            Last_IO_Error:
           Last_SQL_Errno: 0
           Last_SQL_Error:
```

It is important to check that both threads are running (Slave_IO_Running and Slave_SQL_Running), whether there have been any errors (Last_Error), and how many seconds the replica is behind the source. For large databases with an intensive write workload, the replica may take a while to catch up.

Creating a Replica Using the Clone Plugin

MySQL 8.0.17 introduced the clone plugin (*https://oreil.ly/fBWth*), which can be used to make one MySQL server instance a *clone* of another. We refer to the server instance where the CLONE statement is executed as the *recipient* and to the source server instance from which the recipient will clone the data as the *donor*. The donor instance can be local or remote. The cloning process works by creating a physical snapshot of the data and metadata stored in the InnoDB storage engine on the donor, and transferring it to the recipient. Both local and remote instances perform the same clone operation; there is no difference related to the data between the two options.

Let's walk through a real example. We'll show you some additional details along the way, like how to monitor the progress of a long-running CLONE command, the privileges required to clone, and more. The following example uses the classic shell. We'll talk about MySQL Shell, introduced in MySQL 8.0, in Chapter 16.

Choose the MySQL server to clone from and connect to it as the root user. Then install the clone plugin, create a user to transfer the data from the donor server, and grant that user the BACKUP_ADMIN privilege:

```
mysql> INSTALL PLUGIN CLONE SONAME "mysql_clone.so";
mysql> CREATE USER clone_user@'%' IDENTIFIED BY "clone_password";
mysql> GRANT BACKUP_ADMIN ON *.* to clone_user;
```

Next, to observe the progress of the cloning operation, we need to grant that user privileges to view the performance_schema database and execute functions:

```
mysql> GRANT SELECT ON performance_schema.* TO clone_user;
mysql> GRANT EXECUTE ON *.* to clone_user;
```

Now we will move to the recipient server. If you are provisioning a new node, first initialize a data directory and start the server.

Connect to the recipient server as the root user. Then install the clone plugin, create a user to replace the current instance data with the cloned data, and grant that user the CLONE_ADMIN privilege. We'll also provide a list of valid donors that the recipient can clone (here, just one):

```
mysql> INSTALL PLUGIN CLONE SONAME "mysql_clone.so";
mysql> SET GLOBAL clone_valid_donor_list = "127.0.0.1:21122";
mysql> CREATE USER clone_user IDENTIFIED BY "clone_password";
mysql> GRANT CLONE_ADMIN ON *.* to clone_user;
```

We'll grant this user the same privileges we did on the donor side, to observe the progress on the recipient side:

```
mysql> GRANT SELECT ON performance_schema.* TO clone_user;
mysql> GRANT EXECUTE ON *.* to clone_user;
```

We now have everything we need in place, so it's time to start the cloning process. Note that the donor server must be reachable from the recipient. The recipient will connect to the donor with the address and credentials provided and start cloning:

```
mysql> CLONE INSTANCE FROM clone_user@192.168.1.2:3306
    -> IDENTIFIED BY "clone_password";
```

The recipient must shut down and restart itself for the clone operation to succeed. We can monitor the progress with the following query:

```
SELECT STAGE, STATE, CAST(BEGIN_TIME AS TIME) as "START TIME",
CASE WHEN END_TIME IS NULL THEN
LPAD(sys.format_time(POWER(10,12) * (UNIX_TIMESTAMP(now()) -
    UNIX_TIMESTAMP(BEGIN_TIME))), 10,' )
ELSE
LPAD(sys.format_time(POWER(10,12) * (UNIX_TIMESTAMP(END_TIME) -
    UNIX_TIMESTAMP(BEGIN_TIME))), 10, )
END AS DURATION,
LPAD(CONCAT(FORMAT(ROUND(ESTIMATE/1024/1024,0), 0)," MB"), 16, )
AS "Estimate",
CASE WHEN BEGIN_TIME IS NULL THEN LPAD('0%', 7, ' )
WHEN ESTIMATE > 0 THEN
LPAD(CONCAT(CAST(ROUND(DATA*100/ESTIMATE, 0) AS BINARY), "%"), 7, ' ')
WHEN END_TIME IS NULL THEN LPAD('0%', 7, ' )
ELSE LPAD('100%', 7, ' ') END AS "Done(%)"
from performance_schema.clone_progress;
```

This will allow us to observe each state of the cloning process. The output will be similar to this:

```
+-----------+-----------+------------+-----------+----------+---------+
| STAGE     | STATE     | START TIME | DURATION  | Estimate | Done(%) |
+-----------+-----------+------------+-----------+----------+---------+
| DROP DATA | Completed | 14:44:46   |    1.33 s |     0 MB | 100%    |
+-----------+-----------+------------+-----------+----------+---------+
| FILE COPY | Completed | 14:44:48   |    5.62 s | 1,511 MB | 100%    |
+-----------+-----------+------------+-----------+----------+---------+
| PAGE COPY | Completed | 14:44:53   | 95.06 ms  |     0 MB | 100%    |
+-----------+-----------+------------+-----------+----------+---------+
```

```
| REDO COPY | Completed | 14:44:54 |  99.71 ms |    0 MB | 100%  |
+-----------+-----------+-----------+-----------+---------+-------+
| FILE SYNC | Completed | 14:44:54 |    6.33 s |    0 MB | 100%  |
+-----------+-----------+-----------+-----------+---------+-------+
| RESTART   | Completed | 14:45:00 |    4.08 s |    0 MB | 100%  |
+-----------+-----------+-----------+-----------+---------+-------+
| RECOVERY  | Completed | 14:45:04 | 516.86 ms |    0 MB | 100%  |
+-----------+-----------+-----------+-----------+---------+-------+
7 rows in set (0.08 sec)
```

As mentioned previously, there is a restart at the end. Note that replication has not started yet.

In addition to cloning the data, the cloning operation extracts the binary log position and GTID from the donor server and transfers them to the recipient. We can execute the following queries on the donor to view the binary log position or the GTID of the last transaction that was applied:

```
mysql> SELECT BINLOG_FILE, BINLOG_POSITION FROM performance_schema.clone_status;

+-----------------+-----------------+
| BINLOG_FILE     | BINLOG_POSITION |
+-----------------+-----------------+
| mysql-bin.000002 |       816804753 |
+-----------------+-----------------+
1 row in set (0.01 sec)

mysql> SELECT @@GLOBAL.GTID_EXECUTED;

+------------------------+
| @@GLOBAL.GTID_EXECUTED |
+------------------------+
|                        |
+------------------------+
1 row in set (0.00 sec)
```

In this example we are not using GTIDs, so the query does not return anything. Next, we will run the command to start the replication:

```
mysql> CHANGE MASTER TO MASTER_HOST = '192.168.1.2', MASTER_PORT = 3306,
    -> MASTER_USER = 'repl', MASTER_PASSWORD = 'P@ssw0rd!',
    -> MASTER_LOG_FILE = 'mysql-bin.000002',
    -> MASTER_LOG_POSITION = 816804753;
mysql> START SLAVE;
```

As in the previous section, we can check that replication is working correctly by running the SHOW SLAVE STATUS command.

The advantage of this approach is that the clone plugin automates the whole process, and only at the end is it necessary to execute the CHANGE MASTER command. The disadvantage is that the plugin is available only for MySQL 8.0.17 and higher. While it's still relatively new, we believe that in years to come, this process may become the default.

Creating a Replica Using mysqldump

This is what we might call the classic approach. It's the typical option for those who are getting started with MySQL and still learning about the ecosystem. As usual, we assume here that you have performed the necessary setup in "Basic Parameters to Set on the Source and the Replica" on page 492.

Let's see an example of using `mysqldump` to create a new replica. We will execute the backup from the source server:

```
# mysqldump -uroot -p<password> --single-transaction \
    --all-databases --routines --triggers --events \
    --master-data=2 > backup.sql
```

The dump succeeded if the message `Dump completed` appears at the end:

```
# tail -1f backup.sql

-- Dump completed on 2021-04-26 20:16:33
```

With the backup taken, we need to import it in the replica server. For example, you can use this command:

```
$ mysql < backup.sql
```

Once that's done, you'll need to execute the `CHANGE MASTER` command with the coordinates extracted from the dump (for more details about `mysqldump`, revisit "The mysqldump Program" on page 376). Because we used the `--master-data=2` option, the information will be written at the beginning of the dump. For example:

```
$ head -n 35 out
-- MySQL dump 10.13  Distrib 5.7.31-34, for Linux (x86_64)
--
-- Host: 127.0.0.1    Database:
-- ------------------------------------------------------
-- Server version    5.7.33-log

...


--
-- Position to start replication or point-in-time recovery from
--

-- CHANGE MASTER TO MASTER_LOG_FILE='mysql-bin.000001', MASTER_LOG_POS=4089;
```

Or, if you're using GTIDs:

```
--
-- GTID state at the beginning of the backup
-- (origin: @@global.gtid_executed)
--

SET @@GLOBAL.GTID_PURGED=00048008-1111-1111-1111-111111111111:1-16;
```

Next, we are going to execute the command to start the replication. For the GTID scenario, it looks like this:

```
mysql> CHANGE MASTER TO MASTER_HOST='192.168.1.2', MASTER_USER='repl',
    -> MASTER_PASSWORD = 'P@ssw0rd!', MASTER_AUTO_POSITION=1;
mysql> START SLAVE;
```

For traditional replication, you can start replication from the previously extracted binary log file position as follows:

```
mysql> CHANGE MASTER TO MASTER_LOG_FILE='mysql-bin.000001', MASTER_LOG_POS=4089,
    -> MASTER_HOST='192.168.1.2', MASTER_USER='repl',
    -> MASTER_PASSWORD='P@ssw0rd!';
mysql> START SLAVE;
```

To verify that replication is working, execute the SHOW SLAVE STATUS command.

Creating a Replica Using mydumper and myloader

mysqldump is the most common tool used by beginners for performing backups and building replicas. But there is a more efficient method: mydumper. Like mysqldump, this tool generates a logical backup and can be used to create a consistent backup of your database. The main difference between mydumper and mysqldump is that mydumper, when paired with myloader, can dump and restore data in parallel, improving the dump and, especially, restore time. Imagine a scenario where your database has a dump of 500 GB. Using mysqldump, you will have a single huge file. With mydumper, you will have one file per table, allowing the restore process to be executed in parallel later.

Setting up the mydumper and myloader utilities

You can run mydumper directly on the source server or from another server, which in general is better since it will avoid the overhead in the storage system of writing the backup files on the same server.

To install mydumper, download the package specific to the operating system version you are using. You can find the releases in the mydumper GitHub repository (*https://oreil.ly/7hakG*). Let's see an example for CentOS:

```
# yum install https://github.com/maxbube/mydumper/releases/download/v0.10.3/ \
mydumper-0.10.3-1.el7.x86_64.rpm -y
```

Now you should have both the mydumper and myloader commands installed on the server. You can validate this with:

```
$ mydumper --version
mydumper 0.10.3, built against MySQL 5.7.33-36

$ myloader --version
myloader 0.10.3, built against MySQL 5.7.33-36
```

Extracting data from the source

The following command will execute a dump of all databases (except `mysql`, `test`, and the `sys` schema) with 15 simultaneous threads and will also include triggers, views, and functions:

```
# mydumper --regex '^(?!(mysql\.|test\.|sys\.))' --threads=15
--user=learning_user --password='learning_mysql' --host=192.168.1.2 \
    --port=3306 --trx-consistency-only --events --routines --triggers \
    --compress --outputdir /backup --logfile /tmp/log.out --verbose=2
```

You will need to grant at least the SELECT and RELOAD permissions to the mydumper user.

If you check the output directory (`outputdir`), you will see the compressed files. Here's the output on one of the authors' machines:

```
# ls -l backup/
total 5008
-rw...1 vinicius.grippa percona    182 May  1 19:30 metadata
-rw...1 vinicius.grippa percona    258 May  1 19:30 sysbench.sbtest10-schema.sql.gz
-rw...1 vinicius.grippa percona 96568 May  1 19:30 sysbench.sbtest10.sql.gz
-rw...1 vinicius.grippa percona    258 May  1 19:30 sysbench.sbtest11-schema.sql.gz
-rw...1 vinicius.grippa percona 96588 May  1 19:30 sysbench.sbtest11.sql.gz
-rw...1 vinicius.grippa percona    258 May  1 19:30 sysbench.sbtest12-schema.sql.gz
...
```

Decide the number of threads based on the CPU cores of the database server and server load. Doing a parallel dump can consume a lot of server resources.

Restoring data in a replica server

Like with `mysqldump`, we need to have the replica MySQL instance already up and running. Once the data is ready to be imported, we can execute the following command:

```
# myloader --user=learning_user --password='learning_mysql'
--threads=25 --host=192.168.1.3 --port=3306
--directory=/backup --overwrite-tables --verbose 3
```

Establishing the replication

Now that we've restored the data, we will set up replication. We need to find the correct binary log position at the start of the backup. This information is stored in the mydumper metadata file:

```
$ cat backup/metadata
Started dump at: 2021-05-01 19:30:00
SHOW MASTER STATUS:
    Log: mysql-bin.000002
    Pos: 9530779
    GTID:00049010-1111-1111-1111-111111111111:1-319

Finished dump at: 2021-05-01 19:30:01
```

Now, we simply execute the CHANGE MASTER command like we did previously for mysqldump:

```
mysql> CHANGE MASTER TO MASTER_HOST='192.168.1.2', MASTER_USER='repl',
    -> MASTER_PASSWORD='P@ssw0rd!', MASTER_LOG_FILE='mysql-bin.000002',
    -> MASTER_LOG_POS=9530779, MASTER_PORT=49010;
mysql> START SLAVE;
```

Group Replication

It might be a bit controversial to include Group Replication in the asynchronous replication group. The short explanation for this choice is that Group Replication is asynchronous. The confusion here can be explained by the comparison with Galera (discussed in "Galera/PXC Cluster" on page 509), which claims to be synchronous or virtually synchronous.

The more detailed reasoning is that it depends on how we define replication. In the MySQL world, we define replication as the process that enables changes made in one database (the source) to be automatically duplicated in another (the replica). The entire process involves five different steps:

1. Locally applying the change on the source
2. Generating a binlog event
3. Sending the binlog event to the replica(s)
4. Adding the binlog event to the replica's relay log
5. Applying the binlog event from the relay log on the replica

In MySQL Group Replication and Galera (even if the Galera cache primarily replaces the binlog and relay log files), only step 3 is synchronous—the streaming of the binary log event (or write set in Galera) to the replica(s).

Thus, while the process of sending (replicating/streaming) the data to the other servers is synchronous, the *applying* of these changes is still wholly asynchronous.

 Group Replication has been available since MySQL 5.7. However, when the product was released, it was not mature enough, leading to constant performance issues and crashes. We highly recommend using MySQL 8.0 if you want to test Group Replication.

Installing Group Replication

The first advantage of Group Replication compared to Galera is that you don't have to install different binaries. MySQL Server provides Group Replication as a plugin. It's also available for Oracle MySQL and Percona Server for MySQL; for details on installing those, see Chapter 1.

To confirm that the Group Replication plugin is enabled, run the following query:

```
mysql> SELECT PLUGIN_NAME, PLUGIN_STATUS, PLUGIN_TYPE
    -> FROM INFORMATION_SCHEMA.PLUGINS
    -> WHERE PLUGIN_NAME LIKE 'group_replication';
```

The output should show ACTIVE, as you see here:

```
+-------------------+---------------+-------------------+
| PLUGIN_NAME       | PLUGIN_STATUS | PLUGIN_TYPE       |
+-------------------+---------------+-------------------+
| group_replication | ACTIVE        | GROUP REPLICATION |
+-------------------+---------------+-------------------+
1 row in set (0.00 sec)
```

If the plugin is not installed, run the following command to install it:

```
mysql> INSTALL PLUGIN group_replication SONAME 'group_replication.so';
```

With the plugin active, we will set the minimum parameters required on the servers to start Group Replication. Open *my.cnf* on server 1 and add the following:

```
[mysqld]
server_id=175907211
log-bin=mysqld-bin
enforce_gtid_consistency=ON
gtid_mode=ON
log-slave-updates
transaction_write_set_extraction=XXHASH64
master_info_repository=TABLE
relay_log_info_repository=TABLE
binlog_checksum=NONE
```

Let's go over each of those parameters:

`server_id`
> Like with classic replication, this parameter helps to identify each member in the group using a unique ID. You must use a different value for each server participating in Group Replication.

`log_bin`
> In MySQL 8.0 this parameter is enabled by default. It is responsible for recording all the changes in the database in binary log files.

`enforce_gtid_consistency`
> This value must be set to ON to instruct MySQL to execute transaction-safe statements to ensure consistency when replicating data.

`gtid_mode`
> This directive enables global transaction identifier-based logging when set to ON. This is required for Group Replication.

`log_slave_updates`
> This value is set to ON to allow members to log updates from each other. In other words, the directive chains the replication servers together.

`transaction_write_set_extraction`
> This instructs the MySQL server to collect write sets and encode them using a hashing algorithm. In this case, we are using the XXHASH64 algorithm. Write sets are defined by primary keys on each record.

`master_info_repository`
> When set to TABLE, this directive allows MySQL to store details about source binary log files and positions into a table rather than a file to enable faster replication and guarantee consistency using InnoDB's ACID properties. In MySQL 8.0.23 this is the default, and the FILE option is deprecated.

`relay_log_info_repository`
> When set to TABLE, this configures MySQL to store replication information as an InnoDB table. In MySQL 8.0.23 this is the default, and the FILE option is deprecated.

`binlog_checksum`
> Setting this to NONE tells MySQL not to write a checksum for each event in the binary log. The server will instead verify events when they are written by checking their length. In versions of MySQL up to and including 8.0.20, Group Replication cannot make use of checksums. If you're using a later release and want to use checksums, you can omit this setting and use the default, CRC32.

Next, we are going to add some specific parameters for Group Replication:

```
[mysqld]

loose-group_replication_group_name="8dc32851-d7f2-4b63-8989-5d4b467d8251"
loose-group_replication_start_on_boot=OFF
loose-group_replication_local_address="10.124.33.139:33061"
loose-group_replication_group_seeds="10.124.33.139:33061,
10.124.33.90:33061, 10.124.33.224:33061"
loose-group_replication_bootstrap_group=OFF
bind-address = "0.0.0.0"
report_host = "10.124.33.139"
```

 We are using the loose- prefix to instruct the server to start even when the MySQL Group Replication plugin is not installed and configured. This avoids encountering server errors before you finish configuring all the settings.

Let's see what each parameter does:

group_replication_group_name

This is the name of the group that we are creating. We are going to use the built-in Linux uuidgen command to generate a universally unique identifier (UUID). It produces output like this:

$ **uuidgen**

8dc32851-d7f2-4b63-8989-5d4b467d8251

group_replication_start_on_boot

When set to OFF, the value instructs the plugin not to start working automatically when the server starts. You may set this value to ON once you are through with configuring all the group members.

loose-group_replication_local_address

This is the internal IP address and port combination used for communicating with other MySQL server members in the group. The recommended port for Group Replication is 33061.

group_replication_group_seeds

This configures the IP addresses or hostnames of members participating in Group Replication, together with their communication port. New members use the value to establish themselves in the group.

group_replication_bootstrap_group

This option instructs the server whether to create a group or not. We will only enable this option on demand on server 1, to avoid creating multiple groups. So, it will remain off for now.

```
bind_address
```
The value of `0.0.0.0` tells MySQL to listen to all networks.

```
report_host
```
This is the IP address or hostname the group members reports to each other when they are registered in the group.

Setting up MySQL Group Replication

First, we will set up the `group_replication_recovery` channel. MySQL Group Replication uses this channel to transfer transactions between members. Because of this, we must set up a replication user with `REPLICATION SLAVE` permission on each server.

So, on server 1, log in to the MySQL console and execute the following commands:

```
mysql> SET SQL_LOG_BIN=0;
mysql> CREATE USER replication_user@'%' IDENTIFIED BY 'P@ssw0rd!';
mysql> GRANT REPLICATION SLAVE ON *.* TO 'replication_user'@'%';
mysql> FLUSH PRIVILEGES;
mysql> SET SQL_LOG_BIN=1;
```

We first set `SQL_LOG_BIN` to 0 to prevent the new user's details from being logged to the binary log then we reenable it at the end.

To instruct the MySQL server to use the replication user we have created for the `group_replication_recovery` channel, run this command:

```
mysql> CHANGE MASTER TO MASTER_USER='replication_user',
    -> MASTER_PASSWORD='P@ssw0rd!' FOR CHANNEL
    -> 'group_replication_recovery';
```

These settings will allow members joining the group to run the distributed recovery process to get to the same state as the other members (donors).

Now we will start the Group Replication service on server 1. We will bootstrap the group using these commands:

```
mysql> SET GLOBAL group_replication_bootstrap_group=ON;
mysql> START GROUP_REPLICATION;
mysql> SET GLOBAL group_replication_bootstrap_group=OFF;
```

To avoid starting up more groups, we set `group_replication_bootstrap_group` back to `OFF` after successfully starting the group.

To check the status of the new member, use this command:

```
mysql> SELECT * FROM performance_schema.replication_group_members;
```

```
+-------------------------+-----------------------------------------+...
| CHANNEL_NAME            | MEMBER_ID                               |...
+-------------------------+-----------------------------------------+...
| group_replication_applier | d58b2766-ab90-11eb-ba00-00163ed02a2e |...
+-------------+-----------+---------------+-------------+---------+...

...+---------------+-------------+--------------+-------------+----------------+
...| MEMBER_HOST   | MEMBER_PORT | MEMBER_STATE | MEMBER_ROLE | MEMBER_VERSION |
...+---------------+-------------+--------------+-------------+----------------+
...| 10.124.33.139 |        3306 | ONLINE       | PRIMARY     | 8.0.22         |
...+---------------+-------------+--------------+-------------+----------------+
1 row in set (0.00 sec)
```

Great. So far we've bootstrapped and initiated one group member. Let's proceed to the second server. Make sure you have installed the same MySQL version as on server 1, and add the following settings to the *my.cnf* file:

```
[mysqld]
loose-group_replication_group_name="8dc32851-d7f2-4b63-8989-5d4b467d851"
loose-group_replication_start_on_boot=OFF
loose-group_replication_local_address="10.124.33.90:33061"
loose-group_replication_group_seeds="10.124.33.139:33061,
10.124.33.90:33061, 10.124.33.224:33061"
loose-group_replication_bootstrap_group=OFF
bind-address = "0.0.0.0"
```

All we've changed is the `group_replication_local_address`; the other settings remain the same. Note that the other MySQL configurations are required for server 2, and we strongly recommend keeping them the same across all nodes.

With the configurations in place, restart the MySQL service:

```
# systemctl restart mysqld
```

Issue the following commands to configure the credentials for the recovery user on server 2:

```
mysql> SET SQL_LOG_BIN=0;
mysql> CREATE USER 'replication_user'@'%' IDENTIFIED BY 'P@ssw0rd!';
mysql> GRANT REPLICATION SLAVE ON *. TO 'replication_user'@'%';*
mysql> SET SQL_LOG_BIN=1;
mysql> CHANGE MASTER TO MASTER_USER='replication_user',
MASTER_PASSWORD='PASSWORD' FOR CHANNEL
'group_replication_recovery';
```

Next, add server 2 to the group that we bootstrapped earlier:

```
mysql> START GROUP_REPLICATION;
```

And run the query to check the member's state:

```
mysql> SELECT * FROM performance_schema.replication_group_members;
```

```
+-------------------------------+-------------------------------------------+...
| CHANNEL_NAME                  | MEMBER_ID                                 |...
+-------------------------------+-------------------------------------------+...
| group_replication_applier     | 9e971ba0-ab9d-11eb-afc6-00163ec43109      |...
| group_replication_applier     | d58b2766-ab90-11eb-ba00-00163ed02a2e      |...
+-------------+-------------+-------------+---------------+----------+...
...+-------------+-------------+----------------+...
...| MEMBER_HOST   | MEMBER_PORT | MEMBER_STATE |...
...+-------------+-------------+----------------+...
...| 10.124.33.90  |        3306 | ONLINE       |...
...| 10.124.33.139 |        3306 | ONLINE       |...
...+-------------+-------------+----------------+...
...+-------------+----------------+
...| MEMBER_ROLE | MEMBER_VERSION |
...+-------------+----------------+
...| SECONDARY   | 8.0.22         |
...| PRIMARY     | 8.0.22         |
...+-------------+----------------+
2 rows in set (0.00 sec)
```

Now you can follow the same steps for server 3 as we used for server 2, again updating the local address. When you're done, you can validate whether all the servers are responsive by inserting some dummy data:

```
mysql> CREATE DATABASE learning_mysql;

Query OK, 1 row affected (0.00 sec)

mysql> USE learning_mysql

Database changed

mysql> CREATE TABLE test (i int primary key);

Query OK, 0 rows affected (0.01 sec)

mysql> INSERT INTO test VALUES (1);

Query OK, 1 row affected (0.00 sec)
```

Then connect to the other servers to see whether you can visualize the data.

Synchronous Replication

Synchronous replication is used by Galera Clusters, where we have more than one MySQl server, but they act as a single entity for the application. Figure 13-2 illustrates a Galera Cluster with three nodes.

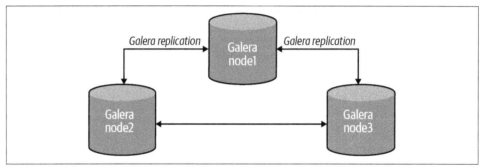

Figure 13-2. In a Galera Cluster, all nodes communicate with each other

The primary difference between synchronous and asynchronous replication is that synchronous replication guarantees that if a change happens on one node in the cluster, then the change will happen on the other nodes in the cluster synchronously, or at the same time. Asynchronous replication gives no guarantees about the delay between applying changes on the source node and propagating those changes to replica nodes. The delay with asynchronous replication can be short or long. This also implies that if the source node crashes in an asynchronous replication topology, some of the latest changes may be lost. This concepts of source and replica do not exist in a Galera Cluster. All nodes can receive reads and writes.

Theoretically, synchronous replication has several advantages over asynchronous replication:

- Clusters utilizing synchronous replication are always highly available. If one of the nodes crashes, then there will be no data loss. Additionally, all cluster nodes are always consistent.

- Clusters utilizing synchronous replication allow transactions to be executed on all nodes in parallel.

- Clusters utilizing synchronous replication can guarantee causality across the whole cluster. This means that if a SELECT is executed on one cluster node after a transaction is executed on another cluster node, it should see the effects of that transaction.

However, there are disadvantages to synchronous replication as well. Traditionally, eager replication protocols coordinate nodes one operation at a time, using a two-phase commit or distributed locking. Increasing the number of nodes in the cluster leads to growth in the transaction response times and the probability of conflicts and deadlocks among the nodes. This is because all nodes need to certify the transaction and reply with an OK message.

For this reason, asynchronous replication remains the dominant replication protocol for database performance, scalability, and availability. Not understanding or underestimating the impact of synchronous replication is one reason companies sometimes give up using Galera Clusters and go back to using asynchronous replication.

At the time of writing, two companies support the Galera Cluster: Percona and MariaDB. The following example shows how to set up a Percona XtraDB Cluster.

Galera/PXC Cluster

Installing Percona XtraDB Cluster (PXC) is similar to installing Percona Server (the difference is the packages), so we won't dive into details for all platforms. You may want to revisit Chapter 1 to review the installation process. The configuration process we'll follow here assumes there are three PXC nodes.

Table 13-1. The three PXC nodes

Node	Host	IP
Node 1	pxc1	172.16.2.56
Node 2	pxc2	172.16.2.198
Node 3	pxc3	172.16.3.177

Connect to one of the nodes and install the repository:

```
# yum install https://repo.percona.com/yum/percona-release-latest.noar
ch.rpm -y
```

With the repository installed, install the binaries:

```
# yum install Percona-XtraDB-Cluster-57 -y
```

Next, you can apply the typical configurations that you would use for a regular MySQL process (see Chapter 11). With the changes made, start the mysqld process and get the temporary password:

```
# 'systemctl start mysqld'
# 'grep temporary password'/var/log/mysqld.log'
```

Use the previous password to log in as root and change the password:

```
$ mysql -u root -p
```

```
mysql> ALTER USER 'root'@'localhost' IDENTIFIED BY 'P@ssw0rd!';
```

Stop the mysqld process:

```
# systemctl stop mysql
```

Repeat the previous steps for the other two nodes.

With the binaries and basic configuration in place, we can start working on the cluster parameters.

We need to add the following configuration variables to *etc/my.cnf* on the first node:

```
[mysqld]
wsrep_provider=/usr/lib64/galera3/libgalera_smm.so
wsrep_cluster_name=pxc-cluster
wsrep_cluster_address=gcomm://172.16.2.56,172.16.2.198,172.16.3.177

wsrep_node_name=pxc1
wsrep_node_address=172.16.2.56

wsrep_sst_method=xtrabackup-v2
wsrep_sst_auth=sstuser:P@ssw0rd!

pxc_strict_mode=ENFORCING

binlog_format=ROW
default_storage_engine=InnoDB
innodb_autoinc_lock_mode=2
```

Use the same configuration for the second and third nodes, except the `wsrep_node_name` and `wsrep_node_address` variables.

For the second node, use:

```
wsrep_node_name=pxc2
wsrep_node_address=172.16.2.198
```

For the third node, use:

```
wsrep_node_name=pxc3
wsrep_node_address=172.16.3.177
```

Like regular MySQL, Percona XtraDB Cluster has many configurable parameters, and the ones we've shown are the minimal settings to start the cluster. We are configuring the node's name and IP address, the cluster address, and the user that will be used for internal communication among the nodes. You can find more detailed information in the documentation (*https://oreil.ly/Ap8Rr*).

We have all the nodes configured at this point, but the `mysqld` process is not running on any node. PXC requires you to start one node in a cluster as a reference point for the others before the other nodes can join and form the cluster. This node must be started in *bootstrap* mode. Bootstrapping is an initial step to introduce one server as a primary component so the others can use it as a reference point to sync up data.

Start the first node with the following command:

```
# systemctl start mysql@bootstrap
```

Before adding other nodes to your new cluster, connect to the node that you just started, create a user for State Snapshot Transfer (SST), and provide the necessary privileges for it. The credentials must match those specified in the `wsrep_sst_auth` configuration that you set previously:

```
mysql> CREATE USER 'sstuser'@'localhost' IDENTIFIED BY 'P@ssw0rd!';
mysql> GRANT RELOAD, LOCK TABLES, PROCESS, REPLICATION CLIENT ON .
    -> TO 'sstuser'@'localhost';
mysql> FLUSH PRIVILEGES;
```

The SST process is used by the cluster to provision nodes by transferring a full data copy from one node to another. When a new node joins the cluster, the new node initiates an SST to synchronize its data with a node that is already part of the cluster.

After this, you can initialize the other nodes regularly:

```
# systemctl start mysql
```

To verify that the cluster is up and running fine, we can perform a few checks, like creating a database on the first node, creating a table and inserting some data on the second node, and retrieving some rows from that table on the third node. First, let's create the database on the first node (pxc1):

```
mysq> CREATE DATABASE learning_mysql;

Query ok, 1 row affected (0.01 sec)
```

On the second node (pxc2), create a table and insert some data:

```
mysql> USE learning_mysql;

Database changed

mysql> CREATE TABLE example (node_id INT PRIMARY KEY, node_name VARCHAR(30));

Query ok, 0 rows affected (0.05 sec)

mysql> INSERT INTO learning_mysql.example VALUES (1, "Vinicius1");

Query OK, 1 row affected (0.02 sec)
```

Then retrieve some rows from that table on the third node:

```
mysql> SELECT * FROM learning_mysql.example;

+---------+-----------+
| node_id | node_name |
+---------+-----------+
|       1 | Vinicius1 |
+---------+-----------+
1 row in set (0.00 sec)
```

Another, more elegant solution is checking the `wsrep_%` global status variables, in particular `wsrep_cluster_size` and `wsrep_cluster_status`:

```
mysql> SHOW GLOBAL STATUS LIKE 'wsrep_cluster_size';

+--------------------+-------+
| Variable_name      | Value |
+--------------------+-------+
| wsrep_cluster_size | 3     |
+--------------------+-------+
1 row in set (0.00 sec)

mysql> SHOW GLOBAL STATUS LIKE 'wsrep_cluster_status';

+----------------------+---------+
| Variable_name        | Value   |
+----------------------+---------+
| wsrep_cluster_status | Primary |
+----------------------+---------+
1 row in set (0.00 sec)
```

The output of these commands tells us that the cluster has three nodes and is in the primary state (it can receive reads and writes).

You might consider using ProxySQL in addition to the Galera Cluster to ensure transparency for the application (see Chapter 15).

The goal of this chapter was just to familiarize you with the different topologies so you know they exist. Cluster maintenance and optimization are advanced topics that are beyond the scope of this book.

## CHAPTER 14

MySQL in the Cloud

"No need to worry, it's in the cloud" is a phrase we often hear. It reminds us of a story about a woman who was worried that, after her iPhone drowned in the toilet, she'd lost all her years' worth of family and travel photos. To her surprise, when she bought a new phone, the device "recovered" all the photos. She was using the iCloud backup solution from Apple to back up her device content to the cloud. (The other surprise may have been the service subscription bill she hadn't realized she was paying.)

As computer engineers, we don't have the luxury of taking risks with regard to whether our data will be recovered or not. Cloud storage is a scalable and reliable solution. In this chapter, we will look at a few options that companies have for using MySQL in the cloud. These range from database-as-a-service (DBaaS) options that are easily scalable and provide automatic backup and high availability features to more traditional choices like EC2 instances, which provide more fine-grained control. In general, startup companies, where the core business is not technology, prefer to use DBaaS options since they are easier to implement and work with. On the other hand, companies that need more strict control over their data might prefer to use an EC2 instance or their own cloud infrastructure.

Database-as-a-Service (DBaaS)

DBaaS is an outsourcing option where companies pay a cloud provider to launch and maintain a cloud database for them. Payment is usually per-usage, and the data owners can access their application data as they please. A DBaaS provides the same functionalities as a standard relational or non-relational database. It's often a good solution for companies trying to avoid configuring, maintaining, and upgrading their databases and servers (although this is not always true). DBaaS lives in the realm of software-as-a-service (SaaS), like platform-as-a-service (PaaS) and infrastructure-as-a-service (IaaS), where products like databases become services.

Amazon RDS for MySQL/MariaDB

The most popular DBaaS is Amazon RDS for MySQL. Getting started with RDS is almost like configuring a new car on a website. You choose the main product and add the options you want until it looks the way you like and then launch. Figure 14-1 shows the products available. In this case, we will go for MySQL (the MariaDB version has similar settings for deployment).

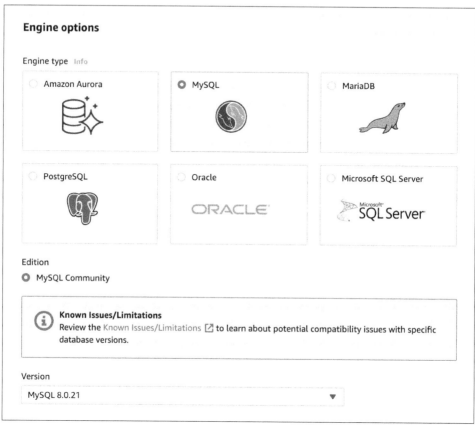

Figure 14-1. Choosing the product

We can also choose the version—here, we've selected 8.0.21. Next, we need to set the master user (similar to `root`) and its password. Make sure to pick a strong password, especially if you will expose your database to the world. Figure 14-2 shows how to define the username and the password for the master user.

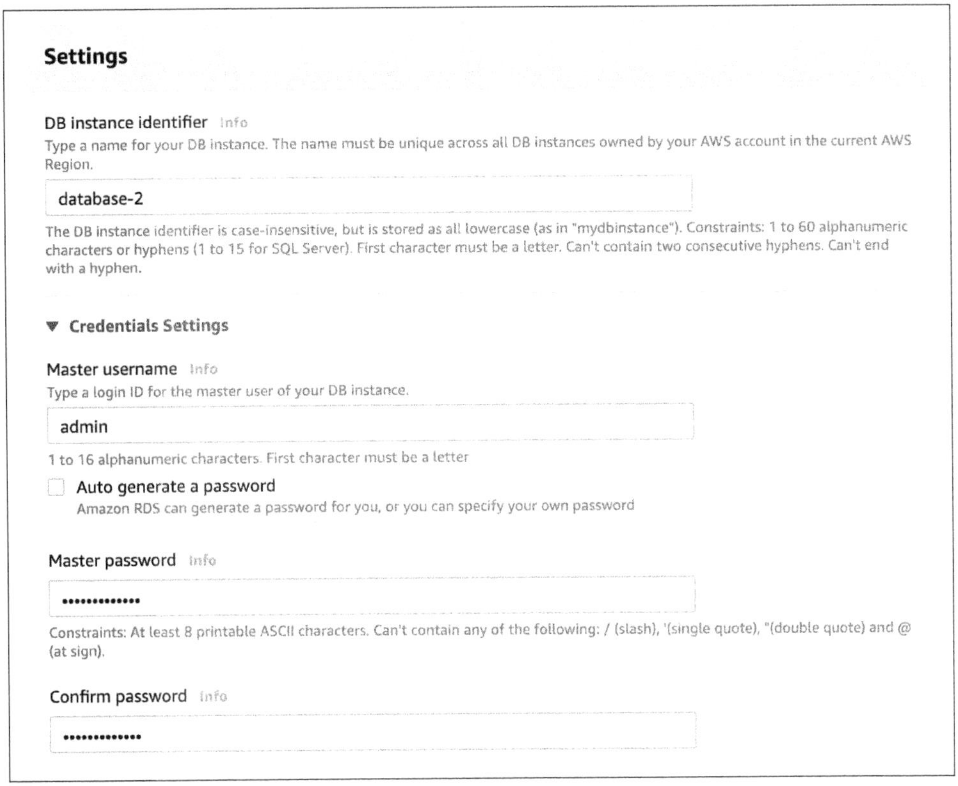

Settings

DB instance identifier Info

Type a name for your DB instance. The name must be unique across all DB instances owned by your AWS account in the current AWS Region.

database-2

The DB instance identifier is case-insensitive, but is stored as all lowercase (as in "mydbinstance"). Constraints: 1 to 60 alphanumeric characters or hyphens (1 to 15 for SQL Server). First character must be a letter. Can't contain two consecutive hyphens. Can't end with a hyphen.

▼ Credentials Settings

Master username Info

Type a login ID for the master user of your DB instance.

admin

1 to 16 alphanumeric characters. First character must be a letter

☐ **Auto generate a password**

Amazon RDS can generate a password for you, or you can specify your own password

Master password Info

••••••••••••

Constraints: At least 8 printable ASCII characters. Can't contain any of the following: / (slash), '(single quote), "(double quote) and @ (at sign).

Confirm password Info

••••••••••••

Figure 14-2. Configuring the master user's username and password

Next is the instance size, which will impact directly on the final price. We will pick a top-level configuration to give you an idea of how costly using a DBaaS can be. Figure 14-3 shows the instance classes that are available; there are several options, with varying costs.

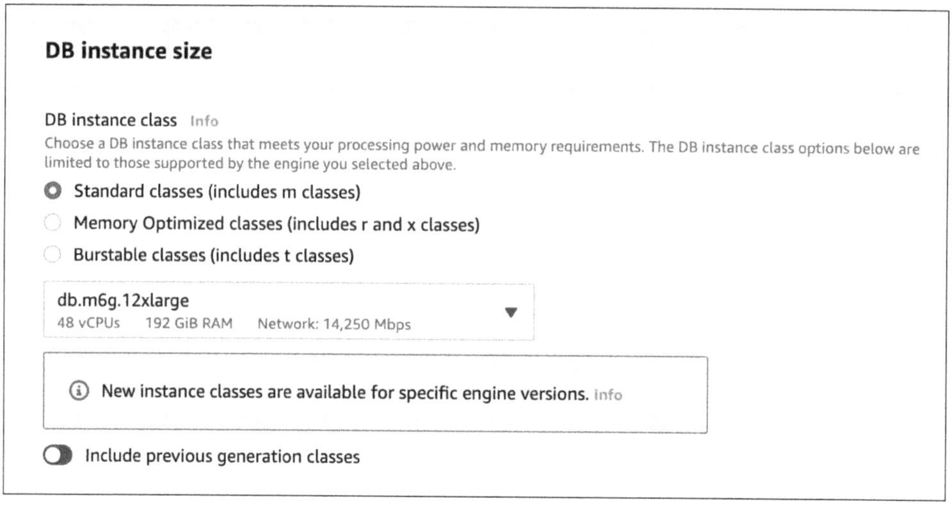

DB instance size

DB instance class   Info
Choose a DB instance class that meets your processing power and memory requirements. The DB instance class options below are limited to those supported by the engine you selected above.

○ Standard classes (includes m classes)
○ Memory Optimized classes (includes r and x classes)
○ Burstable classes (includes t classes)

db.m6g.12xlarge
48 vCPUs   192 GiB RAM   Network: 14,250 Mbps

ⓘ New instance classes are available for specific engine versions. Info

◉ Include previous generation classes

Figure 14-3. Choosing an instance class

Another option that can directly affect the billing is the storage options. Naturally, higher performance (more IOPS) and more storage lead to a higher cost. Figure 14-4 illustrates the choices. You can also select whether to enable autoscaling.

The next option is an important choice: do you want to use multi-AZ deployment or not? The multi-AZ option is all about high availability. When you provision a multi-AZ DB instance, Amazon RDS automatically creates a primary DB instance and synchronously replicates the data to a standby instance in a different Availability Zone (AZ). The AZs are physically distinct and have independent infrastructure, which increases overall availability.

If you don't want to use multi-AZ deployment, RDS will install a single instance. In the event of failure, it will spin up a new one and remount its data volume. This process takes some time, during which your database will not be available. Even big cloud providers are not bulletproof, and disasters can happen, so having a standby server is always recommended. Figure 14-5 shows how to configure the replica.

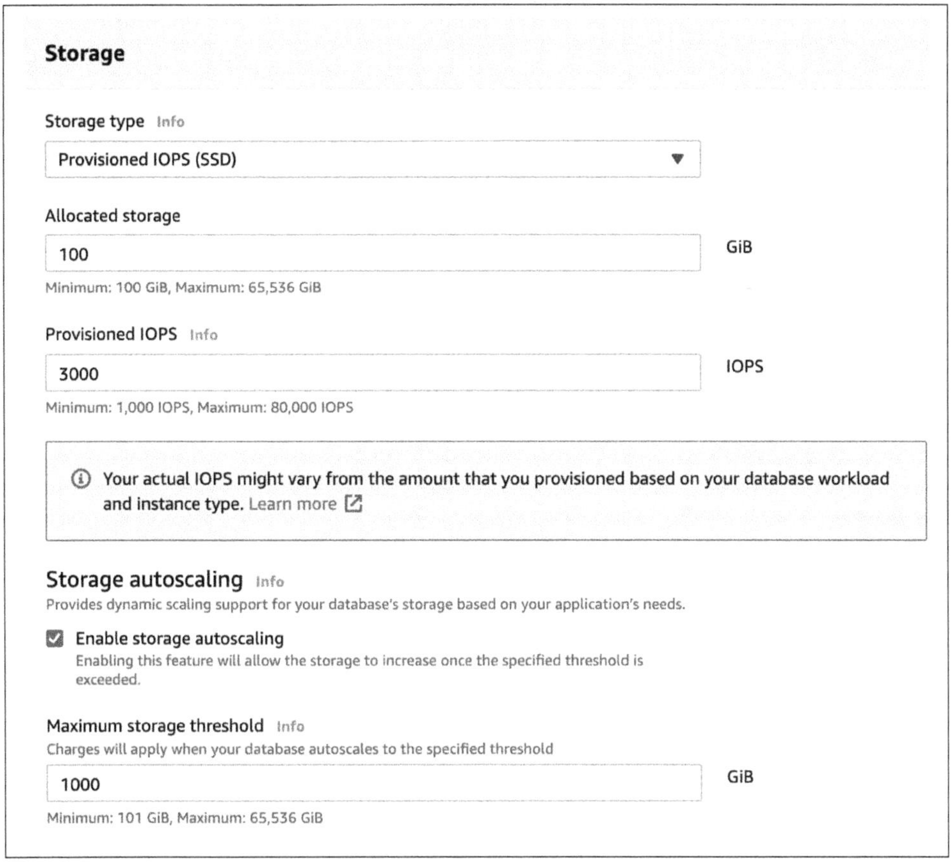

Figure 14-4. Configuring storage size and its IOPS performance

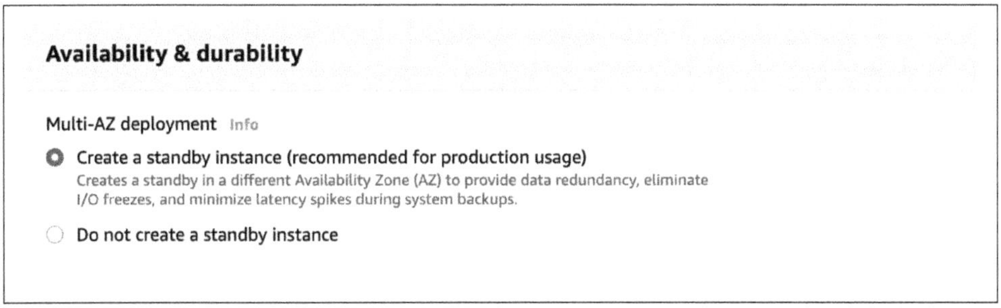

Figure 14-5. Configuring a standby replica

The next part is setting up a general networking configuration. We recommend configuring RDS to use a private network, which only the application servers and developers' IPs can access. Figure 14-6 shows the network options.

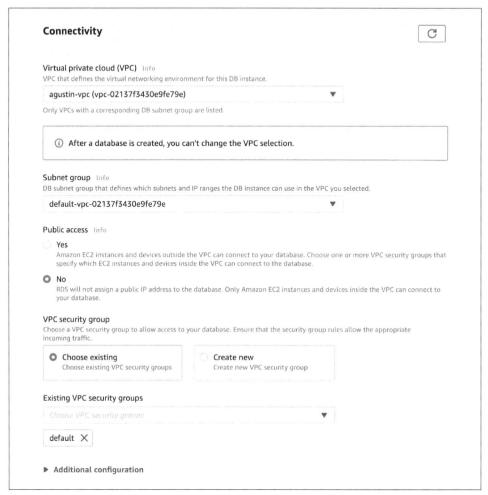

Figure 14-6. Configuring the network settings

Finally, alas, come the estimated costs. Figure 14-7 shows how much you will pay per month for your configured choices.

Estimated monthly costs

DB instance	2663.04 USD
Storage	25.00 USD
Multi-AZ standby instance	2663.04 USD
Provisioned IOPS	300.00 USD
Total	**5651.08 USD**

This billing estimate is based on on-demand usage as described in Amazon RDS Pricing [↗]. Estimate does not include costs for backup storage, IOs (if applicable), or data transfer.

Estimate your monthly costs for the DB Instance using the AWS Simple Monthly Calculator [↗].

Figure 14-7. The bill can reach the stars under certain configurations!

Google Cloud SQL for MySQL

Google Cloud SQL offers managed database services comparable to Amazon RDS (and Azure), but with slight differences. The Google Cloud options for MySQL are more straightforward because there are fewer options to choose from. For example, you cannot choose between MySQL and MariaDB, or choose the MySQL minor version (only the major version). As shown in Figure 14-8, you can get started by either creating a new instance or migrating an existing database to Google Cloud.

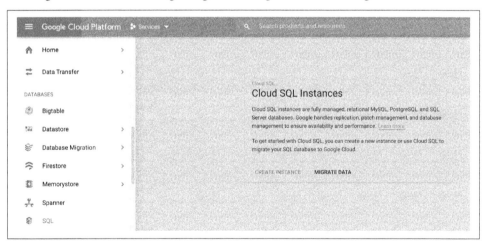

Figure 14-8. Google Cloud SQL

When creating a new instance, you have to fill in a few options. The first step is to choose the product. Figure 14-9 show the options available for MySQL.

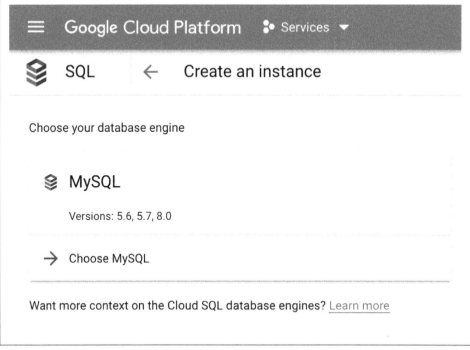

Figure 14-9. Choosing the product

After picking MySQL, you'll need to specify the instance name, `root` password, database version, and location. Figure 14-10 shows how to configure these settings.

Figure 14-10. Setting basic configuration

Next are the settings that can impact the performance, and of course, the cost—it's crucial to find the right balance here. Figure 14-11 shows the storage, memory, and CPU options available.

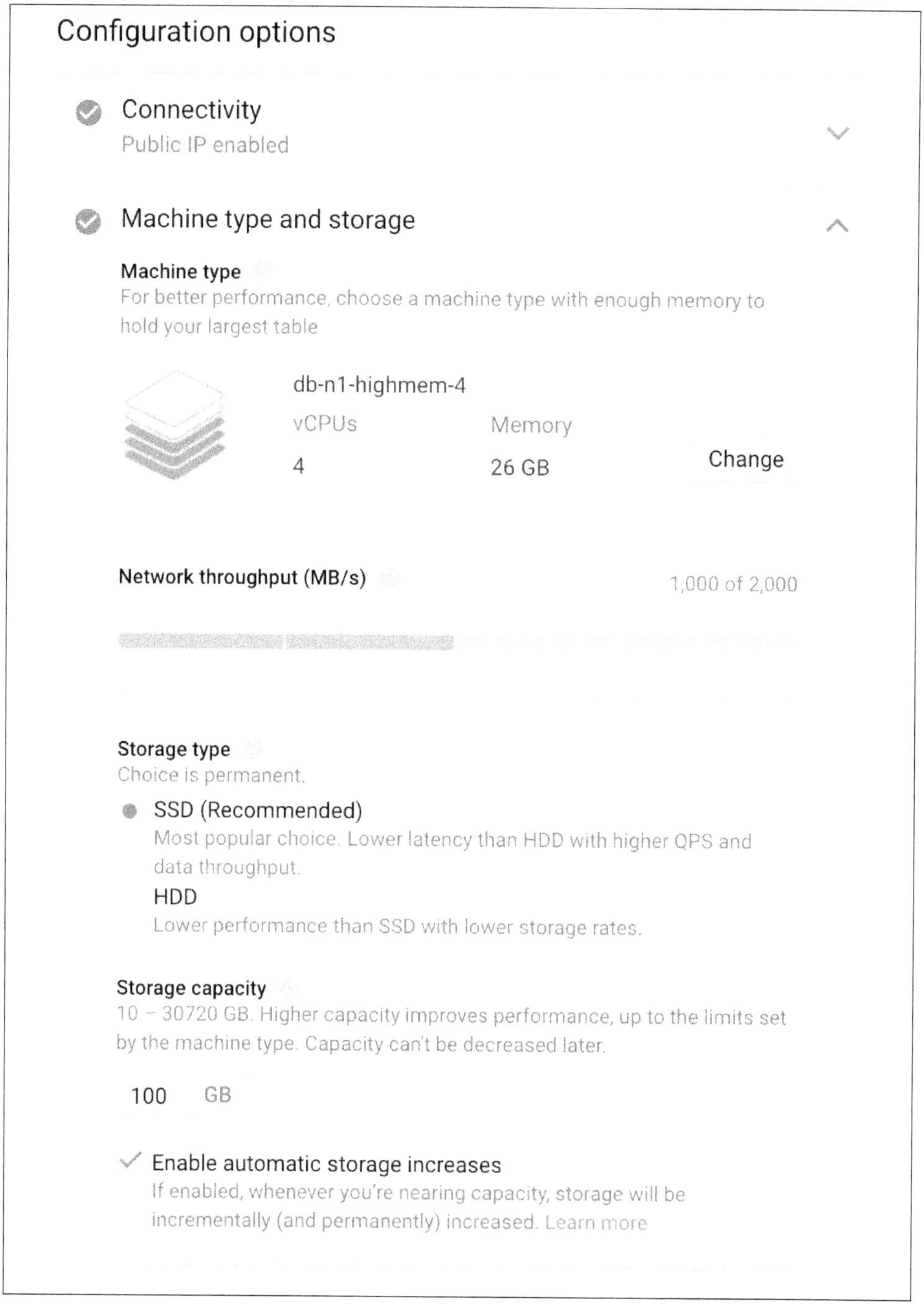

Configuration options

Connectivity
Public IP enabled

Machine type and storage

Machine type
For better performance, choose a machine type with enough memory to hold your largest table

	db-n1-highmem-4		
	vCPUs	Memory	Change
	4	26 GB	

Network throughput (MB/s)   1,000 of 2,000

Storage type
Choice is permanent.

- SSD (Recommended)
  Most popular choice. Lower latency than HDD with higher QPS and data throughput.
  HDD
  Lower performance than SSD with lower storage rates.

Storage capacity
10 – 30720 GB. Higher capacity improves performance, up to the limits set by the machine type. Capacity can't be decreased later.

100   GB

✓ Enable automatic storage increases
If enabled, whenever you're nearing capacity, storage will be incrementally (and permanently) increased. Learn more

Figure 14-11. Configuring the machine type and storage

Now the instance is ready to launch in the Google Cloud.

Azure SQL

The last of the top three cloud service providers is Azure SQL. Figure 14-12 shows the database products available in Azure. You'll want to select "Azure Database for MySQL servers."

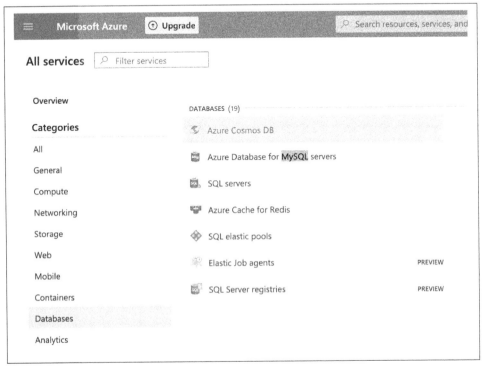

Figure 14-12. Choosing MySQL in Azure

Azure offers two options, to go with a simple server or a more robust solution with high availability in the setup. Figure 14-13 shows the difference between the two options.

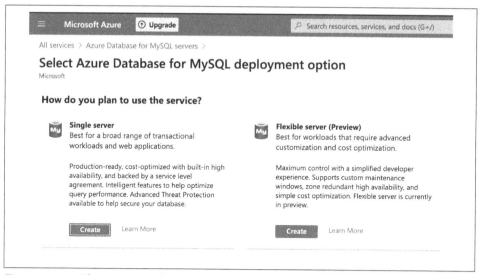

Figure 14-13. Choosing a single server or a flexible server

Those choices are followed by similar configurations regarding the service performance and costs. Figure 14-14 shows the MySQL managed services options.

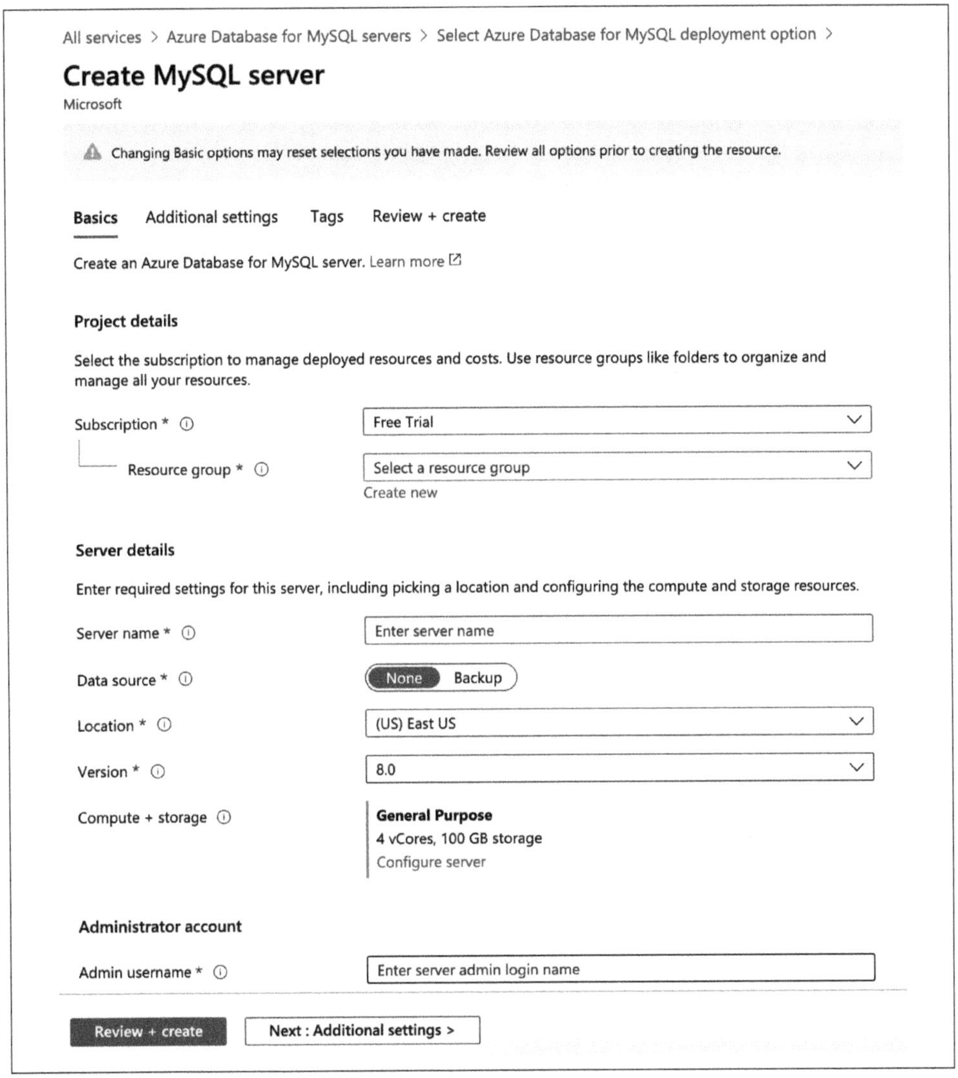
All services > Azure Database for MySQL servers > Select Azure Database for MySQL deployment option >
Create MySQL server
Microsoft
Changing Basic options may reset selections you have made. Review all options prior to creating the resource.
Basics
Additional settings
Tags
Review + create
Create an Azure Database for MySQL server. Learn more
Project details
Select the subscription to manage deployed resources and costs. Use resource groups like folders to organize and manage all your resources.
Subscription *
Free Trial
Resource group *
Select a resource group
Create new
Server details
Enter required settings for this server, including picking a location and configuring the compute and storage resources.
Server name *
Enter server name
Data source *
None
Backup
Location *
(US) East US
Version *
8.0
Compute + storage
General Purpose
4 vCores, 100 GB storage
Configure server
Administrator account
Admin username *
Enter server admin login name
Review + create
Next : Additional settings >

Figure 14-14. Configuring our MySQL managed service instance

Amazon Aurora

Amazon Aurora is a MySQL- and PostgreSQL-compatible relational database solution provided by Amazon under a commercial license. It offers similar features to MySQL, plus a few extra features developed by Amazon.

Two of these features are worth mentioning. First is Aurora Parallel Query (PQ), a feature that parallelizes some of the I/O and computation involved in processing data-intensive queries.

Aurora PQ works by doing a full table scan (the storage level performs the parallel reads). When we use a parallel query, the query does not use the InnoDB buffer pool. Instead, it pushes query processing down to the storage layer and parallelizes it.

The advantage is that moving the processing closer to the data reduces network traffic and latency. However, the feature is not a silver bullet and does not work well for all cases—it works best for analytical queries that need to run over large portions of data.

The PQ feature is not available for all AWS instances. For instances that support this feature, their instance class determines the number of parallel queries that can be active at a given time. The following instances are the ones that support the PQ feature:

- db.r*.large: 1 concurrent parallel query session
- db.r*.xlarge: 2 concurrent parallel query sessions
- db.r*.2xlarge: 4 concurrent parallel query sessions
- db.r*.4xlarge: 8 concurrent parallel query sessions
- db.r*.8xlarge: 16 concurrent parallel query sessions
- db.r4.16xlarge: 16 concurrent parallel query sessions

The other notable feature is the Amazon Aurora Global Database, designed for applications with a global footprint. It allows a single Aurora database to span multiple AWS regions, with fast replication to enable low-latency global reads and disaster recovery from region-wide outages. The Aurora Global Database uses storage-based replication using the dedicated Amazon infrastructure across its data centers worldwide.

MySQL Cloud Instances

A *cloud instance* is nothing but a virtual server. The different cloud providers have different names for these: Amazon Elastic Compute Cloud (EC2) instances, Google Compute Engine instances, and Azure Virtual Machines.

All of them offer different instance types according to the user's business needs, varying from shallow, basic configurations to astounding limits. For example, the Compute Engine `m2-megamem-416` machine type is a monster that has 416 CPUs and 5,888 GB of RAM.

The MySQL installation process for these instances is the standard one described in Chapter 1. In this case, the most significant advantage of using cloud instances compared to DBaaS solutions is the freedom of customizing MySQL and the operating system according to your needs without the limitations that managed databases have.

MySQL in Kubernetes

The most recent option available to deploy MySQL instances is Kubernetes. Kubernetes and the OpenShift platform have added a way to manage containerized systems, including database clusters. The management is achieved by controllers declared in configuration files. These controllers provide automation to create objects, such as a container or a group of containers called a *pod*, to listen for a specific event and perform a task.

This automation adds complexity to the container-based architecture and stateful applications, such as databases. A Kubernetes *operator* is a particular type of controller introduced to simplify complex deployments. The operator extends the Kubernetes API with custom resources.

There are many good books written on how Kubernetes works. To keep this section as concise as possible, we will discuss the significant components relevant to the Percona Kubernetes Operator. For a quick introduction to Kubernetes, you can check out the documentation (*https://oreil.ly/WdWsD*) from the Linux Foundation. Figure 14-15 shows the Percona XtraDB Cluster components in Kubernetes.

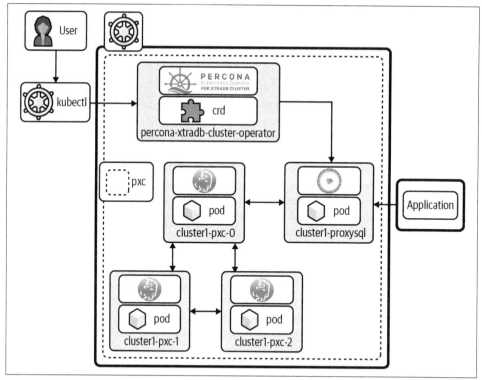

Figure 14-15. The Percona XtraDB Cluster components in Kubernetes

The following section describes how to deploy the Percona Kubernetes Operator for Percona XtraDB Cluster, which is considered production-ready. Other operators are also available. For example:

- Oracle (*https://oreil.ly/wOjgy*) provides a Kubernetes Operator for MySQL InnoDB Cluster. At the time of this writing, the operator is in a preview state, so it is not recommended for production.

- MariaDB (*https://oreil.ly/BkCF9*) has an operator, but at the time of writing it is in the alpha stage, so please check its maturity before using it in production.

- Presslabs (*https://oreil.ly/pgAdN*) has released an operator that deploys MySQL instances along with orchestrator and backup functionalities. This operator is production-ready.

Deploying Percona XtraDB Cluster in Kubernetes

This section will walk you through the steps of deploying a Kubernetes cluster in the Google Cloud using the Google Cloud SDK and the Percona Kubernetes Operator for PXC (*https://oreil.ly/olzY9*):

1. Install the Google Cloud SDK.
   The SDK provides tools and libraries for interacting with Google Cloud products and services. Download the binary appropriate for your platform (*https://oreil.ly/czdsU*) and install it. Here's an example for macOS:

   ```
   $ wget https://dl.google.com/dl/cloudsdk/channels/rapid/downloads/ \
       google-cloud-sdk-341.0.0-darwin-x86_64.tar.gz
   $ tar -xvf google-cloud-sdk-341.0.0-darwin-x86_64.tar.gz
   $ cd google-cloud-sdk/
   $ ./install.sh
   ```

2. Install kubectl with gcloud.
   With gcloud installed, install the kubectl component using the following command:

   ```
   $ gcloud components install kubectl
   ```

3. Create the Kubernetes cluster.
   To create the Kubernetes cluster, first you need to authenticate in the Google Cloud service:

   ```
   $ gcloud auth login
   ```

   Once authenticated, create the cluster. The command accepts a lot of parameters, but in this case, we will go with the basics to create a Kubernetes cluster:

   ```
   $ gcloud container clusters create --machine-type n1-standard-4 \
       --num-nodes 3 --zone us-central1-b --project support-211414 \
       --cluster-version latest vinnie-k8
   ```

    The account needs to have the necessary privileges to create the cluster. Also, you need to replace the project and cluster names used here with your own names. You may also be required to edit the zone location, set to us-central1-b in this example.

The parameters used here are just a small subset of everything available—you can see all the options by running gcloud container clusters --help. For this case, we've just requested a cluster with three nodes of *n1-standard-4* type instances.

This process may take a while, especially if there are a lot of nodes. The output will look like this:

```
Creating cluster vinnie-k8 in us-central1-b... Cluster is being
health-checked (master is healthy)...done.
Created [https://container.googleapis.com/v1/projects/support-211414/
zones/us-central1-b/clusters/vinnie-k8].
To inspect the contents of your cluster, go to:
https://console.cloud.google.com/kubernetes/workload_/gcloud/
us-central1-b/vinnie-k8?project=support-211414
kubeconfig entry generated for vinnie-k8.
+-----------+---------------+------------------+---------------+...
| NAME      | LOCATION      | MASTER_VERSION   | MASTER_IP     |...
+-----------+---------------+------------------+---------------+...
| vinnie-k8 | us-central1-b | 1.19.10-gke.1000 | 34.134.67.128 |...
+-----------+---------------+------------------+---------------+...
...+--------------------------------+-----------+---------+
...| MACHINE_TYPE NODE_VERSION       | NUM_NODES | STATUS  |
...+--------------------------------+-----------+---------+
...| n1-standard-4  1.19.10-gke.1000 | 3         | RUNNING |
...+--------------------------------+-----------+---------+
```

And we can check the pods of our Kubernetes cluster in the Google Cloud:

```
$ kubectl get nodes
NAME                                        STATUS  ROLES   AGE
VERSION
gke-vinnie-k8-default-pool-376c2051-5xgz    Ready   <none>  62s
v1.19.10-gke.1000
gke-vinnie-k8-default-pool-376c2051-w2tk    Ready   <none>  61s
v1.19.10-gke.1000
gke-vinnie-k8-default-pool-376c2051-wxd7    Ready   <none>  62s
v1.19.10-gke.1000
```

It is also possible to use the Google Cloud interface to deploy the cluster, as shown in Figure 14-16.

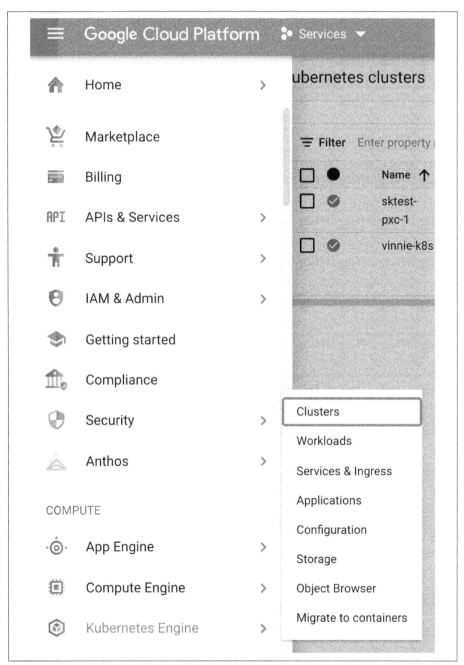

Figure 14-16. From the main menu, select Kubernetes Engine, then Clusters

To create a new cluster, choose the CREATE option shown at the top of Figure 14-17.

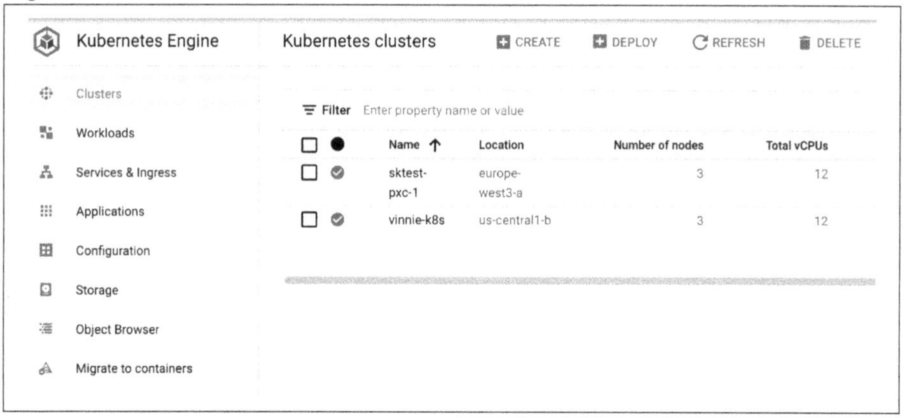

Figure 14-17. Create the Kubernetes cluster by clicking CREATE

The final step is to install the PXC operator. The documentation (*https://oreil.ly/fBJq3*) for deploying the operator has very detailed instructions. We'll follow the recommended steps here.

First, configure Cloud Identity and Access Management (Cloud IAM) to control access to the cluster. The following command will give you the ability to create Roles and RoleBindings:

```
$ kubectl create clusterrolebinding cluster-admin-binding --clusterrole \
    cluster-admin --user $(gcloud config get-value core/account)
```

The return statement confirms the creation:

```
clusterrolebinding.rbac.authorization.k8s.io/cluster-admin-binding created
```

Next, create a namespace and set the context for the namespace:

```
$ kubectl create namespace learning-mysql
$ kubectl config set-context $(kubectl config current-context) \
    --namespace=learning-mysql
```

Now, clone the repository and change to the directory:

```
$ git clone -b v1.8.0 \
    https://github.com/percona/percona-xtradb-cluster-operator
$ cd percona-xtradb-cluster-operator
```

Deploy the operator with the following command:

```
$ kubectl apply -f deploy/bundle.yaml
```

This should return the following confirmation:

```
customresourcedefinition.apiextensions.k8s.io/perconaxtradbclusters.pxc.
percona.com created
customresourcedefinition.apiextensions.k8s.io/perconaxtradbclusterbackups.
pxc.percona.com created
customresourcedefinition.apiextensions.k8s.io/perconaxtradbclusterrestores.
pxc.percona.com created
customresourcedefinition.apiextensions.k8s.io/perconaxtradbbackups.pxc.
percona.com created
role.rbac.authorization.k8s.io/percona-xtradb-cluster-operator created
serviceaccount/percona-xtradb-cluster-operator created
rolebinding.rbac.authorization.k8s.io/service-account-percona-xtradb-
cluster-operator created
deployment.apps/percona-xtradb-cluster-operator created
```

The operator has been started, and you can confirm this by running:

```
$ kubectl get pods
```

Now, create the Percona XtraDB Cluster:

```
$ kubectl apply -f deploy/cr.yaml
```

This step can take some time. After that, you will see all the pods running:

```
$ kubectl get pods
NAME                                READY   STATUS    RESTARTS   AGE
cluster1-haproxy-0                  2/2     Running   0          4m54s
cluster1-haproxy-1                  2/2     Running   0          3m15s
cluster1-haproxy-2                  2/2     Running   0          2m52s
cluster1-pxc-0                      3/3     Running   0          4m54s
cluster1-pxc-1                      3/3     Running   0          3m16s
cluster1-pxc-2                      3/3     Running   0          105s
percona-xtradb-cluster-operator-    1/1     Running   0          7m18s
77bfd8cdc5-d7zll
```

During the previous steps, the operator has generated several secrets, including the password for the root user, which you will need to access the cluster. To get the generated secrets, run the following command:

```
$ kubectl get secret my-cluster-secrets -o yaml
```

You will see output like this:

```
apiVersion: v1
data:
  clustercheck: UFZjdjk0SU4xWGtBSTR2VlVJ
  monitor: ZWZja01mOWhBTXZ4bTB0bUZ4eQ==
  operator: Vm10R0IxbHHA4cVVZTkxqVVI4Mg==
  proxyadmin: VXVFbkx1S3RmUTEzVlNOd1c=
  root: eU53aWlKT3ZXaXJaeG16O0XJK
  xtrabackup: V3VNNWRnWUdIblVWaU1OWGY=
...
secrets/my-cluster-secrets
```

```
  uid: 9d78c4a8-1926-4b7a-84a0-43087a601066
type: Opaque
```

The actual password is base64-encoded, so you'll need to run the following command to get the root password:

```
$ echo 'eU53aWlKT3ZXaXJaeG160XJK' | base64 --decode
yNwiiJOvWirZxmz9rJ
```

Now that you have the password, to check connectivity with the cluster you can create a client pod:

```
$ kubectl run -i --rm --tty percona-client --image=percona:8.0 \
    --restart=Never -- bash -il
```

Then connect to MySQL:

```
$ mysql -h cluster1-haproxy -uroot -pyNwiiJOvWirZxmz9rJ
```

Note that the operator comes with HAProxy, which is a load balancer (we will discuss load balancing in the next chapter).

## CHAPTER 15

Load Balancing MySQL

There are different ways to connect to MySQL. For example, to perform a write test, a connection is created, the statement is executed, and then the connection is closed. To avoid the cost of opening a connection every time it is needed, the concept of the *connection pool* was developed. Connection pooling is a technique of creating and managing a pool of connections that are ready for use by any thread of the application.

Extending the concept of high availability discussed in Chapter 13 to connections in order to improve a production system's resilience, it is possible to use *load balancers* to connect to a database cluster. With load balancing and MySQL high availability, it is possible to keep the application running without interruption (or with only minor downtime). Basically, if the source server or one of the nodes of the database cluster fails, the client just needs to connect to another database node and it can continue to serve requests.

Load balancers were built to provide transparency for clients when connecting to MySQL infrastructure. In this way, the application does not need to be aware of the MySQL topology; whether you're using a classic replication, Group Replication, or Galera Cluster does not matter. The load balancer will provide an online node where it will be possible to read and write queries. Having a robust MySQL architecture and a proper load balancer in place can help DBAs avoid sleepless nights.

Load Balancing with Application Drivers

To connect an application to MySQL, you need a driver. A *driver* is an adapter used to connect the application to a different system type. It is similar to connecting a video card to your computer; you may need to download and install a driver for it to work with your application.

Modern MySQL drivers from commonly used programming languages support connection pooling, load balancing, and failover. Examples include the JDBC driver for MySQL (MySQL Connector/J) (*https://oreil.ly/kaAXI*) and the PDO_MYSQL (*https://oreil.ly/xbC7B*) driver, which implements the PHP Data Objects (PDO) interface to enable access from PHP to MySQL databases.

The database drivers we've mentioned are built to provide transparency for clients when connecting to standalone MySQL Server or MySQL replication setups. We won't show you how to use them in code because that would be outside the scope of this book; however, you should be aware that adding a driver library facilitates code development, since the driver abstracts away a substantial amount of work for the developer.

But for other topologies, such as a clustering setup like Galera Cluster for MySQL or MariaDB, the JDBC and PHP drivers are not aware of internal Galera state information. For instance, a Galera donor node might be in read-only mode while it is helping another node resynchronize (if the SST method is `mysqldump` or `rsync`), or it could be up in non-primary state if split-brain happens. Another solution is to use a load balancer between the clients and the database cluster.

ProxySQL Load Balancer

ProxySQL is a SQL proxy. ProxySQL implements the MySQL protocol, and because of this, it can do things that other proxies cannot do. Here are some of its advantages:

- It provides "intelligent" load balancing of application requests to multiple databases.
- It understands the MySQL traffic that passes through it and can split reads from writes. Understanding the MySQL protocol is especially useful in a source/replica replication setup, where writes should only go to the source and reads to the replicas, or in the case of Galera Cluster for distributing the read queries evenly (linear read scaling).
- It understands the underlying database topology, including whether the instances are up or down, and therefore can route requests to healthy databases.
- It provides query workload analytics and a query cache, which is useful for analyzing and improving performance.
- It provides administrators with robust, rich query rule definitions to efficiently distribute queries and cache data to maximize the database service's efficiency.

ProxySQL runs as a daemon watched by a monitoring process. The process monitors the daemon and restarts it in case of a crash to minimize downtime. The daemon accepts incoming traffic from MySQL clients and forwards it to backend MySQL servers.

The proxy is designed to run continuously without needing to be restarted. Most configurations can be done at runtime using queries similar to SQL statements in the ProxySQL admin interface. These include runtime parameters, server grouping, and traffic-related settings.

While it is common to install ProxySQL on a standalone node between the application and the database, this can affect query performance due to the additional latency from network hops. Figure 15-1 shows ProxySQL as a middle layer.

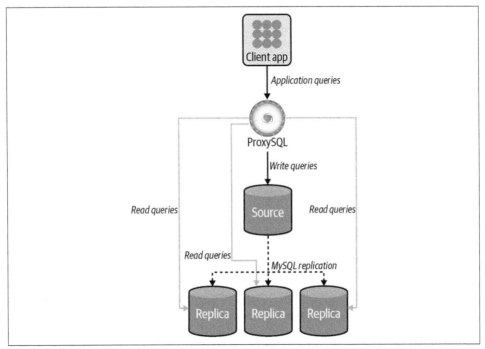

Figure 15-1. ProxySQL between the application and MySQL

To reduce the impact on performance (and avoid the additional network hop), another architecture option is installing ProxySQL on the application servers. The application then connects to ProxySQL (acting as a MySQL server) on localhost using a Unix domain socket, avoiding extra latency. It uses its routing rules to reach out and talk to the actual MySQL servers with their connection pooling. The application doesn't have any idea what happens beyond its connection to ProxySQL. Figure 15-2 shows ProxySQL on the same server as the application.

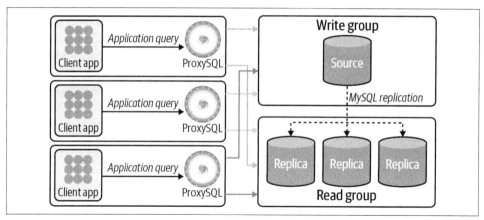

Figure 15-2. ProxySQL on the same server as the application

Installing and Configuring ProxySQL

Let's take a look at how to deploy ProxySQL for a source/replica configuration.

The tool's developers provide official packages for a variety of Linux distributions for all ProxySQL releases on their GitHub releases page (*https://oreil.ly/2EFKJ*), so we'll download the latest package version from there and install it.

Before installing, the following instances are the ones we will use in this process:

```
+-----------------------------------------+----------------------+
| vinicius-grippa-default(mysql)          | 10.124.33.5 (eth0)   |
+-----------------------------------------+----------------------+
| vinicius-grippa-node1(mysql)            | 10.124.33.169 (eth0) |
+-----------------------------------------+----------------------+
| vinicius-grippa-node2(mysql)            | 10.124.33.130 (eth0) |
+-----------------------------------------+----------------------+
| vinicius-grippa-node3(proxysql)         | 10.124.33.170 (eth0) |
+-----------------------------------------+----------------------+
```

To begin, find the proper distribution for your operating system. In this example, we will then install for CentOS 7. First, we will become root, install the MySQL client to connect to ProxySQL, and install ProxySQL itself. We get the URL from the downloads page and refer it to yum:

```
$ sudo su - root
# yum -y install https://repo.percona.com/yum/percona-release-latest.noarch.rpm
# yum -y install Percona-Server-client-57
# yum install -y https://github.com/sysown/proxysql/releases/download/v2.0.15/ \
    proxysql-2.0.15-1-centos7.x86_64.rpm
```

We have all the requirements to run ProxySQL, but the service doesn't automatically start after installation, so we start it manually:

```
# sudo systemctl start proxysql
```

ProxySQL should now be running with its default configuration in place. We can check it by running this command:

```
# systemctl status proxysql
```

The output of the ProxySQL process in the active state should be similar to the following:

```
proxysql.service - High Performance Advanced Proxy for MySQL
   Loaded: loaded (/etc/systemd/system/proxysql.service; enabled; vendor...
   Active: active (running) since Sun 2021-05-23 18:50:28 UTC; 15s ago
  Process: 1422 ExecStart=/usr/bin/proxysql --idle-threads -c /etc/proxysql...
 Main PID: 1425 (proxysql)
   CGroup: /system.slice/proxysql.service
           ├─1425 /usr/bin/proxysql --idle-threads -c /etc/proxysql.cnf
           └─1426 /usr/bin/proxysql --idle-threads -c /etc/proxysql.cnf

May 23 18:50:27 vinicius-grippa-node3 systemd[1]: Starting High Performance...
May 23 18:50:27 vinicius-grippa-node3 proxysql[1422]: 2021-05-23 18:50:27...
May 23 18:50:27 vinicius-grippa-node3 proxysql[1422]: 2021-05-23 18:50:27...
May 23 18:50:27 vinicius-grippa-node3 proxysql[1422]: 2021-05-23 18:50:27...
May 23 18:50:28 vinicius-grippa-node3 systemd[1]: Started High Performance...
```

ProxySQL splits the application interface from the admin interface. This means that ProxySQL will listen on two network ports: the admin interface will listen on 6032, and the application will listen on 6033 (to make it easier to remember, that's the reverse of MySQL's default port, 3306).

Next, ProxySQL needs to communicate with the MySQL nodes to be able to check their condition. To achieve this, ProxySQL needs to connect to each server with a dedicated user.

First, we are going to create the user on the source server. Connect to the MySQL source instance and run these commands:

```
mysql> CREATE USER 'proxysql'@'%' IDENTIFIED by '$3Kr$t';
mysql> GRANT USAGE ON *.* TO 'proxysql'@'%';
```

Next, we will configure ProxySQL parameters to recognize the user. First we connect to ProxySQL:

```
# mysql -uadmin -padmin -h 127.0.0.1 -P 6032
```

And then we set the parameters:

```
proxysql> UPDATE global_variables SET variable_value='proxysql'
       -> WHERE variable_name='mysql-monitor_username';
proxysql> UPDATE global_variables SET variable_value='$3Kr$t'
       -> WHERE variable_name='mysql-monitor_password';
proxysql> LOAD MYSQL VARIABLES TO RUNTIME;
proxysql> SAVE MYSQL VARIABLES TO DISK;
```

Now that we've set the user in the database and ProxySQL, it is time to tell ProxySQL which MySQL servers are present in the topology:

```
proxysql> INSERT INTO mysql_servers(hostgroup_id, hostname, port)
      -> VALUES (10,'10.124.33.5',3306);
proxysql> INSERT INTO mysql_servers(hostgroup_id, hostname, port)
      -> VALUES (11,'10.124.33.169',3306);
proxysql> INSERT INTO mysql_servers(hostgroup_id, hostname, port)
      -> VALUES (11,'10.124.33.130',3306);
proxysql> LOAD MYSQL SERVERS TO RUNTIME;
proxysql> SAVE MYSQL SERVERS TO DISK;
```

The next step is to define who our writer and reader groups. The servers present in the writer group will be able to receive DML operations, while SELECT queries will use the servers in the reader group. In this example, the host group 10 will be the writer, and host group 11 will be the reader:

```
proxysql> INSERT INTO mysql_replication_hostgroups
      -> (writer_hostgroup, reader_hostgroup) VALUES (10, 11);
proxysql> LOAD MYSQL SERVERS TO RUNTIME;
proxysql> SAVE MYSQL SERVERS TO DISK;
```

Next, ProxySQL must have users that can access backend nodes to manage connections. Let's create the user on the backend source server:

```
mysql> CREATE USER 'app'@'%' IDENTIFIED by '$3Kr$t';
mysql> GRANT ALL PRIVILEGES ON *.* TO 'app'@'%';
```

And now we will configure ProxySQL with the user:

```
proxysql> INSERT INTO mysql_users (username,password,default_hostgroup)
      -> VALUES ('app','$3Kr$t',10);
proxysql> LOAD MYSQL USERS TO RUNTIME;
proxysql> SAVE MYSQL USERS TO DISK;
```

The next step is the most exciting because it is here that we define the rules. The rules will tell ProxySQL where to send write and read queries, balancing the load on the servers:

```
proxysql> INSERT INTO mysql_query_rules
      -> (rule_id,username,destination_hostgroup,active,match_digest,apply)
      -> VALUES(1,'app',10,1,'^SELECT.*FOR UPDATE',1);
proxysql> INSERT INTO mysql_query_rules
      -> (rule_id,username,destination_hostgroup,active,match_digest,apply)
      -> VALUES(2,'app',11,1,'^SELECT ',1);
proxysql> LOAD MYSQL QUERY RULES TO RUNTIME;
proxysql> SAVE MYSQL QUERY RULES TO DISK;
```

ProxySQL has a thread responsible for connecting on each server listed in the mysql_servers table and checking the value of the read_only variable. Suppose the replica is showing up in the writer group, like this:

```
proxysql> SELECT * FROM mysql_servers;
```

```
+---------------+----------------+------+-----------+...
| hostgroup_id  | hostname       | port | gtid_port |...
+---------------+----------------+------+-----------+...
| 10            | 10.124.33.5    | 3306 | 0         |...
| 11            | 10.124.33.169  | 3306 | 0         |...
| 11            | 10.124.33.130  | 3306 | 0         |...
+---------------+----------------+------+-----------+...
...+--------+--------+-------------+-----------------+
...| status | weight | compression | max_connections |...
...+--------+--------+-------------+-----------------+...
...| ONLINE | 1      | 0           | 1000            |...
...| ONLINE | 1      | 0           | 1000            |...
...| ONLINE | 1      | 0           | 1000            |...
...+--------+--------+-------------+-----------------+...
...+---------------------+---------+----------------+---------+
...| max_replication_lag | use_ssl | max_latency_ms | comment |
...+---------------------+---------+----------------+---------+
...| 0                   | 0       | 0              |         |
...| 0                   | 0       | 0              |         |
...| 0                   | 0       | 0              |         |
...+---------------------+---------+----------------+---------+
3 rows in set (0.00 sec)
```

Because we do not want ProxySQL writing data to the replica servers, which would cause data inconsistency, we need to set the read_only option in the replica servers, so these servers will serve only read queries.

```
mysql> SET GLOBAL read_only=1;
```

Now we're ready to use our application. Running the following command should return the hostname that ProxySQL connected from:

```
$ mysql -uapp -p'$3Kr$t' -h 127.0.0.1 -P 6033 -e "select @@hostname;"

+----------------------+
| @@hostname           |
+----------------------+
| vinicius-grippa-node1 |
+----------------------+
```

ProxySQL has a lot more features and flexibility than we've shown here; our goal in this section was just to present the tool so you're aware of this option when deciding on an architecture.

 As we mentioned when configuring replication in Chapter 13, we want to reinforce the idea that ProxySQL needs to reach the MySQL servers; otherwise, it won't work.

HAProxy Load Balancer

HAProxy stands for High Availability Proxy, and it is a TCP/HTTP load balancer. It distributes a workload across a set of servers to maximize performance and optimize resource usage.

With the intent to expand your knowledge regarding MySQL architectures and different topologies, we will configure Percona XtraDB Cluster (Galera Cluster) with HAProxy in this section instead of a classic replication topology.

The architecture options are similar to ProxySQL's. HAProxy can be placed together with the application or in a middle layer. Figure 15-3 shows an example where HAProxy is placed on the same server as the application.

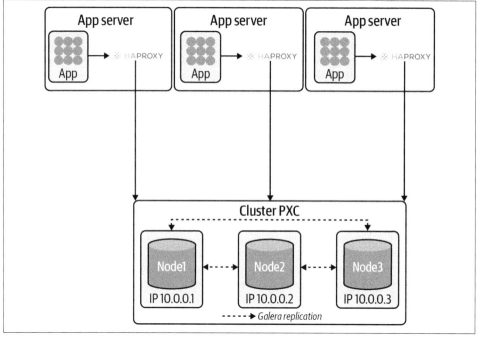

Figure 15-3. HAProxy together with the application

And Figure 15-4 shows a topology with HAProxy in a middle layer.

Again, these are archictectures with different pros and cons. While in the first one we do not have an extra hop (which reduces latency), we add extra load to the application server. Also, you have to configure HAProxy on each application server.

On the other hand, having HAProxy in the middle layer facilitates managing it and increases availability, because the application can connect to any HAProxy server. However, the extra hop adds latency.

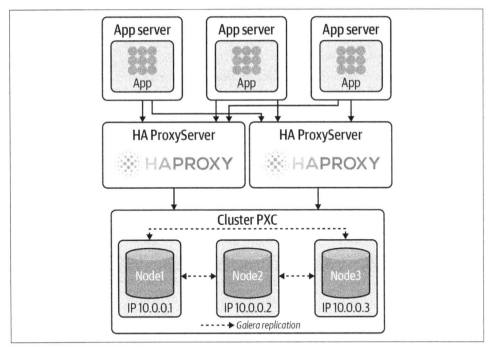

Figure 15-4. HAProxy in a middle layer running in dedicated servers

Installing and Configuring HAProxy

Common operating systems such as Red Hat/CentOS and Debian/Ubuntu provide the HAProxy package, and you can install it using the package manager. The installation process is relatively easy.

For Debian or Ubuntu, use these commands:

```
# apt update
# apt install haproxy
```

For Red Hat or CentOS, use:

```
# sudo yum update
# sudo yum install haproxy
```

When installed, HAProxy will set the default path for the configuration file as */etc/haproxy/haproxy.cfg*.

Before starting HAProxy, we need to configure it. For this demonstration, in our first scenario HAProxy will be located on the same server as the application. Here are the IPs of our three-node Galera Cluster:

```
172.16.3.45/Port:3306
172.16.1.72/Port:3306
172.16.0.161/Port:3306
```

Let's open our *etc/haproxy/haproxy.cfg* file and look at it. There are many parameters to customize, split into three sections:

global
> A section in the configuration file for process-wide parameters

defaults
> A section in the configuration file for default parameters

listen
> A section in the configuration file that defines a complete proxy, including its frontend and backend parts

Table 15-1 shows the basic HAProxy parameters.

Table 15-1. HAProxy options (with links to HAProxy documentation)

Parameter	Description
balance (*https://oreil.ly/Ej25a*)	Defines the load balancing algorithm to be used in a backend.
clitimeout (*https://oreil.ly/HRIC5*)	Sets the maximum inactivity time on the client side
contimeout (*https://oreil.ly/Hjwtm*)	Sets the maximum time to wait for a connection attempt to a server to succeed
daemon (*https://oreil.ly/75stw*)	Makes the process fork into background (recommended mode of operation)
gid (*https://oreil.ly/ikswS*)	Changes the process's group ID to *<number>*
log (*https://oreil.ly/ovcK5*)	Adds a global syslog server
maxconn (*https://oreil.ly/94uQr*)	Sets the maximum per-process number of concurrent connections to *<number>*
mode (*https://oreil.ly/c3CaJ*)	Set the running mode or protocol of the instance
option dontlognull (*https://oreil.ly/DplEm*)	Disable logging of null connections
optiontcplog (*https://oreil.ly/BA2mL*)	Enables advanced logging of TCP connections with session state and timers

To make HAProxy work, we will use the following configuration file based on our settings:

```
global
    log /dev/log    local0
    log /dev/log    local1 notice
    maxconn 4096
    #debug
    #quiet
    chroot      /var/lib/haproxy
    pidfile     /var/run/haproxy.pid
    user        haproxy
    group       haproxy
    daemon

    # turn on stats unix socket
    stats socket /var/lib/haproxy/stats
```

```
#---------------------------------------------------------------------
# common defaults that all the 'listen' and 'backend' sections will
# use if not designated in their block
#---------------------------------------------------------------------
defaults
      log      global
      mode     http
      option   tcplog
      option   dontlognull
      retries 3
      redispatch
      maxconn 2000
      contimeout       5000
      clitimeout       50000
      srvtimeout       50000


#---------------------------------------------------------------------
# round robin balancing between the various backends
#---------------------------------------------------------------------
listen mysql-pxc-cluster 0.0.0.0:3307
      mode tcp
      bind *:3307
      timeout client  10800s
      timeout server  10800s
      balance roundrobin
      option httpchk

      server vinicius-grippa-node2 172.16.0.161:3306 check port 9200
      inter 12000 rise 3 fall 3
      server vinicius-grippa-node1 172.16.1.72:3306 check port 9200 inter 12000

      rise 3 fall 3
      server vinicius-grippa-default 172.16.3.45:3306 check port 9200
      inter 12000 rise 3 fall 3
```

To start HAProxy, we use the `haproxy` command. We can pass any number of configuration parameters on the command line. To use a configuration file, use the `-f` option. For example, we can pass one configuration file:

```
# sudo haproxy -f /etc/haproxy/haproxy.cfg
```

or multiple configuration files:

```
# sudo haproxy -f /etc/haproxy/haproxy.cfg /etc/haproxy/haproxy-2.cfg
```

or a directory:

```
# sudo haproxy -f conf-dir
```

With this configuration, HAProxy will balance the load between three nodes. In this case, it checks only if the `mysqld` process is listening on port 3306, but doesn't take into account the state of the node. So, it could be sending queries to a node that has `mysqld` running even if it's in the `JOINING` or `DISCONNECTED` state.

To check the current status of a node, we need something a little more complex. This idea was taken from Codership's Google group (*https://oreil.ly/7xj0N*).

To implement this setup, we will need two scripts:

- `clustercheck`, located in */usr/local/bin* and a config for `xinetd`
- `mysqlchk`, located in */etc/xinetd.d* on each node

Both scripts are available (*https://oreil.ly/iN1La*) in binaries and source distributions of Percona XtraDB.

Change the */etc/services* file by adding the following line for each node:

```
mysqlchk          9200/tcp                    # mysqlchk
```

If the */etc/services* file does not exist, it's likely that `xinetd` is not installed.

To install it for CentOS/Red Hat, use:

```
# yum install -y xinetd
```

For Debian/Ubuntu, use:

```
# sudo apt-get install -y xinetd
```

Next, we need to create a MySQL user so the script can check if the node is healthy. Ideally, for security reasons, this user should have the minimum privileges required:

```
mysql> CREATE USER 'clustercheckuser'@'localhost' IDENTIFIED BY
               'clustercheckpassword!';
    -> GRANT PROCESS ON *.* TO 'clustercheckuser'@'localhost';
```

To validate how our node is performing on the health check, we can run the following command and observe the output:

```
# /usr/bin/clustercheck

HTTP/1.1 200 OK
Content-Type: text/plain
Connection: close
Content-Length: 40

Percona XtraDB Cluster Node is synced.
```

If we do this for all nodes, we will be ready to test whether our HAProxy setup is working. The easiest way to do this is to connect to it and execute some MySQL commands. Let's run a command that retrieves the hostname from which we are connected:

```
# mysql -uroot -psecret -h 127.0.0.1 -P 3307 -e "select @@hostname"
```

```
+----------------------+
| @@hostname           |
+----------------------+
| vinicius-grippa-node1 |
+----------------------+
```

Running this a second time gives us:

```
$ mysql -uroot -psecret -h 127.0.0.1 -P 3307 -e "select @@hostname"
```

```
mysql: [Warning] Using a password on the command line interface can be
insecure.
+----------------------+
| @@hostname           |
+----------------------+
| vinicius-grippa-node2 |
+----------------------+
```

And the third time we get:

```
$ mysql -uroot -psecret -h 127.0.0.1 -P 3307 -e "select @@hostname"
```

```
mysql: [Warning] Using a password on the command line interface can be
insecure.
+-------------------------+
| @@hostname              |
+-------------------------+
| vinicius-grippa-default |
+-------------------------+
```

As you can see, our HAProxy is connecting in a round-robin fashion. If we shut down one of the nodes, HAProxy will route only to the remaining ones.

MySQL Router

MySQL Router is responsible for distributing the traffic between members of an InnoDB cluster. It is a proxy-like solution to hide the cluster topology from applications, so applications don't need to know which member of a cluster is the primary node and which are secondaries. Note that MySQL Router will *not* work with Galera Clusters; it was developed for *InnoDB Cluster only*.

MySQL Router is capable of performing read/write splitting by exposing different interfaces. A common setup is to have one read/write interface and one read-only interface. This is the default behavior that also exposes two similar interfaces to use the X Protocol (used for CRUD operations and async calls).

The read/write split is done using the concept of *roles*: primary for writes and secondary for read-only. This is analogous to how members of cluster are named. Additionally, each interface is exposed via a TCP port so applications only need to know the IP:port combination used for writes and the one used for reads. Then MySQL

Router will take care of connections to cluster members depending on the type of traffic to the server.

When working in a production environment, the MySQL server instances that make up an InnoDB Cluster run on multiple host machines as part of a network rather than on single machine. So, as with ProxySQL and HAProxy, the MySQL router can be a middle layer in the architecture.

Figure 15-5 illustrates how the production scenario works.

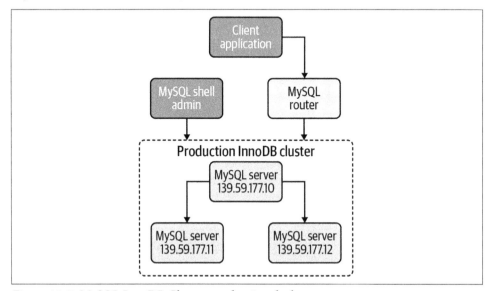

Figure 15-5. MySQL InnoDB Cluster production deployment

Now, to start our example, let's take a look at the MySQL members that are part of the InnoDB Cluster:

```
mysql> SELECT member_host, member_port, member_state, member_role
    -> FROM performance_schema.replication_group_members;

+---------------+-------------+--------------+-------------+
| member_host   | member_port | member_state | member_role |
+---------------+-------------+--------------+-------------+
| 172.16.3.9    |        3306 | ONLINE       | SECONDARY   |
| 172.16.3.127  |        3306 | ONLINE       | SECONDARY   |
| 172.16.3.120  |        3306 | ONLINE       | PRIMARY     |
+---------------+-------------+--------------+-------------+
3 rows in set (0.00 sec)

mysql> SELECT cluster_name FROM mysql_innodb_cluster_metadata.clusters;
```

```
+--------------+
| cluster_name |
+--------------+
| cluster1     |
+--------------+
1 row in set (0.00 sec)
```

Now that we have the configuration of the MySQL nodes and the cluster name, we can start configuring MySQL Router. For performance purposes it's recommended to set up MySQL Router in the same place as the application, supposing we have an instance per application server, so we will place our router on the application server. First, we are going to identify the version of MySQL Router compatible with our OS:

```
# cat /etc/*release
CentOS Linux release 7.9.2009 (Core)
```

Now, we will check the download page (*https://oreil.ly/eCH08*) and install it using yum:

```
# yum install -y https://dev.mysql.com/get/Downloads/MySQL-Router/mysql-
router-community-8.0.23-1.el7.x86_64.rpm
Loaded plugins: fastestmirror
mysql-router-community-8.0.23-1.el7.x86_64.rpm
Examining /var/tmp/yum-root-_ljdTQ/mysql-router-community-8.0.23-1.el7.x
86_64.rpm: mysql-router-community-8.0.23-1.el7.x86_64
Marking /var/tmp/yum-root-_ljdTQ/mysql-router-community-8.0.23-1.el7.x86
_64.rpm to be installed
Resolving Dependencies
--> Running transaction check
...
Running transaction
  Installing : mysql-router-community-8.0.23-1.el7.x86_64
  1/1
  Verifying  : mysql-router-community-8.0.23-1.el7.x86_64
  1/1

Installed:
  mysql-router-community.x86_64 0:8.0.23-1.el7

Complete!
```

Now that MySQL Router is installed, we need to create a dedicated directory for its operation:

```
# mkdir /var/lib/mysqlrouter
```

Next, we are going to bootstrap MySQL Router. The bootstrap will configure the router for operation with a MySQL InnoDB Cluster:

```
# mysqlrouter --bootstrap root@172.16.3.120:3306 \
    --directory /var/lib/mysqlrouter --conf-use-sockets \
```

```
    --account app_router --account-create always \
    --user=mysql

Please enter MySQL password for root:
# Bootstrapping MySQL Router instance at '/var/lib/mysqlrouter'...

Please enter MySQL password for app_router:
- Creating account(s)
- Verifying account (using it to run SQL queries that would be run by
Router)
- Storing account in keyring
- Adjusting permissions of generated files
- Creating configuration /var/lib/mysqlrouter/mysqlrouter.conf

...

## MySQL Classic protocol

- Read/Write Connections: localhost:6446, /var/lib/mysqlrouter/mysql.sock
- Read/Only Connections:  localhost:6447,
/var/lib/mysqlrouter/mysqlro.sock

## MySQL X protocol

- Read/Write Connections: localhost:64460,
/var/lib/mysqlrouter/mysqlx.sock
- Read/Only Connections:  localhost:64470,
/var/lib/mysqlrouter/mysqlxro.sock
```

In the command line, we are telling the router to connect with the user root, in our primary server (172.16.3.120), at port 3306. We are also telling the router to create a socket file so we can connect using it. Finally, we are creating a new user (app_router) to use in our application.

Let's have a look at the contents that the bootstrap process created in our configuration directory (*/var/lib/mysqlrouter*):

```
# ls -l | awk '{print $9}'
```
```
data
log
mysqlrouter.conf
mysqlrouter.key
run
start.sh
stop.sh
```

A generated MySQL Router configuration file (*mysqlrouter.conf*) looks similar to this:

```
# cat mysqlrouter.conf
```
```
# File automatically generated during MySQL Router bootstrap
[DEFAULT]
user=mysql
```

```
logging_folder=/var/lib/mysqlrouter/log
runtime_folder=/var/lib/mysqlrouter/run

...

[rest_routing]
require_realm=default_auth_realm

[rest_metadata_cache]
require_realm=default_auth_realm
```

In this example, MySQL Router configured four ports (two ports to read/write using the regular MySQL protocol, and two to read/write using the X Protocol) and four sockets. Ports are added by default, and sockets were added because we passed in --conf-use-sockets. The InnoDB Cluster named cluster1 is the source of the metadata, and the destinations are using the InnoDB Cluster metadata cache to dynamically configure host information.

By executing the *start.sh* script we can start the MySQL router daemon:

```
# ./start.sh

# PID 1684 written to '/var/lib/mysqlrouter/mysqlrouter.pid'
logging facility initialized, switching logging to loggers specified in
configuration
```

Now, we can observe the process running:

```
# ps -ef | grep -i mysqlrouter

root       1683     1  0 17:36 pts/0    00:00:00 sudo
ROUTER_PID=/var/lib/mysqlrouter/mysqlrouter.pid /usr/bin/mysqlrouter -c
/var/lib/mysqlrouter/mysqlrouter.conf --user=mysql
mysql      1684  1683  0 17:36 pts/0    00:00:17 /usr/bin/mysqlrouter -c
/var/lib/mysqlrouter/mysqlrouter.conf --user=mysql
root       1733  1538  0 17:41 pts/0    00:00:00 grep --color=auto -i
mysqlrouter
```

And the ports open:

```
# netstat -tulnp | grep -i mysqlrouter

tcp   0   0 0.0.0.0:64470   0.0.0.0:*   LISTEN   1684/mysqlrouter
tcp   0   0 0.0.0.0:8443    0.0.0.0:*   LISTEN   1684/mysqlrouter
tcp   0   0 0.0.0.0:64460   0.0.0.0:*   LISTEN   1684/mysqlrouter
tcp   0   0 0.0.0.0:6446    0.0.0.0:*   LISTEN   1684/mysqlrouter
tcp   0   0 0.0.0.0:6447    0.0.0.0:*   LISTEN   1684/mysqlrouter
```

We've configured MySQL Router with the InnoDB Cluster, so now we can test this with read and read/write connections. First, we will connect to the writer port (6446):

```
# mysql -uroot -psecret -h 127.0.0.1 -P 6446 \
    -e "create database learning_mysql;"
# mysql -uroot -psecret -h 127.0.0.1 -P 6446 \
    -e "use learning_mysql; select database()"
```

```
+-----------------+
| database()      |
+-----------------+
| learning_mysql  |
+-----------------+
```

As you can see, it is possible to execute both reads and writes in the writer port.

Now we will check the read port (6447) using a SELECT statement:

```
# mysql -uroot -psecret -h 127.0.0.1 -P 6447 \
    -e "use learning_mysql; select database()"

+-----------------+
| database()      |
+-----------------+
| learning_mysql  |
+-----------------+
```

That's working, but let's try to execute a write:

```
# mysql -uroot -psecret -h 127.0.0.1 -P 6447 \
    -e "create database learning_mysql_write;"

ERROR 1290 (HY000) at line 1: The MySQL server is running with the
--super-read-only option so it cannot execute this statement
```

So, the read port only accepts reads. It is also possible to see the router load-balancing the reads:

```
# mysql -uroot -psecret -h 127.0.0.1 -P 6447 -e "select @@hostname"

+-----------------------+
| @@hostname            |
+-----------------------+
| vinicius-grippa-node1 |
+-----------------------+

# mysql -uroot -psecret -h 127.0.0.1 -P 6447 -e "select @@hostname"

insecure.
+-----------------------+
| @@hostname            |
+-----------------------+
| vinicius-grippa-node2 |
+-----------------------+
```

In this way, if any downtime occurs in one of the MySQL nodes, MySQL Router will route the queries to the remaining active nodes.

## CHAPTER 16

Miscellaneous Topics

The idea of this chapter is to go beyond troubleshooting a query, or an overloaded system, or setting up different MySQL topologies. We want to show you the arsenal of tools available for you to make daily tasks easier or investigate complex issues. Let's start with MySQL Shell.

MySQL Shell

MySQL Shell is an advanced client and code editor for MySQL. It expands the functionality of the traditional MySQL client that most DBAs worked with in MySQL 5.6 and 5.7. MySQL Shell supports programming languages such as Python, JavaScript, and SQL. It also extends functionalities using an API command syntax. For example, it is possible to customize scripts to administer an InnoDB Cluster. From MySQL Shell, you can also start and configure MySQL sandbox instances.

Installing MySQL Shell

For supported Linux distributions, the easiest way to install MySQL Shell is to use the MySQL *yum* or *apt* repository. Let's see how to install it on Ubuntu and CentOS.

Installing MySQL Shell on Ubuntu 20.04 Focal Fossa

Installing MySQL Shell in Ubuntu is relatively easy since it is part of the regular repositories.

First, we need to configure the MySQL repository. We can use these commands to download (*https://oreil.ly/K7eq8*) the *apt* repository to our server and install it:

```
# wget  https://dev.mysql.com/get/mysql-apt-config_0.8.16-1_all.deb
# dpkg -i mysql-apt-config_0.8.16-1_all.deb
```

Once installed, update our package information:

```
# apt-get update
```

Then execute the `install` command to install MySQL Shell:

```
# apt-get install mysql-shell
```

We can now start MySQL Shell using the command line:

```
# mysqlsh
MySQL Shell 8.0.23

Copyright (c) 2016, 2021, Oracle and/or its affiliates.
Oracle is a registered trademark of Oracle Corporation and/or its affiliates.
Other names may be trademarks of their respective owners.

Type '\help' or '\?' for help; '\quit' to exit.
 MySQL  JS >
```

Installing MySQL Shell on CentOS 8

To install MySQL Shell in CentOS 8, we follow the same steps as described for Ubuntu—but first we need to make sure the default MySQL package present in CentOS 8 is disabled:

```
# yum remove mysql-community-release -y
No match for argument: mysql-community-release
No packages marked for removal.
Dependencies resolved.
Nothing to do.
Complete!
```

```
# dnf erase mysql-community-release
No match for argument: mysql-community-release
No packages marked for removal.
Dependencies resolved.
Nothing to do.
Complete!
```

Next, we are going to configure our *yum* repository. We need to get the correct OS version from the download page (*https://oreil.ly/YvW74*):

```
# yum install \
    https://dev.mysql.com/get/mysql80-community-release-el8-1.noarch.rpm -y
```

With the repository installed, we will install the MySQL Shell binary:

```
# yum install mysql-shell -y
```

And we can validate that the installation worked by running it:

```
# mysqlsh
```

```
MySQL Shell 8.0.23

Copyright (c) 2016, 2021, Oracle and/or its affiliates.
Oracle is a registered trademark of Oracle Corporation and/or its affiliates.
Other names may be trademarks of their respective owners.

Type '\help' or '\?' for help; '\quit' to exit.
 MySQL  JS >
```

Deploying a Sandbox InnoDB Cluster with MySQL Shell

MySQL Shell automates the deployment of sandbox instances with AdminAPI, which provides the dba.deploySandboxInstance(*port_number*) command.

By default, the sandbox instances are placed in a directory named *$HOME/mysql-sandboxes/port*. Let's see how to change the directory:

```
# mkdir /var/lib/sandboxes
# mysqlsh

 MySQL  JS > shell.options.sandboxDir='/var/lib/sandboxes'

/var/lib/sandboxes
```

A prerequiste to deploy a sandbox instance is to install the MySQL binaries. If necessary, review Chapter 1 for details. You'll need to enter a password for the root user in order to complete the deployment:

```
 MySQL  JS > dba.deploySandboxInstance(3310)

A new MySQL sandbox instance will be created on this host in
/var/lib/sandboxes/3310

Warning: Sandbox instances are only suitable for deploying and
running on your local machine for testing purposes and are not
accessible from external networks.

Please enter a MySQL root password for the new instance: ******

Deploying new MySQL instance...

Instance localhost:3310 successfully deployed and started.
Use shell.connect('root@localhost:3310') to connect to the instance.
```

We are going to deploy two more instances:

```
 MySQL  JS > dba.deploySandboxInstance(3320)
 MySQL  JS > dba.deploySandboxInstance(3330)
```

The next step is to create the InnoDB Cluster while connected to the seed MySQL Server instance. The *seed* instance is the instance we are connected to via MySQL Shell and that we want to replicate to the other instances. In this example the sandbox instances are all blank instances, so we can choose any instance. In a production setup the seed instance would be the one that contains the existing dataset to be replicated to the other instances in the cluster.

We use this command to connect MySQL Shell to the seed instance, in this case the one at port 3310:

```
MySQL  JS > \connect root@localhost:3310

Creating a session to root@localhost:3310
Please provide the password for root@localhost:3310:
Save password for root@localhost:3310? [Y]es/[N]o/Ne[v]er (default No): Y
Fetching schema names for autocompletion... Press ^C to stop.
Your MySQL connection id is 12
Server version: 8.0.21 Source distribution
No default schema selected; type \use <schema> to set one.
```

Subsequently, we will use the createCluster() method to create the InnoDB Cluster with the currently connected instance as the seed:

```
MySQL localhost:3310 ssl  JS > var cluster = dba.createCluster('learning_mysql')

A new InnoDB cluster will be created on instance 'localhost:3310'.

Validating instance configuration at localhost:3310...
NOTE: Instance detected as a sandbox.
Please note that sandbox instances are only suitable for deploying test clusters
for use within the same host.

This instance reports its own address as 127.0.0.1:3310

Instance configuration is suitable.
NOTE: Group Replication will communicate with other members using
'127.0.0.1:33101'. Use the localAddress option to override.

Creating InnoDB cluster 'learning_mysql' on '127.0.0.1:3310'...

Adding Seed Instance...
Cluster successfully created. Use Cluster.addInstance() to add MySQL instances.
At least 3 instances are needed for the cluster to be able to withstand up to
one server failure.
```

As we can see in the output, three instances are capable of keeping the database online with one server failure, which is why we deployed three sandbox instances.

The next step is to add secondary instances to our learning_mysql InnoDB Cluster. Any transactions that were executed by the seed instance are reexecuted by each secondary instance as it is added.

The seed instance in this example was recently created, so it is nearly empty. Therefore, there is little data that needs to be replicated from the seed instance to the secondary instances. If it's necessary to replicate data, MySQL will use the clone plugin (*https://oreil.ly/VUASS*) (discussed in "Creating a Replica Using the Clone Plugin" on page 495) to configure the instances automatically.

Let's add one secondary to see the process in action. To add the second instance to the InnoDB Cluster:

```
MySQL  localhost:3310 ssl  JS > cluster.addInstance('root@localhost:3320')

...

* Waiting for clone to finish...
NOTE: 127.0.0.1:3320 is being cloned from 127.0.0.1:3310
** Stage DROP DATA: Completed
** Clone Transfer
    FILE COPY  ############################################################
    100%  Completed
    PAGE COPY  ############################################################
    100%  Completed
    REDO COPY  ############################################################
    100%  Completed

NOTE: 127.0.0.1:3320 is shutting down...

* Waiting for server restart... ready
* 127.0.0.1:3320 has restarted, waiting for clone to finish...
** Stage RESTART: Completed
* Clone process has finished: 59.62 MB transferred in about 1 second
(~59.62 MB/s)

State recovery already finished for '127.0.0.1:3320'

The instance '127.0.0.1:3320' was successfully added to the cluster
```

Then add the third instance:

```
MySQL  localhost:3310 ssl  JS > cluster.addInstance('root@localhost:3320')
```

At this point we have created a cluster with three instances: a primary and two secondaries. We can see the status by running the following command:

```
MySQL  localhost:3310 ssl  JS > cluster.status()

{
    "clusterName": "learning_mysql",
    "defaultReplicaSet": {
        "name": "default",
        "primary": "127.0.0.1:3310",
        "ssl": "REQUIRED",
        "status": "OK",
        "statusText": "Cluster is ONLINE and can tolerate up to ONE failure.",
        "topology": {
            "127.0.0.1:3310": {
                "address": "127.0.0.1:3310",
                "mode": "R/W",
```

```
                    "readReplicas": {},
                    "replicationLag": null,
                    "role": "HA",
                    "status": "ONLINE",
                    "version": "8.0.21"
                },
                "127.0.0.1:3320": {
                    "address": "127.0.0.1:3320",
                    "mode": "R/O",
                    "readReplicas": {},
                    "replicationLag": null,
                    "role": "HA",
                    "status": "ONLINE",
                    "version": "8.0.21"
                },
                "127.0.0.1:3330": {
                    "address": "127.0.0.1:3330",
                    "mode": "R/O",
                    "readReplicas": {},
                    "replicationLag": null,
                    "role": "HA",
                    "status": "ONLINE",
                    "version": "8.0.21"
                }
            },
            "topologyMode": "Single-Primary"
        },
        "groupInformationSourceMember": "127.0.0.1:3310"
```

Assuming MySQL Router is already installed (see "MySQL Router" on page 547), the only required step is to bootstrap it with the location of the InnoDB Cluster metadata server.

We observe the router being bootstrapped:

```
# mysqlrouter --bootstrap root@localhost:3310 --user=mysqlrouter

Please enter MySQL password for root:
# Bootstrapping system MySQL Router instance...

- Creating account(s) (only those that are needed, if any)
...

## MySQL Classic protocol

- Read/Write Connections: localhost:6446
- Read/Only Connections:  localhost:6447


...
```

MySQL Shell Utilities

As we've said, MySQL Shell is a powerful, advanced client and code editor for MySQL. Among its many functionalities are utilities to create a logical dump and do a logical restore for the entire database instance, including users. The advantage, compared to `mysqldump`, for example, is that the utility has parallelization capacity, greatly improving the dump and restore speed.

Here are the utilities to execute the dump and restore process:

`util.dumpInstance()`
> Dump an entire database instance, including users

`util.dumpSchemas()`
> Dump a set of schemas

`util.loadDump()`
> Load a dump into a target database

`util.dumpTables()`
> Load specific tables and views

Let's take a closer look at each of these in turn.

util.dumpInstance()

The `dumpInstance()` utility will dump all the databases that are present in the MySQL data directory (see "The Contents of the MySQL Directory" on page 40). It will exclude the `information_schema`, `mysql_`, `ndbinfo`, `performance_schema`, and `sys` schemas while taking the dump.

There's also a dry-run option that allows you to inspect the schemas and view the compatibility issues and then run the dump with the appropriate compatibility options applied to remove the issues. Let's try this now—we'll examine the possible errors and see the options for the dump utility.

To start the dump, run the following command:

```
MySQL  JS > shell.connect('root@localhost:48008');
MySQL  localhost:48008 ssl  JS > util.dumpInstance("/backup",
                         > {ocimds: true, compatibility:
                             dryRun: true})

Acquiring global read lock
Global read lock acquired
Gathering information - done
All transactions have been started
Locking instance for backup
...
NOTE: Database test had unsupported ENCRYPTION option commented out
```

```
ERROR: Table 'test'.'sbtest1' uses unsupported storage engine MyISAM
(fix this with 'force_innodb' compatibility option)
Compatibility issues with MySQL Database Service 8.0.23 were found.
Please use the 'compatibility' option to apply compatibility adaptations
to the dumped DDL.
Util.dumpInstance: Compatibility issues were found (RuntimeError)
```

With the ocimds option set to true, the dump utility will check the data dictionary
and index dictionary. Encryption options in CREATE TABLE statements are commen-
ted out in the DDL files, to ensure that all tables are located in the MySQL data directory and use the default schema encryption. strip_restricted_grants removes
specific privileges that are restricted by MySQL Database Service that would cause an
error during the user creation process. dryRun is self-explanatory: it will perform validation only, and no data will be actually dumped.

So, we have a MyISAM table in the test database. The dry-run option clearly throws
the error.

To fix this error, we are going to use the force_innodb option, which will convert all
unsupported engines to InnoDB in the CREATE TABLE statement:

```
MySQL  localhost:48008 ssl  JS > util.dumpInstance("backup",
                             > {ocimds: true, compatibility:
                             > ["strip_restricted_grants","force_innodb"],
                             dryRun: true})
```

Now the dry run does not throw any errors, and there are no exceptions. Let's run the
dumpInstance() command to take an instance backup. The target directory must be
empty before the export takes place. If the directory does not yet exist in its parent
directory, the utility creates it.

We are going to process the dump in parallel. For this, we will use the option threads
and set a value of 10 threads:

```
MySQL  localhost:48008 ssl  JS > util.dumpInstance("/backup",
                             > {ocimds: true, compatibility:
                             > ["strip_restricted_grants","force_innodb"],
                             > threads : 10 })
```

If we observe the last part of the output, we'll see:

```
1 thds dumping - 100% (10.00K rows / ~10.00K rows), 0.00 rows/s, 0.00 B/s
uncompressed, 0.00 B/s

uncompressed
Duration: 00:00:00s
Schemas dumped: 1
Tables dumped: 10
Uncompressed data size: 1.88 MB
Compressed data size: 598.99 KB
Compression ratio: 3.1
```

```
Rows written: 10000
Bytes written: 598.99 KB
Average uncompressed throughput: 1.88 MB/s
Average compressed throughput: 598.99 KB/s
```

If we were using `mysqldump`, we would have a single file. As we can see here, there are multiple files in the backup directory:

```
@.done.json
@.json
@.post.sql
@.sql
test.json
test@sbtest10@@0.tsv.zst
test@sbtest10@@0.tsv.zst.idx
test@sbtest10.json
test@sbtest10.sql
...
test@sbtest1@@0.tsv.zst
test@sbtest1@@0.tsv.zst.idx
test@sbtest1.json
test@sbtest1.sql
test@sbtest9@@0.tsv.zst
test@sbtest9@@0.tsv.zst.idx
test@sbtest9.json
test@sbtest9.sql
test.sql
```

Let's take a look at these:

- The *@.json* file contains server details and lists of users, database names, and their character sets.

- The *@.post.sql* and *@.sql* files contain MySQL Server version details.

- The *test.json* file contains view, stored procedure, and function names along with a list of tables.

- The *@.users.sql* file (not shown) contains a list of database users.

- The *test@sbtest10.json* file contains column names and character sets. There will be a similiarly named file for each dumped table.

- The *test@sbtest1.sql* file contains a table structure. There will be one for each dumped table.

- The *test@sbtest10@@0.tsv.zst* file is a binary file. It stores data. There will be a similarly named file for each dumped table.

- The *test@sbtest10@@0.tsv.zst.idx* file is a binary file. It stores table index stats. There will be a similarly named file for each dumped table.

- The *@.done.json* file contains the backup end time and data file sizes in KB.

- The *test.sql* file contains a database statement.

util.dumpSchemas()

This utility is similar to dumpInstance(), but it allows us to specify schemas to dump. It supports the same options:

```
MySQL  localhost:48008 ssl  JS > util.dumpSchemas(["test"],"/backup",
                             > {ocimds: true, compatibility:
                             > ["strip_restricted_grants","force_innodb"],
                             > threads : 10 , dryRun: true})
```

If we want to specify multiple schemas, we can do that by running:

```
MySQL  localhost:48008 ssl  JS > util.dumpSchemas(["test","percona",
                                 "learning_mysql"],"/backup",
                             > {ocimds: true, compatibility:
                             > ["strip_restricted_grants","force_innodb"],
                             > threads : 10 , dryRun: true})
```

util.dumpTables()

If we want to extract more granular data, like specific tables, we can use the dumpTables() utility. Again, the big advantage compared to mysqldump is the potential to extract data from MySQL in parallel:

```
MySQL  localhost:48008 ssl  JS > util.dumpTables("test", [ "sbtest1",
                             > "sbtest2" ],"/backup",
                             > {ocimds: true, compatibility:
                             > ["strip_restricted_grants","force_innodb"],
                             > threads : 2 , dryRun: true})
```

util.loadDump(url[, options])

We've seen all the utilities to extract data, but there is one remaining: the one to load data into MySQL.

The loadDump() enables provides data streaming to remote storage, parallel loading of tables or table chunks, and progress state tracking. It also provides resume and reset capabilities and the option of concurrent loading while the dump is still taking place.

Note that this utility uses the LOAD DATA LOCAL INFILE statement, so we need to enable the local_infile (*https://oreil.ly/vm445*) parameter globally while importing.

The loadDump() utility checks whether the sql_require_primary_key system variable (*https://oreil.ly/2Si8y*) is set to ON, and if it is, returns an error if there is a table in the dump files with no primary key:

```
MySQL  localhost:48008 ssl  JS > util.loadDump("/backup",
                             > {progressFile :"/backup
                             > restore.json",threads :12})
```

The last part of the output will be similar to this:

```
[Worker006] percona@sbtest7@@0.tsv.zst: Records: 400000 Deleted: 0  Skipped: 0
Warnings: 0
[Worker007] percona@sbtest4@@0.tsv.zst: Records: 400000 Deleted: 0  Skipped: 0
Warnings: 0
[Worker002] percona@sbtest13@@0.tsv.zst: Records: 220742 Deleted: 0  Skipped: 0
Warnings: 0
Executing common postamble SQL

23 chunks (5.03M rows, 973.06 MB) for 23 tables in 3 schemas were loaded in
1 min 24 sec (avg throughput 11.58 MB/s)
0 warnings were reported during the load.
```

Be sure to check the warnings reported at the end in case any show up.

Flame Graphs

Quoting Brendan Gregg (*https://oreil.ly/STGxb*), determining why CPUs are busy is a routine task for performance analysis, which often involves profiling *stack traces*. Profiling by sampling at a fixed rate is a coarse but effective way to see which code paths are *hot* (busy on the CPU). It usually works by creating a timed interrupt that collects the current program counter, function address, or entire stack trace, and translates these to something human-readable when printing a summary report. *Flame graphs* are a type of visualization for sampled stack traces that allow hot code paths to be identified quickly.

A *stack trace* (also called *stack backtrace* or *stack traceback*) is a report of the active stack frames at a certain point in time during the execution of a program. There are many tools available to collect stack traces. These tools are also known as *CPU profilers*. The CPU profiler we are going to use is perf (*https://oreil.ly/T7qZl*).

perf is a profiler tool for Linux 2.6+–based systems that abstracts away CPU hardware differences in Linux performance measurements and presents a simple command-line interface. perf is based on the perf_events interface exported by recent versions of the Linux kernel.

perf_events is an event-oriented observability tool that can help solve advanced performance and troubleshooting tasks. Questions that can be answered include:

- Why is the kernel on-CPU so much? What code paths are hot?
- Which code paths are causing CPU level 2 cache misses?
- Are the CPUs stalled on memory I/O?
- Which code paths are allocating memory, and how much?
- What is triggering TCP retransmits?

- Is a certain kernel function being called, and how often?
- Why are threads leaving the CPU?

Note that in this book, we are only scratching the surface of `perf`'s capabilities. We highly recommend checking out Brendan Gregg's website (*https://oreil.ly/STGxb*), which contains much more detailed information about `perf` and other CPU profilers.

To produce flame graphs, we need to start collecting the stack trace report with `perf` in the MySQL server. This operation needs to be done on the MySQL host. We will collect data for 60 seconds:

```
# perf record -a -g -F99 -p $(pgrep -x mysqld) -- sleep 60;
# perf report > /tmp/perf.report;
# perf script > /tmp/perf.script;
```

And if we check the */tmp* directory, we will see `perf` files:

```
# ls -l /tmp/perf*
-rw-r--r-- 1 root root  502100 Feb 13 22:01 /tmp/perf.report
-rw-r--r-- 1 root root 7303290 Feb 13 22:01 /tmp/perf.script
```

The next step doesn't need to be executed on the MySQL host; we can copy the files to another Linux host or even macOS.

To produce the flame graphs we can use Brendan's GitHub repository (*https://oreil.ly/llqVS*). For this example, we will clone the Flame Graph repository in the directory where our `perf` report is located:

```
# git clone https://github.com/brendangregg/FlameGraph
# ./FlameGraph/stackcollapse-perf.pl ./perf.script > perf.report.out.folded
# ./FlameGraph/flamegraph.pl ./perf.report.out.folded > perf.report.out.svg
```

We've produced a file named *perf.report.out.svg*. This file can be opened in any browser to be visualized. Figure 16-1 is an example of a flame graph.

Flame graphs show the sample population across the x-axis, and stack depth on the y-axis. Each function (stack frame) is drawn as a rectangle, with the width relative to the number of samples; so the bigger the bar, the more CPU time was spent on that function. The x-axis spans the stack trace collection but does not show the passage of time, so the left-to-right ordering has no special meaning. The ordering is done alphabetically based on the function names, from the root to the leaf of each stack.

The file that's created is interactive, so we can explore where kernel CPU time is spent. In the previous example an `INSERT` operation is consuming 44% of the CPU time, as you can see in Figure 16-2.

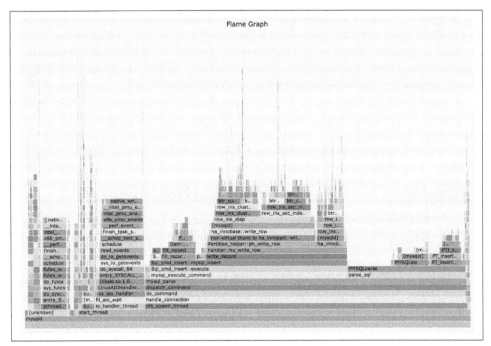

Figure 16-1. An example of a flame graph

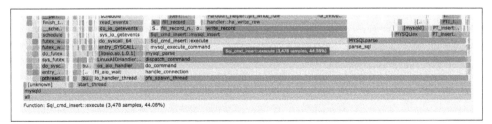

Figure 16-2. 44% of CPU time is used for an INSERT operation

Building MySQL from Source

As Chapter 1 explained, MySQL has a distribution available for most common operating systems. Some companies have also compiled their own MySQL versions, such as Facebook, which worked on the RocksDB engine and integrated it into MySQL. RocksDB is an embeddable, persistent key/value store for fast storage that has several advantages compared with InnoDB with regard to space efficiency.

Despite its advantages, RocksDB does not support replication or a SQL layer. This led the Facebook team to build MyRocks, an open source project that integrates RocksDB as a MySQL storage engine. With MyRocks, it is possible to use RocksDB as backend storage and still benefit from all the features of MySQL. Facebook's project is open source and available on GitHub (*https://oreil.ly/ssWon*).

Another motivation to compile MySQL is the ability to customize its build. For example, for a very specific problem, we can always try to debug MySQL to gather extra information. To do this, we need to configure MySQL with the `-DWITH_DEBUG=1` option.

Building MySQL for Ubuntu Focal Fossa and ARM Processors

Because ARM processors are currently gaining traction (particularly thanks to Apple's M1 chip), we will show you how to compile MySQL for Ubuntu Focal Fossa running on ARM.

First, we are going to create our directories. We will create one directory that will be for the source code, another one for the compiled binaries, and a third for the `boost` library:

```
# cd /
# mkdir compile
# cd compile/
# mkdir build
# mkdir source
# mkdir boost
# mkdir basedir
# mkdir /var/lib/mysql
```

Next, we need to install the additional Linux packages required to compile MySQL:

```
# apt-get -y install dirmngr
# apt-get update -y
# apt-get -y install cmake
# apt-get -y install lsb-release wget
# apt-get -y purge eatmydata || true
# apt-get -y install psmisc pkg-config
# apt-get -y install libsasl2-dev libsasl2-modules libsasl2-modules-ldap || \
    apt-get -y install libsasl2-modules libsasl2-modules-ldap libsasl2-dev
# apt-get -y install dh-systemd || true
# apt-get -y install curl bison cmake perl libssl-dev gcc g++ libaio-dev \
    libldap2-dev libwrap0-dev gdb unzip gawk
# apt-get -y install lsb-release libmecab-dev libncurses5-dev libreadline-dev \
    libpam-dev zlib1g-dev
# apt-get -y install libldap2-dev libnuma-dev libjemalloc-dev libeatmydata \
    libc6-dbg valgrind libjson-perl  libsasl2-dev
# apt-get -y install libmecab2 mecab mecab-ipadic
# apt-get -y install build-essential devscripts libnuma-dev
# apt-get -y install cmake autotools-dev autoconf automake build-essential \
```

```
        devscripts debconf debhelper fakeroot
# apt-get -y install libcurl4-openssl-dev patchelf
# apt-get -y install libeatmydata1
# apt-get install libmysqlclient-dev -y
# apt-get install valgrind -y
```

These packages are related to the CMake flags (*https://oreil.ly/GOnBJ*) that we will run. If we remove or add certain flags, some packages are not necessary to install (for example, if we don't want to compile with Valgrind, we don't need this package).

Next, we will download the source code. For this, we will use MySQL repository (*https://oreil.ly/6Jb4c*) on GitHub:

```
# cd source
# git clone https://github.com/mysql/mysql-server.git
```

The output will be similar to this:

```
Cloning into 'mysql-server'...
remote: Enumerating objects: 1639611, done.
remote: Total 1639611 (delta 0), reused 0 (delta 0), pack-reused 1639611
Receiving objects: 100% (1639611/1639611), 3.19 GiB | 42.88 MiB/s, done.
Resolving deltas: 100% (1346714/1346714), done.
Updating files: 100% (32681/32681), done.
```

To check which version we will compile, we can run the following:

```
# cd mysql-server/
# git branch
```

Next, we will go to our *build* directory and run CMake with our chosen flags:

```
# cd /compile/build
# cmake ../source/mysql-server/  -DBUILD_CONFIG=mysql_release \
    -DCMake_BUILD_TYPE=${CMake_BUILD_TYPE:-RelWithDebInfo} \
    -DWITH_DEBUG=1 \
    -DFEATURE_SET=community \
    -DENABLE_DTRACE=OFF \
    -DWITH_SSL=system \
    -DWITH_ZLIB=system \
    -DCMake_INSTALL_PREFIX="/compile/basedir/" \
    -DINSTALL_LIBDIR="lib/" \
    -DINSTALL_SBINDIR="bin/" \
    -DWITH_INNODB_MEMCACHED=ON \
    -DDOWNLOAD_BOOST=1 \
    -DWITH_VALGRIND=1 \
    -DINSTALL_PLUGINDIR="plugin/" \
    -DMYSQL_DATADIR="/var/lib/mysql/" \
    -DWITH_BOOST="/compile/boost/"
```

Here's what each of these does:

- `DBUILD_CONFIG` configures a source distribution with the same build options as for MySQL releases (we are going to override some of them).

- `DCMake_BUILD_TYPE` with `RelWithDebInfo` enables optimizations and generates debugging information.

- `DWITH_DEBUG` enables the use of the `--debug="d,parser_debug"` option when MySQL is started. This causes the Bison parser used to process SQL statements to dump a parser trace to the server's standard error output. Typically, this output is written to the error log.

- `DFEATURE_SET` indicates we are going to install community features.

- `DENABLE_DTRACE` includes support for DTrace probes. The DTrace probes in the MySQL server are designed to provide information about the execution of queries within MySQL and the different areas of the system being utilized during that process.

- The `DWITH_SSL` option adds support for encrypted connections, entropy for random number generation, and other encryption-related operations.

- `DWITH_ZLIB` enables compression library support for the `COMPRESS()` and `UNCOMPRESS()` functions, and compression of the client/server protocol.

- `DCMake_INSTALL_PREFIX` sets the location of our installation base directory.

- `DINSTALL_LIBDIR` indicates where to install the library files.

- `DINSTALL_SBINDIR` specifies where to install `mysqld`.

- `DWITH_INNODB_MEMCACHED` generates memcached shared libraries (*libmemcached.so* and *innodb_engine.so*).

- `DDOWNLOAD_BOOST` makes CMake download the `boost` library and place it in the location specified with `DWITH_BOOST`.

- `DWITH_VALGRIND` enables Valgrind, exposing the Valgrind API to MySQL code. This is useful for analyzing memory leaks.

- `DINSTALL_PLUGINDIR` defines where the compiler will place the plugin libraries.

- `DMYSQL_DATADIR` defines the location of the MySQL data directory.

- `DWITH_BOOST` defines the directory where CMake will download the `boost` library.

If by mistake you miss a step and the CMake process fails, to prevent old object files or configuration information from being used in the next attempt you'll need to clean up the build directory and the previous configuration. That is, you'll need to run the following commands in the build directory on Unix before rerunning CMake:

```
# cd /compile/build
# make clean
# rm CMakeCache.txt
```

After we run CMake, we are going to compile MySQL using the make command. To optimize the compiling process we will use the -j option, which specifies how many threads we are going to use to compile MySQL. Since in our instance we have 16 ARM cores, we are going to use 15 threads (leaving one for OS activities):

```
# make  -j 15
# make install
```

This process may take a while, and it is very verbose. After it's finished, we can see the binaries in the *basedir* directory:

```
# ls -l /compile/basedir/bin
```

Note that we are not going to find a *mysqld* binary in the */compile/build/bin/* directory, but instead we will see *mysqld-debug*. This is because of the DWITH_DEBUG option we set previously:

```
# /compile/build/bin/mysqld-debug --version
```

```
/compile/build/bin/mysqld-debug  Ver 8.0.23-debug-valgrind for Linux on aarch64
(Source distribution)
```

Now, we can test our binary. For this we are going to manually create the directories and configure the permissions:

```
# mkdir /var/log/mysql/
# mkdir /var/run/mysqld/
# chown ubuntu: /var/log/mysql/
# chown ubuntu: /var/run/mysqld/
```

Then add these settings to */etc/my.cnf*:

```
[mysqld]
pid-file    = /var/run/mysqld/mysqld.pid
socket      = /var/run/mysqld/mysqld.sock
datadir     = /var/lib/mysql
log-error   = /var/log/mysql/error.log
```

Next, we are going to initialize the MySQL data dictionary:

```
# /compile/basedir/bin/mysqld-debug --defaults-file=/etc/my.cnf --initialize \
--user ubuntu
```

Now, MySQL is ready to be started:

```
# /compile/basedir/bin/mysqld-debug --defaults-file=/etc/my.cnf --user ubuntu &
```

A temporary password will be created, and we can extract it from the error log:

```
# grep "A temporary password" /var/log/mysql/error.log

2021-02-14T16:55:25.754028Z 6 [Note] [MY-010454] [Server] A temporary
password is generated for root@localhost: yGldRKoRf0%T
```

Now we can connect using the MySQL client of our preference:

```
# mysql -uroot -p'yGldRKoRf0%T'

mysql: [Warning] Using a password on the command line interface can be
insecure. Welcome to the MySQL monitor. Commands end with ; or \g.
Your MySQL connection id is 8
Server version: 8.0.23-debug-valgrind

Copyright (c) 2000, 2021, Oracle and/or its affiliates.

Oracle is a registered trademark of Oracle Corporation and/or its
affiliates. Other names may be trademarks of their respective
owners.

Type 'help;' or '\h' for help. Type '\c' to clear the current input statement.

mysql>
```

Analyzing a MySQL Crash

We say that MySQL *crashes* when the mysqld process dies without the proper shutdown command. MySQL can crash for a variety of reasons, including these:

- Hardware failure (memory, disk, processor)
- Segmentation faults (invalid memory access)
- Bugs
- Being killed by the OOM process
- Various other causes, such as cosmic rays (*https://oreil.ly/Lq09r*).

The MySQL process can receive a number of signals from Linux. The following are among the most common:

Signal 15 (`SIGTERM`)

Causes the server to shut down. This is like executing a `SHUTDOWN` statement without having to connect to the server (which for shutdown requires an account that has the `SHUTDOWN` privilege). For example, the following two commands result in a regular shutdown:

```
# systemctl stop mysql
# kill -15 -p $(pgrep -x mysqld)
```

Signal 1 (`SIGHUP`)

Causes the server to reload the grant tables and to flush tables, logs, the thread cache, and the host cache. These actions are like various forms of the `FLUSH` statement:

```
mysql> FLUSH LOGS;
```

or:

```
# kill -1 -p $(pgrep -x mysqld)
```

Signal 6 (`SIGABRT`)

Happens because something went wrong. It is commonly used by `libc` and other libraries to abort the program in case of critical errors. For example, `glibc` sends a `SIGABRT` if it detects a double free or other heap corruption. `SIGABRT` will write the crash details in the MySQL error log, like this:

```
18:03:28 UTC - mysqld got signal 6 ;
Most likely, you have hit a bug, but this error can also be caused by...
Thread pointer: 0x7fe6b4000910
Attempting backtrace. You can use the following information to find out
where mysqld died. If you see no messages after this, something went
terribly wrong...
stack_bottom = 7fe71845fbc8 thread_stack 0x46000
/opt/mysql/8.0.23/bin/mysqld(my_print_stacktrace(unsigned char const*...
/opt/mysql/8.0.23/bin/mysqld(handle_fatal_signal+0x323) [0x1032cc3]
/lib64/libpthread.so.0(+0xf630) [0x7fe7244e5630]
/lib64/libc.so.6(gsignal+0x37) [0x7fe7224fa387]
/lib64/libc.so.6(abort+0x148) [0x7fe7224fba78]
/opt/mysql/8.0.23/bin/mysqld() [0xd52c3d]
/opt/mysql/8.0.23/bin/mysqld(MYSQL_BIN_LOG::new_file_impl(bool...
/opt/mysql/8.0.23/bin/mysqld(MYSQL_BIN_LOG::rotate(bool, bool*)+0x35)...
/opt/mysql/8.0.23/bin/mysqld(MYSQL_BIN_LOG::rotate_and_purge(THD*...
/opt/mysql/8.0.23/bin/mysqld(handle_reload_request(THD*, unsigned...
/opt/mysql/8.0.23/bin/mysqld(signal_hand+0x2ea) [0xe101da]
/opt/mysql/8.0.23/bin/mysqld() [0x25973dc]
/lib64/libpthread.so.0(+0x7ea5) [0x7fe7244ddea5]
/lib64/libc.so.6(clone+0x6d) [0x7fe7225c298d]

Trying to get some variables.
Some pointers may be invalid and cause the dump to abort.
```

```
Query (0): Connection ID (thread ID): 0
Status: NOT_KILLED

The manual page at http://dev.mysql.com/doc/mysql/en/crashing.html
contains information that should help you find out what is causing
the crash.
2021-02-14T18:03:29.120726Z mysqld_safe mysqld from pid file...
```

Signal 11 (SIGSEGV)

Indicates a segmentation fault, bus error, or access violation issue. This is generally an attempt to access memory that the CPU cannot physically address, or an access violation. When MySQL receives a SIGSEGV, a core dump will be created if the core-file parameter is configured.

Signal 9 (SIGKILL)

Causes a process to terminate immediately (kills it). This is probably the most famous signal. In contrast to SIGTERM and SIGINT, this signal cannot be caught or ignored, and the receiving process cannot perform any cleanup upon receiving this signal. Besides the chance of corrupting MySQL data, SIGKILL will also force MySQL to perform a recovery process when restarted to bring it to an operational state. The following example shows how to send a SIGKILL manually to the MySQL process:

> **# kill -9 -p $(pgrep -x mysqld)**

Also, the Linux OOM process executes a SIGKILL to terminate with the MySQL process.

Let's try to analyze a crash where MySQL got a signal 11:

```
11:47:47 UTC - mysqld got signal 11 ;
Most likely, you have hit a bug, but this error can also be caused by...
Build ID: Not Available
Server Version: 8.0.22-13 Percona Server (GPL), Release 13, Revision 6f7822f
Thread pointer: 0x7f0e46c73000
Attempting backtrace. You can use the following information to find out
where mysqld died. If you see no messages after this, something went
terribly wrong...
stack_bottom = 7f0e664ecd10 thread_stack 0x46000
/usr/sbin/mysqld(my_print_stacktrace(unsigned char const*, unsigned...
/usr/sbin/mysqld(handle_fatal_signal+0x3c3) [0x1260d33]
/lib/x86_64-linux-gnu/libpthread.so.0(+0x128a0) [0x7f0e7acd58a0]
/usr/sbin/mysqld(Item_splocal::this_item()+0x14) [0xe36ad4]
/usr/sbin/mysqld(Item_sp_variable::val_str(String*)+0x20) [0xe38e60]
/usr/sbin/mysqld(Arg_comparator::compare_string()+0x27) [0xe5c127]
/usr/sbin/mysqld(Item_func_ne::val_int()+0x30) [0xe580e0]
/usr/sbin/mysqld(Item::val_bool()+0xcc) [0xe3ddbc]
/usr/sbin/mysqld(sp_instr_jump_if_not::exec_core(THD*, unsigned int*)+0x2d)...
/usr/sbin/mysqld(sp_lex_instr::reset_lex_and_exec_core(THD*, unsigned int*...
/usr/sbin/mysqld(sp_lex_instr::validate_lex_and_execute_core(THD*, unsigned...
```

```
/usr/sbin/mysqld(sp_head::execute(THD*, bool)+0x5c7) [0x1068e37]
/usr/sbin/mysqld(sp_head::execute_trigger(THD*, MYSQL_LEX_CSTRING const&...
/usr/sbin/mysqld(Trigger::execute(THD*)+0x10b) [0x12288cb]
/usr/sbin/mysqld(Trigger_chain::execute_triggers(THD*)+0x18) [0x1229c98]
/usr/sbin/mysqld(Table_trigger_dispatcher::process_triggers(THD*...
/usr/sbin/mysqld(fill_record_n_invoke_before_triggers(THD*, COPY_INFO*...
/usr/sbin/mysqld(Sql_cmd_update::update_single_table(THD*)+0x1e98) [0x11ec138]
/usr/sbin/mysqld(Sql_cmd_update::execute_inner(THD*)+0xd5) [0x11ec5f5]
/usr/sbin/mysqld(Sql_cmd_dml::execute(THD*)+0x6c0) [0x116f590]
/usr/sbin/mysqld(mysql_execute_command(THD*, bool)+0xaf8) [0x110e588]
/usr/sbin/mysqld(mysql_parse(THD*, Parser_state*, bool)+0x4ec) [0x111327c]
/usr/sbin/mysqld(dispatch_command(THD*, COM_DATA const*...
/usr/sbin/mysqld(do_command(THD*)+0x204) [0x1116554]
/usr/sbin/mysqld() [0x1251c20]
/usr/sbin/mysqld() [0x2620e84]
/lib/x86_64-linux-gnu/libpthread.so.0(+0x76db) [0x7f0e7acca6db]
/lib/x86_64-linux-gnu/libc.so.6(clone+0x3f) [0x7f0e78c95a3f]
Trying to get some variables.
Some pointers may be invalid and cause the dump to abort.
Query (7f0e46cb4dc8): update table1 set c2_id='R', c3_description='testing...
Connection ID (thread ID): 111
Status: NOT_KILLED
Please help us make Percona Server better by reporting any
bugs at https://bugs.percona.com/
```

Sometimes stack may not contain fully resolved symbols or may only have addresses. That depends on whether the mysqld binary is stripped and whether the debug symbols are available. As a rule of thumb, we recommend installing debug symbols, as that has no disadvantage other than using up some disk space. Having debug symbols installed doesn't make your MySQL server run in some slow debug mode. Official MySQL 8.0 builds are always symbolized, however, so you don't need to worry.

The stack trace is analyzed from top to bottom. We can see from the crash that this is a Percona Server v8.0.22. Next, we see the thread being created at the OS level at this point:

```
/lib/x86_64-linux-gnu/libpthread.so.0(+0x76db) [0x7f0e7acca6db]
```

Continuing up through the stack, the code path enters MySQL and starts executing a command:

```
/usr/sbin/mysqld(do_command(THD*)+0x204)...
```

And the code path that crashes is the Item_splocal function:

```
/usr/sbin/mysqld(Item_splocal::this_item()+0x...
```

With a bit of investigation in the MySQL code (*https://oreil.ly/OjTUs*), we discover that Item_splocal is part of the stored procedure code. If we look at the end of the stack trace, we will see a query:

```
Query (7f0e46cb4dc8): update table1 set c2_id='R', c3_description='testing...
```

Triggers can also use the stored procedure path when they contain variables. If we check whether this table has triggers, we see this:

```
CREATE DEFINER=`root`@`localhost` TRIGGER `table1_update_trigger`
BEFORE UPDATE ON `table1` FOR EACH ROW BEGIN
DECLARE vc1_id VARCHAR(2);
SELECT c2_id FROM table1 WHERE c1_id = new.c1_id INTO vc1_id;
IF vc1_id <> P THEN
INSERT INTO table1_hist(
c1_id,
c2_id,
c3_description)
VALUES(
old.c1_id,
old.c2_id,
new.c3_description);
END IF;
END
;;
```

With all this information, we can create a test case and report the bug:

```
USE test;

CREATE TABLE `table1` (
  `c1_id` int primary key auto_increment,
  `c2_id` char(1) NOT NULL,
  `c3_description` varchar(255));

CREATE TABLE `table1_hist` (
  `c1_id` int,
  `c2_id` char(1) NOT NULL,
  `c3_description` varchar(255));
  insert into table1 values (1, T,  test crash);

delimiter ;;

CREATE DEFINER=`root`@`localhost` TRIGGER `table1_update_trigger`
BEFORE UPDATE ON `table1` FOR EACH ROW BEGIN
DECLARE vc1_id VARCHAR(2);
SELECT c2_id FROM table1 WHERE c1_id = new.c1_id INTO vc1_id;
IF vc1_id <> P THEN
INSERT INTO table1_hist(
c1_id,
c2_id,
c3_description)
VALUES(
```

```
old.c1_id,
old.c2_id,
new.c3_description);
END IF;
END
;;
```

To reproduce it, we run multiple commands simultaneously in the same table until the error happens:

```
$ mysqlslap --user=msandbox --password=msandbox \
    --socket=/tmp/mysql_sandbox37515.sock \
    --create-schema=test --port=37515 \
    --query="update table1 set c2_id='R',
    *c3_description='testing crash' where c1_id=1" \
    --concurrency=50 --iterations=200
```

This bug is relatively easy to reproduce, and we recommend you test it. You can find more details about this bug in Percona's Jira system (*https://oreil.ly/cAWbG*).

Also, we can see that Oracle fixed the bug at version 8.0.23 thanks to the release notes (*https://oreil.ly/izg4K*):

> Prepared statements involving stored programs could cause heap-use-after-free memory problems (Bug #32131022, Bug #32045681, Bug #32051928).

Sometimes bugs are not easy to reproduce and can be really frustrating to investigate. Even experienced engineers have problems with this, especially when investigating memory leaks. We hope we have sparked your curiosity to investigate crashes.

Index

About the Authors

Vinicius Grippa is a senior support engineer working for Percona and an Oracle Ace Associate. Vinicius has a bachelor's degree in computer science and has been working with databases for 13 years. He has experience in designing databases for mission-critical applications and, in the last few years, has become a specialist in MySQL and MongoDB ecosystems. Working in the Support team, he has helped Percona customers with hundreds of different cases featuring a vast range of scenarios and complexities. Vinicius is also active in the OS community, participating in virtual rooms like Slack, speaking at meetups, and presenting conferences in Europe, Asia, and North and South America.

Sergey Kuzmichev is a senior support engineer at Percona. He enjoys solving a good technical mystery, working with databases, and building reliable systems. Sergey can often be found contributing code and submitting bug reports to open source projects, and also writes blog posts about MySQL and other open source databases. Before joining Percona, Sergey was a DBA and DevOps engineer for nearly a decade.

Colophon

The animals on the cover of *Learning MySQL* are blue spotted crows (*Euploea midamus*), butterflies found in India and Southeast Asia.

This species of butterfly is mostly black and dark brown, with white spots on the thorax and on the outer part of the wings. The blue patches on their wings are produced by refracted light as a structural color, and are not actually the color of the wing surface.

As with many butterfly species, the caterpillars of blue spotted crows feed mostly on the leaves and stems of a single plant group; in their case, the Apocynaceae/dogbane family. Their eggs are laid on the undersides of plants of this family. Caterpillars evolve through five instars before pupating and emerging as adults. Adult butterflies then feed on the nectar of many flowers, sometimes gathering in large numbers to feed at a single plant. They use their proboscis to funnel flower nectar into their mouths.

The inner membranes of butterfly wings are enclosed in a thin layer of small overlapping scales. The edges of these tiny scales scatter and refract light to create iridescence as well as the color blue (the scales also work functionally, to resist water and help dissipate heat). Studies show that the wings of butterfly genuses (such as *Euploea*) have their own distinct scale patterns. Some butterflies in the *Euploea* genus have also been studied for their ultra-black coloring.

O'REILLY®

There's much more where this came from.

Experience books, videos, live online training courses, and more from O'Reilly and our 200+ partners—all in one place.

Learn more at oreilly.com/online-learning

Milton Keynes UK
Ingram Content Group UK Ltd.
UKHW051950071123
432153UK00004B/6